Alison Balter's Mastering Microsoft® Access 2000 Development

Alison Balter

SAMS

800 East 96th St., Indianapolis, Indiana, 46240 USA

ALISON BALTER'S MASTERING MICROSOFT® ACCESS 2000 DEVELOPMENT

International Standard Book Number: 0-672-31484-3

Library of Congress Catalog Card Number: 98-87340

Printed in the United States of America

First Printing: July 1999

06   05   04   11   10   9   8

TRADEMARKS

WARNING AND DISCLAIMER

EXECUTIVE EDITOR
Rosemarie Graham

ACQUISITIONS EDITOR
Neil Rowe

DEVELOPMENT EDITOR
Robyn Thomas

MANAGING EDITOR
Jodi Jensen

PROJECT EDITOR
Tonya Simpson

COPY EDITOR
Rhonda Tinch-Mize

INDEXER
Greg Pearson

PROOFREADER
Jill Mazurczyk

TECHNICAL EDITORS
Helen Feddema
Bruce Handley
Ken Romero
Eeraj Qaisar

SOFTWARE DEVELOPMENT SPECIALIST
Michael Hunter

INTERIOR DESIGN
Anne Jones

COVER DESIGN
Anne Jones

COPY WRITER
Eric Borgert

LAYOUT TECHNICIANS
Brandon Allen
Stacey DeRome
Timothy Osborn
Staci Somers

CONTENTS AT A GLANCE

CONTENTS

4   What Every Developer Needs to Know About Query Basics   81

ABOUT THE AUTHOR

Alison Balter is the president of Marina Consulting Group LLC, a firm based in Westlake Village, California. Alison is a highly experienced independent trainer and consultant specializing in Windows applications training and development. During her 15 years in the computer industry, she has trained and consulted with many corporations and government agencies. Since Alison founded Marina Consulting Group in 1990, its client base has expanded to include major corporations and government agencies such as Northrop, the Drug Enforcement Administration, Prudential Insurance, Transamerica Insurance, Fox Broadcasting, the United States Navy, and others.

Marina Consulting Group LLC is a Microsoft Certified Solution Provider. Alison is a Microsoft Certified Professional. Alison was one of the first professionals in the computer industry to become a Microsoft Certified Solutions Developer.

Alison is the author of over 200 internationally marketed computer training videos for KeyStone Learning Systems Corporation, including seven Access 2.0 videos, eleven Access 95 videos, thirteen Access 97 videos, nine Visual Basic for Applications videos, and fourteen Visual FoxPro videos. She travels throughout North America giving training seminars in Microsoft Access, Visual Basic, Visual InterDev, and Visual Basic for Applications. She is also featured regularly in live satellite television broadcasts for National Technological University.

Alison is a regular contributing columnist for *Access/Office/VB Advisor* as well as other computer publications. She is also a regular on the Access, Visual Basic, and Visual InterDev national speaker circuits. She was one of four speakers on the Visual Basic 4.0 and 5.0 World Tours, seminar series cosponsored by Application Developers Training Company and Microsoft.

Alison is also a coauthor of three other Access books published by Sams Publishing: *Essential Access 95*, *Access 95 Unleashed*, and *Access 97 Unleashed*.

An active participant in many user groups and other organizations, Alison is a past president of the Independent Computer Consultants Association of Los Angeles, and of the Los Angeles Clipper Users' Group.

On a personal note, Alison keeps herself busy skiing, hiking, traveling, flying, and dancing. She most enjoys spending time with her husband, Dan, and their daughter Alexis.

Alison's firm, Marina Consulting Group LLC, is available for consulting work and on-site training in Microsoft Access, Visual Basic, and Visual InterDev, as well as for Windows NT, Windows 95/98, Windows 2000, PC networking, and Microsoft Exchange Server. Contact Alison by electronic mail at `alison@mcgpc.com`, or visit Marina Consulting Group's Web site at `www.pcvideos.com`.

DEDICATION

I dedicate this book to my husband Dan, my daughter Alexis, "Baby Two" (Brendan or Brianna), my parents Charlotte and Bob, and to my real father, Herman. Dan, you are my partner in life and the wind beneath my wings. Your support over my endeavors is relentless. Without you, my life would never be the same! Alexis, you are the sweet little girl that I always dreamed of. You are everything that I could have ever wanted and so very much more. You make every one of my days a happy one! "Baby Two," you will be born around the time that this book is released. Your kicks late at night when I was writing this book helped keep me awake. I look forward to meeting you and bringing you into our wonderful family! Mom and Dad, without all that you do to help out with life's chores, the completion of this book could never have been possible. Words cannot express my gratitude!

To my real father, Herman, I credit my ability to soar in such a technical field to you. I hope that I inherited just a small part of your intelligence, wit, and fortitude. I am sorry that you did not live to see this accomplishment. I hope that you can see my work and that you are proud of it. I also hope that in some way you share in the joy that Dan and Alexis bring to me. More than anyone else, I dedicate this book to you.

ACKNOWLEDGMENTS

Writing a book is a monumental task. Without the support and understanding of those close to me, my dreams for this book would have never come to fruition. Special thanks go to the following special people who helped to make this book possible:

Dan Balter (My Incredible Husband) for his ongoing support, love, encouragement, friendship, and for staying up many nights proofreading this book. Dan, words cannot adequately express the love and appreciation that I feel for all that you are and all that you do for me. Thank you for being the phenomenal person you are. I enjoy sharing not only our career successes, but even more I enjoy sharing the life of our beautiful child, Alexis. I look forward to our second child being born, and to continuing to reach highs we never dreamed of. There is no one I'd rather spend forever with than you.

Alexis Balter (My Precious Daughter) for giving life a special meaning. Alexis, you make all my hard work worth it. No matter how bad my day, when I look at you, sunshine fills my life. You are the most special gift that anyone has ever given me.

Charlotte and Bob Roman (Mom & Dad) for believing in me and sharing in both the good times and the bad. Mom and Dad, without your special love and support, I never would have become who I am today. Without all your help, I could never get everything done. Words can never express how much I appreciate all that you do!

Roz, Ron, and Charlie Carriere for supporting my endeavors and for encouraging me to pursue my writing. It means a lot to know that you guys are proud of me for what I do.

Steven Chait for being a special brother. I want you to know how much you mean to me. When I was a little girl, I was told about your gift to write. You may not know this, but my desire to write was started as a little girl wanting to be like her big brother.

Sonia Aguilar for being the best nanny that anyone could ever dream of having. You are a person far too special to describe in words. I can't tell you how much it means to know that Alexis has someone so loving and caring to spend her days with. Hugo, Claudia, Gaby, and Little Hugo, you are all special, too. Dan, Alexis, and I are so very lucky to have you in our family.

Shell Forman for being a very special friend. It is so nice to know that even when time goes by when we don't see each other, you are still there. I hope that we are friends forever.

The Marquis Court Clan for providing the best street a family could ever live on. Lori, Gordy, Mimi, Gerry, Karen, Doug, Ellen, Mark, and the rest of the clan, you help so much to make our lives exciting and fun. Thanks for understanding all the times that I had to hide away while spending the many hours writing this book.

Greggory Peck, Clint Argle, and the Folks at Keystone Learning Systems for their contribution to my success in this industry. I believe that the opportunities you have given me have helped me reach a level in this industry that would have been much more difficult for me to reach on my own.

Neil Rowe for doing his best to help make sure that this book was the best it could be. I appreciate you ensuring that deadlines were met, while being as flexible as possible with my schedule. You have been a lot of fun to work with.

TELL US WHAT YOU THINK!

As the reader of this book, *you* are our most important critic and commentator. We value your opinion and want to know what we're doing right, what we could do better, what areas you'd like to see us publish in, and any other words of wisdom you're willing to pass our way.

I welcome your comments. You can email or write me directly to let me know what you did or didn't like about this book—as well as what we can do to make our books stronger.

Please note that I cannot help you with technical problems related to the topic of this book, and that due to the high volume of mail I receive, I might not be able to reply to every message.

When you write, please be sure to include this book's title and author as well as your name and phone or fax number. I will carefully review your comments and share them with the author and editors who worked on the book.

Email: `feedback@samspublishing.com`

Mail: Michael Stephens
           Sams Publishing
           800 East 96th Street
           Indianapolis, IN 46240 USA

INTRODUCTION

Many excellent books about Access are available, so why write another one? In talking to the many students I meet in my travels around the country, I have heard one common complaint. Instead of the several great books available for the user community or the host of wonderful books available for expert Access developers, my students yearn for a book targeted toward the intermediate to advanced developer. They yearn for a book that starts at the beginning, ensures that they have no gaps in their knowledge, and takes them through some of the most advanced aspects of Access development. Along the way, they want to be provided with volumes of practical code that they can easily port into their own applications. *Alison Balter's Mastering Access 2000 Development* is specifically written with those requests in mind.

This book begins by providing you with an introduction to Access development. It alerts you to the types of applications that can be developed in Access and introduces you to the components of an Access application. After you understand what an Access application is and when it is appropriate to develop one, you explore the steps involved in building an actual Access application. Several strategies are covered before the first application component is built. This ensures that you, as the developer of the application, are aware of the design issues that might affect you in your particular environment.

After you have discovered the overall picture, you are ready to venture into the specific details of each object within an Access database. Chapters 2 through 6 cover the basics of tables, relationships, queries, forms, and reports. These chapters are intended to provide you with an approach to developing these database objects from a developer's perspective. Although this text starts at the beginning, it provides many tips, tricks, and caveats not readily apparent from the documentation or from books targeted toward end users.

When you have a strong foundation of knowledge on how to build tables, queries, forms, and reports, you are ready to plunge into coding full-force. Chapters 7 and 8 provide you with an extremely strong grasp of the VBA language. Once again, starting with the basics, you are gently taken to some of the most complex intricacies of the VBA language and Access object model. Many practical examples are provided in the text to ensure that you thoroughly digest each topic.

Chapters 9 through 11 provide you with an advanced discussion of queries, forms, and reports. By the time you reach this point in the text, you should be familiar with all the basics of creating database objects. These chapters combine the basics of table, query, form, and report design with the VBA and object techniques covered in Chapters 7 and 8. The power techniques covered in Chapters 9 through 11 provide you with the expertise that you need to design the most complex types of queries, forms, and reports required by your applications.

Before you are ready to ride through the frontier of the many intricacies of the Access development environment, one basic topic remains. Chapter 12 introduces you to ActiveX data objects and Data Access Objects. After reading Chapter 12, you will understand the differences between ActiveX data objects and Data Access Objects. You will see how you can move away from bound objects, manipulating the data within your database using code.

Unfortunately, things don't always go as planned. No matter what your level of expertise, you will often find yourself stumped over a piece of code and looking for answers. Chapter 13 shows you how to effectively employ the debugger to solve any coding problem you might have. Every aspect of the debugger is covered in the chapter. Even after your application has been thoroughly debugged, you still must responsibly provide a means by which errors are handled within your application. Chapter 14 shows you everything you must know to implement error handling within your application. Included in the text and on the sample code CD-ROM is a generic error handler that you can easily build into any of your own applications.

With the foundation provided by the first 15 chapters, you are ready to move into the more rich and complex aspects of the VBA language and the Access development environment. Chapters 16 through 23 cover all aspects of developing applications for a multi-user or client/server environment. You explore locking strategies, how to interact with non-native Access file formats, and how to use ODBC to design client/server applications. Transaction processing, application optimization, and replication are also covered in these chapters.

As an Access developer, your world is not limited to just Access. To be effective and productive as an Access developer, you must know how to interact with other applications and how to use ActiveX controls, libraries, menu add-ins, wizards, and builders to assist you with the application development process. Chapters 25 through 30 cover OLE, using ActiveX controls, Access and the Internet, managing application development with Visual SourceSafe, and library and add-in techniques. After reading these chapters, you will understand how to employ the use of external objects and functionality to add richness to your applications without too much effort on your part.

At last, you are ready to put the final polish on your application. Chapters 31 through 37 cover the Windows API, security, documentation, maintenance, help, and distribution. You will learn how to properly secure your application so that the investment you have put into the application development process is not compromised in any way. You also discover how easy it is to put into your application the final touches that give it a professional polish and make it stand out from the rest.

The Access development environment is robust and exciting. With the keys to deliver all that it offers, you can produce applications that provide you with much satisfaction as well as many financial rewards. After poring over this hands-on guide and keeping it nearby for handy reference, you too can become masterful at Access 2000 development. This book is dedicated to demonstrating how you can fulfill the promise of making Access 2000 perform up to its lofty capabilities. As you will see, you have the ability to really make Access 2000 shine in the everyday world!

4

THE BASICS OF ACCESS DEVELOPMENT

PART

I

IN THIS PART

ACCESS AS A DEVELOPMENT TOOL

IN THIS CHAPTER

WHAT TYPES OF APPLICATIONS CAN YOU DEVELOP IN ACCESS?

I often find myself explaining exactly what types of applications can be built with Microsoft Access. Access offers a variety of features for different database needs. It can be used to develop six general types of applications:

- Personal applications
- Small Business Applications
- Departmental applications
- Corporation-wide applications
- As a front end for enterprisewide client/server applications
- Intranet/Internet applications

Access as a Development Platform for Personal Applications

At its most basic level, Access can be used to develop simple personal database-management systems. I caution people against this idea, though. People who buy Access hoping to automate everything from their wine collections to their home finances are often disappointed. The problem is that Access is deceptively easy to use. Its wonderful built-in wizards make Access look like a product that anyone can use. After answering a series of questions, you have a finished application—switchboards, data-entry screen, reports, and all. In fact, when Access was first released, many people asked if I was concerned that my business as a computer programmer and trainer would diminish because Access seemed to let absolutely anyone write a database application. Although it's true that the simplest of Access applications can be produced without any thought of design and without a single line of code written by the user, most applications require at least some designing and custom code.

As long as you're satisfied with a wizard-generated personal application with only minor modifications, no problems should occur. It's when you want to substantially customize a personal application that problems can happen.

Access as a Development Platform for Small-Business Applications

Access is an excellent platform for developing an application that can run a small business. Its wizards let developers quickly and easily build the application's foundation; the ability to build code modules allows developers to create code libraries of reusable functions, and the ability to add code behind forms and reports allows them to create powerful custom forms and reports.

The main limitation of using Access for developing a custom small-business application is the time and money involved in the development process. Many people use Access Wizards to begin the development process but find they need to customize their application in ways they can't accomplish on their own. Small-business owners often experience this problem on an even greater scale. The demands of a small-business application are usually much higher than those of a personal application. I have been called in many times after a doctor, attorney, or other professional reaches a dead end in the development process. They're always dismayed at how much money it costs to make their application usable.

Access as a Development Platform for Departmental Applications

Access is perfect for developing applications for departments in large corporations. It's relatively easy to upgrade departmental users to the appropriate hardware—for example, it's much easier to buy additional RAM for 15 users than it is for 4,000! Furthermore, Access's performance is adequate for most departmental applications without the need for client/server technology. Finally, most departments in large corporations have the development budgets to produce well-designed applications.

Fortunately, most departments usually have a PC guru who is more than happy to help design forms and reports. This gives the department a sense of ownership because they have contributed to the development of their application. It also makes my life as a developer much easier. I can focus on the hard-core development issues, leaving some of the form and report design tasks to the local talent.

Access as a Development Platform for Corporation-Wide Applications

Although Access might be best suited for departmental applications, it can also be used to produce applications that are distributed throughout the organization. How successful this endeavor is depends on the corporation. There's a limit to the number of users who can concurrently share an Access application while maintaining acceptable performance, and there's also a limit to the number of records that each table can contain without a significant performance drop. These numbers vary depending on factors such as the following:

- How much traffic already exists on the network.
- How much RAM and how many processors the server has.
- How the server is already being used; for example, are applications such as Microsoft Office being loaded from the server or from local workstations?

- What types of tasks the users of the application are performing; are they querying, entering data, running reports, and so on?
- Where Access and your Access application are run from (the server or the workstation).
- What network operating system is in place?

My general rule of thumb for an Access application that's not client/server is that with more than 10–15 concurrent users and more than 100,000 records, poor performance generally results. Remember, this number varies immensely depending on the factors mentioned, as well as on the definition of acceptable performance by you and your users. The specifics for when to move to a client/server database are covered in Chapter 19, "Client/Server Techniques."

Developers often misunderstand what Access is and what it isn't when it comes to client/server. I'm often asked "Isn't Access client/server?" The answer is that Access is an unusual product because it's a file server application out of the box, but it can act as a front end to a client/server database. In case you're lost, here's an explanation: If you buy Access and develop an application that stores the data on a file server in an Access database, all data processing is performed on the workstation. This means that every time the user runs a query or report, all the data is brought over to the workstation. The query is then run on the workstation machine, and the results are displayed in a datasheet or on a report. This process generates a significant amount of network traffic, particularly if multiple users are running reports and queries at the same time on large Access tables. In fact, such operations can bring the entire network to a crawl.

Access as a Development Platform for Enterprisewide Client/Server Applications

A client/server database, such as Microsoft SQL Server or Oracle, processes queries on the server machine and returns results to the workstation. The server software itself can't display data to the user, so this is where Access comes to the rescue. Acting as a front end, Access can display the data retrieved from the database server in reports, datasheets, or forms. If the data is updated by the user in an Access form, the update is sent to the back-end database. This can either be accomplished by linking to these external databases so that they appear to both you and the user as Access tables, or by using techniques that access client/server data directly.

Using Access Project files (not to be confused with Microsoft Project files), new to Access 2000, you can build an application specifically for a client/server environment. These project files, known as ADP files, contain the program's forms, reports, macros, modules, and data access pages. The project is connected to the back-end database that contains the tables, stored procedures, views, and database diagrams that the program accesses. From within a project file, you can easily modify and manipulate objects stored on the server, using Access's friendly graphical user interface. ADP files help to bring rapid application development to the process of building client/server applications. Because Access 2000 ships with an integrated data store, you can develop a client/server application on the desktop and then easily deploy it to a SQL Server 6.5 or SQL Server 7 database. The alternatives and techniques for developing client/server applications are covered in detail in Chapter 19, "Client/Server Techniques," and in Chapter 20, "Client/Server Strategies."

When you reduce the volume of network traffic by moving the processing of queries to the back end, Access becomes a much more powerful development solution. It can handle huge volumes of data and a large number of concurrent users. The main issue usually faced by developers who want to deploy such a widescale Access application is the type of hardware each user has. Although processing of queries is done at the server, which significantly reduces network traffic, the application itself still must reside in the memory of each user's PC. The hardware requirements for an Access application are covered later in this chapter. Before you decide to deploy a widescale Access application, you need to know the hardware configurations of all your system's users.

Access as a Development Platform for Intranet/Internet Applications

Using data access pages, intranet and Internet users can update your application data from within a browser. Data access pages are HTML documents that are bound directly to data in a database. They are stored outside your database and are used just like standard Access forms except that they are designed to run in Microsoft Internet Explorer 5.0 rather than in Microsoft Access. Internet Explorer 5.0 ships with Office 2000. Data access pages use dynamic HTML in order to accomplish their work. Because they are supported only in Internet Explorer 5.0, data access pages are much more appropriate as an intranet solution than as an Internet solution.

In addition to using data access pages, you can also publish your database objects as either Static or Dynamic HTML pages. Static pages are standard HTML and can be viewed in any browser. Database objects can be published dynamically to either the HTX/IDC file format or to the ASP file format. HTX/IDC files are published dynamically by the Web server and are browser independent. ASP files published by Microsoft Access are also published dynamically by the Web server, but require Internet Explorer 4.0 or higher on the client machine. intranet and Internet development using Microsoft Access are covered in Chapter 31, "Access and the Internet," and Chapter 32, "Using Data Access Pages."

ACCESS AS A SCALABLE PRODUCT

One of Access's biggest strong points is its scalability. An application that begins as a small-business application running on a standalone machine can be scaled to an enterprisewide client/server application. If you design your application properly, scaling can be done with little to no rewriting of your application. This feature makes Access an excellent choice for growing businesses, as well as for applications being tested at a departmental level with the idea that they might eventually be distributed corporationwide.

The great thing about Access is that even acting as both the front end and back end with data stored on a file server in Access tables, it provides excellent security and the ability to establish database rules previously available only on back-end databases. As you will see in Chapters 33, "Database Security Made Easy," and 34, "Advanced Security Techniques," security can be assigned to every object in a database at either a user or group level. Referential integrity rules can be applied at the database level, ensuring that (for example) orders aren't entered for customers who don't exist. Data validation rules can be enforced at either a field or record level, maintaining the integrity of the data in your database. In other words, many of the features previously available only on high-end database servers are now available by using Access's own proprietary data-storage format.

WHAT EXACTLY IS A DATABASE?

The term *database* means different things to different people. For many years, in the world of xBase (dBASE, FoxPro, CA-Clipper), *database* was used to describe a collection of fields and records (this is called a table in Access). In a client/server environment, *database* refers to all the data, schema, indexes, rules, triggers, and stored procedures associated with a system. In Access terms, a database is a collection of all the tables, queries, forms, reports, macros, and modules that compose a complete system.

GETTING TO KNOW THE DATABASE OBJECTS

Access databases are made up of tables, queries, forms, reports, data access pages, macros, and modules. Each of these objects has its own special function. The Access environment also includes several miscellaneous objects, including relationships, command bars, database properties, and import/export specifications. With these objects, you can create a powerful, user-friendly, integrated application. Figure 1.1 shows the Access Database window. Notice the seven categories of objects listed in the database container. The following sections take you on a tour of the objects that make up an Access database.

Tables: A Repository for Your Data

Tables are the starting point for your application. Whether your data is stored in an Access database or you are referencing external data by using linked tables, all the other objects in your database either directly or indirectly reference your tables.

FIGURE 1.1

*The Access
Database window,
with icons for
each type of data-
base object.*

To view all the tables that are contained in the open database, click the Tables icon in the
Objects list. (Note that you won't see any hidden tables unless you have checked the Hidden
Objects check box in the Tools, Options dialog box's View page.) If you want to view the data
in a table, double-click the name of the table you want to view (you can also select the table,
then click the Open button). The table's data is displayed in a datasheet, which includes all the
table's fields and records. (See Figure 1.2.) You can modify many of the datasheet's attributes
and even search for and filter data from within the datasheet. If the table is linked to another
table (like the Northwind Customers and Orders tables), you can also expand and collapse the
subdatasheet to view data stored in child tables. These techniques aren't covered in this book
but can be found in the Access user manual or any introductory Access book, such as *Sams
Teach Yourself Access 2000 in 21 Days.*

FIGURE 1.2

*Datasheet view of
the Customers
table in the
Northwind data-
base.*

	Customer ID	Company Name	Contact Name	Contact Title	
	ALFKI	Alfreds Futterkiste	Maria Anders	Sales Representative	Ob
	ANATR	Ana Trujillo Emparedados y helados	Ana Trujillo	Owner	Av
	ANTON	Antonio Moreno Taquería	Antonio Moreno	Owner	Ma
	AROUT	Around the Horn	Thomas Hardy	Sales Representative	12(
	BERGS	Berglunds snabbköp	Christina Berglund	Order Administrator	Be
	BLAUS	Blauer See Delikatessen	Hanna Moos	Sales Representative	Fo
	BLONP	Blondel père et fils	Frédérique Citeaux	Marketing Manager	24
	BOLID	Bólido Comidas preparadas	Martín Sommer	Owner	C/
	BONAP	Bon app'	Laurence Lebihan	Owner	12
	BOTTM	Bottom-Dollar Markets	Elizabeth Lincoln	Accounting Manager	23
	BSBEV	B's Beverages	Victoria Ashworth	Sales Representative	Fa
	CACTU	Cactus Comidas para llevar	Patricio Simpson	Sales Agent	Ce
	CENTC	Centro comercial Moctezuma	Francisco Chang	Marketing Manager	Si(
	CHOPS	Chop-suey Chinese	Yang Wang	Owner	Ha
	COMMI	Comércio Mineiro	Pedro Afonso	Sales Associate	Av
	CONSH	Consolidated Holdings	Elizabeth Brown	Sales Representative	Be
	DRACD	Drachenblut Delikatessen	Sven Ottlieb	Order Administrator	W:
	DUMON	Du monde entier	Janine Labrune	Owner	67
	EASTC	Eastern Connection	Ann Devon	Sales Agent	35
	ERNSH	Ernst Handel	Roland Mendel	Sales Manager	Kir
	FAMIA	Familia Arquibaldo	Aria Cruz	Marketing Assistant	Ru
	FISSA	FISSA Fabrica Inter. Salchichas S.A.	Diego Roel	Accounting Manager	C/
	FOLIG	Folies gourmandes	Martine Rancé	Assistant Sales Agent	18.

Record: 1 of 91

As a developer, you most often want to view the table's design, which is the blueprint or template for the table. To view a table's design, click Design with the table selected. (See Figure 1.3.) In Design view, you can view or modify all the field names, data types, and field and table properties. Access gives you the power and flexibility you need to customize the design of your tables. These topics are covered in Chapter 2, "What Every Developer Needs to Know About Tables."

FIGURE 1.3

The design of the Customers table.

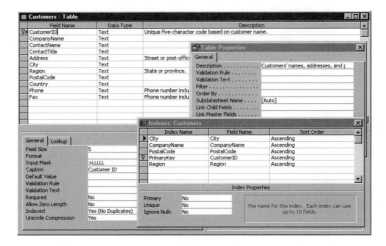

Relationships: Tying the Tables Together

To properly maintain your data's integrity and ease the process of working with other objects in the database, you must define relationships among the tables in your database. This can be done by using the Relationships window. To view the Relationships window, with the Database window active, select Tools|Relationships or click Relationships on the toolbar. (See Figure 1.4.) In this window, you can view and maintain the relationships in the database. If you or a fellow developer have set up some relationships, but you don't see any in the Relationships dialog box, select Relationships|Show All to unhide any hidden tables and relationships.

Notice that many of the relationships in Figure 1.4 have a join line between tables with a number *1* and an infinity symbol. This indicates a one-to-many relationship between the tables. If you double-click on the join line, the Edit Relationships dialog box opens. (See Figure 1.5.) In this dialog box, you can specify the exact nature of the relationship between tables. The relationship between Customers and Orders, for example, is a one-to-many relationship with referential integrity enforced. This means that orders can't be added for customers who don't exist. Notice that the check box to Cascade Update Related Fields is checked. This means that if a

CustomerID is updated, all records containing that CustomerID in the Orders table are also updated. Because Cascade Delete Related Records is not checked, customers cannot be deleted from the Customers table if they have corresponding orders in the Orders table.

FIGURE 1.4
The Relationships window, where you view and maintain the relationships in the database.

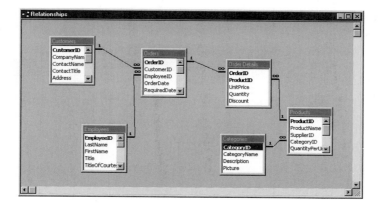

FIGURE 1.5
The Edit Relationships dialog box, which lets you specify the nature of the relationship between tables.

Chapter 3, "Relationships: Your Key to Data Integrity," extensively covers the process of defining and maintaining relationships. For now, remember that relationships should be established both conceptually and literally as early in the design process as possible. They are integral to successfully designing and implementing your application.

Queries: Stored Questions or Actions to be Applied to Your Data

Queries in Access are powerful and multifaceted. Select queries allow you to view, summarize, and perform calculations on the data in your tables. Action queries let you add to, update, and delete table data. To run a query, select Queries from the Objects list and then double-click the query you want to run, or click to select the query you want to run, and then click Open. When you run a select query, a datasheet appears, containing all the fields specified in the query and all the records meeting the query's criteria. (See Figure 1.6.) When you run an action query, the specified action is run, such as making a new table or appending data to an existing table. In general, the data in a query result can be updated because the result of a query is actually a dynamic set of records, called a *dynaset*, based on your tables' data.

FIGURE 1.6

The result of running the Employee Sales by Country query.

When you store a query, only its definition, layout or formatting properties, and datasheet are actually stored in the database. Access offers an intuitive, user-friendly tool for you to design your queries. Figure 1.7 shows the Query Design window. To open this window, select the Queries from the Objects list in the Database window, choose the query you want to modify, and click Design. The query pictured in the figure selects data from Employees, Orders, and Order Subtotals. It displays the Country, LastName, and FirstName from the Employees table, the ShippedDate and OrderID from the Orders table, and the Subtotal from the Order Subtotals query. Only records within a specific Shipped Date range are displayed in the query's output. This special type of query is called a *parameter query*. It prompts for criteria at runtime, using the criteria entered by the user to determine which records are included in the output. Queries are covered in Chapters 4, "What Every Developer Needs to Know About Query Basics," and 11, "Advanced Query Techniques." Because queries are the foundation for most forms and reports, they're covered throughout this book as they apply to other objects in the database.

Forms: A Means of Displaying, Modifying, and Adding Data

Although you can enter and modify data in a table's Datasheet view, you can't control the user's actions very well, nor can you do much to facilitate the data-entry process. This is where forms come in. Access forms can take on many traits, and they're very flexible and powerful.

FIGURE 1.7

The design of a query that displays data from the Employees and Orders tables and the Order Subtotals Query.

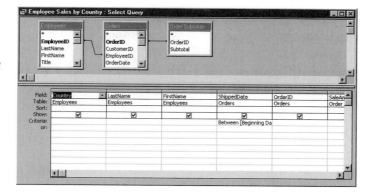

To view any form, select Forms from the Objects list. Then double-click the form you want to view, or click to select the form you want to view, and then click Open. Figure 1.8 illustrates a form in Form view. This form is actually three forms in one: one main form and two subforms. The main form displays information from the Customers table, and the subforms display information from the Orders table and the Order Details table. As the user moves from customer to customer, the orders associated with that customer are displayed. When the user clicks to select an order, the products included on that order are displayed.

FIGURE 1.8

The Customer Orders form includes customer, order, and order detail information.

Like tables and queries, forms can also be viewed in Design view. To view the design of a form, select the Forms icon from the Objects list, choose the form whose design you want to modify, and then click Design. Figure 1.9 shows the Customer Orders form in Design view. Notice the two subforms within the main form. Forms are officially covered in Chapters 5, "What Every Developer Needs to Know About Forms," and 9, "Advanced Form Techniques." They're also covered throughout this text as they apply to other examples of building an application.

Reports: Turning Data into Information

Forms allow you to enter and edit information, but with reports, you can display information, usually to a printer. Figure 1.10 shows a report being previewed. To preview any report, select Reports from the Objects list; then double-click the report you want to preview or choose the report you want to preview, and then click Preview. Notice the graphic in the report, as well as other details, such as the shaded line. Like forms, reports can be elaborate and exciting yet contain valuable information.

FIGURE **1.10**

A preview of the Catalog report.

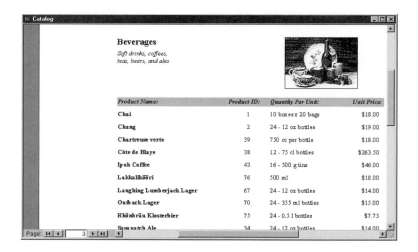

If you haven't guessed yet, reports can be viewed in Design view, as shown in Figure 1.11. To view the design of any report, select Reports from the Objects list and click Design after selecting the report you want to view. Figure 1.11 illustrates a report with many sections; you can see a Report Header, Page Header, CategoryName Group Header, and Detail section—just a few of the many sections available on a report. Just as a form can contain subforms, a report can contain subreports. Reports are covered in Chapters 6, "What Every Developer Needs to Know About Reports," and 10, "Advanced Report Techniques," and throughout the book as they apply to other examples.

FIGURE 1.11

Design view of the Catalog report.

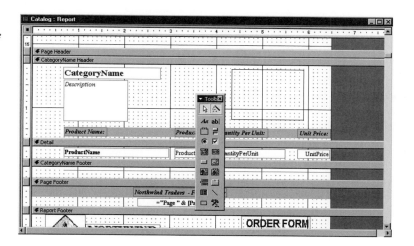

Data Access Pages: Forms Viewed in a Browser

Data access pages, discussed earlier in the chapter, are new to Access 2000. They allow you to view and update the data in your database from within a browser. Although they are stored outside the Access database (.mdb) file, they are created and maintained in a manner similar to that of forms. Figure 1.12 shows a data access page being viewed within Access. Although data access pages are targeted toward a browser, they can also be previewed within the Access application environment.

Data Access Pages can also be viewed and modified in Design view. Figure 1.13 shows a data access page in Design view. As you can see, the Design view of a data access page is similar to that of a form. This makes working with data access pages, and the deployment of your application over an intranet, very easy.

FIGURE 1.12

An example of a Data Access Page based on the Employees table.

FIGURE 1.13

A Data Access Page shown in Design view.

Macros: A Means of Automating Your System

Macros in Access aren't like the macros in other languages. They can't be recorded, as they can in Microsoft Word or Excel, and they aren't saved as VBA code. With Access macros, you can perform most of the tasks that you can manually perform from the keyboard, menus, and toolbars. Macros provide for conditions, allowing you to build logic into your application flow. Generally, you use VBA (Visual Basic for Applications) code contained in modules, rather than macros, to do the tasks your application must perform. This is because VBA code modules give you more flexibility and power than macros do. Although in earlier versions of Access certain tasks could be performed only by using macros, they are rarely used by developers today. The development of applications using macros is therefore not covered in this book.

To run a macro, select Macros from the Objects list, click the macro you want to run, then click Run. The actions in the macro are then executed. To view a macro's design, select Macros from the Objects list, select the macro you want to modify, and click Design to open the Macro Design window. (See Figure 1.14.) The macro pictured has four columns. The first column is the Macro Name column where you can specify the name of a subroutine within a macro. The second column allows you to specify a condition. The action in the macro's third column won't execute unless the condition for that action evaluates to true. The fourth column lets you document the macro. In the bottom half of the Macro Design window, you specify the arguments that apply to the selected action. In Figure 1.14, the selected action is `MsgBox`, which accepts four arguments: `Message`, `Beep`, `Type`, and `Title`.

FIGURE 1.14

The design of the Customers macro, containing macro names, conditions, actions, and comments.

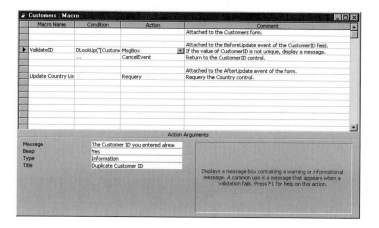

Modules: The Foundation to the Application Development Process

Modules, the foundation of any application, let you create libraries of functions that can be used throughout your application. Modules are usually made up of subroutines and functions. Functions always return a value; subroutines do not. By using Code modules, you can do the following:

- Perform error handling
- Declare and use variables
- Loop through and manipulate recordsets
- Call Windows API and other library functions

- Create and modify system objects, such as tables and queries
- Perform transaction processing
- Perform many functions not available with macros
- Test and debug complex processes
- Create library databases

These are just a few of the tasks you can accomplish with modules. To view the design of an existing module, click Modules in the Objects list, choose the module you want to modify, and click Design to open the Module Design window. (See Figure 1.15.) The global code module in Figure 1.15 contains a General Declarations section and one function called IsLoaded. Modules and VBA are discussed in Chapters 7, "VBA—An Introduction," and 24, "Advanced VBA Techniques," and are covered extensively throughout this book.

FIGURE 1.15

The Global Code module in Design view, showing the General Declarations section and IsLoaded *function.*

OBJECT NAMING CONVENTIONS

Finding a set of naming conventions—and sticking to it—is one of the keys to successful development in Access or any other programming language. When you're choosing a set of naming conventions, look for three characteristics:

- Ease of use
- Readability
- Acceptance in the developer community

The Reddick naming convention, proposed by Greg Reddick, is by far the best set of naming conventions currently published in the development world.

The Reddick naming conventions supply a standardized approach for naming objects. They were derived from the Leszynski/Reddick naming conventions that were prominent in Access versions 1.x and 2.0. These standards were adopted and used extensively by the development community and can be found in most good development books and magazine articles written in the past couple of years. The new Reddick naming conventions have been revised to deal with issues faced by people developing concurrently in Access, Visual Basic, Excel, and other Microsoft products that use the VBA language. These conventions give you an easy-to-use, consistent methodology for naming the objects in all these environments.

A summarized and slightly modified version of the Reddick conventions for naming objects is published in Appendix B, "Naming Conventions." I'll be using them throughout the book and highlighting certain aspects of them as they apply to each chapter.

HARDWARE REQUIREMENTS

One of the downsides of Access is the amount of hardware resources it requires. The requirements for a developer are different from those for an end user, so I have broken the system requirements into two parts. As you read through these requirements, be sure to note actual versus recommended requirements.

What Hardware Does the Developer's System Require?

According to Microsoft documentation, these are the *official* minimum requirements to run Microsoft Access 2000:

- 386DX processor (486 recommended)
- Windows 95 or Windows NT 3.51 or later
- 12MB of RAM on a Windows 95 machine
- 16MB of RAM on a Windows NT machine
- VGA or higher resolution (SVGA 256-color recommended)
- pointing device

As if all that hardware isn't enough, my personal recommendations for a development machine are much higher because you'll probably be running other applications along with Microsoft Access. You also want to greatly reduce the chance of hanging or other problems caused by low-memory conditions. I recommend the following for a development machine (in addition to Microsoft's requirements):

- Pentium 133 or higher
- 64MB of RAM for Windows 95 or Windows 98, 64MB for Windows NT (or even higher if you like to run multiple applications simultaneously)
- High-resolution monitor—the larger, the better, and SVGA if possible

CAUTION

A word of caution: If you're developing on a high-resolution monitor, you should design your forms so that they will display properly on the lowest common denominator monitor. Although you can take advantage of the high resolution in your development endeavors, don't forget that many of your users might be running your application at a lower resolution.

The bottom line for hardware is the more, the better. You just can't have enough memory or hard drive capacity. The more you have, the happier you will be using Access.

What Hardware Does the User's System Require?

Although the user's PC doesn't need to be as sophisticated as the developer's, I still recommend the following in addition to Microsoft's requirements:

- Pentium 133 or higher processor
- 48MB of RAM for Windows 95 or Windows 98, 64MB for Windows NT (or even higher if your application supports OLE or your user will be running your application along with other programs)

HOW DO I GET STARTED DEVELOPING AN ACCESS APPLICATION?

Many developers believe that because Access is such a rapid application-development environment, there's absolutely no need for system analysis or design when creating an application. I couldn't disagree more. As mentioned earlier in this chapter, Access applications are deceptively easy to create, and without proper planning, they can become a disaster.

Task Analysis

The first step in the development process is *task analysis*, or considering each and every process that occurs during the user's workday—a cumbersome but necessary task. When I first started working for a large corporation as a mainframe programmer, I was required to carefully follow a task-analysis checklist. I had to find out what each user of the system did to complete his or her daily tasks, document each procedure and determine the flow of each task to the next, relate each task of each user to his or her other tasks as well as to the tasks of every other user of the system, and tie each task to corporate objectives. In this day and age of rapid application development and changing technology, this step in the development process seems to have gone out the window. I maintain that if care isn't taken to complete this process at least at some level, the developer will have to rewrite large parts of the application.

Data Analysis and Design

After you have analyzed and documented all the tasks involved in the system, you're ready to work on the data analysis and design phase of your application. In this phase, you must identify each piece of information needed to complete each task. These data elements must be assigned to subjects, and each subject will become a separate table in your database. For example, a subject might be a client; then every data element relating to that client would become a field in the client table. The name, address, phone, credit limit, and any other pertinent information about the client would become fields within the client table.

You should determine the following for each data element:

- Appropriate data type
- Required size
- Validation rules

You should also determine whether each data element can be updated and whether it's entered or calculated; then you can figure out whether your table structures are normalized.

Normalization Made Easy

Normalization is a fancy term for the process of testing your table design against a series of rules that ensure that your application will operate as efficiently as possible. These rules are based on set theory and were originally proposed by Dr. E. F. Codd. Although you could spend years studying normalization, its main objective is an application that runs efficiently with as little data manipulation and coding as possible. Here are six of the rules:

1. Fields should be atomic; that is, each piece of data should be broken down as much as possible. For example, rather than creating a field called Name, you would create two fields: one for the first name and the other for the last name. This method makes the data much easier to work with. If you need to sort or search by first name separately from the last name, for example, you can do so without any extra effort.

2. Each record should contain a unique identifier so that you have a way of safely identifying the record. For example, if you're changing customer information, you can make sure you're changing the information associated with the correct customer. This unique identifier is called a *primary key*.

3. The primary key is a field or fields that uniquely identify the record. Sometimes you can assign a natural primary key. For example, the social security number in an employee table should serve to uniquely identify that employee to the system. At other times, you

might need to create a primary key. Because two customers could have the same name, for example, the customer name might not uniquely identify the customer to the system. It might be necessary to create a field that would contain a unique identifier for the customer, such as a customer ID.

4. A primary key should be short, stable, and simple. Short means it should be small in size (not a 50-character field); stable means the primary key should be a field whose value rarely, if ever, changes. For example, although a customer ID would rarely change, a company name is much more likely to change. Simple means it should be easy for a user to work with.

5. Every field in a table should supply additional information about the record the primary key serves to identify. For example, every field in the customer table describes the customer with a particular customer ID.

6. Information in the table shouldn't appear in more than one place. For example, a particular customer name shouldn't appear in more than one record.

Take a look at an example. The datasheet shown in Figure 1.16 is an example of a table that hasn't been normalized. Notice that the CustInfo field is repeated for each order, so if the customer address changes, it has to be changed in every order assigned to that customer. In other words, the CustInfo field is not atomic. If you want to sort by city, you're out of luck because the city is in the middle of the CustInfo field. If the name of an inventory item changes, you need to make the change in every record where that inventory item was ordered. Probably the worst problem in this example involves items ordered. With this design, you must create four fields for each item the customer orders: name, supplier, quantity, and price. This design would make it extremely difficult to build sales reports and other reports your users need to effectively run the business.

FIGURE 1.16

A table that hasn't been normalized.

Order#	CustInfo	OrderTotal	OrderDate	Item1Name	Item1Supplier	Item1Quantity	Item1Price
1	12 AnyStreet, Anywhere, CA	$350.00	1/5/98	Widget	Good Supplier	5	$1.50
1	12 AnyStreet, Anywhere, CA	$350.00	1/5/98	Gadget	Bad Supplier	2	$2.20
1	12 AnyStreet, Anywhere, CA	$350.00	1/5/98	Nut	Okay Supplier	7	$7.70
1	12 AnyStreet, Anywhere, CA	$350.00	1/5/98	Bolt	Another Supplier	9	$3.00
2	45 AnyStreet, Somewhere	$200.00	3/1/98	Pencil	Good Supplier	2	$1.50
2	45 AnyStreet, Somewhere	$200.00	3/1/98	Eraser	Someone	4	$2.20
0		$0.00				0	$0.00

Record: 1 of 6

Figure 1.17 shows the same data normalized. Notice that it's been broken out into several different tables: tblCustomers, tblOrders, tblOrderDetails, and tblSuppliers. The tblCustomers table contains data that relates only to a specific customer. Each record is uniquely identified by a contrived CustID field, which is used to relate the orders table, tblOrders, to tblCustomers. The tblOrders table contains only information that applies to the entire order, rather than to a particular item that was ordered. This table contains the CustID of the customer who placed the order and the date of the order, and it's related to the tblOrderDetails table based on the OrderID. The tblOrderDetails table holds information about each item ordered for a particular OrderID. There's no limit to the potential number of items that can be ordered. As many items can be ordered as needed, simply by adding more records to the tblOrderDetails table. Finally, supplier information has been placed in a separate table, tblSuppliers, so that if any of the supplier information changes, it has to be changed in only one place.

FIGURE 1.17

Data normalized into four separate tables.

Prototyping

Although the task analysis and data analysis phases of application development haven't changed much since the days of mainframes, the prototyping phase has changed. In working with mainframes or DOS-based languages, it was important to develop detailed specifications for each screen and report. I remember requiring users to sign off on every screen and report. Even a change such as moving a field on a screen meant a change order and approval for additional hours. After the user signed off on the screen and report specifications, the programmers would go off for days and work arduously to develop each screen and report. They would return to the user after many months only to hear that everything was wrong. This meant back to the drawing board for the developer and many additional hours before the user could once again review the application.

The process is quite different now. As soon as the tasks have been outlined and the data analysis finished, the developer can design the tables and establish relationships among them. The form and report prototype process can then begin. Rather than the developer going off for weeks or months before having further interaction with the user, the developer needs only a few days, using the Access Wizards to quickly develop form prototypes.

Testing

As far as testing goes, you just can't do enough. I recommend that if your application is going to be run in Windows 95, Windows 98, and Windows NT, you test in all environments. I also suggest you test your application extensively on the lowest common denominator piece of hardware—the application might run great on your machine but show unacceptable performance on your users' machines.

It usually helps to test your application both in pieces and as an integrated application. Recruit several people to test your application and make sure they range from the most savvy of users to the least computer-adept person you can find. These different types of users will probably find completely different sets of problems. Most important, make sure you're not the only tester of your application because you're the least likely person to find errors in your own programs.

Implementation

Your application is finally ready to go out into the world, or at least you hope so! Distribute your application to a subset of your users and make sure they know they're the test case. Make them feel honored to participate as the first users of the system, but warn them that problems might occur and it's their responsibility to make you aware of them. If you distribute your application on a widescale basis and it doesn't operate exactly as it should, it will be difficult to regain the confidence of your users. That's why it is so important to roll out your application slowly.

Maintenance

Because Access is such a rapid application-development environment, the maintenance period tends to be much more extended than the one for a mainframe or DOS-based application. Users are much more demanding; the more you give them, the more they want. For a consultant, this is great. Just don't get into a fixed bid situation—due to the scope of the application changing, you could very well end up on the losing end of that deal.

There are three categories of maintenance activities: bug fixes, specification changes, and frills. Bug fixes need to be handled as quickly as possible. The implications of specification changes need to be clearly explained to the user, including the time and cost involved in making the requested changes. As far as frills, try to involve the users as much as possible in adding frills by teaching them how to enhance forms and reports and by making the application as flexible and user defined as possible. Of course, the final objective of any application is a happy group of productive users.

PRACTICAL EXAMPLES

A Practical Example of Application Design: A Computer Consulting Firm

Your goal throughout this book is to build an application that will be a time and billing system for a computer consulting firm. First, look at the application from a design perspective.

The system will track client contacts and the projects associated with those clients. It will allow the users to record all hours billed to and expenses associated with each client and project. It will also let users track pertinent information about each employee or subcontractor. The tables in the system are based on the tables produced by the Database Wizard. They have been modified somewhat, and their names have been changed to follow the Reddick naming conventions. The system you build will be far more powerful and flexible than the one supplied by the Database Wizard. Ten tables will be included in the system. Some of these tables are built in Chapter 2, and they can all be found in the application databases on the sample code CD-ROM:

- tblClients—This table contains all the pertinent information about each client; it's related to tblProjects, the table that will track the information about each project associated with a client.

- tblProjects—This table holds all the pertinent information about each project; it's related to several other tables: tblClients, tblPayments, tblEmployees, tblTimeCardHours, and tblTimeCardExpenses.

- tblTimeCardHours—This table is used to track the hours associated with each project and employee; it's related to tblProjects, tblTimeCards, and tblWorkCodes.

- tblPayments—This table is used to track all payments associated with a particular project; it's related to tblProjects and tblPaymentMethods.

- tblTimeCardExpenses—This table is used to track the expenses associated with each project and employee; it's related to tblProjects, tblTimeCards, and tblExpenseCodes.

- tblEmployees—This table is used to track employee information; it's related to tblTimeCards and tblProjects.

- tblTimeCards—This table is used to track each employee's hours; it's actually a bridge between the many-to-many relationship between Employees and Time Card Expenses, as well as between Employees and Time Card Hours, and it's related to tblEmployees, tblTimeCardHours, and tblTimeCardExpenses.

- tblExpenseCodes—This table is a lookup table for valid expense codes; it's related to tblTimeCardExpenses.

- tblWorkCodes—This table is a lookup table for valid work codes; it's related to tblTimeCardHours.

- tblPaymentMethods—This table is a lookup table for valid payment methods; it's related to tblPayments.

The relationships among the tables are covered in more detail in Chapter 3, but they're shown in Figure 1.18.

FIGURE 1.18

Relationships among tables in the time and billing system.

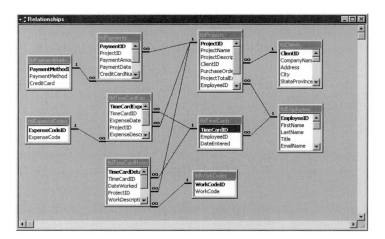

SUMMARY

Before you learn about the practical aspects of Access development, you need to understand what Access is and how it fits into the application development world. Access is an extremely powerful product with a wide variety of uses; Access applications can be found on everything from the home PC to the desks of many corporate PC users going against enterprisewide client/server databases.

After you understand what Access is and what it does, you're ready to learn about its many objects. Access applications are made up of tables, queries, forms, reports, data access pages, macros, modules, command bars, ActiveX controls, relationships, and other objects. When designed properly, an Access application effectively combines these objects to give the user a powerful, robust, utilitarian application.

WHAT EVERY DEVELOPER NEEDS TO KNOW ABOUT TABLES

IN THIS CHAPTER

BUILDING A NEW TABLE

There are several ways to add a new table to an Access 2000 database: using a wizard to help you with the design process, designing the table from scratch, building the table from a spreadsheet-like format, importing the table from another source, and linking to an external table. The process of designing a table from scratch is discussed in this chapter; importing and linking are covered extensively throughout this book. Because the other two options are not appropriate for most business solutions, they are not discussed here.

Regardless of which method you choose, start by selecting the Tables icon from the list of objects in the Database window. Icons appear allowing you to create a table in Design view, create a table using a wizard, and create a table by entering data (see Figure 2.1).

FIGURE 2.1

To create a new table, click the Tables icon of the Database window.

Designing a Table from Scratch

Designing tables from scratch offers flexibility and encourages good design principles. It is almost always the best choice when creating a custom business solution. To design a table from scratch, select Tables from the list of objects, and double-click the Create Table in Design View icon. The Table Design view window, pictured in Figure 2.2, appears. Follow these steps:

1. Define each field in the table by typing its name in the Field Name column. If you prefer, you can click the build button on the toolbar (the button with the ellipsis) to open the Field Builder dialog box, shown in Figure 2.3. This builder lets you select from predefined fields with predefined properties. Of course, the properties can be modified at any time.

FIGURE 2.2

The Table Design view window is used to enter field names, data types, and descriptions for all the fields in a table.

FIGURE 2.3

The Field Builder dialog box lets you select from predefined fields with predefined properties.

2. Tab to the Data Type column. Select the default field type, which is Text, or use the drop-down combo box to select another field type. You can find details on which field type is appropriate for your data in the "Selecting the Appropriate Field Type for Your Data" section of this chapter. Note that if you use the Field Builder, it sets a field type value for you that you can modify.

3. Tab to the Description column. What you type in this column appears on the status bar when the user is entering data into the field. This column is also great for documenting what data is actually stored in the field.

4. Continue entering fields. If you need to insert a field between two existing fields, click the Insert Rows button on the toolbar. The new field is inserted above the field you were on. To delete a field, click the Delete Rows button.

5. To save your work click the Save tool on the toolbar. The Save As dialog shown in Figure 2.4 appears. Enter a Table Name and click OK. A dialog appears, recommending that you establish a primary key. Every table should have a primary key. Primary keys are discussed in the section "The All-Important Primary Key," later in this chapter.

FIGURE 2.4

Use the Save As dialog box to name a table.

NOTE

The naming conventions for table names are similar to those for field names, except the standard for table names is that they should begin with the tag *tbl*. Naming conventions are covered in detail in Chapter 1, "Access as a Development Tool," and in Appendix B, "Naming Conventions."

NOTE

Field names can be up to 64 characters long. For practical reasons, you should try to limit them to 10–15 characters—enough to describe the field without making the name difficult to type.

Field names can include any combination of letters, numbers, spaces, and other characters, excluding periods, exclamation points, accents, and brackets. I recommend that you stick to letters. Spaces in field names can be inconvenient when you're building queries, modules, and other database objects. Don't be concerned that your users will see the field names without the spaces. The Caption property of a field, discussed later in this chapter, allows you to designate the text that is displayed for your users.

Field names can't begin with leading spaces. As mentioned, field names shouldn't contain any spaces, so this shouldn't be a problem.

Try not to duplicate property names, keywords, function names, or the names of other Access objects when naming your fields. Although your code might work in some circumstances, you'll get unpredictable results in others.

To make a potential move to client/server as painless as possible, you should be aware that not all field types are supported by every back-end database. Furthermore, most back-end databases impose stricter limits than Access does on the length of field names and the characters that are valid in field names. To reduce the number of problems you'll encounter if you migrate your tables to a back-end database server, these issues should be considered when you're naming the fields in your Access tables.

> **NOTE**
>
> Adding descriptions to your table, query, form, report, macro, and module objects goes a long way toward making your application self-documenting. This helps you, or anyone who modifies your application, perform any required maintenance on the application's objects. Documenting your application is covered in detail in Chapter 35, "Documenting Your Application."

SELECTING THE APPROPRIATE FIELD TYPE FOR YOUR DATA

The data type you select for each field can greatly affect the performance and functionality of your application. Several factors can influence your choice of data type for each field in your table:

- The type of data that's stored in the field
- Whether the field's contents need to be included in calculations
- Whether you need to sort the data in the field
- The way you want to sort the data in the field
- How important storage space is to you

The type of data you need to store in a field has the biggest influence on which data type you select. For example, if you need to store numbers beginning with leading zeros, you can't select a Number field because leading zeros entered into a Number field are ignored. This rule affects data such as zip codes (some begin with leading zeros) and department codes.

> **NOTE**
>
> If it is unimportant that leading zeros are stored in a field, and you simply need them to appear on forms and reports, this can be accomplished using the Format property of the field. The Format property is covered in the "Working with Field Properties" section of this chapter.

If the contents of a field need to be included in calculations, you must select a Number or Currency data type. You can't perform calculations on the contents of fields defined with the other data types. The only exception to this rule is the Date field, which can be included in date/time calculations.

You also must consider whether you will sort or index the data in a field. Memo, OLE, and Hyperlink fields can't be sorted, so don't select these field types if the data in the field must be sorted or indexed. Furthermore, you must think about the *way* you want the data to be sorted. For example, in a Text field, a set of numbers would be sorted in the order in which they appear (that is, 1, 10, 100, 2, 20, 200) because data in the Text field is sorted in a standard ASCII sequence. On the other hand, in a Number or Currency field the numbers would be sorted as expected (that is, 1, 2, 10, 20, 100, 200). You might think you would never want data sorted in a standard ASCII sequence, but sometimes it makes sense to sort certain information, such as department codes, in this fashion.

Finally, you should consider how important disk space is to you. Each field type takes up a different amount of storage space on your hard disk, which could be a factor when you're selecting a data type for a field.

Nine field types are available in Access: Text, Memo, Number, Date/Time, Currency, AutoNumber (known as Counter in Access 2.0), Yes/No, OLE Object, and Hyperlink. Table 2.1 summarizes information on the appropriate uses for each field type and the amount of storage space each type needs.

TABLE 2.1 APPROPRIATE USES AND STORAGE SPACE FOR ACCESS FIELD TYPES

Field Type	Appropriate Uses	Storage Space
Text	Data containing text, a combination of text and numbers, or numbers that don't need to be included in calculations; examples are names, addresses, department codes, phone numbers	Based on what's actually stored in the field; ranges from 0 to 255 bytes
Memo	Long text and numeric strings; examples are notes and descriptions	Ranges from 0 to 64,000 bytes
Number	Data that's included in calculations (excluding money); examples are ages, codes, such as employee ID, or payment methods	1, 2, 4, or 8 bytes, depending on the field size selected (or 16 bytes for replication ID)
Date/Time	Dates and times; examples are date ordered and birthdate	8 bytes
Currency	Currency values; examples are amount due and price	8 bytes

Field Type	Appropriate Uses	Storage Space
AutoNumber	Unique sequential or random numbers; examples are invoice numbers and project numbers	4 bytes (16 bytes for replication ID)
Yes/No	Fields that contain one of two values (yes/no, true/false); examples are indicating bills paid and tenure status	1 bit
OLE Object	Objects like Word documents or Excel spreadsheets; examples are employee reviews and budgets	0 bytes to 1 gigabyte, depending on what's stored within the field
Hyperlink	Text, or a combination of text and numbers, stored as text and used as a hyperlink address; examples are Web pages or network files	0 to 2048 bytes for each of the three parts that compose the address (up to 64,000 characters total)

2

WHAT YOU NEED TO KNOW ABOUT TABLES

NOTE

The Hyperlink field type contains a hyperlink object. The hyperlink object consists of three parts. The first part is called the *displaytext*; it's the text that appears in the field or control. The second part is the actual *file path* (UNC) or *page* (URL) the field is referring to. The third part is the *subaddress*, a location within the file or page.

The most difficult part of selecting a field type is knowing which type is best in each situation. The following detailed descriptions of each field type and when they are used should help you with this process.

Text Fields: The Most Common Field Type

Most fields are Text fields. Many developers don't realize that it's best to use Text fields for any numbers not used in calculations. Examples are phone numbers, part numbers, and zip codes. Although the default size for a Text field is 50 characters, up to 255 characters can be stored in a Text field. Because Access allocates disk space dynamically, a large field size doesn't use hard-disk space, but you can improve performance if you allocate the smallest field size possible. The maximum number of characters allowed in a Text field can be controlled by the FieldSize property.

Memo Fields: For Those Long Notes and Comments

Memo fields can store up to 64K of text, which can hold up to 16 pages of text for each record. Memo fields are excellent for any types of notes you want to store with table data. Remember, you can't sort by a Memo field.

Number Fields: When You Need to Calculate

Number fields are used to store data that must be included in calculations. If currency amounts are included in calculations or if your calculations require the highest degree of accuracy, you should use a Currency field rather than a Number field. The Number field is actually several types of fields in one because Access 2000 offers six sizes of numeric fields. Byte can store integers from 0–255, Integer can hold whole numbers from –32768–32767, and Long Integer can hold whole numbers ranging from less than –2 billion to just over 2 billion. Although all three of these sizes offer excellent performance, each type requires an increasingly larger amount of storage space. Two of the other numeric field sizes, Single and Double, offer floating decimal points and, therefore, much slower performance. Single can hold fractional numbers to seven significant digits; Double extends the precision to 14 significant digits. The final size, Replication ID, supplies a unique identifier required by the data synchronization process.

Date/Time Fields: Tracking When Things Happened

The Date/Time field type is used to store valid dates and times. Date/Time fields allow you to perform date calculations and make sure dates and times are always sorted properly. Access actually stores the date or time internally as an 8-byte floating-point number. Time is represented as a fraction of a day.

> **NOTE**
>
> Any date and time settings you establish in the Windows Control Panel are reflected in your data. For example, if you modify the Short Date Style in Regional Settings within the Control Panel, your forms, reports, and datasheets will immediately reflect those changes.

Currency Fields: Storing Money

The Currency field type is a special type of number field used when currency values are being stored in a table. Currency fields prevent rounding off data during calculations. They hold 15 digits of whole dollars, plus accuracy to the hundredths of a cent. Although very accurate, this type of field is quite slow.

> **NOTE**
>
> Any changes to the currency format made in the Windows Control Panel are reflected in your data. Of course, Access doesn't automatically perform any actual conversion of currency amounts. As with dates, if you modify the currency symbol in Regional Settings within Control Panel, your forms, reports, and datasheets will immediately reflect those changes.

AutoNumber Fields: For Unique Record Identifiers

The AutoNumber field in Access 2000 is equivalent to the Counter field in Access 2.0. AutoNumber field values are automatically generated when a record is added. In Access 2.0, counter values had to be sequential. The AutoNumber field type in Access 2000 can be either sequential or random. The random assignment is useful when several users are adding records offline because it's unlikely that Access will assign the same random value to two records. A special type of AutoNumber field is a Replication ID. This randomly produced, unique number helps with the replication process by generating unique identifiers used to synchronize database replicas.

You should note a few important points about sequential AutoNumber fields. If a user deletes a record from a table, its unique number is lost forever. Likewise, if a user is adding a record but cancels, the unique counter value for that record is lost forever. If this behavior is unacceptable, you can generate your own counter values. This process is covered in Chapter 17, "Developing Multiuser Applications."

Yes/No Fields: When One of Two Answers Is Correct

You should use Yes/No fields to store a logical true or false. What's actually stored in the field is -1 for Yes, 0 for No, or Null for no specific choice. The display format for the field determines what the user actually sees (normally Yes/No, True/False, On/Off, or a third option—Null—if you set the TripleState property to True). Yes/No fields work efficiently for any data that can have only a true or false value. Not only do they limit the user to valid choices, but also they take up only 1 bit of storage space.

OLE Object Fields: The Place to Store Just About Anything

OLE Object fields are designed to hold data from any OLE server application registered in Windows, including spreadsheets, word processing documents, sound, and video. There are many business uses for OLE fields, such as storing resumes, employee reviews, budgets, or videos. However, in many cases it is more efficient to use a Hyperlink field to store a link to the document rather than store the document itself in an OLE Object field.

Hyperlink Fields: Your Link to the Internet

Hyperlink fields are used to store uniform resource locator addresses (URLs), which are links to World Wide Web pages on the Internet, or Universal Naming Convention paths (UNCs), which are links to a file path. The Hyperlink field type is broken into three parts: (1) what the user sees, (2) the URL or UNC, and (3) a subaddress, such as a range name or bookmark. After an entry is placed in a Hyperlink field, the entry serves as a direct link to the file or page it's referring to. Hyperlinks are covered in more detail later in this chapter, in the section "Access Tables and the Internet."

WORKING WITH FIELD PROPERTIES

After you have added fields to your table, you need to customize their properties. Field properties let you control how data is stored as well as what data can be entered into the field. The available properties differ depending on which field type is selected. The most comprehensive list of properties is found under the Text field type. (See Figure 2.5.) The following sections describe each field property.

FIGURE 2.5

Field properties available for a Text field.

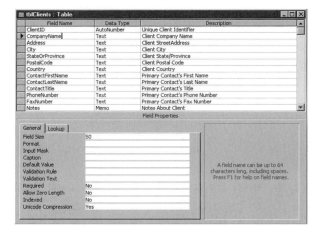

Field Size: Limiting What's Entered into a Field

The first property is Field Size, available for Text and Number fields only. As mentioned previously, it's best to set the field size to the smallest value possible. For Number fields, a small size means lower storage requirements and faster performance.

TRY IT Build a table with the following fields and types:

> CompanyID: AutoNumber
> CompanyName: Text
> State: Text
> PhoneNumber: Text
> ContactDate: Date/Time
> CreditLimit: Currency

1. To set the Field Size property of the State field to two characters, click anywhere in the field; then type 2 in the Field Size property.

2. Switch to Datasheet view. You are prompted to save the table. Name it tblCustomers. Because you have not assigned a primary key, you are prompted. When you try to enter data into the State field, notice that only two characters can be entered.

NOTE

 This example, and all others in this chapter, can be found in the Chap2TryIt.MDB file included on the book's sample code CD-ROM. Refer to this file if you want to verify that your table structures are correct.

Format: Determining How Data Is Displayed

The second property is Format, available for all but OLE Object fields. It allows you to specify how Access displays your data. Access lets you select from predefined formats or create your own custom formats. The available formats differ depending on the field's data type. For example, with Access you can select from a variety of Date/Time formats, including Short Date (7/7/96), Long Date (Sunday, July 7, 1996), Short Time (7:17), and Long Time (7:17:11AM). The formats for a Currency field include Currency ($1,767.25), Fixed (1767.25), and Standard (1,767.25).

| TRY | IT | Set the Format property of the ContactDate field to Medium Date. Switch to Datasheet view and enter some dates in different formats, such as 07/08/96 and July 8, 1996. Notice that no matter how you enter the dates, as soon as you tab away from the field, they appear in the format dd/mm/yy as 08-Jul-96.

Input Mask: Determining What Data Goes into a Field

Another important property is Input Mask, available for Text, Number, Date/Time, and Currency fields. The Format property affects how data is displayed, but the Input Mask property controls what data is stored in a field. You can use the Input Mask property to control, on a character-by-character basis, what type of character (numeric, alphanumeric, and so on) can be stored and whether a particular character is required. The Input Mask Wizard, shown in Figure 2.6, helps you create commonly used input masks for Text and Date fields only. To access the Input Mask Wizard, click the button to the right of the Input Mask field.

| **NOTE** |

The Input Mask Wizard is available only if you selected the Advanced Wizards component during setup.

FIGURE 2.6

The Input Mask Wizard helps you enter an input mask.

For example, the input mask 000-00-0000;;_ (converted to 000\-00\-0000;;_ as soon as you tab away from the property) forces the entry of a valid social security number. Everything that precedes the first semicolon designates the actual mask. The zeros force the entry of the digits 0 through 9. The dashes are literals that appear within the control as the user enters data. The character you enter between the first and second semicolon determines whether literal characters (the dashes in this case) are stored in the field. If you enter a 0 in this position, literal characters are stored in the field; if you enter a 1 or leave this position blank, the literal characters aren't stored. The final position (after the second semicolon) indicates what character is displayed to indicate the space where the user types the next character (in this case, the underscore).

Here's a more detailed example: In the mask `\(999") "000\-0000;;_`, the first backslash causes the character that follows it (the parenthesis) to be displayed as a literal. The three nines allow optional numbers or spaces to be entered. The parenthesis and space within the quotation marks are displayed as literals. The first three zeros require values `0` through `9`. The dash that follows the next backslash is displayed as a literal. Four additional numbers are then required. The two semicolons have nothing between them, so the literal characters aren't stored in the field. The second semicolon is followed by an underscore, so an underscore is displayed to indicate the space where the user types the next character.

TRY IT Use the Input Mask Wizard to add a mask for the PhoneNumber field, which you should have set up as a Text field.

1. To do this, click anywhere in the PhoneNumber field, and then click the Input Mask property.

2. Click the ellipsis to the right of the Input Mask property.

3. Select Phone Number from the list of available masks and choose not to store the literal characters in the field.

4. Switch to Datasheet view and enter a phone number. Notice how your cursor skips over the literal characters. Try leaving the area code blank; Access should allow you to do this.

5. Now try to enter a letter in any position—Access should prohibit you from doing this.

6. Next, try to leave any character from the seven-digit phone number blank. Access shouldn't let you do this, either.

TIP

When you use an input mask, the user is always in Overtype mode. This behavior is a feature of the product and can't be altered.

Caption: A Great Timesaver

The next available property is Caption. The text placed in this property becomes the caption for fields in Datasheet view. It's also used as the caption for the attached label added to data-bound controls when you add them to forms and reports. The Caption property becomes important whenever you name your fields without spaces. Whatever is in the Caption property overrides the field name for use in Datasheet view, on forms, and on reports.

NOTE

The term *data-bound control* is used to refer to a control that is bound to a field in a table or query. The term *attached label* is used to refer to the label attached to a data-bound control.

TIP

It's important to set the Caption property for fields *before* you build any forms or reports that use them. When a form or report is produced, Access looks at the current caption. If the caption is added or modified at a later time, captions for that field on existing forms and reports aren't modified.

Default Value: Saving Data-Entry Time

Another important property is the Default Value property, used to specify the default value that Access will place in the field when the user adds new records to the table. Default values, which can be either text or expressions, can save the data-entry person a lot of time. However, they do not in any way validate what's entered into a field.

TIP

Default values are automatically carried into any queries and forms containing the field. Unlike what happens with the Caption property, this occurs whether the default value was created before or after the query or form.

TRY IT Enter the following default values for the State, ContactDate, and CreditLimit fields:

State: CA

ContactDate: =Date()

CreditLimit: 1000

Switch to Datasheet view and add a new record. Notice that default values appear for the State, ContactDate, and CreditLimit fields. You can override these defaults, if you want.

2
WHAT YOU NEED TO KNOW ABOUT TABLES

Validation Rule: Controlling What's Entered in a Field

The Default Value property suggests a value to the user, but the Validation Rule property actually limits what the user can place in the field. Validation rules can't be violated; the database engine strictly enforces them. As with the Default Value property, this property can contain either text or a valid Access expression, but user-defined functions can't be included in the Validation Rule property. You also can't include references to forms, queries, or tables in the Validation Rule property.

TIP

If you set the Validation Rule property but not the Validation Text property, Access automatically displays a standard error message whenever the validation rule is violated. To display a custom message, you must enter your message text in the Validation Text property.

TRY IT   Add the following validation rules to the fields in your table (Access will place quotes around the state abbreviations as soon as you tab away from the property):

State: `In (CA, AZ, NY, MA, UT)`

ContactDate: `<= Date()`

CreditLimit: `Between 0 And 5000`

1. Switch to Datasheet view. If the table already contains data, when you save your changes the message shown in Figure 2.7 appears.

FIGURE 2.7

The message box asking whether you want to validate existing data.

If you select Yes, Access tries to validate all existing data using the new rules. If any errors are found, you're notified that errors occurred, but you aren't informed of the offending records. (See Figure 2.8.) You have to build a query to find all the records violating the new rules.

FIGURE 2.8

A warning that all data did not validate successfully.

If you select No, Access doesn't try to validate your existing data, and you aren't warned of any problems.

2. After you have entered Datasheet view, try to enter an invalid state in the State field; you should see the message box displayed in Figure 2.9. As you can see, this isn't the most friendly message, which is why you should create a custom message by using the Validation Text property.

FIGURE 2.9

The message displayed when a validation rule is violated and no validation text has been entered.

TIP

Validation rules entered at a table level are automatically applied to forms and queries built from the table. This occurs whether the rule was entered before or after the query or form was built. If you create a validation rule for a field, Access won't allow Null values to be entered in the field, which means the field can't be left blank. If you want to allow the field to be left Null, you must add the Null to the validation expression:

```
In (CA, AZ, NY, MA, UT) or Is Null
```

Validation Text: Providing Error Messages to the User

Use the Validation Text property to specify the error message users see when they violate the validation rule. The Validation Text property must contain text; expressions aren't valid in this property.

TRY IT — Add the following to the Validation Text properties of the State, ContactDate, and CreditLimit fields:

State: `The State Must Be CA, AZ, NY, MA, or UT`

ContactDate: `The Contact Date Must Be On or Before Today`

CreditLimit: `The Credit Limit Must Be Between 0 and 5000`

Try entering invalid values for each of the three fields, and observe the error messages.

Required: Make the User Enter a Value

The Required property is very important—it determines whether you require that a value be entered into the field. This property is useful for foreign key fields, when you want to make sure data is entered into the field. It's also useful for any field containing information that's needed for business reasons (company name, for example).

> **NOTE**
>
> A foreign key field is a field that is looked up in another table. For example, in the case of a Customers table and an Orders table, both might contain a CustomerID field. In the Customers table the CustomerID is the primary key field. In the Orders table, the CustomerID is the foreign key field because its value is looked up in the Customer table.

TRY IT — Set the Required property of the CompanyName and PhoneNumber fields to `Yes`. Switch to Datasheet view and try to add a new record, leaving the CompanyName and PhoneNumber fields blank. Make sure you enter a value for at least one of the other fields in the record. When you try to move off the record, the error message shown in Figure 2.10 appears.

FIGURE 2.10

A message appears when you leave a field blank with the Required property set to Yes.

Allow Zero Length: Accommodate Situations with Nonexistent Data

The Allow Zero Length property is similar to the Required property. Use it to determine whether you allow the user to enter a zero-length string (""). A zero-length string isn't the same as a Null (absence of an entry); it indicates that the data doesn't exist for that particular field. For example, a foreign employee might not have a social security number. By entering a zero-length string, the data-entry person can indicate that the social security number doesn't exist.

TRY IT Add a new field called ContactName and set its Required property to Yes. Try to add a new record and enter two quotes ("") in the ContactName field. You should get the error message shown in Figure 2.11. Return to the design of the table. Change the Allow Zero Length Property to Yes; then go to Datasheet view and try to enter two quotes in the ContactName field. This time you should be successful. Your zero-length string will appear blank when you move off the field.

FIGURE 2.11

The result of entering "" when the Allow Zero Length property is set to No.

TIP

Don't forget that if you want to cancel changes to the current field, press Esc once. To abandon all changes to a record, press Esc twice.

TIP

The Required and Allow Zero Length properties interact with each other. If the Required property is set to Yes and the Allow Zero Length property is set to No, you're being as strict as possible with your users. Not only must they enter a value, but also that value can't be a zero-length string.

If the Required property is set to Yes and the Allow Zero Length property is set to Yes, you're requiring users to enter a value, but that value can be a zero-length string. However, if the Required property is set to No and the Allow Zero Length property is set to No, you're allowing users to leave the field Null (blank), but not allowing them to enter a zero-length string.

Finally, if you set the Required property to No and the Allow Zero Length property to Yes, you're being the most lenient with your users. In this case, they can leave the field Null or enter a zero-length string.

Indexes: Speeding Up Searches

Indexes are used to improve performance when the user searches a field. Although it's generally best to include too many indexes rather than too few, indexes do have downsides (see the Tip following the example). A general rule is to provide indexes for all fields regularly used in searching, sorting, and as criteria for queries.

TRY IT Set the Indexed property of the CompanyName, ContactName, and State fields to Yes—(Duplicates OK). Click the Indexes button on the toolbar. Your screen should look like Figure 2.12.

FIGURE 2.12

The Indexes window shows you all the indexes defined for a table.

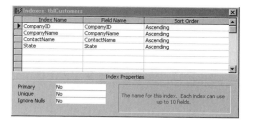

TIP

To create nonprimary-key multifield indexes, you must use the Indexes window; you create an index with one name and more than one field. See Figure 2.13, which shows an index called StateByCredit that's based on the combination of the CreditLimit and State fields. Notice that only the first field in the index has an index name. The second field, State, appears on the line below the first field but doesn't have an index name.

Indexes speed up searching, sorting, and grouping data. The downside is that they take up hard-disk space and slow down the process of editing, adding, and deleting data. Although the benefits of indexing outweigh the detriments in most cases, you should not index every field in each table. Create indexes only for fields, or combinations of fields, on which the user will search or sort. Do not create indexes for fields that contain highly repeated data, such as a field that can contain only two different values. Finally, never index Yes/No fields. They are only 1 bit in storage size and can take on only one of two values. For these reasons, indexes offer no benefits with Yes/No fields.

FIGURE 2.13

A multifield index called StateByCredit, based on a combination of the CreditLimit and State fields.

Unicode Compression

The final property is Unicode Compression. The Unicode Compression property applies to Text and Memo fields only. This property is used to designate whether or not you want the data in the field to be compressed using Unicode compression. Prior to Access 2000, data was stored in the DBCS format. The DBCS format was used to store character data for certain languages such as Chinese. With Access 2000, all character data is stored in the Unicode 2-byte representation format. Although this format requires more space for each character (2 bytes rather than 1 byte), the Unicode Compression property allows the data to be compressed if possible. If the character set being used allows compression, and the Unicode Compression property is set to Yes, the data in the column is stored in a compressed format.

THE ALL-IMPORTANT PRIMARY KEY

The most important index in a table is called the Primary Key index; it ensures uniqueness of the fields that make up the index and also gives the table a default order. You must set a primary key for the fields on the one side of a one-to-many relationship. To create a Primary Key index, select the fields you want to establish as the primary key, and then click the Primary Key button on the toolbar.

Figure 2.14 shows the tblCustomer table with a Primary Key index established based on the CompanyID field. Notice that the Index Name of the field designated as the Primary Key of the table is called PrimaryKey. Note that the Primary and Unique properties for this index are both set to True.

FIGURE 2.14

A Primary Key index based on the CompanyID field.

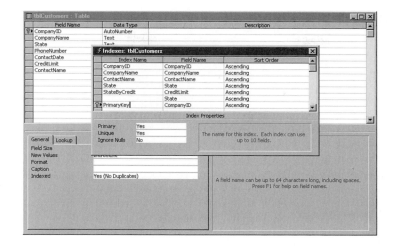

WORKING WITH THE LOOKUP FEATURE

Using the Lookup Wizard, you can instruct a field to look up its values in another table or query or from a fixed list of values. You can also display the list of valid values in a combo or list box. A lookup is generally created from the foreign key (many side) to the primary key (one side) of a one-to-many relationship.

The Lookup Wizard can be invoked by selecting Lookup Wizard from the list of data types for the field. The first dialog box of the wizard asks whether you want to look up the values in a table or query or whether you want to input the values. I recommend that you always look up the values in a table or query; this makes your application easy to maintain. The second dialog box asks you to indicate the table or query used to look up the values. Select a table or query and click Next to open the third dialog box. This step of the Lookup Wizard asks you which field in the table or query will be used for the lookup. The fourth step of the Lookup Wizard, shown in Figure 2.15, gives you the opportunity to control the width of the columns in your combo or list box.

FIGURE 2.15

In the fourth step of the Lookup Wizard, you adjust the column widths.

TIP

To work through the previous example, it is best that you use the Chap2.MDB sample database file. All the lookup tables have already been added to the sample database.

NOTE

If you select more than one field for your lookup and one is a key column, such as an ID, the Hide Key Column check box appears. You should leave this checked; it automatically hides the key column in the lookup, even though the end result will be bound to the key field.

Finally, the wizard lets you specify a title for your combo box. When you click Finish, you will be prompted to save the table and all the appropriate properties are filled in by the wizard; they appear on the Lookup tab of the field. (See Figure 2.16.) The Display Control property is set to Combo Box, indicating that a combo box is used to display the valid values. This occurs whether the user is in Datasheet view or in a form. The Row Source Type indicates that the source for the combo box is a table or query and shows the actual SQL Select statement used to populate the combo box. Other properties show which column in the combo box is bound to data, how many columns are in the combo box, the width of the combo box, and the width of each column in the combo box. These properties are covered in more detail in Chapter 5, "What Every Developer Needs to Know About Forms." You can modify the SQL statement for the combo box later, if necessary.

FIGURE 2.16

*The field proper-
ties set by the
Lookup Wizard.*

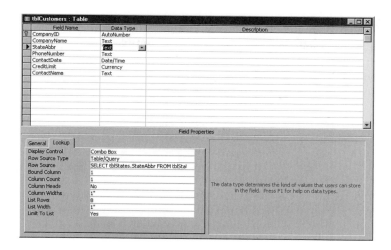

WORKING WITH TABLE PROPERTIES

In addition to field properties, you can specify properties that apply to the table as a whole. To
access the table properties, click the Properties button on the toolbar while in a table's Design
view. The available table properties are shown in Figure 2.17. The Description property is used
mainly for documentation purposes. The Validation Rule property is used to specify validations
that must occur at a record level rather than a field level. For example, credit limits might differ depending on what state a customer is in. In that case, what's entered in one field depends
on the value in another field. By entering a table-level validation rule, it doesn't matter in what
order the user enters the data. A table-level validation rule ensures that the proper dependency
between fields is enforced. The validation rule might look something like this:

```
[State] In ("CA","NY") And [CreditLimit]<=2500 Or _
    [State] In ("MA","AZ") And [CreditLimit]<=3500 Or _
    [State] Not In ("CA", "NY", "MA", "AZ")
```

This validation rule requires a credit limit of $2,500 or less for California and New York and a
limit of $3,500 or less for Massachusetts and Arizona, but it doesn't specify a credit limit for
any other states. Table-level validation rules can't be in conflict with field-level validation
rules.

The Validation Text property determines the message that appears when the user violates the
validation rule. If it's left blank, a default message appears.

FIGURE 2.17

Viewing the available table properties.

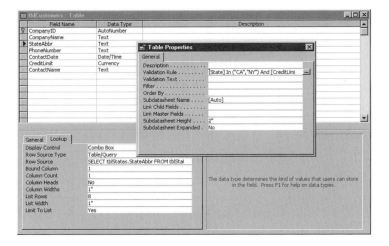

The Filter property is used to indicate a subset of records that appears in a datasheet, form, or query. The Order By property is used to specify a default order for the records. The Filter and Order By properties aren't generally applied as properties of a table.

The Subdatasheet Name property identifies the name of a table used as a drill-down. If set to Auto, the drill-down table is automatically detected based on relationships established in the database. The Link Child Fields and Link Master Fields properties are implemented to designate the fields, which are used to link the current table with the table specified in the Subdatasheet Name property. These properties should be left blank when Auto is selected for the Subdatasheet Name. The Subdatasheet Height is used to specify the maximum height of the subdatasheet, and the Subdatasheet Expanded property is used to designate whether the subdatasheet is automatically displayed in an expanded state.

USING INDEXES TO IMPROVE PERFORMANCE

As previously mentioned, indexes can help you improve your application's performance. You should create indexes on any fields you sort, group, join, or set criteria for, unless those fields contain highly repeated data. Queries can greatly benefit from indexes, especially when indexes are created for fields included in your criteria, fields used to order the query, and fields used to join two tables that are not permanently related but are joined in a query. In fact, you should always create indexes for fields on both sides of a join. If your users are using the Find dialog box, indexes can help reduce the search time. Remember, the downsides to indexes are the disk space they require and the amount of time it takes to update them when adding, deleting, and updating records. You should always perform benchmarks with your own application, but you will probably find indexes helpful in many situations.

ACCESS TABLES AND THE INTERNET

Microsoft has made it easier to develop Internet-aware applications by adding a Hyperlink field type and by allowing users to save table data as HTML. The Hyperlink field type lets your users easily store UNC or URL addresses within their tables. The ability to save table data as HTML makes it easy for you or your users to publish table data on an Internet or intranet site. These features are covered in the following sections.

The Hyperlink Field Type

By using the Hyperlink field type, your users can store a different UNC or URL address for each record in the table. Although a UNC or URL address can be typed directly into a field, it's much easier to enter the address by using the Insert Hyperlink dialog box. (See Figure 2.18.) Here, users can graphically browse hyperlink addresses and subaddresses, and the address is entered automatically when they exit the dialog box. To invoke the Insert Hyperlink dialog box, choose Insert | Hyperlink with the cursor placed in the Hyperlink field, or click the Insert Hyperlink button.

FIGURE 2.18

With the Insert Hyperlink dialog box, users can select or create a Hyperlink object for the field.

The Text to Display text box is used to enter the text the user will see when viewing the field data in datasheet view, in a form, or on a report. The hyperlink can be to any of the following:

- An existing file or Web page
- Another object in the current database
- A new data access page
- An email address

To select an existing file or Web page, click the appropriate Link To icon and either type the file or Web page name or select it from the list of Recent Files, Browsed Pages, or Inserted Links. The File button is used to browse for an existing file, and the Web Page button is used to browse for an existing Web page.

To link to an object in the current database, click the appropriate Link To icon. Click a plus (+) sign to expand the list of tables, queries, forms, reports, pages, macros, or modules. Then click the database object to which you want to link.

To link to a new data access page that you create, click the appropriate Link To icon. Enter the name of the new page and designate whether you want to edit the new page now or later.

To designate an email address you want to link to, click the appropriate Link To icon. Enter the email address and subject, or select from the list of recently used email addresses.

After all the required information has been entered, the link is established and the hyperlink is entered in the field. If a UNC was entered, clicking the hyperlink invokes the application associated with the file. The selected file is opened, and the user is placed in the part of the document designated in the subaddress. If a URL is entered, and the user is logged onto the Internet or connected to his or her company's intranet, the user is taken directly to the designated page. If the user isn't currently connected to the Internet or an intranet, the Connect To dialog appears, allowing him or her to log on to the appropriate network.

Saving Table Data as HTML

Table data can be easily saved as HTML so that it can be published on an Internet or intranet site. You can save a file as HTML by using the File | Export menu item. The steps are as follows:

1. Choose File | Export.
2. Select HTML Documents (*.html; *.htm) from the Save as Type combo box.
3. Select a name and location for the .HTM file and click Save. Saving a file as HTML with this procedure does not load the browser.

Figure 2.19 shows you how your published Access table might look, and Figure 2.20 displays the underlying HTML that can be edited by using any HTML editor.

FIGURE 2.19

Viewing an HTML document in Internet Explorer after a table was saved as HTML (note the ugly gaps for fields lacking data).

FIGURE 2.20

Viewing HTML generated when a table is saved as HTML.

> **NOTE**
>
> Building applications for the Internet is covered extensively in Chapters 31, "Access and the Internet," and 32, "Using Data Access Pages."

PRACTICAL EXAMPLES

Designing the Tables Needed for the Computer Consulting Firm's Time and Billing Application

Now create a new database and try designing a few of the tables needed by the computer consulting firm's Time and Billing application. You will build tblClients and tblProjects; tblClients is the main table for the application. It will be used to track the key information about each client. The second table, tblProjects, will be used to hold all the key information users need to store on the projects they're working on for each client. Table 2.2 shows the field names, data types, and sizes for each field in tblClients. You should include indexes for all fields except Notes. Table 2.3 shows the properties that need to be set for these fields. Table 2.4 shows the fields, data types, and sizes for the fields in tblProjects, and Table 2.5 shows the properties that need to be set for these fields. You should include indexes for all fields except ProjectDescription.

TABLE 2.2   FIELD NAMES, DATA TYPES, AND SIZES FOR THE FIELDS IN TBLCLIENTS

Field Name	Data Type	Size
ClientID	AutoNumber	Long integer (stored as 4)
CompanyName	Text	50
Address	Text	255
City	Text	30
StateProvince	Text	20
PostalCode	Text	20
Country	Text	20
ContactFirstName	Text	30
ContactLastName	Text	50
ContactTitle	Text	50
OfficePhone	Text	30
Fax	Text	30

Field Name	Data Type	Size
Cellular	Text	30
Home	Text	30
EMailAddress	Text	30
ReferredBy	Text	30
AssociatedWith	Text	30
IntroDate	Date/Time	Stored as 8
DefaultRate	Currency	Stored as 8
Notes	Memo	-
HomePage	Hyperlink	-

TABLE 2.3 PROPERTIES THAT NEED TO BE SET FOR THE FIELDS IN TBLCLIENTS

Field Name	Property	Value
ClientID	Caption	Client ID
ClientID	Set as primary key	
CompanyName	Caption	Company Name
CompanyName	Required	Yes
StateProvince	Caption	State/Province
StateProvince	DefaultValue	CA
StateProvince	Input Mask	>LL (if only U.S. data will be entered)
PostalCode	Caption	Postal Code
PostalCode	Input Mask	00000-9999;;_ (if only U.S. data will be entered)
ContactFirstName	Caption	Contact First Name
ContactLastName	Caption	Contact Last Name
ContactTitle	Caption	Contact Title
OfficePhone	Caption	Office Phone
OfficePhone	Input Mask	!\(999\)000\-0000
Fax	Input Mask	!\(999\)000\-0000
Cellular	Input Mask	!\(999\)000\-0000
Home	Input Mask	!\(999\)000\-0000

continues

TABLE 2.3 CONTINUED

Field Name	Property	Value
EMailAddress	Caption	Email Address
ReferredBy	Caption	Referred By
AssociatedWith	Caption	Associated With
IntroDate	Caption	Intro Date
IntroDate	Default Value	=Date()
IntroDate	Validation Rule	<=Date()
IntroDate	Validation Text	Date Entered Must Be On Or Before Today
IntroDate	Required	Yes
DefaultRate	Caption	Default Rate
DefaultRate	Default Value	125
DefaultRate	Validation Rule	Between 75 and 150
DefaultRate	Validation Text	Rate Must Be Between 75 and 150
DefaultRate	Format	Currency
HomePage	Caption	Home Page

TABLE 2.4 FIELD NAMES, DATA TYPES, AND SIZES FOR THE FIELDS IN TBLPROJECTS

Field Name	Data Type	Size
ProjectID	AutoNumber	Long integer (stored as 4)
ProjectName	Text	50
ProjectDescription	Memo	-
ClientID	Number	Long integer (stored as 4)
PurchaseOrderNumber	Text	30
ProjectTotalEstimate	Currency	8
EmployeeID	Number	Long integer (stored as 4)
ProjectBeginDate	Date/Time	Stored as 8
ProjectEndDate	Date/Time	Stored as 8

TABLE 2.5   PROPERTIES THAT NEED TO BE SET FOR THE FIELDS IN TBLPROJECTS

Field Name	Property	Value
ProjectID	Caption	Project ID
ProjectID	Set as primary key	
ProjectName	Caption	Project Name
ProjectName	Required	Yes
ProjectDescription	Caption	Project Description
ClientID	Caption	Client ID
ClientID	Set lookup to ClientID in tblClients	
ClientID	Required	Yes
PurchaseOrderNumber	Caption	Purchase Order Number
ProjectTotalEstimate	Caption	Project Total Estimate
ProjectTotalEstimate	Format	Currency
EmployeeID	Caption	Employee ID
ProjectBeginDate	Caption	Project Begin Date
ProjectEndDate	Caption	Project End Date

The rest of the tables needed by the Time and Billing application are listed in Appendix A, "Table Structures." The finished table structures can be found in CHAP2.MDB; this file, and all files referred to in this book, can be found on the book's sample code CD-ROM.

SUMMARY

Tables are the foundation for your application. A poorly designed table structure can render an otherwise well-designed application useless. This chapter begins by walking you through several methods for creating tables. It then discusses theoretical issues, such as selecting the correct field type and effectively using field properties. Each property, and its intended use, is discussed in detail. Finally, table properties and indexes are covered. After reading this chapter, you should be ready to harness the many features the Access table designer has to offer.

2

WHAT YOU NEED
TO KNOW ABOUT
TABLES

RELATIONSHIPS: YOUR KEY TO DATA INTEGRITY

IN THIS CHAPTER

A relationship exists between two tables when a key field(s) from one table is matched to a key field(s) in another table. The fields in both tables usually have the same name, data type, and size. Relationships are a necessary by-product of the data normalization process. Data normalization is covered in Chapter 1, "Access as a Development Tool;" it is the process of eliminating duplicate information from your system by splitting information into several tables, each containing a unique value (primary key). Although data normalization brings many benefits, you need to relate the tables in your system so that your users can view the data in the system as a single entity. After you define relationships between tables, you can build queries, forms, reports, and data access pages that combine information from multiple tables. In this way, you can reap all the benefits of data normalization while ensuring that your system provides users with all the information they need.

EXAMINING THE TYPES OF RELATIONSHIPS

Three types of relationships can exist between tables in a database: one-to-many, one-to-one, and many-to-many. Setting up the proper type of relationship between two tables in your database is imperative. The right type of relationship between two tables ensures

- Data integrity
- Optimal performance
- Ease of use in designing system objects

The reasons behind these benefits are covered throughout this chapter. Before you can understand the benefits of relationships, though, you must understand the types of relationships available.

One-to-Many

A one-to-many relationship is by far the most common type of relationship. In a *one-to-many relationship*, a record in one table can have many related records in another table. A common example is a relationship set up between a Customers table and an Orders table. For each customer in the Customers table, you want to have more than one order in the Orders table. On the other hand, each order in the Orders table can belong to only one customer. The Customers table is on the *one side* of the relationship, and the Orders table is on the *many side*. In order for this relationship to be implemented, the field joining the two tables on the one side of the relationship must be unique. In the Customers and Orders tables example, the CustomerID field that joins the two tables must be unique within the Customers table. If more than one customer in the Customers table has the same customer ID, it is not clear which customer belongs to an order in the Orders table. For this reason, the field that joins the two tables on the one side of the one-to-many relationship must be a primary key or have a unique index. In almost all cases, the field relating the two tables is the primary key of the table on the one side of the relationship. The field relating the two tables on the many side of the relationship is called a *foreign key*.

One-to-One

In a one-to-one relationship, each record in the table on the one side of the relationship can have only one matching record in the table on the many side of the relationship. This relationship is not common and is used only in special circumstances. Usually, if you have set up a one-to-one relationship, you should have combined the fields from both tables into one table. The following are the most common reasons why you should create a one-to-one relationship:

- The amount of fields required for a table exceeds the number of fields allowed in an Access table.
- Certain fields that are included in a table need to be much more secure than other fields included in the same table.
- Several fields in a table are required for only a subset of records in the table.

The maximum number of fields allowed in an Access table is 255. There are very few reasons why a table should ever have more than 255 fields. In fact, before you even get close to 255 fields, you should take a close look at the design of your system. On the rare occasion when having more than 255 fields is appropriate, you can simulate a single table by moving some of the fields to a second table and creating a one-to-one relationship between the two tables.

The second reason to separate into two tables data that logically would belong in the same table involves security. An example is a table containing employee information. Certain information, such as employee name, address, city, state, zip code, home phone, and office extension, might need to be accessible by many users of the system. Other fields, including the hire date, salary, birth date, and salary level, might be highly confidential. Field-level security is not available in Access. You can simulate field-level security by using a special attribute of queries called *Run with Owner's permissions*. This feature is covered in Chapter 11, "Advanced Query Techniques." The alternative to this method is to place all the fields that can be accessed by all users in one table and the highly confidential fields in another. Only a special Admin user (a user with special security privileges, not one actually named Admin) is given access to the table containing the confidential fields. *Data Access Objects* (DAO) code is used to display the fields in the highly confidential table when needed. This is done using a query with Run with Owner's permissions, based on the special Admin user's permission to the highly secured table. This technique is covered in Chapter 34, "Advanced Security Techniques."

The last reason to define one-to-one relationships is when certain fields in a table are going to be used for only a relatively small subset of records. An example is an Employee table and a

3

RELATIONSHIPS: YOUR KEY TO DATA INTEGRITY

Vesting table. Certain fields are required only for employees who are vested. If only a small percentage of the company's employees are vested, it is not efficient, in terms of performance or disk space, to place all the fields containing information about vesting in the Employee table. This is especially true if the vesting information requires a large volume of fields. By breaking the information into two tables and creating a one-to-one relationship between them, you can reduce disk-space requirements and improve performance. This improvement is particularly pronounced if the Employee table is large.

Many-to-Many

In a *many-to-many relationship*, records in both tables have matching records in the other table. A many-to-many relationship cannot be directly defined in Access; you must develop this type of relationship by adding a table called a *junction table*. The junction table is related to each of the two tables as one-to-many relationships. An example is an Orders table and a Products table. Each order probably will contain multiple products, and each product is found on many different orders. The solution is to create a third table called Order Details. The Order Details table is related to the Orders table in a one-to-many relationship based on the OrderID field. It is related to the Products table in a one-to-many relationship based on the ProductID field.

ESTABLISHING RELATIONSHIPS

Relationships between Access tables are established in the Relationships window, as shown in Figure 3.1. To open the Relationships window, click Relationships on the toolbar with the Database window active or choose Relationships from the Tools menu. If no relationships have been established, the Show Table dialog appears. The Show Table dialog allows you to add tables to the Relationships window. Looking at the Relationships window, you can see the type of relationship that exists for each table. All the one-to-many and one-to-one relationships defined in a database are represented with a join line. If referential integrity has been enforced between the tables involved in a one-to-many relationship, the join line between the tables appears with the number *1* on the one side of the relationship and with an infinity symbol on the many side of the relationship. One-to-one relationships appear with a 1 on both ends of the join line.

FIGURE 3.1

The Relationships window enables you to view, add, modify, and remove relationships between tables

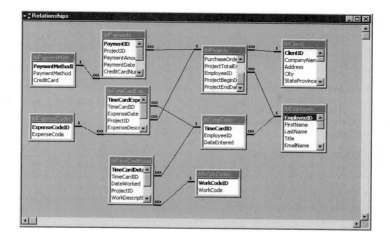

Establishing a Relationship Between Two Tables

To establish a relationship between two tables, follow these six steps:

1. Open the Relationships window.

2. If you have never opened the Relationships window of a particular database, the Show Table dialog box appears. Select each table you want to relate and click Add.

3. If you have already established relationships in the current database, the Relationships window appears. If the tables you want to include in the relationship do not appear, click the Show Table button on the toolbar or choose Show Table from the Relationships menu. To add the desired tables to the Relationships window, click to select a table, and then click Add. Repeat this process for each table you want to add. To select multiple tables at once, press Shift while clicking to select contiguous tables or press Ctrl while clicking to select noncontiguous tables; then click Add. Click Close when you are done.

4. Click and drag the field from one table to the matching field in the other table. The Edit Relationships dialog box appears, as shown in Figure 3.2.

FIGURE 3.2

The Edit Relationships dialog box enables you to view and modify the relationships between the tables in a database.

5. Determine whether you want to establish referential integrity, and whether you want to cascade update related fields or cascade delete related records by enabling the appropriate check boxes. These topics are covered in the section, "Establishing Referential Integrity."

6. Click Create.

Looking at Guidelines for Establishing Relationships

You must remember a few important things when establishing relationships. If you are not aware of these important gotchas, you could find yourself in some pretty hairy situations.

- It is important to understand the correlation between the Relationships window and the actual relationships you have established within the database. The Relationships window lets you view and modify the existing relationships. When you establish relationships, the actual relationship is created the moment you click Create. You can delete the tables from the Relationships window (by selecting them and pressing Delete), but the relationships still will exist (permanently removing relationships is covered in the "Modifying an Existing Relationship" section of this chapter). The Relationships window provides a visual blueprint of the relationships that have been established. If you modify the layout of the window by moving around tables, adding tables to the window, or removing tables from the window, you are prompted to save the layout after you close the Relationships window. Access is not asking whether you want to save the relationships you have established; it is simply asking whether you want to save the visual layout of the window.

- When adding tables to the Relationships window using the Show Tables dialog box, it is easy to accidentally add the same table to the window many times. This is because the tables you are adding can hide behind the Show Tables dialog box, or they can appear below the portion of the Relationships window you are viewing. If this occurs, you'll see multiple occurrences of the same table when you close the Show Tables dialog box. Each occurrence of the table is given a different alias. You must remove the extra occurrences.

- You also can add queries to the Relationships window by using the Show Tables dialog box. Although rarely used, this might be useful if you regularly include the same queries within other queries and want to permanently establish a relationship between them.

- If you remove tables from the Relationships window (this does not delete the relationships) and you want to once again show all relationships that exist in the database, click Show All Relationships on the toolbar or choose Show All from the Relationships menu. This button shows all existing relationships.

- To delete a relationship, click the join line and press Delete.

TRY IT Create a new database and add a table called tblCustomers, another called tblOrders, and another called tblOrderDetails. Each table should have the following fields:

> tblCustomers: CustomerID, CompanyName, Address, City, State, ZipCode
>
> tblOrders: OrderID, CustomerID, OrderDate, ShipVIA
>
> tblOrderDetails: OrderID, LineNumber, ItemID, Quantity, Price

1. In the tblCustomers table, set the CustomerID field as the primary key. Set the size of the field to 5. All other fields can be left with their default properties.

2. In the tblOrders table, set OrderID to the AutoNumber field type. Make the OrderID the primary key field. Set the length of the CustomerID field to 5. Set the field type of the OrderDate field to Date.

3. In the tblOrderDetails table, set the field type of the OrderID field to Number and make sure that the size is Long Integer. Set the type of the LineNumber field to Number with a size of Long Integer. The primary key of the table should be based on the combination of the OrderID and LineNumber fields. The ItemID and Quantity fields should be Number type with a size of Long Integer. The Price field should be Currency type.

4. To open the Relationships window, click Relationships on the toolbar with the Database window active. With the tblCustomers table in the Show Table dialog box selected, hold down your Shift key and click to select the tblOrders table. Click Add. All three tables should be added to the Relationships window. Click Close. Click and drag from the CustomerID field in the tblCustomers table to the CustomerID field in the tblOrders table. After the Relationships dialog box appears, click Create. Repeat the process, clicking and dragging the OrderID field from the tblOrders table to the OrderID field in the tblOrderDetails table.

NOTE

 You can find this example, and all examples included in this chapter, in the Chap3TryIt.MDB file included with the sample code on the accompanying CD-ROM.

Modifying an Existing Relationship

Modifying an existing relationship is easy. Access gives you the capability to delete an existing relationship or to simply modify the nature of the relationship. To permanently remove a relationship between two tables, follow these three steps:

1. With the Database window active, click Relationships on the toolbar.

2. Click the line joining the two tables whose relationship you want to delete.

3. Press Delete. You are asked to verify your actions. Click Yes.

You often will want to modify the nature of a relationship rather than remove it. To modify a relationship, follow these four steps:

1. With the Database window active, click Relationships on the toolbar.

2. Double-click on the line joining the two tables whose relationship you want to modify.

3. Make the required changes.

4. Click OK. All the normal rules regarding the establishment of relationships will apply.

ESTABLISHING REFERENTIAL INTEGRITY

As you can see, establishing a relationship is quite easy. Establishing the right kind of relationship is a little more difficult. When you attempt to establish a relationship between two tables, Access makes some decisions based on a few predefined factors:

- A one-to-many relationship is established if one of the related fields is a primary key or has a unique index.

- A one-to-one relationship is established if both the related fields are primary keys or have unique indexes.

- An indeterminate relationship is created if neither of the related fields is a primary key and neither has a unique index. Referential integrity cannot be established in this case.

Referential integrity consists of a series of rules that are applied by the Jet Engine to ensure that the relationships between tables are maintained properly. At the most basic level, referential integrity rules prevent the creation of orphan records in the table on the many side of the one-to-many relationship. After establishing a relationship between a Customers table and an Orders table, for example, all orders in the Orders table must be related to a particular customer in the Customers table. Before you can establish referential integrity between two tables, the following conditions must be met:

- The matching field on the one side of the relationship must be a Primary Key field or must have a unique index.

- The matching fields must have the same data types (for linking purposes, AutoNumber fields match Long Integer fields). With the exception of Text fields, they also must have the same size. Number fields on both sides of the relationship must have the same size (Long Integer, for example).

- Both tables must be part of the same Access database.

- Both tables must be stored in the proprietary Access file (.MDB) format (they cannot be external tables from other sources).

- The database containing the two tables must be open.

- Existing data within the two tables cannot violate any referential integrity rules. All orders in the Orders table must relate to existing customers in the Customers table, for example.

CAUTION

Although Text fields involved in a relationship do not have to be the same size, it is prudent to make them the same size. Otherwise, you will degrade performance as well as risk the chance of unpredictable results when creating queries based on the two tables.

After referential integrity is established between two tables, the following rules are applied:

- You cannot enter a value in the foreign key of the related table that does not exist in the primary key of the primary table. For example, you cannot enter a value in the CustomerID field of the Orders table that does not exist in the CustomerID field of the Customers table.

- You cannot delete a record from the primary table if corresponding records exist in the related table. For example, you cannot delete a customer from the Customers table, if related records exist in the Orders table (records with the same value in the CustomerID field).

- You cannot change the value of a primary key on the one side of a relationship if corresponding records exist in the related table. For example, you cannot change the value in the CustomerID field of the Customers table if corresponding orders exist in the Orders table.

If any of the previous three rules are violated and referential integrity is being enforced between the tables, an appropriate error message is displayed, as shown in Figure 3.3.

FIGURE 3.3

An error message when attempting to add an order for a customer who doesn't exist.

3

**RELATIONSHIPS:
YOUR KEY TO
DATA INTEGRITY**

Access's default behavior is to prohibit the deletion of parent records that have associated child records and to prohibit the change of a primary key value of a parent record when that parent has associated child records. You can override these restrictions by using the two check boxes available in the Relationships dialog box when you establish or modify a relationship.

TRY IT

1. To open the Relationships window, select the Database window and click Relationships on the toolbar. Double-click on the join line between tblCustomers and tblOrders. Enable the Enforce Referential Integrity check box. Click OK. Repeat the process for the relationship between tblOrders and tblOrderDetails.

2. Go into tblCustomer and add a couple of records. Take note of the CustomerIDs. Go into tblOrders. Add a couple of records, taking care to assign customer IDs of customers that exist in the tblCustomers table. Now try to add an order for a customer whose customer ID does not exist in tblCustomers. You should get an error message.

3. Attempt to delete a customer from tblCustomers who does not have any orders. You should get a warning message, but you should be allowed to complete the process. Now try to delete a customer who does have orders. You should be prohibited from deleting the customer. Attempt to change the customer ID of a customer who has orders. You should not be able to do this.

Cascade Update Related Fields

The Cascade Update Related Fields option is available only if referential integrity has been established between the tables. With this option selected, the user is not prohibited from changing the primary key value of the record on the one side of the relationship. Instead, when an attempt is made to modify the field joining the two tables on the one side of the relationship, the change is cascaded down to the Foreign Key field on the many side of the relationship.

NOTE

There is no need to select the Cascade Update Related Fields option when the related field on the one side of the relationship is an AutoNumber field. An AutoNumber field can never be modified. The Cascade Update Related Fields option has no effect on AutoNumber fields.

> **CAUTION**
>
> It is very easy to accidentally introduce a loophole into your system. If you create a one-to-many relationship between two tables but forget to set the Required property of the Foreign Key field to Yes, you allow the addition of orphan records. Figure 3.4 illustrates this point. An order was added to tblOrders without a customer ID being entered. This record is an orphan record because no records in tblCustomers have a customer ID of Null. The problem is eliminated by setting the Required property of the Foreign Key field to Yes.

FIGURE 3.4

An orphan record with Null in the Foreign Key field.

Cascade Delete Related Records

The Cascade Delete Related Records option is available only if referential integrity has been established between the tables. With this option selected, the user can delete a record on the one side of a one-to-many relationship, even if related records exist in the table on the many side of the relationship. A customer can be deleted even if the customer has existing orders, for example. Referential integrity is maintained between the tables because Access automatically deletes all related records in the child table.

If you attempt to delete a record from the table on the one side of a one-to-many relationship and no related records exist in the table on the many side of the relationship, you get the usual warning message, as shown in Figure 3.5. On the other hand, if you attempt to delete a record from the table on the one side of a one-to-many relationship and related records exist in the child table, you are warned that you are about to delete the record from the parent table as well as any related records in the child table (see Figure 3.6).

FIGURE 3.5

A message that appears after the user attempts to delete a parent record without related child records.

FIGURE 3.6

A message that appears after the user attempts to delete a parent record with related child records.

TIP

The Cascade Delete Related Records option is not always appropriate. It is an excellent feature, but you should use it prudently. Although it is usually appropriate to cascade delete from an Orders table to an Order Details table, for example, it generally is not appropriate to cascade delete from a Customers table to an Orders table. This is because you generally do not want all your order history deleted from the Orders table if for some reason you wanted to delete a customer. Deleting the order history causes important information, such as your profit and loss history, to change. It therefore is appropriate to prohibit this type of deletion and handle the customer in some other way, such as marking him as inactive. On the other hand, if you delete an order because it was canceled, you probably want the corresponding order detail information to be removed as well. In this case, the Cascade Delete Related Records option is appropriate. You need to make the appropriate decision in each situation, based on business needs. The important thing is to carefully consider the implications of each option before making your decision.

TRY IT

1. Modify the relationship between tblCustomers and tblOrders. Enable the Cascade Update Related Fields check box. Modify the relationship between tblOrders and tblOrderDetails. Enable the Cascade Delete Related Records check box. There is no need to enable Cascade Update Related Fields because the OrderID field in tblOrders is an AutoNumber field.

2. Attempt to delete a customer who has orders. You still should be prohibited from doing this because you did not enable Cascade Delete Related Records. Change the customer

ID in tblCustomers of a customer who has orders. This change should be allowed. Take a look at the tblOrders table. The customer ID of all corresponding records in the table now should be updated to reflect the change in the parent record.

3. Add some order details to the tblOrderDetails table. Try to delete any order that has details within the tblOrderDetails table. You should receive a warning, but you should be allowed to complete the process.

LOOKING AT THE BENEFITS OF RELATIONSHIPS

The primary benefit of relationships is the data integrity they provide. Without the establishment of relationships, users are free to add records to child tables without regard to entering required parent information. After referential integrity is established, you can enable Cascade Update Related Fields or Cascade Delete Related Records, as appropriate, which will save you quite a bit of code in maintaining the integrity of the data in your system. Most relational database management systems require that you write the code to delete related records when a parent record is deleted or to update the foreign key in related records when the primary key of the parent is modified. By enabling the Cascade Update and Cascade Delete check boxes, you are sheltered from having to write a single line of code to accomplish these common tasks.

Relationships automatically are carried into your queries. This means that each time you build a new query, the relationships between the tables within it automatically are established, based on the relationships you have set up in the Relationships window. Furthermore, each time you build a form or report, relationships between the tables included on the form or report are used to assist with the design process. Whether you delete or update data using a datasheet or a form, all referential integrity rules automatically apply, even if the relationship is established after the form is built.

EXAMINING INDEXES AND RELATIONSHIPS

The field that joins two tables on the one side of a one-to-many relationship must be a Primary Key field or must have a unique index so that referential integrity can be maintained. If the index on the one side of the relationship is not unique, there is no way to determine to which parent a child record belongs.

In Access 2000, it is not necessary to create an index for the field on the many side of the relationship. Access 2000 will create an internal index for you. If you do create an index on the many side of the relationship, make sure that you set the index to Yes (Duplicates OK); otherwise, you will have a one-to-one rather than a one-to-many relationship.

PRACTICAL EXAMPLES

Establishing the Relationships Between the Tables Included in the Time and Billing Database

In this example, you'll establish the relationships you need to set up for the tables included in the time and billing database. If you would like to build the relationships yourself, open the database that you created in Chapter 2.

- tblClients to tblProjects—tblClients and tblProjects need to be related in a one-to-many relationship based on the ClientID field. You must enforce referential integrity to ensure that projects cannot be added for nonexistent clients. There is no need to set Cascade Update Related Fields because the client ID that relates the two tables is an AutoNumber field in tblClients. You do not want to enable Cascade Delete Related Records because you do not want any billing information to change if a client is deleted. Instead, you want to prohibit the deletion of clients who have projects by establishing referential integrity between the two tables.

- tblProjects to tblPayments—tblProjects and tblPayments need to be related in a one-to-many relationship based on the ProjectID field. You must enforce referential integrity to ensure that payments cannot be added for nonexistent projects. There is no need to set Cascade Update Related Fields because the ProjectID that relates the two tables is an AutoNumber field in tblProjects. You do not want to enable Cascade Delete Related Records because you do not want any payment information to change if a client is deleted. Prohibit the deletion of clients who have payments by establishing referential integrity between the two tables.

- tblProjects to tblTimeCardHours—tblProjects and tblTimeCardHours need to be related in a one-to-many relationship based on the ProjectID field. You must enforce referential integrity to ensure that hours cannot be added for nonexistent projects. There is no need to set Cascade Update Related Fields because the ProjectID that relates the two tables is an AutoNumber field in tblProjects. Enable Cascade Delete Related Records so that hours are deleted if a project is deleted.

- tblProjects to tblTimeCardExpenses—tblProjects and tblTimeCardExpenses need to be related in a one-to-many relationship based on the ProjectID field. You must enforce referential integrity to ensure that expenses cannot be added for nonexistent projects. There is no need to set Cascade Update Related Fields because the ProjectID that relates the two tables is an AutoNumber field in tblProjects. Enable Cascade Delete Related Records so that expenses are deleted if a project is deleted.

- tblEmployees to tblTimeCards—tblEmployees and tblTimeCards need to be related in a one-to-many relationship based on the EmployeeID field. You must enforce referential integrity to ensure that time cards cannot be added for nonexistent employees. There is no need to set Cascade Update Related Fields because the EmployeeID that relates the two tables is an AutoNumber field in tblEmployees. You do not want to enable Cascade Delete Related Records because if an employee is deleted, all the employee's time cards are deleted.

- tblEmployees to tblProjects—tblEmployees and tblProjects need to be related in a one-to-many relationship based on the EmployeeID field. You must enforce referential integrity to ensure that projects cannot be assigned to nonexistent employees. There is no need to set Cascade Update Related Fields because the employee ID that relates the two tables is an AutoNumber field in tblEmployees. You do not want to enable Cascade Delete Related Records because if an employee is deleted, all the employee's projects would be deleted, which is generally not desirable.

- tblTimeCards to tblTimeCardHours—tblTimeCards and tblTimeCardHours need to be related in a one-to-many relationship based on the TimeCardID field. You must enforce referential integrity to ensure that time card hours cannot be added for nonexistent time cards. There is no need to set Cascade Update Related Fields because the time card ID that relates the two tables is an AutoNumber field in tblTimeCards. You do want to enable Cascade Delete Related Records because if a time card is deleted, you want the corresponding hours to be deleted.

- tblTimeCards to tblTimeCardExpenses—tblTimeCards and tblTimeCardExpenses need to be related in a one-to-many relationship based on the TimeCardID field. You must enforce referential integrity to ensure that time card expenses cannot be added for nonexistent time cards. There is no need to set Cascade Update Related Fields because the time card ID that relates the two tables is an AutoNumber field in tblTimeCards. You do want to enable Cascade Delete Related Records because if a time card is deleted, you want the corresponding expenses to be deleted.

- tblExpenseCodes to tblTimeCardExpenses—tblExpenseCodes and tblTimeCardExpenses need to be related in a one-to-many relationship based on the ExpenseCodeID field. You must enforce referential integrity to ensure that time card expenses cannot be added with nonexistent expense codes. There is no need to set Cascade Update Related Fields because the expense code ID that relates the two tables is an AutoNumber field in tblExpenseCodes. You do not want to enable Cascade Delete Related Records because if an expense code is deleted, you do not want the corresponding expenses to be deleted.

- tblWorkCodes to tblTimeCardHours—tblWorkCodes and tblTimeCardHours need to be related in a one-to-many relationship based on the WorkCodeID field. You must enforce referential integrity to ensure that time card hours cannot be added with invalid work codes. There is no need to set Cascade Update Related Fields because the work code ID that relates the two tables is an AutoNumber field in tblWorkCodes. You do not want to enable Cascade Delete Related Records because if a work code is deleted, you do not want the corresponding hours to be deleted.

- tblPaymentMethods to tblPayments—tblPaymentMethods and tblPayments need to be related in a one-to-many relationship based on the PaymentMethodID field. You must enforce referential integrity to ensure that payments cannot be added with an invalid payment method. There is no need to set Cascade Update Related Fields because the PaymentMethodID that relates the two tables is an AutoNumber field in tblPaymentMethods. You do not want to enable Cascade Delete Related Records because if a payment method is deleted, you do not want the corresponding payments to be deleted.

SUMMARY

Relationships enable you to normalize your database. Using relationships, you can divide your data into separate tables, once again combining the data at runtime. This chapter begins by describing the types of relationships that can be defined. It then covers the details of establishing and modifying relationships between tables and describes all the important aspects of establishing relationships.

The capability to easily establish and maintain referential integrity between tables is an important strength of Microsoft Access. This chapter describes the referential integrity options and highlights when each option is appropriate. Finally, this chapter summarizes the benefits of relationships.

WHAT EVERY DEVELOPER NEEDS TO KNOW ABOUT QUERY BASICS

IN THIS CHAPTER

WHAT IS A QUERY AND WHEN SHOULD YOU USE ONE?

A *Select query* is a stored question about the data stored in your database's tables. Select queries are the foundation of much of what you do in Access. They underlie most of your forms and reports, allowing you to view the data you want, when you want. You use a simple Select query to define the tables and fields whose data you want to view and also to specify the criteria to limit the data the query's output displays. A Select query is simply a query of a table or tables that just displays data; it doesn't modify data in any way. More advanced Select queries are used to summarize data, supply the results of calculations, or cross tabulate your data. You can use Action queries to add, edit, or delete data from your tables, based on selected criteria, but this chapter covers Select queries. Other types of queries are covered in Chapter 11, "Advanced Query Techniques."

EVERYTHING YOU NEED TO KNOW ABOUT QUERY BASICS

Creating a basic query is easy because Microsoft has given us a user-friendly, drag-and-drop interface. There are three ways to start a new query in Access 2000. The first way is to select the Queries icon from the Objects list in the Database window; then double-click the Create Query in Design view icon or the Create Query by Using Wizard icon. (See Figure 4.1.) The second method is to select the Queries icon from the Objects list in the Database window and then click the New command button. The New Query dialog appears (see Figure 4.2). This dialog box lets you select whether you want to build the query from scratch or use one of the wizards to help you. The Simple Query Wizard walks you through the steps for creating a basic query. The other wizards help you create three specific types of queries: Crosstab, Find Duplicates, or Find Unmatched.

FIGURE 4.1

Select the Queries icon from the Objects list to create a query in Design view or to create one using a wizard.

Adding Tables to Your Queries

If you select Design View rather than one of the wizards, the Show Table dialog box appears.
(See Figure 4.3.) Here, you can select the tables or queries that supply data to your query.
Access doesn't care whether you select tables or queries as the foundation for your queries.
You can select them by double-clicking the name of the table or query you want to add or by
clicking the table and then clicking Add. You can select multiple tables or queries by using the
Shift key to select a contiguous range of tables or the Ctrl key to select noncontiguous tables.
When you have selected the tables or queries you want, click Add and then click Close. This
brings you to the Query Design window shown in Figure 4.4.

FIGURE 4.3

*Selecting Design
view displays the
Show Table dialog
that allows you to
select the tables
and queries on
which your query
is based.*

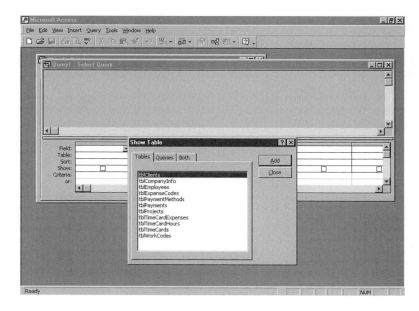

4

QUERY BASICS

FIGURE 4.4

The Query Design window is an easy-to-use (and learn) Query By Design grid.

TIP

An alternative to the method just described is to first select Tables from the Objects list in the Database window. Then select the table on which you want the query to be based. With the table selected, select New Query from the New Object drop-down list on the toolbar or choose Query from the Insert menu. This is an efficient method of starting a new query based on only one table because the Show Table dialog box never appears.

Adding Fields to Your Query

You're now ready to select the fields you want to include in the query. The query shown in Figure 4.4 is based on the tblClients table included in the CHAP4.MDB database on the sample code CD-ROM. Notice that the query window is divided into two sections. The top half of the window shows the tables or queries that underlie the query you're designing; the bottom half shows any fields that will be included in the query output. A field can be added to the query design grid on the bottom half of the query window in several ways:

- Double-click the name of the field you want to add.
- Click and drag a single field from the table in the top half of the query window to the query grid below.
- Select multiple fields at the same time by using your Shift key (for a contiguous range of fields) or your Ctrl key (a noncontiguous range). You can double-click the title bar of the field list to select all fields; then click and drag any one of the selected fields to the query grid.

TIP

You can double-click the asterisk to include all fields within the table in the query result. Although very handy in that changes to the table structure magically affect the query's output, I believe that this "trick" is dangerous. When the asterisk is selected, all table fields are included in the query result whether or not they are needed. This can cause major performance problems in a LAN, WAN, or client/server application.

TRY IT Open the Northwind database that comes with Access. If you want to prevent the Startup form from appearing, hold down your Shift key as you open the database. Click the Query icon and then click New. Select Design View from the New Query dialog. Add the Customers table to the query. Follow these steps to select the CustomerID, CompanyName, ContactName, ContactTitle, Region, and Phone fields from Customers:

1. Click the CustomerID field.

2. Hold down your Shift key and click the ContactTitle field. This should select the CustomerID, CompanyName, ContactName, and ContactTitle fields.

3. Scroll down the list of fields, using the vertical scrollbar, until the Region field is visible.

4. Hold down your Ctrl key and click the Region field.

5. With the Ctrl key still held down, click the Phone field. All six fields should now be selected.

Click and drag any of the selected fields from the table on the top half of the query window to the query grid on the bottom. All six fields should appear in the query grid. You might need to use the horizontal scrollbar to view some of the fields on the right.

TIP

The easiest way to run a query is to click the Run button on the toolbar (which looks like an exclamation point). You can click the Query View button to run a query, but this method works only for Select queries, not for Action queries. The Query View button has a special meaning for Action queries (explained in Chapter 11). Clicking Run is preferable because you don't have to worry about what type of query you're running. After running a Select query, you should see what looks like a datasheet, with only the fields you selected. To return to the query's design, click the Query View button.

4

QUERY BASICS

Removing a Field from the Query Grid

To remove a field from the query grid, follow these steps:

1. Find the field you want to remove.

2. Click the small horizontal gray button (column selector) immediately above the name of the field. The entire column of the query grid should become black. (See Figure 4.5.)

FIGURE 4.5

Removing a field from the query grid.

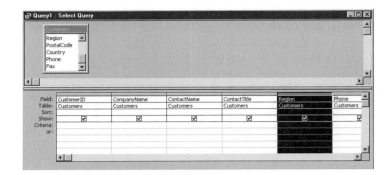

3. Press the Delete key or select Delete from the Edit menu.

TRY IT Assume that you have decided to remove the Region field from the query grid. Use the horizontal scrollbar to see the Region field on the query grid.

1. Click the column selector immediately above the Region field. The entire column of the query grid should become black, and the cursor turns into a downward-pointing arrow.

2. Press the Delete key to remove the Region field from the query grid.

Inserting a Field After the Query Is Built

The process for inserting a field after a query is built differs, depending on where you want the new field to be inserted. If you want the new field to be inserted after the existing fields, it's easiest to double-click the name of the field you want to add. If you prefer to insert the new field between two existing fields, it's best to click and drag the field you want to add, dropping it on the column you want to appear to the right of the inserted column.

TRY IT To insert the Country field between the ContactTitle and Phone fields, click and drag the Country field from the table until it's on top of the Phone field. This inserts the field in the correct place. To run the query, click Run on the toolbar.

Moving a Field to a Different Location on the Query Grid

Although the user can move a column while in a query's Datasheet view, sometimes you want to permanently alter the position of a field in the query output. This can be done as a convenience to the user or, more important, because you will use the query as a foundation for forms and reports. The order of the fields in the query becomes the default order of the fields on any forms and reports you build using any of the wizards. You can save yourself quite a bit of time by setting up your queries effectively.

To move a single column, follow these steps:

1. To select a column while in the query's Design view, click its column selector (the button immediately above the field name).

2. Click the selected column a second time; then drag it to a new location on the query grid.

Follow these steps to move more than one column at a time:

1. Drag across the column selectors of the columns you want to move.

2. Click any of the selected columns a second time; then drag them to a new location on the query grid.

TRY IT Move the ContactName and ContactTitle fields so that they appear before the CompanyName field. Do this by clicking and dragging from ContactName's column selector to ContactTitle's column selector. Both columns should be selected. Click again on the column selector for either column; then click and drag until the thick black line jumps to the left of the CompanyName field.

NOTE

Moving a column in the Datasheet view doesn't modify the query's underlying design. If you move a column in Datasheet view, subsequent reordering in the Design view isn't reflected in the Datasheet view. In other words, Design view and Datasheet view are no longer synchronized, and you must reorder both by hand. This actually serves as an advantage in most cases. As you will learn later, if you want to sort by the Country field and then by the CompanyName field, the Country field must appear to the left of the CompanyName field in the design of the query. If you want the CompanyName to appear to the left of the Country in the query's result, you make that change in Datasheet view. The fact that the order of the columns is maintained separately in both views allows you to easily accomplish both objectives.

4

QUERY BASICS

Saving and Naming Your Query

To save your query at any time, click the Save button on the toolbar. If the query is a new one, you're then prompted to name your query. Query names should begin with the tag *qry* so that you can easily recognize and identify them as queries. It's important to understand that when you save a query, you're saving only the query's definition, not the actual query result.

> **TRY IT** Return to the design of the query. To save your work, click Save on the toolbar. When prompted for a name, call the query qryCustomers.

ORDERING YOUR QUERY RESULT

When you run a new query, notice that the query output appears in no particular order, but generally, you want to order it. You can do this by using the Sort row of the query grid.

To order your query result, follow these steps:

1. Click within the query grid in the Sort cell of the column you want to sort. (See Figure 4.6.)

FIGURE 4.6

Changing the order of the query result.

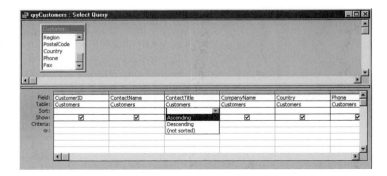

2. Use the drop-down combo box to select an ascending or descending sort.

> **TRY IT** To sort in ascending order by the ContactTitle field, follow these steps:

1. Click in the Sort row of the query grid for the ContactTitle field.
2. Open the Sort drop-down combo box.
3. Select Ascending.
4. Run your query and view the results. Your records should now be in order by the ContactTitle field.
5. If you want to return to the query's design, click View on the toolbar.

Sorting by More than One Field

Quite often you want to sort your query output by more than one field. The columns you want to sort must be placed in order from left to right on the query grid, with the column you want to act as the primary sort on the far left and the secondary, tertiary, and any additional sorts following to the right. If you want the columns to appear in a different order in the query output, they need to be moved manually in Datasheet view after the query is run.

| TRY | IT | Sort the query output by the Country field and, within country, by the ContactTitle field. Because sorting always occurs from left to right, you must place the Country field before the ContactTitle field. Therefore, you must move the Country field. Follow these steps:

1. Select the Country field from the query grid by clicking the thin gray button above the Country column.
2. After you have selected the Country field, move your mouse back to the thin gray button and click and drag to the left of ContactTitle. A thick gray line should appear to the left of the ContactTitle field.
3. Release the mouse button.
4. Change the sort of the Country field to Ascending.
5. Run the query. The records should be in order by country and, within country, by contact title.

REFINING YOUR QUERY WITH CRITERIA

So far, you have learned how to select the fields you want and how to indicate the sort order for your query output. One of the important features of queries is the ability to limit your output by selection criteria. Access allows you to combine criteria by using any of several operators to limit the criteria for one or more fields. The operators and their meanings are covered in Table 4.1.

TABLE 4.1 ACCESS OPERATORS AND THEIR MEANINGS

Operator	Meaning	Example	Result
=	Equal to	="Sales"	Finds only those records with "Sales" as the field value.
<	Less than	<100	Finds all records with values less than 100 in that field.
<=	Less than or equal to	<=100	Finds all records with values less than or equal to 100 in that field.

continues

TABLE 4.1 CONTINUED

Operator	Meaning	Example	Result
>	Greater than	>100	Finds all records with values greater than 100 in that field.
>=	Greater than or equal to	>=100	Finds all records with values greater than or equal to100 in that field.
<>	Not equal to	<>"Sales"	Finds all records with values other than Sales in the field.
And	Both conditions must be true	Created by adding criteria on the same line of the query grid to more than one field	Finds all records where the conditions in both fields are true.
Or	Either condition can be true	"CA" or "NY" or "UT"	Finds all records with the value of "CA", "NY", or "UT" in the field.
Like	Compares a string expression to a pattern	Like "Sales*"	Finds all records with the value of "Sales" at the beginning of the field.
Between	Finds a range of values	Between 5 and 10	Finds all records with the values of 5–10 (inclusive) in the field.
In	Same as Or	In("CA", "NY","UT")	Finds all records with the value of "CA", "NY", or "UT" in the field.
Not	Same as not equal	Not "Sales"	Finds all records with values other than Sales in the field.
Is Null	Finds nulls	Is Null	Finds all records where no data has been entered in the field.
Is Not Null	Finds all records not null	Is Not Null	Finds all records where data has been entered in the field.

Criteria entered for two fields on a single line of the query grid are considered an And, which means that both conditions need to be true for the record to appear in the query output. Entries made on separate lines of the query grid are considered an Or, which means that either condition can be true for the record to be included in the query output. Take a look at the example in Figure 4.7; this query would output all records in which the ContactTitle field begins with either Marketing or Owner, regardless of the customer ID. It outputs the records in which the ContactTitle field begins with Sales only for the customers whose IDs begin with the letters *M* through *R* inclusive.

FIGURE 4.7

Adding AND *and* OR *conditions to a query.*

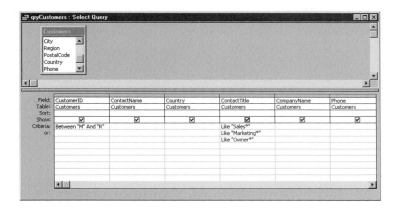

Design a query to find all the sales agents in Brazil or France. The criteria you
TRY IT build should look like those in Figure 4.8.

1. Notice that the criteria for the Country field is `"Brazil" Or "France"` because you want both Brazil and France to appear in the query output. The criteria for the ContactTitle field is `"Sales Agent"`. Because the criteria for both the Country and ContactTitle fields are entered on the same line of the query grid, both must be true for the record to appear in the query output. In other words, the customer must be in either Brazil or France and must also be a sales agent.

2. Modify the query so that you can output all the customers for whom the contact title begins with Sales. Try changing the criteria for the ContactTitle field to Sales. Notice that no records appear in the query output because no contact titles are just Sales. You must enter `"Like Sales*"` for the criteria. Now you get the Sales Agents, Sales Associates, Sales Managers, and so on. You still don't see the Assistant Sales Agents because their titles don't begin with Sales. Try changing the criteria to `"Like *Sales*"`. Now all the Assistant Sales Agents appear.

4

QUERY BASICS

FIGURE 4.8

The criteria to select sales agents whose country is either Brazil or France.

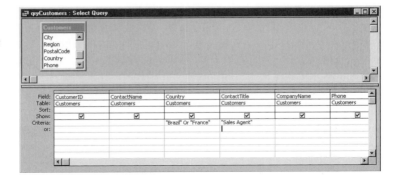

WORKING WITH DATES IN CRITERIA

Access gives you significant power for adding date functions and expressions to your query criteria. Using these criteria, you can find all records in a certain month, on a specific weekday, or between two dates. Table 4.2 lists several examples.

TABLE 4.2   SAMPLE DATE CRITERIA

Expression	Meaning	Example	Result
`Date()`	Current date	`Date()`	Records with the current date within a field.
`Day(Date)`	The day of a date	`Day ([OrderDate])=1`	Records with the order date on the first day of the month.
`Month(Date)`	The month of a date	`Month ([OrderDate])=1`	Records with the order date in January.
`Year(Date)`	The year of a date	`Year ([OrderDate]) =1991`	Records with the order date in 1991.
`Weekday(Date)`	The weekday of a date	`Weekday ([OrderDate])=2`	Records with the order date on a Monday.
`Between Date And Date`	A range of dates	`Between #1/1/95# and #12/31/95#`	All records in 1995.
`DatePart (Interval, Date)`	A specific part of a date	`DatePart ("q", [OrderDate])=2`	All records in the second quarter.

The `Weekday(Date, [FirstDayOfWeek])` function works based on your locale and how your system defines the first day of the week. `Weekday()` used without the optional `FirstDayOfWeek` argument defaults to `vbSunday` as the first day. A value of `0` defaults the `FirstDayOfWeek` to the system definition. Other values can be set also. (See the online help for `Weekday()`.)

Figure 4.9 illustrates the use of a date function. Notice that `DatePart("q",[OrderDate])` is entered as the expression, and the value of `2` is entered for the criteria. `Year([OrderDate])` is entered as another expression with the number `1995` as the criteria. Therefore, this query outputs all records in which the order date is in the second quarter of 1995.

FIGURE 4.9

Using the
`DatePart()` *and*
`Year()` *functions*
in a query.

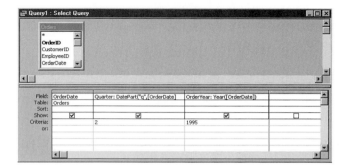

UNDERSTANDING HOW QUERY RESULTS CAN BE UPDATED

If you haven't realized it yet, the results of your query can usually be updated. This means that if you modify the data in the query output, the data in the tables underlying the query is permanently modified.

Build a query based on the Customers table. Add the CustomerID, CompanyName, Address, City, and Region fields to the query grid; then run the query. Change the address of a particular customer, and make a note of the customer ID of the customer whose address you changed. Make sure you move off the record so that the change is written to disk. Close the query, open the actual table in Datasheet view, and find the record whose address you modified. Notice that the change you made was written to the original table—this is because a query result is a dynamic set of records that maintains a link back to the original data. This happens whether you're on a standalone machine or on a network.

4

QUERY BASICS

> | **CAUTION**
> |
> | It's essential that you understand how query results are updated; otherwise, you
> | might mistakenly update table data without even realizing you did so. Updating mul-
> | titable queries is covered later in this chapter in the sections "Pitfalls of Multitable
> | Queries" and "Row Fix-Up in Multitable Queries."

BUILDING QUERIES BASED ON MULTIPLE TABLES

If you have properly normalized your table data, you probably want to bring the data from
your tables back together by using queries. Fortunately, you can do this quite easily with
Access queries.

The query in Figure 4.10 joins the Customers, Orders, and Order Details tables, pulling fields
from each. Notice that the CustomerID and CompanyName fields are selected from the
Customers table, the OrderID and OrderDate from the Orders table, and the UnitPrice and
Quantity from the Order Details table. After running this query, you should see the results
shown in Figure 4.11. Notice that you get a record in the query's result for every record in the
Order Details table. In other words, there are 2,155 records in the Order Details table, and
that's how many records appear in the query output. By creating a multitable query, you can
look at data from related tables, along with the data from the Order Details table.

FIGURE 4.10

*A query joining
the Customers,
Orders, and
Order Details
tables.*

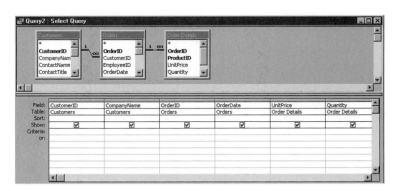

FIGURE 4.11

The results of querying multiple tables.

Build a query that combines information from the Customers, Orders, and Order Details tables. To do this, build a new query by following these steps:

1. Select the Query tab from the Database window.

2. Click New.

3. Select Design view.

4. From the Show Table dialog box, select Customers, Orders, and Order Details by holding down the Ctrl key and clicking on each table name. Then select Add.

5. Click Close.

6. Some of the tables included in the query might be hiding below. If so, scroll down with the vertical scrollbar to view any tables that aren't visible. Notice the join lines between the tables; they're based on the relationships set up in the Relationships window.

7. Select the following fields from each table:

   Customers: Country, City

   Orders: Order Date

   Order Details: UnitPrice, Quantity

8. Sort by Country and then City. Your finished query design should look like the one in Figure 4.12.

9. Run the query. Data from all three tables should be included in the query output.

4

QUERY BASICS

FIGURE 4.12

*The query design
from the example.*

NOTE

To remove a table from a query, click anywhere on the table in the top half of the query grid and press the Delete key. You can add tables to the query at any time by clicking the Show Table button from the toolbar. If you prefer, you can select the Database window and then click and drag tables directly from the Database window to the top half of the query grid.

Pitfalls of Multitable Queries

You should be aware of some pitfalls of multitable queries; they concern updating as well as which records you see in the query output.

It's important to remember that certain fields in a multitable query can't be updated—these are the join fields on the "one" side of a one-to-many relationship (unless the Cascade Update referential integrity feature has been activated). You also can't update the join field on the "many" side of the relationship after you've updated data on the "one" side. More important, which fields can be updated, and the consequences of updating them, might surprise you. If you update the fields on the "one" side of a one-to-many relationship, you must be aware of that change's impact. You're actually updating that record in the original table on the "one" side of the relationship; several records on the "many" side of the relationship will be affected.

For example, Figure 4.13 shows the result of a query based on the Customers, Orders, and Order Details tables. I have changed `"Alfreds Futterkiste"` to `"Waldo Futterkiste"` on a specific record of my query output. You might expect this change to affect only that specific order detail item. Pressing the down-arrow key to move off the record shows that all records associated with Alfreds Futterkiste have been changed. (See Figure 4.14.) This happened because all the orders for Alfreds Futterkiste were actually getting their information from one record in the Customers table—the record for customer ID ALFKI. This is the record I modified while viewing the query result.

FIGURE 4.13

Changing a record on the "one" side of a one-to-many relationship. After updating the company name, all records with the same customer ID are affected.

FIGURE 4.14

The result of changing a record on the "one" side of a one-to-many relationship. Notice that the Company Name field has been updated for all records with ALFKI as the customer ID.

TRY IT To get this experience firsthand, try changing the data in the City field for one of the records in the query result. Notice that the record (as well as several other records) is modified. This happens because the City field actually represents data from the "one" side of the one-to-many relationship. In other words, when you're viewing the Country and City fields for several records in the query output, the data for the fields might be originating from one record. The same goes for the Order Date field because it's also on the "one" side of a one-to-many relationship. The only field in the query output that can't be modified is TotalPrice, a calculated field. Practice modifying the data in the query result; then returning to the original table and noticing what data has changed.

The second pitfall of multitable queries is figuring out which records result from such a query. So far, you have learned how to build only inner joins. Join types are covered in detail in Chapter 11, but for now, it's important to understand that the query output contains only customers who have orders and orders that have order detail. This means that not all the customers

4

QUERY BASICS

or orders might be listed. In Chapter 11, you learn how to build queries in which you can list all customers, regardless of whether they have orders. You'll also learn how to list only the customers without orders.

Row Fix-Up in Multitable Queries

The row fix-up feature is automatically available to you in Access. As you fill in key values on the "many" side of a one-to-many relationship in a multitable query, the non-key values are automatically looked up in the parent table. Most database developers refer to this as *enforced referential integrity*. A foreign key must first exist on the "one" side of the query to be entered successfully on the "many" side. As you can imagine, you don't want to be able to add an order to your database for a nonexistent customer.

For example, the query in Figure 4.15 is based on the Customers and Orders tables. The fields included in the query are CustomerID from the Orders table; CompanyName, Address, and City from the Customers table; and OrderID and OrderDate from the Orders table. If the CustomerID associated with an order is changed, the CompanyName, Address, and City are looked up from the Customers table and immediately displayed in the query result. Notice in Figure 4.16 how the information for Alfreds Futterkiste is displayed in the query result. Figure 4.17 shows that the CompanyName, Address, and City change automatically when the CustomerID is changed. Don't be confused by the combo box used to select the customer ID. The presence of the combo box within the query is a result of Access's auto-lookup feature, covered in Chapter 2, "What Every Developer Needs to Know About Tables." The customer ID associated with a particular order is actually being modified in the query. If a new record is added to the query, the customer information is filled in as soon as the customer ID associated with the order is selected.

FIGURE 4.15

This query illustrates the use of Auto Fix Up in a query with multiple tables.

FIGURE 4.16

The query result before selecting another customer ID.

FIGURE 4.17

The result of an auto-lookup after the customer ID is changed. The information on the "one" side of the relationship is "fixed up" to display information for the appropriate customer.

CREATING CALCULATED FIELDS

One of the rules of data normalization is that the results of calculations shouldn't be included in your database. You can output the results of calculations by building those calculations into your queries, and you can display the results of the calculations on forms and reports by making the query the foundation for a form or report. You can also add controls to your forms and reports containing the calculations you want. In certain cases, this can improve performance. (This topic is covered in more depth in Chapter 15.)

The columns of your query result can hold the result of any valid expression, including the result of a user-defined function. This makes your queries extremely powerful. For example, the following expression could be entered:

```
Left([FirstName],1) & "." & Left([LastName],1) & "."
```

This expression would give you the first character of the first name followed by a period, the first character of the last name, and another period. An even simpler expression would be this one:

```
[UnitPrice]*[Quantity]
```

This calculation would simply take the UnitPrice field and multiply it by the Quantity field. In both cases, Access would automatically name the resulting expression. For example, the calculation that results from concatenating the first and last initials is shown in Figure 4.18. Notice that in the figure, the expression has been given a name. To give the expression a name, such as Initials, you must enter it as follows:

```
Initials: Left([FirstName],1) & "." & Left([LastName],1) & "."
```

Thetext preceding the colon is the name of the expression—in this case, Initials. If you don't explicitly give your expression a name, it defaults to Expr1.

FIGURE 4.18

The result of the expression
`Initials:Left`
`([FirstName],1)`
`& "." &`
`Left([LastName],`
`1) & "."` *in the query.*

TRY IT Follow these steps to add a calculation that shows the unit price multiplied by the quantity:

1. Scroll to the right on the query grid until you can see a blank column.

2. Click in the Field row for the new column.

3. Type `TotalPrice:UnitPrice*Quantity`. If you want to see more easily what you're typing, press Shift+F2 (Zoom). The dialog box shown in Figure 4.19 appears. (Access will supply the space after the colon and the square brackets around the field names if you omit them.)

4. Click OK to close the Zoom window.

5. Run the query. The total sales amount should appear in the far-right column of the query output. The query output should look like the one in Figure 4.20.

FIGURE 4.19

Expanding the field with the Zoom function (Shift+F2).

FIGURE 4.20

The result of the total price calculation.

> NOTE
>
> You can enter any valid expression in the Field row of your query grid. Notice that field names included in an expression are automatically surrounded by square brackets. This happens automatically unless your field name has spaces. If a field name includes any spaces, you must enclose the field name in brackets; otherwise, your query won't run properly, which is just one of the many reasons why field and table names shouldn't contain spaces.

GETTING HELP FROM THE EXPRESSION BUILDER

The Expression Builder is a helpful tool for building expressions in your queries, as well as in many other situations in Access. To invoke the Expression Builder, click in the Field cell of your query grid and then click Build on the toolbar. (See Figure 4.21.) Notice that the

4

QUERY BASICS

Expression Builder is divided into three columns. The first column shows the objects in the database. After selecting an element in the left column, select the elements you want to paste from the middle and right columns.

FIGURE 4.21

The Expression Builder makes it easier for you to create expressions in your query.

The example in Figure 4.22 shows Functions selected in the left column. Within Functions, both user-defined and built-in functions are listed; here, the Functions object is expanded with `Built-In Functions` selected. In the center column, `Date/Time` is selected. After selecting Date/Time, all the built-in date and time functions appear in the right column. If you double-click a particular function—in this case, the `DatePart` function—the function and its parameters are placed in the text box at the top of the Expression Builder window. Notice that the `DatePart` function has four parameters: `Interval`, `Date`, `FirstWeekDay`, and `FirstWeek`. If you know what needs to go into each of these parameters, you can simply replace the parameter place markers with your own values. If you need more information, you can invoke help on the selected function and learn more about the required parameters. In Figure 4.23, two parameters are filled in: the interval and the name of the field being evaluated. After clicking OK, the expression is placed in theField cell of the query.

FIGURE 4.22

The Expression Builder with the DatePart *function selected and pasted in the expression box.*

FIGURE 4.23

A function pasted by Expression Builder with the parameters updated with appropriate values.

SUMMARIZING DATA WITH TOTALS QUERIES

With Totals queries, you can easily summarize numeric data. Totals queries can be used to calculate the Sum, Average, Count, Minimum, Maximum, and other types of summary calculations for the data in your query result. These queries let you calculate one value for all the records in your query result or group the calculations as desired. For example, you could determine the total sales for every record in the query result, as shown in Figure 4.24, or you could output the total sales by country and city. (See Figure 4.25.) You could also calculate the total, average, minimum, and maximum sales amounts for all customers in the United States. The possibilities are endless.

FIGURE 4.24

Total sales for every record in the query result.

4

QUERY BASICS

To create a Totals query:

1. Add to the query grid the fields or expressions you want to summarize. It's important that you add the fields in the order in which you want them grouped. For example, Figure 4.26 shows a query grouped by country, then city.

2. Click Totals on the toolbar or select View | Totals to add a Total row to the query. By default, each field in the query has Group By in the total row.

FIGURE 4.25

Total sales by country and city.

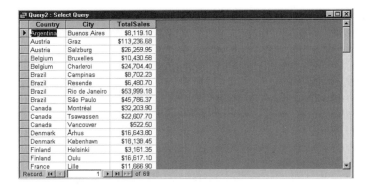

3. Click in the Total row on the design grid.

4. Open the combo box and choose the calculation you want. (See Figure 4.26.)

5. Leave `Group By` in the Total cell of any fields you want to group by, as shown in Figure 4.26. Remember to place the fields in the order in which you want them grouped. For example, if you want the records grouped by country, and then by sales representative, the Country field must be placed to the left of the Sales Representative field on the query grid. On the other hand, if you want records grouped by sales representative, and then by country, the Sales Representative field must be placed to the left of the Country field on the query grid.

FIGURE 4.26

Selecting the type of calculation for the Totals row from a drop-down list.

6. Add the criteria you want to the query.

Figure 4.27 shows the design of a query that finds the total, average, maximum, and number of sales by country and city; Figure 4.28 shows the results of running the query. As you can see, Totals queries can give you valuable information.

FIGURE 4.27

A query that finds the total, average, maximum, and number of sales by country and city.

FIGURE 4.28

The result of running a query with many aggregate functions.

If you save this query and reopen it, you'll see that Access has made some changes to its design. The Total cell for the Sum is changed to Expression, and the Field cell is changed to the following:

```
TotalSales: Sum([UnitPrice]*[Quantity])
```

If you look at the Total cell for the Avg, it's also changed to Expression. The Field cell is changed to the following:

```
AverageSales: Avg([UnitPrice]*[Quantity])
```

Access modifies the query in this way when it determines you're using an aggregate function on an expression having more than one field. You can enter the expression either way. Access stores and resolves the expression as noted.

4

QUERY BASICS

TRY IT Modify the query to show the total sales by country, city, and order date. Before you continue, save your query as qryCustomerOrderInfo, then close it. With the Query tab of the Database window visible, click qryCustomerOrderInfo. Choose Copy from the toolbar and then Paste. Access should prompt you for the name of the new query. Type qryCustomerOrderSummary and click OK. With qryCustomerOrderSummary selected, click the Design command button. Delete both the UnitPrice and Quantity fields from the query output. To turn your query into a Totals query, follow these steps:

1. Click Totals on the toolbar. Notice that an extra line, called the Total line, is added to the query grid; this line says Group By for all fields.

2. Group by country, city, and order date but total by the total price (the calculated field). Click the Total row for the TotalPrice field and use the drop-down list to select Sum. (Refer to Figure 4.26.)

3. Run the query. Your result should be grouped and sorted by country, city, and order date, with a total for each unique combination of the three fields.

4. Return to the query's design and remove the order date from the query grid.

5. Rerun the query. Notice that now you're summarizing the query by country and city.

6. Change the Total row to Avg. Now you're seeing the average price times quantity for each combination of country and city. Change it back to Sum, and save the query.

As you can see, Totals queries are both powerful and flexible. Their output can't be edited, but you can use them to view the sum, minimum, maximum, average, and count of the total price, all at the same time. You can easily modify whether you're viewing this information by country, country and city, and so on, all at the click of your mouse.

EXCLUDING FIELDS FROM THE OUTPUT

At times, you need to include a column in your query that you don't want displayed in the query output; this is often the case with columns used solely for criteria. Figure 4.29 shows an example. If this query were run, you would get the total, average, and maximum sales grouped by both country and order date. However, you want to group only by country and use the order date only for criteria. Therefore, you need to set the Total row of the query to Where, as shown in Figure 4.30. The column used in the Where has been excluded from the query result. This is easily determined by noting that the check box in the Show row of the OrderDate column is unchecked.

FIGURE 4.29

A query with criteria for the order date, before excluding fields from the query output.

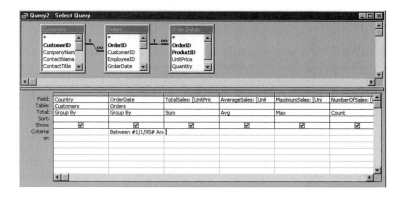

FIGURE 4.30

The Total row of the OrderDate field is set to Where, *excluding the field from the query result.*

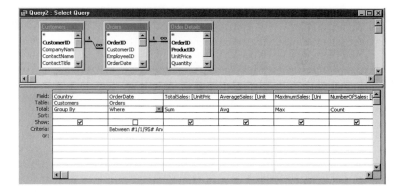

NULLS AND QUERY RESULTS

Null values in your table's fields can noticeably affect query results. A Null value is different from a zero or a zero-length string; a field contains a Null value when no value has yet been stored in the field. As discussed in Chapter 2, a zero-length string is entered in a field by typing two quotation marks.

Null values can affect the results of multitable queries, queries including aggregate functions (Totals queries), and queries with calculations. By default, when a multitable query is built, only records that have non-Null values on the "many" side of the relationship appear in the query result (discussed earlier in this chapter, in the "Pitfalls of Multitable Queries" section).

Null values can also affect the result of aggregate queries. For example, if you perform a count on a field containing Null values, only records having non-Null values in that field are included in the count. If you want to get an accurate count, it's best to perform the count on a Primary Key field or some other field that can't have Null values.

Probably the most insidious problem with Nulls happens when they're included in calculations. A Null value, when included in a calculation containing a numeric operator (+, -, /, *, and so on), results in a Null value. In Figure 4.31, for example, notice that the query includes a calculation that adds the values in both the Parts and Labor fields. These fields have been set to have no default value and, therefore, contain Nulls unless something has been explicitly entered into them. Running the query gives you the results shown in Figure 4.32. Notice that all the records having Nulls in either the Parts or Labor fields contain a Null in the result.

FIGURE 4.31

The Design view of a query that propagates Nulls in the query result.

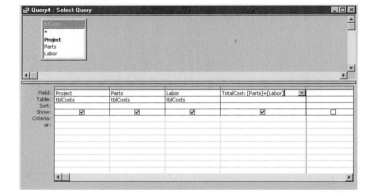

FIGURE 4.32

The result of running a query illustrating Nulls.

The solution to this problem is constructing an expression that converts the Null values to zero. The expression looks like this:

```
TotalCost: NZ([Parts])+NZ([Labor])
```

The NZ function determines whether the Parts field contains a Null value. If the Parts field contains a Null value, it's converted to a zero and included in the calculation; otherwise, the field's value is used in the calculation. The same expression is used to evaluate the Labor field. The result of the modified query is shown in Figure 4.33.

FIGURE 4.33

The query with an expression to eliminate Nulls.

Project	Parts	Labor	TotalCost
Project 1	$10.00	$4.00	$14.00
Project 2	$5.00		$5.00
Project 3		$6.00	$6.00
Project 4	$11.00	$5.00	$16.00
Project 5		$8.00	$8.00
Project 6		$7.00	$7.00
Project 7	$20.00	$15.00	$35.00
Project 8	$4.00		$4.00
Project 9	$4.00	$6.00	$10.00
*	$0.00	$0.00	

Record: 1 of 9

CAUTION

Nulls really cause trouble when the results of one query containing Nulls are used in another query—a snowball effect occurs. It's easy to miss the problem and output reports with inaccurate results. Using the IsNull() function eliminates this kind of problem. You can use the IsNull() function to replace the Null values with zeros or zero-length strings. Be careful when doing this, though, because it might affect other parts of your query that use this value for another calculation. Also, be sure to use any function in a query on the top level of the query tree only because functions at lower levels might hinder query performance. A *query tree* refers to the fact that a query can be based on other queries. Placing the criteria at the top of the query tree means that if queries are based on other queries, the criteria should be placed in the highest-level queries.

REFINING YOUR QUERIES WITH FIELD, FIELD LIST, AND QUERY PROPERTIES

Field and query properties can be used to refine and control the behavior and appearance of the columns in your query and of the query itself. Here's how:

1. Click in a field to select the field, click in a field list to select the field list, or click in the Query Design window anywhere outside a field or the field list to select the query.

2. Click Properties on the toolbar.

3. Modify the desired property.

Field Properties: Changing the Behavior of a Field

The properties of a field in your query include the Description, Format, Input Mask, and Caption of the column. The Description property is used for documentation and to control what appears on the status bar when the user is in that column in the query result. The Format property is the same as the Format property in a table's field; it controls the display of the field in the query result. The Input Mask property, like its table counterpart, actually controls how data is entered and modified in the query result. Just as the Caption property of a field sets the caption for the column in Datasheet view and the default label for forms and reports, the Caption property in the query does the same thing.

You might be wondering how the properties of the fields in a query interact with the same properties of a table. For example, how does the Caption property of a table's field interact with the Caption property of the same field in a query? All properties of a table's field are automatically inherited in your queries. Properties explicitly modified in the query override those same properties of the table's fields. Any objects based on the query inherit the properties of the query, not of the original table.

> **NOTE**
>
> In the case of the Input Mask property, it is important that the Input Mask in the query is not in conflict with the Input Mask of the table. The Input Mask of the query can be used to further restrict the Input Mask of the table, but not to override it. If the Input Mask of the query conflicts with the Input Mask of the table, the user will not be able to enter data into the table.

Field List Properties: Changing the Properties of the Field List

Field List properties are used to specify attributes of each table participating in the query. The two Field List properties are Source. The Alias property is used most often when the same table is used more than once in the same query. This is done in self-joins, covered in Chapter 11. The Source property is used to specify a connection string or database name when you're dealing with external tables that aren't linked to the current database.

Query Properties: Changing the Behavior of the Overall Query

Microsoft offers many properties, shown in Figure 4.34, that allow you to affect the behavior of the overall query. Some of the properties are discussed here; the rest are covered as applicable throughout this book.

FIGURE **4.34**

Query properties that affect the behavior of a given query.

The Description property is used to document what the query does. Top Values lets you specify the top *x* number or *x* percent of values in the query result. Output All Fields shows all the fields in the query results, regardless of the contents of the Show check box in each field. Filter displays a subset that you determine, rather than the full result of the query. Order By determines the sort order of the query. The Unique Values and Unique Records properties are used to determine whether only unique values or unique records are displayed in the query's output. (These properties are also covered in detail in Chapter 11, "Advanced Query Techniques.") The Recordset Type property determines whether updates can be made to the query output. By default, this is set to the Dynaset type allowing updates to the underlying data. The Run Permissions property has to do with security and is covered in Chapter 34, "Advanced Security Techniques." Source Database, Source Connect String, ODBC Timeout,

4

QUERY BASICS

and MaxRecords all have to do with client/server issues and are covered in Chapter 19, "Client/Server Techniques." The Record Locks property concerns multiuser issues and is covered in Chapter 17, "Developing for a Multiuser Environment." The Subdatasheet Name property allows you to specify the name of the table or query that will appear as a subdatasheet within the current query. After the Subdatasheet property is set, the Link Child Fields and Link Master Fields properties are used to designate the fields from the child and parent tables or queries that are used to link the current query to its subdatasheet. Finally, the Subdatasheet Height is used to set the maximum height for a subdatasheet and the Subdatasheet Expanded property determines whether the subdatasheet automatically appears in an expanded state.

BUILDING PARAMETER QUERIES WHEN YOU DON'T KNOW THE CRITERIA AT DESIGN TIME

You, or your application's user, might not always know the parameters for the query output when designing the query. Parameter queries let you specify different criteria at runtime so that you don't have to modify the query each time you want to change the criteria.

For example, say you have a query, like the one shown in Figure 4.35, for which you want users to specify the date range they want to view each time they run the query. The following clause has been entered as the criteria for the OrderDate field:

```
Between [Enter Starting Date] And [Enter Ending Date]
```

FIGURE 4.35

This Parameter query prompts for a starting date and an ending date.

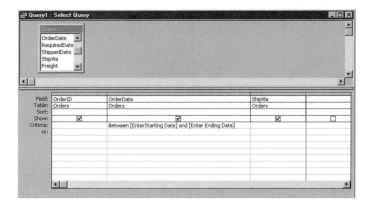

This criterion causes two dialog boxes to appear when the query is run. The first one, shown in Figure 4.36, prompts the user with the text in the first set of brackets. The text the user types is substituted for the bracketed text. A second dialog box appears, prompting the user for whatever is in the second set of brackets. The user's responses are used as criteria for the query.

FIGURE 4.36

This dialog box appears when the Parameter query is run.

TRY IT Add a parameter to the query qryCustomerOrderSummary so that you can view only TotalPrice summaries within a specific range. Go to the criteria for TotalPrice and type `Between [Please Enter Starting Value] and [Please Enter Ending Value]`. This allows you to view all the records in which the total price is within a specific range. The bracketed text is replaced by actual values when the query is run. Click OK and run the query. You're then prompted to enter both a starting and an ending value.

To make sure Access understands what type of data should be placed in these parameters, you must define the parameters. Do this by selecting Parameters from the Query menu to open the Parameters window. Another way to display the Query Parameters window is to right-click a gray area in the top half of the query grid; then select Parameters from the context-sensitive pop-up menu.

The text that appears within the brackets for each parameter must be entered in the Parameter field of the Query Parameters dialog. The type of data in the brackets must be defined in the Data Type column. Figure 4.37 shows an example of a completed Query Parameters dialog box.

FIGURE 4.37

This completed Query Parameters dialog box declares two date parameters.

You can easily create parameters for as many fields as you want, and parameters are added just as you would add more criteria. For example, the query shown in Figure 4.38 has parameters for the Title, HireDate, and City fields in the Employees table from the Northwind database. Notice that all the criteria are on one line of the query grid, which means that all the parameters entered must be satisfied for the records to appear in the output. The criteria for the title is `[Please Enter a Title]`. This means that the records in the result must match the title entered when the query is run. The criteria for the HireDate field is `>=[Please Enter Starting Hire Date]`. Only records with a hire date on or after the hire date entered when

4

QUERY BASICS

the query is run will appear in the output. Finally, the criteria for the City field is [Please Enter a City]. This means that only records with the City entered when the query is run will appear in the output.

The criteria for a query can also be the result of a function; this technique is covered in Chapter 11.

FIGURE 4.38

The Query Design window showing a query with parameters for three fields.

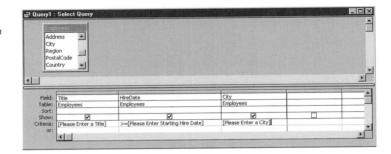

NOTE

Parameter queries offer significant flexibility; they allow the user to enter specific criteria at runtime. What's typed in the Query Parameters dialog box must exactly match what's typed within the brackets; otherwise, Access prompts the user with additional dialog boxes.

TIP

You can add as many parameters as you like to a query, but the user might become bothered if too many dialog boxes appear. Instead, build a custom form that feeds the Parameter query. This technique is covered in Chapter 10.

PRACTICAL EXAMPLES

Building Queries Needed by the Time and Billing Application for the Computer Consulting Firm

Build a query based on tblTimeCardHours. This query gives you the total billing amount by project for a specific date range. The query's design is shown in Figure 4.39. Notice that it's a Totals query that groups by project and totals by using the following expression:

```
BillAmount: Sum([BillableHours]*[BillingRate])
```

The DateWorked field is used as the `Where` clause for the query; here's the criteria for the `Where` clause:

```
Between [Enter Start Date] And [Enter End Date]
```

FIGURE 4.39

The design of the qryBillAmountBy Project query.

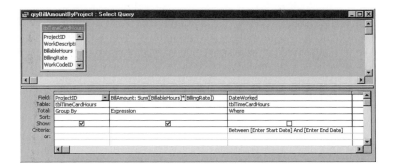

The two parameters of the criteria are declared in the Parameters dialog box. (See Figure 4.40.) Save this query as `qryBillAmountByProject`.

FIGURE 4.40

The Parameters window for qryBillAmountBy Project.

The second query is based on tblClients, tblProjects, and tblTimeCardHours. This query gives you the total billing amount by client for a specific date range. The query's design is shown in Figure 4.41. This query is a Totals query that groups by the company name from the tblClients table and totals by using the following expression:

```
BillAmount: Sum([BillableHours]*[BillingRate])
```

As with the first query, the DateWorked field is used as the `Where` clause for the query, and the parameters are defined in the Parameters window. Save this query as `qryBillAmountByClient`.

 These queries are included on the sample CD-ROM in a database called CHAP4.MDB. You will build many other queries as part of the computer consulting firm's time and billing system.

FIGURE 4.41

The design of the qryBillAmountBy Client query.

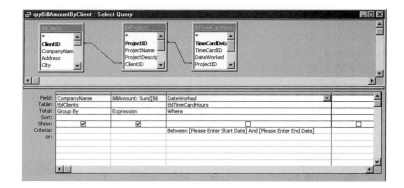

SUMMARY

This chapter covers the foundations of perhaps the most important function of a database: getting data from the database in a usable form. You have learned about the Select query used to retrieve data from a table, how to retrieve data from multiple tables, and how to use functions in your queries to make them more powerful by synthesizing data. In later chapters, you will extend your abilities with Action queries and queries based on other queries (also known as *nested queries*).

WHAT EVERY DEVELOPER NEEDS TO KNOW ABOUT FORMS

CHAPTER

5

IN THIS CHAPTER

USES OF FORMS

Developers often think that forms exist solely for the purpose of data entry. To the contrary, forms serve many different purposes in Access 2000:

- Data entry—Displaying and editing data
- Application flow—Navigating through your application
- Custom dialog boxes—Providing messages to your user
- Printing information—Providing hard copies of data-entry information

Probably the most common use of an Access form is as a vehicle for displaying and editing existing data or for adding new data. Fortunately, Access offers many features that allow you to build forms that ease data entry for your users. Access also makes it easy for you to design forms that let your users view and modify data, view data but not modify it, or add new records only.

Although not everyone immediately thinks of an Access form as a means of navigating through an application, forms are quite strong in this area. Figure 5.1 shows a form created with the Switchboard Manager in Access 2000; Figure 5.2 shows a "home-grown" switchboard form. Although the Switchboard Manager makes designing a switchboard form very simple, you will find any type of switchboard easy to develop. You can be creative with switchboard forms by designing forms that are both utilitarian and exciting. Switchboard forms are covered in detail in Chapter 9, "Advanced Form Techniques."

FIGURE 5.1

A form created with the Switchboard Manager.

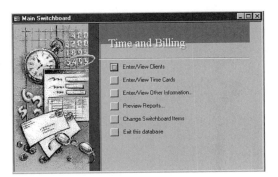

You can also use Access to create custom dialog boxes used to display information or retrieve information from your users. The custom dialog box shown in Figure 5.3 gets the information needed to run a report. The user must fill in the required information before he or she can proceed.

FIGURE 5.2

A custom switch-board with tooltips and bitmaps.

FIGURE 5.3

A custom dialog box that lets the user specify a date range for a report.

Another strength of Access is its capability to produce professional-looking printed forms. With many other products, it's difficult to print a data-entry form; sometimes the entire form needs to be re-created as a report. In Access, printing a form is simply a matter of clicking a button with a little code placed under it. You have the option of creating a report that displays the information your user is entering or of printing the form itself.

Access offers many styles of forms. The data in a form can be displayed one record at a time, or you can let the user view several records at once. Forms can be displayed *modally*, meaning that the user must respond and close the form before continuing, or displayed so that the user can move through the open forms at will. The important thing to remember is that there are many uses and styles of forms. You will learn about them throughout this chapter, in Chapter 9, and throughout the book. As you read this chapter, remember that your forms are limited only by your imagination.

ANATOMY OF A FORM

Access forms are comprised of a few different sections; each one has its own function and behavior. These are the three main sections of an Access form:

- Header
- Detail
- Footer

5

FORMS

The Detail section of a form is the main section; it's the one used to display the data of the table or query underlying the form. As you will see, the Detail section can take on many different looks. It's quite flexible and robust.

The Header and Footer sectionsof the form are used to display information that doesn't change from record to record. Command buttons—such as one used to let users view all the projects associated with a particular client—that control the form are often placed in the form's header or footer. Controls can also be used to help the user navigate around the records associated with the form. In the example shown in Figure 5.4, the user can select from a valid list of clients. After a client has been selected from the combo box, the user is moved to the appropriate record.

FIGURE 5.4

Record navigation using a combo box placed in the form header.

CREATING A NEW FORM

You can create a new form in several ways. The most common way is to select the Forms icon from the Objects list in the Database window. You can then select the Create Form in Design View icon or the Create Form By Using the Wizard icon. Another way to create a form is to click Forms in the Objects list and then click the New command button. If you create a form using this method, the New Form dialog box appears. The New Form dialog allows you to select from the multitude of options available for creating a new form. (See Figure 5.5.) Forms can be created from scratch by using Design view, or they can be created with the help of any one of six wizards. The wizards will be covered briefly before you move on to the process of creating a form from scratch. Even the most experienced developers use the Form Wizard to perform certain tasks.

FIGURE 5.5

The New Form dialog box lets you specify the table or query to underlie the form and choose the method for creating the form.

Creating a Form with the Form Wizard

To create a form with the Form Wizard, select the Create form by using the wizard icon with the Forms icon selected in the Objects list, or select Form Wizard from the New Form dialog and click OK. The first step of the Form Wizard prompts you for the name of the table or query you want to use as the form's foundation. Whether you're creating a form with Form Wizard or from Design view, it's generally better to base a form on a query. Using a query as the foundation for a form offers better performance (unless your form requires all fields and all records), allows for more flexibility, and lets you create a form based on data from several tables.

Figure 5.6 shows the Tables/Queries drop-down list. You can see that all the tables are listed, followed by all the queries. After you select a particular table or query, its fields are displayed in the list box on the left. (See Figure 5.7.) To select the fields you want to include on the form, double-click the name of the field or click on the field; then click the > button. In the example shown in Figure 5.7, several fields have been selected from the qryClients query.

FIGURE 5.6

A list of available tables and queries available for use in the Form Wizard.

FIGURE 5.7

Selected fields from qryClients.

After you've selected the fields you want, click Next. The second step of the Form Wizard allows you to specify the layout for the form you're designing. You can select from Columnar, Tabular, Datasheet, or Justified; the most common choice is Columnar. Click Next after selecting a form layout. In the third step of the Form Wizard, you can select a style for your form from several predefined styles. (See Figure 5.8.) Although all the properties set by the wizard can be modified in Design view after the form has been created, to save time, it's best to select the appropriate style now. Click Next after selecting a style.

FIGURE 5.8

Selecting a form style.

In the final step of the Form Wizard, supply a title for your form (if you just accept the default, the form will have the same name as the underlying table or query, which could be confusing). Unfortunately, the form's title becomes the name of the form as well. For this reason, type the text you want to use as the name of the form. If you want to follow standard naming conventions, you should begin the name of the form with the tag *frm*. You can worry about changing the title in Design view of the form. This step of the Form Wizard also lets you specify whether you want to view the results of your work or open the form in Design view. It's usually best to view the results and then modify the form's design after you have taken a peek at what the Form Wizard has done.

Creating a Form from Design View

Although the Form Wizards are both powerful and useful, in many cases you'll prefer building a form from scratch, especially if you're building a form that's not bound to data. To create a form without using a wizard, click Forms in the Objects list. Double-click the Create Form in Design View icon or click New to open the New Form dialog box and select Design view (the default choice). If you clicked New to open the New Form dialog, and your form will be bound to data, use the drop-down list in the New Form dialog box to select the table or query that will serve as the form's foundation. Click OK, and the Form Design window appears. (See Figure 5.9.)

FIGURE 5.9

Use the Form Design window to build and customize a form.

WORKING WITH THE FORM DESIGN WINDOW

The Form Design window is used to build and customize a form. Using this window, you can add objects to a form and customize them by using the Properties window. Microsoft has supplied many form and control properties. After gaining a command of these properties, you can customize the look and feel of your forms.

5

FORMS

Understanding and Working with the Form Design Tools

Even the best developer needs the right tools for the job. Fortunately, Microsoft has given you tools to help you build exciting and utilitarian forms. The Form Design window includes a toolbar, a toolbox, and the actual form you're designing. Other tools are available to help you with the design process, including the Field List and Properties window.

By default, two toolbars appear when you're in a form's Design view: the Form Design toolbar and the Formatting toolbar. The Form Design toolbar has buttons you use to save, print, copy, cut, paste, and perform other standard Windows tasks within the form. It also includes buttons that allow you to toggle the different design windows (such as the toolbox). The Formatting toolbar contains tools for graphically modifying the form's properties and objects. You can modify the font, font size, and color of selected objects on the form. With the Formatting toolbar, you can also add bold, underline, and italic; change the alignment; and add special effects to the selected objects.

Toggling the Tools to Get What You Want

Many windows are available to help you with the design process when you're in a form's Design view. Depending on whether you have a high-resolution monitor, you'll probably find it annoying to have all the windows open at once. In fact, with all the windows open at once on a low-resolution monitor, the form is likely to get buried underneath all the windows. This is why Microsoft has made each window open and close in a toggle-switch–like fashion. The Form Design toolbar has tools for the Field List, Toolbox, and Properties windows, and each of these toolbar buttons is a toggle. Clicking once on the button opens the appropriate window; clicking a second time closes it.

Figure 5.10 shows a form with the Field List, Toolbox, and Properties windows open. Although each of these windows can be sized however you want (and the toolbox can be docked to a window edge), the design environment in this low-resolution display is rather cluttered with all these windows open. One of the tricks in working with Access is knowing when it's appropriate to have each set of tools available. The goal is to have the right windows open at the right time as often as possible.

> **NOTE**
>
> The Field List, Toolbox, and Properties windows can be closed by using the toolbar buttons. In addition, they can be closed by using the Close button on each window or toggled with the View menu.

FIGURE 5.10

The Form Design toolbar with Design windows visible.

Adding Fields to the Form

Fields can be easily added to a form by using the Field List window, which contains all the fields that are part of the form's record source. The *record source* for the form is the table or query that underlies the form. For example, in Figure 5.10, the form's record source is qryClients. The fields listed in the Field List window are the fields that are part of the query. To add fields to a form, use these two steps:

1. Make sure the Field List window is visible. If it isn't, click the Field List button on the toolbar.
2. Locate the field you want to add to the form; then click and drag the field from the field list to the place on the form where you want it to appear. The location you select becomes the upper-left corner of the text box, and the attached label appears to the left of where you dropped the control.

NOTE

A *control* is an object that you add to a form or report. Types of controls include text boxes, combo boxes, list boxes, and check boxes.

> **NOTE**
>
> To add multiple fields to a form at the same time, select several fields from the field list. Use the Ctrl key to select noncontiguous fields or the Shift key to select contiguous fields. For example, hold down your Ctrl key and click on three noncontiguous fields. Each field will be selected. Now click a field, hold down your Shift key, and click another field. All fields between the two fields will be selected. If you want to select all fields, double-click the field list title bar. Click and drag any of the selected fields to the form, and all of them will be added to the form at once.

Selecting, Moving, Aligning, and Sizing Form Objects

You must know several important tricks of the trade when selecting, moving, aligning, and sizing form objects. These tips will save you hours of frustration and wasted time.

Selecting Form Objects

The easiest way to select a single object on a form is to click it. After the object is selected, you can move it, size it, or change any of its properties. Selecting multiple objects is a bit trickier, but can be done in several ways. Different methods are more efficient in different situations. To select multiple objects, you can hold down the Shift key and click each object you want to select. Each selected object is surrounded by selection handles, indicating that it's selected.

Figure 5.11 shows a form with four selected objects; it's important to understand which objects are actually selected. The ClientID text box, the Address label and text box, and the Company Name label are all selected; however, the Client ID label and CompanyName text box aren't selected. If you look closely at the figure, you can see that the selected objects are completely surrounded by selection handles. The Client ID label and CompanyName text box have single selection handles because they're attached to objects that are selected. If you change any properties of the selected objects, the Client ID label and CompanyName text box will be unaffected.

FIGURE 5.11

Selecting objects on a form.

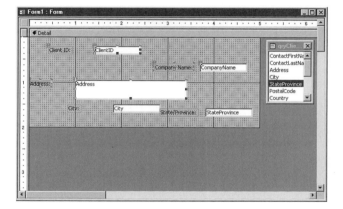

You can also select objects by lassoing them. To lasso objects, they must be located adjacent to one another on the form. Place your mouse pointer on a blank area of the form (not over any objects); then click and drag. You can see a thin line around the objects your mouse pointer is encircling. When you let go, any objects that were within the lasso, including those only partially surrounded, are selected. If you want to deselect any of these objects to exclude them, hold down your Shift key and click on the object you want to deselect.

One of my favorite ways to select multiple objects is to use the horizontal and vertical rulers that appear at the edges of the Form Design window. Click and drag within the ruler. Notice that as you click and drag on the vertical ruler, two horizontal lines appear, indicating which objects are selected. As you click and drag across the horizontal ruler, two vertical lines appear, indicating the selection area. When you let go of your mouse, any objects within the lines are selected. As with the process of lassoing, to remove any objects from the selection, hold down your Shift key and click on the object you want to deselect.

Moving Things Around

To move a single control with its attached label, you don't need to select it first. Place your mouse over the object and click and drag. An outline appears, indicating the object's new location. When the object reaches the position you want, release the mouse. The attached label automatically moves with its corresponding control.

To move more than one object at a time, you must first select the objects you want to move. Select the objects using one of the methods outlined in the previous section. Place your mouse over any of the selected objects and click and drag. An outline appears, indicating the proposed new position for the objects. Release the mouse when you have reached the position you want for the objects.

Sometimes you want to move a control independent of its attached label, which requires a special technique. If you click on a control, such as a text box, as you move your mouse over the border of the control, a hand icon with five fingers pointing upward appears. If you click and drag, both the control and the attached label move as a unit, and the relationship between them is maintained. If you place your mouse pointer over the larger handle in the upper-left corner of the object, the mouse pointer appears as a hand with only the index finger pointing upward. If you click and drag here, the control moves independently of its attached label, and the relationship between the objects changes.

Aligning Objects to One Another

Access makes it easy to align objects. Figure 5.12 shows several objects that aren't aligned. Notice that the attached labels of three of the objects are selected. If you align the attached labels, the controls (in this case, text boxes) remain in their original positions. If you select the text boxes as well, they will try to align with the attached labels. Because Access doesn't allow the objects to overlap, the text boxes end up immediately next to their attached labels. To left-align any objects (even objects of different types), select the objects you want to align and then choose Format, Align, Left or right-click one of the objects and select Align, Left. The selected objects are then aligned. (See Figure 5.13.) You can align the left, right, top, or bottom edges of any objects on a form.

TIP

It is helpful to add to the toolbar the design tools you commonly use.

FIGURE 5.12

The form before aligning objects.

FIGURE 5.13

The form after aligning objects.

NOTE

Don't confuse the Format, Align feature with the Align tools on the Formatting toolbar. The Format, Align feature aligns objects one to the other, but the Align tools on the Formatting toolbar align the text of an object within its borders.

Snap to Grid

The Snap to Grid feature determines whether objects snap to the gridlines on the form as you move and size them. This feature is found under the Format menu. If you turn this feature off (it's a toggle), objects can be moved and sized without regard for the gridlines.

> **TIP**
>
> I prefer to leave the Snap to Grid feature on at all times. I use a special trick to temporarily deactivate the feature when needed—hold down your Ctrl key as you click and drag to move objects. The Snap to Grid setting is then ignored.

Power Sizing Techniques

Just as there are several ways to move objects, you have several options for sizing objects. When an object is selected, each handle, except for the handle in the upper-left corner of the object, can be used to size the object. The handles at the top and bottom of the object allow you to change the object's height, and the handles at the left and right of the object let you change the object's width. You can use the handles in the upper-right, lower-right, and lower-left corners of the object to change the width and height of the object simultaneously. To size an object, place your mouse pointer over a sizing handle and click and drag. You can select several objects and size them at once. Each of the selected objects increases or decreases in size by the same amount; their relative sizes stay intact.

Access offers several powerful methods of sizing multiple objects, found under the Format, Size menu:

- **To Fit:** Sizes the selected objects to fit the text within them
- **To Grid:** Sizes the selected objects to the nearest gridlines
- **To Tallest:** Sizes the selected objects to the height of the tallest object in the selection
- **To Shortest:** Sizes the selected objects to the height of the shortest object in the selection
- **To Widest:** Sizes the selected objects to the width of the widest object in the selection
- **To Narrowest:** Sizes the selected objects to the width of the narrowest object in the selection

Probably the most confusing of the options is Format, Size, To Fit. This option is somewhat deceiving because it doesn't perfectly size text boxes to the text within them. In today's world of proportional fonts, it isn't possible to perfectly size a text box to the largest possible entry it contains. Generally, however, you can visually size text boxes to a sensible height and width. Use the field's Size property to limit what's typed in the text box. If the entry is too large to fit in the allocated space, the user can scroll to view the additional text. As the tip indicates, the Format, Size, To Fit option is much more appropriate for labels than it is for text boxes.

> **Tip**
>
> To quickly size a label to fit the text within it, select the label and then double-click any of its sizing handles, except the sizing handle in the upper-left corner of the label.

Controlling Object Spacing

Access gives you excellent tools for spacing the objects on your form an equal distance from one another. Notice in Figure 5.14 that the ClientID, Address, and City text boxes aren't equally spaced vertically from one another. To make the vertical distance between selected objects equal, choose Format, Vertical Spacing, Make Equal. In Figure 5.15, you can see the result of using this command on the selected objects in Figure 5.14.

Figure 5.14

The form before modifying vertical spacing.

The horizontal distance between objects can be made equal by choosing Format, Horizontal Spacing, Make Equal. Other related commands that are useful are Format, Vertical Spacing, Increase (or Decrease) and Format, Horizontal Spacing, Increase (or Decrease). These commands maintain the relationship between objects while proportionally increasing or decreasing the distance between them.

Modifying Object Tab Order

The tab order for the objects on a form is determined by the order in which you add the objects to the form. However, this order isn't necessarily appropriate for the user. You might need to modify the tab order of the objects on the form. To do so, select View, Tab Order to open the Tab Order dialog box, shown in Figure 5.16. This dialog box offers two options. Use the Auto Order command button to tell Access to set the tab order based on each object's location in a section on the form. However, if you want to customize the order of the objects, click and drag the gray buttons to the left of the object names listed under the Custom Order heading to specify the objects' tab order.

FIGURE 5.15

The form after modifying vertical spacing.

> **NOTE**
>
> You must set the tab order for the objects in each section of the form separately. To do this, select the appropriate section from the Tab Order dialog box, and then set the order of the objects in the section. If your selected form doesn't have a header or footer, the Form Header and Form Footer sections are unavailable.

FIGURE 5.16

Use the Tab Order dialog box to select the tab order of the objects in each section of a form.

SELECTING THE CORRECT CONTROL FOR THE JOB

Windows programming in general, and Access programming in particular, isn't limited to just writing code. Your ability to design a user-friendly interface can make or break the success of your application. Access and the Windows programming environment offer a variety of controls, and each one is appropriate in different situations. The following sections discuss each control, outlining when and how it should be used.

Labels

Labels are used to display information to your users. Attached labels are automatically added to your form when you add other controls, such as text boxes, combo boxes, and so on, and they can be deleted or modified as necessary. Their default captions are based on the Caption property of the field that underlies the control they're attached to. If nothing has been entered into the field's Caption property, the field name is used for the label's caption.

The Label tool, found in the toolbox, can be used to add any text to the form. Click the Label tool; then click and drag the label to place it on the form. Labels are often used to provide a description of the form or to supply instructions to users. Labels can be customized by modifying their font, size, color, and so on. Although developers can use VBA code to modify label properties at runtime, users don't have this ability.

TIP

Sometimes attached labels get detached from their associated text boxes. This means that the label will no longer move, size, and become selected with the text box that it applies to. To re-associate the label with the text box, cut the label (Ctrl+x), click to select the text box, and then press Ctrl+v to paste.

If you purposely want to disassociate a label from its attached control, simply cut the label and then paste it back on the form *without* selecting the control that it was attached to. This allows you to perform tasks such as hiding the control without hiding the label.

Text Boxes

Text boxes are used to get information from the user. Bound text boxes display and retrieve field information stored in a table; unbound text boxes gather information from the user that's not related to a specific field in a specific record. For example, a text box can be used to gather information about report criteria from a user.

Text boxes are automatically added to a form when you click and drag a field from the field list to the form and the Display control for the field is set to Text Box (the Display control is the default control type for an object, and is set in the design of the underlying table). Another way to add a text box is to select the Text Box tool from the toolbox; then click and drag to place the text box on the form. This process adds an unbound text box to the form. If you want to bind the text box to data, you must set its Control Source property.

Combo Boxes

Access offers several easy ways to add a combo box to a form. If a field's Display Control property has been set to Combo Box, a combo box is automatically added to a form when the field is added. The combo box automatically knows the source of its data as well as all its other important properties.

If a field's Display Control property hasn't been set to Combo Box, the easiest way to add a combo box to a form is to use the Control Wizard. The Control Wizard, when selected, helps you add combo boxes, list boxes, option groups, and subforms to your forms. Although all the properties set by the Combo Box Wizard can be set manually, using the wizard saves both time and energy. If you want the Combo Box Wizard to be launched when you add a combo box to the form, make sure the Control Wizards tool in the toolbox has been clicked (switched on) before you add the combo box.

To add a combo box to a form, select the Combo Box tool in the toolbox, and then click and drag to place the combo box on the form. This launches the Combo Box Wizard; its first step is shown in Figure 5.17. You're asked whether you want the combo box to look up the values in a table or query, whether you prefer to type the values yourself, or whether the combo box is going to be used to search for a particular record. Use the first option if your combo box will select the data that's stored in a field, such as the state associated with a particular client. I rarely, if ever, use the second option, which requires that you type the values for the combo box, because populating a combo box this way makes it difficult to maintain. Every time you want to add an entry to the combo box, your application must be modified. The third and final option is appropriate when you want the combo box to be used as a tool to find a specific record. For example, a combo box can be placed in the form's header to display a list of valid customers. After selecting a customer, the user is then moved to the appropriate record. This option is available only when the form is bound to a record source.

FIGURE 5.17

The first step of the Combo Box Wizard: selecting the source of the data.

In the second step of the Combo Box Wizard, you select a table or query to populate the combo box. For optimal performance, you should select a query. The third step of the Combo Box Wizard allows you to select the fields that appear in your combo box. (See Figure 5.18.) The combo box being built in the example will be used to select the client associated with a particular project. Although the CompanyName field will be the only field visible in the combo box, ClientID and CompanyName have both been selected because ClientID is a necessary element of the combo box. After a company name has been selected from the combo box, the client ID associated with the company name will be stored in the ClientID field of the tblProjects table.

FIGURE 5.18

The third step of the Combo Box Wizard: selecting fields.

The fourth step of the Combo Box Wizard lets you specify the width of each field in the combo box. Notice in Figure 5.19 that Access recommends that the key column, ClientID, be hidden. The idea is that the user will see the meaningful English description while Access worries about storing the appropriate key value into the record.

FIGURE 5.19

The fourth step of the Combo Box Wizard: setting column widths.

In the Combo Box Wizard's fifth step, you specify whether you want Access to simply remember the selected value or store it in a particular field in a table. In the example shown in Figure 5.20, the selected combo box value will be stored in the ClientID field of the tblProjects table.

FIGURE 5.20

The fifth step of the Combo Box Wizard: indicating where the selected value will be stored.

The sixth and final step of the Combo Box Wizard prompts for the text that will become the attached label for the combo box. The Finish button completes the process, building the combo box and filling in all its properties with the appropriate values.

Although the Combo Box Wizard is a helpful tool, it's important to understand the properties it sets. Figure 5.21 shows the Properties window for a combo box. Many of the Combo Box properties are covered in other chapters, but take a moment to go over the properties set by the Combo Box Wizard here.

The Control Source property indicates the field in which the selected entry is stored. In Figure 5.21, the selected entry will be stored in the ClientID field of the tblProjects table. The Row Source Type property specifies whether the source used to populate the combo box is a table/query, value list, or field list. In the example, the Row Source Type is Table/Query. The Row Source is the name of the actual table or query used to populate the combo box. In the example, the Row Source is tblClients. The Column Count property designates how many columns are in the combo box, and the Column Widths property indicates the width of each column. In the example, the width of the first column is zero, which renders the column invisible. Finally, Bound Column is used to specify which column in the combo box is being used to store data into the Control Source. In the example, this is column 1.

FIGURE 5.21

Properties of a combo box, showing that the ClientID field has been selected as the control source for the Combo5 combo box.

Combo boxes are very powerful controls, but you need to know many other things about them to leverage their power. The advanced aspects of combo boxes are covered in Chapter 9.

List Boxes

List boxes are similar to combo boxes, but differ from them in three major ways:

- They consume more screen space.
- They allow you to select only from the list that's displayed. This means you can't type new values into a list box (as you can with a combo box).
- They can be configured to let you select multiple items.

As with a combo box, the Display Control of a field can be set to List Box. If the Display Control has been set to List Box, a list box is added to the form when the field is clicked and dragged from the field list to the form.

The List Box Wizard is almost identical to the Combo Box Wizard. After running the List Box Wizard, the List Box properties affected by the wizard are the same as the Combo Box properties. Advanced list box techniques are covered in Chapter 9.

Check Boxes

Check boxes are used when you want to limit your user to entering one of two values. The values entered can be limited to Yes/No, True/False, or On/Off. You can add a check box to a form in several ways:

- Set the Display Control of the underlying field to Check Box; then click and drag the field from the field list to the form.
- Click the Check Box tool in the toolbox; then click and drag a field from the field list to the form. This method adds a check box to the form even if the Display Control of the underlying field isn't a check box.

- Click the Check Box tool in the toolbox; then click and drag to add a check box to the form. The check box you have added will be unbound. To bind the check box to data, you must set the control's Control Source property.

> **TIP**
>
> You can use the `Triple` state property of a check box to allow a third value, `Null`, to the possible choices for the check box value.

Option Buttons

Option buttons can be used alone or as part of an option group. An option button alone can be used to display a True/False value, but this isn't a standard use of an option button (check boxes are standard for this purpose). As part of an option group, option buttons force the user to select from a mutually exclusive set of options, such as choosing from American Express, MasterCard, Visa, or Discover for a payment type. This use of option buttons is covered in the section, "Option Groups."

Toggle Buttons

Like option buttons, toggle buttons can be used alone or as part of an option group. A toggle button by itself can display a True/False value, but this isn't a standard use. Toggle buttons are more commonly used as part of an option group, as discussed in the next section.

Option Groups

Option groups allow the user to select from a mutually exclusive set of options. They can include check boxes, toggle buttons, or option buttons, but the most common implementation of an option group is option buttons.

The easiest way to add an option group to a form is to use the Option Group Wizard. To ensure that the Option Group Wizard will run, make sure the Control Wizards button in the toolbox is selected. Click Option Group in the toolbox, and then click and drag to add the option group to the form; this launches the Option Group Wizard.

The first step of the Option Group Wizard, shown in Figure 5.22, allows you to type the text associated with each item in the option group. The second step gives you the option of selecting a default choice for the option group. This choice comes into effect when a new record is added to the table underlying the form. The third step of the wizard lets you select values associated with each option button. (See Figure 5.23.) The text displayed with the option button isn't stored in the record; instead, the underlying numeric value is stored in the record. In the example shown in Figure 5.23, the number 2 is stored in the field if Check is selected. The fourth step of the Option Group Wizard asks whether you want to remember the option group value for later use or store the value in a field. In the example in Figure 5.24, the option group value is stored in the PaymentMethodID field. In the fifth step of the Option Group Wizard, you can select from a variety of styles for the option group buttons, including option buttons, check boxes, and toggle buttons. You can also select from etched, flat, raised, shadowed, or sunken effects for your buttons. The wizard lets you preview each option. The sixth and final step of the wizard allows you to add an appropriate caption to the option group. The completed group of option buttons is shown in Figure 5.25.

FIGURE 5.22

Step 1 of the Option Group Wizard: adding text to options.

FIGURE 5.23

Step 3 of the Option Group Wizard: selecting values for options.

FIGURE 5.24

Step 4 of the Option Group Wizard: tying the group to data.

FIGURE 5.25

The results of running the Option Group Wizard.

It's important to understand that the Option Group Wizard sets properties of the frame, the option buttons within the frame, and the labels attached to the option buttons. The properties of the frame are shown in Figure 5.26. The control source of the frame and default value of the option group are set by the Option Group Wizard. Each individual option button is assigned a value, and the caption of the attached labels associated with each button is set.

FIGURE 5.26

An option group frame, showing the properties of the selected button.

CONTROL MORPHING

When you first build a form, you might not always choose the best type of control to display each field on the form, or you might make what you think is the best choice for the control, only to find out later that it wasn't exactly what your user had in mind. In Access, it's easy to "morph," or convert, the type of control. For example, you can morph a list box into a combo box.

Morphing a Text Box to a Combo Box

One of the most common types of conversions is from a text box to a combo box. To morph a text box to a combo box, right-click on the text box. Choose Change To, and then select the type of control you want to morph the text box to. The types of controls available depend on the type of control you're morphing. For example, a text box can be converted to a label, list box, or combo box. (See Figure 5.27.)

5

FORMS

FIGURE 5.27

Morphing a text box.

After morphing a text box to a combo box, you modify the appropriate Control properties. The Row Source, Bound Column, Column Count, and Column Widths properties need to be filled in. For the row source, you must select the appropriate table or query. If you select a table and then click the ellipse, you are prompted to create a query based on the table. After selecting Yes, you can build a query containing only the fields you want to include in the combo box. You're then ready to select the bound column, which is used to store data in the underlying table. For example, the user might select the name of a project that a payment is being applied to, but the ProjectID will be stored in the Payments table. Set the column count to the number of columns selected in the underlying query; the column widths can be set so that the key column is hidden.

Combo Box to a List Box

Converting a combo box to a list box is a much simpler process than converting a text box to a combo box or list box because combo boxes and list boxes share so many properties. To morph a combo box to a list box, simply right-click on the combo box and choose Change To, List Box.

CONDITIONAL FORMATTING

New to Access 2000 is conditional formatting. Using conditional formatting, data meeting specified criteria is displayed differently. To conditionally format data displayed within a control, follow these steps:

1. Select the control you want to conditionally format.
2. Select Format | Conditional Formatting. The Conditional Formatting dialog appears.
3. Select Field Value Is, Expression Is, or Field Has Focus from the first combo box.
4. Select the appropriate operator from the second combo box.
5. Enter the values you are testing for in the text boxes that appear on the right.
6. Select the formatting (bold, italic, background color, and so on) that you want to apply when the conditional criteria is met.
7. Click Add to add additional formats.
8. Click OK to apply the conditional formatting.

WHAT FORM PROPERTIES ARE AVAILABLE AND WHY USE THEM?

Forms have many properties that can be used to affect their look and behavior. The properties are broken down into categories: Format, Data, Event, and Other. To view a form's properties, you must select the form in one of two ways:

- Click the Form Selector (the small gray button at the intersection of the horizontal and vertical rulers).
- Choose Edit, Select Form.

Working with the Properties Window

After a form has been selected, click the Properties button on the toolbar to view its properties. The Properties window, shown in Figure 5.28, consists of five tabs: Format, Data, Event, Other, and All. Many developers prefer to view all properties at once, but a form has a total of 81 properties! Rather than viewing all 81 properties at once, try viewing the properties by category. The Format category includes all the physical attributes of the form, the ones that affect the form's appearance (such as background color, for example). The Data category includes all the properties that relate to the data the form is bound to, such as the form's underlying record source. The Event category contains all the Windows events to which a form can respond. For example, you can write code that executes in response to the form being loaded, becoming active, displaying a different record, and so on. The Other category has a few properties that don't fit into the other three categories.

FIGURE 5.28

*Viewing the
Format properties
of a form.*

Working with the Important Form Properties

As mentioned, forms have 81 properties, and of those, 32 are Event properties, covered in Chapter 9. This section covers the Format, Data, and Other properties of forms.

Format Properties of a Form

The Format properties of a form affect its physical appearance. Forms have 26 Format properties:

Caption: The Caption property sets the text that appears on the form's title bar. This property can be customized at runtime. For example, you could include the name of the current user or specify the name of the client for whom an invoice is being generated.

Default View: The Default View property allows you to select three options:

- SINGLE FORM—Only one record can be viewed at a time

- CONTINUOUS FORMS—As many records as will fit within the form window are displayed at one time, each displayed as the detail section of a single form

- DATASHEET—Displays the records in a spreadsheet-like format, with the rows representing records and the columns representing fields

The selected option becomes the default view for the form.

Views Allowed: The Views Allowed property determines whether the user is allowed to switch from Form view to Datasheet view or vice versa. The Default View property determines the default display mode for the form, but Views Allowed determines whether the user is permitted to switch out of the default view.

Scroll Bars: The Scroll Bars property determines whether scrollbars appear if the controls on the form don't fit within the form's display area. You can select from vertical and horizontal, neither vertical nor horizontal, just vertical, or just horizontal.

Record Selectors: A record selector is the gray bar to the left of a record in Form view or the gray box to the left of each record in Datasheet view. It's used to select a record to be copied or deleted. The Record Selectors property determines whether the record selectors appear. If you give the user a custom menu, you can opt to remove the record selector to make sure the user copies or deletes records using only the features specifically built into your application.

Navigation Buttons: Navigation buttons are the controls that appear at the bottom of a form; they allow the user to move from record to record within the form. The Navigation Buttons property determines whether the navigation buttons are visible. You should set it to No for any dialog forms, and you might want to set it to No for data-entry forms, too, and add your own toolbar or command buttons that enhance or limit the standard buttons' functionality. For example, in a client/server environment, you might not want to give users the ability to move to the first or last record because that type of record movement can be inefficient in a client/server architecture.

Dividing Lines: The Dividing Lines property indicates whether you want a line to appear between records when the default view of the form is set to Continuous Forms.

Auto Resize: The Auto Resize property determines whether the form is automatically sized to display a complete record.

Auto Center: The Auto Center property specifies whether you want the form to automatically be centered within the Application window whenever it's opened.

Border Style: The Border Style property is far more powerful than its name implies. The options for the Border Style property are None, Thin, Sizable, and Dialog. The border style is often set to None for splash screens, which means the form has no border. A Thin border is not resizable; the Size command isn't available in the Control menu. This setting is a good choice for pop-up forms, which remain on top even when other forms are given the focus. A Sizable border is standard for most forms. It includes all the standard options in the Control menu. A Dialog border looks like a Thin border. A form with a border style of Dialog can't be maximized, minimized, or resized. Once the border style of a form is set to Dialog, the Maximize, Minimize, and Resize options aren't available in the form's Control menu. The Dialog border is often used along with the Pop Up and Modal properties to create custom dialog boxes.

Control Box: The Control Box property determines whether a form has a Control menu. You should use this option sparingly. One of your responsibilities as an Access programmer is to make your applications comply with Windows standards. If you look at the Windows programs you use, you'll find very few forms without Control menu boxes. This should tell you something about how to design your own applications.

5

Min Max Buttons: The Min Max Buttons property indicates whether the form has minimize and maximize buttons. The available options are None, Min Enabled, Max Enabled, and Both Enabled. If you remove one or both buttons, the appropriate options also become unavailable in the Control menu. The Min Max property is ignored for forms with a border style of None or Dialog. As with the Control Box property, I rarely use this property. To make my applications comply with Windows standards, I set the Border Style property, and then inherit the standard attributes for each border style.

Close Button: The Close Button property determines whether the user can close the form by using the Control menu or double-clicking the Control icon. If you set the value of this property to No, you must give your user another way to close the form; otherwise, the user might have to reboot his or her computer to close your application.

Whats This Button: The Whats This Button property specifies whether you want the Whats This button added to the form's title bar. This feature works only when the form's Min Max Buttons property is set to No. When the Whats This Button property is set to Yes, the user can click on the Whats This button and then click on an object on the form to display Help for that object. If the selected object has no Help associated with it, Help for the form is displayed, and if the form has no Help associated with it, Microsoft Access Help is displayed.

Width: The Width property is used to specify the form's width. This option is most often set graphically by clicking and dragging to select an appropriate size for the form. You might want to set this property manually when you want more than one form to be the exact same size.

Picture, Picture Type, Picture Size Mode, Picture Alignment, and Picture Tiling: The Picture properties let you select and customize the attributes of a bitmap used as the background for a form.

Grid X, Grid Y: The Grid X and Grid Y properties can be used to modify the spacing of the horizontal and vertical lines that appear in the form when in Design view. By setting these properties, you can affect how precisely you place objects on the form when the Snap to Grid option is active.

Layout for Print: The Layout for Print property specifies whether screen or printer fonts are used on the form. If you want to optimize the form for printing rather than display, set this property to Yes.

SubdatasheetHeight: The SubdatasheetHeight property is used to designate the maximum height for a subdatasheet.

SubdatasheetExpanded: The SubdatasheetExpanded property allows you to designate whether a subdatasheet is initially displayed in an expanded format. When set to False, the subdatasheet initially appears collapsed. When set to True, the subdatasheet appears in an expanded format.

Palette Source: The Palette Source property determines the source for selecting colors for a form.

Data Properties of a Form

The Data properties of a form are used to control the source for the form's data, what sort of actions the user can take on the data in the form, and how the data in the form is locked in a multiuser environment. There are 10 Data properties of a form.

Record Source: The Record Source property indicates the Table, Stored Query, or SQL statement on which the form's records are based. After you have selected a record source for a form, the controls on the form can be bound to the fields in the record source.

> **NOTE**
>
> The Field List window is unavailable until the record source of the form has been set.

> **TIP**
>
> The record source of a form can be changed at runtime. With this aspect of the Record Source property, you can create generic, reusable forms for many situations.

Filter: The Filter property is used to automatically load a stored filter along with the form. I prefer to base a form on a query that limits the data displayed on the form. The query can be passed parameters at runtime to customize exactly what data is displayed.

Order By: The Order By property specifies in what order the records on a form appear. This property can be modified at runtime to change the order in which the records appear.

Allow Filters: The Allow Filters property allows you to control whether records can be filtered at runtime. When this option is set to No, all filtering options become disabled to the user.

Allow Edits, Allow Deletions, Allow Additions: These properties let you specify whether the user can edit data, delete records, or add records from within the form. These options can't override any permissions that have been set for the form's underlying table or queries. Security is covered in Chapters 33, "Database Security Made Easy," and 34, "Advanced Security Techniques."

Data Entry: The Data Entry property determines whether your users can only add records within a form. Set this property to Yes if you don't want your users to view or modify existing records but want them to be able to add new records.

Recordset Type: The Recordset Type property gives you three options: Dynaset, Dynaset (Inconsistent Updates), and Snapshot. Each offers different performance and updating capability. The Dynaset option creates a fully updateable recordset. The only exceptions to this rule involve records or fields that can't be updated for some other reason. An example is a form based on a query involving a one-to-many relationship. The join field on the "one" side of the relationship can be updated only if the Cascade Update Related Records feature has been enabled. The Dynaset (Inconsistent Updates) option allows all tables and bound data to be edited. This might result in inconsistent updating of data in the tables involved in the query. The Snapshot option doesn't allow any updating.

Record Locks: The Record Locks property specifies the locking mechanism to be used for the data underlying the form's recordset. Three options are available. The No Locks option—the least restrictive locking mechanism—provides *optimistic locking*; that is, Access doesn't try to lock the record until the user moves off it. This option can lead to potential conflicts when two users simultaneously make changes to the same record. The All Records option locks all records underlying the form the entire time the form is open. This is the most restrictive option and should be used only when it's necessary for the form's user to make sure other users can view, but not modify, the form's underlying recordset. The Edited Record option locks a 2KB page of records as soon as a user starts editing the data in the form. This option provides *pessimistic locking*. Although it averts conflicts by prohibiting two users from modifying a record at the same time, it can lead to potential locking conflicts. These three locking options are covered in detail in Chapter 17, "Developing Multiuser Applications."

Other Properties of a Form

Pop Up: The Pop Up property indicates whether the form always remains on top of other windows. This property is often set to Yes, along with the Modal property, for custom dialog boxes.

Modal: The Modal property indicates whether focus can be removed from a form while it's open. When the Modal property is set to Yes, the form must be closed before the user can continue working with the application. As mentioned, this property is used with the Pop Up property to create custom dialog boxes.

Cycle: The Cycle property controls the behavior of the Tab key in the form. The options are All Records, Current Record, and Current Page. When the Cycle property is set to All Records, the user is placed on the next record when he or she presses Tab from the last control on the form. With Current Record, the user is moved from the last control on a form to the first control on the same record. The Current Page option refers only to multipage forms;

when the Cycle property is set to `Current Page`, the user tabs from the last control on the page to the first control on the same page. All three options are affected by the tab order of the objects on the form.

Menu Bar: The Menu Bar property specifies a menu bar associated with the form. The menu bar, sometimes referred to as a command bar in Access 2000, is created by using the Customize dialog box, available by choosing Toolbars from the View menu and then selecting Customize. Menus are covered in Chapter 9.

Toolbar: The Toolbar property designates a toolbar associated with the form. The toolbar, sometimes referred to as a *command bar* in Access 2000, is created by using the Customize dialog box. The toolbar you select is displayed whenever the form has the focus. Toolbars are covered in Chapter 9.

Shortcut Menu, Shortcut Menu Bar: The Shortcut Menu property indicates whether a shortcut menu is displayed when the user clicks with the right mouse button over an object on the form. The Shortcut Menu Bar property lets you associate a custom menu with a control on the form or with the form itself. As with a standard menu bar, a shortcut menu bar is created by choosing Toolbars from the View menu and then selecting Customize. Shortcut menus are covered in Chapter 9.

Fast Laser Printing: The Fast Laser Printing property determines whether lines and rectangles print along with the form. When this property is set to `Yes`, you'll notice a definite improvement when printing the form to a laser printer.

Help File, Help Context ID: The Help File and Help Context ID properties are used to associate a specific Help file and topic with a form.

Tag: The Tag property is an extra property used to store miscellaneous information about the form. This property is often set and monitored at runtime to store necessary information about the form. An example would be to add a tag to each of several forms that should be unloaded as a group.

Has Module: The Has Module property determines whether the form has a class module. If no code is associated with your form, setting this property to `No` can noticeably decrease load time and improve your form's performance while decreasing the database's size.

Allow Design Changes: The Allow Design Changes property determines whether changes can be made to the design of the form while viewing form data. If this property is set to All Views, the Properties window is available in Form view, and changes made to form properties while in Form view are permanent if the form is saved.

5

FORMS

WHAT CONTROL PROPERTIES ARE AVAILABLE AND WHY USE THEM?

Available Control properties vary quite a bit, depending on the type of control that's been selected. The more common properties are covered in this section; individual properties are covered throughout the book as they apply to a specific topic.

Format Properties of a Control

Format: The Format property of a control determines how the data in the control is displayed. A control's format is automatically inherited from its underlying data source. This property is used in three situations:

- When the Format property is not set for the underlying field
- When you want to override the Format setting set for the field
- When you want to apply a format to an unbound control

You can select from a multitude of predefined values for a control's format, or you can create a custom format. I often modify this property at runtime to vary the format of a control depending on a certain condition. For example, the format for a Visa card number is different from the format for an ATM card number.

Decimal Places: The Decimal Places property specifies how many decimal places you want to appear in the control. This property is used with the Format property to determine the control's appearance.

Caption: The Caption property is used to specify information helpful to the user. It's available for labels, command buttons, and toggle buttons.

Hyperlink Address: The Hyperlink Address property is available only for command buttons, images, and unattached labels. It contains a string used to specify the UNC (path to a file) or URL (Web page address) associated with the control. When the form is active and the cursor is placed over the control, clicking the control displays the specified object or Web page.

Hyperlink SubAddress: Like the Hyperlink Address property, the Hyperlink SubAddress property is available only for command buttons, images, and unattached labels. The Hyperlink SubAddress property is a string representing a location in the document specified in the Hyperlink Address property.

Visible: The Visible property indicates whether a control is visible. This property can be toggled at runtime, depending on specific circumstances. For example, a question on the form might apply only to records in which the gender is set to Female; if the gender is set to Male, the question shouldn't be visible.

Display When: The Display When property is used when you want certain controls on the form to be sent only to the screen or only to the printer. The three options are Always, Print Only, or Screen Only. An example of the use of the Display When property is a label containing instructions. You might want the instructions to appear on the screen but not on the printout.

Scroll Bars: The Scroll Bars property determines whether scrollbars appear when the data in the control doesn't fit within the control's size. The options are None and Vertical. I often set the Scroll Bars property to Vertical when the control is used to display data from a Memo field. The scrollbar makes it easier for the user to work with a potentially large volume of data in the Memo field.

Can Grow, Can Shrink: The Can Grow and Can Shrink properties apply only to the form's printed version. The Can Grow property, when set to Yes, expands the control when printing so that all the data in the control fits on the printout. The Can Shrink property applies when no data has been entered into the control. When this property is set to Yes, the control shrinks when no data has been entered so that blank lines won't be printed.

Left, Top, Width, Height: These properties are used to set the control's position and size.

Back Style, Back Color: The Back Style property can be set to Normal or Transparent. When set to Transparent, the form's background color shows through the control. This is often the preferred setting for an option group. The control's Back Color property specifies the background color (as opposed to text color) for the control.

CAUTION

If the Back Style of a control is set to Transparent, the control's back color is ignored.

Special Effect: The Special Effect property adds 3D effects to a control. The options for this property are Flat, Raised, Sunken, Etched, Shadowed, and Chiseled. Each of these effects gives the control a different look.

Border Style, Border Color, Border Width: These properties affect the look, color, and thickness of a control's border. The border style options are Transparent, Solid, Dashes, Short Dashes, Dots, Sparse Dots, Dash Dot, and Dash Dot Dot. The Border Color property specifies the color of the border; you can select from a variety of colors. The Border Width property can be set to one of several point sizes.

CAUTION

If the Border Style of a control is set to Transparent, the control's Border Color and Border Width are ignored.

Fore Color, Font Name, Font Size, Font Weight, Font Italic, Font Underline: These properties control the appearance of the text in a control. As their names imply, they let you select a color, font, size, and thickness for the text and determine whether the text is italicized or underlined. These properties can be modified in response to a runtime event, such as modifying a control's text color if the value in that control exceeds a certain amount. The font weight selections generally exceed what is actually available for a particular font and printer—normally, you have a choice of only Regular and Bold, whatever value you select for this property.

Text Align: The Text Align property is often confused with the ability to align controls. The Text Align property affects how the data is aligned *within* a control.

Left Margin, Top Margin, Right Margin, Bottom Margin: These properties determine how far the text appears from the left, top, right, and bottom of the control. They are particularly useful with controls such as text boxes based on memo fields, where the size of the control is large.

Line Spacing: The Line Spacing property is used to determine the spacing between lines of text in a multiline control. This property is most commonly used with a text box based on a memo field.

Is Hyperlink: This property, when set to Yes, formats the data in the control as a hyperlink. If the data in the control is a relevant link (that is, http:\\microsoft.com) the data will function as a hyperlink.

Data Properties of a Control

Control Source: The Control Source property specifies the field from the record source that's associated with a particular control. A control source can also be any valid Access expression.

Input Mask: The Format and Decimal Places properties affect the appearance of the control, but the Input Mask property affects what data can be entered into the control. The input mask of the field underlying the control is automatically inherited into the control. If no input mask is entered as a field property, the input mask can be entered directly in the form. If the input mask of the field is entered, the input mask of the associated control on a form can be used to further restrict what is entered into that field via the form.

Default Value: The Default Value property of a control determines the value assigned to new records entered in the form. This property can be set within the field properties. A default value set at the field level is automatically inherited into the form. The default value set for the control overrides the default value set at the field level.

Validation Rule, Validation Text: The validation rule and validation text of a control perform the same function as they do for a field.

Enabled: The Enabled property determines whether you allow a control to get focus. If set to No, the control appears dimmed.

Locked: The Locked property determines whether the data in the control can be modified. When the Locked property is set to Yes, the control can get focus but can't be edited. The Enabled and Locked properties of a control interact with one another. Table 5.1 summarizes their interactions.

TABLE 5.1 HOW ENABLED AND LOCKED PROPERTIES INTERACT

Enabled	Locked	Effect
Yes	Yes	The control can get focus; its data can be copied but not modified.
Yes	No	The control can get focus, and its data can be edited.
No	Yes	The control can't get focus.
No	No	The control can't get focus; its data appears dimmed.

Filter Lookup: The Filter Lookup property indicates whether you want the values associated with a bound text box to appear in the Filter By Form window.

Other Properties of a Control

Name: The Name property allows you to name the control. This name is used when you refer to the control in code and is also displayed in various drop-down lists that show all the controls on a form. It's important to name your controls because named controls improve your code's readability and make working with Access forms and other objects easier. The naming conventions for controls are in Appendix B, "Naming Conventions."

Status Bar Text: The Status Bar Text property specifies the text that appears in the status bar when the control gets focus. This property setting overrides the Description property that can be set in a table's design.

Enter Key Behavior: The Enter Key Behavior property determines whether the Enter key causes the cursor to move to the next control or add a new line in the current control. This setting is often changed for text boxes used to display the contents of Memo fields.

Allow AutoCorrect: The Allow AutoCorrect property specifies whether the AutoCorrect feature is available in the control. The AutoCorrect feature automatically corrects common spelling errors and typos.

Vertical: The Vertical property is used to control whether the text in the control is displayed horizontally or vertically. The default is No, or horizontal. When vertical is selected, the text within the control is rotated 90 degrees.

Auto Tab: The Auto Tab property, when set to Yes, automatically advances the cursor to the next control when the last character of an input mask has been entered. Some users like this option and others find it annoying, especially if they must tab out of some fields but not others.

Default: The Default property applies to a command button or ActiveX control and specifies whether the control is the default button on a form.

Cancel: The Cancel property applies to a command button or ActiveX control. It indicates that you want the control's code to execute when the Esc key is pressed while the form is active.

Auto Repeat: The Auto Repeat property specifies whether you want an event procedure or macro to execute repeatedly while the command button is being pressed.

Status Bar Text: The Status Bar Text property specifies the message that appears in the status bar when the control has the focus.

Tab Stop: The Tab Stop property determines whether the Tab key can be used to enter a control. It's appropriate to set this property to No for controls whose values rarely get modified. The user can always opt to click in the control when necessary.

Tab Index: The Tab Index property sets the tab order for the control. I generally set the Tab Index property by using View, Tab Order, rather than by setting the value directly in the control's Tab Index property.

Shortcut Menu Bar: The Shortcut Menu Bar attaches a specific menu to a control. The menu bar appears when the user right-clicks the control.

ControlTip Text: The ControlTip Text property specifies the tooltip associated with a control. The tooltip automatically appears when the user places the mouse pointer over the control and leaves it there for a moment.

Help Context ID: The Help Context ID property designates the Help topic associated with a particular control.

Tag: The Tag property is an extra property you can use to store information about a control. Your imagination determines how you use this property. The Tag property can be read and modified at runtime.

BOUND, UNBOUND, AND CALCULATED CONTROLS

There are important differences between bound and unbound controls. *Unbound controls* display information to the user or gather information from the user that's not going to be stored in your database. Here are some examples of unbound controls:

- A label providing instructions to the user
- A logo placed on a form
- A combo or text box placed on a form so that the user can enter report criteria
- A rectangle placed on the form to logically group several controls

Bound controls are used to display and modify information stored in a database table. A bound control automatically appears in the form specified in its Display Control property; the control automatically inherits many of the attributes assigned to the field the control is bound to.

NOTE

The Display Control property is set in the design of the underlying table. It is located on the Lookup tab of the Table Design window. It determines the default control type that is used when a control is added to a form or report.

A *Calculated control* is a special type of control that displays the results of an expression. The data in a Calculated control can't be modified by the user. The control's value automatically changes as the values in its expression are changed. For example, the Sales Total changes as the Price or Quantity is changed.

USING EXPRESSIONS TO ENHANCE YOUR FORMS

As mentioned in the previous section, a control can contain any valid expression as its control source. When entering an expression as a control source, the expression must be preceded by an equal sign. The control source can be manually typed, or you can use the Expression Builder to make the process easier.

To add an expression to a control source, start by adding an unbound control to the form. To use the Expression Builder, click the control's Control Source property, and then click the ellipsis. The Expression Builder appears. (See Figure 5.29.) In the list box on the left, select the type of object you want to include in the expression. The middle and right list boxes let you select the specific element you want to paste into your expression. The Expression Builder is useful when you're not familiar with the specific syntax required for the expression. An expression can also be entered directly into the text box for the Control Source property. To view the expression more easily, you can use the Zoom feature (Shift+F2). The Zoom dialog box for the control source is pictured in Figure 5.30; the expression shown in the figure evaluates the PaymentAmount. If the PaymentAmount is greater than or equal to 1,000, the message "Big Hitter" is displayed; otherwise, nothing is displayed.

FIGURE 5.29

The Expression Builder helps you add an expression as a control's control source.

FIGURE 5.30

The Zoom dialog box for a control source.

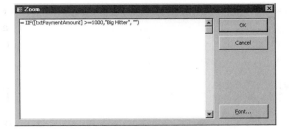

THE COMMAND BUTTON WIZARDS: PROGRAMMING WITHOUT TYPING

With the Command Button Wizard, you can quickly and easily add functionality to your forms. It writes the code to perform 33 commonly required tasks. The tasks are separated into record navigation, record operations, form operations, report operations, application operations, and other miscellaneous tasks. The Command Button Wizard is automatically invoked when a command button is added with the Control Wizards tool selected. The first step of the Command Button Wizard is shown in Figure 5.31; here, you specify the category of activity and specific action you want the command button to perform. The subsequent wizard steps vary, depending on the category and action you select.

FIGURE 5.31

The first step of the Command Button Wizard.

Figure 5.32 shows the second step of the Command Button Wizard when the Form Operations category and Open Form action are selected in the first step. Notice that this step asks which form you want to open. After selecting a form and clicking Next, you're asked whether you want Access to open the form and find specific data to display or whether you want the form to be opened and all records displayed. If you indicate that you want only specific records displayed, the dialog box shown in Figure 5.33 appears. This dialog box asks you to select fields relating the two forms. In the next step of the wizard, select text or a picture for the button. The final step of the wizard asks you to name the button.

FIGURE 5.32

The Command Button Wizard requesting the name of a form to open.

FIGURE 5.33

The Command Button Wizard asking for the fields that relate each form.

What's surprising about the Command Button Wizard is how much it varies depending on the features you select. It allows you to add somewhat sophisticated functionality to your application without writing a single line of code. The code generated by the example just outlined is shown in Figure 5.34; it will make a lot more sense after you read the next couple of chapters. The advantage to the code generated by the Command Button Wizard is that it can be fully modified after it's written; this means you can have Access do some of the dirty work for you, and then customize the work to your liking.

FIGURE 5.34

The code generated from the Command Button Wizard.

```
Private Sub cmdViewProjects_Click()
On Error GoTo Err_cmdViewProjects_Click

    Dim stDocName As String
    Dim stLinkCriteria As String

    stDocName = "frmProjects"

    stLinkCriteria = "[ClientID]=" & Me![txtClientID]
    DoCmd.OpenForm stDocName, , , stLinkCriteria

Exit_cmdViewProjects_Click:
    Exit Sub

Err_cmdViewProjects_Click:
    MsgBox Err.Description
    Resume Exit_cmdViewProjects_Click

End Sub
```

BUILDING FORMS BASED ON MORE THAN ONE TABLE

Many forms are based on more than one table. A form, for example, that shows a customer at the top and the orders associated with that customer at the bottom is considered a One-to-Many form. Forms can also be based on a query that joins more than one table. Rather than seeing a one-to-many relationship in such a form, you see the two tables displayed as one, with each record on the "many" side of the relationship appearing with its parent's data.

Creating One-to-Many Forms

There are several ways to create One-to-Many forms. As with many other types of forms, you can use a wizard to help you or build the form from scratch. Because all the methods for creating a form are useful to users and developers alike, the available options are covered in this section.

Building a One-to-Many Form by Using the Form Wizard

Building a One-to-Many form by using the Form Wizard is a simple process with 10 steps:

1. Click Forms in the Objects list and double-click the Create Form by Using Wizard icon.
2. Use the Tables/Queries drop-down list to select the table or query that will appear on the "one" side of the relationship.
3. Select the fields you want to include from the "one" side of the relationship.
4. Use the Tables/Queries drop-down list to select the table or query that will appear on the "many" side of the relationship.
5. Select the fields you want to include from the "many" side of the relationship.
6. Click Next.
7. Select whether you want the parent form to appear with subforms or the child forms to appear as linked forms. (See Figure 5.35.) Click Next.

FIGURE 5.35

The Form Wizard creating a One-to-Many form.

8. If you select the Subform option, indicate whether you want the subform to appear in a tabular format or as a datasheet (this option is not available if Linked forms was selected in step 7). Click Next.

9. Select a style for the form; then click Next.

10. Name both the form and the subform and click Finish.

The result is a main form that contains a subform. An example is shown in Figure 5.36.

FIGURE 5.36

The result of creating a One-to-Many form with the Form Wizard.

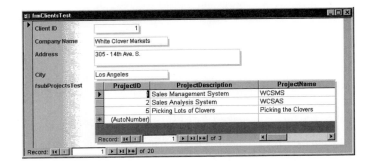

Building a One-to-Many Form with the Subform/Subreport Wizard

A One-to-Many form can also be created by building the parent form; then adding a Subform/Subreport control, which is found in the toolbox. If you want to use the Subform/Subreport Wizard, make sure the Control Wizards tool is selected before you add the Subform/Subreport control to the main form. Then follow these six steps:

1. Click to select the Subform/Subreport control.

2. Click and drag to place the Subform/Subreport control on the main form; this invokes the Subform/Subreport Wizard.

3. Indicate whether you want to use an existing form as the subform or build a new subform from a table or query.

4. If you select Table/Query, the next step of the Subform/Subreport Wizard prompts you to select a table or query and which fields you want to include from it. (See Figure 5.37.) Select the fields; then click Next.

FIGURE 5.37

Selecting fields to include in the subform

5. The next step of the Subform/Subreport Wizard prompts you to select the relationship between the fields in the two forms. You can select from the suggested relationships or define your own. (See Figure 5.38.) Select the appropriate relationship and click Next.

FIGURE 5.38

Defining the relationship between the main form and the subform.

6. Name the subform and click Finish.

The resulting form should look similar to the form created with the Form Wizard. Creating a One-to-Many form this way is simply an alternative to the Form Wizard.

TIP

Another way to add a subform to a main form is to click and drag a form from the Database window onto the main form. Access then tries to identify the relationship between the two forms.

Working with Subforms

Once a subform has been added, you need to understand how to work with it. To begin, familiarize yourself with a few properties of a Subform control, as follows:

Source Object: The name of the form that's being displayed in the control.

Link Child Fields: The fields from the child form that link the child form to the master form.

Link Master Fields: The fields from the master form that link the child form to the master form.

You should also understand how to make changes to the subform. One option is to open the subform as you would open any other form. After closing and saving the form, all the changes automatically appear in the parent form. The other choice is to modify the subform from within the main form. With the main form open the subform is visible. Any changes made to the design of the subform from within the main form are permanent.

The default view of the subform is Datasheet or Continuous Forms, depending on how you added the subform and what options you selected. If you want to modify the default view, simply change the subform's Default View property.

NOTE

When a subform is displayed in Datasheet view, the order of the fields in the subform has no bearing on the datasheet that appears in the main form. The order of the columns in the datasheet depends on the tab order of the fields in the subform. You must therefore modify the tab order of the fields in the subform to change the order of the fields in the resulting datasheet.

BASING FORMS ON QUERIES: THE WHY AND HOW

One strategy when building forms is to base them on queries; by doing this, you generally get optimal performance and flexibility. Rather than bringing all fields and all records over the network, you bring only the fields and records you need. The benefits are even more pronounced in a client/server environment where the query is run on the server. Even in an environment where data is stored in the proprietary Access file format (.MDB) on a file server, a form based on a stored query can better take advantage of Access's indexing and paging features. By basing a form on a query, you also have more control over which records are included in the form and in what order they appear. Finally, you can base a form on a query containing a one-to-many join, viewing parent and child information as if it were one record. Notice in Figure 5.39 that the client and project information appear on one form as if they were one record.

FIGURE 5.39

A form based on a one-to-many query.

Embedding SQL Statements Versus Stored Queries

In earlier versions of Access, stored queries offered better performance than embedded SQL statements. This is because when a query is saved, Access compiles the query and creates a query plan, which has information on the best way to execute the query based on available indexes and the volume of data. In earlier versions of Access, if a form was based on an embedded SQL statement, the SQL statement was compiled and optimized each time the form was opened. With Access 2000, embedded SQL statements are compiled just like stored queries. You might ask yourself the question whether with Access 2000 it is better to base a query on a stored query or on a SQL statement. My personal preference is as follows: If I plan to use the same or a similar query with multiple forms and reports, I build a query and base multiple forms and reports on that query. This keeps me from having to duplicate my efforts in building the query. If I have a query that is unique to the form, I build it as an embedded SQL statement. This eliminates the extra "clutter" of the query in the database container.

> **NOTE**
>
> A query plan can sometimes be inaccurate because the query plan optimizes the query based on the amount of data in the underlying tables. If the amount of data in the tables underlying a form changes significantly, it is necessary to rebuild the query plan. This can be accomplished by opening, running, and saving the query, or by compacting the database.

ACCESS FORMS AND THE INTERNET

Microsoft has made it easier to develop Internet-aware applications by adding hyperlinks to forms and allowing you to save an Access form as HTML or in the Microsoft IIS 1-2 format. These features are covered in the following sections.

Adding a Hyperlink to a Form

Hyperlinks can be added to unattached labels (labels not attached to a text box or other object), command buttons, and image controls. Once added, they let the user jump to a document (UNC) or home page (URL) simply by clicking the control containing the hyperlink. To add a hyperlink to a label, command button, or image control, follow these steps:

1. Click to select the control.
2. View the control's properties.
3. Select the Format tab of the Properties window.
4. Click in the Hyperlink Address property.
5. Click the build button (the ellipsis) to open the Insert Hyperlink dialog box. (See Figure 5.40.)

FIGURE 5.40

Establishing a link to a file or URL by using the Insert Hyperlink dialog box.

6. With Existing File or Web Page selected as the Link To, you can enter a file path or URL in the text box or click File to locate a file or Web Page to locate a URL. You can also click to insert hyperlinks to Recent Files, Browsed Pages, or Inserted Links. With Object in This Database selected as the Link To, you can link to an object in the current database (see Figure 5.41). Select Create New Page to create a new data access page and select Email Address to link to an email address.

FIGURE 5.41

Setting the location within an Access database for your hyperlink.

7. Click OK to finish the process. The contents of the Link to File or URL combo box become the Hyperlink Address, and the object name becomes the Hyperlink SubAddress. (See Figure 5.42.)

FIGURE 5.42

Hyperlink address and subaddress defined for a label control.

TIP

Using a hyperlink address to open an object in an Access database, rather than using the `Click` event of the command button and VBA code, allows you to remove the class module associated with the form (if that is the only procedure you need for the form), thereby optimizing the form's performance.

Saving a Form as HTML

Forms can be saved as HTML documents in one of two ways. The first method is to save a form as HTML by choosing File, Export (you can also right-click the form in the database container [Database window] and select Export). The Export Form dialog appears. Select

HTML Documents (*.html*.htm) from the Save as Type drop-down. Enter a filename for the HTML document. If you want the system's default browser to load after the HTML document is saved, click Autostart. Click Save All. The HTML Output Options dialog appears. If desired, click Browse to locate an HTML template file. Click OK to close the HTML Output Options dialog. Only the datasheet associated with the form is saved as HTML; the format of the form itself isn't saved.

The other method is to choose File, Save As. Select Data Access Page from the As drop-down. See Chapter 32, "Utilizing Active Data Pages," for more detailed information.

Saving a Form as Microsoft IIS 1-2 or Microsoft Active Server Pages

Forms can also be saved in the Microsoft IIS 1-2 format or as Active Server Pages. Both of these options create dynamic forms. With Microsoft IIS 1-2, Microsoft Information Server uses the .HTX and .IDC files to build an .HTM file with the current data. The .IDC file contains data source information, including the data source name, user name, password, and the query that returns the record source of the form being created. The .HTX file is an HTML file that includes merge codes indicating where the data being returned should be inserted. With Active Server Pages, Microsoft Information Server also builds an .HTM file with the current data.

> **NOTE**
>
> These topics, and others on creating Access applications for the Internet, are covered in more detail in Chapter 31, "Access and the Internet."

> **PRACTICAL EXAMPLES**

Designing Forms for Your Application

 Several forms are required by the Time and Billing application. The more important ones are designed in this section; they're included in the CHAP5.MDB file on the CD-ROM.

> **NOTE**
>
> The forms created in this section are somewhat complex. If you prefer, you can review the completed forms in CHAP5.MDB rather than build them yourself.

Designing the Clients Form

Figure 5.43 shows the frmClients form, a One-to-Many form containing a subform called fsubClients. The main form is based on a query called qryClients, and the subform is based on a query called qryClientsSub.

FIGURE 5.43

The frmClients form shows all the projects associated with the selected client.

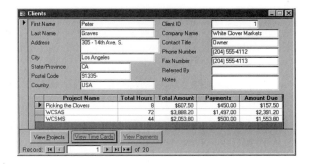

The form footer has three command buttons. The View Projects command button opens the frmProjects form with a `Where` condition, showing only the projects associated with the client being displayed on the main form. The View Payments command button opens the frmPayments form for the project selected in the fsubClients subform. Rather than use a `Where` condition on the `OpenForm` statement, the criteria is set in the query underlying the frmPayments form. A hyperlink is used to open the frmPayments form. The frmTimeCards form is opened without regard for the selected client by clicking the View Time Cards command button. It allows time cards to be entered for any project, regardless of the client. It's also opened with a hyperlink.

Now take a look at the steps required for adding a command button, such as the View Projects command button. It can be added by using the Command Button Wizard. Select the category Form Operations and the action Open Form. Make sure that you open the frmProjects form with a `Where` condition by selecting Open the Form and Find Specific Data to Display on the third step of the Command Button Wizard. Name the command button `cmdProjects`.

One important line needs to be added to the piece of code the Command Button Wizard wrote. To add this line of code, click the command button whose code you want to modify while you're in Design view for frmClients. View the command button's Event properties, and then click the ellipsis to the right of the `Click` event for the command button. Add the following line of code before the `stDocNAme = "frmProjects"` line:

```
DoCmd.RunCommand acCmdSaveRecord
```

5

FORMS

This line of code saves the current client record before opening any of the other forms. An example of the completed routine looks like this:

```
Sub cmdProjects_Click()
On Error GoTo Err_cmdProjects_Click

    Dim stDocName As String
    Dim stLinkCriteria As String

    DoCmd.RunCommand acCmdSaveRecord

    stDocName = "frmProjects"

    stLinkCriteria = "[ClientID]=" & Me![txtClientID]
    DoCmd.OpenForm stDocName, , , stLinkCriteria

Exit_cmdProjects_Click:
    Exit Sub

Err_cmdProjects_Click:
    MsgBox Err.Description
    Resume Exit_cmdProjects_Click

End Sub
```

Name the other two buttons cmdPayments and cmdTimeCards. Fill in the Hyperlink Address property for each command button to refer to the current database. Set the Hyperlink SubAddress property of cmdPayments to open the frmPayment form and the Hyperlink SubAddress property of cmdTimeCards to open the frmTimeCards form.

Designing the Time Cards Form

The frmTimeCards form is based on a query called qryTimeCards and contains two subforms. (See Figure 5.44.) The first subform is fsubTimeCards and the second is fsubTimeCardsExpenses. The fsubTimeCards subform is based on a query called qrySubTimeCards and has a Calculated control in its footer. The control is called txtTotalHoursWorked and holds the expression =Sum(BillableHours), which totals the billable hours in the subform. The fsubTimeCardsExpenses subform is based on a query called qrySubTimeCardsExpenses and has a Calculated control in its footer. The control is called txtTotalExpenses and holds the expression =Sum(ExpenseAmount), which totals the expense amounts in the subform.

FIGURE 5.44

The frmTimeCards form shows all the time and expenses entered for a particular employee.

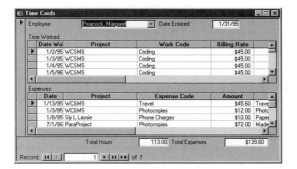

The footer of the frmTimeCards form contains two controls: txtTotalBillableHours and txtTotalExpenses. The txtTotalBillableHours control contains the following expression:

```
=[fsubTimeCards].[Form]![txtTotalHoursWorked]
```

This expression pulls the result of the calculation of the txtTotalHoursWorked control on the fsubTimeCards subform. The txtTotalExpenses control contains the following expression:

```
=[fsubTimeCardsExpenses].[Form]![txtTotalExpenses]
```

This expression pulls the result of the calculation of the txtTotalExpenses control on the fsubTimeCardsExpenses form.

Designing the Payments Form

The frmPayments form is based on a query called qryPayments, which contains the following criteria for the ProjectID:

```
[Forms]![frmClients]![fsubClients].[Form]![ProjectID]
```

This criteria looks at the ProjectID field from the subform fsubClients that's part of the frmClients form. It ensures you'll be looking only at payments relating to the selected project. The Payments form is shown in Figure 5.45. The Project Name text box contains this expression:

```
=[Forms]![frmClients]![fsubClients].[Form]![txtProject Name]
```

This expression displays the ProjectName from the subform called fsubClients on the frmClients form.

Designing the Projects Form

The frmProjects form is more complex than the others; it contains two subforms, one on top of the other. The View Expenses button is a toggle that lets the user view both expenses and hours. (See Figure 5.46.)

FIGURE 5.45

The frmPayments form is used to enter payments associated with a project.

FIGURE 5.46

The frmProjects form allows the user to view the expenses and hours associated with the selected project.

The frmProjects form is based on a query called qryProjects, which has the following expression as the criterion for the ClientID:

```
[Forms]![frmClients]![txtClientID]
```

This means that only projects with the ClientID displayed in the frmClients form are shown. The two subforms are fsubProjects and fsubProjectExpenses. The code that toggles their visibility is covered in Chapter 8, "Objects, Properties, Methods, and Events Explained." The fsubProjects form is based on qrySubProjects, and the fsubProjectExpenses form is based on qrySubProjectExpenses. The frmProjects form, as well as the subforms, contains several Calculated controls.

What's Ahead

The application you're building is modeled after the time and billing application created by the Database Wizard. You will build the application from scratch so you can learn about all its components. You'll also be adding considerably more functionality to the application. When you're finished, your application will be far more powerful than the application built by the Database Wizard.

SUMMARY

Microsoft Access gives you rich, powerful tools you can use to build even the most sophisticated form. This chapter gives you an overview of what Access forms are capable of and shows you the many options you have for creating a new form.

Regardless of how a form has been created, you need to know how to modify all the attributes of a form and its controls. This chapter shows you how to work with form objects, modifying both their appearance and how they're tied to data. Each control type and its properties have been discussed in detail, and all the properties of the form itself have been covered. Using the techniques in this chapter, you can control both the appearance and functionality of a form and its objects.

WHAT EVERY DEVELOPER NEEDS TO KNOW ABOUT REPORTS

IN THIS CHAPTER

TYPES OF REPORTS AVAILABLE

The reporting engine of Microsoft Access is very powerful, with a wealth of features. Many types of reports are available in Access 2000:

- Detail reports
- Summary reports
- Cross-tabulation reports
- Reports containing graphics and charts
- Reports containing forms
- Reports containing labels
- Reports including any combination of the preceding

Detail Reports

A Detail report supplies an entry for each record included in the report. As you can see in Figure 6.1, there's an entry for each order in the Orders table during the specified period (1995 and 1996). The report's detail is grouped by country and within country by salesperson and gives you subtotals by salesperson and country. The bottom of the report has grand totals for all records included in the report. The report is based on a Parameter query that limits the data displayed on the report based on criteria supplied by the user at runtime.

FIGURE 6.1

An example of a Detail report.

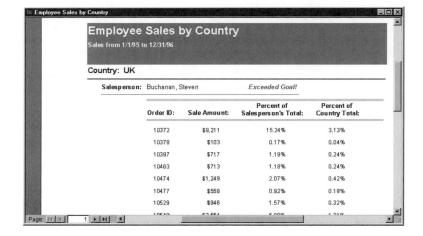

Summary Reports

A Summary report gives you summary data for all the records included in the report. In Figure 6.2, only total sales by quarter and year are displayed in the report. The underlying detail records that compose the summary data aren't displayed in the report. The report is based on a query that summarizes the net sales by OrderID. The report itself contains no controls in its Detail section. All controls are placed in report Group Headers and Footers that are grouped on the quarter and year of the ship date. Because no controls are found in the report's Detail section, Access prints summary information only.

FIGURE 6.2

An example of a Summary report.

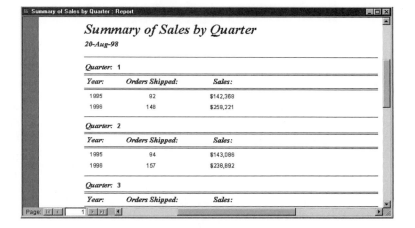

Cross Tabulation Reports

Cross Tabulation reports display summarized data grouped by one set of information on the left side of the report and another set across the top. The report shown in Figure 6.3 shows total sales by product name and employee. The report is based on a Crosstab query and is generated using a fair amount of VBA code. This code is required because each time the report is run, a different number of employees might need to be displayed in the report's columns. In other words, the number of columns needed might be different each time the report is run. This report and the techniques needed to produce it are covered in Chapter 10, "Advanced Report Techniques."

FIGURE 6.3

An example of a Cross Tabulation report.

ProductName	Buchanan	Callahan	Davolio	Dodsworth	Fuller	Kin
Konbu	0	720	312	216	593	43
Lakkalikööri	720	3,456	4,140	1,163	1,260	7
Laughing Lumberjack Lager	0	0	0	0	980	37
Longlife Tofu	0	200	128	0	550	
Louisiana Fiery Hot Pepper Sauce	653	84	904	842	1,094	71
Louisiana Hot Spiced Okra	0	0	0	816	0	40
Manjimup Dried Apples	3,413	1,293	13,409	0	3,710	2,65
Mascarpone Fabioli	0	2,080	192	128	1,760	2,24
Maxilaku	0	1,220	1,040	560	1,280	84
Mishi Kobe Niku	0	0	0	4,850	1,552	29
Mozzarella di Giovanni	4,543	2,366	1,384	278	1,183	2,60
Nord-Ost Matjeshering	1,812	2,392	1,729	906	777	77
Northwoods Cranberry Sauce	0	2,400	2,240	2,800	0	40
NuNuCa Nuß-Nougat-Creme	630	204	358	252	546	21
Original Frankfurter grüne Soße	650	634	1,716	689	949	64
Outback Lager	0	1,389	1,500	765	1,110	1,41

Reports with Graphics and Charts

Although the statement "A picture paints a thousand words" is a cliché, it's also quite true—research proves that you retain data much better when it's displayed as pictures rather than numbers. Fortunately, Access makes including graphics and charts in your reports quite easy. As shown in Figure 6.4, a report can be designed to combine both numbers and charts. The report in Figure 6.4 shows the sales by product, both as numbers and as a bar chart. The main report is grouped by product category and contains a subreport based on a query that summarizes sales by CategoryID, CategoryName, and ProductName for a specific date range. The chart totals product sales by product name, displaying the information graphically.

FIGURE 6.4

An example of a report with a chart.

Reports with Forms

Users often need a report that looks like a printed form. The Access Report Builder, with its many graphical tools, allows you to quickly produce reports that emulate the most elegant data-entry form. The report shown in Figure 6.5 produces an invoice for a customer. The report is based on a query that draws information from the Customers, Orders, Order Details, Products, Employees, and Shippers tables. The report's Filter property is filled in, limiting the data that appears on the report to the last six records in the Orders table. Using graphics, color, fonts, shading, and other special effects gives the form a professional look.

FIGURE 6.5

An example of a report containing a form.

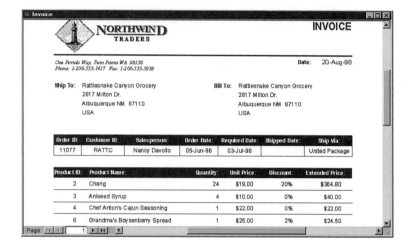

Reports with Labels

Creating mailing labels in Access 2000 is easy using the Label Wizard. Mailing labels are simply a special type of report with a page setup indicating the number of labels across the page and the size of each label. An example of a mailing label report created by using the Label Wizard is shown in Figure 6.6. This report is based on the Customers table but could have just as easily been based on a query that limits the mailing labels produced.

ANATOMY OF A REPORT

Reports can have many parts. These parts are referred to as *sections* of the report. A new report is automatically made up of the following three sections, shown in Figure 6.7:

- Page Header Section
- Detail Section
- Page Footer Section

FIGURE 6.6

An example of a report containing mailing labels.

FIGURE 6.7

Sections of a report.

The Detail section is the main section of the report; it's used to display the detailed data of the table or query underlying the report. Certain reports, such as Summary reports, have nothing in the Detail section. Instead, Summary reports contain data in Group Headers and Footers (discussed at the end of this section).

The Page Header is the portion that automatically prints at the top of every page of the report. It often includes information such as the report's title. The Page Footer automatically prints at the bottom of every page of the report and usually contains information such as the page number and date. Each report can have only one Page Header and one Page Footer.

In addition to the three sections automatically added to every report, a report can have the following sections:

- Report Header
- Report Footer
- Group Headers
- Group Footers

A Report Header is a section that prints once, at the beginning of the report; the Report Footer prints once, at the end of the report. Each Access report can have only one Report Header and one Report Footer. The Report Header is often used to create a cover sheet for the report. It can include graphics or other fancy effects, adding a professional look to a report. The most common use of the Report Footer is for grand totals, but it can also include any other summary information for the report.

In addition to Report and Page Headers and Footers, an Access report can have up to 10 Group Headers and Footers. Report groupings separate data logically and physically. The Group Header prints before the detail for the group, and the Group Footer prints after the detail for the group. For example, you can group customer sales by country and city, printing the name of the country or city for each related group of records. If you total the sales for each country and city, you can place the country and city names in the country and city Group Headers and the totals in the country and city Group Footers.

CREATING A NEW REPORT

You can create a new report in several ways—the most common is to select Reports from the Objects list in the Database window and double-click the Create Report by Using a Wizard icon. If you prefer, you can click New to open the New Report dialog box. (See Figure 6.8.) Here, you can select from many options available for creating reports. Reports can be created from scratch by using Design view; they can also be created with the help of five wizards. Three of the wizards help you build standard reports, one helps you build reports with charts, and the last wizard automates the process of creating mailing labels. The Report Wizards are so powerful that I use one of them to build the initial foundation for almost every report I create.

FIGURE 6.8

In the New Report dialog box, you can designate Design view or select from one of five wizards.

Creating a Report with the Report Wizard

To create a report with the Report Wizard, click Reports in the Objects list and then double-click the Create Report by Using a Wizard icon. This launches the Report Wizard. The first step is to select the table or query that will supply data to the report. I prefer to base my reports on queries. This generally improves performance because it returns as small a dataset as possible. In a client/server environment, this is particularly pronounced because the query is usually run on the server and only the results are sent over the network wire. Basing reports on queries also enhances your ability to produce reports based on varying criteria.

After you have selected a table or query, you can select the fields you want to include on the report. The fields included in the selected table or query are displayed in the list box on the left. To add fields to the report, double-click the name of the field you want to add or click the field name and click the > button. In the example in Figure 6.9, six fields have been selected from the tblClients table.

FIGURE 6.9

The first step of the Report Wizard: table/field selection.

After you have selected a table or query and the fields you want to include on the report, click Next. You're then prompted to add group levels, which add report groupings, to the report. Add group levels if you need to visually separate groups of data or include summary calculations (subtotals) in your report. Report groupings are covered later in this chapter. If your report doesn't require groupings, click Next.

In the third step of the Report Wizard, you choose sorting levels for your report. Because the order of a query underlying a report is overridden by any sort order designated in the report, it's a good idea to designate a sort order for the report. You can add up to four sorting levels with the wizard. In the example shown in Figure 6.10, the report is sorted by the ClientID field. After you select the fields you want to sort on, click Next.

FIGURE 6.10

The third step of the Report Wizard: sorting report data.

In the fourth step of the Report Wizard, you decide on the report's layout and orientation. The layout options vary depending on what selections have been made in the wizard's previous steps. The orientation can be Portrait or Landscape. This step of the Report Wizard also allows you to specify whether you want Access to try to adjust the width of each field so that all the fields fit on each page. After supplying Access with this information, click Next.

You choose a style for your report in the Report Wizard's fifth step. The available choices are Bold, Casual, Compact, Corporate, Formal, and Soft Gray. You can preview each look before you make a decision. Any of the style attributes applied by the Report Wizard, as well as other report attributes defined by the wizard, can be modified in Report Design view any time after the wizard has produced the report. After you have selected a style, click Next.

The final step of the Report Wizard prompts you for the report's title. This title is used as both the name and the caption for the report. I supply a standard Access report name and modify the caption after the Report Wizard has finished its process. You're then given the opportunity to preview the report or modify the report's design. If you opt to modify the report's design, you're placed in Design view. (See Figure 6.11.) The report can then be previewed at any time.

FIGURE 6.11

Design view of a completed report.

Creating a Report from Design View

Although you usually get started with most of your reports by using a Report Wizard, you should understand how to create a new report from Design view. To create a report without using a wizard, click Reports in the Objects list and then double-click the Create Report in Design View icon. The Report Design window appears. You must then set the Record Source of the report to the table or query upon which you want the report to be based. Another way to create a report from Design view is to click Reports in the Objects list and then click New to open the New Report dialog box. Click Design view, use the drop-down list to select the table or query on which the report will be based; then click OK. The Report Design window appears.

WORKING WITH THE REPORT DESIGN WINDOW

The Report Design window is used to build and modify a report. Using this window, you can add objects to a report and modify their properties. Microsoft provides numerous Report, Report Grouping, and Control properties. By modifying these properties, you can create reports with diverse looks and functionality.

Understanding the Report Design Tools

To help you with designing reports, several report design tools are available, including the Properties, Toolbox, Field List, and Sorting and Grouping windows. Two toolbars are also available to make developing and customizing your reports easier: the Report Design toolbar and the Formatting toolbar. The Report Design toolbar offers tools for saving, previewing, and printing your report and for cutting, copying, and pasting report objects. The Formatting toolbar is specifically designed to help you customize the look of your report. It includes tools for changing the font, font size, alignment, color, shading, and other physical attributes of the report objects.

The Properties, Toolbox, Field List, and Sorting and Grouping windows are all designed as toggles. This means that buttons on the Report Design toolbar alternately hide and show these valuable windows. If you have a high-resolution monitor, you might want to leave the windows open at all times. If you have a low-resolution monitor, you need to get a feel for when it's most effective for each window to be opened or closed.

Adding Fields to the Report

Fields can most easily be added to a report by using the Field List window. With the Field List window open, click and drag a field from the field list onto the appropriate section of the report. Several fields can be added at one time, just as they can in forms. Use the Ctrl key to select noncontiguous fields, use the Shift key to select contiguous fields, or double-click the field list's title bar to select all the fields; then click and drag them to the report as a unit.

CAUTION

One problem with adding fields to a report is that both the fields and the attached labels are placed in the same section of the report. This means that if you click and drag fields from the Field List window to the Detail section of the report, both the fields and the attached labels appear in the Detail section. If you're creating a tabular report, this isn't acceptable, so you must cut the attached labels and paste them into the report's Page Header section.

Selecting, Moving, Aligning, and Sizing Report Objects

Microsoft Access offers several techniques to help you select, move, align, and size report objects. Different techniques are effective in different situations. Experience will tell you which technique you should use and when. Selecting, moving, aligning, and sizing report objects are quite similar to performing the same tasks with form objects. The techniques are covered briefly in this chapter; for a more detailed explanation of each technique, refer to Chapter 5, "What Every Developer Needs to Know About Forms."

Selecting Report Objects

To select a single report object, click it; selection handles appear around the selected object. After the object is selected, you can modify any of its attributes (properties), or you can size, move, or align it.

To select multiple objects so you can manipulate them as a unit, use one of the following techniques:

- Hold down the Shift key as you click multiple objects. Each object you click is then added to the selection.
- Place your mouse pointer in a blank area of the report. Click and drag to lasso the objects you want to select. When you let go of the mouse, any object even partially within the lasso is selected.
- Click and drag within the horizontal or vertical ruler. As you click and drag, lines appear indicating the potential selection area. When you release the mouse, all objects within the lines are selected.

> **NOTE**
>
> Make sure that you understand which objects are actually selected; attached labels can cause some confusion. Figure 6.12 shows a report with four objects selected: the rptClients label, the Contact First Name label, the City text box, and the ContactFirstName text box. The City label is *not* selected. It's surrounded by one selection handle because it's attached to the City text box. If you were to modify the properties of the selected objects, the City label would be unaffected.

Moving Things Around

If you want to move a single control along with its attached label, click the object and drag it to a new location. The object and the attached label move as a unit. To move multiple objects, use one of the methods explained in the previous section to select the objects you want to move. After the objects are selected, click and drag any of them; the selected objects and their attached labels move as a unit.

Moving an object without its attached label is a trickier process. When placed over the center or border of a selected object (not on a sizing handle), the mouse pointer looks like a hand with all five fingers pointing upward. This indicates that the selected object and its attached label move as a unit, maintaining their relationship to one another. However, if you place your mouse pointer directly over the selection handle in the object's upper-left corner, the mouse pointer looks like a hand with the index finger pointing upward. This indicates that the object and the attached label move independently of one another so that you can alter the distance between them.

Aligning Objects with One Another

To align objects with one another, you must select them first. Choose Format|Align; then select Left, Right, Top, Bottom, or To Grid. The selected objects then align in relation to each other.

CAUTION

Watch out for a few "gotchas" when you're aligning report objects. If you select several text boxes and their attached labels and align them, Access tries to align the left sides of the text boxes with the left sides of the labels. To avoid this problem, you have to align the text boxes separately from their attached labels.

During the alignment process, Access never overlaps objects. For this reason, if the objects you're aligning don't fit, Access can't align them. For example, if you try to align the bottom of several objects horizontally and they don't fit across the report, Access aligns only the objects that fit on the line.

Using Snap to Grid

The Snap to Grid feature is a toggle found under the Format menu. When Snap to Grid is selected, all objects that you're moving or sizing snap to the report's grid lines. To temporarily disable the Snap to Grid feature, hold down your Ctrl key while sizing or moving an object.

Using Power Sizing Techniques

Access offers many techniques to help you size report objects. A selected object has eight sizing handles, and all of them, except for the upper-left handle, can be used to size the object. Simply click and drag one of the sizing handles. If multiple objects are selected, they are sized by the same amount.

The Format | Size menu can also help you size objects. It has six options: To Fit, To Grid, To Tallest, To Shortest, To Widest, and To Narrowest. These options are discussed in detail in Chapter 5.

> **TIP**
>
> Access offers a great trick that can help size labels fit. Simply double-click any sizing handle, and the object is automatically sized to fit the text within it.

Controlling Object Spacing

Access also makes it easy for you to control object spacing. Both the horizontal and vertical distances between selected objects can be made equal. Select the objects; then choose Format | Horizontal Spacing | Make Equal or Format | Vertical Spacing | Make Equal. You can also maintain the relative relationship between selected objects while increasing or decreasing the space between them. To do this, choose Format | Horizontal/Vertical Spacing | Increase/Decrease.

SELECTING THE CORRECT CONTROL FOR THE JOB

Reports usually contain labels, text boxes, lines, rectangles, image controls, and bound and unbound object frames. The other controls are generally used for reports that emulate data-entry forms. The different controls that can be placed on a report, as well as their uses, are discussed briefly in the following sections.

Labels

Labels are used to display information to your users. They're commonly used as report headings, column headings, or group headings for your report. Although the text they display can be modified at runtime by using VBA code, they can't be directly bound to data.

To add a label to a report, select the Label tool in the toolbox; then click and drag to place the label on the report.

Text Boxes

Text boxes are used to display field information or the result of an expression. They are used throughout a report's different sections. For example, in a Page Header, a text box might contain an expression showing the date range that's the criteria for the report. In a Group Header, a text box might be used to display a heading for the group. The possibilities are endless because a text box can hold any valid expression.

To add a text box to a report, select the Text Box tool from the toolbox. Click and drag the text box to place it on the report. A text box can also be added to a report by dragging a field from the field list to a report. This works as long as the field's Display control property is a text box.

Lines

Lines can be used to visually separate objects on your report. For example, a line can be placed at the bottom of a section or underneath a subtotal. To add a line to a report, click the Line tool to select it; then click and drag to place the line on your report. When added, the line has several properties that can be modified to customize its look.

> **TIP**
>
> To make sure the line you draw is perfectly straight, hold down the Shift key while you click and drag to draw the line.

Rectangles

Rectangles can be used to visually group items on the report that logically belong together. They can also be used to make certain controls on your report stand out. I often draw rectangles around important subtotal or grand total information that I want to make sure the report's reader notices.

To add a rectangle to a report, select the Rectangle tool from the toolbox; then click and drag to place the rectangle on the report.

> **CAUTION**
>
> The rectangle might obscure objects that have already been added to the report. To rectify this problem, the rectangle's Back Style property can be set to Transparent. This setting is fine unless you want the rectangle to have a background color. If so, choose Format | Send to Back to layer the objects so that the rectangle lies behind the other objects on the report.

Bound Object Frames

Bound object frames let you display the data in OLE fields, which contain objects from other applications, such as pictures, spreadsheets, and word processing documents.

To add a bound object frame to a report, click the Bound Object Frame tool in the toolbox; then click and drag the frame onto the report. Set the Control Source property of the frame to the appropriate field. You can also add a bound object frame to a report by dragging and dropping an OLE field from the field list onto the report.

Unbound Object Frames

Unbound object frames can be used to add logos and other pictures to a report. Unlike bound object frames, however, they aren't tied to underlying data.

To add an unbound object frame to a report, click the Unbound Object Frame tool in the toolbox. Click and drag the object frame to place it on the report. This opens the Insert Object dialog box, shown in Figure 6.13, which you use to create a new OLE object or insert an existing OLE object from a file on disk. If you click Create From File, the Insert Object dialog box changes to look like Figure 6.14. Click Browse and locate the file you want to include in the report. The Insert Object dialog box gives you the option of linking to or embedding an OLE object. If you select Link, a reference is created to the OLE object. Only the bitmap of the object is stored in the report, and the report continues to refer to the original file on disk. If you don't select Link, the object you select is copied and embedded in the report and becomes part of the Access MDB file; no link to the original object is maintained.

FIGURE 6.13

Use the Insert Object dialog box to insert a new or existing object into an unbound object frame.

> **NOTE**
>
> It's usually preferable to use an image control rather than an unbound object frame for static information like a logo because the image control requires much fewer resources than does an unbound object frame. Image controls are covered in the next section; Figure 6.15 shows a report with an image control.

FIGURE 6.14

The Insert Object dialog box with Create from File selected.

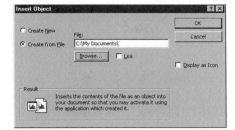

FIGURE 6.15

A report with an unbound object frame.

Image Controls

Image controls are your best option for displaying static images, such as logos, on a report. An unbound object can be modified after it is placed on a report, but you can't open the object application and modify an image when it's placed on a report. This limitation, however, means far fewer resources are needed, so performance improves noticeably.

Other Controls

As mentioned earlier in this section, it's standard to include mostly labels and text boxes on your reports, but other controls can be added when appropriate. To add any other type of control, click to select the control; then click and drag to place it on the report.

WHAT REPORT PROPERTIES ARE AVAILABLE AND WHY USE THEM

Reports have many different properties that can be modified to change how the report looks and performs. Like Form properties, Report properties are divided into categories: Format, Data, Event, and Other. To view a report's properties, first select the report, rather than a section of the report, in one of two ways:

- Click the Report Selector, which is the small gray button at the intersection of the horizontal and vertical rulers.
- Choose Edit | Select Report.

When a report has been selected, you can view and modify its properties.

Working with the Properties Window

When the report is selected, the Properties window shows all the properties associated with the report. To select the report and open the Properties window at the same time, double-click the Report Selector. A report has 37 properties available on the property sheet (there are additional properties available only from code) broken down into the appropriate categories in the Properties window. Thirty of the properties relate to the report's format, data, and other special properties; the remaining seven relate to the events that occur when a report is run. The format, data, and other properties are covered here, and the event properties are covered in Chapter 10, "Advanced Report Techniques."

The Report's Format Properties

A report has the following 15 Format properties for changing the report's physical appearance:

Caption: The Caption property of the report is the text that appears in the Report window's title bar when the user is previewing the report. It can be modified at runtime to customize it for a particular situation.

Page Header, Page Footer: The Page Header and Page Footer properties determine on what pages these sections appear. The options are `All Pages`, `Not with Rpt Hdr`, `Not with Rpt Ftr`, and `Not with Rpt Hdr/Ftr`. Because you might not want the Page Header or Page Footer to print on the Report Header or Report Footer pages, these properties give you control over where those sections print.

Grp Keep Together: In Access, you can keep a group of data together on the same page by using the Grp Keep Together property. The `Per Page` option forces the group of data to remain on the same page, and the `Per Column` option forces the group of data to remain within a column. A *group of data* refers to all the data within a report grouping (for example, all the customers in a city).

Width: The Width property specifies the width of the report sections.

Picture, Picture Type, Picture Size Mode, Picture Alignment, Picture Tiling, and Picture Pages: The background of a report can be a picture. The Picture properties determine what picture is used as a background for the report and what attributes are applied to it.

Grid X / Grid Y: The Grid X and Grid Y properties determine the density of the gridlines in the Report Design window.

Layout for Print: The Layout for Print property specifies whether screen or printer fonts are used in the report. If you want to optimize reports for preview, select No; if you want to optimize reports for the printer, select Yes. This option is not as important if you select TrueType fonts because TrueType fonts usually print equally well to the screen and printer.

Palette Source: The Palette Source property determines the source for the report's selectable color.

The Report's Data Properties

A report has the following five Data properties used to supply information about the data underlying the report:

Record Source: The Record Source property specifies the table or query whose data underlies the report. The record source of a report can be modified at runtime. This aspect of the Record Source property makes it easy for you to create generic reports that use different record sources in different situations.

Filter: The Filter property allows you to open the report with a specific filter set. I usually prefer to base a report on a query rather than apply a filter to it. At other times, it's more appropriate to base the report on a query but then apply and remove a filter as required, based on the report's runtime conditions.

Filter On: The Filter On property determines whether a report filter is applied. If the value of this property is set to No, the Filter property of the report is ignored.

Order By: The Order By property determines how the records in a report are sorted when the report is opened.

Order By On: The Order By On property determines whether the Order By property of the report is used. If the value of this property is No, the report's Order By property is ignored.

Other Report Properties

A report has 10 Other properties; these miscellaneous properties, shown in the following, allow you to control other important aspects of the report:

Record Locks: The Record Locks property determines whether the tables used in producing the report are locked while the report is being run. The two values for this property are No Locks and All Records. No Locks is the default value; it means that no records in the tables underlying the report are locked while the report is being run. Users can modify the underlying data as the report is run, which can be disastrous when running sophisticated reports. The data in the report can be changed as the report is being run, which would make figures for totals and percent of totals invalid. Although the All Records option for this property locks all records in all tables included in the report (thereby preventing data entry while the report is being run), it might be a necessary evil for producing an accurate report.

Date Grouping: The Date Grouping property determines how grouping of dates occurs in your report. The US Defaults option means that Access uses United States defaults for report groupings; therefore, Sunday is the first day of the week, the first week begins January 1, and so on. The Use System Settings option means that date groupings are based on the locale set in the Control Panel's Regional Settings, rather than on U.S. defaults.

Menu Bar: The Menu Bar property allows you to associate a custom menu bar with the report that's visible when the user is previewing the report. Adding a custom menu to your report lets you control what the user can do while the report is active.

Toolbar: The Toolbar property lets you associate a custom toolbar with the report that's visible when the user is previewing the report.

Shortcut Menu Bar: The Shortcut Menu Bar property determines what shortcut menu is associated with the report while the report is being previewed. The shortcut menu bar appears when the user clicks the right mouse button over the preview window.

Fast Laser Printing: The Fast Laser Printing property determines whether lines and rectangles are replaced with text character lines when you print a report with a laser printer. If fast printing is your objective and you're using a laser printer, you should set this property to Yes.

Help File, Help Context ID: The Help File and Help Context ID properties let you associate a help file and help topic with the report.

Tag: The Tag property is an extra property for storing information defined by the user at either design time or runtime. It is Microsoft Access's way of giving you an extra property. Access makes no use of this property; if you don't take advantage of it, it will never be used.

Has Module: The Has Module property determines whether the report contains an associated class module. If no code will be included in the report, eliminating the class module can both improve performance and reduce the size of the application database. A report without a class module is considered a "lightweight object," which loads and displays faster than an object with an associated class module.

> **CAUTION**
>
> A couple of the Has Module property's behaviors deserve special attention. When a report is created, the default value for the Has Module property is No. Access automatically sets the Has Module property to Yes as soon as you try to view a report's module. If you set the Has Module property of an existing report to No, Access deletes the object's class module and all the code it contains!

WHAT CONTROL PROPERTIES ARE AVAILABLE AND WHY USE THEM

Just as reports have properties, so do controls. Most control properties can be changed at design time or at runtime, allowing you to easily build flexibility into your reports. For example, certain controls are visible only when specific conditions are true.

The Control's Format Properties

You can modify several formatting properties of the selected objects by using the formatting toolbar. If you prefer, you can set all the properties in the Properties window.

Format: The Format property determines how the data in the control is displayed. This property is automatically inherited from the underlying field. If you want the control's format on the report to differ from the underlying field's format, you must set the Format property of the control.

Caption: The Caption property specifies the text displayed for labels and command buttons. A caption is a string containing up to 2,048 characters.

Hyperlink Address: The Hyperlink Address property is a string representing the path to a UNC (network path) or URL (Web page). Command buttons, image controls, and labels all contain the Hyperlink Address property.

Hyperlink SubAddress: The Hyperlink SubAddress property is a string representing a location within the document specified in the Hyperlink Address property. Command buttons, image controls, and labels all contain the Hyperlink SubAddress property.

Decimal Places: The Decimal Places property defines the number of decimal places displayed for numeric values.

Visible: The Visible property determines whether a control is visible. In many cases, you want to toggle the visibility of a control in response to different situations.

Hide Duplicates: The Hide Duplicates property hides duplicate data values in a report's Detail section. Duplicate data values occur when one or more consecutive records in a report contain the same value in one or more fields.

Can Grow, Can Shrink: The Can Grow property, when set to `Yes`, allows a control to expand vertically to accommodate all the data in it. The Can Shrink property eliminates blank lines when no data exists in a field for a particular record. For example, if you have a second address line on a mailing label, but there's no data in the Address2 field, you don't want a blank line to appear on the mailing label.

Left, Top, Width, Height: These properties set the size and position of the controls on a report.

Back Style, Back Color: The Back Style property can be set to `Normal` or `Transparent`. When set to `Transparent`, the color of the report shows through to the control. When set to `Normal`, the control's Back Color property determines the object's color.

Special Effect: The Special Effect property adds 3D effects to a control.

Border Style, Border Color, Border Width: These properties set the physical attributes of a control's border.

Font Color, Font Name, Font Size, Font Weight, Font Italic, Font Underline: The border properties affect the control's border, but the font properties affect the appearance of the text within the control.

Text Align: The Text Align property sets the alignment of the text within the control. It can be set to Left, Center, Right, or Distribute. When set to Distribute, text is justified.

Left Margin, Top Margin, Right Margin, Bottom Margin: These properties are used to determine how far the text within the control prints from the left, top, right, and bottom of the control. These properties are particularly useful for large controls containing a lot of text, such as a memo on an invoice.

Line Spacing: The Line Spacing property is used to control the spacing between lines of text within a control. The Line Spacing property is designated in inches.

Is Hyperlink: The Is Hyperlink property is used to determine whether the text within the control is displayed as a hyperlink. If the Is Hyperlink property is set to `Yes`, and the text within the control is a relevant link, the text will serve as a hyperlink. (This is useful only if you save the report in HTML format.)

The Control's Data Properties

The Data properties of a control specify information about the data underlying a particular report control.

Control Source: The Control Source property specifies the field in the report's record source that's used to populate the control. A control source can also be a valid expression.

Running Sum: The Running Sum property (unique to reports) is quite powerful. It can be used to calculate a record-by-record or group-by-group total. It can be set to `No`, `Over Group`, or `Over All`. When set to `Over Group`, the value of the text box accumulates from record to record within the group but is reset each time the group value changes. An example is a report that shows deposit amounts for each state with a running sum for the amount deposited within the state. Each time the state changes, the amount deposited is set to zero. When set to `Over All`, the sum continues to accumulate over the entire report.

The Other Control Properties

The Other properties of a control designate properties that don't fit into any other category.

Name: The Name property gives you an easy and self-documenting way to refer to the control in VBA code and in many other situations. You should name all your controls. Naming conventions for report controls are the same as those for form controls. Refer to Appendix B, "Naming Conventions," for more detailed information.

Vertical: The Vertical property is used to determine whether the text within the control is displayed vertically. The default value for this property is `No`.

Tag: Like the Tag property of a report, the Tag property of a control gives you a user-defined slot for the control. You can place any extra information in the Tag property.

CAUTION

A common mistake many developers make is giving controls names that conflict with Access names. This type of error is very difficult to track down. Make sure you use distinctive names for both fields and controls. Furthermore, don't give a control the same name as the name of a field within its expression. For example, the expression `=ClientName & Title` shouldn't have the name "ClientName"; that would cause an `#error#` message when the report is run. Finally, don't give a control the same name as its control source. Access gives bound controls the same name as their fields, so you need to change them to avoid problems. Following these simple warnings will spare you a lot of grief!

INSERTING PAGE BREAKS

Page breaks can be set to occur before, within, or at the end of a section. The way you set each type of page break is quite different. To set a page break within a section, you must use the Page Break tool in the toolbox. Click the Page Break tool in the toolbox, and then click the report where you want the page break to occur. To set a page break before or after a section, set the Force New Page property of the section to Before Section, After Section, or Before & After. The Force New Page property applies to Group Headers, Group Footers, and the report's Detail section.

UNBOUND, BOUND, AND CALCULATED CONTROLS

Three types of controls can be placed on a report: Bound, Unbound, and Calculated. Unbound controls, such as logos placed on reports, aren't tied to data. Bound controls are tied to data within a field of the table or query underlying the report. Calculated controls contain valid expressions; they can hold anything from a page number to a sophisticated financial calculation. Most complex reports have a rich combination of Bound, Unbound, and Calculated controls.

USING EXPRESSIONS TO ENHANCE YOUR REPORTS

Calculated controls use expressions as their control sources. To create a Calculated control, you must first add an Unbound control to the report. Expressions must be preceded by an equal sign (=); an example of a report expression is =Sum([BillableHours]). This expression, if placed in the Report Footer, totals the contents of the BillableHours control for all detail records in the report. You can build an expression by typing it directly into the control source or by using the Expression Builder, covered in Chapter 5, "What Every Developer Needs to Know About Forms."

BUILDING REPORTS BASED ON MORE THAN ONE TABLE

The majority of reports you create will probably be based on more than one table. This is because a properly normalized database usually requires that you bring table data back together to give your users valuable information. For example, a report that combines data from a Customers table, an Orders table, an Order Details table, and a Product table can supply the following information:

- Customer information: company name and address
- Order information: order date and shipping method
- Order detail information: quantity ordered, price
- Product table: product description

A multitable report can be based directly on the tables whose data it displays, or it can be based on a query that has already joined the tables, providing a flat table structure.

Creating One-to-Many Reports

You can create one-to-many reports by using a Report Wizard, or you can build the report from scratch. Different situations require different techniques, some of which are covered in the following sections.

Building a One-to-Many Report with the Report Wizard

Building a one-to-many report with the Report Wizard is quite easy; just follow these steps:

1. Click Reports in the Objects list and double-click Create Report by Using Wizard.

2. Use the Tables/Queries drop-down list to select the first table or query whose data will appear on the report.

3. Select the fields you want to include from that table.

4. Select each additional table or query you want to include on the report, selecting the fields you need from each.

5. Click Next after selecting all the fields you want to include from all the tables and queries. Step 2 of the Report Wizard offers a suggested layout for your data. (See Figure 6.16.) You can accept Access's suggestion, or you can choose from any of the available layout options. Click Next.

FIGURE 6.16

Step 2 of the Report Wizard: selecting a layout.

6. Step 3 of the Report Wizard asks whether you want to add any grouping levels. Grouping levels can be used to visually separate data and to provide subtotals. In the example in Figure 6.17, the report is grouped by city and company name. After you select grouping levels, click Next.

FIGURE 6.17

Step 3 of the Report Wizard: selecting groupings.

7. Step 4 of the Report Wizard lets you select how you want the records in the report's Detail section to be sorted. (See Figure 6.18.) This step of the wizard also allows you to specify any summary calculations you want to perform on the data. (See Figure 6.19.) Click the Summary Options to specify the summary calculations. Using the button you can even opt to include the percent of total calculations.

FIGURE 6.18

Step 4 of the Report Wizard: selecting a sort order.

FIGURE 6.19

Adding summary calculations.

8. In Step 5 of the Report Wizard, you select the layout and orientation of your report. Layout options include Stepped, Blocked, Outline 1, Outline 2, Align Left 1, and Align Left 2.

9. Step 6 of the Report Wizard lets you select from predefined styles for your report. The styles include Bold, Casual, Compact, Corporate, Formal, and Soft Gray. You can preview each style to see what it looks like.

10. In Step 7 of the Report Wizard, you select a title for your report. The title also becomes the name for the report. I select an appropriate name and change the title after the wizard is finished. The final step also allows you to determine whether you want to immediately preview the report or to see the report's design first.

The report created in the previous example is shown in Figure 6.20. Notice that the report is sorted and grouped by City and CompanyName. The report's data is in order by OrderDate and ProductName within a CompanyName grouping.

FIGURE 6.20

A completed one-to-many report.

This method of creating a one-to-many report is by far the easiest. In fact, the "background join" technology that the wizards use when they allow you to pick fields from multiple tables, figuring out how to build the complex queries needed for the report or form, was one of the major enhancements in Access for Windows 95. It's a huge timesaver and helps hide unnecessary complexity from you as you build a report. Although you should take advantage of this feature, it's important that, as a developer, you know what's happening under the covers. The following two sections give you this necessary knowledge.

Building a Report Based on a One-To-Many Query

Another popular method of building a one-to-many report is from a one-to-many query. A one-to-many report built in this way is constructed as though it were based on the data within a single table. First, you build the query that will underlie the report. (See Figure 6.21.)

FIGURE 6.21

An example of a query underlying a one-to-many report.

When you have finished the query, you can select it rather than select each individual table (as done in the previous section). After the query is selected, creating the report is the same process as the one used for the previous report.

Building a One-to-Many Report with the Subreport Wizard

A one-to-many report can also be created by building the parent report and then adding a Subform/Subreport control. This is often the method used to create reports such as invoices that show the report's data in a one-to-many relationship rather than in a denormalized format (as shown in Figure 6.20). If you want to use the Subform/Subreport Wizard, you must make sure that the Control Wizards tool is selected before you add the Subform/Subreport control to the main report. Here is the process:

1. Click to select the Subform/Subreport control tool.

2. Click and drag to place the Subform/Subreport control on the main report. The Subform/Subreport control is usually placed in the report's Detail section. When you have placed the Subform/Subreport control on the report, the Subform/Subreport Wizard is invoked.

3. Indicate whether you want the subreport to be based on an existing report or form or you want to build a new subreport based on a query or table. Click Next.

4. If you select Table or Query, you have to select the table or query on which the subreport will be based. You can then select the fields you want to include on the subreport. You can even select fields from more than one table or query. When you're finished, click Next.

5. The next step of the Subform/Subreport Wizard suggests a relationship between the main report and the subreport. (See Figure 6.22.) You can accept the selected relationship, or you can define your own. When you're finished, click Next.

6. The final step of the Subform/Subreport Wizard asks you to name the subreport. To follow standards, the name should begin with the prefix *rsub*. Click Finish when you're finished.

FIGURE 6.22

The Subform/ Subreport Wizard: identifying the relationship.

As you can see in Figure 6.23, the one-to-many relationship between two tables is clearly highlighted by this type of report. In the example, each customer is listed. All the detail records reflecting the orders for each customer are listed immediately following each customer's data.

FIGURE 6.23

A completed one-to-many report created with the Subform/Subreport Wizard.

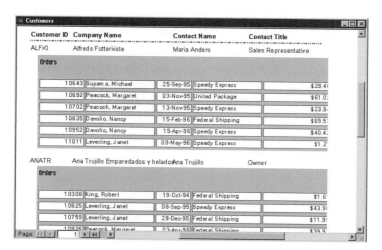

Working with Subreports

When a subreport has been added to a report, it's important to understand what properties have been set by the Subform/Subreport Wizard so that you can modify the Subreport control, if needed. You should become familiar with a few properties of a subreport:

Source Object: The name of the report or other object that's being displayed within the control.

Link Child Fields: The fields from the child report that links the child report to the master report.

Link Master Fields: The fields from the master report that links the master report to the child report.

Can Grow: Determines whether the control can expand vertically to accommodate data in the subreport.

Can Shrink: Determines whether the control can shrink to eliminate blank lines when no data is found in the subreport.

Not only should you know how to work with the properties of a Subreport object, but you should also be able to easily modify the subreport from within the main report. You can always modify the subreport by selecting it within the list of reports in the Database window. To do this, click the report you want to modify; then click Design. You can also modify a subreport by selecting its objects directly within the parent report.

WORKING WITH SORTING AND GROUPING

As opposed to sorting within forms, sorting the data within a report isn't determined by the underlying query. In fact, the underlying query affects the report's sort order only when no sort order has been specified for the report. Any sort order specified in the query is completely overwritten by the report's sort order, which is determined by the report's Sorting and Grouping window. (See Figure 6.24.) The sorting and grouping of the report is affected by what options you select when you run a Report Wizard. The Sorting and Grouping window can then be used to add, remove, or modify sorting and grouping options for the report. Sorting simply affects the order of the records on the report. Grouping adds Group Headers and Footers to the report.

FIGURE 6.24

The Sorting and Grouping window, showing grouping by city and company name and sorting by order date and product name.

Adding Sorting and Grouping

Often, you want to add sorting or grouping to a report. To do so, follow these four steps:

1. Click Sorting and Grouping on the Report Design toolbar to open the Sorting and Grouping window.

2. Click the selector of the line above where you want to insert the sorting or grouping level. In Figure 6.25, a sorting or grouping level is being added above the City grouping. Press the Insert key to insert a blank line in the Sorting and Grouping window.

FIGURE 6.25

Inserting a sorting or grouping level.

3. Click in the Field/Expression field and use the drop-down list to select the field on which you want to sort or group.

4. Set the properties to determine the nature of the sorting or grouping (see the next section).

NOTE

To remove a sorting or grouping that has been added, click the selector on the line of the field in the Sorting and Grouping window you want to delete; then press the Delete key. You will be warned that any controls in the Group Header or Footer will be lost.

Sorting and Grouping Properties

Each grouping in a report has properties that define the group's attributes. Each group has five properties that determine whether the field or expression is used for sorting, grouping, or both. (See Figure 6.26.) They are also used to specify details about the grouping options. Here are the Sorting and Grouping properties:

Group Header: The Group Header property specifies whether the selected group contains a header band. When you set the Group Header property to Yes, an additional band appears in the report that can be used to display information about the group. For example, if you're grouping by country, the Group Header is used to display the name of the country you're about to print. If the Group Header and Group Footer properties are both set to No, the field is used only to determine the sort order of the records in the report.

FIGURE 6.26

The Sorting and Grouping window, showing the five sorting and grouping properties.

Group Footer: The Group Footer property specifies whether the selected group contains a footer band. When you set the Group Footer property to Yes, an additional band appears in the report. The Group Footer band can be used to display summary information about the group; it's often used to display subtotals for the group.

Group On: The Group On property specifies what constitutes a new group. It's often used for situations such as departmental roll-ups. Rather than grouping on the entire department number, you might want to group on the first three digits, for example.

The Group On choices for text fields are Each Value and Prefix Characters. For Date fields, the choices are much more complex. They include Each Value, Year, Qtr, Month, Week, Day, Hour, and Minute. This means you could group by a Date field and have Access subtotal and begin a new group each time the week changes in the field. For AutoNumber, Currency, and Number fields, the choices are Each Value and Interval.

Group Interval: The Group Interval property is used with the Group On property to specify an interval value by which data is grouped. If, for example, the Group On property for a text field is set to Prefix Characters, and the Group Interval is set to 3, the field's data is grouped on the first three characters.

Keep Together: The Keep Together property determines whether Access tries to keep an entire group together on one page. The three choices for the property are No, Whole Group, and With First Detail. The Whole Group option means that Access tries to keep the entire group together on one page. This includes the Group Header, Group Footer, and Detail section. The With First Detail option means that Access prints the group header on a page only if it can also print the first detail record on the same page.

> **NOTE**
>
> If you have set Keep Together to Whole Group, and the group is too large to fit on a page, Access ignores the property setting. Furthermore, if you set Keep Together to With First Detail and either the group header or detail record is too large to fit on one page, that setting is ignored too.

What Are Group Header and Footer Properties and Why Use Them?

Each Group Header and Footer has its own properties that determine the behavior of the Group Header or Footer:

Force New Page: The Force New Page property can be set to None, Before Section, After Section, or Before & After. When set to None, no page break occurs either before or after the report section. If set to Before Section, a page break occurs before the report section prints; if set to After Section, a page break occurs after the report section prints. When set to Before and After, a page break occurs before the report section prints as well as after it prints.

New Row or Col: The New Row or Col property determines whether a column break occurs whenever the report section prints. This property applies only to multicolumn reports. The choices are None, Before Section, After Section, and Before & After. Like the Force New Page property, this property determines whether the column break occurs before the report section prints, after it prints, or before and after or whether it's affected by the report section break at all.

Keep Together: The Keep Together property specifies whether you want Access to try to keep an entire report section together on one page. If this property is set to Yes, Access starts printing the section at the top of the next page if it can't print the entire section on the current page. When set to No, Access prints as much of the section as possible on the current page, inserting each page break as necessary. If a section exceeds the page length, Access starts printing the section on a new page and continues printing it on the following page.

Visible: The Visible property indicates whether the section is visible. It's common to hide the visibility of a particular report section at runtime in response to different situations. This can easily be done by changing the value of the report section's Visible property with VBA code, usually on the Format event.

Can Grow, Can Shrink: The Can Grow property determines whether the section stretches vertically to accommodate the data in it. The Can Shrink property specifies whether you want the section to shrink vertically, eliminating blank lines.

Repeat Section: The Repeat Section property is a valuable property; it lets you specify whether the group header is repeated on subsequent pages if a report section needs more than one page to print.

IMPROVING PERFORMANCE AND REUSABILITY BY BASING REPORTS ON STORED QUERIES

It's usually best to base your Access reports on queries. This option offers you several benefits:

- The query underlying the report can be used by other forms and reports.
- Sophisticated calculations need to be built only once—they don't need to be re-created for each report (or form).

With earlier versions of Access, reports based on stored queries opened faster than reports based on embedded SQL statements. This is because when you build and save a query, Access compiles and creates a query plan. This query plan is a plan of execution that's based on the amount of data in the query's tables as well as all the indexes available in each table. In earlier version of Access, if you ran a report based on an embedded SQL statement, the query was compiled, and the query plan was built at runtime, slowing the query's execution. With Access 2000, query plans are built for embedded SQL statements when the form or report is saved. Query plans are stored with the associated form or report.

So what are the benefits of basing a report on a stored query instead of an embedded SQL statement? Often, you want to build several reports and forms all based on the same information. An embedded SQL statement can't be shared by multiple database objects. At the very least, you must copy the embedded SQL statement for each form and report you build. Basing reports and forms on stored queries eliminates this problem. You build the query once and modify it once if changes need to be made to it. Many forms and reports can all use the same query (including its criteria, expressions, and so on).

Reports often contain complex expressions. If a particular expression is used in only one report, nothing is lost by building the expression into the embedded SQL statement. On the other hand, many complex expressions are used in multiple reports and forms. By building these expressions into queries on which the reports and forms are based, you have to create the expression only one time.

> **TIP**
>
> It's easy to save an embedded SQL statement as a query. This allows you to use the Report Wizard to build a report using several tables; you can then save the resulting SQL statement as a query. With the report open in Design view, bring up the Properties window. Click the Data tab; then click in the Record Source property and click the ellipsis. The embedded SQL statement appears as a query. Select File Save As/Export, enter a name for the query, and click OK. Close the Query window, indicating that you want to update the Record Source property. Your query is now based on a stored query instead of an embedded SQL statement.

ACCESS REPORTS AND THE INTERNET

Microsoft has made it easier to develop Internet-aware applications by adding hyperlinks to reports and by allowing you to save an Access report as an HTML document. These features are covered in the following sections.

Adding a Hyperlink to a Report

Hyperlinks can be added to reports in the form of labels. When added, they serve as a direct link to a UNC or URL. To add a hyperlink to a report, follow these steps:

1. With the report open in Design view, add a label to the report.
2. Set the Hyperlink Address property to the UNC or URL you want to link to. The easiest way to do this is to click in the Hyperlink Address property; then click the ellipsis to open the Insert Hyperlink dialog box.
3. Enter the UNC or URL in the Type the File or Web Page Name text box. You can use the File button to browse for a UNC or the Web Page button to locate a URL.
4. If you want to enter a Hyperlink SubAddress, click Bookmark. The Hyperlink SubAddress can be a range name, bookmark, slide number, or any other recognized location in the document specified in the Link to File or URL combo box.
5. Click OK. The Hyperlink Address and Hyperlink SubAddress properties are filled in with the information supplied in the Insert Hyperlink dialog box.

The Hyperlink Address and Hyperlink SubAddress properties come into play only when a report is saved as HTML and viewed in a Web browser, such as Internet Explorer 5.0. Saving a report as an HTML document is covered in the following section.

Saving a Report as HTML

To save a report as HTML | choose File, Export. Use the Save As Type drop-down list to select HTML documents (*.htm, *.html). Pick a location and name for the file; then click Export. The document is saved as HTML and assigned the name and location you specified. Click Autostart to display the report in the default Web browser after the HTML is generated.

PRACTICAL EXAMPLES

Building Reports Needed for Your Application

The Time and Billing application requires several reports that you'll design throughout the book. A couple of the simpler ones are built here.

Designing the rptClientListing Report

The rptClientListing report lists all the clients in the tblClients table. The report includes the company name, contact name, city, state, zip code, and office phone of each customer and is sorted by company name.

The rptClientListing report is based on a query called qryClientListing, which is shown in Figure 6.27. The query includes the CompanyName, City, State, OfficePhone, and Fax fields. It also includes an expression called Contac¡tName that concatenates the ContactFirstName and ContactLastName fields. The expression looks like this:

```
ContactName: [ContactFirstName] & " " & [ContactLastName]
```

FIGURE 6.27

The qryClientListing query—a foundation for the rptClientListing report.

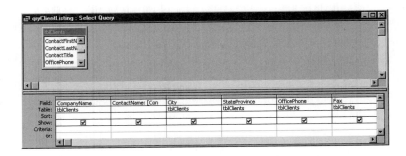

To build the report, follow these steps:

1. Select Reports from the Objects list and double-click Create Report by Using Wizard.

2. Use the drop-down list to select the qryClientListing query. (See Figure 6.28.) Click OK.

FIGURE 6.28

Selecting the qryClientListing query.

3. Click the >> button to designate that you want to include all the fields in the query within the report. Click Next.

4. Do not add any grouping to the report. Click Next.

5. Use the drop-down list to select CompanyName as the sort field. (See Figure 6.29.) Click Next.

FIGURE 6.29

Selecting CompanyName as the sort order.

6. Select Landscape for the Orientation and click Next.

7. Select a style for the report and click Next.

8. Give the report the title rptClientListing; then click Finish.

9. The completed report should look like Figure 6.30. Click Design to open the report in Design view. Notice that both the name and title of the report are rptClientListing. Modify the title of the report so that it reads Client Listing by Company Name. (See Figure 6.31.)

FIGURE 6.30

A preview of the completed report.

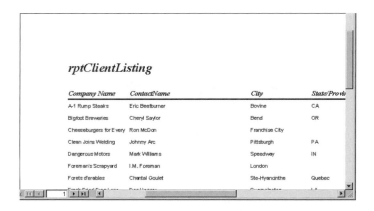

FIGURE 6.31

Changing the report title.

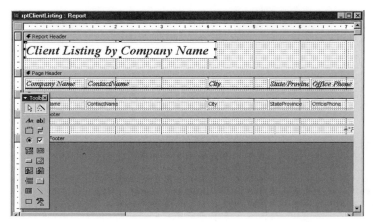

Designing the rptTimeSheet Report

The rptTimeSheet report is much more complex than the rptClientListing report. It includes two subreports: rsubTimeSheet and rsubTimeSheetExpenses.

The rptTimeSheet report is shown in Figure 6.32. It's based on a query called qryTimeSheet. (See Figure 6.33.) It contains fields from both tblTimeCards and tblEmployees.

FIGURE 6.32
The rptTimeSheet report in Design view.

FIGURE 6.33
The qryTimeSheet query in Design view.

The rptTimeSheet report has a Page Header that includes the title of the report, but nothing else is found within the Page Header. The TimeCardID header contains the EmployeeName and DateEntered from the qryTimeSheet query. The report's Detail section contains the two subreports rsubTimeSheet and rsubTimeSheetExpenses. The Page Footer holds two expressions, one for the date and another for the page number. They look like this:

```
=Now()
="Page " & [Page] & " of " & [Pages]
```

The rsubTimeSheet report is based on qrySubTimeSheet; this query contains the following fields from the tblProjects and tblTimeCardHours tables:

> tblProjects: ProjectName
>
> tblTimeCardsHours: TimeCardID, TimeCardDetailID, DateWorked, WorkDescription, BillableHours, BillingRate, and the expression `HourlyBillings:`
> `[tblTimeCardHours].[BillingRate]*[BillableHours]`

The design of rsubTimeSheet is shown in Figure 6.34. This subreport can easily be built from a wizard. Select all fields except TimeCardID and TimeCardDetailID from qrySubTimeSheets. View the data by tblTimeCardHours. Don't add any groupings, and don't sort the report. When you're finished with the wizard, modify the design of the report. Remove the caption from the Report Header, and move everything from the Page Header to the Report Header. Collapse the Page Header, remove everything from the Page Footer, and add a Report Footer with the expression =Sum([HourlyBillings]).

FIGURE 6.34

The rsubTimeSheet report in Design view.

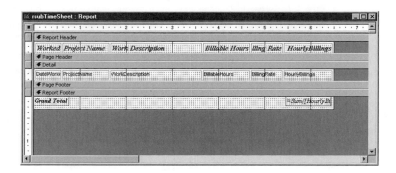

Change the format of the HourlyBillings and the TotalHourlyBillings controls to Currency. Use the Sorting and Grouping window to sort by TimeCardID and TimeCardDetailID.

The rsubTimeSheetExpenses report is based on qrySubTimeSheetExpense, which contains the following fields from the tblProjects, tblExpenseCodes, and tblTimeCardExpenses tables:

> tblProjects: ProjectName
>
> tblTimeCardsExpenses: TimeCardID, TimeCardExpenseID, ExpenseDate, ExpenseDescription, and ExpenseAmount
>
> tblExpenseCodes: ExpenseCode

The design of rsubTimeSheetExpenses is shown in Figure 6.35. This subreport can easily be built from a wizard. Select all fields except TimeCardID and TimeCardExpenseID from qrySubTimeSheetExpense. View the data by tblTimeCardExpenses. Don't add any groupings, and don't sort the report. When you're finished with the wizard, modify the design of the report. Remove the caption from the Report Header, and move everything from the Page Header to the Report Header. Collapse the Page Header, remove everything from the Page Footer, and add a Report Footer with the expression =Sum([ExpenseAmount]).

FIGURE 6.35

The rsubTimeSheet-Expenses report in Design view.

Change the format of the ExpenseAmount and the TotalExpenseAmount controls to Currency, and use the Sorting and Grouping window to sort by TimeCardID and TimeCardExpenseID.

SUMMARY

Reports give you valuable information about the data stored in your database. Many types of reports can be built in Access 2000, including Detail reports, Summary reports, reports that look like printed forms, and reports containing graphs and other objects. Access offers many properties for customizing the look and behavior of each report to fit your users' needs. Understanding how to work with each property is integral to the success of your application-development projects.

VBA: AN INTRODUCTION

IN THIS CHAPTER

VBA EXPLAINED

Visual Basic for Applications (VBA) is the development language for Microsoft Access 2000. It offers a consistent language for application development in the Microsoft Office suite, including Outlook for the first time. The core language, its constructs, and the environment are the same in Microsoft Access 2000, Microsoft Visual Basic, Microsoft Excel, Microsoft Word, Microsoft Outlook (for application-wide programming), and Microsoft Project. What differs among these environments are the built-in objects specific to each application. For example, Access has a CurrentProject object, but Excel has a Workbook object. Each application's objects have appropriate properties (attributes) and methods (actions) associated with them (and in some cases, events). This chapter gives you an overview of the VBA language and its constructs.

Unlike macros in Word or Excel, Access macros are not Sub procedures in modules; instead, they are a different type of database object, with their own interface. Because of this, you can't use Access macros to learn to program in VBA, as you can by recording a Word or Excel macro and then examining its VBA code.

Simple Access applications can be written by using macros. Although macros are okay for quick prototyping and very basic application development, most serious Access development is done by using the VBA language. Unlike macros, VBA gives you the ability to do the following:

- Work with complex logic structures (case statements, loops, and so on)
- Use constants and variables
- Take advantage of functions and actions not available in macros
- Loop through and perform actions on recordsets
- Perform transaction processing
- Programmatically create and work with database objects
- Implement error handling
- Create libraries of user-defined functions
- Call Windows API functions
- Perform complex DDE and OLE automation commands

The VBA language enables you to use complex logic structures. Macros allow you to perform only simple If...Then...Else logic, but the VBA language offers a wealth of logic and looping constructs, which are covered later in this chapter.

The VBA language also lets you declare and work with variables and constants. These variables can be scoped appropriately and passed as parameters to subroutines and functions. As you will see later in this chapter, variables and constants are an integral part of any Access application.

Many important features of the VBA language aren't available through macro actions. If you try to develop an application using only macros, you can't take advantage of many of the rich features available in the VBA language. In addition, many of the actions available in both macros and modules can be done much more efficiently with VBA code.

Complex Access applications often require you to loop through a recordset, performing some action on each member of the set. There's no way to do this by using Access macros. However, with the VBA language and ActiveX Data Objects, you can add, delete, update, and manipulate data. ActiveX Data Objects are covered in Chapter 12, "What Are ActiveX Data Objects and Data Access Objects and Why Are They Important?"

When manipulating sets of records, you want to ensure that all processing finishes successfully before your data is permanently updated. Macros don't enable you to protect your data with transaction processing. Using the BeginTrans, CommitTrans, and Rollback methods, you can make sure your data is updated only if all parts of a transaction finish successfully. Transaction processing, if done properly, can substantially improve your application's performance because no data is written to disk until the process is finished. Transaction processing and its benefits are covered in Chapter 22, "Transaction Processing."

With Access macros, you can't create or modify database objects at runtime. Using VBA, you can create databases, tables, queries, and other database objects; you can also modify existing objects. There are many practical applications of this capability to create or modify database objects (discussed in more detail in Chapter 12). When users are able to build queries on-the-fly, for example, you might want to give them the capability to design a query by using a front-end form you provide and to store the query so they can run it again later.

Access macros don't allow you to implement error handling. If an error occurs while an Access macro is executing in Access's runtime version, the user is exited out of the application (and, therefore, the Access runtime). By using error-handling techniques, you can determine exactly what will happen when an error occurs during the execution of your application. Error handling is covered in more depth in Chapter 14, "Error Handling: Preparing for the Inevitable."

VBA also makes it easier for you to write code libraries of reusable functions, design and debug complex processes, and even write your own add-ins. If you're developing even moderately complex applications, you want to be able to create generic function libraries that can be used with all your Access applications. It's extremely difficult, if not impossible, to do this using macros.

Many powerful functions not available within the VBA language are available as part of Windows itself. The Windows API (Application Programming Interface) refers to the nearly

7

**VBA: AN
INTRODUCTION**

1,000 Windows functions Microsoft exposes for use by Access programmers. You can't take advantage of these functions from an Access macro; however, by using VBA code, you can declare and call these functions, improving both the performance and functionality of your applications. The Windows API is covered in Chapter 27, "Exploiting the Power of the Windows API."

DDE (Dynamic Data Exchange) and Automation enable you to communicate between your Access applications and other applications. Although DDE is an older technology than Automation, it's still used to communicate with a few applications that don't support Automation. Automation is used to control Automation server applications, such as Excel and Project, and their objects (all Microsoft Office applications are Automation servers). Automation is covered in Chapter 26, "Automation: Communicating with Other Applications."

Although macros can offer a quick fix to a simple problem, their limitations make the VBA language the only real option for developing complex solutions. To make the transition from macros to modules easier, Microsoft has given you a feature that enables you to convert any macro to VBA code.

WHAT ARE ACCESS CLASS MODULES, STANDARD MODULES, FORM MODULES, AND REPORT MODULES?

VBA code is written in units called subroutines and functions that are stored in modules. Microsoft Access modules are either Standard modules or Class modules. Standard modules are created by selecting the Modules icon in the Database window, and then clicking New. Class modules can be standalone objects or can be associated with a form or report. To create a standalone Class module, you choose the Class Module command from the Insert menu. In addition, whenever you add code behind a form or report, Microsoft Access creates a Class module associated with that form or report that contains the code you create.

Modules specific to a form or report are generally called *Form and Report Class modules*, and their code is often referred to as Code Behind Forms (CBF). CBF is created and stored in that form or report and triggered from events occurring within it.

A *subroutine* (subprocedure) is a routine that responds to an event or performs some action. An *event procedure* is a special type of subroutine that automatically executes in response to an event like a mouse click on a command button or the loading of a form. A *function* is a special type of routine because it can return a value; a subroutine can't return a value. Like a subroutine, a function can be triggered from an event.

Where Is VBA Code Written?

All VBA Code is written in the Visual Basic Editor, also known as the VBE. You are placed in the VBE any time that you attempt to access the code in a standard or Class module. The Visual Basic Editor is pictured in Figure 7.1. The VBE environment in Microsoft Access is now consistent with the other Microsoft Office products. The VBE is a separate window from that of Microsoft Access and is comprised of a Menu Bar, Tool Bar, Project window, Properties window, Immediate window, Locals window, Watch window, Object Browser, and Code windows. The various components of the VBE are discussed as appropriate in this chapter and throughout the book.

FIGURE 7.1

The Visual Basic Editor (VBE).

The Anatomy of a Module

Whether you're dealing with a Standard module or a Class module, all modules contain a General Declarations section. (See Figure 7.2.) As the name implies, this is where you can declare variables and constants that you want to be visible to all the functions and subroutines in the module, and also set options. These variables are referred to as *module-level* or *Private variables*. You can also declare Public variables in the General Declarations section of a module. Public variables can be seen and modified by any function or procedure in any module in the database.

FIGURE 7.2

The General Declarations section of a module is used to declare Private and Public variables.

NOTE

Public variables in Access 2000 replace Access 2.0's Global variables. Although Global variables are still supported in Access 2000, there are subtle differences between Public and Global variables. These differences are discussed later in this chapter.

A module is also made up of user-defined subroutines and functions. Figure 7.3 shows a subroutine called SayHello. Notice the drop-down list in the upper-left portion of the window titled Chap7Ex - Module1 (Code). This is referred to as the Object drop-down list. Subroutines and functions are sometimes associated with a specific object, such as a form or a control within a form. This is where such an association is noted. In this case, our subroutine named SayHello is not associated with any object, so the Object drop-down list contains (General).

FIGURE 7.3

An example of a user-defined subroutine called SayHello.

TIP

Access 2000 has an environment option called Full Module View. This option, when checked, enables you to see several subroutines and functions in a module at one time. Notice the difference between Figure 7.3 and Figure 7.4. In the code window shown in Figure 7.3, only one subroutine is visible at a time. The code window shown in Figure 7.4 illustrates the effects of Full Module View—multiple subroutines are visible, each separated by a thin horizontal line. Full Module View is the default in Access 2000. To change the Full Module View environment setting, with the Microsoft Visual Basic Editor (VBE) active, choose Tools | Options, click the Editor tab, and check Default to Full Module View. If you want to temporarily change to Procedure view, click the Procedure view button in the lower-left corner of a module window and then click the Full Module View button to return to Full Module View.

FIGURE 7.4

In Full Module View, you can view several procedures simultaneously.

Option Explicit

Option Explicit is a statement that can be included in the General Declarations section of any module, including the Class module of a form, or report. When Option Explicit is used, all variables in that module must be declared before they're used, or an error saying that a variable is undefined will occur when the module is compiled. If an undeclared variable is encountered when compiling a module without Option Explicit, VBA will simply treat it as a new variable and continue without warning. It might appear at first glance that because Option Explicit can cause compiler errors that would otherwise not occur, it might be better to avoid the use of this option. However, just the opposite is true. You should use Option Explicit in every module, without exception. For example, look at the following code:

```
intAmount = 2
intTotal = intAmont * 2
```

Clearly the intent of this code is to multiply the value contained in the variable intAmount, in this case 2, by 2. Notice however, that the variable name is misspelled on the second line. If

`Option Explicit` has not been set, VBA views `intAmount` as a new variable and simply continues its processing. The variable `intTotal` will be set to 0 instead of 4, and no error indication is given at all. This kind of result can be totally avoided by using `Option Explicit`.

> ## TIP
>
> In Access 2.0, you had to manually enter the `Option Explicit` statement into each module, form, and report. Starting with Access 97, developers have had the option of globally instructing Access to insert the `Option Explicit` statement in all new modules. To do this in Access 2000, with the Visual Basic Editor (VBE) active, choose Tools | Options. Under the Editor tab, click Require Variable Declaration. It's important that the `Option Explicit` statement be placed in all your modules, so make sure you set this option to True. The default when installing Microsoft Access 2000 is False! `Option Explicit` will save you hours of debugging and prevent your beeper from going off after your application has been distributed to your users.

In addition to a General Declarations section and user-defined procedures, forms, and reports, Class modules also contain event procedures that are associated with a particular object on a form. Notice in Figure 7.5 that the Object drop-down list says `cmdHello`. This is the name of the object whose event routines you are viewing. The drop-down list on the right shows all the events that can be coded for a command button; each of these events creates a separate event routine. You will have the opportunity to write many event routines as you read through this book.

FIGURE 7.5

An event procedure for the `Click` *event of the* `cmdHello` *command button.*

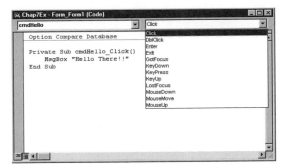

Creating Event Procedures

Event procedures are automatically created when you write event code for an object. For example, the routine `Private Sub cmdHello_Click` is created when you place code in the

Click event of the cmdHello command button, shown in Figure 7.5. To get to the event code of an object, follow these steps:

1. Click on the object in Design view and click the Properties button on the toolbar, or right-click on the object and choose Properties from the context-sensitive menu.
2. Click on the Event properties tab.
3. Select the property you want to write code for (for example, the On Click event).
4. Select [Event Procedure] from the drop-down list.
5. Click on the ellipsis button, which places you in the Visual Basic Editor (VBE) within the event code for that object.

> **NOTE**
>
> As discussed at the beginning of the chapter, the Visual Basic Editor, also known as the VBE, opens in a separate window. It provides a programming environment consistent with all the other Microsoft Office applications. Modules added in the VBE will not appear in the database container until they are saved within the VBE.

Creating Functions and Subroutines

You can also create your own procedures that aren't tied to a particular object or event. Depending on how and where they're declared, they can be called from anywhere in your application or from a particular code module, form module, or report module.

Creating a User-Defined Routine in a Code Module

1. Click Modules within the Objects list in the Database window.
2. Click New to create a new module or select an existing module and click Design. The VBE appears.
3. Select Procedure from the Insert drop-down on the toolbar (second icon from the left) or choose Procedure from the Insert menu. The Add Procedure dialog shown in Figure 7.6 appears.
4. Type the name of the procedure.
5. Select Sub, Function, or Property as the Type of procedure.
6. To make the procedure available to your entire application, select Public as the Scope; to make the procedure private to this module select Private.
7. Finally, indicate whether you want all the variables in the procedure to be static. (Static variables are discussed in this chapter under "Scope and Lifetime of Variables: Exposing Your Variables as Little as Possible.") Then click OK.

FIGURE 7.6

In the Add Procedure dialog box, you specify the name, type, and scope of the procedure you're creating.

Creating a User-Defined Routine in a Form or Report Class Module

1. While in Design view of a form or report, select View from the menu. Notice the icon beside the Code menu entry. This same icon is also available on the toolbar. You may view the code behind the form or report by clicking on this icon on the toolbar or by selecting Code from the View menu. You are placed in the VBE.

2. Select Procedure from the Insert drop-down list on the toolbar (second icon from the left) or choose Procedure from the Insert menu to open the Insert Procedure dialog box.

3. Type the name of the procedure.

4. Select Sub, Function, or Property as the Type of procedure.

5. To make the procedure available to your entire application, select Public as the Scope; to make the procedure private to this module, select Private.

6. Finally, indicate whether you want all the variables in the procedure to be static. (Static variables are discussed in this chapter under "Scope and Lifetime of Variables: Exposing Your Variables as Little as Possible.") When you're finished, click OK.

TIP

Whether you're creating a procedure in a Standard module or a Class module, you're now ready to enter the code for your procedure. A great shortcut for creating a procedure is to type directly in the code window the name of the new procedure, preceded by its designation as either a Sub or a Function. Example: *Sub Whatever* or *Function Whatever*. This creates a new subroutine or function as soon as you press Return.

Calling Event and User-Defined Procedures

Event procedures are automatically called when an event occurs for an object. For example, when a user clicks a command button, the `Click` event code for that command button executes.

The standard method for calling user-defined procedures is to use the `Call` keyword—Call `SayHello`, for example. You can also call the same procedure without using the `Call` keyword: `SayHello`.

Although not required, using the `Call` keyword makes the statement self-documenting and easier to read. A user-defined procedure can be called from an event routine or from another user-defined procedure or function.

Scope and Lifetime of Procedures

The scope of a procedure can be declared Public or Private. A procedure's scope determines how widely it can be called from other procedures. In addition to a procedure's scope, the placement of a procedure can noticeably affect your application's functionality and performance.

Another attribute of a procedure has to do with the lifetime of any variables that are declared within the procedure. By default, the variables declared within a procedure have a lifetime; that is, they have value and meaning only while the procedure is executing. When the procedure completes execution, the variables it declared are destroyed. This default lifetime can be altered by using the `Static` keyword.

Public Procedures

A Public procedure placed in a code module can be called from anywhere in the application. Procedures declared in a module are automatically Public. This means that unless you specify otherwise, procedures you place in any code module can be called from anywhere within your application.

 You might think that two Public procedures can't have the same name. Although this was true in earlier versions of Access, it isn't true in Access 2000. If two Public procedures share a name, the procedure that calls them must explicitly state which of the two routines it's calling. This is illustrated by the following code snippet found in frmHello's Class module in the sample database, Chap7ex.mdb:

```
Private Sub cmdSayGoodBye_Click()
   Call basUtils.SayGoodBye
End Sub
```

The SayGoodBye routine is found in two Access code modules; however, the prefix basUtils indicates that the routine you want to execute is in the Standard module named basUtils.

Procedures declared in Form or Report Class modules are also automatically Public, so they can be called from anywhere within the application. The procedure called cbfIAmPublic, shown in Figure 7.7, is found in the form called frmHello. Although the procedure is found in the form, it can be called from anywhere within the application. The only requirement is that the form containing the procedure must be open in form view. The cbfIAmPublic procedure can be called from anywhere within the application by using the following syntax (found in the Standard module basHello):

```
Sub CallPublicFormProc()
    Call Forms.frmHello.cbfIAmPublic
End Sub
```

FIGURE 7.7

A Public form procedure is visible to any subroutine or function in the database.

Private Procedures

As mentioned, all user-defined procedures are automatically Public. If you want a procedure declared in a module to have the scope of that module only, meaning that it can be called only from another routine within the module, you must explicitly declare it as Private. (See Figure 7.8.)

FIGURE 7.8

A Private procedure is visible only to subroutines and functions in the basUtils *module.*

The procedure shown in Figure 7.8, called IAmPrivate, is in the Standard module named basUtils. Because the procedure is Private, it can be called only from other procedures in the basUtils module.

Scope Precedence

Private procedures always take precedence over Public procedures. If a Private procedure has the same name as a Public procedure, the Private procedure's code is executed if it's called by any routine in the module where it was declared. Naming conflicts don't occur between Public and Private procedures.

TIP

Developers often wonder where to place code: in form or report Class modules or in Standard modules? There are pros and cons to each method. Placing code in Standard modules means that the code can be easily called from anywhere in your application, without loading a specific form or report. Public routines placed in Standard modules can also be called from other databases. For this reason, Standard modules are a great place to put generic routines that you want readily available as part of a library.

Access 2000 loads modules on a demand-only basis, which means that procedures no longer take up memory unless they're being used. This is especially true if you plan your modules carefully (see Chapter 15, "Optimizing Your Application"). Regardless of when the code is loaded, an advantage of placing code behind forms and reports

continues

7

VBA: AN
INTRODUCTION

(rather than within modules) is that the form or report is self-contained and, there-fore, portable. You can import the form or report into any other database and it still operates as expected. This object-oriented approach means that the form requires nothing from the outside world.

As you can see, there are pluses and minuses to each method. As a general rule, if a routine is specific to a particular form or report, place that routine in the form or report; if it's widely used, place it in a module.

Static Procedures

If a procedure is declared as Static, all the variables declared in the procedure maintain their values between calls to the procedure. This is an alternative to explicitly declaring each vari-able in the procedure as Static. Here's an example of a Static procedure, found in basVariable:

```
Static Sub IncrementThem()
    Dim intCounter1 As Integer
    Dim intCounter2 As Integer
    Dim intCounter3 As Integer
    intCounter1 = intCounter1 + 1
    intCounter2 = intCounter2 + 1
    intCounter3 = intCounter3 + 1
    MsgBox intCounter1 & " - " & intCounter2 & " - " & intCounter3
End Sub
```

Ordinarily, each variable in this procedure would be reinitialized to zero each time the proce-dure is run. This means that all 1s would appear in the message box each time the procedure is run. Because the procedure is declared as Static, the variables in it retain their values from call to call. That means each time the procedure is run, the values in the message box increase. This behavior should become much clearer after the discussion of variables later in this chapter.

WORKING WITH VARIABLES

You must consider many issues when creating VBA variables. The way you declare a variable determines its scope, its lifetime, and more. The following topics will help you better under-stand declaring variables in VBA.

Declaring Variables

There are several ways to declare variables in VBA: three are nonstandard and one is standard. For example, you could simply declare x=10. With this method of variable declaration, you really aren't declaring your variables at all; you're essentially declaring them as you use them. This method is quite dangerous; it lends itself to typos and other problems. If you follow the practice, recommended previously, of always using the `Option Explicit` statement, Access will not allow you to declare variables in this manner.

You could also type `Dim intCounter`; the `Dim` statement declares the variable. The only problem with this method is that you haven't declared the type of the variable to the compiler, so it's declared as a variant variable.

Another common mistake is declaring multiple variables on the same line, as in this example:

```
Dim intCounter, intAge, intWeight As Integer.
```

In this line, only the last variable is explicitly declared as an integer variable. The other variables are implicitly declared as variants. If you're going to declare multiple variables on one line, make sure each variable is specifically declared, as in the following example:

```
Dim intCounter As Integer, intAge As Integer, intWeight As Integer
```

The most efficient and bug-proof way to declare your variables is to strong type them to the compiler and declare only one variable per line of code, as in this example:

```
Dim intCounter As Integer
Dim strName As String
```

As you can see, strong typing declares the name of the variable as well as the type of data it can contain. This enables the compiler to catch errors, such as storing a string into an integer variable, before your program runs. If implemented properly, this method can also reduce the resources needed to run your programs by selecting the smallest practical data type for each variable.

7

VBA: AN INTRODUCTION

NOTE

You should try to eliminate using variants whenever possible. Besides requiring a significant amount of storage space, variants are also slow because they must be resolved by the compiler at runtime. However, certain situations warrant using a variant. One example is when you want the variable to contain different types of data at different times. Another case occurs when you want to be able to differentiate between an empty variable (one that hasn't been initialized) and a variable having a zero or a zero-length string. Also, variant variables are the only type of variable that can hold the special value of `null`. Empty and `null` values are covered in Chapter 24, "Advanced VBA Techniques."

VBA Data Types

VBA offers several data types for variables. Table 7.1 shows a list of the available data types, the standard for naming them, the amount of storage space they require, the data they can store, and their default values.

TABLE 7.1 DATA TYPES AND NAMING CONVENTIONS

Data Type	Naming Conv Example	Storage of Data	Range	Default Value
Byte	bytValue	1 byte	0 to 255	0
Boolean	boolAnswer	2 bytes	True or False	False
Integer	intCounter	2 bytes	-32768 to 32767	0
Long Integer	lngAmount	4 bytes	-2,147,483,648 to 2,147,483,647	0
Single	sngAmount	4 bytes	-3.402823E38 to -1.401298E-45 for negative values; from 1.401298E-45 to 3.402823E38 for positive values	0
Double	dblValue	8 bytes	-1.79769313486231E308 to -4.94065645841247E-324 for negative values; from 4.94065645841247E-324 to 1.79769313486232E308 for positive values	0
Currency	curSalary	8 bytes	-922,337,203,685,477.5808 to 922,337,203,685,477.5807	0
Date	dtmStartDate	8 bytes	1/1/100 to 12/31/9999	
Object Reference	objExcel	4 bytes	Any object	
Fixed String	strName	varies	Up to 65,526 characters	" "
Variable String	strName	varies	Up to approximately 2 billion characters	" "

Data Type	Naming Conv Example	Storage of Data	Range	Default Value
Variant	varData	varies	Can contain any of the other datatypes except Fixed String	Empty
User-Defined Data Type	typEmp	varies	Based on Elements	
Decimal	decTaxAmount	12 bytes	+/- 79,228,162,514,264,337, 593,543,950,335 with 0 decimal places +/-7.9228162514264337593543950335 with 28 decimal places	0

Scope and Lifetime of Variables: Exposing Your Variables as Little as Possible

You have read about the different types of variables available in VBA. Like procedures, variables also have a scope. A variable can be declared as Local, Private (Module), or Public in scope. You should try to use Local variables in your code because they're shielded from being accidentally modified by other routines.

Variables also have an attribute referred to as their lifetime. The lifetime of a variable reflects the time during which the variable actually exists, and therefore the time during which its value is retained. In the following sections, we take a closer look at how you can set the scope and lifetime of variables.

Local Variables

Local variables are available only in the procedure where they are declared. Consider this example (not included in Chap7ex):

```
Private Sub cmdOkay_Click
  Dim strAnimal As String
  strAnimal = "Dog"
  Call ChangeAnimal
  Debug.Print strAnimal ''Still Dog
End Sub
```

```
Private Sub ChangeAnimal
  strAnimal = "Cat"
End Sub
```

This code can behave in one of three ways. If `Option Explicit` were in effect, meaning that all variables must be declared before they're used, this code would generate a compiler error. If the `Option Explicit` statement isn't used, `strAnimal` would be changed to `Cat` only within the context of the subroutine `ChangeAnimal`. If the `Dim strAnimal As String` statement is moved to the Declarations section of the module, the variable's value is changed to `"Cat"`.

NOTE

Notice the `Debug.Print` statement in `cmdOkay_Click` event routine shown above. The expression that follows the `Debug.Print` statement is printed in the Immediate window. The Immediate window is a tool that helps you to troubleshoot your applications. You can invoke the Immediate window from almost anywhere within your application. The easiest way to activate the Immediate window is with the Ctrl+G keystroke combination. You are placed in the Visual Basic Editor within the Immediate window. You can then view the expressions that were printed to the Immediate window. The Immediate window is discussed in detail in Chapter 13, "Debugging: Your Key to Successful Development."

Static Variables: A Special Type of Local Variable

The following examples illustrate the difference between Local and Static variables. Local variables are reinitialized each time the code is called. The following procedure can be run by opening the form named frmScopeAndLifeTime and clicking the Local Age button. Notice that each time you run the procedure, the numeral 1 is displayed in the txtNewAge text box.

```
Private Sub cmdLocalAge_Click()
  Dim intAge As Integer
  intAge = intAge + 1
  Me.txtNewAge = intAge
End Sub
```

Each time this code runs, the `Dim` statement reinitializes `intAge` to zero. This is quite different from the following code, which illustrates the use of a Static variable:

```
Private Sub cmdStaticAge_Click()
  Static sintAge As Integer
  sintAge = sintAge + 1
  Me.txtNewAge = sintAge
End Sub
```

Each time this code executes, the variable called sintAge is incremented and its value retained. You can test this by opening the form named frmScopeAndLifeTime and clicking the Static Age button.

Private Variables

So far, this discussion has been limited to variables that have scope within a single procedure. Private (module-level) variables can be seen by any routine in the module they were declared in, but not from other modules. Thus, they are Private to the module. Private variables are declared by placing a Private statement, such as the following, in the General Declarations section of a Form, Report, or Access module:

```
[General Declarations]
Option Explicit
Private mintAge As Integer
```

The value of a variable declared as Private can be changed by any subroutine or function within that module. For example, the following subroutine increments the value of the Private variable mintAge by 1. You can run this code by opening the form frmScopeAndLifeTime and clicking the Module Age button.

```
Private Sub cmdModuleAge_Click()
  mintAge = mintAge + 1
  Me.txtNewAge = mintAge
End Sub
```

Notice the naming convention of using the letter m to prefix the name of the variable, which denotes the variable as a Private module-level variable. You should use Private declarations only for variables that need to be seen by multiple procedures in the same module; aim for making most of your variables Local to make your code modular and more bullet-proof.

Public Variables

Public variables can be accessed from any VBA code in your application. They're usually limited to things such as login IDs, environment settings, and other variables that must be seen by your entire application. Declarations of Public variables can be placed in the General Declarations section of a module. The declaration of a Public variable looks like this:

```
Option Explicit
Public gintAge As Integer
```

Notice the prefix g (a relic of the old Global variables), the proper prefix for a Public variable declared in a Standard module. This standard is used because Public variables declared in a

Standard module are visible not only to the module they were declared in, but also to other modules. The following code, placed in the `Click` event of the cmdPublic command button, increments the Public variable `gintCounter` by 1. You can run this code by opening the form frmScopeAndLifeTime and clicking the Public Age button.

```
Private Sub cmdPublicAge_Click()
  gintAge = gintAge + 1
  Me.txtNewAge = gintAge
End Sub
```

ADDING COMMENTS TO YOUR CODE

Comments, which have been color-coded since Access 97, are added to modules by using an apostrophe. The keyword `Rem` can also be used, but the apostrophe is generally preferred. The apostrophe can be placed at the beginning of the line of code or anywhere within it. Anything following the apostrophe is considered a comment. Figure 7.9 shows code containing comments.

FIGURE 7.9

Code containing comments that clarify what the subroutine is doing.

USING THE LINE CONTINUATION CHARACTER

Access Basic code, used in Access 2.0, didn't have a line continuation character. Therefore, you had to scroll a lot, as well as pull out a bag of tricks to simulate continuing a line of code. With VBA, Access 97 and 2000 solves this problem; the line continuation character is an underscore. Figure 7.10 illustrates the use of this character.

FIGURE 7.10

The line continuation character is used to improve the readability of a long line of code.

USING THE VBA CONTROL STRUCTURES

VBA gives the developer several different constructs for looping and decision processing. The most commonly used ones are covered in the following sections and are found in the form called frmControlStructures.

If...Then...Else

The If...Then...Else construct evaluates whether a condition is true. In the following example, anything between If and Else will occur if the statement evaluates to True, and any code between Else and End If will be executed if the statement evaluates to False. The Else is optional.

```
Private Sub cmdIfThenElse_Click()
 If IsNull(Me.txtName) or IsNull(Me.txtAge) Then
    MsgBox "Name or Age is Blank"
  Else
    MsgBox "Your Name Is " & Me.txtName _
        & " And Your Age Is " & Me.txtAge
  End If
End Sub
```

This code tests whether the text box called txtName or the text box txtAge contains a null. A different message is displayed depending on whether one of the text boxes contains a null value.

One-line If statements are also permitted; they look like this:

```
If IsNull(Me.txtvalue) Then MsgBox "You must Enter a Value"
```

However, this format for an If statement isn't recommended because it reduces readability.

Another useful form of an `If` statement is `ElseIf`, which enables you to evaluate an unlimited number of conditions in one `If` statement. The following code gives you an example (this example is not included in Chap7Ex):

```
Sub MultipleIfs(intNumber As Integer)
    If intNumber = 1 Then
        MsgBox "You entered a One"
    ElseIf intNumber = 2 Then
        MsgBox "You entered a Two"
    ElseIf intNumber >= 3 And intNumber <= 10 Then
        MsgBox "You entered a Number Between 3 and 10"
    Else
        MsgBox "You Entered Some Other Number"
    End If
End Sub
```

The conditions in an `If` statement are evaluated in the order in which they appear. For this reason, it's best to place the most common conditions first. After a condition is met, execution continues immediately after `End If`. If no conditions are met, and there's no `Else` statement, execution will also continue immediately after `End If`.

> **NOTE**
>
> If multiple conditions exist, it's almost always preferable to use a `Select Case` statement, described later in this chapter, rather than an `If` statement. `Case` statements generally make your code easier to read and maintain.

Immediate If (IIf)

An Immediate If (`IIf`) is a variation of an `If` statement; it's actually a built-in function that returns one of two values, depending on whether the condition being tested is true or false. Here's an example (this code is not included in Chap7Ex):

```
Function EvalSales(curSales As Currency) As String
    EvalSales = IIf(curSales >= 100000, "Great Job", "Keep Plugging")
End Function
```

This function evaluates the `curSales` parameter to see whether its value is greater than or equal to $100,000. If it is, the string `"Great Job"` is returned from the function; otherwise, the string `"Keep Plugging"` is returned.

CAUTION

Both the true and false portions of the IIf are evaluated, so if there's a problem with either part of the expression (for example, a divide-by-zero condition), an error occurs.

The IIf function is most often used in a calculated control on a form or report or to create a new field in a query. Probably the most common example is an IIf expression that determines whether the value of a control is null. If it is, you can have the expression return a zero or an empty string; otherwise, you can have the expression return the value in the control. The following expression, for example, evaluates the value of a control on a form:

```
=IIf(IsNull(Forms!frmOrders.txtFreight),0,Forms!frmOrders.txtFreight)
```

This expression displays either a zero or the value for freight in the control called txtFreight.

NOTE

Although the IIF function can be used to handle Nulls, the built-in NZ function is a more efficient solution to this problem and avoids the inherent pitfalls of IIF.

The Conditional If: Conditional Compilation

Conditional compilation enables you to selectively execute blocks of code. This feature is useful in several situations:

- When you want certain blocks of code to execute in the demo version of your product and other blocks to execute in your product's retail version

- When you're distributing your application in different countries and want certain blocks of code to apply to some countries but not to others

- When you want certain blocks of code to execute only during the testing of your application

Conditional compilation is done by using the `#If...Then...#Else` directive, as shown here and found under the Conditional Compilation command button on the frmControlStructures form:

```
Sub cmdConditionalCompilation_Click()
    #If Language = "Spanish" Then
        MsgBox "Hola, Que Tal?"
    #Else
        MsgBox "Hello, How Are You?"
    #End If
End Sub
```

The compiler constant, in this case, `Language`, can be declared in one of two places: in a module's General Declarations section or in the Project Properties dialog. A compiler constant declared in the General Declarations section of a module looks like this:

```
#Const Language = "Spanish"
```

The disadvantage of this constant is that it can't be declared as Public. It isn't possible to create Public compiler constants by using the `#Const` directive. This means that any compiler constants declared in a module's Declarations section can be used only within that module. The major advantage of declaring this type of compiler constant is that it can contain a string. For example, the compiler constant `Language`, defined in the previous paragraph, is given the value `"Spanish"`.

Public compiler constants can be declared by modifying the Project Properties. Because they are Public in scope, compiler constants declared in the Project Properties can be referred to from anywhere in your application. The major limitation of compiler directives set up in Project Properties is that they can contain only integers. For example, you would have to enter `Language = 1`.

To define compiler constants using the Project Properties dialog, right-click within the Project window and select *projectx* Properties, where *projectx* is the name of the project you are working with. You may now enter the values you need into the text box labeled Conditional Compilation Arguments. You may enter several arguments by separating them with a colon, such as `Language = 1 : Version = 2`.

With the compiler directive `Language=1`, the code would look like this:

```
Sub ConditionalIf()
    #If Language = 1 Then
        MsgBox "Hola, Que Tal?"
    #Else
        MsgBox "Hello, How Are You?"
    #End If
End Sub
```

> **NOTE**
>
> For this code to execute properly, you must remove the constant declaration from the previous example.

Notice that ConditionalIf now evaluates the constant Language against the integer of 1.

It's important to understand that using conditional constants isn't the same as using regular constants or variables with the standard If...Then...Else construct. Regular constants or variables are evaluated at runtime, which requires processing time each time the application is run. Conditional constants and conditional If...Then...Else statements control which sections of code are actually compiled. All resolution is completed at compile time; this eliminates the need for unnecessary processing at runtime.

Select Case

Rather than using multiple If...Then...Else statements, it's often much clearer to use a Select Case statement, as shown here and found under the Select Case command button of the frmControlStructures form:

```
Private Sub cmdCase_Click()
    Dim intAge As Integer
    IntAge = Nz(Me![txtAge]
    Select Case intAge
      Case 0
        MsgBox "You Must Enter a Number"
      Case 1 To 18
        MsgBox "You Are Just a Kid"
      Case 19, 20, 21
        MsgBox "You are Almost an Adult"
      Case 22 to 40
        MsgBox "Good Deal"
      Case Is > 40
        MsgBox "Getting Up There!"
      Case Else
        MsgBox "You Entered an Invalid Number"
    End Select
End Sub
```

This subroutine first uses the Nz function to convert a null or empty value in the txtAge control to 0; otherwise, the value in txtAge is stored in intAge. The Select Case statement then evaluates intAge. If the value is 0, a message box is displayed with You Must Enter a Number. If the value is between 1 and 18 inclusive, a message box is displayed saying You Are Just a Kid. If the user enters 19, 20, or 21, the message You are Almost an Adult is displayed. If the user enters a value between 22 and 40 inclusive, the message Good Deal is displayed. If a value greater than 40 is displayed, the message Getting Up There is displayed; otherwise, the user gets a message indicating that he or she entered an invalid number.

Looping

Several looping structures are available in VBA; most are discussed in this section. Take a look at the following example of a looping structure (found under the Do While...Loop command button of the frmControlStructures form):

```
Sub cmdDoWhileLoop_Click()

    Do While Nz(Me!txtAge)< 35

        Me.txtAge = Nz(Me!txtAge) + 1
    Loop
End Sub
```

In this structure, if txtAge is greater than or equal to 35, the code in the loop is not executed. If you want the code to execute unconditionally at least one time, you need to use the following construct (found under the Do...Loop While command button of the frmControlStructures form:

```
Sub cmdDoLoopWhile_Click()

    Do

        Me.txtAge = Nz(Me!txtAge) + 1
    Loop While Nz(Me!txtAge) < 35
End Sub
```

This code will execute one time, even if txtAge is set to 35. The Do While...Loop in the previous example evaluates before the code is executed, so it doesn't ensure code execution. The Do...Loop While is evaluated at the end of the loop and it, therefore, guarantees execution.

Alternatives to the Do While...Loop and the Do...Loop While are Do Until...Loop and Do...Loop Until. Do Until...Loop (found under the Do Until...Loop command button of the frmControlStructures form) works like this:

```
Sub cmdDoUntil_Click()

    Do Until Nz(Me!txtAge) = 35

        Me!txtAge = Nz(Me!txtAge) + 1
    Loop
End Sub
```

This loop continues to execute until `txtAge` becomes equal to 35. The `Do...Loop Until` construct (found under the `Do...Loop Until` command button of the frmControlStructures form) is another variation:

```
Sub cmdLoopUntil_Click()

    Do

        Me.txtAge = Nz(Me!txtAge) + 1
    Loop Until Nz(Me!txtAge) = 35
End Sub
```

As with the `Do...Loop While` construct, the `Do...Loop Until` construct doesn't evaluate the condition until the end of the loop, so the code in the loop is guaranteed to execute at least once.

CAUTION

It's easy to unintentionally cause a loop to execute endlessly, as shown in this example (this code is not included in Chap7Ex):

```
Sub EndlessLoop()
    Dim intCounter As Integer
    intCounter = 5
    Do
        Debug.Print intCounter
        intCounter = intCounter + 1
    Loop Until intCounter = 5
End Sub
```

This code snippet sets `intCounter` equal to 5. The code in the loop increments `intCounter`, then tests to see whether `intCounter` equals 5. If it doesn't, the code in the loop executes another time. Because `intCounter` will never become equal to 5 (it starts at 6 within the `Do` loop), the loop executes endlessly. You need to use Ctrl+Break to exit out of the loop; however, Ctrl+Break doesn't work in Access's run-time version.

For...Next

The `For...Next` construct is used when you have an exact number of iterations you want to perform. It looks like this and is found under the `For...Next` command button of the frmControlStructures form:

```
Sub cmdForNext_Click()
    Dim intCounter As Integer
```

```
    For intCounter = 1 To 5
        Me!txtAge = Nz(Me!txtAge) + 1
    Next intCounter
End Sub
```

Note that `intCounter` is self-incrementing. The start value and the stop value can both be variables. A `For...Next` construct can also be given a step value, as shown here (the counter is incremented by the value of `Step` each time the loop is processed):

```
Sub ForNextStep()
' Note that this code is not in database Chap7ex.mdb
    Dim intCounter As Integer
    For intCounter = 1 To 5 Step 2
        Me!txtAge = Nz(Me!txtAge) + 1
    Next intCounter
End Sub
```

With...End With

The `With...End With` statement executes a series of statements on a single object. Here's an example (found under the `With...End With` command button of the frmControlStructures form):

```
Private Sub cmdWithEndWith_Click()
    With Me!txtAge
        .BackColor = 16777088
        .ForeColor = 16711680
        .Value = "40"
        .FontName = "Arial"
    End With
End Sub
```

This code performs four operations on the txtAge text box, found on the form it's run on. The `BackColor`, `ForeColor`, `Value`, and `FontName` properties of the txtAge text box are all modified by the code.

TIP

The `With...End With` statement offers two main benefits. The first is simply less typing—you don't need to repeat the object name for each action you want to perform on the object. The more important benefit involves performance. Because the object is referred to once rather than multiple times, this code runs much more efficiently. The benefits are even more pronounced when the `With...End With` construct is found in a loop.

For Each...Next

The For Each...Next statement executes a group of statements on each member of an array or collection. The following example (found under the For Each...Next command button of the frmControlStructures form illustrates the use of this powerful construct:

```
Private Sub cmdForEachNext_Click()

    Dim ctl As Control
    For Each ctl In Controls
        With ctl
            .ForeColor = 16711680
            .FontName = "Arial"
            .FontSize = 14
        End With
    Next ctl
End Sub
```

This code loops through each control on a form; the ForeColor, FontName, and BackColor properties of each control on the form are modified. As in the preceding example, the With...End With construct is often used with the For Each...Next construct. Here's an example of the With...End With construct (found under the With...End With command button of the frmControlStructures form):

```
Private Sub cmdForEachWith_Click()
    With Me.txtAge
        .BackColor = 16777088
        .ForeColor = 16711680
        .Value = "Hello World"
        .FontName = "Arial"

    End With

End Sub
```

This code modifies three properties of the txtAge control: ForeColor, FontName, and FontSize.

> **CAUTION**
>
> Before you put all this good information to use, remember that no error handling has been implemented in the code yet. If one of the controls on the form in the example doesn't have a ForeColor, FontName, or FontSize property, the code would cause an error. In Chapter 8, you will learn how to determine the type of an object before you perform a command on it. Knowing the type of an object before you try to modify its properties can help you prevent errors.

PASSING PARAMETERS AND RETURNING VALUES

Both subroutines and functions can receive arguments (parameters), but only functions can return values. The following subroutine (found under the Pass Parameters command button of the frmParametersAndReturnValues form) receives two parameters, txtFirst and txtLast. It then displays a message box with the first character of each of the parameters that was passed.

```
Private Sub cmdPassParameters_Click()
  Call Initials(Nz(Me!txtFirstName), Nz(Me!txtLastName))
End Sub

Sub Initials(strFirst As String, strLast As String)
' This procedure can be found by selecting General in
' the Object drop-down list in the VBE window
  MsgBox "Your Initials Are: " & Left$(strFirst, 1) _
    & Left$(strLast, 1)
End Sub
```

Notice that the text in the controls txtFirstName and txtLastName from the current form (represented by the Me keyword) is passed to the subroutine called Initials. The parameters are received as strFirst and strLast. The first left character of each parameter is displayed in the message box.

The preceding code simply passes values and then operates on those values. This next example (found under the Return Values command button of the frmParametersAndReturnValues form) uses a function to return a value.

```
Private Sub cmdReturnValues_Click()
    Dim strInitials As String
    strInitials = ReturnInit(Nz(Me!txtFirstName), _
        Nz(Me!txtLastName))
    MsgBox "Your initials are: " & strInitials
End Sub
```

```
Function ReturnInit(strFName As String, strLName As String) As String
' This procedure can be found by selecting General in
' the Object drop-down list in the VBE window
    ReturnInit = Left$(strFName, 1) & Left(strLName, 1)
End Function
```

Notice that this example calls the function `ReturnInit`, sending values contained in the two text boxes as parameters. The function sets `ReturnInit` (the name of the function) equal to the first two characters of the strings. This returns the value to the calling routine (`cmdReturnValues _Click`) and sets `strInitials` equal to the return value.

> **NOTE**
>
> Notice that the function `ReturnInit` is set to receive two string parameters. You know this because of the `As String` keywords that follow each parameter. The function is also set to return a string. You know this because the keyword `As String` follows the list of the parameters, outside the parentheses. If you don't explicitly state that the function should return a particular type of data, it returns a variant.

EXECUTING PROCEDURES FROM THE MODULE WINDOW

It's easy to test procedures from the Module window in Access 2000—simply click anywhere inside the procedure you want to execute, then press the F5 key or click the Run Sub/UserForm button on the toolbar. The procedure you're in will execute as though you had called it from code or from the Immediate pane of the Debug window.

THE DoCmd OBJECT: PERFORMING MACRO ACTIONS

The Access environment is rich with objects that have built-in properties and methods. By using VBA code, you can modify the properties and execute the methods. One of the objects available in Access is the `DoCmd` object, used to execute macro actions in Visual Basic procedures. The macro actions are executed as methods of the `DoCmd` object. The syntax looks like this:

```
DoCmd.ActionName [arguments]
```

Here's a practical example:

```
DoCmd.OpenReport strReportName, acPreview
```

The `OpenReport` method is a method of the `DoCmd` object; it runs a report. The first two parameters the `OpenReport` method receives are the name of the report you want to run and the view in which you want the report to appear (Preview, Normal, or Design). The name of the report and the view are both arguments of the `OpenReport` method.

Most macro actions have corresponding `DoCmd` methods that can be found in Help, but some don't. They are `AddMenu`, `MsgBox`, `RunApp`, `RunCode`, `SendKeys`, `SetValue`, `StopAllMacros`, and `StopMacro`. The `SendKeys` method is the only one that has any significance to you as a VBA programmer. The remaining macro actions either have no application to VBA code or can be performed more efficiently by using VBA functions and commands. The VBA language includes a `MsgBox` function, for example, that's far more robust than its macro action counterpart.

Many of the `DoCmd` methods have optional parameters. If you don't supply an argument, its default value is assumed. You can use commas as place markers to designate the position of missing arguments, as shown here:

```
DoCmd.OpenForm "frmOrders", , ,"[OrderAmount] > 1000"
```

The `OpenForm` method of the `DoCmd` object receives seven parameters; the last six parameters are optional. In the example, two parameters are explicitly specified. The first is the name of the form, a required parameter. The second and third parameters have been omitted, meaning that you're accepting their default values. The commas, used as place markers for the second and third parameters, are necessary because one of the parameters following them is explicitly designated. The fourth parameter is the `Where` condition for the form, which has been designated as the record in which the `OrderAmount` is greater than 1,000. The remaining parameters haven't been referred to, so default values are used for these parameters.

If you prefer, you can use named parameters to designate the parameters that you are passing. Named parameters, covered later in this chapter, can greatly simplify the preceding syntax. With named parameters, the arguments don't need to be placed in a particular order, nor do you need to worry about counting commas. The preceding syntax can be changed to the following:

```
DoCmd.OpenForm FormName:="frmOrders", WhereCondition:=
"[OrderAmount] > 1000"
```

WORKING WITH BUILT-IN FUNCTIONS

Visual Basic for Applications has a rich and comprehensive function library as well as tools to assist in their use.

Built-In Functions

Some of the more commonly used functions and examples are listed in the following sections. On some rainy day, go through the online Help or the *Microsoft Access Visual Basic Language Reference* to become familiar with the rest.

Format

The `Format` function formats expressions in the style specified. The first parameter is the expression you want to format; the second is the type of format you want to apply. Here's an example of using the `Format` function:

```
Sub FormatData()
   Debug.Print Format$(50, "Currency")
   'Prints $50.00
   Debug.Print Format$(Now, "Short Date")
   'Prints the current date
   Debug.Print Format$(Now, "DDDD")
   'Displays the word for the day
   Debug.Print Format$(Now, "DDD")
   'Displays 3 - CHAR Day
   Debug.Print Format$(Now, "YYYY")
   'Displays 4 - digit Year
   Debug.Print Format$(Now, "WW")
   'Displays the Week Number
End Sub
```

Instr

The `Instr` function returns the position where one string begins within another string:

```
Sub InstrExample()
  Debug.Print InStr("Alison Balter", "Balter") 'Returns 8
  Debug.Print InStr("Hello", "l") 'Returns 3
End Sub
```

Left

Left returns the left-most number of characters in a string:

```
Sub LeftExample()
  Debug.Print Left$("Hello World", 7) 'Prints Hello W
End Sub
```

Right

Right returns the right-most number of characters in a string:

```
Sub RightExample()
 Debug.Print Right$("Hello World", 7) 'Prints o World
End Sub
```

Mid

Mid returns a substring of a specified number of characters in a string. This example starts at the fourth character and returns five characters:

```
Sub MidExample()
    Debug.Print Mid$("Hello World", 4, 5) ''Prints lo Wo
End Sub
```

UCase

UCase returns a string that is all uppercase:

```
Sub UCaseExample()
    Debug.Print UCase$("Hello World") 'Prints HELLO WORLD
End Sub
```

DatePart

DatePart returns the specified part of a date:

```
Sub DatePartExample()
    Debug.Print DatePart("YYYY", Now)
    'Prints the Year
    Debug.Print DatePart("M", Now)
    'Prints the Month Number
    Debug.Print DatePart("Q", Now)
    'Prints the Quarter Number
    Debug.Print DatePart("Y", Now)
    'Prints the Day of the Year
    Debug.Print DatePart("WW", Now)
    'Prints the Week of the Year
End Sub
```

DateDiff

DateDiff returns the interval of time between two dates:

```
Sub DateDiffExample()
  Debug.Print DateDiff("d", Now, "12/31/99")
  ''Days until 12/31/99
  Debug.Print DateDiff("m", Now, "12/31/99")
  ''Months until 12/31/99
  Debug.Print DateDiff("yyyy", Now, "12/31/99")
```

```
    ''Years until 12/31/99
    Debug.Print DateDiff("q", Now, "12/31/99")
    ''Quarters until 12/31/99
End Sub
```

DateAdd

DateAdd returns the result of adding or subtracting a specified period of time to a date:

```
Sub DateAddExample()
    Debug.Print DateAdd("d", 3, Now)
    'Today plus 3 days
    Debug.Print DateAdd("m", 3, Now)
    'Today plus 3 months
    Debug.Print DateAdd("yyyy", 3, Now)
    'Today plus 3 years
    Debug.Print DateAdd("q", 3, Now)
    'Today plus 3 quarters
    Debug.Print DateAdd("ww", 3, Now)
    'Today plus 3 weeks
End Sub
```

Functions Made Easy with the Object Browser

With the Object Browser, you can view members of an ActiveX component's type library. In plain English, the Object Browser enables you to easily browse through a component's methods, properties, and constants. You can also copy information and add it to your code. It even adds a method's parameters for you. The following steps let you browse among the available methods, copy the method you want, and paste it into your code:

1. With the VBE active, select View | Object Browser from the menu (note that the menu line also shows an icon that you can use from the toolbar) or press F2 to open the Object Browser window. (See Figure 7.11.)

FIGURE 7.11

The Object Browser showing all the classes in the Chap7ex database and all the members in the basUtils module.

2. The Object Browser window is divided into two parts; the upper part of the window and the lower part of the window. The drop-down list at the upper-left of the window is used to filter the items to be displayed in the lower part of the window. Use this drop-down list to select the project or library whose classes and members you want to view in the lower part of the window.

3. In the lower portion of the window, select the class from the left list box, which lists Class modules, templates for new objects, standard modules, and modules containing subroutines and functions.

4. Select a related property, method, event, constant, function, or statement from the Members Of list box. In Figure 7.11, the basUtils module is selected from the list box on the left. Notice that the subroutines and functions included in basUtils appear in the list box on the right.

5. Click the Copy to Clipboard button (third from the right in the upper toolbar within the Object Browser window) to copy the function and its parameters to the Clipboard so that you can easily paste it into your code.

The example in Figure 7.11 shows choosing a user-defined function selected from a module in a database, but you can also select any built-in function. Figure 7.12 shows an example in which the `DatePart` function is selected from the Visual Basic for Applications library. The Object Browser exposes all libraries referred to by the database and is covered in more detail in Chapters 8, "Objects, Properties, Methods, and Events Explained" and Chapter 26, "Automation: Communicating with Other Applications."

FIGURE 7.12

The Object Browser with the VBA library selected.

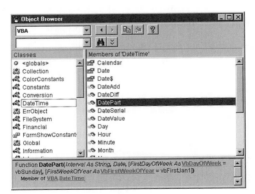

WORKING WITH CONSTANTS

A *constant* is a meaningful name given to a meaningless number or string. Constants can be used only for values that don't change at runtime. A tax rate or commission rate, for example, might be constant throughout your application. There are three types of constants in Access:

- Symbolic
- Intrinsic
- System-Defined

Symbolic constants, created by using the `Const` keyword, are used to improve the readability of your code and make code maintenance easier. Rather than referring to the number `.0875` every time you want to refer to the tax rate, you can refer to the constant `mccurTaxRate`. If the tax rate changes, and you need to modify the value in your code, you'll make the change in only one place. Furthermore, unlike the number `.0875`, the name `mccurTaxRate` is self-documenting.

Intrinsic constants are built into Microsoft Access; they are part of the language itself. As an Access programmer, you can use constants supplied by Microsoft Access, Visual Basic, DAO, and Active Data Objects (ADO). You can also use constants provided by any object libraries you're using in your application.

There are only three system-defined constants, available to all applications on your computer: `True`, `False`, and `Null`.

Working with Symbolic Constants

As mentioned, a symbolic constant is declared by using the `Const` keyword. A constant can be declared in a subroutine or function or in the General section of a Form or Report module. Constants can be strong-typed in Access 2000. The declaration and use of a Private constant would look like this:

```
Private Const TAXRATE As Currency = .0875
```

This code, when placed in a module's Declarations section, creates a Private constant called TAXRATE and sets it equal to `.0875`. Here's how the constant is used in code:

```
Function TotalAmount(curSaleAmount As Currency)
   TotalAmount = curSaleAmount * TAXRATE
End Function
```

This routine multiplies the curSaleAmount, received as a parameter, by the constant TAXRATE. It returns the result of the calculation by setting the function name equal to the product of the two values. The advantage of the constant in this example is that the code is more readable than TotalAmount = curSaleAmount * .0875 would be.

Scoping Symbolic Constants

Just as regular variables have scope, user-defined constants have scope. In the preceding example, you created a Private constant. The following statement, when placed in a module's Declarations section, creates a Public constant:

```
Public Const TAXRATE = 0.0875 As Currency
```

Because this constant is declared as Public, it can be accessed from any subroutine or function (including event routines) in your entire application. To better understand the benefits of a Public constant, take a case where you have many functions and subroutines all making reference to the constant TAXRATE. Imagine what would happen if the tax rate were to change. If you hadn't used a constant, you would need to search your entire application, replacing the old tax rate with the new tax rate. However, because your Public constant is declared in one place, you can easily go in and modify the one line of code where this constant is declared.

> **NOTE**
>
> By definition, the values of constants cannot be modified at runtime. If you try to modify the value of a constant, you get this VBA compiler error:
>
> ```
> Assignment to constant not permitted
> ```
>
> Figure 7.13 illustrates this message box. You can see that an attempt is made to modify the value of the constant called TAXRATE, which results in a compile error.
>
> If you need to change the value at runtime, you should consider storing the value in a table rather than declaring it as a constant. You can read the value into a variable when the application loads, then modify the variable if needed. If you choose, you can write the new value back to the table.

Working with Intrinsic Constants

Microsoft Access declares a number of intrinsic constants that can be used in Code, Form, and Report modules. Because they're reserved by Microsoft Access, you can't modify their values or reuse their names; however, they can be used at any time without being declared.

You should use intrinsic constants whenever possible in your code. Besides making your code more readable, they make your code more portable to future releases of Microsoft Access.

Microsoft might change the value associated with a constant, but it isn't likely to change the constant's name. All intrinsic constants appear in the Object Browser; to activate it, simply click the Object Browser tool on the Visual Basic toolbar. To view the constants that are part of the Access library, select Access from the Object Browser's Project/Library drop-down list. Click Constants in the Classes list box, and a list of those constants is displayed in the Members Of 'Constants' list box. (See Figure 7.14.)

FIGURE 7.13

Trying to modify the value of a constant.

FIGURE 7.14

Using the Object Browser to view intrinsic constants.

In the list shown in Figure 7.14, all the constant names begin with *ac*. All VBA constants are prefixed with vb, all Data Access Object constants are prefixed with db, and all constants that are part of the Access language are prefixed with ac. To view the Visual Basic language constants, select VBA from the Project/Library drop-down list and Constants from the Classes list

7

VBA: AN INTRODUCTION

box. If the project you are working with has a reference to the ActiveX Data Object library, you may view these constants by selecting ADODB from the Project/Library drop-down list. Click <globals>. A list of the ADODB constants appears (these constants have the prefix ad).

Another way to view constants is within the context of the parameter you're working with in the Code window. Left-click the name of a parameter to display the constants associated with the parameter. This feature was shown earlier in this chapter.

TOOLS FOR WORKING IN THE VISUAL BASIC EDITOR

Effectively using the tips and tricks of the trade, many of which are highlighted in this chapter, can save you hours of time. These tricks help you to navigate around the coding environment, as well as to modify your code quickly and easily. They include the capability to easily zoom to a user-defined procedure, search and replace within modules, get help on VBA functions and commands, and split the Code window so that two procedures can be viewed simultaneously.

The Access 97 and Access 2000 development environments are better than their predecessors. Several features have been added to make coding easier and more pleasant for you. These enhancements include the capability to do the following:

- List properties and methods
- List constants
- Get quick information on a command or function
- Get parameter information
- Enable Access to finish a word for you
- Get a definition of a function

All these features that help you with coding are available with a right-click when you place your cursor within the Module window.

List Properties and Methods

With the List Properties and Methods feature, you can view all the objects, properties, and methods available for the current object. To invoke this feature, right-click after the name of the object and select List Properties, Methods (you can also press Ctrl+J). The applicable objects, properties, and methods appear in a list box. (See Figure 7.15.) To find the appropriate object, property, or method in the list, use one of these methods:

1. Begin typing the name of the object, property, or method.
2. Use the up-arrow and down-arrow keys to move through the list.
3. Scroll through the list and select your choice.

FIGURE 7.15

A list of properties and methods for the TextBox object.

Use one of these methods to insert your selection:

- Double-click the entry.
- Click to select the entry. Then press Tab to insert or Enter to insert and move to the next line.

TIP

The Auto List Members option, available on the Editor tab of the Options dialog box, causes the List Properties and Methods feature, as well as the List Constants feature, to be invoked automatically each time you type the name of an object or property.

List Constants

The List Constants feature opens a drop-down list displaying valid constants for a property you have typed and for functions with arguments that are constants. It works in a similar manner to the List Properties and Methods feature. To invoke it, right-click after the name of the property or argument (in cases where multiple arguments are available, the previous argument must be delimited with a comma) and select List Constants (or press Ctrl+Shift+J). A list of valid constants appears. (See Figure 7.16.) You can use any of the methods listed in the previous section to select the constant you want.

FIGURE 7.16

A list of constants for the `vbMsgBoxStyle` *parameter.*

Quick Info

The Quick Info feature gives you the full syntax for a function, statement, procedure, method, or variable. To use this feature, right-click after the name of the function, statement, procedure, method, or variable and select Quick Info (or press Ctrl+I). A tip appears, showing the valid syntax for the item. (See Figure 7.17.) As you type each parameter in the item, it's displayed in boldface type until you type the comma that delineates it from the next parameter.

FIGURE 7.17

The syntax for the `MsgBox` *function.*

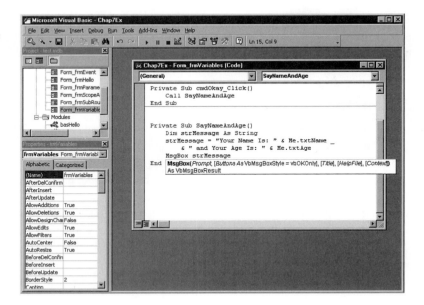

TIP

The Auto Quick Info option, available in the Options dialog box, causes the Quick Info feature to be invoked automatically each time you type the name of an object or property.

Parameter Information

The Parameter Info feature gives you information about the parameters of a function, a statement, or method. To use this feature, after the delimiter that denotes the end of the function, statement or method name, right-click and select Parameter Info (or press Ctrl+Shift+I). A pop-up list appears with information about the parameters of the function or statement. This list doesn't close until all the required parameters are entered, the function is completed without any optional parameters, or the Esc key is pressed.

NOTE

The Parameter Info feature supplies information about the initial function only. If parameters of a function are themselves functions, you must use Quick Info to find information about the embedded functions.

Complete Word

The Complete Word feature completes a word you're typing. To use this feature, you must first type enough characters for Visual Basic to recognize the word you want. Next, right-click and select Complete Word (or press Ctrl+Spacebar). Visual Basic then finishes the word you're typing.

Definition

The Definition feature shows the place in the Code window where the selected variable or procedure is defined. To get a definition of a variable or procedure, right-click in the name of the variable or procedure of interest, and select Definition (or press Shift+F2). Your cursor is moved to the module and location where the variable or procedure was defined.

As you become more advanced with VBA, you can create libraries of VBA functions and sub-routines. When you're viewing a call to a particular subroutine or function, you usually want to view the code behind that function. Fortunately, VBA gives you a quick and easy way to navigate from procedure to procedure. Assume that the following code appears in your application:

```
Private Sub cmdOkay_Click()
    Dim iAgeInTen As Integer
    If IsNull(Me!txtName) Or IsNull(Me!txtAge) Then
        MsgBox "You must fill in name and age"
        Exit Sub
    Else
        MsgBox "Your Name Is: " & Me!txtName & " _
        and Your Age Is: " & Nz(Me!txtAge)
        Call EvaluateAge(Nz(Me!txtAge))
        iAgeInTen = AgePlus10(Fix(Val(Me!txtAge)))
        MsgBox "In 10 Years You Will Be " & iAgeInTen
    End If
End Sub
```

If you want to quickly jump to the procedure called EvaluateAge, all you need to do is place your cursor anywhere within the name, EvaluateAge, and then press Shift+F2. This immediately moves you to the EvaluateAge procedure. Ctrl+Shift+F2 takes you back to the routine you came from (in this case, cmdOkay_Click). This procedure works for both functions and subroutines.

TIP

If you prefer, you can right-click the name of the routine you want to jump to and select Definition. To return to the original procedure, right-click again and select Last Position.

NOTE

If the definition is in a referenced library, the Object Browser is invoked and the definition is displayed.

Mysteries of the Coding Environment Solved

If you're a developer who's new to VBA, you might be confused by the Visual Basic Editor. We will begin by talking about the Code window. The Code window has two combo boxes, shown in Figure 7.18. The combo box on the left lists objects. For a form or report, the list includes all its objects; for a standard module, which has no objects, only (General) appears.

FIGURE 7.18

*The Code window
with the Object
combo box.*

The combo box on the right lists all the event procedures associated with a particular object. Figure 7.19 shows all the event procedures associated with a command button. Notice that the Click event is the only one that appears in bold because it's the only event procedure that has been coded.

FIGURE 7.19

*The Code window
with the
Procedure
combo box.*

The Project Window

The Project window, shown in Figure 7.20, enables you to easily maneuver between the modules behind the objects within your database. The elements of your Project are displayed hierarchically in a tree view within the Project window. All elements of the project are divided into Microsoft Access Classes and Modules. All Form, Report, and Class modules are found within the Microsoft Access Classes. All standard modules are found within Modules. To view the code behind an object, simply double-click the object within the Project window. To view the object, such as a form, single-click the name of the form in the Project window and then click the View Object tool (the second icon from the left on the Project Window toolbar). You are returned to Microsoft Access with the selected object active.

FIGURE 7.20

The Project window showing all the classes and modules contained within the Chap7ex project.

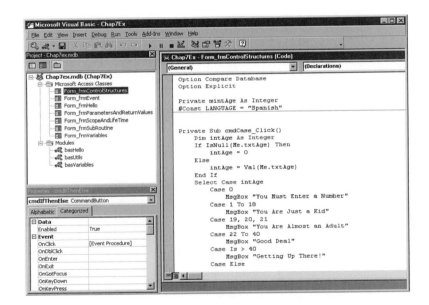

The Properties Window

The Properties window, pictured in Figure 7.21, enables you to view and modify object properties from within the VBE. At the top of the Properties window is a combo box that allows you to select the object whose properties you wish to modify. The objects listed in the combo box include the parent object selected in the Project window (for example, the form) and the objects contained within the parent object (for example, the controls). After an object is selected, its properties can be modified within the list of properties. The properties can be viewed either alphabetically or categorically. In the example, the command button cmdIfThenElse is selected. The properties of the command button are shown by category.

FIGURE 7.21
The Properties window showing the properties of a command button displayed categorically.

The View Microsoft Access Tool

If at any time you want to return to the Access application environment, simply click the View Microsoft Access icon (the left icon) on the toolbar. You can then return to the VBE using the taskbar, or using one of the methods covered earlier in this chapter.

Find and Replace

Often, you name a variable only to decide later that you want to change the name. VBA comes with an excellent find-and-replace feature to help you with this change. You can simply search for data, or you can search for a value and replace it with some other value. To invoke the Find dialog box, shown in Figure 7.22, choose Edit|Find or use Ctrl+F.

FIGURE 7.22

The Find dialog box is set up to search for strMessage *in the current module.*

Type the text you want to find in the Find What text box. Notice that you can search in the Current Procedure, Current Module, Current Project, or Selected Text. The option Find Whole Word Only doesn't find the text if it's part of another piece of text. For example, if you check Find Whole Word Only, then search for *Count*, VBA doesn't find *Counter*. Other options include toggles for case sensitivity and pattern matching.

You can also use the Replace dialog box to search for text and replace it with another piece of text. (See Figure 7.23.) This dialog can be invoked by selecting Edit | Replace from the menu or by pressing Ctrl+H (or Alt+E, E). It offers all the features of the Find dialog box, but also enables you to enter Replace With text. In addition, you can select Replace or Replace All. Replace asks for confirmation before each replacement, but Replace All replaces text without this prompt. I recommend you take the time to confirm each replacement because it's all too easy to miscalculate the pervasive effects of a global search-and-replace.

FIGURE 7.23

The Replace dialog box is set to find strMessage *and replace it with* strNewMessage *in the current project.*

Help

A very useful but little-known feature of VBA is getting context-sensitive help while coding. With your cursor placed anywhere in a VBA command or function, press the F1 key to get context-sensitive help on that command or function. Most of the help topics let you view practical examples of the function or command within code. Figure 7.24 shows help on the With...End With construct. Notice that the Help window includes the syntax for the command, a detailed description of each parameter included in the command, and remarks about using the command. At the top of the window, you can see hypertext links to related topics (See Also), as well as a link to an example of using the With...End With construct. If you click on Example, a specific example of the construct appears that you can copy and place into a module. (See Figure 7.25.) This feature is a great way to learn about the various parts of the VBA language.

FIGURE 7.24

Help on
`With...End With.`

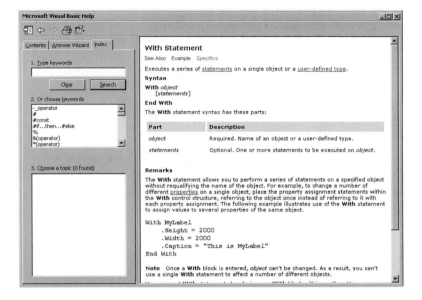

FIGURE 7.25

An example of
`With...End With.`

Splitting the Code Window

The VBA Code window can be split so that you can look at two routines in the same module at the same time. This option is useful if you're trying to solve a problem involving two procedures or event routines in a large module. An example of a split Code window is shown in Figure 7.26. To split your Code window, choose Window | Split.

FIGURE 7.26

A split Code window lets you view two routines.

```
Chap7Ex - Form_frmControlStructures [Code]
cmdForNext                              Click

    Private Sub cmdCase_Click()
        Dim intAge As Integer
        If IsNull(Me.txtAge) Then
            intAge = 0
        Else
            intAge = Val(Me.txtAge)
        End If
        Select Case intAge
            Case 0
                MsgBox "You Must Enter a Number"
            Case 1 To 18
                MsgBox "You Are Just a Kid"
            Case 19, 20, 21

    Private Sub cmdForNext_Click()
        Dim intCounter As Integer
        For intCounter = 1 To 5
            Me.txtAge = Me.txtAge + 1
        Next intCounter
    End Sub

    Private Sub cmdIfThenElse_Click()
        If IsNull(Me.txtName) Or IsNull(Me.txtAge) Then
            MsgBox "Name or Age Is Blank"
        Else
            MsgBox "Your Name Is " & Me.txtName _
```

Notice the splitter. Place your mouse cursor on the gray splitter button just above the Code window's vertical scrollbar. By clicking and dragging, you can size each half of the window. The window can be split into only two parts. After it has been split, you can use the Object and Procedure drop-down lists to navigate to the procedure of your choice. The drop-down lists will work for either of the two panes of the split window, depending on which pane was last selected.

NOTE

Only routines in the same module can be viewed in a particular Code window, but several Code windows can be open at the same time. Each time you open an Access, Form, or Report module, you're placed in a different window. Each module window can then be sized, moved, and split.

Using Bookmarks to Save Your Place

The Access 2000 coding environment enables you to create place markers—called *bookmarks*—so that you can easily return to key locations in your modules. To add a bookmark, right-click on the line of code where the bookmark will be placed and choose Toggle | Bookmark or choose Bookmarks | Toggle Bookmark from the Edit menu. You can add as many bookmarks as you like.

To navigate between bookmarks, choose Edit | Bookmarks | Next Bookmark or Edit | Bookmarks | Previous Bookmark. A bookmark is a toggle. To remove one, you simply choose Toggle | Bookmark from the shortcut menu or Bookmarks | Toggle Bookmark from the Edit menu. If you want to clear all bookmarks, choose Edit | Bookmarks | Clear All Bookmarks. Bookmarks are not saved when you close the database.

7

VBA: AN
INTRODUCTION

> **NOTE**
>
> Do not confuse the bookmarks discussed in this section with recordset bookmarks. Recordset bookmarks are covered in Chapter 12, "What Are ActiveX Data Objects and Data Access Objects and Why Are They Important?"

CUSTOMIZING THE VBE

Access 2000 provides Access programmers with significant opportunity to customize the look and behavior of the Visual Basic Editor (VBE). To view and customize the environment options, choose Tools | Options with the VBE active. Figure 7.27 shows the Options dialog; its different aspects are discussed in detail in the rest of this section.

FIGURE 7.27

The Options dialog box.

Coding Options—The Editor Tab

The coding options available to you are found under the Editor tab of the Options dialog. They include Auto Indent, Tab Width, Auto Syntax Check, Require Variable Declaration, Auto List Members, Auto Quick Info, and Auto Data Tips. The Auto Indent feature invokes the automatic indenting of successive lines of code. This means that when you indent one line, all other lines are indented to the same position until you specify otherwise.

The Auto Syntax Check feature determines whether Access performs a syntax check each time you press Enter after typing a single line of code. Many developers find this option annoying. It's not uncommon to type a line of code and notice a typo in a previous line of code. You want to rectify the error before you forget, so you move off the incomplete line of code you're typing, only to get an error message that your syntax is incorrect.

The Require Variable Declaration option is a must. If this option is turned on, all variables must be declared before they are used. This important feature, when set, places the Option Explicit line in the Declarations section of every module. You're then forced to declare all variables before they're used. Many innocent typos are identified by the compiler at compile time rather than by your users at runtime.

The Auto List Members option determines whether the List Properties/Methods and List Constants features are automatically invoked as you type code in the Code window. They help you in your coding endeavors by presenting a valid list of properties, methods, and constants. For more about these features, see Chapter 8.

The Auto Quick Info feature determines whether the syntax of a procedure or method is automatically displayed. If this option is selected, the syntax information is displayed as soon as you type a procedure or method name followed by a space, period, or opening parenthesis.

The Auto Data Tips feature is used when you're debugging. It displays the current value of a selected value when you place your mouse pointer over the variable in Break mode. This feature is discussed in Chapter 13, "Debugging: Your Key to Successful Development."

Code Color, Fonts, and Sizes—The Editor Format Tab

In Access 2000, you can customize code colors, font, and size within the coding environment. You can also specify the foreground and background colors for the Code window text, selection text, syntax error text, comment text, keyword text, and more. You can select from any of the Windows fonts and sizes for the text in the Code window. For a more readable code window, select the FixedSys font.

General Options—The General Tab

The General tab contains miscellaneous options that affect the behavior of the development environment. For example, the Show Grid option determines whether a form grid is displayed, and the Grid Units are used to designate the granularity of the gridlines. The other options on this tab are discussed in Chapter 24, "Advanced VBA Techniques."

Docking Options—The Docking Tab

The docking tab enables you to specify whether the windows within the VBE are dockable. A window is said to be dockable if you can lock it along side another dockable window. It is not dockable when you can move it anywhere and leave it there. The windows you can dock include the Immediate, Locals, Watch, Project, Properties, and Object Browser windows.

> **CAUTION**
>
> All the customization options that have been discussed apply to the entire Access environment. This means that, when set, they affect all your databases.

PRACTICAL EXAMPLES

Event Routines, User-Defined Functions, and Subroutines Needed for the Time and Billing Application

 This example, available in the sample database CHAP7.MDB, uses a form, a query, and a report to retrieve criteria and then preview sales information by client for a specific date range. The rptClientInformationByProject report is based on a query called qryBillingDetailByClient; this query requires information from a form named frmPrintClientBilling. The frmPrintClientBilling form, shown in Figure 7.28, must be open for the process to finish successfully because the criteria for the query is gathered from the form. The code for the two command buttons, found on the form frmPrintClientBilling, looks like this:

```
Sub cmdRunReport_Click()
   If IsNull(Me.txtStartDate) Or IsNull(Me.txtEndDate) Then
      MsgBox "Both the Start Date and End Date Must Be Filled In"
   Else
      Call RunReport("rtpClientInformationByProject")
   End If
End Sub
```

```
Sub cmdClose_Click()
    DoCmd.Close
End Sub
```

FIGURE 7.28

*The Report
Criteria form,
requesting
required informa-
tion for the query
underlying the
Billing Detail
Report.*

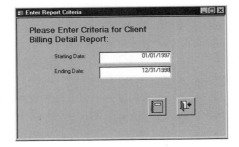

The first routine evaluates the two text boxes to make sure they're filled in. If either text box contains a null, a message is displayed. If neither box has a null, a user-defined routine called RunReport is executed. The second routine simply closes the criteria form.

The RunReport subroutine is included in a module called basUtils; RunReport looks like this:

```
Sub RunReport(strReportName As String)
    DoCmd.OpenReport strReportName, acPreview
End Sub
```

This routine receives the name of any report as a parameter and runs the report whose name is passed as the parameter.

The other code, found in the report named rptClientInformationByClient, is placed in the report's Open event and looks like this:

```
Private Sub Report_Open(Cancel As Integer)
    If Not IsLoaded("frmPrintClientBilling") Then
        MsgBox "Print Client Billing Form Must Be Open to Run _
        This Report",
            vbCritical, "Error!!"
        Cancel = True
    End If
End Sub
```

This routine calls the user-defined function IsLoaded. If the function returns a false, indicating that the required criteria form isn't open, a message is displayed and the report is canceled. The IsLoaded function, found in the basUtils module, looks like this:

```
Function IsLoaded(ByVal strFormName As String) As Integer
    Const CLOSED = 0
    Const DESIGN = 0
```

```
    If SysCmd(acSysCmdGetObjectState, acForm, strFormName) <> CLOSED Then
        If Forms(strFormName).CurrentView <> DESIGN Then
            IsLoaded = True
        End If
    End If
End Function
```

This function uses the built-in function SysCmd to determine if a form is loaded. When passed the argument acSysCmdGetObjectState, the type of object whose state you want to evaluate, and the name of the object whose state you want to evaluate, SysCmd returns a True or False. This True or False value is compared with a user-defined constant CLOSED, which is equal to 0 or False. If the form is not closed, the CurrentView property of the form is used to determine if the form is open in design view. If the form is not open in Design view, it must be open in Form or Datasheet view and True is returned from the function.

NOTE

If the range of dates entered does not return any rows, #Error appears on the report. This problem can be rectified using the NoDate event of a report. The NoDate event is covered in Chapter 10, "Advanced Report Techniques."

SUMMARY

A strong knowledge of the VBA language is imperative for the Access developer. This chapter has covered all the basics of the VBA language. You have learned the differences between Code, Form, and Report modules and how to effectively use each. You have also learned the difference between event procedures and user-defined subroutines and functions. To get the most mileage out of your subroutines and functions, you have learned how to pass parameters to and receive return values from procedures.

Variables are used throughout your application code. Declaring each variable with the proper scope and lifetime helps make your application bullet-proof and easy to maintain. Furthermore, selecting an appropriate variable type ensures that the minimal amount of memory is consumed and that your application code protects itself. Effectively using control structures and built-in functions gives you the power, flexibility, and functionality required by even the most complex of applications. Finally, a strong command of the Visual Basic Editor (VBE) is imperative to a successful development experience!

OBJECTS, PROPERTIES, METHODS, AND EVENTS EXPLAINED

CHAPTER

8

IN THIS CHAPTER

UNDERSTANDING ACCESS'S OBJECT MODEL

Objects are the components of a database. They include the tables, queries, forms, reports, data access pages, macros, and modules that appear in the database window. They also include the controls (text boxes, list boxes, and so on) on a form or report. The key to successful programming lies in your ability to manipulate the database objects by using VBA code at runtime. It's also very useful to be able to add, modify, and remove application objects at runtime.

> **NOTE**
>
> The examples in this chapter are included in the Chap8Ex database located on the sample code CD-ROM.

The `Application` Object

An overview of the superficial Access Object Model is shown in Access help. At the top of the model, you can see the `Application` object, which refers to the active Access application. It contains all Access's other objects and collections, including the Forms collection, the Reports collection, the DataAccessPages collection, the Modules collection, the `CurrentData` object, the `CurrentProject` object, the `CodeProject` object, the `CodeData` object, the `Screen` object, and the `DoCmd` object. The `Application` object can be used to modify the properties of, or execute commands on, the Access application itself, such as specifying whether Access's built-in toolbars are available while the application is running.

> **NOTE**
>
> This object model can be found in Access 2000 help under the Programming Information/MS Access VB Language Reference Help folder.

The Forms Collection

The Forms collection contains all the currently open forms in the database. Using the Forms collection, you can perform an action, such as changing the color, on each open form.

> **NOTE**
>
> The Forms collection isn't the same as the list of all forms in the database; that list is part of the `CurrentProject` object discussed later in this chapter.

The code that follows iterates through the Forms collection, printing the name of each form. It is found in the basApplicationObject module within the Chap8Ex database. It begins by establishing a form object variable. It then uses the `For Each...Next` construct to loop through each form in the Forms collection (the collection of open forms), printing its name. Before running the code, open a few forms. Run the code and then take a look in the Immediate window. Close a couple of the forms and rerun the code. The list of forms displayed in the Immediate window should change.

> **NOTE**
>
> The Immediate window and its uses are covered in Chapter 13, "Debugging: Your Key to Successful Development."

```
Sub IterateOpenForms()
    Dim frm As Form
    For Each frm In Forms
        Debug.Print frm.Name
    Next frm
End Sub
```

> **NOTE**
>
> Notice that it is not necessary to refer to `Application.Forms`. This is because the `Application` object is always assumed when writing VBA code within Access.

The Reports Collection

Just as the Forms collection contains all the currently open forms, the Reports collection contains all the currently open reports. Using the Reports collection, you can perform an action on each open report.

The code that follows iterates through the Reports collection, printing the name of each report. It is found in basApplicationObject. It begins by establishing a report object variable. It then uses the `For Each...Next` construct to loop though each report in the reports collection (the collection of reports open in print preview), printing its name.

```
Sub IterateOpenReports()
    Dim rpt As Report
    For Each rpt In Reports
        Debug.Print rpt.Name
    Next rpt
End Sub
```

The DataAccessPages Collection

Just as the Forms collection contains all the currently open forms and the Reports collection contains all the currently open reports, the DataAccessPages collection contains all the currently open data access pages. Using the DataAccessPages collection, you can perform an action on each open data access page.

The Modules Collection

The Modules collection contains all the standard and class modules that are open. All open modules are included in the Modules collection, regardless of whether they're compiled and whether they contain code that's currently running.

The `CurrentProject` Object

The `CurrentProject` object returns a reference to the current project. The `CurrentProject` contains properties such as Name, Path, and Connection. It contains the following collections: AllDataAccessPages, AllForms, AllMacros, AllModules, and AllReports. These collections are used to iterate through all the data access pages, forms, macros, modules, and reports stored in the database. These collections differ from the DataAccessPages, Forms, Macros, Modules, and Reports collections in that they refer to all objects stored in the current project, rather than to just the open objects.

The following code retrieves the Name and Path properties of the current project. It uses the `With...End With` construct to retrieve the properties of the `CurrentProject` object.

```
Sub CurrentProjectObject()
    With CurrentProject
        Debug.Print .Name
        Debug.Print .Path
    End With
End Sub
```

As previously mentioned, the `CurrentProject` object contains collections that refer to the various objects in your database. The following code iterates through the AllForms collection of the `CurrentProject`, printing the name of each form.

```
Sub IterateAllForms()
    Dim vnt As Variant
    With CurrentProject
        For Each vnt In .AllForms
            Debug.Print vnt.Name
        Next vnt
    End With
End Sub
```

NOTE

> **NOTE**
>
> It's easy to confuse the AllForms collection of the `CurrentProject` object with the Forms collection. The AllForms collection of the `CurrentProject` object comprises all the saved forms that are part of the database; the Forms collection comprises only the forms currently running in memory. If you want to see a list of all the forms that make up a database, you must use the AllForms collection of the `CurrentProject` object, but if you want to change the caption of all the open forms, you must use the Forms collection.

The `CurrentData` Object

Whereas the `CurrentProject` object is used to access and manipulate the application components of your database, the `CurrentData` object is used to reference the data elements of the database. The `CurrentData` object contains five collections: AllDatabaseDiagrams, AllQueries, AllStoredProcedures, AllTables, and AllViews. These collections are used to iterate through and manipulate all the database diagrams, queries, stored procedures, and views stored in the database.

The following code iterates through the AllTables collection of the `CurrentData` object. It prints the name of each table in the database.

```
Sub IterateAllTables()
    Dim vnt As Variant
    With CurrentData
        For Each vnt In .AllTables
            Debug.Print vnt.Name
        Next vnt
    End With
End Sub
```

The `CodeProject` Object

The `CodeProject` object is used when your database implements code libraries. It is similar to the `CurrentProject` object, but is used to reference the properties and collections stored within the library database. Library databases are covered in Chapter 29, "Creating Your Own Libraries."

The `CodeData` Object

Just as the `CodeProject` is used to reference the application objects stored within a library database, the `CodeData` object is used to reference the data elements of a code library. These include the database diagrams, queries, stored procedures, tables, and views stored within the library.

The `Screen` Object

The `Screen` object can be used to refer to the form, datasheet, report, data access page, or control that has the focus. The `Screen` object contains properties that refer to the active form, active report, active control, and previous control. Using these properties, you can manipulate the currently active form, report, or control, as well as the control that was active just before the current control. If you try to refer to the `Screen` object when no form or report is active, a runtime error occurs.

The `DoCmd` Object

The `DoCmd` object is used to perform macro commands or Access actions from VBA code; it's followed by a period and the name of an action. Most of the `DoCmd` actions—the `OpenQuery` action, for example—also require arguments. The `OpenQuery` action is used to execute an Access query. It receives the following arguments:

- Query Name—The name of the query you want to execute
- View—Datasheet, Design, or Print preview
- Data Mode—Add, edit, or read-only

Here's an example of the `OpenQuery` action of the `DoCmd` object:

```
DoCmd.OpenQuery "qryCustomers", acNormal, acReadOnly
```

The `OpenQuery` action is performed by the `DoCmd` object. The first argument, the query name, is `"qryCustomers"`. This is the name of the query that's opened in Datasheet view (rather than Design view or Print preview). It's opened in read-only mode, meaning the resulting data can't be modified.

UNDERSTANDING OBJECTS, PROPERTIES, EVENTS, AND METHODS

Many people, especially those used to a procedural language, don't understand the concept of objects, properties, and events. You need a thorough knowledge of Access's objects, their properties, and the events each object can respond to if you want to be a productive and successful Access programmer.

What Exactly Are Objects?

As mentioned earlier in this chapter, *objects* are all the things that make up your database. They include tables, queries, forms, reports, data access pages, macros, and modules, as well as the components of those objects. For example, a Table object contains Field and Index objects. A Form contains various controls (text boxes, combo boxes, list boxes, and so on). Each object in the database has specific properties that determine its appearance or behavior. Each object also has specific methods, which are actions that can be taken upon it.

What Exactly Are Properties?

A *property* is an attribute of an object, and each object has many properties. Often, different types of objects share the same properties; at other times, an object's properties are specific to that particular object. Forms, combo boxes, and text boxes all have Width properties, for example, but a form has a RecordSource property that the combo box and text box don't have.

Most properties can be set at design time and modified at runtime; however, some can't be modified at runtime, and others can't be accessed at design time (just modified at runtime). Access's built-in Help for each property tells you one of the following:

- You can set the property in the object's property sheet, a macro, or Visual Basic.
- You can set this property only in Design view.
- You can access this property by using Visual Basic or a macro.

Each of these descriptions indicates when the property can be modified.

As a developer, you set the values of many objects' properties at design time; the ones you set at design time are the starting values at runtime. Much of the VBA code you write modifies the values of these properties at runtime in response to different situations. For example, a text box has a Visible property. If a client is paying by cash, you might not want the text box for the credit-card number to be visible. If he's paying by credit card, you might want to set the Visible property of the text box with the credit-card number to True. This is just one of the many things you can do to modify the value of an object's property at runtime in response to an event or action that has occurred.

You might wonder how you can determine all the properties associated with a particular object (both those that can be modified at design time and those that can be modified at runtime). Of course, to view the properties that can be set at design time, you can select the object and then view its property sheet. Viewing all the properties associated with an object is actually quite easy to do; just invoke Help by pressing F1. Click the Index tab in the help topics dialog box and type the name of the object whose properties you want to view. In Figure 8.1, Combo has been typed into the text box. Click Search. Notice that one of the entries in the list box at the bottom of the dialog box is Combo Box Control Properties. If you click that entry, information about the Combo Box Control Properties appears in the right pane. (See Figure 8.2.) To find out about a specific property, click the property you want to view. In Figure 8.3, the Column property has been selected. You can also use the Object Browser to quickly and easily view all properties associated with an object.

FIGURE 8.1
The Help Topics dialog box.

FIGURE 8.2
A list of the combo box control properties.

FIGURE 8.3

Help associated with a combo box's Column property.

What Exactly Are Events?

Windows is an event-driven operating system; in other words, the operating system responds to many events that are triggered by actions the user takes and by the operating system itself. Access exposes many of these events through its Object Model. An *event* in an Access application is something your application can respond to. Events include mouse movements, changes to data, a form opening, a record being added, and much more. Users initiate events, as does your application code. It's up to you to determine what happens in response to the events that are occurring. You respond to events by using macros or VBA code. Each Access object responds to different events. If you want to find out all the events associated with a particular object, take the following steps:

1. Select the object (for example, a text box).
2. Open the Properties window.
3. Click the Event tab, shown in Figure 8.4.
4. Scroll through the available list of events.

FIGURE 8.4

The list of events associated with a text box.

What Exactly Are Methods?

Methods are actions that can be taken on the objects in your database. As with properties and events, different objects have different methods associated with them. A method is like a function or subroutine, except that it's specific to the object it applies to. For example, a form has a GoToPage method that doesn't apply to a text box or any other object. If you search for help on methods, you see that the Choose a Topic list box fills with a list of topics. (See Figure 8.5.) If you select Methods Reference in the list of topics, the Methods Reference appears. (See Figure 8.6.) The methods are grouped by object. When a particular object is selected, you get specific help on that object. You can then click Methods to invoke the Topics Found dialog with a list of methods that apply to that object. (See Figure 8.7.) If you click the Applies To Hypertext entry, you get a list of all objects the selected method applies to. You can click the Example Hypertext entry to view sample code that includes an appropriate implementation of the selected method.

FIGURE 8.5

Getting help on methods.

FIGURE 8.6

The Methods Reference provides help on all Access methods and collections.

FIGURE 8.7

The Topics Found dialog shows all methods associated with the Form object.

USING THE OBJECT BROWSER TO LEARN ABOUT ACCESS'S OBJECTS

The Object Browser is a powerful tool that can help you learn about and work with the objects that are part of both Access 2000 and the Microsoft Windows environment. The Object Browser displays information about Microsoft Access and other objects and can help you with coding by showing you all the properties and methods associated with a particular object.

Access objects are complex—they have many properties and methods. The Object Browser helps you to understand and use objects, properties, and methods by doing the following:

- Displaying the types of objects available
- Allowing you to quickly navigate between application procedures
- Displaying the properties and methods associated with a particular object
- Finding and pasting code into your application

How to Use the Object Browser

The Object Browser can easily be invoked from the Visual Basic Editor. You can click the Object Browser button on the toolbar, press F2, or choose View | Object Browser. The dialog box shown in Figure 8.8 appears.

FIGURE 8.8

The Object Browser dialog box with the database object selected.

The Object Browser displays two levels of information about the selected library or database. With the Chap8Ex database open, if you select Chap8Ex.MDB from the Project/Library drop-down (the top drop-down), your screen will look similar to Figure 8.8. The Classes list box displays all modules, including Form and Report modules, in the database. The Members of list box displays any procedures that have been defined in the selected module. Notice the basUtils module, which is part of the CHAP8Ex.MDB database. Looking at the list box on the right, you can see the functions included in the basUtils module. You can click to select each Form and Report module in the list box on the left and view the associated methods and properties in the list box on the right.

You can use the Project/Library drop-down list to select a different object library (provided you have set a reference to it). The Classes list box displays the types of objects available in the selected library or database. The Members of list box displays the methods, properties, and data elements defined for the selected object. (See Figure 8.9.) The Access item has been selected from the Library combo box, so the list box on the left shows all Access 2000's classes. The list box on the right shows all the members of the selected object—in this case, the `Application` object. You can even add other libraries to the Library drop-down list by referring to other type libraries. This method is covered in Chapter 26, "Automation: Communicating with Other Applications."

FIGURE 8.9

Selecting the Access 2000 library in the Object Browser.

Pasting Code Templates into a Procedure

After you have located the method or property you're interested in, you have the option of pasting it into your application. With the method or property selected, simply click the Copy to Clipboard button in the Object Browser; then paste it in the appropriate module. If you want to get more information about a particular method or property, just click the Help button in the Object Browser or press F1.

REFERRING TO OBJECTS

Access objects are categorized into *collections*, which are groupings of objects of the same type. The Forms collection, for example, is a grouping of all the open forms in a database. Each form has a Controls collection that includes all the controls on that form. Each control is an object, and you must refer to an object through the collection to which it belongs. For example, you refer to a form through the Forms collection. VBA offers three ways to refer to an object; if you want to refer to the frmProjects form, for example, you can choose from the following options:

- `Forms!frmProjects`
- `Forms("frmProjects")`
- `Forms(0)`

Referring to the form as `Forms(0)` assumes that `frmProjects` was the first form opened. However, you need to understand that although an element number is assigned as each form is loaded, this element number changes as forms are loaded and unloaded at runtime. For example, the third form that's loaded can initially be referred to as element two, but if the second form is unloaded, that third form becomes element one. In other words, you can't rely on the element number assigned to a form; that number is a moving target.

You must refer to a control on a form first through the Forms collection and then through the specific form. The reference looks like this:

`Forms!frmProjects.txtClientID`

In this example, `Forms` is the name of the collection, `frmProjects` is the name of the specific form, and `txtClientID` is the name of a control on the `frmProjects` form. If this code is found in the Code module of `frmProjects`, it could be rewritten like this:

`Me.txtClientID`

`Me` refers to the current form or report. It's generic because the code could be copied to any form having a `txtClientID` control and it would still run properly. Referring to a control on a report is very similar to referring to a control on a form. Here's an example:

`Reports!rptTimeSheet.txtHoursBilled`

This example refers to the txtHoursBilled text box on the rptTimeSheet report, part of the Reports collection. After you know how to refer to an object, you're ready to write code that modifies its properties and executes its methods.

PROPERTIES AND METHODS MADE EASY

To modify an object's properties and execute its methods, you must refer to the object and then supply an appropriate property or method, as shown in this example:

`Forms!frmHello.cmdHello.Visible = False`

This line of code refers to the Visible property of `cmdHello`, found in the `frmHello` form, which is in the Forms collection. Notice that you must identify the object name `frmHello` as being associated with the Forms collection. If you want to change the Caption property of `frmHello` to say `"Hello World"`, you would use the following code:

```
Forms!frmHello.Caption = "Hello World"
```

TIP

You might be confused about whether you're looking at an object's property or method, but there are a couple of quick ways to tell. A property is always used in some type of an expression. For example, you might be setting a property equal to some value:

```
Forms!frmClients.txtAddress.Visible = False
```

Here, you're setting the Visible property of the txtAddress text box on the frmClients form from True to False. You also might retrieve the value of a property and place it in a variable:

```
strFirstName = Forms!frmClients.txtFirstName.Value
```

You also might use the value of a property in an expression, as in the following example:

```
MsgBox Forms!frmClients.txtFirstName.Value
```

The pattern here is that a property is always used somewhere in an expression. It can be set equal to something, something can be set equal to its value, or it's otherwise used in an expression.

A method, however, is an action taken on an object. The syntax for a method is Object.Method. A method isn't set equal to something; however, you frequently create an object variable and then set it by invoking a method. A method looks like this:

```
Forms!frmHello.txtHelloWorld.SetFocus
```

In this example, the SetFocus method is being executed on the text box called txtHelloWorld.

A method that returns an object variable looks like this:

```
Dim cbr As CommandBar
Set cbr = CommandBars.Add("MyNewCommandBar")
```

In this example, the CommandBars collection Add method is used to set the value of the CommandBar object variable named cbr. For more information, see the section "Declaring and Assigning Object Variables," later in this chapter.

> **NOTE**
>
> Many people are confused about when to use a bang (!) and when to use a period. You can use a bang whenever you're separating an object from its collection, as shown in these two examples:
>
> ```
> Forms!frmClients
> ```
>
> ```
> Forms!frmClients!txtClientID
> ```
>
> In the first example, `frmClients` is part of the Forms collection. In the second example, `txtClientID` is part of the Controls collection of the `frmClients` form.
>
> In most cases, you can also use a period to separate an object from its collection. This is because the expression `Me!txtClientId` is actually a shortcut to the complete reference `Me.Controls!txtClientID`. Because Controls is the default collection for a form, you can omit Controls from the statement. The expression can be abbreviated to `Me.txtClientID`. The advantage of using the dot over the bang is that the dot provides you with Intellisense. To test this, create a form and add a control called txtFirstName. Go to the code behind the form and try typing `Me!`. Notice that Intellisense is not invoked. Next type `Me.` and watch Intellisense get invoked. Intellisense facilitates the development process by providing a list box containing valid properties, methods, constants, and so on as appropriate.
>
> In addition to separating an object from its collection, the period is also used to separate an object from a property or method. The code looks like this:
>
> ```
> Forms!frmClients.RecordSource = "tblClients"
> ```
>
> ```
> Forms!frmClients!txtClientID.Visible = False
> ```
>
> The first example sets the RecordSource property of `frmClients` to `tblClients`, and the second example sets the Visible property of the `txtClientID` on the `frmClients` form to `False`.

Default Properties

Each object has a default property, and if you're working with an object's default property, you don't have to explicitly refer to it in code. Take a look at the following two code samples:

```
Forms!frmHello.txtHello.Value = "Hello World"
```

```
Forms!frmHello.txtHello = "Hello World"
```

The Value property is the default property of a text box, so you don't need to explicitly refer to it in code. However, I prefer to explicitly state the property—it is a practice that contributes to the code's readability and keeps novice Access programmers who work with my code from having to guess which property I'm changing.

DECLARING AND ASSIGNING OBJECT VARIABLES

Object variables are variables that reference an object of a specific type, such as databases, recordsets, forms, controls, and even objects created in other applications. They allow you to create shortcut references to objects and pass objects to subroutines and functions. You can use them to streamline code by using short names to refer to objects with long names and to optimize code by supplying a direct pointer to a particular object.

First, you must declare an object variable; then, you assign—or *point*—the object variable to a particular object, as shown in the following code:

```
Private Sub cmdChangeCaption_Click()
    Dim cmdAny As CommandButton
    Set cmdAny = Me!cmdHello
    cmdAny.Caption = "Hello"
End Sub
```

This code creates an object variable called `cmdAny` of the type `CommandButton`. You then use the `Set` statement to point your `CommandButton` object variable toward the `cmdHello` object on the current form, using the `Me` keyword. Finally, you modify the caption of the `cmdAny` object variable. Because an object variable is a reference to the original object, you're actually changing the caption of the `cmdHello` command button.

Object Variables Versus Regular Variables

The difference between object variables and regular variables is illustrated by the following code:

```
Dim intVar1 As Integer
Dim intVar2 As Integer
intVar1 = 5
intVar2 = intVar1
intVar1 = 10
Debug.Print intVar1 'Prints 10
Debug.Print intVar2 'Prints 5
```

This code uses ordinary variables. When you dimension these variables, each one is assigned a separate memory location. Although `intVar2` is initially assigned the value of `intVar1`, changing the value of `intVar1` has no effect on `intVar2`. This differs from the following code, which uses an object variable:

```
Private Sub Command5_Click()
    Dim ctlText As TextBox
    Set ctlText = Forms!frmSales!txtProductID
    ctlText.Text = "New Text"
    Debug.Print Forms!frmSales!txtProductID.Text 'Prints New Text
End Sub
```

This routine creates an object variable called `ctlText` of type `TextBox`. It then associates the object variable with `Forms!frmSales!txtProductID`. Next, it modifies the Text property of the object variable. Because the object variable is actually pointing to the text box on the form, the `Debug.Print` statement prints the new text value.

Generic Versus Specific Object Variables

Access supports the use of generic object variables, including `Application`, `Control`, `Form`, and `Report`. Generic object variables can be used to refer to any object of that generic type:

```
Private Sub ChangeVisible_Click()
    Dim ctlAny As Control
    Set ctlAny = Me!txtCustomerID
    ctlAny.Visible = False
End Sub
```

In this example, `ctlAny` can be used to point to any control. Compare that with the following code:

```
Private Sub cmdChangeVisible_Click()
    Dim txtAny As TextBox
    Set txtAny = Me!txtCustomerID
    txtAny.Visible = False
End Sub
```

Here, your object variable can be used only to point to a text box.

Cleaning Up After Yourself

When you're finished working with an object variable, you should set its value to `Nothing`. As used in the following example, this statement frees up all memory and system resources associated with the object:

```
Set frmNew = Nothing
```

UNDERSTANDING THE DIFFERENCES BETWEEN OBJECTS AND COLLECTIONS

Many people get confused about the differences between an object and a collection. Think of an object as a member of a collection. For example, `frmHello` is a form that's a member of the Forms collection; `cmdHello`, a command button on `frmHello`, is a member of the Controls collection of `frmHello`. Sometimes you want to manipulate a specific object, but other times you want to manipulate a collection of objects.

Manipulating a Single Object

You have already learned quite a bit about manipulating a single object, such as setting the Enabled property of a text box:

```
txtCustomerID.Enabled = False
```

This line of code affects only one text box and only one of its properties. However, when you're manipulating a single object, you might want to affect several properties at the same time. In that case, it's most efficient to use the With...End With construct, explained in the following section.

With...End With: Performing Multiple Commands on an Object

One method you can use to modify several properties of an object is to modify the value of each property, one at a time:

```
txtCustomerID.Enabled = False
txtCustomerID.SpecialEffect = 1
txtCustomerID.FontSize = 16
txtCustomerID.FontWeight = 700
```

Contrast this with the following code:

```
With txtCustomerID
    .Enabled = False
    .SpecialEffect = 1
    .FontSize = 16
    .FontWeight = 700
End With
```

This code uses the With...End With statement to assign multiple properties to an object. In addition to improving the readability of your code, the With...End With construct results in a slight increase in performance.

Manipulating a Collection of Objects

A *collection* is like an array of objects. What makes the array special is that it's defined and maintained by Access. Every collection in Microsoft Access is an object, each with its own properties and methods. The VBA language makes it easy for you to manipulate Access's collections of objects; you simply use the For Each...Next construct, covered in the following section.

For...Each: Performing the Same Command on Multiple Objects

In the "Determining the Type of a Control" section later in this chapter, you learn how to loop through the collection of controls on a form, performing actions on all the command buttons. This illustrates a practical use of a collection. In the following example, you loop through all the open forms, changing the caption of each form:

```
Sub FormCaptions()
    Dim frm As Form
    For Each frm In Forms
        frm.Caption = frm.Caption & " - " & CurrentUser
    Next frm
End Sub
```

This routine uses the For...Each construct to loop through each form in the Forms collection, setting the caption of each form to the form's caption concatenated with the current username. As you travel through the loop, the code frm.Caption refers to each individual member of the Forms collection.

PASSING OBJECTS TO SUBROUTINES AND FUNCTIONS

 Just as you can pass a string or a number to a subroutine or function, you can also pass an object to a subroutine or function. The code, found in the basExamples module in the Chap8Ex database, looks like this:

```
Sub ChangeCaption(frmAny as Form)
    frmAny.Caption = frmAny.Caption & ": " & CurrentUser
End Sub
```

The ChangeCaption routine receives a reference to a form as a parameter. The caption of the form referenced by the procedure is modified to include the name of the current user. The ChangeCaption routine is called like this:

```
Private Sub cmdChangeCaption_Click()
    Call ChangeCaption(Me)
End Sub
```

In this example, the click event of the cmdChangeCaption command button calls the ChangeCaption routine, sending a reference to the form that the command button is contained within. This code is found in the form frmChangeCaption.

DETERMINING THE TYPE OF A CONTROL

When writing generic code, you might need to determine the type of a control. For example, you might want to loop through all the controls on a form and flip the Enabled property of all the command buttons. To do this, use the ControlType property of a control. Here's an example of how it's used (you can find this in CHAP8EX.MDB in the module called basExamples):

```
Sub FlipEnabled(frmAny As Form, ctlAny As Control)
    Dim ctl As Control
    'Loop through the Controls collection using the For..Each Construct
    ctlAny.Enabled = True
    ctlAny.SetFocus
    For Each ctl In frmAny.Controls
        'Evaluate the type of the control
        If ctl.ControlType = acCommandButton Then
            'Make sure that we don't try to disable the command button _
            that invoked this routine
            If ctl.Name <> ctlAny.Name Then
                ctl.Enabled = Not ctl.Enabled
            End If
        End If
    Next ctl
End Sub
```

The FlipEnabled procedure is called from the form frmTypeOf. Each command button on the form (Add, Edit, Delete, and so on) sends the form and the name of a control to the FlipEnabled routine. The control that it sends is the one that you want to receive the focus after the routine executes. In the example that follows, the cmdSave command button is sent to the FlipEnabled routine. The FlipEnabled routine sets focus to the Save button:

```
Private Sub cmdAdd_Click()
    Call FlipEnabled(Me, Me!cmdSave)
End Sub
```

The FlipEnabled routine receives the form and control as parameters. It begins by enabling the command button that was passed to it and setting focus to it. The FlipEnabled routine then uses the VBA construct For...Each to loop through all the controls on a form. The For...Each construct repeats a group of statements for each object in an array or collection— in this case, the Controls collection. The code evaluates each control on the form to determine whether it's a command button. If it is, and it isn't the command button that was passed to the routine, the routine flips the control's Enabled property. The following VBA intrinsic controls are used when evaluating the `ControlType` property of a control:

Intrinsic Constant	Type of Control
acLabel	Label
acRectangle	Rectangle
acLine	Line
acImage	Image
acCommandButton	Command button
acOptionButton	Option button
acCheckBox	Check box
acOptionGroup	Option group
acBoundObjectFrame	Bound object frame
acTextBox	Text box
acListBox	List box
acComboBox	Combo box
acSubform	Subform/subreport
acObjectFrame	Unbound object frame or chart
acPageBreak	Page break
acPage	Page
acCustomControl	ActiveX (custom) control
acToggleButton	Toggle button
acTabCtl	Tab

SPECIAL PROPERTIES THAT REFER TO OBJECTS

VBA offers the convenience of performing actions on the active control, the active form, and other specially recognized objects. The following is a list of special properties that refer to objects in the Access Object Model:

- The `ActiveControl` property refers to the control that has focus on a screen object, form, or report.
- The `ActiveForm` property refers to the form that has focus.
- The `ActiveReport` property refers to the report that has focus.
- The `Form` property refers to the form that a subform is contained in or to the form itself.
- `Me` refers to the form or report where code is currently executing.

- `Module` refers to the module of a form or report.

- The `Parent` property refers to the form, report, or control that contains a control.

- `PreviousControl` refers to the control that had focus immediately before the ActiveControl.

- `RecordsetClone` refers to a clone of the form's underlying recordset.

- The `Report` property refers to the report that a subform is contained in or to the report itself.

- The `Section` property refers to the section in a form or report where a particular control is located.

The following example using the `Screen.ActiveForm` property shows how a subroutine can change the caption of the active form:

```
Sub ChangeCaption()
    Screen.ActiveForm.Caption = Screen.ActiveForm.Caption & _
        " - " & CurrentUser()
End Sub
```

This subroutine modifies the caption of the active form, appending the value of the `CurrentUser` property onto the end of the existing caption.

PRACTICAL EXAMPLES

Working with Objects

 Objects are used throughout the Time and Billing application. Almost every aspect of the application uses the skills explained in this chapter. The example that follows applies the technique you learned to enable and disable command buttons in response to the user making changes to the data on the `frmClients` form, located in CHAP8.MDB on the sample code CD-ROM.

Enabling and Disabling Command Buttons

When a user is in the middle of modifying form data, there's really no need for her to use the Project, Time Cards, Payments, and Invoice portions of the application. It makes sense to disable these features until the user has opted to save the changes to the Client data. The clean form begins with the Project, Time Cards, Payments, and Invoice command buttons enabled and the Save button disabled. The `KeyPreview` property of the form is set to `Yes` so that the form previews all keystrokes before the individual controls process them. The `KeyDown` event of the form looks like this:

```
Private Sub Form_KeyDown(KeyCode As Integer, Shift As Integer)
    If Not cmdSave.Enabled Then
        If ImportantKey(KeyCode, Shift) Then
            Call FlipEnabled(Me, ActiveControl)
            Me.NavigationButtons = False
        End If
    Else
        If KeyCode = vbKeyPageDown Or _
        KeyCode = vbKeyPageUp Then
            KeyCode = 0
        End If
    End If
End Sub
```

The `KeyDown` event automatically receives the code of the key that was pressed and whether Shift, Alt, or Ctrl was pressed along with that key. The event routine checks to determine whether the Save button is already enabled. If it is, there's no reason to continue; the Enabled property of the command buttons has already been flipped. If Save isn't already enabled, the `ImportantKey` function is called. It receives the key that was pressed and whether Shift, Alt, or Control was used. The `ImportantKey` function looks like this:

```
Function ImportantKey(KeyCode, Shift)
    ImportantKey = False
    If Shift = 4 Then
        Exit Function
    End If
    If KeyCode = vbKeyDelete Or KeyCode = vbKeyBack Or (KeyCode > 31 _
    And KeyCode < 256) Then
        If KeyCode  = vbKeyRight or KeyCode = vbKeyLeft or _
            KeyCode = vbKeyUp or KeyCode = vbKeyDown or _
            KeyCode = vbKeyPageUp or KeyCode = vbKeyPageDown Then

        Else
            ImportantKey = True
        End If
    End If
End Function
```

This generic function, found in basUtils, sets its default return value to `False`. It tests to see whether the Alt key was pressed. If so, the user was accessing a menu or accelerator key, which means there's no reason to flip the command buttons, so the function is exited. If Alt wasn't pressed, the key that was pressed is evaluated. If the Delete key, Backspace key, or any key with an ANSI value between 31 and 256 (excluding the left, right, up, and down arrow keys, and page up or page down) was pressed, a True is returned from this function. The Keydown event of the form then calls the FlipEnabled routine. It looks like this:

```
Sub FlipEnabled(frmAny As Form, ctlAny As Control)
   Dim ctl As Control
   If TypeOf ctlAny Is CommandButton Then
      ctlAny.Enabled = True
      ctlAny.SetFocus
   End If
   For Each ctl In frmAny.Controls
      If TypeOf ctl Is CommandButton Then
         If ctl.Name <> ctlAny.Name Then
            ctl.Enabled = Not ctl.Enabled
         End If
      End If
   Next ctl
End Sub
```

This generic routine, also found in basUtils, flips the Enabled property of every command button in the form except the one that was passed to it. The FlipEnabled routine receives a form and a control as parameters. It begins by creating a control object variable; then tests to see whether the type of control that was passed to it is a command button. If so, it enables the control and sets focus to it. The routine then loops through every control on the form that was passed to it. It tests to see whether each control is a command button. If it finds a command button, and the name of the command button isn't the same as the name of the control that was passed to it, it flips the Enabled property of the command button. The idea is this: When the user clicks Save, you can't immediately disable the Save button because it still has focus. You must first enable a selected control (the one that was passed to the routine) and set focus to the enabled control. After the control is enabled, you don't want to disable it again, so you need to eliminate it from the processing loop.

After the FlipEnabled routine is executed, the NavigationButtons property of the form is set to False. This is an important step because it is imperative that the user not be able to move from record to record while editing the form data.

You need a way to flip the command buttons back the other way. The Click event of the Save button has the following code:

```
Private Sub cmdSave_Click()
   DoCmd.RunCommand Command:=acCmdSaveRecord
   Call FlipEnabled(Me, Me!Projects)
   Me.NavigationButtons = True
End Sub
```

8

OBJECTS, PROP-ERTIES, METHODS, AND EVENTS

This code saves the current record and calls the `FlipEnabled` routine. The `FlipEnabled` routine flips the command buttons back to their original state. You probably want to add a Cancel button that issues an `Undo` and also flips the command buttons. You should also either prohibit users from moving to other records until they select Save or flip the command buttons if the Save button is enabled and the user moves to another record. If you fail to do this, users move to another record, their changes are automatically saved (by Access), and the command buttons still reflect a dirty state of the form.

SUMMARY

The ability to successfully work with objects and understand their properties, methods, and events is fundamental to your success as an Access programmer. Working with properties involves setting properties at design time and changing their values in response to events that occur at runtime. The ability to create multiple form instances and pass forms and other objects to subroutines and functions makes the VBA language extremely robust and flexible.

ADVANCED FORM TECHNIQUES

IN THIS CHAPTER

THIS CHAPTER IS IMPORTANT

Access's graphical environment, your development efforts are often centered on forms, so you must understand all the Form and Control events and know which event you should code to perform each task. You should also know what types of forms are available and how you can get the look and behavior you want for them.

Often, you won't need to design your own form because you can make use of one of the built-in dialog boxes that are part of the VBA language or supplied as part of the Microsoft Office 2000 Developer Edition tools. Whatever types of forms you create, you should take advantage of all the tricks and tips of the trade covered throughout this chapter, including adding menu bars and toolbars to your forms.

WHAT ARE THE FORM EVENTS AND WHEN DO YOU USE THEM?

Microsoft Access traps for 30 Form events, each of which has a distinct purpose. Access also traps events for Form sections and controls. The following sections cover the Form events and when you should use them.

Current

A form's Current event is one of the more commonly coded events. It happens each time focus moves from one record to another. The Current event is a great place to put code you want to execute whenever a record is displayed. For example, you might want the company name to appear with a special background if the client is an important one. The following code is placed in the Current event of the frmClients form that's part of the Time and Billing application:

```
Private Sub Form_Current()
    If IsNull(Me.txtClientID) Then
        Me.txtContactFirstName.SetFocus
    End If

End Sub
```

This code moves focus to the txtContactFirstName control if the txtClientID of the record the user is moving to happens to be Null; this happens if the user is adding a new record.

BeforeInsert

The BeforeInsert event occurs when the first character is typed in a new record, but before the new record is actually created. If the user is typing in a text or combo box, the

BeforeInsert event occurs even before the Change event of the text or combo box. The frmProjects form of the Time and Billing application has an example of a practical use of the BeforeInsert event:

```
Private Sub Form_BeforeInsert(Cancel As Integer)
    Me.ClientID = Forms.frmClients.txtClientID
End Sub
```

The frmProjects form is always called from the frmClients form. The BeforeInsert event of frmProjects sets the value of the txtClientID text box equal to the value of the txtClientID text box on frmClients.

AfterInsert

The AfterInsert event occurs after the record has actually been inserted. It can be used to requery a recordset when a new record is added.

> **NOTE**
>
> Here's the order of form events when a user begins to type data into a new record:
>
> BeforeInsert?BeforeUpdate?AfterUpdate-AfterInsert
>
> The BeforeInsert event occurs when the user types the first character, the BeforeUpdate event happens when the user updates the record, the AfterUpdate event takes place when the record is updated, and the AfterInsert event occurs when the record that's being updated is a new record.

BeforeUpdate

The BeforeUpdate event runs before a record is updated. It occurs when the user tries to move to a different record (even a record on a subform) or when the Records|Save Record command is executed. The BeforeUpdate event can be used to cancel the update process when you want to perform complex validations. When a user adds a record, the BeforeUpdate event occurs after the BeforeInsert event. The Northwind database that comes with Access has an excellent example of using a BeforeUpdate event:

```
Private Sub Form_BeforeUpdate(Cancel As Integer)

' If number of digits entered in PostalCode text box is incorrect for
' value in Country text box, display message and undo PostalCode value.

    Select Case Me!Country
        Case IsNull(Me![Country])
```

```
                Exit Sub
    Case "France", "Italy", "Spain"
        If Len(Me![PostalCode]) <> 5 Then
            MsgBox "Postal Code must be 5 characters", _
                0, "Postal Code Error"
            Cancel = True
            Me![PostalCode].SetFocus
        End If
    Case "Australia", "Singapore"
        If Len(Me![PostalCode]) <> 4 Then
            MsgBox "Postal Code must be 4 characters", _
                0, "Postal Code Error"
            Cancel = True
            Me![PostalCode].SetFocus
        End If
    Case "Canada"
        If Not Me![PostalCode] _
            Like "[A-Z][0-9][A-Z] [0-9][A-Z][0-9]" Then
            MsgBox "Postal Code not valid. " & _
             "Example of Canadian code:" _
             & " H1J 1C3", 0, "Postal Code Error"
            Cancel = True
            Me![PostalCode].SetFocus
        End If

End Select


End Sub
```

This code from the Suppliers form determines whether the zip code entered is appropriate for the selected country. If it is not, a message is displayed and the Cancel parameter is set to True, canceling the update process. As a convenience to the user, focus is placed in the postal code control.

NOTE

Notice that the examples from the Northwind database do not adhere to the naming and programming standards that I follow in this book. To avoid confusion when you are viewing the code in the Northwind database that ships with Access 2000, I have kept all Northwind examples as is, rather than modifying them to adhere to the Reddick naming standards.

AfterUpdate

The `AfterUpdate` event occurs after the changed data in a record is updated. You might use this event to requery combo boxes on related forms or perhaps log record changes. Here's an example:

```
Private Sub Form_AfterUpdate()
    Me.cboSelectProduct.Requery
End Sub
```

This code requeries the cboSelectProduct combo box after the current record is updated.

Dirty

The `Dirty` event occurs when the contents of the form, or of the text portion of a combo box, changes. It also occurs when you programmatically change the Text property of a control. Here's an example:

```
Private Sub Form_Dirty(Cancel As Integer)
    Call FlipEnabled(Me, ActiveControl)
    Me.NavigationButtons = False
End Sub
```

This code, located in the frmClients form of the Time and Billing application, calls FlipEnabled to flip the command buttons on the form. This has the effect of enabling the Save and Cancel command buttons and disabling the other command buttons on the form. The code also removes the navigation buttons, prohibiting the user from moving to other records while the data is in a "dirty" state.

Delete

The `Delete` event occurs when a user tries to delete a record, but before the record is actually removed from the table. This is a great way to place code that allows deleting a record only under certain circumstances. If the `Delete` event is canceled, the `BeforeDelConfirm` and `AfterDelConfirm` events never execute, and the record is never deleted.

> **TIP**
>
> When the user deletes multiple records, the `Delete` event happens after each record is deleted. This allows you to evaluate a condition for each record and decide whether each record should be deleted.

BeforeDelConfirm

The `BeforeDelConfirm` event takes place after the `Delete` event, but before the Delete Confirm dialog box is displayed. If you cancel the `BeforeDelConfirm` event, the record being deleted is restored from the delete buffer, and the Delete Confirm dialog box is never displayed.

AfterDelConfirm

The `AfterDelConfirm` event occurs after the record is actually deleted, or when the deletion is canceled. If the `BeforeDelConfirm` is *not* canceled, the `AfterDelConfirm` event takes place after the Confirmation dialog box is displayed.

Open

The `Open` event occurs when a form is opened but before the first record is displayed. With this event, you can control exactly what happens when the form first opens. The `Open` event of the Time and Billing application's frmProjects form looks like this:

```
Private Sub Form_Open(Cancel As Integer)
    If Not IsLoaded("frmClients") Then
        MsgBox "Open the Projects form using the " & _
            "Projects button on the Clients Form"
        Cancel = True
    End If
End Sub
```

This code checks to make sure the frmClients form is loaded. If it isn't, a message box is displayed, and the `Cancel` parameter is set to `True`, which prohibits the form from loading.

Load

The `Load` event happens when a form is opened and the first record is displayed; it occurs after the `Open` event. A form's `Open` event can cancel the opening of a form, but the `Load` event can't. The following routine is placed in the `Load` event of the Time and Billing application's frmExpenseCodes form:

```
Private Sub Form_Load()
    If Me.DataEntry And Not (IsNull(Me.OpenArgs)) Then
        Me.txtExpenseCode = Me.OpenArgs
    End If
End Sub
```

This routine looks at the string that's passed as an opening argument to the form. If the `OpenArg` string is not `Null`, and the form is opened in data entry mode, the txtExpenseCode text box is set equal to the opening argument. In essence, this code allows the form to be used for two purposes. If the form is opened from the database container, no special processing occurs. On the other hand, if the form is opened from the fsubTimeCardsExpenses subform, the form is opened in data entry mode, and the expense code that the user specified is placed in the txtExpenseCode text box.

Resize

The Resize event takes place when a form is opened or whenever the form's size changes.

Unload

The Unload event happens when a form is closed, but before the form is actually removed from the screen. It's triggered when the user chooses Close from the File menu, quits the application by choosing End Task from the task list, quits Windows, or when your code closes the form. You can place code that makes sure it's okay to unload the form in the Unload event, and you can also use the Unload event to place any code you want executed whenever the form is unloaded. Here's an example:

```
Private Sub Form_Unload(Cancel As Integer)
    If Me.cmdSave.Enabled Then
        Select Case MsgBox("Do You Want To Save", _
            vbYesNoCancel + vbCritical, _
            "Please Respond")
            Case vbYes
                DoCmd.RunCommand Command:=acCmdSaveRecord
                Cancel = False
            Case vbNo
                On Error Resume Next
                DoCmd.RunCommand Command:=acCmdUndo
                Cancel = False
            Case vbCancel
                Cancel = True
        End Select
    End If
End Sub
```

This code is placed in the Unload event of the frmClients form from the Time and Billing application. It checks whether the Save button is enabled. If it is, the form is in a dirty state. The user is asked whether he wants to save changes to the record. If he responds affirmatively, the data is saved and the form is unloaded. If he responds no, changes to the record are canceled and the form is unloaded. Finally, if he opts to cancel, the value of the Cancel parameter is set to False and the form is not unloaded.

9

ADVANCED FORM TECHNIQUES

Close

The Close event occurs when a form is closed and removed from the screen, *after* the Unload event. Remember, you can cancel the Unload event but not the Close event.

The following code is placed in the Close event of the frmClients form that's part of the Time and Billing database:

```
Private Sub Form_Close()
    If IsLoaded("frmProjects") Then
        DoCmd.Close acForm, "frmProjects"
    End If
End Sub
```

When the frmClients form is closed, the code tests whether the frmProjects form is open. If it is, the code closes it.

Activate

The Activate event takes place when the form gets focus and becomes the active window. It's triggered when the form is opened, when a user clicks on the form or one of its controls, and when the SetFocus method is applied by using VBA code. The following code, found in the Activate event of the Time and Billing application's frmClients form, requeries the fsubClients subform whenever the frmClients main form is activated:

```
Private Sub Form_Activate()
    Me.fsubClients.Requery
End Sub
```

Deactivate

The Deactivate event occurs when the form loses focus, which happens when a table, query, form, report, macro, module, or the Database window becomes active. However, the Deactivate event isn't triggered when a dialog, pop-up form, or another application becomes active. The following is an example of the use of the Deactivate event:

```
Private Sub Form_Deactivate()
    ' Use AllowEdits property setting to determine which toolbar to hide.
    ' Show Form View toolbar.
    If Me.AllowEdits = True Then
        DoCmd.ShowToolbar "Enter Or Edit Products 2", acToolbarNo
    Else
        DoCmd.ShowToolbar "Enter Or Edit Products 1", acToolbarNo
    End If
    DoCmd.ShowToolbar "Form View", acToolbarWhereApprop
End Sub
```

This code evaluates the AllowEdits property to determine which custom toolbar is currently active. It hides the appropriate toolbar and shows the standard Form View toolbar.

GotFocus

The GotFocus event happens when a form gets focus, but only if there are no visible, enabled controls on the form. This event is rarely used for a form.

LostFocus

The LostFocus event occurs when a form loses focus, but only if there are no visible, enabled controls on the form. This event, too, is rarely used for a form.

Click

The Click event takes place when the user clicks on a blank area of the form, on a disabled control on the form, or on the form's record selector.

DblClick

The DblClick event happens when the user double-clicks on a blank area of the form, on a disabled control on the form, or on the form's record selector.

MouseDown

The MouseDown event occurs when the user clicks on a blank area of the form, on a disabled control on the form, or on the form's record selector, but it happens *before* the Click event fires. It can be used to determine which mouse button was pressed.

MouseMove

The MouseMove event takes place when the user moves the mouse over a blank area of the form, over a disabled control on the form, or over the form's record selector. It's generated continuously as the mouse pointer moves over the form. The MouseMove event occurs *before* the Click event fires.

MouseUp

The MouseUp event occurs when the user releases the mouse button. Like the MouseDown event, it happens before the Click event fires and can be used to determine which mouse button was pressed.

KeyDown

The `KeyDown` event happens if there are no controls on the form or if the form's `KeyPreview` property is set to `Yes`; if the latter condition is true, all keyboard events are previewed by the form and occur for the control that has focus. If the user presses and holds down a key, the `KeyDown` event occurs repeatedly until the key is released. Here's an example:

```
Private Sub Form_KeyDown(KeyCode As Integer, Shift As Integer)
    If Me.Dirty Then
        If KeyCode = vbKeyPageDown Or _
            KeyCode = vbKeyPageUp Then
            KeyCode = 0
        End If
    End If
End Sub
```

This code, found in the frmClients form that is part of the Time and Billing application, tests to see if the form is in a "dirty" state. If it is, and Page Down or Page Up is pressed, the keystroke is ignored. This prevents the user from moving to other records without first clicking the Save or Cancel command buttons.

KeyUp

Like the `KeyDown` event, the `KeyUp` event occurs if there are no controls on the form or if the form's `KeyPreview` property is set to `Yes`. The `KeyUp` event takes place only once, though, regardless of how long the key is pressed. The keystroke can be canceled by setting `KeyCode` to `Zero`.

KeyPress

The `KeyPress` event occurs when the user presses and releases a key or key combination that corresponds to an ANSI code. It takes place if there are no controls on the form or if the form's `KeyPreview` property is set to `Yes`. The keystroke can be canceled by setting `KeyCode` to `Zero`.

Error

The `Error` event is triggered whenever an error happens while the user is in the form. Microsoft Jet Engine errors are trapped, but Visual Basic errors aren't. This event can be used to suppress the standard error messages. Visual Basic errors must be handled by using standard `On Error` techniques. Both the `Error` event and handling Visual Basic errors are covered in Chapter 14, "Error Handling: Preparing for the Inevitable."

Filter

The `Filter` event takes place whenever the user selects the Filter By Form or Advanced Filter/Sort options. You can use this event to remove the previous filter, enter default settings for the filter, invoke your own custom filter window, or prevent certain controls from being available in the Filter By Form window.

ApplyFilter

The `ApplyFilter` event occurs when the user selects the Apply Filter/Sort, Filter By Selection, or Remove Filter/Sort options. It also takes place when the user closes the Advanced Filter/Sort window or the Filter By Form window. You can use this event to make sure the filter being applied is correct, to change the form's display before the filter is applied, or to undo any changes you made when the `Filter` event occurred.

Timer

The `Timer` event and a form's `TimerInterval` property work hand in hand. The `TimerInterval` property can be set to any value between 0 and 2,147,483,647. The value used determines the frequency, expressed in milliseconds, at which the `Timer` event will occur. For example, if the `TimerInterval` property is set to 0, the `Timer` event will not occur at all; if set to 5000 (5000 milliseconds) the `Timer` event will occur very 5 seconds. In the following example the `Timer` event is used to alternately change the visibility of a label on the form. This produces a flashing effect. The `TimerInterval` property could be initially set to any valid value other than 0, but will be reduced by 50 milliseconds each time the code executes. This has the effect of making the control flash faster and faster. The `Timer` events continue to occur until the `TimerInterval` property is finally reduced to 0.

```
Private Sub Form_Timer()
If Me.Label2.Visible = True Then
    Me.Label2.Visible = False
Else
    Me.Label2.Visible = True
End If

Me.TimerInterval = Me.TimerInterval - 50

If Me.TimerInterval = 0 Then
    Me.Label2.Visible = True
End If
End Sub
```

9

ADVANCED FORM
TECHNIQUES

Understanding the Sequence of Form Events

One of the mysteries of events is the order in which they occur. One of the best ways to figure this out is to place `Debug.Print` statements in the events you want to learn about. This technique is covered in Chapter 13, "Debugging: Your Key to Successful Development." Keep in mind that event order isn't an exact science; it's nearly impossible to guess when events will happen in all situations. It's helpful, though, to understand the basic order in which certain events do take place.

What Happens When a Form Is Opened?

When the user opens a form, the following events occur:

```
Open->Load->Resize->Activate->Current
```

After these Form events take place, the `Enter` and `GotFocus` events of the first control occur. Remember that the `Open` event is the only place you can cancel opening the form.

What Happens When a Form Is Closed?

When the user closes a form, the following events take place:

```
Unload->Deactivate->Close
```

Before these events occur, the `Exit` and `LostFocus` events of the active control are triggered.

What Happens When a Form Is Sized?

When the user resizes a form, what happens depends on whether the form is minimized, restored, or maximized. When the form is minimized, here's what happens:

```
Resize->Deactivate
```

When the user restores a minimized form, these events take place:

```
Activate->Resize
```

When the user maximizes a form or restores a maximized form, just the `Resize` event occurs.

What Happens When Focus Shifts from One Form to Another?

When the user moves from one form to another, the `Deactivate` event occurs for the first form; then the `Activate` event occurs for the second form. Remember that the `Deactivate` event doesn't take place if focus moves to a dialog box, a pop-up form, or another application.

What Happens When Keys Are Pressed?

When the user types a character and the form's `KeyPreview` property is set to `True`, the following events occur:

```
KeyDown->KeyPress->Dirty->KeyUp
```

If you trap the KeyDown event and set the KeyCode to Zero, the remaining events never happen. The KeyPress event captures only ANSI keystrokes. This event is the easiest to deal with; however, you must handle the Keydown and KeyUp events when you need to trap for non-ANSI characters, such as Shift, Alt, and Ctrl.

What Happens When Mouse Actions Take Place?

When the user clicks the mouse button, the following events occur:

```
MouseDown->MouseUp->Click
```

WHAT ARE THE SECTION AND CONTROL EVENTS AND WHEN DO YOU USE THEM?

Sections have only five events: Click, DblClick, MouseDown, MouseMove, and MouseUp. These events rarely play a significant role in your application.

Each control type has its own set of events it responds to. Many events are common to most controls, but others are specific to certain controls. Furthermore, some controls respond to very few events. The following sections cover all the Control events. As each event is covered, you learn which controls the event applies to.

BeforeUpdate

The BeforeUpdate event applies to text boxes, option groups, combo boxes, list boxes, and bound object frames. It occurs before changed data in the control is updated. The following code example is found in the BeforeUpdate event of the CustomerID control on the Orders form from the Northwind database:

```
Private Sub CustomerID_BeforeUpdate(Cancel As Integer)
' Display message if CustomerID combo box is blank.

    Dim strMsg As String, strTitle As String
    Dim intStyle As Integer

    If IsNull(Me!CustomerID) Or Me!CustomerID = "" Then
        strMsg = "You must pick a value from the Bill To list."
        strTitle = "Bill To Customer Required"
        intStyle = vbOKOnly
        MsgBox strMsg, intStyle, strTitle
        Cancel = True
    End If

End Sub
```

This code tests whether the value of the CustomerID control is `Null` or a zero-length string. If it is, a message box is displayed, and the `Update` event is canceled.

AfterUpdate

The `AfterUpdate` event applies to text boxes, option groups, combo boxes, list boxes, and bound object frames. It occurs after changed data in the control is updated. The following code example is from the `AfterUpdate` event of the `txtBeginDate` control on the frmPrintInvoice form found in the Time and Billing database:

```
Private Sub txtBeginDate_AfterUpdate()
    Me.fsubPrintInvoiceTime.Requery
    Me.fsubPrintInvoiceExpenses.Requery
End Sub
```

This code requeries both the fsubPrintInvoiceTime subform and the fsubPrintInvoiceExpenses subform when the txtBeginDate control is updated. This ensures that the subforms display the time and expenses appropriate for the selected date range.

Updated

The `Updated` event applies to a bound object frame only. It occurs when the OLE (Object Linking and Embedding) object's data has been modified.

Change

The `Change` event applies to text and combo boxes and takes place when data in the control changes. For a text box, this event occurs when a character is typed; for a combo box, it happens when a character is typed or a value is selected from the list. You use this event when you want to trap for something happening on a character-by-character basis.

NotInList

The `NotInList` event applies only to a combo box and happens when the user enters a value in the text box portion of the combo box that's not in the combo box list. By using this event, you can allow the user to add a new value to the combo box list. For this event to be triggered, the `LimitToList` property must be set to `Yes`. Here's an example from the Time and Billing application's frmPayments form:

```
Private Sub cboPaymentMethodID_NotInList _
    (NewData As String, Response As Integer)
    If MsgBox("Payment Method Not Found, Add?", _
        vbYesNo + vbQuestion, _
```

```
        "Please Respond") = vbYes Then
        DoCmd.OpenForm "frmPaymentMethods", _
            Datamode:=acFormAdd, _
            WindowMode:=acDialog, _
            OpenArgs:=NewData
        If IsLoaded("frmPaymentMethods") Then
            Response = acDataErrAdded
            DoCmd.Close acForm, "frmPaymentMethods"
        Else
            Response = acDataErrContinue
        End If
    Else
        Response = acDataErrContinue
    End If

End Sub
```

This code is executed when the user enters a payment method that's not in the cboPaymentMethodID combo box. It asks the user if he wants to add the entry. If he responds yes, the frmPaymentMethods form is displayed. Otherwise, the user must select another entry from the combo box. The NotInList event is covered in more detail later in the "Handling the NotInList Event" section.

Enter

The Enter event applies to text boxes, option groups, combo boxes, list boxes, command buttons, object frames, and subforms. It occurs before a control actually gets focus from another control on the same form and takes place *before* the GotFocus event. Here's an example from the Time and Billing application's frmTimeCards form:

```
Private Sub fsubTimeCards_Enter()
    If IsNull(Me.cboEmployeeID) Then
        MsgBox "Enter employee before entering time or expenses"
        CboEmployeeID.SetFocus
    End If
End Sub
```

When the user moves into the fsubTimeCards subform control, its Enter event tests whether the EmployeeID has been entered on the main form. If it hasn't, a message box is displayed, and focus is moved to the cboEmployeeID control on the main form.

Exit

The Exit event applies to text boxes, option groups, combo boxes, list boxes, command buttons, object frames, and subforms. It occurs just before the LostFocus event.

GotFocus

The `GotFocus` event applies to text boxes, toggle buttons, options buttons, check boxes, combo boxes, list boxes, and command buttons. It takes place when focus moves to a control in response to a user action or when the `SetFocus`, `SelectObject`, `GoToRecord`, `GoToControl`, or `GoToPage` methods are issued in code. Controls can get focus only if they're visible and enabled.

LostFocus

The `LostFocus` event applies to text boxes, toggle buttons, options buttons, check boxes, combo boxes, list boxes, and command buttons. It occurs when focus moves away from a control in response to a user action or when the `SetFocus`, `SelectObject`, `GoToRecord`, `GoToControl`, or `GoToPage` methods are issued in code.

> **NOTE**
>
> The difference between `GotFocus`/`LostFocus` and `Enter`/`Exit` lies in when they occur. If focus is moved to another form or returned to the current form, the control's `GotFocus` and `LostFocus` events are triggered. The `Enter` and `Exit` events don't take place when the form loses or regains focus. Finally, it is important to note that none of these events take place when menu selections are made or toolbars are clicked.

Click

The `Click` event applies to labels, text boxes, option groups, combo boxes, list boxes, command buttons, and object frames. It occurs when the user presses, and then releases a mouse button over a control. Here's an example from the Time and Billing application's frmProjects form:

```
Private Sub cmdToggleView_Click()
    If Me.cmdToggleView.Caption = "&View Expenses" Then
        Me.fsubProjects.Visible = False
        Me.fsubProjectExpenses.Visible = True
        Me.cmdToggleView.Caption = "&View Hours"
    Else
        Me.fsubProjectExpenses.Visible = False
        Me.fsubProjects.Visible = True
        Me.cmdToggleView.Caption = "&View Expenses"
    End If
End Sub
```

This code checks the caption of the cmdToggleView command button. If the caption reads "&View Expenses" (with the ampersand indicating a hotkey), the fsubProjects subform is hidden, the fsubProjectExpenses subform is made visible, and the caption of the cmdToggleView command button is modified to read "&View Hours". Otherwise, the fsubProjectsExpenses subform is hidden, the fsubProjects subform is made visible, and the caption of the cmdToggleView command button is modified to read "&View Expenses".

NOTE

The Click event is triggered when the user clicks the mouse over an object, as well as in the following situations:

- When the spacebar is pressed while a command button has focus
- When a command button's Default property is set to Yes and the Enter key is pressed
- When a command button's Cancel property is set to Yes and the Escape key is pressed
- When an accelerator key for a command button is used

DblClick

The DblClick event applies to labels, text boxes, option groups, combo boxes, list boxes, command buttons, and object frames. It occurs when the user presses, and then releases the left mouse button twice over a control. Here's an example from the Time and Billing application's fsubTimeCards form:

```
Private Sub cboWorkCodeID_DblClick(Cancel As Integer)
On Error GoTo Err_cboWorkCodeID_DblClick
    Dim lngWorkCodeID As Long

    If IsNull(Me.cboWorkCodeID) Then
        Me.cboWorkCodeID.Text = ""
    Else
        lngWorkCodeID = Me.cboWorkCodeID
        Me.cboWorkCodeID = Null
    End If
    DoCmd.OpenForm "frmWorkCodes", , , , , acDialog, "GotoNew"
    Me.cboWorkCodeID.Requery
    If lngWorkCodeID <> 0 Then Me.cboWorkCodeID = lngWorkCodeID
```

```
Exit_cboWorkCodeID_DblClick:
    Exit SubErr_cboWorkCodeID_DblClick:


    MsgBox Err.Description
    Resume Exit_cboWorkCodeID_DblClick
End Sub
```

In this example, the code evaluates the cboWorkCodeID combo box control to see whether it's Null. If it is, the text of the combo box is set to a zero-length string. Otherwise, a long integer variable is set equal to the combo box value, and the combo box value is set to Null. The frmWorkCodes form is opened modally. When it's closed, the cboWorkCodeID combo box is requeried. If the long integer variable doesn't contain a zero, the combo box value is set equal to the long integer value.

MouseDown

The MouseDown event applies to labels, text boxes, option groups, combo boxes, list boxes, command buttons, and object frames. It takes place when the mouse button is pressed over a control, *before* the Click event fires.

MouseMove

The MouseMove event applies to labels, text boxes, option groups, combo boxes, list boxes, command buttons, and object frames. It occurs as the mouse is moved over a control.

MouseUp

The MouseUp event applies to labels, text boxes, option groups, combo boxes, list boxes, command buttons, and object frames. It occurs when the mouse is released over a control, *before* the Click event fires.

KeyDown

The KeyDown event applies to text boxes, toggle buttons, option buttons, check boxes, combo boxes, list boxes, and bound object frames. It happens when the user presses a key while within a control and occurs repeatedly until the key is released. It can be canceled by setting KeyCode equal to Zero.

KeyUp

The KeyUp event applies to text boxes, toggle buttons, option buttons, check boxes, combo boxes, list boxes, and bound object frames. It occurs when a key is released within a control. It occurs only once, no matter how long a key is pressed down.

KeyPress

The KeyPress event applies to text boxes, toggle buttons, option buttons, check boxes, combo boxes, list boxes, and bound object frames. It occurs when the user presses and releases an ANSI key while the control has focus. It can be canceled by setting KeyCode equal to Zero.

Understanding the Sequence of Control Events

Just as Form events take place in a certain sequence when the form is opened, activated, and so on, Control events occur in a specific sequence. When writing the event code for a control, you need to understand the order in which Control events happen.

What Happens When Focus Is Moved to or from a Control?

When focus is moved to a control, the following events occur:

```
Enter->GotFocus
```

If focus is moving to a control as the form is opened, the Form and Control events take place in the following sequence:

```
Open(form)->Activate(form)->Current(form)->Enter(control)
➡GotFocus(control)
```

When focus leaves a control, the following events occur:

```
Exit->LostFocus
```

When focus leaves the control because the form is closing, the following events happen:

```
Exit(control)->LostFocus(control)->Unload(form)->Deactivate(form)
➡Close(form)
```

What Happens When the Data in a Control Is Updated?

When you change data in a control and then move focus to another control, the following events occur:

```
BeforeUpdate->AfterUpdate->Exit->LostFocus
```

After every character that's typed in a text or combo box, the following events take place before focus is moved to another control:

```
KeyDown->KeyPress->Change->KeyUp
```

For a combo box, if the NotInList event is triggered, it occurs after the KeyUp event.

REFERRING TO Me

The Me keyword is like an implicitly declared variable; it's available to every procedure in a Form or Report module. Using Me is a great way to write generic code in a form or report. You can change the name of the form or report, and the code will be unaffected. Here's an example:

```
Me.RecordSource = "qryProjects"
```

It's also useful to pass Me (the current form or report) to a generic procedure in a module, as shown in the following example:

```
Call ChangeCaption(Me)
```

The ChangeCaption procedure looks like this:

```
Sub ChangeCaption(frmAny As Form)
    If IsNull(frmAny.Caption) Then
        frmAny.Caption = "Form For - " & CurrentUser
    Else
        frmAny.Caption = frmAny.Caption & " - " & CurrentUser
    End If
End Sub
```

The ChangeCaption procedure in a Code module receives any form as a parameter. It evaluates the caption of the form that was passed to it. If the caption is Null, ChangeCaption sets the caption to "Form for -", concatenated with the user's name. Otherwise, it takes the existing caption of the form passed to it and appends the user's name.

WHAT TYPES OF FORMS CAN I CREATE AND WHEN ARE THEY APPROPRIATE?

You can design a variety of forms with Microsoft Access. By working with the properties available in Access's form designer, you can create forms with many different looks and types of functionality. This chapter covers all the major categories of forms, but remember that you can create your own forms. Of course, don't forget to maintain consistency with the standards for Windows applications.

Single Forms: Viewing One Record at a Time

One of the most common types of forms allows you to view one record at a time. The form shown in Figure 9.1, for example, lets the user view one customer record then move to other records as needed.

FIGURE 9.1

A single form.

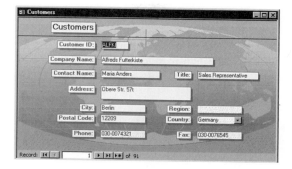

Creating a Single form is easy—simply set the form's Default View property to `Single Form`. (See Figure 9.2.)

FIGURE 9.2

Setting the form's Default View property.

Continuous Forms: View Multiple Records at a Time

Often, the user wants to be able to view multiple records at a time. which requires creating a Continuous form, like the one shown in Figure 9.3. To do this, just set the Default View property to `Continuous Forms`.

FIGURE 9.3

A continuous form.

9

ADVANCED FORM
TECHNIQUES

A subform is a common use of a Continuous form; generally, you should show multiple records in a subform. The records displayed in the subform are all the records that relate to the record displayed in the main form. An example is pictured in Figure 9.4, which shows two sub-forms, each with its Default View property set to `Continuous Forms`. One subform shows all the orders relating to a specific customer, and the other shows all the order detail items for the selected order.

FIGURE 9.4

A form containing two continuous subforms.

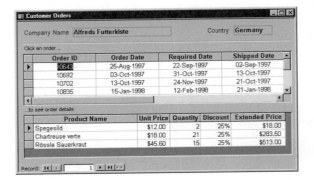

Multipage Forms: When Everything Doesn't Fit on One Screen

Scarcity of screen real-estate is a never-ending problem, but a multipage form can be a good solution. Figures 9.5 and 9.6 show the two pages of the multipage Employee form, which can be found in the Northwind.MDB database. When looking at the form in Design view, you can see a Page Break control placed just before the 3-inch mark on the form. (See Figure 9.7.) To insert a Page Break control, select it from the toolbox, and then click and drag to place it on the form.

FIGURE 9.5

The first page of a multipage form.

FIGURE 9.6

The second page of a multipage form.

FIGURE 9.7

A multipage form in Design view.

When creating a multipage form, remember a few important steps:

- Set the Default View property of the form to `Single Form`.
- Set the Scrollbars property of the form to `Neither` or `Horizontal Only`.
- Set the AutoResize property of the form to `No`.
- Place the Page Break control exactly halfway down the form's Detail section if you want the form to have two pages. If you want more pages, divide the total height of the Detail section by the number of pages and place Page Break controls at the appropriate positions on the form.
- Size the Form window to fit exactly one page of the form.

Tabbed Forms: Conserving Screen Real-Estate

A tabbed form is an alternative to a multipage form. Access 97 and Access 2000 include a built-in Tab control that allows you to easily group sets of controls together. A tabbed form could, for example, show customers on one tab, orders for the selected customer on another tab, and order detail items for the selected order on a third tab.

The form shown in Figure 9.8 uses a Tab control. This form, called Employees, is included in the Northwind database. It shows the employee's company information on one tab and the selected employee's personal information on the second tab. No code is needed to build the example.

FIGURE 9.8

A multipage tabbed form.

Adding a Tab Control and Manipulating Its Pages

To add a Tab control to a form, simply select it from the toolbox and drag and drop it onto the form. By default, two tab pages appear. To add more tabs, right-click the control and select Insert Page. To remove tabs, right-click the page you want to remove and select Delete Page. To change the order of pages, right-click any page and select Page Order.

Adding Controls to Tab Pages

You can add controls to each tab just as you would add them directly to the form. However, remember to select a tab by clicking it before you add the controls. If you don't select a specific tab, the controls you add will appear on every page.

Modifying the Tab Order of Controls

The controls on each page have their own tab order. To modify their tab order, right-click the page and select Tab Order. You can then reorder the controls in whatever way you want on the page.

Changing the Properties of the Tab Control

To change the properties of the Tab control, click to select it rather than a specific page. You can tell whether you've selected the Tab control because the words `Tab Control` appear in the upper-left corner of the Title Bar of the Properties window. (See Figure 9.9.) A Tab control's properties include its name, the text font on the tabs, and more.

FIGURE 9.9

Viewing properties of a Tab control.

Changing the Properties of Each Page

To change the properties of each page, select a specific page of the Tab control. You can tell whether you've selected a specific page because the word `Page` is displayed in the upper-left corner of the Title Bar of the Properties window. (See Figure 9.10.) Here you can select a name for the page, the page's caption, a picture for the page's background, and more.

FIGURE 9.10

Viewing properties of a Tab page.

Switchboard Forms: Controlling Your Application

A Switchboard form is a great way to control your application. A Switchboard form is simply a form with command buttons that allow you to navigate to other Switchboard forms or to the forms and reports that make up your system.

The form shown in Figure 9.11 is a Switchboard form. The form lets the user work with different components of the database. What differentiates a Switchboard form from other forms is that its purpose is limited to navigating through the application. It usually has a border style of

9

ADVANCED FORM TECHNIQUES

Dialog, and it has no scrollbars, record selectors, or navigation buttons. Other than these characteristics, a Switchboard form is a normal form. There are many styles of Navigation forms; which one you use depends on your users' needs.

FIGURE 9.11

An example of a Switchboard form.

Splash Screen Forms: A Professional Opening to Your Application

Splash screens add professional polish to your applications and give your users something to look at while your programming code is setting up the application. Just follow these steps to create a Splash Screen form:

1. Create a new form.
2. Set the Scrollbars property to Neither, the Record Selectors property to No, the Navigation Buttons property to No, the Auto Resize property to Yes, the AutoCenter property to Yes, and the Border Style to None.
3. Make the form Pop-up and Modal.
4. Add a picture to the form and set the picture's properties.
5. Add any text you want to put on the form.
6. Set the form's timer interval to the number of seconds you want the splash screen to be displayed.
7. Code the form's Timer event for DoCmd.Close.
8. Code the form's Unload event to open your main Switchboard form.

Because the Timer event of the Splash Screen form closes the form after the amount of time specified in the timer interval, the Splash Screen form unloads itself. While it's unloading, it loads the Switchboard form. The Splash Screen form included in CHAP9EX.MDB is called frmSplash. When it unloads, it opens the frmSwitchboard form.

You can implement your Splash Screen form in many other ways. For example, you can call the Splash Screen form from a Startup form; its Open event simply needs to open the Splash

Screen form. The problem with this method is that if your application loads and unloads the switchboard while the application is running, the splash screen is displayed again.

> **TIP**
>
> You can also display a splash screen by including a bitmap file with the same name as your database (MDB) in the same directory as the database file. When the application is loaded, the splash screen is displayed for a couple of seconds. The only disadvantage to this method is that you have less control over when, and how long, the splash screen is displayed.

Dialog Forms: Gathering Information

Dialog forms are typically used to gather information from the user. What makes them Dialog forms is that they're modal, meaning that the user can't go ahead with the application until the form is handled. Dialog forms are generally used when you must get specific information from your user before your application can continue processing. A custom Dialog form is simply a regular form that has a Dialog border style and has its Modal property set to Yes. Remember to give users a way to close the form; otherwise, they might close your modal form with the famous "Three-Finger Salute" (Ctrl+Alt+Del) or, even worse, by using the PC's Reset button. The frmArchivePayments form in CHAP9EX.MDB is a custom Dialog form.

> **TIP**
>
> Although opening a form with its BorderStyle property set to Dialog and its Modal property set to Yes will prevent the user from clicking outside the form (thereby continuing the application), it does not halt the execution of the code that opened the form. Suppose the intent is to open a dialog form to gather parameters for a report, and then open the report based on those parameters. In this case, the OpenForm method used to open the form must include the acDialog option in its Windowmode argument. Otherwise the code will continue after the OpenForm method and open the report before the parameters are collected from the user.

USING BUILT-IN DIALOG BOXES

Access comes with two built-in dialog boxes: the standard Windows message box and the input box. The Microsoft Office Developer also includes the Common Dialog ActiveX control, which gives you access to other commonly used dialog boxes.

Message Boxes

A message box is a predefined dialog box that you can incorporate into your applications; however, it can be customized by using parameters. The VBA language has a MsgBox statement—that just displays a message—and a MsgBox function, which can display a message and return a value based on the user's response.

The message box in the VBA language is the same message box that's standard in most Windows applications, so it's already familiar to most Windows users. Rather than create your own dialog boxes to get standard responses from your users, you can use an existing, standard interface.

The MsgBox Function

The MsgBox function receives five parameters. The first parameter is the message you want to display. The second is a numeric value indicating which buttons and icon you want to display. Tables 9.1 and 9.2 list the values that can be numerically added to create the second parameter. The intrinsic constants in the table can be substituted for the numeric values, if you want. The third parameter is the message box's title. The fourth and fifth parameters are the Help file and context ID you want available if the user selects Help while the dialog box is displayed. The MsgBox function looks like this:

```
MsgBox "This is a Message", vbInformation, "This is a Title"
```

This example displays the message "This is a Message" and the information icon. The title for the message box is "This is a Title". The message box also has an OK button that's used to close the dialog box.

The MsgBox function is normally used to display just an OK button, but it can also be used to allow you to select from a variety of standard button combinations. When used in this way, it returns a value indicating which button the user selected.

TABLE 9.1 VALUES INDICATING THE BUTTONS YOU WANT TO DISPLAY

Buttons	Value	Intrinsic Constant
OK button only	0	vbOKOnly
OK and Cancel	1	vbOKCancel
Abort, Retry, and Ignore	2	vbAbortRetryIgnore
Yes, No, and Cancel	3	vbYesNoCancel
Yes and No	4	vbYesNo
Retry and Cancel	5	vbRetryCancel

The values in Table 9.1 must be numerically added to one of the values in Table 9.2 if you want to include an icon other than the dialog box's default icon.

TABLE 9.2 VALUES INDICATING THE ICONS YOU WANT TO DISPLAY

Icon	Value	Intrinsic Constant
Critical (Stop Sign)	16	vbCritical
Warning Query (Question)	32	vbQuestion
Warning Exclamation (!)	48	vbExclamation
Information (I)	64	vbInformation

In the following example, the message box displays Yes, No, and Cancel buttons:

```
Sub MessageBoxFunction()
    Dim intAnswer As Integer
    intAnswer = MsgBox("Are You Sure?", vbYesNoCancel + vbQuestion, _
        "Please Respond")
End Sub
```

This message box also displays the Question icon. (See Figure 9.12.) The Function call returns a value stored in the Integer variable intAnswer.

FIGURE 9.12

The dialog box displayed by the MsgBox function.

After you have placed the return value in a variable, you can easily introduce logic into your program to respond to the user's selection, as shown in this example:

```
Sub MessageBoxAnswer()
    Dim intAnswer As Integer
    intAnswer = MsgBox("Are You Sure?", vbYesNoCancel + vbQuestion, _
        "Please Respond")
    Select Case intAnswer
        Case vbYes
            MsgBox "I'm Glad You are Sure!!"
        Case vbNo
            MsgBox "Why Aren't You Sure??"
        Case vbCancel
            MsgBox "You Coward! You Bailed Out!!"
    End Select
End Sub
```

This code evaluates the user's response and displays a message based on her answer. Of course, in a real-life situation, the code in the `Case` statements would be more practical. Table 9.3 lists the values returned from the `MsgBox` function, depending on which button the user selected.

TABLE 9.3   VALUES RETURNED FROM THE `MsgBox` FUNCTION

Response	*Value*	*Intrinsic Constant*
OK	1	vbOK
Cancel	2	vbCancel
Abort	3	vbAbort
Retry	4	vbRetry
Ignore	5	vbIgnore
Yes	6	vbYes
No	7	vbNo

Input Boxes

The `InputBox` function displays a dialog box containing a simple text box. It returns the text the user typed in the text box and looks like this:

```
Sub InputBoxExample()
   Dim strName As String
   strName = InputBox("What is Your Name?", _
                  "This is the Title", "This is the Default")
   MsgBox "You Entered " & strName
End Sub
```

This subroutine displays the input box shown in Figure 9.13. Notice that the first parameter is the message, the second is the title, and the third is the default value. The second and third parameters are optional.

FIGURE 9.13

An example of using the InputBox *function to gather information.*

Common Dialog Boxes

As mentioned, the Common Dialog control is an OCX control that's included as part of the ODE. You can use it to display Windows common dialog boxes, including File Save, File Open, File Print, File Print Setup, Fonts, and Colors. The Common Dialog control is covered in Chapter 25, "Using ActiveX Controls."

ADDING CUSTOM MENUS, TOOLBARS, AND SHORTCUT MENUS TO YOUR FORMS

You can create custom menus to display with your forms and reports; there's no limit on how many you can use. Each menu can be attached to one or more forms or reports. Quite often, you want to restrict what users can do while they're working with a form or report. By creating a custom menu, you can restrict and customize what they're allowed to do.

Designing a Menu

Prior to Access 97, you created a custom menu bar by setting the `MenuBar` property to the name of a menu bar macro. This function is supported for backward compatibility only. In Access 97 and Access 2000, custom menu bars, toolbars, and pop-up menus are all referred to as *command bars*. To create any of these three objects, choose View | Toolbars and then select Customize. After a custom menu bar, toolbar, or pop-up menu has been created, you can easily associate it with forms and reports by using the Menubar, Toolbar, and Shortcut Menu Bar properties.

Follow these steps to create a custom menu bar:

1. Choose View | Toolbars and click Customize, or right-click any toolbar and select Customize.
2. When the Customize dialog box opens, click the Toolbars tab and then click New. (See Figure 9.14.)

FIGURE 9.14
Using the Customize dialog box to create a new command bar.

3. Assign a name to the new menu bar, toolbar, or pop-up menu. The new command bar then appears.

4. Click the Properties button on the Customize dialog box to view the properties for your newly created toolbar. In the Toolbar Properties dialog box, you name the toolbar, select the toolbar type, indicate the type of docking that's allowed, and set other options for the command bar. The Type drop-down list allows you to select Menu Bar, Toolbar, or Pop-up. The Docking options are Allow Any, Can't Change, No Vertical, and No Horizontal. You can also choose whether the user will be allowed to customize or move the menu or toolbar.

5. Select the options you want and click Close.

Now you're ready to add items to the toolbar, menu bar, or pop-up menu. The process differs slightly, depending on which type of command bar you selected. To add items to a command bar, click the Commands tab of the Customize dialog box, shown in Figure 9.15, and drag and drop command icons onto your new command bar.

FIGURE 9.15

Use the Commands tab to add items to a command bar.

Here are some tips to help you to create custom menu bars, toolbars, and pop-up menus:

- To add an entire built-in menu to the menu bar, select Built-in Menus from the Categories list box. Click and drag a menu pad from the Commands list box over to the menu bar to add the entire built-in menu pad to the custom menu.

- To create a custom menu pad, select New Menu from the Categories list box. Click and drag the New Menu option to the menu bar. To modify the text on the menu pad, right-click the menu pad and type a new value in the Name text box.

- To add a built-in command to the menu, select a category from the Categories list box, and then click and drag the appropriate command to the menu pad. The new item will appear underneath the menu pad.

- To add a separator bar to a menu, right-click on the menu item that will follow the separator bar and select Begin a Group. To remove the separator bar, select Begin a Group again.

- Menu items can contain Text Only or Image and Text. To select one, right-click a menu item and select Default Style, Text Only (Always), Text Only (in Menus), or Image and Text. To customize an image, right-click a menu item and select Change Button Image. Choose one of the available images. To modify the button image, right-click a menu item and select Edit Button Image; this opens the Button Editor dialog box. (See Figure 9.16.) If you want to reset the button to its original image, right-click the menu item and select Reset Button Image.

FIGURE 9.16

Modifying or creating button images with the Button Editor.

- If you want to modify several properties of a menu item at once, you can right-click the menu item and select Properties to open the File Control Properties dialog box. (See Figure 9.17.) Here you can select attributes for the menu item, such as the Caption, Tooltip, Style, Help File, and Help Context ID. You can also associate an action with a custom menu item (covered in the next section).

9

ADVANCED FORM
TECHNIQUES

FIGURE **9.17**

Modifying menu item properties with the File Control Properties dialog box.

Associating a Command with a Menu Item

In Access, it's easy to customize your menus with both built-in commands and custom-built functions. For built-in commands, you can simply drag and drop commands onto your command bars. To have a command bar item run a custom-built function, you need to create a custom item and set its properties, as explained in the following steps:

1. Select the File category from the Categories list box in the Customize dialog box.
2. Click and drag the Custom option from the Commands list box to the position you want for the menu.
3. Right-click the new menu item and select Properties.
4. Type the name of the function or subroutine you want to call in the On Action drop-down list. If the procedure you're calling is a function, you must precede the function name with an equal sign and include any parameters in parentheses following the function name.
5. Click Close to close the Control Properties dialog box.
6. Click Close to close the Customize dialog box.

Deleting and Renaming Menus

You can also use the Customize dialog box to delete and rename menus by following these steps:

1. Right-click any command bar and select Customize.
2. Click in the Toolbars list box to select the command bar you want to delete or rename.
3. Click Delete to delete the command bar or Rename to rename it.

Manipulating Command Bars by Using Code

Command bars can be added, modified, and removed, all by using VBA code, which allows you to build flexibility into your application. You can easily modify a command bar in response to different conditions in your application. You can even give your user a front end to customize the command bars in your application, as shown in this example located in the basExamples module in Chap9Ex.mdb.

```
Sub CreateCustomCommandBar()
    On Error Resume Next
    Dim cbr As CommandBar
    Dim btn As CommandBarButton

    Set cbr = CommandBars("My Command Bar")
    If Err <> 0 Then
        Set cbr = CommandBars _
          .Add(Name:="My Command Bar", Position:=msoBarTop)
    End If

    Set btn = cbr.Controls("Are You Sure?")

    If Err <> 0 Then
        ' Custom button doesn't already exist, so create it.
        Set btn = cbr.Controls.Add(msoControlButton, , , , True)
    End If
    With btn
        .Caption = "Are You Sure?"
        .BeginGroup = True
        .OnAction = "MessageBoxAnswer"
        .Style = msoButtonCaption
    End With
End Sub
```

This code illustrates that by using the VBA language, you have full control over command bar objects. It begins by creating `CommandBar` and `CommandBarButton` object variables; then sets the `CommandBar` object variable to a command bar called "My Command Bar." If this causes an error, you know that the "My Command Bar" command bar doesn't exist. The `Add` method is used to add the command bar, which will be placed at the top of the screen. The routine then tries to point at a command bar button called "Are You Sure?". If this causes an error, the `Add` method of the Controls collection of the `CommandBar` object is used to add a command button to the collection. The button's caption is set to `"Are You Sure?"`, a group is added, and the command button's action is set to call the subroutine `MessageBoxAnswer`. The command button's style is set to display just a caption.

9

ADVANCED FORM TECHNIQUES

TAKING ADVANTAGE OF BUILT-IN FORM-FILTERING FEATURES

Access has several form-filtering features that are part of the user interface. You can opt to include these features in your application, omit them from your application entirely, or control their behavior. For your application to control their behavior, it needs to respond to the `Filter` event, which it does by detecting when a filter is placed on the data in the form. When it has detected the filter, the code in the `Filter` event executes.

Sometimes you might want to alter the standard behavior of a filter command. You might want to display a special message to the user, for example, or take a specific action in your code. You might also want your application to respond to a `Filter` event because you want to alter the form's display before the filter is applied. For example, if a certain filter is in place, you might want to hide or disable certain fields. When the filter is removed, you could then return the form's appearance to normal.

Fortunately, Access not only lets you know that the `Filter` event occurred, but it also lets you know how the filter was invoked. Armed with this information, you can intercept and change the filtering behavior as needed.

When a user chooses Filter By Form or Advanced Filter/Sort, the `FilterType` parameter is filled with a value that indicates how the filter was invoked. If the user invokes the filter by selecting Filter By Form, the `FilterType` parameter equals the constant `acFilterByForm`; however, if she selects Advanced Filter/Sort, the `FilterType` parameter equals the constant `acFilterAdvanced`. The following code demonstrates how to use these constants:

```
Private Sub Form_Filter(Cancel As Integer, FilterType As Integer)
    Select Case FilterType
        Case acFilterByForm
            MsgBox "You Just Selected Filter By Form"
        Case acFilterAdvanced
            MsgBox "You Are Not Allowed to Select Advanced Filter/Sort"
            Cancel = True
    End Select
End Sub
```

This code, placed in the form's `Filter` event, evaluates the filter type. If Filter By Form was selected, a message box is displayed and the filtering proceeds as usual, but if the user selects Advanced Filter/Sort, she's told she can't do this and the filter process is canceled.

Not only can you check how the filter was invoked, but you can also intercept the process when the filter is applied. You do this by placing code in the form's `ApplyFilter` event, as shown in this example:

```
Private Sub Form_ApplyFilter(Cancel As Integer, ApplyType As Integer)
    Dim intAnswer As Integer
    If ApplyType = acApplyFilter Then
        intAnswer = MsgBox("You just selected the criteria: & _
                    Chr(13) & Chr(10) & Me.Filter & _
                    Chr(13) & Chr(10) & Are You Sure You Wish _
                    to Proceed?", vbYesNo + vbQuestion)
        If intAnswer = vbNo Then
            Cancel = True
        End If
    End If
End Sub
```

This code evaluates the value of the `ApplyType` parameter. If it's equal to the constant `acApplyFilter`, a message box is displayed, verifying that the user wants to apply the filter. If the user responds Yes, the filter is applied; otherwise, the filter is canceled.

INCLUDING OBJECTS FROM OTHER APPLICATIONS: LINKING VERSUS EMBEDDING

Microsoft Access is an ActiveX client application, meaning that it can contain objects from other applications. Access 97 and Access 2000 are also ActiveX server applications. Using Access as an ActiveX server is covered in Chapter 26, "Automation: Communicating with Other Applications." Access's ability to control other applications with programming code is also covered in Chapter 26. In the following sections, you learn how to link to and embed objects in your Access forms.

Bound OLE Objects

Bound OLE objects are tied to the data in an OLE field within a table in your database. An example is the Photo field that's part of the Employees table in the Northwind database. The field type of the Employees table that supports multimedia data is OLE object. This means that each record in the table can contain a unique OLE object. The Employees form contains a bound OLE control whose control source is the Photo field from the Employees table.

If you double-click the photo of an employee, the OLE object can be edited *In-Place*. The picture of the employee is actually embedded in the Employees table. This means that the data associated with the OLE object is actually stored as part of the Access database (MDB) file, within the Employees table. Embedded objects, if they support the OLE 2.0 standard, can be modified In-Place. This is called *In-Place activation.*

To insert a new object, take the following steps:

1. Move to the record that will contain the OLE object.

2. Right-click the OLE Object control and select Insert Object to open the Insert Object dialog box.

3. Select an object type. Select Create New if you want to create an embedded object, or select Create from File if you want to link to or embed an existing file.

4. If you select Create from File, the Insert Object dialog box changes to look like the one shown in Figure 9.18.

FIGURE 9.18

The Insert Object dialog box as it appears when you select Create from File.

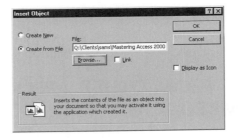

5. Select Link if you want to link to the existing file. Don't click Link if you want to embed the existing file. If you link to the file, the Access table will have a reference to the file as well as presentation data (a bitmap) for the object. If you embed the file, Access copies the original file, placing the copy in the Access table.

6. Click Browse and select the file you want to link to or embed.

7. Click OK.

If you double-click a linked object, you launch its source application; you don't get In-Place activation. (See Figure 9.19.)

Unbound OLE Objects

Unbound OLE objects aren't stored in your database. Instead, they are part of the form they were created in. Like bound OLE objects, unbound OLE objects can be linked or embedded. You create an unbound OLE object by adding an unbound object frame to the form.

FIGURE 9.19

Editing a linked object.

OpenArgs

The OpenArgs property gives you a way to pass information to a form as it's being opened. The OpenArgs argument of the OpenForm method is used to populate a form's OpenArgs property at runtime. It works like this:

```
DoCmd.OpenForm "frmPaymentMethods", _
            Datamode:=acFormAdd, _
            WindowMode:=acDialog, _
            OpenArgs:=NewData
```

This code is found in the Time and Billing application's frmPayments form. It opens the frmPaymentMethods form when a new method of payment is added to the cboPaymentMethodID combo box. It sends the frmPaymentMethods form an OpenArg of whatever data is added to the combo box. The Load event of the frmPaymentMethods form looks like this:

```
Private Sub Form_Load()
    If Not IsNull(Me.OpenArgs) Then
        Me.txtPaymentMethod.Value = Me.OpenArgs
    End If
End Sub
```

This code sets the txtPaymentMethod text box value to the value passed as the opening argument. This occurs only when the frmPaymentMethods form is opened from the frmPayments form.

SWITCHING A FORM'S RECORD SOURCE

Many developers don't realize how easy it is to switch a form's RecordSource property at runtime. This is a great way to use the same form to display data from more than one table or query containing the same fields. It's also a great way to limit the data that's displayed in a form at a particular moment. Using the technique of altering a form's RecordSource property at runtime, as shown in Listing 9.1, you can dramatically improve performance, especially for a client/server application. Here's an example found in the frmShowSales form of the Chap9Ex database. (See Figure 9.20.)

FIGURE 9.20

Changing the RecordSource property of a form at runtime.

LISTING 9.1   ALTERING A FORM'S RECORDSOURCE AT RUNTIME

```
Private Sub cmdShowSales_Click()

    'Check to see that Ending Date is later than Beginning Date.
    If Me.txtEndingDate < Me.txtBeginningDate Then
        MsgBox "The Ending Date must be later than the Beginning Date."
        txtBeginningDate.SetFocus
        Exit Sub
    End If

    '  Create an SQL statement using search criteria entered by user and
    '  set RecordSource property of ShowSalesSubform.

    Dim strSQL As String
    Dim strRestrict As String
    Dim lngX As Long
```

```
lngX = Me.optSales.Value
strRestrict = ShowSalesValue(lngX)

'   Create SELECT statement.
strSQL = "SELECT DISTINCTROW tblCustomers.CompanyName,_
  qryOrderSubtotals.OrderID, "
strSQL = strSQL & "qryOrderSubtotals.Subtotal ," & _
    "tblOrders.ShippedDate "
strSQL = strSQL & "FROM tblCustomers INNER JOIN _
  (qryOrderSubtotals INNER JOIN tblOrders ON "
strSQL = strSQL & "qryOrderSubtotals.OrderID = " & _
    "tblOrders.OrderID) ON "
strSQL = strSQL & "tblCustomers.CustomerID = tblOrders.CustomerID "
strSQL = strSQL & "WHERE (tblOrders.ShippedDate _
Between Forms!frmShowSales!txtBeginningDate "
strSQL = strSQL & "And Forms!frmShowSales!txtEndingDate) "
strSQL = strSQL & "And " & strRestrict
strSQL = strSQL & " ORDER BY qryOrderSubtotals.Subtotal DESC;"

'   Set RecordSource property of ShowSalesSubform.
Me.fsubShowSales.Form.RecordSource = strSQL

'   If no records match criteria, reset subform's
'   RecordSource property,
'   display message, and move focus to BeginningDate text box.
If Me.fsubShowSales.Form.RecordsetClone.RecordCount = 0 Then
    Me.fsubShowSales.Form.RecordSource = _
    "SELECT CompanyName FROM tblCustomers WHERE False;"
    MsgBox "No records match the criteria you entered.", _
     vbExclamation, "No Records Found"
    Me.txtBeginningDate.SetFocus
Else
    '   Enable control in detail section.
    EnableControls Me, acDetail, True
    '   Move insertion point to ShowSalesSubform.
    Me.fsubShowSales!txtCompanyName.SetFocus
End If

End Sub

Private Function ShowSalesValue(lngOptionGroupValue As Long) As String

'   Return value selected in Sales option group.

'   Define constants for option group values.
Const conSalesUnder1000 = 1
```

continues

9

**ADVANCED FORM
TECHNIQUES**

LISTING 9.1 CONTINUED

```
    Const conSalesOver1000 = 2
    Const conAllSales = 3

    ' Create restriction based on value of option group.
    Select Case lngOptionGroupValue
        Case conSalesUnder1000:
            ShowSalesValue = "qryOrderSubtotals.Subtotal < 1000"
        Case conSalesOver1000:
            ShowSalesValue = "qryOrderSubtotals.Subtotal >= 1000"
        Case Else
            ShowSalesValue = "qryOrderSubtotals.Subtotal = True"
    End Select
End Function
```

This code begins by storing the value of the optSales option group on the frmShowSales main form into a Long Integer variable. It then calls the ShowSalesValue function, which declares three constants; then evaluates the parameter that was passed to it (the Long Integer variable containing the option group value). Based on the value of the option group, it builds a selection string for the subtotal value. This selection string becomes part of the SQL statement used for the subform's record source and limits the range of sales values displayed on the subform.

The ShowSales routine then builds a string containing a SQL statement, which selects all required fields from the tblCustomers table and qryOrderSubtotals query. It builds a WHERE clause that includes the txtBeginningDate and txtEndingDate from the main form as well as the string returned from the ShowSalesValue function.

When the SQL statement has been built, the RecordSource property of the fsubShowSales subform control is set equal to the SQL statement. The RecordCount property of the RecordsetClone (the form's underlying recordset) is evaluated to determine whether any records meet the criteria specified in the RecordSource. If the record count is zero, no records are displayed in the subform and the user is warned that no records met the criteria. However, if records are found, the form's Detail section is enabled, and focus is moved to the subform.

POWER COMBO BOX AND LIST BOX TECHNIQUES

Combo and list boxes are very powerful. Being able to properly respond to a combo box's NotInList event, to populate a combo box by using code, and to select multiple entries in a list box are essential skills of an experienced Access programmer. They're covered in detail in the following sections.

Handling the `NotInList` Event

As discussed, the `NotInList` event occurs when a user types a value in the text box portion of a combo box that's not found in the combo box list. This event takes place only if the `LimitToList` property of the combo box is set to `True`. It's up to you whether you want to respond to this event.

You might want to respond with something other than the default error message when the `LimitToList` property is set to `True` and the user tries to add an entry. For example, if a user is entering an order and she enters the name of a new customer, you could react by displaying a message box asking whether she really wants to add the new customer. If the user responds affirmatively, you can display a customer form.

After you have set the `LimitToList` property to `True`, any code you place in the `NotInList` event is executed whenever the user tries to type an entry that's not found in the combo box. The following is an example:

```
Private Sub cboPaymentMethodID_NotInList(NewData As String, _
    Response As Integer)
    If MsgBox("Payment Method Not Found, Add?", _
        vbYesNo + vbQuestion, _
        "Please Respond") = vbYes Then
        DoCmd.OpenForm "frmPaymentMethods", _
            Datamode:=acFormAdd, _
            WindowMode:=acDialog, _
            OpenArgs:=NewData
        If IsLoaded("frmPaymentMethods") Then
            Response = acDataErrAdded
            DoCmd.Close acForm, "frmPaymentMethods"
        Else
            Response = acDataErrContinue
        End If
    Else
        Response = acDataErrContinue
    End If

End Sub
```

When this code is placed in the `NotInList` event procedure of your combo box, it displays a message asking the user whether she wants to add the payment method. If the user responds No, she is returned to the form without the standard error message being displayed, but she still must enter a valid value in the combo box. If the user responds Yes, she is placed in the `frmPaymentMethods` form, ready to add the payment method whose name she typed.

9

ADVANCED FORM TECHNIQUES

The NotInList event procedure accepts a response argument, which is where you can tell VBA what to do *after* your code executes. Any one of the following three constants can be placed in the response argument:

- acDataErrAdded—This constant is used if your code adds the new value into the record source for the combo box. This code requeries the combo box, adding the new value to the list.

- AcDataErrDisplay—This constant is used if you want VBA to display the default error message.

- AcDataErrContinue—This constant is used if you want to suppress VBA's own error message, using your own instead. Access still requires that a valid entry be placed in the combo box.

Working with a Pop-Up Form

The NotInList technique just described employs the use of a pop-up form. When the user opts to add the new payment method, the frmPaymentMethod form displays modally. This halts execution of the code in the form that loads the frmPaymentMethod form (in this case the frmPayments form.) What deems the frmPaymentMethod form a pop-up form is the fact that the form is modal, that it uses information from the frmPayments form, and that the frmPayments form reacts to whether the OK or Cancel button is selected. The code in the Load event of the frmPaymentMethods form in the Time and Billing database appears as follows:

```
Private Sub Form_Load()
    Me.txtPaymentMethod.Value = Me.OpenArgs
End Sub
```

This code uses the information received as an opening argument to populate the txtPaymentMethod text box. No further code executes until the user clicks either the OK or the Cancel command button. If the OK button is clicked, the following code executes:

```
Private Sub cmdOK_Click()
    Me.Visible = False
End Sub
```

Notice that the preceding code hides, rather than closes the frmPaymentMethod form. If the Cancel button is clicked, this code executes:

```
Private Sub cmdCancel_Click()
    DoCmd.RunCommand acCmdUndo
    DoCmd.Close
End Sub
```

The code under the cancel button first undoes the changes that the user made. It then closes the `frmPaymentMethod` form. Once back in the `NotInList` event of the `cboPaymentMethod` combo box on the `frmPayments` form, the code that follows executes:

```
If IsLoaded("frmPaymentMethods") Then
        Response = acDataErrAdded
        DoCmd.Close acForm, "frmPaymentMethods"
Else
        Response = acDataErrContinue
End If
```

The code evaluates whether the `frmPaymentMethods` form is still loaded. If it is, the user must have clicked OK. The `Response` parameter is set to `acDataErrAdded`, designating that the new entry has been added to the combo box and to the underlying data source. The `frmPaymentMethods` form is then closed.

If the `frmPaymentMethods` form is not loaded, the user must have clicked Cancel. The user is returned to the combo box where she must select another combo box entry. In summary, the steps are as follows:

1. Open the pop-up form modally (with the `WindowMode` parameter equal to `acDialog`).

2. Pass an `OpenArgs` parameter, if desired.

3. When control returns to the original form, check to see if the pop-up form is still loaded.

4. If the pop-up form is still open, use its information and then close it.

Populating a Combo or List Box with a `Callback` Function

As you know, it's easy to populate a combo or list box by setting the control's properties. This method is enough for many situations; however, there are times when you might want to populate a combo or list box programmatically—with values from an array, for example. You might also want to populate the box with table or report names or some other database component.

To populate a combo or list box using code, you create a `Callback` function, which tells Access how many rows and columns will be in the combo or list box and what data will be used to fill the box. This function becomes the Row Source type for your combo or list box. Access calls the function; then uses its information to populate the combo or list box. The example in Listing 9.2 is found in the frmSendToExcel form that's part of the Chap9Ex database.

9

ADVANCED FORM TECHNIQUES

LISTING 9.2 FILLING A LIST BOX BY USING A Callback FUNCTION

```
Function FillWithTableList(ctl As Control, vntID As Variant, _
        lngRow As Long, lngCol As Long, intCode As Integer) _
        As Variant

    Dim cat As ADOX.Catalog
    Dim tdf As ADOX.Table
    Dim qdf As ADOX.View
    Dim intCounter As Integer
    Static sastrTables() As String
    Static sintNumTables As Integer
    Dim varRetVal As Variant

    varRetVal = Null

    Select Case intCode
        Case acLBInitialize          ' Initialize.
        Set cat = New ADOX.Catalog
        cat.ActiveConnection = CurrentProject.Connection
        'Determine the Total Number of Tables + Queries
        sintNumTables = cat.Tables.Count + cat.Views.Count
        ReDim sastrTables(sintNumTables - 2)
        'Loop through each Table adding its name to
        'the List Box
        For Each tdf In cat.Tables
            If Left(tdf.Name, 4) <> "MSys" Then
                sastrTables(intCounter) = tdf.Name
                intCounter = intCounter + 1
            End If
        Next tdf
        'Loop through each Query adding its name to
        'the List Box
        For Each qdf In cat.Views
            sastrTables(intCounter) = qdf.Name
            intCounter = intCounter + 1
        Next qdf
        varRetVal = sintNumTables
        Case acLBOpen                'Open
            varRetVal = Timer         'Generate unique ID for control.
        Case acLBGetRowCount         'Get number of rows.
            varRetVal = sintNumTables
        Case acLBGetColumnCount      'Get number of columns.
            varRetVal = 1
        Case acLBGetColumnWidth      'Get column width.
            varRetVal = -1            '-1 forces use of default width.
```

```
        Case acLBGetValue              'Get the data.
            varRetVal = sastrTables(lngRow)
        End Select
        FillWithTableList = varRetVal
End Function
```

The function must contain five predetermined arguments. The first argument must be declared as a control, and the remaining arguments must be declared as variants. The function itself must return a variant. The parameters are listed in Table 9.4.

TABLE 9.4 FIVE PREDETERMINED ARGUMENTS OF A Callback FUNCTION

Argument	Description
fld	A control variable that refers to the combo or list box being filled.
id	A unique value that identifies the control being filled. It's useful when you're using the same function to populate more that one combo or list box.
row	The row being filled (zero-based).
col	The column being filled (zero-based).
code	A value specifying the information being requested.

The List function is called several times. Each time it's called, Access automatically supplies a different value for the code, indicating the information it's requesting. The code item can have the values shown in Table 9.5.

TABLE 9.5 CODE ITEM VALUES

Code	Intrinsic Constant	Meaning	Returns
0	acLBInitialize	Initialize	Nonzero if the function can fill the list; False or Null if a problem occurs
1	acLBOpen	Open	Nonzero ID value if the function can fill the list; False or Null if a problem occurs
3	acLBGetRowCount	Number of rows	Number of rows in the list
4	acLBGetColumnCount	Number of columns	Number of columns in the list
5	acLBGetColumnWidth	Column width	Width of the column specified

continues

TABLE 9.5 CONTINUED

Code	Intrinsic Constant	Meaning	Returns
6	acLBGetValue	List entry	List entry to be displayed in the column and row specified
7	acLBGetFormat	Format string	Format string used to format the list entry
8	acLBClose	Not used	
9	acLBEnd	End (last call)	Nothing

The function is automatically called once for codes 0, 1, 3, and 4. These calls initiate the process and determine the number of rows and columns that the combo or list box contains. The function is called twice for code 5: once to determine the total width of the box, and again to set the column width. The number of times that codes 6 and 7 are executed varies depending on the number of rows contained in the box (code 3). Code 9 is called when the form is closed or the combo or list box is queried.

Armed with this knowledge, you can take a good look at the FillWithTableList function, the Callback function that's used to populate the list box. The purpose of this function is to populate the list box with a list of tables and queries contained in the current database. When the user selects a table or query and clicks the Send To Excel command button, the data from the selected table or query is sent to Excel.

The Callback function uses ADO code to count all the tables and queries found in the current database. ADO (ActiveX Data Objects) is covered in Chapter 12, "What Are ActiveX Data Objects and Data Access Objects and Why Are They Important?" Each element of the case structure seen in the routine is called as each code is sent by Access. Here's what happens:

- When Access sends the code of 0, the tables and views are counted. The code loops through each table and query in the database. If it is not a system table, its name is added to the sastrTables array. The return value of the function is the number of tables and views in the database.
- When Access sends the code of 1, the return value is a unique value equal to the return value of the Timer function.
- When Access sends the code of 3, the return value is set equal to the count of tables and queries in the database.
- When Access sends the code of 4, the return value is set to 1 (one column).

- When Access sends the code of 5, the return value is set to -1, forcing a default width for the combo or list box.

- Access then automatically calls code 6 by the number of times that was returned for the number of rows in the combo or list box. Each time code 6 is called, the form object variable is set equal to a different element of the form collection. The table or query name is returned from the function. The table or query name is the value that's added to the list box.

All this work might seem difficult at first. After you have populated a couple of combo or list boxes, though, it's quite easy. In fact, all you need to do is copy the case structure you see in the FillWithTableList function and use it as a template for all your Callback routines.

Handling Multiple Selections in a List Box

Access 97 and Access 2000 list boxes have a Multiselect property. When set to True, this property lets the user select multiple elements from the list box. Your code can then evaluate which elements are selected and perform some action based on the selected elements. The frmReportEngine form, found in the Chap9Ex database, illustrates an example of the use of a multiselect list box. The code under the Click event of the Run Reports button looks like Listing 9.3.

LISTING 9.3   EVALUATING WHICH ITEMS ARE SELECTED IN THE MULTISELECT LIST BOX

```
Private Sub cmdRunReports_Click()
    Dim varItem As Variant
    Dim lst As ListBox

    Set lst = Me.lstReports
    ' Single select is 0, Simple multi-select is 1,
    ' and extended multi-select is 2.
    If lst.MultiSelect > 0 Then
        ' Loop through all the elements
        ' of the ItemsSelected collection, and use
        ' the Column array to retrieve the
        ' associated value.
        If lst.ItemsSelected.Count > 0 Then
            For Each varItem In lst.ItemsSelected
                DoCmd.OpenReport lst.ItemData(varItem), acViewPreview
            Next varItem
        End If
    End If

End Sub
```

9

ADVANCED FORM TECHNIQUES

This code first checks to ensure that the list box is a multiselect list box. If it is, and at least one report is selected, the code loops through all the selected items in the list box. It prints each report that is selected.

POWER SUBFORM TECHNIQUES

Many new Access developers don't know the ins and outs of creating and modifying a subform and referring to subform controls, so first look at some important points you should know when working with subforms:

- The easiest way to add a subform to a main form is to open the main form, and then drag and drop the subform onto the main form.
- The subform control's `LinkChildFields` and `LinkMasterFields` properties determine which fields in the main form link to which fields in the subform. A single field name, or a list of fields separated by semicolons, can be entered into these properties. When they are properly set, these properties make sure all records in the child form relate to the currently displayed record in the parent form.

Referring to Subform Controls

Many developers don't know how to properly refer to subform controls. You must refer to any objects on the subform through the subform control on the main form, as shown in this example:

```
Forms.frmCustomer.fsubOrders
```

This example refers to the fsubOrders control on the frmCustomer form. If you want to refer to a specific control on the fsubOrders subform, you can then point at its controls collection. Here's an example:

```
Forms.frmCustomer.fsubOrders!txtOrderID
```

You can also refer to the control on the subform implicitly, as shown in this example:

```
Forms!frmCustomer!subOrders!txtOrderID
```

Both of these methods refer to the txtOrderID control on the form in the fsubOrder control on the frmCustomer form. To change a property of this control, you would extend the syntax to look like this:

```
Forms.frmCustomer.fsubOrders!txtOrderID.Enabled = False
```

This code sets the Enabled property of the txtOrderID control on the form in the fsubOrders control to `False`.

SYNCHRONIZING A FORM WITH ITS UNDERLYING RECORDSET

A form's `RecordsetClone` property is used to refer to its underlying recordset. You can manipulate this recordset independently of what's currently being displayed on the form. Here's an example:

```
Private Sub cboCompany_AfterUpdate()
   Me.RecordsetClone.FindFirst "[ClientID] = " & cboCompany.Value
   If Me.RecordsetClone.NoMatch Then
      MsgBox "Client Not Found"
   Else
      Me.Bookmark = Me.RecordsetClone.Bookmark
   End If
End Sub
```

This example issues the `FindFirst` method on the form's `RecordsetClone`. It searches for a record in the form's underlying recordset whose `ClientID` is equal to the current combo box value. If a match is found, the form's bookmark is synchronized with the bookmark of the form's underlying recordset. This code can be rewritten, using an object variable to point at the `RecordsetClone`:

```
Private Sub cboCompany_AfterUpdate()
   Dim rs As DAO.Recordset
   Set rs = Me.RecordsetClone
   rs.FindFirst "[ClientID] = " & cboCompany.Value
   If rs.NoMatch Then
      MsgBox "Client Not Found"
   Else
      Me.Bookmark = rs.Bookmark
   End If
End Sub
```

This code creates an object variable that points at the form's `RecordsetClone`. The recordset object variable can then be substituted for `Me.RecordsetClone` because it references the form's underlying recordset.

CREATING CUSTOM PROPERTIES AND METHODS

Forms and reports are called *Class modules*, which means they act as templates for objects you create instances of at runtime. Public procedures of a form and report become Custom properties and methods of the form object at runtime. Using VBA code, you can set the values of a form's Custom properties and execute its methods.

Creating Custom Properties

Custom properties of a form or report can be created in one of two ways:

- Create Public variables in the form or report.
- Create PropertyLet and PropertyGet routines.

Creating and Using a Public Variable as a Form Property

The following steps are used to create and access a Custom form or report property based on a Public variable. The example is included in CHAP9EX.MDB in the forms frmPublicProperties and frmChangePublicProperty:

1. Begin by creating the form that will contain the Custom property (Public variable).
2. Place a Public variable in the General Declarations section of the form or report. (See Figure 9.21.)

FIGURE 9.21

Creating a Public variable in the Declarations section of a Class module.

3. Place code in the form or report that accesses the Public variable. The code in Figure 9.21 creates a Public variable called CustomCaption. The code behind the Click event of the cmdChangeCaption command button sets the form's (frmPublicProperties) Caption property equal to the value of the Public variable.
4. Create a form, report, or module that modifies the value of the Custom property. Figure 9.22 shows a form called frmChangePublicProperty.

FIGURE 9.22

Viewing the form frmChangePublic Property.

5. Add the code that modifies the value of the Custom property. The code behind the ChangeCaption button, as seen in Figure 9.21, modifies the value of the Custom property called CustomCaption that's found on the form called frmPublicProperties.

 To test the Custom property created in the preceding example, run the form called frmPublicProperties, which is in the database called CHAP9EX.MDB, found on your sample code CD-ROM. Click the Change Form Caption command button. Nothing happens because the value of the Custom property hasn't been set. Open the form called frmChangePublicProperty and click the Change Form Property command button. Return to frmPublicProperties and again click the Change Form Caption command button. The form's caption should now change.

Close the frmPublicProperties form and try clicking the Change Form Property command button. A runtime error occurs, indicating that the form you're referring to is not open. You can eliminate the error by placing the following code in the Click event of cmdPublicFormProperty:

```
Private Sub cmdPublicFormProperty_Click()
    Form_frmPublicProperties.CustomCaption = _
        "This is a Custom Caption"
    Forms!frmPublicProperties.Visible = True
End Sub
```

This code modifies the value of the Public property by using the syntax Form_FormName.Property. If the form isn't loaded, this syntax loads the form but leaves it hidden. The next command sets the form's Visible property to True.

Creating and Using Custom Properties with PropertyLet and PropertyGet Routines

A PropertyLet routine is a special type of subroutine that automatically executes whenever the property's value is changed. A PropertyGet routine is another special subroutine that automatically executes whenever the value of the Custom property is retrieved. Instead of using a Public variable to create a property, you insert two special routines: PropertyLet and PropertyGet. This example is found in CHAP9EX.MDB in the frmPropertyGetLet and frmChangeWithLet forms. To insert the PropertyLet and PropertyGet routines, follow these steps:

1. Choose Insert | Procedure. The dialog box shown in Figure 9.23 appears.
2. Type the name of the procedure in the Name text box.
3. Select Property from the Type option buttons.
4. Select Public as the Scope so that the property is visible outside the form.
5. Click OK. The PropertyGet and PropertyLet subroutines are inserted in the module. (See Figure 9.24.)

FIGURE 9.23

Starting a new procedure with the Add Procedure dialog box.

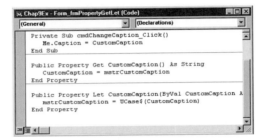

FIGURE 9.24

Subroutines created using the Add Procedure dialog.

Notice that the `Click` event code for the cmdChangeCaption command button hasn't changed. The `PropertyLet` routine, which automatically executes whenever the value of the `CustomCaption` property is changed, takes the uppercase value of what it's being sent and places it in a Private variable called `mstrCustomCaption`. The `PropertyGet` routine takes the value of the Private variable and returns it to whomever asked for the value of the property. The sequence of events is as follows—the following code is placed in the form called frmChangeWithLet:

```
Private Sub cmdPublicFormProperty_Click()
   Form_frmPropertyGetLet.CustomCaption = "This is a Custom Caption"
   Forms!frmPropertyGetLet.Visible = True
End Sub
```

This routine tries to set the value of the Custom property called `CustomCaption` to the value `"This is a Custom Caption"`. Because the property's value is being changed, the `PropertyLet` routine in frmPropertyGetLet is automatically executed. It looks like this:

```
Public Property Let CustomCaption(ByVal CustomCaption As String)
   mstrCustomCaption = UCase$(CustomCaption)
End Property
```

The `PropertyLet` routine receives the value `"This is a Custom Caption"` as a parameter. It uses the `UCase` function to manipulate the value it was passed and convert it to uppercase. It then places the manipulated value into a Private variable called `mstrCustomCaption`. The `PropertyGet` routine isn't executed until the user clicks the cmdChangeCaption button in the frmPropertyGetLet form. The `Click` event of cmdChangeCaption looks like this:

```
Private Sub cmdChangeCaption_Click()
   Me.Caption = CustomCaption
End Sub
```

Because this routine needs to retrieve the value of the Custom property `CustomCaption`, the `PropertyGet` routine automatically executes:

```
Public Property Get CustomCaption() As String
   CustomCaption = mstrCustomCaption
End Property
```

The `PropertyGet` routine takes the value of the Private variable, set by the `PropertyLet` routine, and returns it as the value of the property.

You might wonder why this method is preferable to declaring a Public variable. Using the `UCase` function within `PropertyLet` should illustrate why. Whenever you expose a Public variable, you can't do much to validate or manipulate the value you receive. The `PropertyLet` routine gives you the opportunity to validate and manipulate the value the property is being set to. By placing the manipulated value in a Private variable and then retrieving the Private variable's value when the property is returned, you gain full control over what happens internally to the property.

> **NOTE**
>
> This section provides an introduction to custom properties and methods. A comprehensive discussion of custom classes, properties, and methods is found in Chapter 28, "Exploiting the Power of Class Modules."

9

Creating Custom Methods

Custom methods are simply Public functions and subroutines placed in a form module or a report module. As you will see, they can be called by using the `Object.Method` syntax. Here are the steps involved in creating a Custom method; they are found in CHAP9EX.MDB in the forms frmMethods and frmExecuteMethod:

1. Open the form or report that will contain the Custom method.
2. Create a Public function or subroutine. (See Figure 9.25.)

FIGURE 9.25

Using the custom method ChangeCaption.

3. Open the form module, report module, or code module that executes the Custom method.

4. Use the Object.Method syntax to invoke the Custom method. (See Figure 9.26.)

FIGURE 9.26

The Click *event code behind the Execute Method button.*

Figure 9.25 shows the Custom method ChangeCaption found in the frmMethods form. The method changes the form's caption. Figure 9.26 shows the Click event of cmdExecuteMethod found in the frmExecuteMethod form. It issues the ChangeCaption method of the frmMethods form, and then sets the form's Visible property to True.

PRACTICAL EXAMPLES

Applying Advanced Techniques to Your Application

Many examples in this chapter are taken directly from the Time and Billing application. To polish your application, build a startup form that displays a splash screen and then performs some setup functions. The CHAP9.MDB file contains these changes.

Getting Things Going with a Startup Form

The frmSwitchboard form is responsible both for displaying the splash screen, and for performing necessary setup code. The code in the Load event of the frmSwitchboard form looks like this:

```
Private Sub Form_Load()
    DoCmd.Hourglass True
    DoCmd.OpenForm "frmSplash"
    Call GetCompanyInfo
    DoCmd.Hourglass False
End Sub
```

The Form_Load event first invokes an hourglass. It then opens the frmSplash form. Next it calls the GetCompanyInfo routine to fill in the CompanyInfo type structure that is eventually used throughout the application. Type structures are covered in Chapter 24, "Advanced VBA Techniques." Finally, it turns off the hourglass.

Building a Splash Screen

The splash screen, shown in Figure 9.27, is called frmSplash. Its timer interval is set to 3000 milliseconds (3 seconds), and its Timer event looks like this:

```
Private Sub Form_Timer()
    DoCmd.Close acForm, Me.Name
End Sub
```

FIGURE 9.27

Using an existing form as a splash screen.

9

The Timer event unloads the form. The frmSplash Pop-up property is set to Yes, and its border is set to None. Record selectors and navigation buttons have been removed.

SUMMARY

Forms are the centerpiece of most Access applications, so it's vital that you're able to fully harness their power and flexibility. The techniques covered in this chapter have shown you how to work with Form and Control events. You have seen many examples of when and how to leverage the event routines associated with forms and specific controls. You have also learned about the types of forms available, their uses in your applications, and how you can build them. Finally, you have learned several power techniques that will help you develop complex forms.

ADVANCED REPORT TECHNIQUES

IN THIS CHAPTER

WHY THIS CHAPTER IS IMPORTANT

Chapter 6, "What Every Developer Needs to Know About Reports," covers all the basics of report design. Reports are an integral part of almost every application, so fortunately for you, the Access 2000 report design tool is very powerful. Although it's easy to create most reports, as you mature as an Access developer, you'll probably want to learn the intricacies of Access report design. This chapter covers report events, advanced techniques, and tips and tricks of the trade.

EVENTS AVAILABLE FOR REPORTS AND WHEN TO USE THEM

Although report events aren't as plentiful as form events, the report events you can trap for allow you to control what happens as your report runs. This topic discusses report events, and the topic "Events Available for Report Sections and When to Use Them" covers events specific to report sections.

The Open Event

The Open event is the first event that occurs for a report, before the report begins printing or displaying. In fact, it happens even before the query underlying the report is run. Here's an example of using the Open event:

```
Private Sub Report_Open(Cancel As Integer)
    On Error Resume Next
    DoCmd.OpenForm "frmReportDateRange", _
        WindowMode:=acDialog, _
        OpenArgs:="rptProjectBillingsbyWorkCode"
    If Not IsLoaded("frmReportDateRange") Then
        MsgBox "Criteria Form Not Successfully Loaded, " & _
            "Canceling Report"
        Cancel = True
    End If
End Sub
```

 This code can be found in rptProjectBillingsByWorkCode in CHAP10.MDB on the sample code CD-ROM. It tries to open the frmReportDateRange form, the criteria form used to supply the parameters for the query underlying the report. If the form can't be loaded, the report is canceled.

The `Close` Event

The `Close` event occurs as the report is closing, before the `Deactivate` event occurs. The following example illustrates the use of the `Close` event:

```
Private Sub Report_Close()
    DoCmd.Close acForm, "frmReportDateRange"
End Sub
```

 This code is found in the rptProjectBillingsByWorkCode report in CHAP10.MDB on the sample code CD-ROM. It closes the criteria form frmReportDateRange when the report is closing, in case the form is still open.

The `Activate` Event

A report's `Activate` event happens when the report becomes the active window. It occurs after the `Open` event and before the report starts printing. It is often used to display a custom toolbar that will be visible whenever the report is active. Here's an example:

```
Private Sub Report_Activate()

'  Hide built-in Print Preview toolbar.
    '   Show Custom Print Preview toolbar.
    DoCmd.ShowToolbar "Print Preview", acToolbarNo
    DoCmd.ShowToolbar "Custom Print Preview", acToolbarYes

End Sub
```

This code hides the Print Preview toolbar and shows the custom toolbar called Custom Print Preview. As you will see, this event works with the `Deactivate` event to show and hide the custom report toolbars when the report becomes the active window and the user moves the focus to another window.

The `Deactivate` Event

The `Deactivate` event occurs when you move to another Access window or close the report, *not* when focus is moved to another application. Here's an example of how the `Deactivate` event is used:

```
Private Sub Report_Deactivate()

    '  Hide Custom Print Preview toolbar.
    '  Show built-in Print Preview toolbar.
    DoCmd.ShowToolbar "Custom Print Preview", acToolbarNo
    DoCmd.ShowToolbar "Print Preview", acToolbarWhereApprop

End Sub
```

This routine hides the custom toolbar displayed during the `Activate` event and indicates that the Print Preview toolbar should once again display where appropriate. You don't want to show the Print Preview toolbar here; instead, you just reset it to display whenever Access's default behavior would tell it to display. The `acToolbarWhereApprop` constant accomplishes this task.

> **NOTE**
>
> The sample code used in the sections on the `Activate` and `Deactivate` events illustrates one way to hide and show custom toolbars. The Toolbar property of a report can be used to perform the same task. However, when you need to display more than one toolbar while the report is active, you must place the code to hide and show the toolbars in the `Activate` and `Deactivate` events.

The `NoData` Event

If no records meet the criteria of the recordset underlying a report's `RecordSource`, the report prints without any data and displays `#Error` in the report's Detail section. To eliminate this problem, you can code the `NoData` event of the report, as shown here:

```
Private Sub Report_NoData(Cancel As Integer)
    MsgBox "There is no data for this report. Canceling report..."
    Cancel = True
End Sub
```

 This code is found in the `NoData` event of rptProjectBillingsByWorkCode in CHAP10.MDB on the sample code CD-ROM. In case no data is returned by the report's underlying recordset, a message is displayed to the user and Cancel is set equal to `True`. This exits the report without running it.

The `Page` Event

The `Page` event gives you the opportunity to do something immediately before the formatted page is sent to the printer. An example of the use of the `Page` event would be to place a border around a page. Here's an example:

```
Private Sub Report_Page()
    Me.Line (0, 0)-(Me.ScaleWidth, Me.ScaleHeight - 10), _
        RGB(255, 0, 0), _
        B
End Sub
```

This code is found in the rptTimeSheet report, in CHAP10.MDB. It draws a red line on the report, starting in the upper-left corner and going to the lower-right corner. It uses the `ScaleWidth` and `ScaleHeight` properties to determine where the lower-right corner of the report's printable area is. The `B` in the third parameter creates a rectangle by using the coordinates as opposite corners of the rectangle.

The `Error` Event

If a Jet Engine error occurs when the report is formatting or printing, the `Error` event is triggered. This error usually occurs if there's no `RecordSource` for the report or if someone else has exclusive use over the report's `RecordSource`. Here's an example:

```
Private Sub Report_Error(DataErr As Integer, Response As Integer)
    If DataErr = 2580 Then
        MsgBox "Record Source Not Available for This Report"
        Response = acDataErrContinue
    End If
End Sub
```

This code responds to a `DataErr` of `2580`, which means that the report's `RecordSource` isn't available. A custom message is displayed to the user, and the Access error is suppressed.

ORDER OF EVENTS FOR REPORTS

It's important to understand the order of events for reports. When the user opens a report, previews it, and then closes it, the following sequence of events occurs:

```
Open->Activate->Close->Deactivate
```

When the user switches to another report or to a form, the following sequence occurs:

```
Deactivate(Current Report)->Activate(Form or Report)
```

> **NOTE**
>
> The `Deactivate` event doesn't occur when the user switches to a dialog box, to a form whose `PopUp` property is set to `Yes`, or to a window of another application.

EVENTS AVAILABLE FOR REPORT SECTIONS AND WHEN TO USE THEM

Just as the report itself has events, so does each section of the report. The three section events are the `Format` event, `Print` event, and `Retreat` event, covered in the following sections.

The Format Event

The Format event happens after Access has selected the data to be included in a report section, but before it formats or prints the data. With the Format event, you can affect the layout of the section or calculate the results of data in the section, before the section actually prints. Listing 10.1 shows an example.

LISTING 10.1 AN EXAMPLE OF USING THE Format EVENT TO AFFECT THE REPORT LAYOUT

```
Private Sub Detail2_Format(Cancel As Integer, FormatCount As Integer)

    '  Determine whether to print detail record or "Continued."

    '  Show Continued text box if at maximum number of
    '  detail records for page.
    If (Me.txtRow = Me.txtOrderPage * (Me.txtRowsPerPage - 1) + 1) _
        And Me.txtRow <> Me.txtRowCount Then
        Me.txtContinued.Visible = True
    End If

    ' Show page break and hide controls in detail record.
    With Me
        If .txtContinued.Visible Then
            .txtDetailPageBreak.Visible = True
            .txtProductID.Visible = False
            .txtProductName.Visible = False
            .txtQuantity.Visible = False
            .txtUnitPrice.Visible = False
            .txtDiscount.Visible = False
            .txtExtendedPrice.Visible = False

            ' Increase value in Order Page.
            .NextRecord = False
            .txtOrderPage = Me.txtOrderPage + 1
        Else
            ' Increase row count if detail record is printed.
            .txtRow = Me.txtRow + 1
        End If
    End With

End Sub
```

This code is found in the rptInvoice report included in the CHAP10EX.MDB database found on your sample code CD. The report has controls that track how many rows of detail records should be printed on each page. If the maximum number of rows has

been reached, a control with the text Continued on Next Page... is visible. If the control is visible, the page break control is also made visible, and all the controls that display the detail for the report are hidden. The report is kept from advancing to the next record.

 Another example of the Format event is found in the Page Header of the rptEmployeeSales report, found in the CHAP10EX.MDB database. Because the report is an unbound report whose controls are populated by using VBA code at runtime, the report needs to determine what's placed in the report header. This varies depending on the result of the Crosstab query on which the report is based. The code appears in Listing 10.2.

LISTING 10.2 AN EXAMPLE OF USING THE Format EVENT TO POPULATE UNBOUND CONTROLS AT RUNTIME

```
Private Sub PageHeader0_Format(Cancel As Integer, FormatCount As Integer)

    Dim intX As Integer

    '  Put column headings into text boxes in page header.
    For intX = 1 To mintColumnCount
        Me("Head" + Format(intX)) = mrstReport(intX - 1).Name
    Next intX

    '  Make next available text box Totals heading.
    Me("Head" + Format(mintColumnCount + 1)) = "Totals"

    '  Hide unused text boxes in page header.
    For intX = (mintColumnCount + 2) To conTotalColumns
        Me("Head" + Format(intX)).Visible = False
    Next intX
End Sub
```

The code loops through each column of the recordset that results from executing the Crosstab query (in the Open event of the report). The controls in the report's Page Header are populated with the name of each column in the query result. The final column header is set equal to Totals. Finally, any remaining (extra) text boxes are hidden. More examples of using the Format event are covered throughout this chapter.

TIP

By placing logic in the Format event of a report's Detail section, you can control what happens as each line of the Detail section is printed.

The `Print` Event

The code in the `Print` event is executed when the data has been formatted to print in the section, but before it's actually printed. The `Print` event occurs at the following times for different sections of the report:

Detail Section: Just before the data is printed.

Group Headers: Just before the Group Header is printed; the Group Header's `Print` event has access to both the Group Header and the first row of data in the group.

Group Footers: Just before the Group Footer is printed; the `Print` event of the Group Footer has access to both the Group Footer and the last row of data in the group.

 Listing 10.3 is found in the `Print` event of the rptEmployeeSales report's Detail section; this report is included in the CHAP10EX.MDB database.

LISTING 10.3 AN EXAMPLE OF USING THE `Print` EVENT TO CALCULATE COLUMN AND ROW TOTALS

```
Private Sub Detail1_Print(Cancel As Integer, PrintCount As Integer)

    Dim intX As Integer
    Dim lngRowTotal As Long

    '  If PrintCount is 1, initialize rowTotal variable.
    '  Add to column totals.
    If Me.PrintCount = 1 Then
        lngRowTotal = 0

        For intX = 2 To mintColumnCount
            '  Starting at column 2 (first text box with crosstab value),
            '  compute total for current row in detail section.
            lngRowTotal = lngRowTotal + Me("Col" + Format(intX))
            '  Add crosstab value to total for current column.
            mlngRgColumnTotal(intX) = mlngRgColumnTotal(intX) + _
                Me("Col" + Format(intX))
        Next intX

        '  Place row total in text box in detail section.
        Me("Col" + Format(mintColumnCount + 1)) = lngRowTotal
        '  Add row total for current row to grand total.
        mlngReportTotal = mlngReportTotal + lngRowTotal
    End If
End Sub
```

The code begins by evaluating the `PrintCount` property. If it's equal to one, meaning this is the first time the `Print` event has occurred for the Detail section, the row total is set equal to `0`. The code then loops through each control in the section, accumulating totals for each column of the report and a total for the row. After the loop has been exited, the routine places the row total in the appropriate control and adds the row total to the report's grand total. The report's Detail section is now ready to be printed.

NOTE

Many people are confused about when to place code in the `Format` event and when to place code in the `Print` event. If you're doing something that doesn't affect the page layout, you should use the `Print` event. However, if you're doing something that affects the report's physical appearance (the layout), use the `Format` event.

The `Retreat` Event

Sometimes Access needs to move back to a previous section when printing, such as when a group's `Keep Together` property is set to `With First Detail` or `Whole` in the Sorting and Grouping dialog box. Access needs to format the Group Header and the first detail record or, in the case of `Whole`, the entire group. It then determines whether it can fit the section on the current page. It retreats from the two sections, and then formats and prints them; a `Retreat` event occurs for each section. Here's an example of the `Retreat` event for a report's Detail section:

```
Private Sub Detail1_Retreat()

    ' Always back up to previous record when detail section retreats.
    mrstReport.MovePrevious

End Sub
```

 This code is placed in the `Retreat` event of the rptEmployeeSales report that's part of the CHAP10EX.MDB. Because the report is an unbound report, it needs to return to the previous record in the recordset whenever the `Retreat` event occurs.

CAUTION

Whenever you're working with an unbound report, you need to be careful that the record pointer remains synchronized with the report. For example, if the record pointer has been advanced and the `Retreat` event occurs, the record pointer must be moved back to the previous record.

Order of Section Events

Just as report events have an order, report sections also have an order of events. All the `Format` and `Print` events for each section happen after the report's `Open` and `Activate` events, but before the report's `Close` and `Deactivate` events. The sequence looks like this:

```
Open(Report)->Activate(Report)->Format(Report Section)->
Print(Report Section)->Close(Report)->Deactivate(Report)
```

SPECIAL REPORT PROPERTIES

Several report properties are available only at runtime. They let you refine your report's processing significantly. These properties are covered in the sections that follow. Examples are provided in the section of this chapter titled "Practical Applications of Report Events and Properties."

MoveLayout

The `MoveLayout` property indicates to Access whether it should move to the next printing location on the page. By setting the property to `False`, the printing position is not advanced.

NextRecord

The `NextRecord` property specifies whether a section should advance to the next record. By setting this property to `False`, you suppress advancing to the next record.

PrintSection

The `PrintSection` property indicates whether the section is printed. By setting this property to `False`, you can suppress printing the section.

Interaction of MoveLayout, NextRecord, and PrintSection

By using the `MoveLayout`, `NextRecord`, and `PrintSection` properties in combination, you can determine exactly where, how, and whether data is printed. Table 10.1 illustrates this point.

TABLE 10.1 INTERACTION OF MoveLayout, NextRecord, AND PrintSection

MoveLayout	NextRecord	PrintSection	*Effect*
True	True	True	Move to the next position, get the next record, and print the data.
True	False	True	Move to the next position, remain on the same record, and print the data.
True	True	False	Move to the next position, get the next record, and don't print the data. This has the effect of skipping a record and leaving a blank space.
True	False	False	Move to the next position, remain on the same record, and don't print. This causes a blank space to appear without moving to the next record.
False	True	True	Remain in the same position, get the next record, and print the data. This has the effect of over-laying one record on another.
False	False	True	Not allowed.
False	True	False	Remain in the same position, get the next record, and refrain from printing. This has the effect of skipping a record without leaving a blank space.
False	False	False	Not allowed.

FormatCount

The FormatCount property evaluates the number of times the Format event has occurred for the report's current section. The Format event happens more than once whenever the Retreat event occurs. By checking the FormatCount property, you can make sure that complex code placed in the Format event is executed only once.

10

ADVANCED
REPORT
TECHNIQUES

PrintCount

The PrintCount property identifies the number of times the Print event has occurred for the report's current section. The Print event happens more than once whenever the Retreat event occurs. By checking the value of the PrintCount property, you can make sure that logic in the Print event is executed only once.

HasContinued

The HasContinued property determines whether part of the current section is printed on a previous page. You can use this property to hide or show certain report controls (for example, Continued From...), depending on whether the section is continued.

WillContinue

The WillContinue property determines whether the current section continues on another page. You can use this property as you do the HasContinued property to hide or display certain controls when a section continues on another page.

PRACTICAL APPLICATIONS OF REPORT EVENTS AND PROPERTIES

When developing reports, you should make sure the report can be used in as many situations as possible—that you build as much flexibility into the report as you can. Instead of managing several similar reports, making changes to each one whenever something changes, you can manage one report that handles different situations. Using the events and properties covered in this chapter will help you do just that. This might involve changing the report's RecordSource at runtime; using the same report to print summary data, detail data, or both; changing the print position; or even running a report based on a Crosstab query with unbound controls. All these aspects of report design are covered in the following sections.

Changing a Report's RecordSource

There are many times when you might want to change a report's RecordSource at runtime. By doing this, you can allow your users to alter the conditions for your report and transparently modify the query on which the report is based. The rptClientListing report in CHAP10.MDB has the code in Listing 10.4 in its Open event.

LISTING 10.4 AN EXAMPLE OF USING THE REPORT OPEN EVENT TO MODIFY A REPORT'S
RecordSource

```
Private Sub Report_Open(Cancel As Integer)
    On Error Resume Next
    DoCmd.OpenForm "frmClientListingCriteria", WindowMode:=acDialog
    If Not IsLoaded("frmClientListingCriteria") Then
        MsgBox "Criteria form not successfully loaded, " & _
            "Canceling Report"
        Cancel = True
    Else
        Select Case Forms!frmClientListingCriteria.optCriteria.Value
            Case 1
                Me.RecordSource = "qryClientListingCity"
            Case 2
                Me.RecordSource = "qryClientListingStateProv"
            Case 3
                Me.RecordSource = "qryClientListing"
        End Select
    End If
End Sub
```

This code begins by opening the frmClientListingCriteria form, if it isn't already loaded. It
loads the form modally and waits for the user to select the report criteria. (See Figure 10.1.)
After the user clicks to preview the report, the form sets its own Visible property to False.
This causes execution to continue in the report, but leaves the form in memory so that its controls can be accessed with VBA code. The value of the form's optCriteria option button is
evaluated. Depending on which option button is selected, the report's RecordSource property is
set to the appropriate query. The following code is placed in the Close event of the report:

```
Private Sub Report_Close()
    DoCmd.Close acForm, "frmClientListingCriteria"
End Sub
```

FIGURE 10.1

*The criteria selec-
tion used to deter-
mine the
RecordSource.*

10

This code closes the criteria form as the report is closing. The frmClientListingCriteria form has some code that's important to the processing of the report. It's found in the AfterUpdate event of the optCriteria option group (see Listing 10.5).

LISTING 10.5 THE AfterUpdate EVENT OF OPTCRITERIACOMBO HIDES AND SHOWS COMBO BOXES AS APPROPRIATE

```
Private Sub optCriteria_AfterUpdate()
   Select Case optCriteria.Value
      Case 1
         Me.cboCity.Visible = True
         Me.cboStateProv.Visible = False
      Case 2
         Me.cboStateProv.Visible = True
         Me.cboCity.Visible = False
      Case 3
         Me.cboCity.Visible = False
         Me.cboStateProv.Visible = False
   End Select
End Sub
```

This code evaluates the value of the option group. It hides and shows the visibility of the cboCity and cboState combo boxes, depending on which option button is selected. The cboCity and cboState combo boxes are then used as appropriate criteria for the queries that underlie the rptClientListing report.

Using the Same Report to Display Summary, Detail, or Both

Many programmers create three reports for their users: one that displays summary only, one that displays detail only, and another that displays both. This is totally unnecessary. Because report sections can be optionally hidden or displayed at runtime, you can create one report that meets all three needs. The rptClientBillingsByProject report included in the CHAP10.MDB database illustrates this point. Place the code shown in Listing 10.6 in the report's Open event.

LISTING 10.6 THE REPORT Open EVENT IS USED TO HIDE AND SHOW REPORT SECTIONS AS APPROPRIATE

```
Private Sub Report_Open(Cancel As Integer)
   DoCmd.OpenForm "frmReportDateRange", WindowMode:=acDialog, _
   OpenArgs:= "rptClientBillingsbyProject"
   If Not IsLoaded("frmReportDateRange") Then
      Cancel = True
```

```
      Else
         Select Case Forms!frmReportDateRange.optDetailLevel.Value
            Case 1
               Me.Caption = Me.Caption & " - Summary Only"
               Me.lblTitle.Caption = Me.lblTitle.Caption & _
               " - Summary Only"
               Me.Detail.Visible = False
            Case 2
               Me.Caption = Me.Caption & " - Detail Only"
               Me.lblTitle.Caption = Me.lblTitle.Caption & " - Detail Only"
               Me.GroupHeader0.Visible = False
               Me.GroupFooter1.Visible = False
               Me.CompanyNameDet.Visible = True
            Case 3
               Me.Caption = Me.Caption & " - Summary and Detail"
               Me.lblTitle.Caption = Me.lblTitle.Caption & " - Summary and _
               Detail"
               Me.CompanyNameDet.Visible = False
         End Select
      End If
End Sub
```

The code begins by opening frmReportDateRange included in CHAP10.MDB. (See Figure 10.2.) The form has an option group asking users whether they want a Summary report, Detail report, or report that contains both Summary and Detail. If Summary is selected, the caption of the Report window and the lblTitle label are modified, and the Visible property of the Detail section is set to False. If the user selects Detail, the captions of the Report window and the lblTitle label are modified, and the Visible property of the Group Header and Footer sections is set to False. A control in the Detail section containing the company name is made visible. The CompanyName control is visible in the Detail section when the Detail Only report is printed, but it's invisible when the Summary and Detail report is printed. When Both is selected as the level of detail, no sections are hidden. The captions of the Report window and the lblTitle label are modified, and the CompanyName control is hidden.

FIGURE 10.2

The criteria selection used to determine detail level.

The code behind the form's Preview button looks like Listing 10.7.

LISTING 10.7   CODE THAT VALIDATES THE DATE RANGE ENTERED BY THE USER

```
Private Sub cmdPreview_Click()
    If IsNull(Me.txtBeginDate) Or IsNull(Me.txtEndDate) Then
        MsgBox "You must enter both beginning and ending dates."
        Me.txtBeginDate.SetFocus
    Else
        If Me.txtBeginDate > Me.txtEndDate Then
            MsgBox "Ending date must be greater than Beginning date."
            Me.txtBeginDate.SetFocus
        Else
            Me.Visible = False
        End If
    End If
End Sub
```

This code makes sure that both the beginning date and the ending date are filled in, and that the beginning date comes before the ending date. If both of these rules are fulfilled, the `Visible` property of the form is set to `False`. Otherwise, an appropriate error message is displayed.

Printing Multiple Labels

Many times, users want to print multiple copies of the same label. This can be done by using the report's `MoveLayout`, `NextRecord`, `PrintSection`, and `PrintCount` properties. The form shown in Figure 10.3 is called frmClientLabelCriteria and is found in CHAP10.MDB. It asks that the users select a company and the number of labels they want to print for that company. The code for the Print Labels command button looks like Listing 10.8.

LISTING 10.8   CODE THAT PRINTS THE LBLCLIENTMAILINGLABELS REPORT FOR THE SELECTED COMPANY

```
Sub cmdPrintLabels_Click()
On Error GoTo Err_cmdPrintLabels_Click

    Dim strDocName As String

    strDocName = "lblClientMailingLabels"
    DoCmd.OpenReport strDocName, acPreview, , "CompanyName = '" _
            & Me.cboCompanyName.Value & "'"
```

```
Exit_cmdPrintLabels_Click:
    Exit Sub

Err_cmdPrintLabels_Click:
    MsgBox Err.Description
    Resume Exit_cmdPrintLabels_Click

End Sub
```

FIGURE 10.3

The criteria selection used to specify company name and number of labels to print.

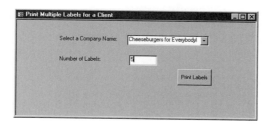

Notice that the routine uses the company name selected from the combo box as a criterion to run the lblClientMailingLabels report. The Open event of lblClientMailingLabels looks like this:

```
Private Sub Report_Open(Cancel As Integer)
    If Not IsLoaded("frmClientLabelCriteria") Then
        MsgBox "You Must Run This Report From Label Criteria Form"
        Cancel = True
    End If
End Sub
```

This code tests to make sure the frmClientLabelCriteria form is open. If it's not, a message is displayed and the report is canceled. The key to the whole process is found in the Detail section's Print event:

```
Private Sub Detail_Print(Cancel As Integer, PrintCount As Integer)
    If PrintCount < Forms!frmClientLabelCriteria.txtNumberOfLabels Then
        Me.NextRecord = False
    End If
End Sub
```

This code compares the PrintCount property to the number of labels the user wants to print. As long as the PrintCount is less than the number of labels requested, the record pointer is not advanced. This causes multiple labels to be printed for the same record.

Determining Where a Label Prints

Users often want to print several copies of the same label, but they might also want to print mailing labels in a specific position on the page. This is done so that they can begin the print process on the first unused label. The frmClientLabelPosition form from CHAP10.MDB lets the user specify the first label location on which to print by designating the number of labels that need to be skipped. (See Figure 10.4.) The Open event of the lblClientMailLabelsSkip looks like this:

```
Private Sub Report_Open(Cancel As Integer)
    If Not IsLoaded("frmClientLabelPosition") Then
        MsgBox "You Must Run This Report From Label Criteria Form"
        Cancel = True
    Else
        mboolFirstLabel = True
    End If
End Sub
```

FIGURE 10.4

The criteria selection used to indicate the number of labels to skip.

The code tests to make sure that the frmClientLabelPosition form is loaded. It also sets a private variable, mboolFirstLabel, equal to True. The Detail section's Print event looks like this:

```
Private Sub Detail_Print(Cancel As Integer, PrintCount As Integer)
    If PrintCount <= Forms!frmClientLabelPosition.txtLabelsToSkip _
                And mboolFirstLabel = True Then
        Me.NextRecord = False
        Me.PrintSection = False
    Else
        mboolFirstLabel = False
    End If
End Sub
```

This routine checks to see whether the PrintCount property of the report is less than or equal to the number of the labels to skip. It also checks to make sure that the mboolFirstLabel variable is equal to True. If both conditions are True, the report doesn't move to the next record and doesn't print anything. The print position is advanced. When the PrintCount becomes greater than the number of labels to skip, the mboolFirstLabel variable is set to False and printing proceeds as usual. If `mboolFirstLabel` is not set to `False`, the designated number of labels is skipped between each record. One additional event makes all this work—the `Print` event of the Report Header:

```
Private Sub ReportHeader_Format(Cancel As Integer, FormatCount As Integer)
    mboolFirstLabel = True
End Sub
```

The `ReportHeader Format` event sets `mboolFirstLabel` back to `True`. You must include this step in case the user previews and then prints the labels. If the `mboolFirstLabel` variable is not reset to `True`, the selected number of labels isn't skipped on the printout because the condition that skips the labels is never met.

Building a Report from a Crosstab Query

It's difficult to base a report on the results of a Crosstab query because its number of columns usually varies. Take a look at the example shown in Figure 10.5. Notice that the employee names appear across the top of the report as column headings, and the products are listed down the side of the report. This report is based on the Crosstab query called qxtabEmployeeSales, part of the CHAP10EX.MDB database found on the sample code CD. (See Figure 10.6.) The problem is that the number of employees—and, therefore, column headings—can vary. This report is coded to handle such an eventuality.

FIGURE 10.5

A report based on a Crosstab query.

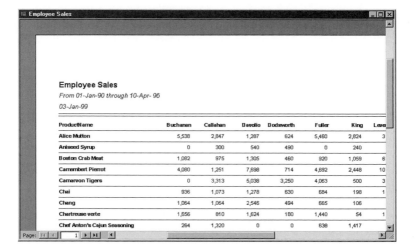

FIGURE 10.6

A Crosstab query underlying a report.

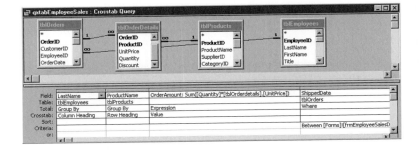

When the rptEmployeeSales (located in Chap10Ex) report runs, its Open event is executed (see Listing 10.9).

LISTING 10.9 CODE THAT OBTAINS CRITERIA INFORMATION FOR THE REPORT AND THEN BUILDS A RECORDSET THAT UNDERLIES THE REPORT

```
Private Sub Report_Open(Cancel As Integer)

    '   Create underlying recordset for report using criteria entered in
    '   EmployeeSalesDialogBox form.

    Dim intX As Integer
    Dim db As DAO.Database
    Dim qdf As DAO.QueryDef
    Dim frm As Form

    Set db = CurrentDb

    '   Don't open report if EmployeeSalesDialogBox form isn't loaded.
    If Not (IsLoaded("frmEmployeeSalesDialogBox")) Then
        Cancel = True
        MsgBox "To preview or print this report, you must open " _
        & "EmployeeSalesDialogBox in Form view.", vbExclamation, _
        "Must Open Dialog Box"
        Exit Sub
    End If

    Set frm = Forms!frmEmployeeSalesDialogBox
    '   Open qxtabEmployeeSales Query.
    Set qdf = db.QueryDefs("qxtabEmployeeSales")
    ' Set parameters for query based on values entered
    ' in EmployeeSalesDialogBox form.
    qdf.Parameters("Forms!frmEmployeeSalesDialogBox!txtBeginningDate") _
        = frm!txtBeginningDate
```

```
qdf.Parameters("Forms!frmEmployeeSalesDialogBox!txtEndingDate") _
    = frm!txtEndingDate

'  Open Recordset object.
Set mrstReport = qdf.OpenRecordset

'  Set a variable to hold number of columns in crosstab query.
mintColumnCount = mrstReport.Fields.Count

End Sub
```

The Open event sets a database object variable to the current database. It then checks to make sure the criteria form, frmEmployeeSalesDialogBox, is open. This form supplies the criteria for the qxtabEmployeeSales query that underlies the report. It opens the qxtabEmployeeSales query definition and passes it the parameters from the frmEmployeeSalesDialogBox criteria form. Next, it opens a recordset based on the query definition, using the criteria found on the frmEmployeeSalesDialogBox form. The number of columns returned from the Crosstab query is very important; this number is stored in a Private variable called mintColumnCount and is used throughout the remaining functions to determine how many columns to fill with data.

> **NOTE**
>
> This book focuses on the use of ADO (ActiveX Data Objects) rather than DAO (Data Access Objects). You might wonder why this example uses DAO rather than ADO. The query that underlies this example is a Crosstab query. The ADO command object does not recognize Crosstab queries. It was therefore necessary to use DAO in this example.

Next, the Report Header Format event occurs. It moves to the first record in the recordset created during the Open event. It also calls an InitVars routine:

```
Private Sub ReportHeader3_Format(Cancel As Integer, _
FormatCount As Integer)

    '  Move to first record in recordset at beginning of report
    '  or when report is restarted. (A report is restarted when
    '  you print a report from Print Preview window, or when you return
    '  to a previous page while previewing.)
    mrstReport.MoveFirst

    'Initialize variables.
    Call InitVars

End Sub
```

The `InitVars` routine initializes some variables used in the report:

```
Private Sub InitVars()

    Dim intX As Integer

    ' Initialize lngReportTotal variable.
    mlngReportTotal = 0

    ' Initialize array that stores column totals.
    For intX = 1 To conTotalColumns
        mlngRgColumnTotal(intX) = 0
    Next intX

End Sub
```

The `mlngReportTotal` variable is used for the report grand total (all products, all salespeople), and the `mlngRgColumnTotal` array contains the total for each salesperson. After the `Report Header Format` event occurs, the `Page Header Format` event takes place:

```
Private Sub PageHeader0_Format(Cancel As Integer, FormatCount As Integer)

    Dim intX As Integer

    '  Put column headings into text boxes in page header.
    For intX = 1 To mintColumnCount
        Me("Head" + Format$(intX)) = mrstReport(intX - 1).Name
    Next intX

    '  Make next available text box Totals heading.
    Me("Head" + Format$(mintColumnCount + 1)) = "Totals"

    '  Hide unused text boxes in page header.
    For intX = (mintColumnCount + 2) To conTotalColumns
        Me("Head" + Format$(intX)).Visible = False
    Next intX
End Sub
```

The `PageHeader Format` event uses the names of the fields in the query results as column headings for the report. This essential routine is "smart" because, after it fills in all the column headings, it hides all the extra controls on the report.

Next, the `Detail Section Format` event occurs:

```
Private Sub Detail1_Format(Cancel As Integer, FormatCount As Integer)
'   Place values in text boxes and hide unused text boxes.

    Dim intX As Integer
    '  Verify that not at end of recordset.
    If Not mrstReport.EOF Then
        '  If FormatCount is 1, place values from recordset into text boxes
        '  in detail section.
      If Me.FormatCount = 1 Then
          For intX = 1 To mintColumnCount
              '  Convert Null values to 0.
              Me("Col" + Format(intX)) = xtabCnulls(mrstReport(intX - 1))
          Next intX

          '  Hide unused text boxes in detail section.
          For intX = mintColumnCount + 2 To conTotalColumns
              Me("Col" + Format(intX)).Visible = False
          Next intX

          '  Move to next record in recordset.
          mrstReport.MoveNext
      End If
    End If


End Sub
```

The `Detail Section Format` event checks the recordset's `EOF` property to determine whether the last record in the query has already been read. If not, the section's `FormatCount` property is tested to see whether it's equal to 1. If so, each column in the current record of the recordset is read. Each control in the Detail section is filled with data from a column in the recordset, and any unused text boxes in the report's Detail section are hidden. Finally, the code moves to the next record in the recordset, readying the report to print the next line of detail. The `xtabCnulls` function, which converts `Null` values into zeros, is called each time the recordset underlying the report is read:

```
Private Function xtabCnulls(varX As Variant)

    '  Test if a value is null.
    XtabCnulls = NZ(varX,0)

End Function
```

10

The `xtabCnulls` function evaluates each value sent to it to check whether the value is `Null`. If so, a zero is returned from the function; otherwise, the value that was passed to the function is returned.

After the `Detail Section Format` event is executed, the `Detail Section Print` event occurs:

```
Private Sub Detail1_Print(Cancel As Integer, PrintCount As Integer)

    Dim intX As Integer
    Dim lngRowTotal As Long

    '  If PrintCount is 1, initialize rowTotal variable.
    '  Add to column totals.
    If Me.PrintCount = 1 Then
        lngRowTotal = 0

        For intX = 2 To mintColumnCount
            '  Starting at column 2 (first text box with crosstab value),
            '  compute total for current row in detail section.
            lngRowTotal = lngRowTotal + Me("Col" + Format(intX))
            '  Add crosstab value to total for current column.
            mlngRgColumnTotal(intX) = mlngRgColumnTotal(intX) + _
                Me("Col" + Format(intX))
        Next intX

        '  Place row total in text box in detail section.
        Me("Col" + Format(mintColumnCount + 1)) = lngRowTotal
        '  Add row total for current row to grand total.
        mlngReportTotal = mlngReportTotal + lngRowTotal
    End If
End Sub
```

The `Detail Print` event generates the row total value, placing it in the last column of the report, accumulating column totals, and accumulating the `mlngReportTotal` value, which is the grand total for all columns and rows. It does this by making sure the `PrintCount` of the section is 1. If so, it resets the `lngRowTotal` variable to `0`. Starting at column 2 (column 1 contains the product name), it begins accumulating a row total by looking at each control in the row, adding its value to `lngRowTotal`. As it traverses each column in the row, it also adds the value in each column to the appropriate element of the `mlngRgColumnTotal` private array, which maintains all the column totals for the report. It prints the row total and adds the row total to the report's grand total.

When the `Retreat` event occurs, the following code executes:

```
Private Sub Detail1_Retreat()

    ' Always back up to previous record when Detail section retreats.
    mrstReport.MovePrevious

End Sub
```

This code forces the record pointer to be moved back to the previous record in the recordset. Finally, the report footer prints, which causes the `Report Footer Format` event to execute:

```
Private Sub ReportFooter4_Print(Cancel As Integer, PrintCount As Integer)

    Dim intX As Integer

    '   Place column totals in text boxes in report footer.
    '   Start at column 2 (first text box with crosstab value).
    For intX = 2 To mintColumnCount
        Me("Tot" + Format(intX)) = mlngRgColumnTotal(intX)
    Next intX

    '   Place grand total in text box in report footer.
    Me("Tot" + Format(mintColumnCount + 1)) = mlngReportTotal

    '   Hide unused text boxes in report footer.
    For intX = mintColumnCount + 2 To conTotalColumns
        Me("Tot" + Format(intX)).Visible = False
    Next intX
End Sub
```

The `Report Footer Format` event loops through each control in the footer, populating each control with the appropriate element of the `mlngRgColumnTotal` array. This gives you the column totals for the report. Finally, the grand total is printed in the next available column. Any extra text boxes are hidden from display.

Printing the First and Last Page Entries in the Page Header

Another useful technique is printing the first and last entries from a page in the report's header. This is illustrated in the rptCustomerPhoneList report, found in the CHAP10EX.MDB database located on the sample code CD. (See Figure 10.7.) The code for this report relies on Access making two passes through the report. During the first pass, a variable called `gboolLastPage` is equal to `False`. The `gboolLastPage` variable becomes `True` only when the Report Footer's `Format` event is executed at the end of the first pass through the report. Keep this in mind as you review the code behind the report.

FIGURE 10.7

The first and last entry printed in the report header.

The first routine that affects the report processing is the `Report Header Format` event routine:

```
Private Sub PageHeader0_Format(Cancel As Integer, FormatCount As Integer)

    ' During second pass, fill in FirstEntry and LastEntry text boxes.
    If gboolLastPage = True Then
        Reports!rptCustomerPhoneList.txtFirstEntry = _
            Reports!rptCustomerPhoneList.txtCompanyName
        Reports!rptCustomerPhoneList.txtLastEntry = _
            gstrLast(Reports!rptCustomerPhoneList.Page)
    End If

End Sub
```

The `Page Header Format` routine tests to see whether the `gboolLastPage` variable is equal to `True`. During the first pass through the report, the `gboolLastPage` variable is equal to `False`. During the second pass, the `txtFirstEntry` and `txtLastEntry` text boxes (both of which appear in the report's header) are populated with data. The `txtFirstEntry` text box is filled with the value in the `txtCompanyName` control of the current record (the first record on the page), and the `txtLastEntry` text box is populated with the appropriate element number from the `CustomerPhoneList` array. Each element of the `CustomerPhoneList` array is populated by the `Format` event of the Page Footer for that page during the first pass through the report.

Next, the `Page Footer Format` event is executed:

```
Private Sub PageFooter2_Format(Cancel As Integer, FormatCount As Integer)

    ' During first pass, increase size of array and enter last record on
    ' page into array.
    If Not gboolLastPage Then
        ReDim Preserve gstrLast(Reports!rptCustomerPhoneList.Page + 1)
        gstrLast(Reports!rptCustomerPhoneList.Page) = _
            Reports!rptCustomerPhoneList.txtCompanyName
    End If

End Sub
```

The `Page Footer Format` event determines whether the `gboolLastPage` variable is equal to `False`. If so (which it is during the first pass through the report) the `gstrLast` array is redimensioned to add an element. The value from the `txtCompanyName` control of the last record on the page is stored in the new element of the `gstrLast` array. This value eventually appears in the Page Header of that page as the last company name that appears on the page. Finally, the `Report Footer Format` event executes:

```
Private Sub ReportFooter4_Format(Cancel As Integer, _
FormatCount As Integer)

    Dim rst As ADODB.Recordset
    Set rst = New ADODB.Recordset

    ' Set flag after first pass has been completed.
    gboolLastPage = True

    ' Open recordset for report.
    rst.Open "tblCustomers", CurrentProject.Connection, adOpenStatic
    ' Move to last record in recordset.
    rst.MoveLast
    ' Enter last record into array.
    ReDim Preserve gstrLast(Reports!rptCustomerPhoneList.Page + 1)
    gstrLast(Reports!rptCustomerPhoneList.Page) = rst!CompanyName

End Sub
```

The `Report Footer` routine sets the `gboolLastPage` variable equal to `True` and opens a recordset based on the Customers table. This is the recordset on which the report is based. It moves to the last record in the recordset and adds the `CompanyName` value from the recordset's last record in an additional element of the array.

Now the first pass of the report has finished. As the user moves to each page of the report during a print preview, or as each page is printed to the printer, the Format event executes for the Page Header. The company name from the first record on the page is placed in the txtFirstEntry control, and the appropriate element from the gstrLast array is placed in the txtLastEntry control.

Creating a Multifact Crosstab Report

By nature, Crosstab queries are limited because they don't allow you to place multiple rows of data in the result. For example, you can't display months as column headings and then show the minimum, average, and maximum sales for each employee as row headings. The rptSalesAverages report, found in the Chap10Ex database, and shown in Figure 10.8, solves this problem.

FIGURE 10.8

An example of a multifact crosstab report.

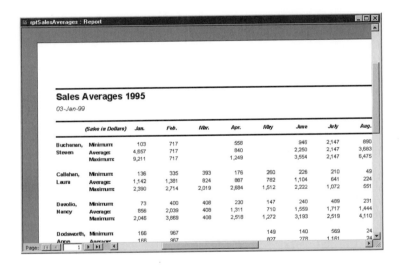

Each time the Format event of the Page Header executes, the value of a control on the report, called txtPrintWhat, is reset to 0:

```
Private Sub PageHeader1_Format(Cancel As Integer, FormatCount As Integer)

    ' Set PrintWhat text box to 0 at top of page.
    Me.txtPrintWhat = 0

End Sub
```

After the `Page Header Format` event executes, the `Group Header Format` event launches:

```
Private Sub GroupHeader2_Format(Cancel As Integer, _
FormatCount As Integer)
    ' Print information in row headings in correct order.

    ' Print SalespersonLastName and FirstName text boxes,
    ' hide Minimum, Average, and Maximum labels,
    ' set PrintWhat text box to -1, and don't advance to next record.
    With Me
        If .txtPrintWhat = 0 Then
            .txtSalespersonLastName.Visible = True
            .txtFirstName.Visible = True
            .lblMinimum.Visible = False
            .lblAverage.Visible = False
            .lblMaximum.Visible = False
            .txtPrintWhat = True
            .NextRecord = False

        ' Hide SalespersonLastName and FirstName text boxes,
        ' print Minimum, Average, and Maximum labels,
        ' and set PrintWhat text box to 0.
        Else
            .txtSalespersonLastName.Visible = False
            .txtFirstName.Visible = False
            .lblMinimum.Visible = True
            .lblAverage.Visible = True
            .lblMaximum.Visible = True
            .txtPrintWhat = 0
        End If
    End With
End Sub
```

The first time the `Format` event for LastName Group Header (GroupHeader2) executes, the value of the `txtPrintWhat` control is equal to `False`. The `txtSalePersonLastName` and the `txtFirstName` controls are made visible, and the `lblMinimum`, `lblAverage`, and `lblMaximum` controls are hidden. The `txtPrintWhat` control's value is set to `True`, and movement to the next record is suppressed by setting the value of the `NextRecord` property to `False`.

The second time the `Format` event for the LastName Group Header executes, the `txtSalepersonLastName` and `txtFirstName` controls are hidden. The `lblMinimum`, `lblAverage`, and `lblMaximum` controls are made visible, and the value of the `txtPrintWhat` control is reset to `False`.

10

The only other code for the report is in the Format event of the Shipped Date Header (GroupHeader3):

```
Private Sub GroupHeader3_Format(Cancel As Integer, _
FormatCount As Integer)
    '  Print data in correct column.

    ' Don't advance to next record or print next section.
    If Me.Left < Me.txtLeftMargin + (Month(Me.ShippedDate) + 1) _
        * Me.txtColumnWidth Then
        Me.NextRecord = False
        Me.PrintSection = False
    End If
End Sub
```

This code compares the report's Left property to the result of an expression. The Left property is the amount that the current section is offset from the page's left edge. This number is compared with the value in the txtLeftMargin control added to the current month plus one, and then it's multiplied by the value in the txtColumnWidth control. If this expression evaluates to True, the NextRecord and PrintSection properties of the report are both set to False. This causes the printer to move to the next printing position, but to remain on the same record and not print anything, which forces a blank space in the report. You might wonder what the complicated expression is all about. Simply put, it's an algorithm that makes sure printing occurs and that Access moves to the next record only when the data for January is ready to print.

PRACTICAL EXAMPLES

The rptEmployeeBillinsByProject Report

Almost every report in the Time and Billing application implements at least one of the techniques discussed in this chapter. In fact, the rptClientListing, rptClientBillingsByProject, lblClientMailingLabels, and lblClientMailingLabelsSkip reports discussed in this chapter are an integral part of the Time and Billing application.

One report not covered in the chapter is the rptEmployeeBillingsByProject report. This report has the following code in its NoData event:

```
Private Sub Report_NoData(Cancel As Integer)
    MsgBox "There is no data for this report. Canceling report..."
    Cancel = True
End Sub
```

If there's no data in the report's `RecordSource`, a message box is displayed and the report is canceled. The `Open` event of the report looks like this:

```
Private Sub Report_Open(Cancel As Integer)
    DoCmd.OpenForm "frmReportDateRange", _
        WindowMode:=acDialog, _
        OpenArgs:="Employee Billings by Project"
    If Not IsLoaded("frmReportDateRange") Then
        Cancel = True
    End If
End Sub
```

The report's `Open` event opens a form called frmReportDateRange. (See Figure 10.9.) This form is required because it supplies criteria to the query underlying the report. If the form isn't loaded successfully, the report is canceled.

FIGURE 10.9

A criteria selection form.

Finally, the report's `Close` event looks like this:

```
Private Sub Report_Close()
    DoCmd.Close acForm, "frmReportDateRange"
End Sub
```

The report cleans up after itself by closing the criteria form.

SUMMARY

To take full advantage of what the Access report writer has to offer, you must understand—and be able to work with—report and section events. This chapter has gone through the report and section events, giving you detailed examples of when to use each event.

In addition to the report events, several special properties are available to you only at runtime. By manipulating these properties, you can have more control over your reports' behavior. After covering the report and section events, this chapter has covered the properties you can manipulate only at runtime. Examples have been given to highlight the appropriate use of each property.

There are many tips and tricks of the trade that help you do things you might otherwise think are impossible to accomplish. This chapter has given you several practical examples of these tips and tricks, making it easy for you to use them in your own application development.

ADVANCED QUERY TECHNIQUES

IN THIS CHAPTER

You learned the basics of query design in Chapter 4, "What Every Developer Needs to Know About Queries," but Access has a wealth of query capabilities. In addition to the relatively simple Select queries covered in Chapter 4, you can create Crosstab queries, Union queries, Self-Join queries, and many other complex selection queries. You can also easily build Access queries that modify information, rather than retrieve it. This chapter covers these topics and the more advanced aspects of query design.

ACTION QUERIES

With Action queries, you can easily modify data without writing any code. In fact, action queries are often a more efficient method than using code. Four types of action queries are available: Update, Delete, Append, and Make Table. You use Update queries to modify data in a table, Delete queries to remove records from a table, Append queries to add records to an existing table, and Make Table queries to create an entirely new table. Each type of query and its appropriate uses are explained in the following sections.

Update Queries

Update queries are used to modify all records or any records meeting specific criteria. An update query can be used to modify the data in one field or several fields (or even tables) at one time (for example, a query that increases the salary of everyone in California by 10 percent). As mentioned, using Update queries is usually more efficient than performing the same task with VBA code, so they're considered a respectable way to modify table data.

To build an Update query, follow these steps:

1. Click Queries in the Objects list from the Database window.

2. Double-click the Create Query in Design view icon.

3. In the Show Table dialog box, select the tables or queries that will participate in the Update query and click Add. Click Close when you're ready to continue.

4. To let Access know you're building an Update query, open the Query Type drop-down list on the toolbar and select Update Query. You can also choose Query | Update Query from the menu.

5. Add fields to the query that will either be used for criteria or be updated as a result of the query. In Figure 11.1, StateProvince has been added to the query grid because it will be used as criteria for the update. DefaultRate has been included because it's the field that's being updated.

6. Add any further criteria, if you want. In Figure 11.1, the criteria for StateProvince has been set to CA.

7. Add the appropriate Update expression. In Figure 11.1, the DefaultRate is being increased by 10 percent.

FIGURE 11.1

An Update query that increases the DefaultRate for all clients in California.

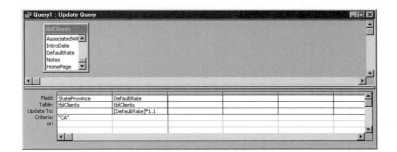

8. Click Run on the toolbar. The message box shown in Figure 11.2 appears. (See the section "Special Notes About Action Queries" later in this chapter for how to suppress this message by programming.) Click Yes to continue. All records meeting the selected criteria are updated.

FIGURE 11.2

The confirmation message you see when running an Update query.

Access Update queries should be named with the prefix qupd. Each type of Action query should be given a prefix indicating what type of query it is. Table 11.1 lists all the proper prefixes for Action queries.

TABLE 11.1 NAMING PREFIXES FOR ACTION QUERIES

Type of Query	Prefix	Example
Update	qupd	qupdDefaultRate
Delete	qdel	qdelOldTimeCards
Append	qapp	qappArchiveTimeCards
Make Table	qmak	qmakTempSales

NOTE

Each type of action query is displayed in the Database window with a distinctive icon.

All Access queries are stored as SQL (Structured Query Language) statements. (Access SQL is discussed later in this chapter in the "Understanding SQL" section.) The SQL for a query can be displayed by selecting SQL View from the View drop-down on the toolbar. The SQL behind an Access Update query looks like this:

```
UPDATE tblClients SET tblClients._
    DefaultRate = [DefaultRate]*1.1
     WHERE (((tblClients.StateProvince)="CA"));
```

CAUTION

The actions taken by an Update query, as well as by all Action queries, can't be reversed. You must exercise extreme caution when running any Action query.

CAUTION

It's important to remember that if the Cascade Update Related Fields Referential Integrity setting is turned on and the Update query tried to modify a primary key field, the foreign key of all corresponding records in related tables is updated. If the Cascade Update Related Fields option isn't turned on and referential integrity is being enforced, the Update query doesn't allow the offending records to be modified.

Delete Queries

Rather than simply modify table data, Delete queries permanently remove from a table any records meeting specific criteria; they're often used to remove old records. You might want to delete all orders from the previous year, for example.

To build a Delete query, follow these steps:

1. While in a query's Design View, use the Query Type drop-down list on the toolbar to select Delete Query. You can also choose Query | Delete Query from the menu.

2. Add the criteria you want to the query grid. The query shown in Figure 11.3 deletes all time cards more than 365 days old.

FIGURE 11.3

A Delete query used to delete all time cards entered more than a year ago.

3. Click Run on the toolbar. The message box shown in Figure 11.4 appears. You can suppress this message using the programming techniques explained later in this chapter in the section "Special Notes About Action Queries."

FIGURE 11.4

The Delete query confirmation message box.

4. Click Yes to permanently remove the records from the table.

The SQL behind a Delete query looks like this:

```
DELETE tblTimeCards.DateEntered
    FROM tblTimeCards
    WHERE (((tblTimeCards.DateEntered)<Date()-365));
```

> **NOTE**
>
> It's often useful to view the results of an Action query before you actually affect the records included in the criteria. To view the records affected by the Action query, click the Query View button on the toolbar before you select Run. All records that will be affected by the Action query appear in Datasheet view. If necessary, you can temporarily add key fields to the query to get more information about the records that are about to be affected.

CAUTION

Remember that if the Cascade Delete Related Records Referential Integrity setting is turned on, all corresponding records in related tables are deleted. If the Cascade Delete Related Records option isn't turned on and referential integrity is being enforced, the Delete query doesn't allow the offending records to be deleted. If you want to delete the records on the One side of the relationship, first you need to delete all the related records on the Many side.

Append Queries

With Append queries, you can add records to an existing table. This is often done during an archive process. First, the records to be archived are appended to the history table by using an Append query. Next, they're removed from the master table by using a Delete query.

To build an Append query, follow these steps:

1. While in Design View of a query, use the Query Type drop-down list on the toolbar to select Append Query or choose Query | Append Query from the menu. The dialog box shown in Figure 11.5 appears.

FIGURE 11.5

Identifying which table to which data will be appended and the database containing that table.

2. Select the table to which you want the data appended.

3. Drag all the fields whose data you want included in the second table to the query grid. If the field names in the two tables match, Access automatically matches the field names in the source table to the corresponding field names in the destination table. (See Figure 11.6.) If the field names in the two tables don't match, you need to explicitly designate which fields in the source table match which fields in the destination table.

FIGURE 11.6

An Append query that appends the TimeCardID, EmployeeID, and DateEntered of all employees entered in the year 1995 to another table.

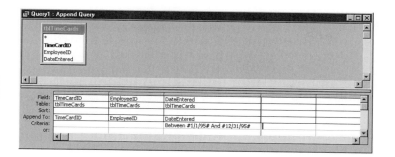

4. Enter any criteria in the query grid. Notice in Figure 11.6 that all records with a DateEntered in 1995 are appended to the destination table.

5. To run the query, click Run on the toolbar. The message box shown in Figure 11.7 appears.

6. Click Yes to finish the process.

FIGURE 11.7

The Append Query confirmation message box.

The SQL behind an Append query looks like this:

```
INSERT INTO tblTimeCardsArchive ( TimeCardID, EmployeeID, DateEntered )
    SELECT tblTimeCards.TimeCardID, tblTimeCards.EmployeeID,
    tblTimeCards.DateEntered
    FROM tblTimeCards
    WHERE (((tblTimeCards.DateEntered) Between #1/1/95# And #12/31/95#));
```

NOTE

Append queries don't allow you to introduce any primary key violations. If you're appending any records that duplicate a primary key value, the message box shown in Figure 11.8 appears. If you go ahead with the append process, only those records without primary key violations are appended to the destination table.

Make Table Queries

An Append query adds records to an existing table, but a Make Table query creates a new table, which is often a temporary table used for intermediary processing. A temporary table is often created to freeze data while a report is being run. By building temporary tables and running the report from those tables, you make sure users can't modify the data underlying the report during the reporting process. Another common use of a Make Table query is to supply a subset of fields or records to another user.

To build a Make Table query, follow these steps:

1. While in the query's Design view, use the Query Type drop-down list on the toolbar to select Make Table Query or choose Query | Make Table Query from the menu. The dialog box shown in Figure 11.9 appears.

FIGURE 11.9
Enter a name for the new table and select which database to place it in.

2. Enter the name of the new table and click OK.

3. Move all the fields you want included in the new table to the query grid. The result of an expression is often included in the new table. (See Figure 11.10.)

FIGURE 11.10
Add an expression to a Make Table query.

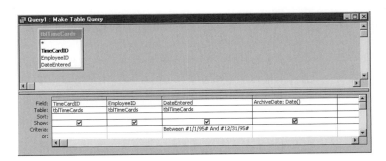

4. Add the criteria you want to the query grid.

5. Click Run on the toolbar to run the query. The message shown in Figure 11.11 appears.

FIGURE 11.11
The Make Table query confirmation message box.

6. Click Yes to finish the process.

CAUTION

If you try to run the same Make Table query more than one time, the table with the same name as the table you're creating is permanently deleted. (See the warning message in Figure 11.12.)

FIGURE 11.12
The Make Table query warning message displayed when a table already exists with the same name as the table to be created.

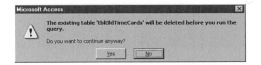

The SQL for a Make Table query looks like this:

```
SELECT tblTimeCards.TimeCardID, tblTimeCards.EmployeeID,
    tblTimeCards.DateEntered, [DateEntered]+365 AS ArchiveDate
    INTO tblOldTimeCards
    FROM tblTimeCards
    WHERE (((tblTimeCards.TimeCardID) Between 1 And 10));
```

Special Notes About Action Queries

Additional warning messages, such as the one shown in Figure 11.13, appear when you're running Action queries from the Database window or using code. This message, and all other query messages, can be suppressed programmatically by using the SetWarnings method of the DoCmd object. The code looks like this:

```
DoCmd.SetWarnings False
```

TIP

I strongly suggest that Docmd.SetWarnings True be used to restore the warning messages immediately after running your Action query. Failure to do so could result in accidental deletion or alteration of data at some later time, without any warning.

FIGURE **11.13**

A warning message you might see when running an Action query from code.

To suppress warnings by modifying the Access environment, choose Tools | Options and click the Edit/Find tab. Remove the checkmark from the Action Queries Confirm checkbox.

NOTE

There's a major difference between suppressing warnings by using the DoCmd object and doing so by choosing Tools | Options. Suppressing warnings by using the DoCmd object centralizes control within the application. On the other hand, using Tools | Options to suppress warnings affects all applications run by a particular user.

Action Queries Versus Processing Records with Code

As mentioned, Action queries can be far more efficient than VBA code. Take a look at this example:

```
Sub ModifyRate()
    Dim rst As ADODB.Recordset

    Set rst = New ADODB.Recordset

    With rst
        .CursorType = adOpenKeyset
        .LockType = adLockOptimistic
        .Open "tblEmployees", CurrentProject.Connection

        Do Until .EOF
            !BillingRate = !BillingRate + 1
            .Update
            .MoveNext
```

```
    Loop
  End With
End Sub
```

This subroutine loops through tblEmployees. It increases the billing rate by 1. Compare the ModifyRate subroutine to the following code:

```
Sub RunActionQuery()
    DoCmd.OpenQuery "qupdBillingRate"
End Sub
```

As you can see, the RunActionQuery subroutine is much easier to code. The qupdBillingRate query, shown in Figure 11.14, performs the same tasks as the ModifyRate subroutine. In most cases, the Action query runs more efficiently.

FIGURE 11.14

The qupdBillingRate query increments the BillingRate by 1.

SPECIAL QUERY PROPERTIES

Access 2000 queries have several properties that can dramatically change their behavior. To look up a query's properties, right-click on a blank area in the top half of the Query window and select Properties to open the Properties window. (See Figure 11.15.) Many of these properties are discussed in Chapter 4 "What Every Developer Needs to Know About Query Basics," but unique values, unique records, and top values are covered in the following sections.

FIGURE 11.15

Viewing the general properties for a query.

Unique Values

The Unique Values property, when set to Yes, causes the query output to contain no duplicates for the combination of fields included in it. Figure 11.16, for example, shows a query that includes the Country and City fields from tblClients. The Unique Values property in this example is set to No, its default value. Notice that many combinations of countries and cities appear more than once. This happens whenever more than one client is found in a particular country and city. Compare this with Figure 11.17, in which the Unique Values property is set to Yes. Each combination of country and city appears only once.

FIGURE 11.16

A query with the Unique Values property set to No.

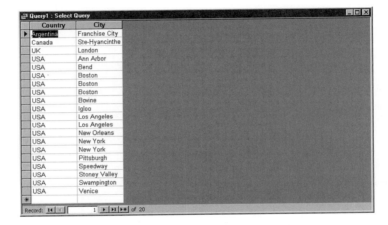

FIGURE 11.17

A query with the Unique Values property set to Yes.

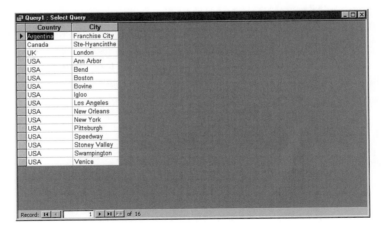

Unique Records

In Access 2000 (a departure from previous versions), the default value for the Unique Records property is No. Setting it to Yes causes the DISTINCTROW statement to be included in the SQL statement underlying the query. The *Unique Records* property applies only to multitable queries; it's ignored for queries that include only one table. The DISTINCTROW statement allows the results of a multitable query to be updated by making sure each record in the query output is unique.

Top Values

The Top Values property enables you to specify a certain percentage or a specific number of records that the user wants to view in the query result. For example, you can build a query that outputs the country/city combinations which have the top 10 sales amounts. You can also build a query that shows the country/city combinations whose sales rank in the top 50 percent. You can specify the Top Values property in a few different ways. Here are two examples:

- Click Top Values combo box on the toolbar and choose from the predefined list of choices (this combo box is not available for certain field types).

- Type a number or a number with a percent sign directly into the Top Values property in the Query Properties window, or select one of the predefined entries from the drop-down list for the property.

Figure 11.18 illustrates the design of a query showing the companies with the top 25 percent of sales. This Totals query summarizes the result of the BillableHours multiplied by the BillingRate for each company. Notice that the Top Values property is set to 25%. The output of the query is sorted in descending order by the result of the TotalAmount calculation. (See Figure 11.19.) If the SaleAmount field were sorted in ascending order, the bottom 10 percent of the sales amount would be displayed in the query result. Remember that the field being used to determine the top values must appear as the left-most field in the query's sort order.

NOTE

You might be surprised to discover that the Top Values property doesn't always seem to accurately display the correct number of records in the query result. All records with values that match the value in the last record are returned as part of the query result. In a table with 100 records, for example, the query asks for the top 10 values. Twelve records will appear in the query result if the 10th, 11th, and 12th records all have the same value in the field being used to determine the top value.

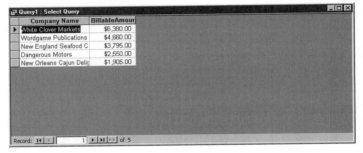

OPTIMIZING QUERIES

The Microsoft Jet Engine includes an Optimizer that looks at how long it takes to perform each task needed to produce the required query results. It then produces a plan for the shortest path to getting the results you want. This plan is based on several statistics:

- The amount of data in each table included in the query
- How many data pages are in each table
- The location of each table included in the query
- What indexes are available in each table
- Which indexes are unique
- Other statistics

Understanding the Query Compilation Process

The statistics just listed are updated whenever the query is compiled. For a query to be compiled, it must be flagged as needing to be compiled. The flag can be any of the following occurrences:

- Changes are saved to the query.
- Changes are saved to any tables underlying a query.
- The database is compacted.

After a query has been flagged as needing to be compiled, it isn't compiled until the next time the query is run. During compiling, which takes one to four seconds, all statistics are updated, and a new optimization or Query Plan is produced.

NOTE

Because a Query Plan is based on the number of records in each table included in the query, you should open and save your queries each time the volume of data in a table changes significantly. This is especially true when you're moving your query from a test environment to a production environment. If you test your application with a few records in each table and the table's production data soon grows to thousands of records, your query will be optimized for only a few records and won't run efficiently. I handle this problem by compacting the production database on a regular basis.

Analyzing a Query's Performance

When you're analyzing the time it takes for a particular query to run, it's important to time two tasks:

- How long it takes for the first screen of data to display
- How long it takes to get the last record in the query result

The first measurement is fairly obvious; it measures the amount of time it takes from the moment the Run button is clicked on the toolbar until the first screen of data is displayed. The second measurement is a little less obvious; it involves waiting until the N value in Record 1 of N displays at the bottom of the query result. The two measurements might be the same, if the query returns only a small number of records. The Jet Engine decides whether it's more efficient to run the query and then display the query results, or to display partial query results while the query continues to run in the background.

> **TIP**
>
> The Performance Analyzer can analyze your queries to determine whether additional indexes will improve query performance. It's important to run the Performance Analyzer with the same volume of data that will be present in the production version of your tables. The Performance Analyzer is covered in Chapter 15, "Optimizing Your Application."

Things You Can Do to Improve a Query's Performance

You can do many things to improve a query's performance. These include, but aren't limited to, the following techniques:

- Index fields on both sides of a join. If you establish a permanent relationship between two tables, the foreign key index is automatically created for you.

- Add to the query grid only the fields you actually need in the query results. If a field is required for criteria, but it doesn't need to appear in the query result, clear the Show check box on the query grid.

- Add indexes for any fields that you are using in the sort order of the query result.

- Always index on fields used in the criteria of the query.

- Compact the database often. During compacting, Access tries to reorganize a table's records so that they reside in adjacent database pages, ordered by the table's primary key. The query plans are also rebuilt, based on the current amount of data. These side effects of the compacting process improve performance when the table is being scanned during a query.

- When running a multitable query, test to see whether the query runs faster with the criteria placed on the One side or the Many side of the join.

- Avoid adding criteria to calculated or nonindexed fields.

- Select the smallest field types possible for each field. For example, create a Long Integer CustID field rather than specifying the CompanyName field as the primary key for the table.

- Avoid calculated fields in nested queries. It's always preferable to add calculations to the higher-level queries.

- Rather than including all expressions in the query, consider placing some expressions in the control source of form and report controls. If you do this, the expression will need to be repeated and maintained on each form and report.

- Use Make Table queries to build tables out of query results based on tables that rarely change. In a State table, for example, rather than displaying a unique list of states on all the states currently included in the Customer table, build a separate State table and use that in your queries.

- When using `Like` in the query criteria, try to place the asterisk at the end of the character string rather than at the beginning. When the asterisk is placed at the end of a string, as in `Like Th*`, an index can be used to improve query performance. If the asterisk is placed at the beginning of a string, as in `Like *Sr`, no index can be used.

- Use `Count(*)` rather than `Count([fieldname])` when counting how many records meet a particular set of criteria. `Count(*)` simply tallies up the total number of records, but `Count([fieldname])` actually checks to see whether the value is `Null`, which would exclude the record from the total computation. Furthermore, as mentioned in the next section on Rushmore technology, the `Count(*)` function is highly optimized by Rushmore.

- Use `Group By` as little as possible. When possible, use `First` instead. For example, if you're totaling sales information by order date and order number, you can use `First` for the order date and group by order number. This is because all records for a given order number automatically occur on the same order date.

- Use Rushmore technology to speed query performance whenever possible. Rushmore technology—a data-access technology "borrowed" from Microsoft's FoxPro PC database engine—improves the performance of certain queries. Rushmore technology is discussed in the following section.

Probably one of the most important things to learn about the tips listed here is that they shouldn't be followed blindly. Query optimization is an art rather than a science. What helps in some situations might actually do harm in others, so it's important to do benchmarks with your actual system and data.

Rushmore Technology

As mentioned, Rushmore is a data-access technology that can help improve processing queries. Rushmore technology can be used only when certain types of expressions are included in the query criteria. It won't automatically speed up all your queries. A query must be constructed in a certain way for the query to benefit from Rushmore.

A query with an expression and comparison operator as the criteria for an Indexed field can be optimized by Rushmore. The comparison operator must be <, >, =, <=, >=, <>, `Between`, `Like`, or `In`.

The expression can be any valid expression, including constants, functions, and fields from other tables. Here are some examples of expressions that can be optimized:

```
[Age] > 50
[OrderDate] Between #1/1/98# And #12/31/98#
[State] = "CA"
```

Rushmore can also be used to optimize queries that include complex expressions combining the And and Or operators. If both expressions are fully optimizable, the query will be fully optimized. However, if only one expression is fully optimizable, and the expressions are combined with an And, the query will be partially optimized. If only one expression is fully optimizable, and the expressions are combined with an Or, the query won't be optimized.

Important Notes About Rushmore

You should remember a few important notes about Rushmore:

- Queries containing the Not operator can't be optimized.
- The Count(*) function is highly optimized by Rushmore.
- Descending indexes cannot be used by Rushmore unless the expression is =.
- Queries on ODBC data sources can't use Rushmore.
- Multifield indexes can be used by Rushmore only when the criteria is in the order of the index. For example, if an index exists for the LastName field in combination with the FirstName field, the index can be used to search on LastName or on a combination of LastName and FirstName, but it can't be used in an expression based on the FirstName field.

CROSSTAB QUERIES

A Crosstab query summarizes query results by displaying one field in a table down the left side of the datasheet and additional facts across the top of the datasheet. A Crosstab query can, for example, summarize the dollars sold by a salesperson to each company. The name of each company can be placed in the query output's left-most column, and each salesperson can be displayed across the top. The dollars sold appear in the appropriate cell of the query output. (See Figure 11.20.)

Crosstab queries are probably one of the most complex and difficult queries to create. For this reason, Microsoft offers a Crosstab Query Wizard. The methods for creating a Crosstab query with and without the Crosstab Query Wizard are explained in the following sections.

FIGURE **11.20**

An example of a Crosstab query that shows the dollars sold to each company by salesperson.

Company Name	Balter, Dan	Callahan, Laura	Davolio, Nancy	Fuller, Andrew	Leverling, Janet
A-1 Rump Steaks				$8,500.00	
Bigfoot Breweries			$2,500.00		$4,000.00
Cheeseburgers for Everybody!	$250,000.00				
Clean Joins Welding					
Dangerous Motors				$2,000.00	
Foreman's Scrapyard		$700.00			
Forets d'erables			$3,700.00		
Fresh Fried Frog Legs					$5,250.00
Grandma Kelly's Homestead					
Hartley Clinic		$2,500.00			
Li'l Green Onion Farm					
New England Seafood Cannery	$30,000.00	$5,000.00			
New Orleans Cajun Delights	$15,000.00		$3,000.00		
Parasailing Promotions	$2,700.00				
Parker's Rock-Climbing Adventu		$2,400.00			
Polar Building Materials	$3,000.00				
Skull Island Cruises		$0.00			

Record: ◄ ◄ 1 ► ►I ►* of 20

Creating a Crosstab Query with the Crosstab Query Wizard

Follow these steps to design a Crosstab query with the Crosstab Query Wizard:

1. Select Queries from the Objects list in the Database window and click New.

2. Select Crosstab Query Wizard and click OK.

3. Select the table or query that will act as a foundation for the query. If you want to include fields from more than one table in the query, you'll need to base the Crosstab query on another query that has the tables and fields you want. Click Next.

4. Select the fields whose values you want to use as the row headings for the query output. In Figure 11.21, the ProductName and CustomerID fields are selected as the row headings. Click Next.

FIGURE **11.21**

Specifying the rows of a Crosstab query.

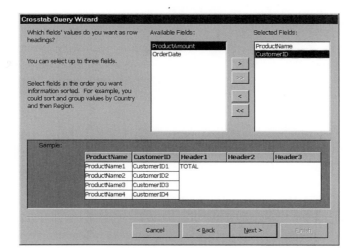

5. Select the field whose values you want to use as the column headings for the query output. In Figure 11.22, the OrderDate field is selected as the column heading. Click Next.

FIGURE **11.22**

Specifying the columns of a Crosstab query.

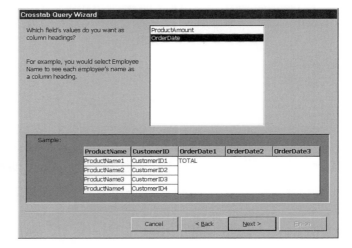

6. If the field you selected for a heading is a Date field, the Crosstab Query Wizard asks that you specify the interval you want to group by. In Figure 11.23, the OrderDate field is grouped by quarter. Select the desired date interval and click Next.

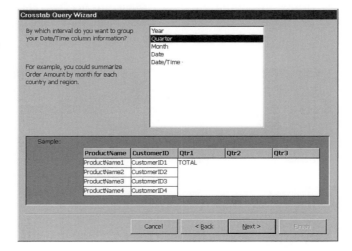

7. The next step of the Crosstab Query Wizard asks you to specify what field stores the number you want to use to calculate the value for each column and row intersection. In

Figure 11.24, the ProductAmount field is totaled by quarter for each product and customer. Click Next.

FIGURE 11.24

Specifying the field you want the Crosstab query to use for calculating.

8. In the final step of the wizard, you specify a name for your query. When you're finished, click Finish.

Figure 11.25 shows a completed Crosstab query in Design View; take a look at several important attributes. Notice the Crosstab row of the query grid. The ProductName and CustomerID fields are specified as row headings and are used as Group By columns for the query. The following expression is included as a Column Heading:

```
"Qtr" & Format([OrderDate], "q")
```

FIGURE 11.25

A completed Crosstab query in Design View.

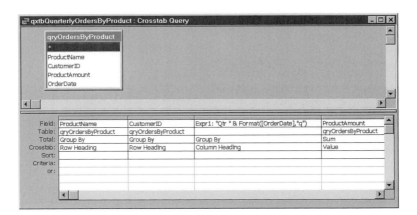

This expression returns the order date formatted to display only the quarter. This expression is also used as a Group By for the query. The ProductAmount is specified as a value. The Total cell for the column indicates that this field will be summed (as opposed to being counted, averaged, and so on).

Notice the column labeled Total of ProductAmount. This column displays the total of all the columns in the query. It's identical to the column containing the value except for the alias in the field name and the fact that the Crosstab cell is set to Row Heading rather than Value, as shown in Figure 11.26.

FIGURE 11.26

A Row Total column in a Crosstab query in Design View.

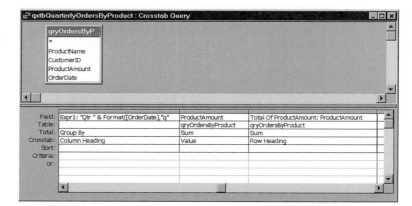

Creating a Crosstab Query Without the Crosstab Query Wizard

Although you can create many of your Crosstab queries by using the Crosstab Query Wizard, you should know how to build one without the wizard. This knowledge lets you modify existing Crosstab queries and gain ultimate control over creating new queries.

To build a Crosstab query without using the Crosstab Query Wizard, follow these steps:

1. Click Queries in the Objects list of the Database window and click New.
2. Double-click Create a Query Design View.
3. Select the table or query that will be included in the query grid. Click Add to add the table or query. Click Close.
4. Use the Query Type drop-down list to select Crosstab Query.
5. Add to the query grid the fields you want to include in the query output.

6. Click the Crosstab row of each field you want to include as a row heading. Select Row Heading from the drop-down list.

7. Click the Crosstab row of the field you want to include as a column heading. Select Column Heading from the drop-down list.

8. Click the Crosstab row of the field whose values you want to cross-tabulate. Select Value from the Crosstab drop-down list.

9. Select the appropriate aggregate function from the Total drop-down list.

10. Add any date intervals or other expressions you want to include.

11. Specify any criteria for the query.

12. Change the sort order of any of the columns, if you like.

13. Run the query when you're ready.

Figure 11.27 shows a query in which the column heading is set to the month of the ProjectBeginDate field; the row heading is set to the EmployeeName field. The sum of the ProjectTotalEstimate field is the value for the query. The OrderDate is also included in the query grid as a WHERE clause for the query. Figure 11.28 shows the results of running the query.

FIGURE 11.27

A Crosstab query, designed without a wizard, showing the project total estimate by employee and month.

FIGURE 11.28

The result of running the Crosstab query shown in Figure 11.27.

Creating Fixed Column Headings

If you don't use fixed column headings, all the columns are included in the query output in alphabetical order. For example, if you include month names in the query result, they appear as Apr, Aug, Dec, Feb, and so on. By using fixed column headings, you tell Access the order in which each column appears in the query result. Column headings can be specified by setting the query's Column Headings. (See Figure 11.29.)

FIGURE 11.29

A query's Column Headings property.

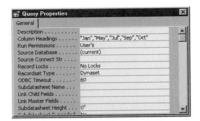

> **NOTE**
>
> All fixed column headings must match the underlying data exactly; otherwise, information will be omitted inadvertently from the query result. For example, if the column heading for the month of June was accidentally entered as June and the data output by the format statement included data for the month of Jun, all June data would be omitted from the query output.

Important Notes About Crosstab Queries

Regardless of how Crosstab queries are created, you should be aware of some special caveats when working with them:

- You can select only one value and one column heading for a Crosstab query, but you can select multiple row headings.
- The results of a Crosstab query can't be updated.

- You can't define criteria on the Value field. If you do, you get the error message You can't specify criteria on the same field for which you enter Value in the Crosstab row. If you must specify criteria for the Value field, you must first build another query that includes your selection criteria, and base the Crosstab query on the first query.

- All parameters used in a Crosstab query must be explicitly declared in the Query Parameters dialog box.

OUTER JOINS

Outer joins are used when you want the records on the One side of a one-to-many relationship to be included in the query result, regardless of whether there are matching records in the table on the Many side. With a Customers table and an Orders table, for example, users often want to include only customers with orders in the query output. An Inner Join (the default join type) does this. In other situations, users want all customers to be included in the query result, whether they have orders or not. This is when an outer join is necessary.

NOTE

There are two types of outer joins: left outer joins and right outer joins. A left outer join occurs when all records on the One side of a one-to-many relationship are included in the query result, regardless of whether any records exist on the Many side. A right outer join means all records on the Many side of a one-to-many relationship are included in the query result, regardless of whether there are any records on the One side. A right outer join should never occur if referential integrity is being enforced.

To establish an outer join, you must modify the join between the tables included in the query:

1. Double-click the line joining the tables in the query grid.
2. The Join Properties window appears. (See Figure 11.30.) Select the type of join you want to create. To create a left outer join between the tables, select Option 2 (Option 3 if you want to create a right outer join). Notice in Figure 11.30 that the description is "Include ALL records from tblClients and only those records from tblProjects where the joined fields are equal."

FIGURE **11.30**

Establishing a left outer join.

3. Click OK to accept the join. An outer join should be established between the tables. Notice that the line joining the two tables now has an arrow pointing to the many side of the join.

The SQL statement produced when a left outer join is established looks like this:

```
SELECT DISTINCTROW tblClients.ClientID, tblClients.CompanyName
FROM tblClients
LEFT JOIN tblProjects ON tblClientss.ClientID = tblProjects.ClientID;
```

A left outer join can also be used to identify all the records on the One side of a join that don't have any corresponding records on the Many side. To do this, simply enter `Is Null` as the criteria for any field on the Many side of the join. In the query shown in Figure 11.31, only clients without projects are displayed in the query result.

FIGURE **11.31**

A query showing clients without projects.

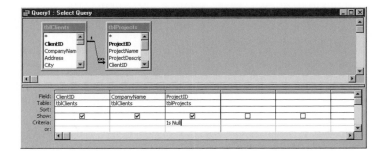

SELF JOINS

A self join enables you to join a table to itself. This is often done so that information in a single table can appear to exist in two separate tables. A classic example is seen with employees and supervisors. Two fields are included in the Employees table; one field includes the EmployeeID of the employee being described in the record, and the other field specifies the

EmployeeID of the employee's supervisor. If you want to see a list of employee names and the names of their supervisors, you'll need to use a self join.

To build a self-join query, follow these steps:

1. Click the Queries tab of the Database window and then click New.

2. Select Design View and click OK.

3. From the Show Tables dialog box, add the table to be used in the self join to the query grid two times. Click Close. Notice that the second instance of the table appears with an underscore and the number 1.

4. To change the alias of the second table, right-click on top of the table in the query grid and select Properties. Change the Alias property as desired. In Figure 11.32, the alias has been changed to Supervisors.

FIGURE 11.32
Building a self join.

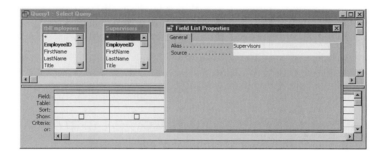

5. To establish a join between the table and its alias, click and drag from the field in one table that corresponds to the field in the aliased table. In Figure 11.33, the SupervisorID field of the tblEmployees table has been joined with the EmployeeID field from the aliased table.

6. Drag the appropriate fields to the query grid. In Figure 11.33, the FirstName and LastName fields are included from the tblEmployees table. The SupervisorName expression (a concatenation of the supervisor's first and last names) is supplied from the copy of the table with the Supervisors alias.

TIP

Self-relationships can be permanently defined in the Relationships window. This is often done so that referential integrity can be established between two fields in the same table. In the example of employees and supervisors, a permanent relationship with referential integrity can be established to make sure supervisor ID numbers aren't entered with employee ID numbers that don't exist.

FIGURE 11.33

Establishing a self join between the table and its alias.

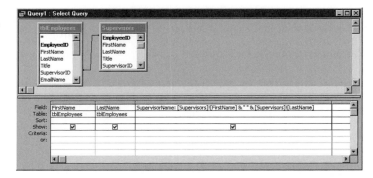

UNDERSTANDING SQL

Access SQL is the language that underlies Access queries, so you need to understand a little bit about it, where it came from, and how it works. Access SQL enables you to construct queries without using the Access QBE (Query By Example) grid. For example, you must build a SQL statement on-the-fly in response to user interaction with your application. Furthermore, certain operations supported by Access SQL aren't supported by the graphical QBE grid. You must build these SQL statements in the Query Builder's SQL view.

What Is SQL and Where Did It Come From?

SQL is a standard from which many different dialects have emerged. It was developed at an IBM research laboratory in the early 1970s and first formally described in a research paper released in 1974 at an Association for Computing Machinery meeting. Jet 4.0, the version of the Jet Engine provided with Access 2000, has two modes, one of which supports Access SQL and the other SQL-92.

What Do You Need to Know About SQL?

At the very least, you need to understand SQL's basic constructs, which enable you to select, update, delete, and append data by using SQL commands and syntax. SQL is actually made up of very few verbs. The most commonly used verbs are discussed in the following sections.

SQL Syntax

SQL is easy to learn. When retrieving data, you simply build a SELECT statement. SELECT statements are composed of clauses that determine the specifics of how the data is selected. When they're executed, SELECT statements select rows of data and return them as a recordset.

The SELECT Clause

The SELECT clause specifies what columns you want to retrieve from the table whose data is being returned to the recordset. The simplest SELECT clause looks like this:

```
SELECT *
```

This SELECT clause retrieves all columns from a table. Here's another example that retrieves only the ClientID and CompanyName columns from a table:

```
SELECT ClientID, CompanyName
```

Not only can you include columns that exist in your table, you can include expressions in a SELECT clause. Here's an example:

```
SELECT ClientID, [City] & ", " & [State] & "  " & [PostalCode] AS Address
```

This SELECT clause retrieves the ClientID column as well as a pseudo-column called Address, which includes an expression that concatenates the City, State, and PostalCode columns.

The FROM Clause

The FROM clause specifies the tables or queries from which the records should be selected. It can include an alias you use to refer to the table. The FROM clause looks like this:

```
FROM tblClients AS Clients
```

In this case, the name of the table is tblClients, and the alias is Clients. If you combine the SELECT clause with the FROM clause, the SQL statement looks like this:

```
SELECT ClientID, CompanyName FROM tblClients
```

This SELECT statement retrieves the ClientID and CompanyName columns from the tblClients table.

The WHERE Clause

The WHERE clause limits the records retrieved by the SELECT statement. A WHERE clause can include up to 40 columns combined by the keywords AND and OR. A simple WHERE clause looks like this:

```
WHERE Country = "USA"
```

Using an AND to further limit the criteria, the WHERE clause looks like this:

```
WHERE Country = "USA" AND ContactTitle Like "Sales*"
```

This WHERE clause limits the records returned to those in which the country is equal to USA and the ContactTitle begins with Sales. Using an OR, the SELECT statement looks like this:

```
WHERE Country = "USA" OR Country = "Canada"
```

This WHERE clause returns all records in which the country is equal to either USA or Canada. Compare that with the following example:

```
WHERE Country = "USA" OR ContactTitle Like "Sales*"
```

This WHERE clause returns all records in which the country is equal to USA or the ContactTitle begins with Sales. For example, the salespeople in China will be returned from this WHERE clause because their ContactTitle begins with Sales. The WHERE clause combined with the SELECT and FROM clauses looks like this:

```
SELECT ClientID, CompanyName FROM tblClients
    WHERE Country = "USA" OR Country = "Canada"
```

The ORDER BY Clause

The ORDER BY clause determines the order in which the returned rows are sorted. It's an optional clause and looks like this:

```
ORDER BY ClientID
```

The ORDER BY clause can include more than one field:

```
ORDER BY Country, ClientID
```

When more than one field is specified, the left-most field is used as the primary level of sort. Any additional fields are the lower sort levels. Combined with the rest of the SELECT statement, the ORDER BY clause looks like this:

```
SELECT ClientID, CompanyName FROM tblClients
    WHERE Country = "USA" OR Country = "Canada"
    ORDER BY ClientID
```

The JOIN Clause

Often you'll need to build SELECT statements that retrieve data from more than one table. When building a SELECT statement based on more than one table, you must join the tables with a JOIN clause. The JOIN clause differs depending on whether you join the tables with an INNER JOIN, a LEFT OUTER JOIN, or a RIGHT OUTER JOIN. Here's an example of an INNER JOIN:

```
SELECT DISTINCTROW tblClients.ClientID,
    tblClients.CompanyName, tblProjects.ProjectName,
    tblProjects.ProjectDescription
    FROM tblClients
    INNER JOIN tblProjects ON tblClients.ClientID = tblProjects.ClientID
```

Notice that four columns are returned in the query result. Two columns are from tblClients and two are from tblProjects. The SELECT statement uses an INNER JOIN from tblClients to tblProjects based on the ClientID field. This means that only clients who have projects are displayed in the query result. Compare this with the following SELECT statement:

```
SELECT DISTINCTROW tblClients.ClientID,
    tblClients.CompanyName, tblProjects.ProjectName,
    tblProjects.ProjectDescription
    FROM tblClients
    LEFT JOIN tblProjects ON tblClients.ClientID = tblProjects.ClientID
```

This SELECT statement joins the two tables using a LEFT JOIN from tblClients to tblProjects based on the ClientID field. All clients are included in the resulting records, whether they have projects or not.

NOTE

The word OUTER is assumed in the LEFT JOIN clause used when building a left outer join.

ALL, DISTINCTROW, and DISTINCT Clauses

The ALL clause of a SELECT statement means that all rows meeting the WHERE clause are included in the query result. When the DISTINCT keyword is used, Access eliminates duplicate rows, based on the fields included in the query result. This is the same as setting the Unique Values property to Yes in the graphical QBE grid. When the DISTINCTROW keyword is used, Access eliminates any duplicate rows based on all columns of all tables included in the query (whether they appear in the query result or not). This is the same as setting the Unique Records property to Yes in the graphical QBE grid.

The GROUP BY Clause

The GROUP BY clause is used to calculate summary statistics; it's created when you build a Totals query by using the graphical QBE grid. In the following example, the SELECT statement returns the country, city, and total freight for each country/city combination:

```
SELECT DISTINCTROW tblCustomers.Country, tblCustomers.City,
    Sum(tblOrders.Freight) AS SumOfFreight
    FROM tblCustomers
    INNER JOIN tblOrders ON tblCustomers.CustomerID = tblOrders.CustomerID
    GROUP BY tblCustomers.Country, tblCustomers.City
```

The GROUP BY clause indicates that detail for the selected records isn't displayed. Instead, the fields indicated in the GROUP BY clause are displayed uniquely. One of the fields in the SELECT statement must include an aggregate function. This result of the aggregate function is displayed along with the fields specified in the GROUP BY clause.

The HAVING Clause

A HAVING clause is similar to a WHERE clause, but it differs in one major respect: It's applied after the data is summarized rather than before. In the following example, the criteria > 1000 will be applied after the aggregate function SUM is applied to the grouping:

```
SELECT DISTINCTROW tblCustomers.Country, tblCustomers.City,
    Sum(tblOrders.Freight) AS SumOfFreight
    FROM tblCustomers
    INNER JOIN tblOrders ON tblCustomers.CustomerID = tblOrders.CustomerID
    GROUP BY tblCustomers.Country, tblCustomers.City
    HAVING (((Sum(tblOrders.Freight))>1000))
```

Applying What You Have Learned

You can practice entering and working with SQL statements in two places:

- In a query's SQL View window
- In VBA code

Now take a look at both these techniques.

Using the Graphical QBE Grid as a Two-Way Tool

A great place to practice writing SQL statements is in the SQL View window of a query. It works like this:

1. Start by building a new query.
2. Add a couple of fields and maybe even some criteria.
3. Use the Query View drop-down list on the Query Design toolbar to select SQL View.
4. Try changing the SQL statement, using what you have learned in this chapter.
5. Use the Query View drop-down list on the Query Design toolbar to select Design View. As long as you haven't violated any Access SQL syntax rules, you can easily switch to the query's Design View and see the graphical result of your changes. If you've introduced any syntax errors into the SQL statement, an error occurs when you try to return to the query's Design View.

Including SQL Statements in VBA Code

SQL statements can also be executed directly from VBA code. You can run a SQL statement from VBA code in two ways:

- You can build a temporary query and execute it.
- You can open a recordset with the SQL statement as the foundation for the recordset.

The VBA language enables you to build a query on-the-fly, execute it, and never store it. The parentheses are omitted in the following CurrentDB function because VBA doesn't require parentheses with functions that have no arguments. You can decide whether to include them. The code looks like this:

```
Sub CreateTempQuery()
    Dim cmd As ADODB.Command
    Dim rst As ADODB.Recordset

    Set cmd = New ADODB.Command
    With cmd
        .ActiveConnection = CurrentProject.Connection
        .CommandText = "Select ProjectID, ProjectName from " & _
            "tblProjects Where ProjectTotalEstimate > 30000"
        .CommandType = adCmdText
        .Prepared = True
        Set rst = .Execute
    End With

    Do Until rst.EOF
        Debug.Print rst!ProjectID, rst!ProjectName
        rst.MoveNext
    Loop

End Sub
```

Working with recordsets is covered extensively in Chapter 12, "What Are Data Access Objects and Why Are They Important?" For now, you need to understand that this code creates a temporary query definition using a SQL statement. In this example, the query definition is never added to the database. Instead, the SQL statement is executed but never stored.

A SQL statement can also be provided as part of the recordset's Open method. The code looks like this:

```
Sub OpenRWithSQL()
    Dim rst As ADODB.Recordset

    Set rst = New ADODB.Recordset

    rst.Open "Select ProjectId, ProjectName from " & _
        "tblProjects Where ProjectTotalEstimate > 30000", _
        CurrentProject.Connection

    Do Until rst.EOF
        Debug.Print rst!ProjectID, rst!ProjectName
        rst.MoveNext
    Loop
End Sub
```

Again, this code is discussed more thoroughly in Chapter 12. Notice that the Open method of the recordset object receives two parameters: The first is a SELECT statement, and the second is the Connection object.

UNION QUERIES

A Union query enables you to combine data from two tables with similar structures; data from each table is included in the output. For example, say you have a tblTimeCards table containing active time cards and a tblTimeCardsArchive table containing archived time cards. The problem occurs when you want to build a report that combines data from both tables. To do this, you must build a Union query as the record source for the report:

1. Click Queries in the list of objects in the Database window and double-click Create Query in Design View.
2. Click Close from the Show Tables dialog box without selecting a table.
3. Choose Query | SQL Specific | Union to open a SQL window.
4. Type in the SQL UNION clause. Notice that you can't switch back to the query's Design View. (See Figure 11.34.)
5. Click the Run button on the toolbar to execute the query.

FIGURE **11.34**

An example of a Union query that joins tblTimeCards with tblTimeCards-Archive.

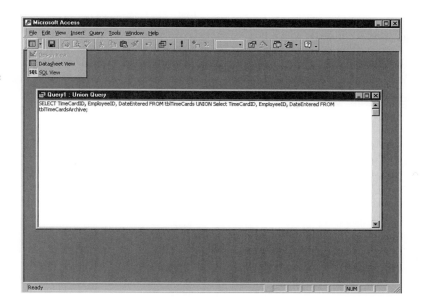

PASS-THROUGH QUERIES

Pass-Through queries enable you to send uninterpreted SQL statements to your back-end database when you're using something other than the Jet Engine. These uninterpreted statements are in the SQL that's specific to your particular back-end. Although the Jet Engine sees these SQL statements, it makes no attempt to parse or modify them. Pass-Through queries are used in several situations:

- The action you want to take is supported by your back-end database server, but not by Access SQL or ODBC SQL.
- Access or the ODBC driver is doing a poor job parsing the SQL statement and sending it in an optimized form to the back-end database.
- You want to execute a stored procedure on the back-end database server.
- You want to make sure the SQL statement is executed on the server.
- You want to join data from more than one table residing on the database server. If you execute the join without a Pass-Through query, the join is done in the memory of the user's PC after all the required data has been sent over the network.

Although Pass-Through queries offer many advantages, they aren't a panacea. They do have a few disadvantages:

- Because you're sending SQL statements specific to your particular database server, you'll need to rewrite all the SQL statements if you switch to another back-end.
- The results returned from a Pass-Through query can't be updated.
- The Jet Engine does no syntax checking of the query before passing it on to the back-end.

Now that you know all the advantages and disadvantages of Pass-Through queries, you can learn how to build one:

1. Click Queries in the list of objects in the Database window, then and double-click Create Query in Design View.
2. Click Close from the Show Tables dialog box without selecting a table.
3. Choose Query | SQL Specific | Pass-Through to open the SQL Design window.
4. Type in the SQL statement in the dialect of your back-end database server.
5. View the Query Properties window and enter an ODBC connect string. (See Figure 11.35.)

FIGURE 11.35

A SQL Pass-Through query that selects specific fields from the Sales table, which resides in the PublisherInfo data source.

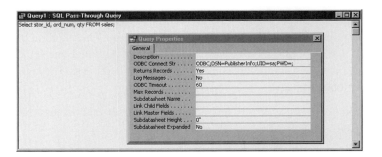

6. Click the Run button on the toolbar to run the query.

THE PROPAGATION OF Nulls AND QUERY RESULTS

Null values can wreak havoc with your query results because they propagate. Take a look at the query in Figure 11.36. Notice that when parts and labor are added, and either the parts or labor field contains a `Null`, the result of adding the two fields is `Null`. In Figure 11.37, the problem is rectified. Notice the expression that adds the two values:

```
TotalPrice: Nz([Parts]) + Nz([Labor])
```

This expression uses the `Nz` function to convert the `Null` values to zero before the two field values are added together.

FIGURE 11.36

Propagation of `Null`s *in a query result.*

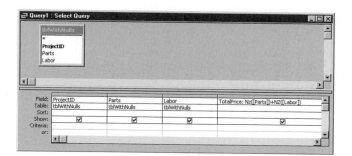

FIGURE 11.37

A solution to eliminate propagation of `Null`s.

SUBQUERIES

Subqueries allow you to embed one `SELECT` statement within another. By placing a subquery in a query's criteria, you can base one query on the result of another. Figure 11.38 shows an example. The query pictured finds all the clients without projects. The SQL statement looks like this:

```
SELECT DISTINCTROW tblClients.ClientID,
    tblClients.CompanyName FROM tblClients
    WHERE tblClients.ClientID Not In (Select ClientID from tblProjects)
```

This query first runs the `SELECT` statement `Select ClientID from` `tblProjects`. It uses the result as criteria for the first query.

FIGURE 11.38

A query containing a subquery.

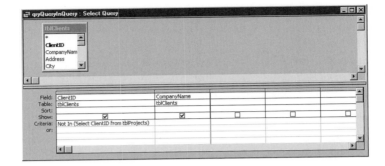

USING THE RESULT OF A FUNCTION AS THE CRITERIA FOR A QUERY

Many people are unaware that the result of a function can serve as an expression in a query or as a parameter to a query. The query shown in Figure 11.39 evaluates the result of a function called `Initials`. The return value from the function is evaluated with criteria to determine whether the employee is included in the query result. The `Initials` function shown below (it's also in the basUtils module of CHAP11EX.MDB, found on the sample code CD-ROM) receives two strings and returns the first character of each string followed by a period:

```
Function Initials(strFirstName As String, _
    strLastName As String) As String
  Initials = Left(strFirstName, 1) & "." & _
    Left(strLastName, 1) & "."
End Function
```

FIGURE 11.39

A query that uses the result of a function as an expression.

The return value from a function can also be used as the criteria for a query. (See Figure 11.40.) The query in the figure uses a function called `HighlyPaid` to determine which records appear in the query result. Here's what the `HighlyPaid` function looks like. (It's also in the basUtils module of CHAP12EX.MDB, found on the sample code CD-ROM.)

```
Function HighlyPaid(strTitle) As Currency
   Dim curHighRate As Currency
   Select Case strTitle
      Case "Sr. Programmer"
         curHighRate = 60
      Case "Systems Analyst"
         curHighRate = 80
      Case "Project Manager"
         curHighRate = 100
      Case Else
         curHighRate = 50
   End Select
   HighlyPaid = curHighRate
End Function
```

The function receives the employee's title as a parameter. It then evaluates the title and returns a threshold value to the query that's used as the criteria for the query's Billing Rate column.

FIGURE 11.40

A query that uses the result of a function as criteria.

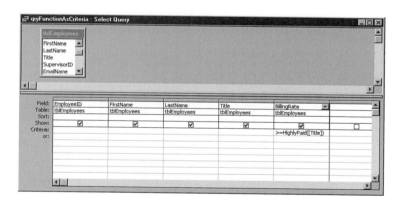

PASSING PARAMETER QUERY VALUES FROM A FORM

The biggest frustration with Parameter queries occurs when multiple parameters are required to run the query. The user is confronted with multiple dialog boxes, one for each parameter in the query. The following steps explain how to build a Parameter query that receives its parameter values from a form:

1. Create a new unbound form.
2. Add text boxes or other controls to accept the criteria for each parameter added to your query.
3. Name each control so that you can readily identify the data it contains.
4. Add a command button to the form and instruct it to call the Parameter query. (See Figure 11.41.)

FIGURE 11.41

The Click *event code of the command button that calls the Parameter query.*

5. Save the form.
6. Create the query and add the parameters to it. Each parameter should refer to a control on the form. (See Figure 11.42.)

FIGURE 11.42

Parameters that refer to controls on a form.

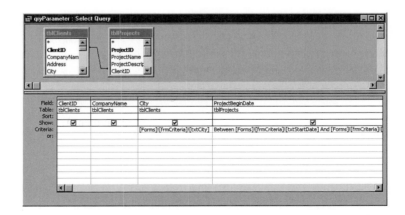

7. Right-click the top half of the Query Design grid and select Parameters. Define a data type for each parameter in the Parameters dialog box. (See Figure 11.43.)

FIGURE 11.43

The Parameters dialog box lets you select the data type for each parameter in the query.

8. Save and close the query.

9. Fill in the values on the criteria form and click the command button to execute the query. It should execute successfully.

PRACTICAL EXAMPLES

Applying These Techniques in Your Application

The advanced query techniques you have learned will be used while you're creating the Time and Billing application. Take a look at several practical applications of these advanced techniques.

NOTE

The examples shown in this section are included in the CHAP11.MDB database on the sample code CD-ROM.

Archive Payments

After a while, you might need to archive some of the data in the tblPayment table. Two queries archive the payment data. The first, called qappAppendToPaymentArchive, is an Append query that sends all data in a specified date range to an archive table called tblPaymentsArchive. (See Figure 11.44.) The second query, called qdelRemoveFromPayments, is a Delete query that deletes all the data archived from the tblPayments table. (See Figure 11.45.) The archiving is run from a form called frmArchivePayments, where the date range can be specified by the user at runtime. (See Figure 11.46.)

FIGURE 11.44

The Append query qappAppendTo-PaymentArchive.

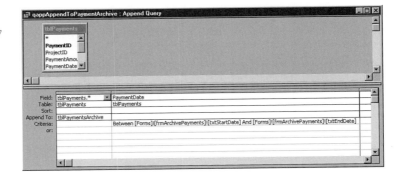

FIGURE 11.45

The Delete query qdelRemoveFrom-Payments.

FIGURE 11.46

The form that supplies criteria for the archive process.

Show All Payments

At times, you might want to combine data from both tables. To do this, you'll need to create a Union query that joins tblPayments to tblPaymentsArchive. The query's design is shown in Figure 11.47.

FIGURE 11.47

Using a Union query to join tblPayments to tblPayments-Archive.

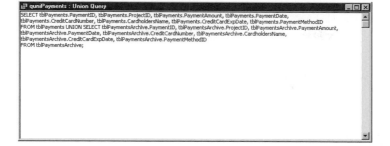

Create State Table

Because you'll regularly be looking up the states and provinces, you want to build a unique list of all the states and provinces your clients are currently located in. The query needed to do this is shown in Figure 11.48. The query uses the tblClients table to come up with all the unique values for the StateProvince field. The query is a `Make Table` query that takes the unique list of values and outputs it to a tblStateProvince table.

FIGURE 11.48

A Make Table query that creates a tblStateProvince table.

SUMMARY

As you can see, Microsoft gives you a sophisticated query builder for constructing complex and powerful queries. Action queries let you modify table data without writing code; these highly efficient queries can be used to add, edit, or delete table data. The Unique Values and Top Values properties of a query offer you flexibility in determining exactly what data is returned in your query result.

Many things can be done to improve your queries' efficiency. A little attention to the details covered in this chapter can give you dramatic improvements in your application's performance.

Other special types of queries covered in this chapter include Crosstab queries, outer joins, and self joins. Whatever can't be done by using the graphical QBE grid can be accomplished by typing the required SQL statement directly into the SQL View window. In this window, you can type Access SQL statements or use SQL Pass-Through to type SQL statements in the SQL dialect that's specific to your back-end database.

WHAT ARE ACTIVEX DATA OBJECTS AND DATA ACCESS OBJECTS AND WHY ARE THEY IMPORTANT?

IN THIS CHAPTER

UNDERSTANDING DATA ACCESS OBJECTS

ActiveX Data Objects (ADO) and Data Access Objects (DAO) are used to create, modify, and remove Jet Engine objects via code. They give you the flexibility to move beyond the user interface to manipulate data stored in the Jet Engine and other formats. You can use either ActiveX Data Objects or Data Access Objects to perform these tasks:

- Analyze the structure of an existing database
- Add or modify tables and queries
- Create new databases
- Change the underlying definitions for queries by modifying the SQL on which the query is based
- Traverse through sets of records
- Modify table data

USING ACTIVEX DATA OBJECTS VERSUS DATA ACCESS OBJECTS

The previous editions of this book referred only to Data Access Objects (DAO). There was no mention of ActiveX Data Objects (ADO). This is because ActiveX Data Objects were only in their infancy when Access 97 was released. When I began writing this book, I was faced with a decision as to whether to cover ADO, DAO, or both. I pondered the question for quite some time. Although I recommend that all new development be done using ADO, it is premature to entirely remove coverage of DAO from this book. I made the decision to cover both ADO and DAO in this chapter. The first half of this chapter covers ADO. If you are developing a new application or have the liberty of rebuilding an existing application, the first half of the chapter is for you. If you are unfamiliar with DAO and need to work with existing applications, the second half of the chapter provides you with the basics of DAO. Finally, if you are already familiar with DAO and want to compare and contrast DAO and ADO, this chapter shows you how to perform each task using both data access methodologies.

> **NOTE**
>
> Although DAO is covered in this chapter, the remainder of the book uses ADO to perform all necessary data access tasks. If you want further information on DAO, consult *Alison Balter's Mastering Access 97 Development*.

EXAMINING THE ACTIVEX DATA OBJECT MODEL

Figure 12.1 shows an overview of the Microsoft ActiveX Data Object (ADO) model. Unlike the Data Access Object (DAO) model, the ADO object model is not hierarchical.

FIGURE 12.1

The ADO object model.

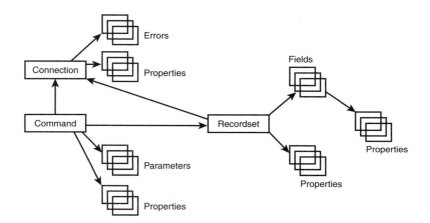

The `Connection` Object

The `Connection` object defines a session for a user for a data source. Although the ADO object model is not considered to be hierarchical, the `Connection` object is considered the highest-level ADO object. After you have established a `Connection` object, you can use it with multiple recordsets. This improves performance and greatly simplifies your programming code.

A `Connection` object must be declared before it is used. The declaration looks like this:

```
Dim cnn as ADODB.Connection
```

After the `Connection` object has been declared, a new `Connection` object must be instantiated. The code looks like this:

```
Set cnn = New ADODB.Connection
```

The `Connection` must then be opened. The `Open` method of the `Connection` object receives a connection string, and optionally a user ID, password, and options as a parameter. The following is an example of the simplest use of the `Open` method:

```
cnn.Open CurrentProject.Connection
```

This example uses the `Open` method of the `Connection` object to open the connection. The connection string parameter is supplied by a connection string that is returned from the

Connection property of the CurrentProject object. This opens a connection based on the connection associated with the current database. The reference to the connection associated with the current project can be changed to look like this:

```
cnn.Open "Provider=Microsoft.Jet.OLEDB.4.0;" & _
    "Persist Security Info=False;" & _
    "User ID=Admin;" & _
    "Data Source=Q:\Clients\sams\" & _
        "Mastering Access 2000 Development\Databases" & _
    "\Chap12Ex.mdb;"
```

The complete routine required to establish a connection appears in Listing 12.1.

LISTING 12.1   CREATING A Connection OBJECT

```
Sub CreateConnection()
    Dim cnn As ADODB.Connection
    Set cnn = New ADODB.Connection
    cnn.Open CurrentProject.Connection
    cnn.Close
    Set cnn = Nothing
End Sub
```

NOTE

Listing 12.1 and most code in this chapter is located in the CHAP12EX.MDB file included with this book's CD-ROM.

The Recordset Object

A Recordset object is used to look at records as a group. A Recordset object refers to the set of rows returned from a request for data. As with a Connection object, to use a Recordset object, you must first declare it. The code looks like this:

```
Dim rst as ADODB.Recordset
```

After the Recordset object has been declared, it must be instantiated. The code looks like this:

```
Set rst = New ADODB.Recordset
```

As with a Connection object, the Open method is used to point the Recordset object at a set of records. The code looks like this:

```
rst.Open "Select * From tblClients", CurrentProject.Connection
```

The first parameter of the Open method is the source of the data. The source can be a table name, a SQL statement, a stored procedure name, a Command object variable name, or the file name of a persisted recordset. In the example, the source is a SQL select statement.

The second parameter of the Open method must be either a valid connection string, or the name of a Connection object. In the example, the Connection property of the CurrentProject object returns a string. The string is used as the connection string. The completed code appears in Listing 12.2.

LISTING 12.2   CREATING A RECORDSET USING A CONNECTION STRING

```
Sub CreateRecordset1()
    Dim rst As ADODB.Recordset
    Set rst = New ADODB.Recordset
    rst.Open "Select * From tblClients", CurrentProject.Connection
    Debug.Print rst.GetString
    rst.Close
    Set rst = Nothing
End Sub
```

12

Notice that after the recordset is opened, the result of the GetString method of the Recordset object is printed to the Immediate window. The GetString method of the Recordset object builds a string based on the data contained in the recordset. For now, this is a simple way of verifying that your code works as expected. Also note that the Close method of the Recordset object is used to close the recordset. The Close method, when applied to either a Connection object, or to a Recordset object, has the effect of freeing the associated system resources. The Close method does not eliminate the object from memory. Setting the Recordset object equal to Nothing eliminates the object from memory.

Although this syntax works quite well, I prefer to set the parameters of the Open method as properties of the Recordset object, before the Open method is issued. You will see that this makes your code much more readable as you add parameters to the Open method. The code appears in Listing 12.3.

LISTING 12.3   CREATING A RECORDSET USING THE ActiveConnection PROPERTY

```
Sub CreateRecordset2()
    Dim rst As ADODB.Recordset
    Set rst = New ADODB.Recordset
    rst.ActiveConnection = CurrentProject.Connection
    rst.Open "Select * From tblClients"
    Debug.Print rst.GetString
    rst.Close
    Set rst = Nothing
End Sub
```

Finally, a Connection object can be used instead of the Connection string. The same Connection object can be used for multiple recordsets. The code appears in Listing 12.4.

LISTING 12.4   CREATING A RECORDSET USING A Connection OBJECT

```
Sub CreateRecordset3()
    Dim cnn As ADODB.Connection
    Dim rst1 As ADODB.Recordset
    Dim rst2 As ADODB.Recordset

    Set cnn = New ADODB.Connection
    Set rst1 = New ADODB.Recordset
    Set rst2 = New ADODB.Recordset

    cnn.ConnectionString = CurrentProject.Connection
    cnn.Open

    rst1.ActiveConnection = cnn
    rst1.Open "Select * From tblClients"
    rst2.ActiveConnection = cnn
    rst2.Open "Select * From tblPayments"

    Debug.Print rst1.GetString
    Debug.Print rst2.GetString

    rst1.Close
    rst2.Close
    cnn.Close

    Set rst1 = Nothing
    Set rst2 = Nothing
    Set cnn = Nothing

End Sub
```

Notice that both rst1 and rst2 use the same Connection object.

The Command Object

The ADO Command object represents a query, SQL statement, or stored procedure that is executed against a data source. Although not always necessary, a Command object is particularly useful when executing parameterized queries and stored procedures. Just as with the Connection object and the Recordset object, the Command object must be declared before it is used:

```
Dim cmd as ADODB.Command
```

Next the `Command` object must be instantiated:

```
Set cmd = New ADODB.Command
```

After the `Command` object has been instantiated, you must set its `ActiveConnection` property and its `CommandText` property. As with a `Recordset` object, the `ActiveConnection` property can be either a connection string or a reference to a `Connection` object. The `CommandText` property is the SQL statement or stored procedure used by the `Command` object. The `ActiveConnection` and the `CommandText` properties look like this:

```
cmd.ActiveConnection = CurrentProject.Connection
cmd.CommandText = "tblClients"
```

The completed code appears in Listing 12.5.

LISTING 12.5   USING A `Command` OBJECT

```
Sub CommandObject()
    Dim rst As ADODB.Recordset
    Dim cmd As ADODB.Command

    Set cmd = New ADODB.Command

    cmd.CommandText = "Select * from tblClients"
    cmd.ActiveConnection = CurrentProject.Connection

    Set rst = cmd.Execute
    Debug.Print rst.GetString

    rst.Close

    Set cmd = Nothing
    Set rst = Nothing
End Sub
```

In the example, the `Command` object is instantiated. The `CommandText` property is set to a SQL `Select` statement and the `ActiveConnection` property is pointed to the connection associated with the current database. The `Execute` method of the `Command` object is used to return the results of the SQL statement into the `Recordset` object.

UNDERSTANDING ADO RECORDSET TYPES

There are three parameters of the `Open` method of a `Recordset` object that affect the type of recordset that is created. They are the `CursorType`, the `LockType`, and the `Options` parameters.

These parameters combine to determine the types of movements that can be executed within a recordset, when changes other users make to data underlying the recordset are seen, and whether the recordset's data is updateable.

The `CursorType`

By default, when you open a recordset, the `CursorType` parameter is set to `adOpenForwardOnly`. This means that you can only move forward through the records in the recordset. You will not see any adds, edits, or deletions that other users make. Furthermore, many properties and methods, such as the `RecordCount` property and the `MovePrevious` method, are unavailable.

Three other values are available for the `CursorType`. They are `adOpenStatic`, `adOpenKeyset`, and `adOpenDynamic`. The `adOpenStatic` option allows forward and backward movement through the records in the recordset, but changes that other users make to the underlying data are not seen by the recordset. The `adOpenKeyset` option offers everything offered by the `adOpenStatic` option, but in addition, edits that other users make are seen by the recordset. Finally, with the `adOpenDynamic` option, adds, edits, and deletions made by other users are seen by the recordset.

The `CursorType` property of the recordset can be set in one of two ways. It can be set as a parameter of the `Open` method of the `Recordset` object. Listing 12.6 illustrates this.

LISTING 12.6 SUPPLYING THE `CursorType` AS A PARAMETER OF THE `Open` METHOD

```
Sub StaticRecordset1()
    Dim rst As ADODB.Recordset
    Set rst = New ADODB.Recordset

    rst.ActiveConnection = CurrentProject.Connection
    rst.Open "Select * from tblClients", _
        CursorType:=adOpenStatic
    Debug.Print rst.RecordCount

    rst.Close
    Set rst = Nothing


End Sub
```

Notice that in Listing 12.6, the `CursorType` appears as a parameter of the `Open` method. Contrast Listing 12.6 with Listing 12.7.

LISTING 12.7 SUPPLYING THE CursorType AS A PROPERTY OF THE Recordset OBJECT

```
Sub StaticRecordset2()
    Dim rst As ADODB.Recordset
    Set rst = New ADODB.Recordset

    rst.ActiveConnection = CurrentProject.Connection
    rst.CursorType = adOpenStatic
    rst.Open "Select * from tblClients"
    Debug.Print rst.RecordCount

    rst.Close
    Set rst = Nothing

End Sub
```

In Listing 12.7 the CursorType is set as a property of the Recordset object, prior to the execution of the Open method. Separating the properties from the Open method improves readability of the code.

The LockType

Although the CursorType property of a Recordset object determines how movements can occur within the recordset, and whether other users' changes are seen, the CursorType in no way affects the updateability of the recordset's data. In fact, when a recordset is opened, it is opened as read-only by default. It is only by changing the LockType property that you can make the recordset updateable.

The options for lock type are adLockReadOnly, adLockPessimistic, adLockOptimistic, and adLockBatchOptimistic. The default, adLockReadOnly, does not allow changes to be made to the recordset. The other options all provide updateability for the recordset's data. The differences lie in when the records are locked. With the adLockPessimistic option, the record is locked as soon as the editing process begins. With the adLockOptimistic option, the record is locked when the Update method is issued. Finally, with the adLockBatchOptimistic, you can postpone locking until a batch of records are updated. All these options are discussed further in Chapter 17, "Developing Multiuser Applications."

As with the CursorType property, the LockType property can be set as a parameter of the Open method or as a property of the Recordset object. Listing 12.8 shows the configuration of the lock type as a property of the Recordset object.

LISTING 12.8 CONFIGURATION OF THE LockType PROPERTY

```
Sub OptimisticRecordset()
    Dim rst As ADODB.Recordset
    Set rst = New ADODB.Recordset

    rst.ActiveConnection = CurrentProject.Connection
    rst.CursorType = adOpenStatic
    rst.LockType = adLockOptimistic
    rst.Open "Select * from tblClients"
    rst!City = "Westlake Village"
    rst.Update
    Debug.Print rst!City

    rst.Close
    Set rst = Nothing

End Sub
```

In Listing 12.8, the LockType property is set to adLockOptimistic. The record is locked when the Update method of the Recordset object is issued.

The Options Parameter

The Options parameter determines how the provider should establish the source argument. The valid choices are illustrated in Table 12.1.

TABLE 12.1 VALID CHOICES FOR THE Options PARAMETER

Value	Description
adCmdText	The provider evaluates the source as a command
adCmdTable	A SQL query is generated to return all rows from the table named in the source
adCmdTableDirect	The provider returns all rows in the table named in the source
adCmdStoredProc	The provider evaluates the source as a stored procedure
adCmdUnknown	The type of command in the source is unknown
adCmdFile	The source is evaluated as a persisted recordset
adAsyncExecute	The source is executed asynchronously
adAsyncFetch	The initial quantity specified in the Initial Fetch Size property is fetched
adAsyncFetchNonBlocking	The main thread never blocks when fetching

The default for the `Options` parameter is `adCmdUnknown`. If the `Options` parameter is not explicitly specified, the provider attempts to evaluate it while the code is running. This degrades performance. It is therefore important to specify the parameter. Listing 12.9 illustrates the use of the `Options` parameter of the `Open` method.

LISTING 12.9   THE `Options` PARAMETER OF THE `Open` METHOD

```
Sub OptionsParameter()
    Dim rst As ADODB.Recordset
    Set rst = New ADODB.Recordset

    rst.ActiveConnection = CurrentProject.Connection
    rst.CursorType = adOpenStatic
    rst.LockType = adLockOptimistic
    rst.Open "Select * from tblClients", _
        Options:=adCmdText
    rst!City = "Westlake Village"
    rst.Update
    Debug.Print rst!City

    rst.Close
    Set rst = Nothing


End Sub
```

In Listing 12.9, the `Options` parameter is set to `adCmdText`. This causes the source to be evaluated as a SQL command.

WORKING WITH ADO RECORDSET PROPERTIES AND METHODS

The ADO `Recordset` object is rich with properties and methods. These properties and methods allow you to move through a recordset, sort, filter, and find data, as well as update data contained with the recordset. The most commonly used properties and methods are covered in the sections that follow.

Examining Record-Movement Methods

When you have a `Recordset` object variable set, you probably want to manipulate the data in the recordset. Table 12.2 shows several methods you can use to traverse through the records in a recordset.

TABLE 12.2   METHODS FOR MOVING THROUGH THE RECORDS IN A RECORDSET

Method	*Moves*
MoveFirst	To the first record in a recordset
MoveLast	To the last record in a recordset
MovePrevious	To the previous record in a recordset
MoveNext	To the next record in a recordset

Listing 12.10 shows an example of using the record-movement methods on a `Recordset` object.

LISTING 12.10   Recordset MOVEMENT METHODS

```
Sub RecordsetMovements()
    Dim rst As ADODB.Recordset

    Set rst = New ADODB.Recordset
    rst.ActiveConnection = CurrentProject.Connection
    rst.CursorType = adOpenStatic
    rst.Open "Select * from tblProjects"

    Debug.Print rst!ProjectID
    rst.MoveNext
    Debug.Print rst!ProjectID
    rst.MoveLast
    Debug.Print rst!ProjectID
    rst.MovePrevious
    Debug.Print rst!ProjectID
    rst.MoveFirst
    Debug.Print rst!ProjectID
    rst.Close
    Set rst = Nothing
End Sub
```

This code opens a recordset based on the tblProjects table. When the recordset is open, the ProjectID of the first record is printed to the Immediate window. The `MoveNext` method of the `Recordset` object is used to move to the next record in the recordset. The ProjectID of the record is printed. The `MoveLast` method of the `Recordset` object is used to move to the last record in the recordset. Once again, the ProjectID is printed. The `MovePrevious` method moves the record pointer back one record and the ProjectID is printed again. Finally, the `MoveFirst` method moves the record pointer to the first record and the ProjectID is printed. The recordset is closed and the `Recordset` object is destroyed.

Detecting the Limits of a Recordset

Before you begin to traverse through recordsets, you must understand two recordset properties: BOF and EOF. The names of these properties are outdated acronyms that stand for *beginning of file* and *end of file*. They determine whether you have reached the limits of your recordset. The BOF property is True when the record pointer is before the first record, and the EOF property is True when the record pointer is after the last record.

You commonly will use the EOF property when moving forward through your recordset with the MoveNext method. This property becomes True when your most recent MoveNext has moved you beyond the bounds of the recordset. Similarly, BOF is most useful when using the MovePrevious method.

You must keep in mind some important characteristics of the BOF and EOF properties:

- If a recordset contains no records, both the BOF and EOF properties evaluate to True.
- When you open a recordset containing at least one record, the BOF and EOF properties are set to False.
- If the record pointer is on the first record in the recordset and the MovePrevious method is issued, the BOF property is set to True. If you attempt to use MovePrevious again, a runtime error occurs.
- If the record pointer is on the last record in the recordset and the MoveNext method is issued, the EOF property is set to True. If you attempt to use MoveNext again, a runtime error occurs.
- When the BOF and EOF properties are set to True, they remain True until you move to a valid record.
- When the only record in a recordset is deleted, the BOF and EOF properties remain False until you attempt to move to another record.

Listing 12.11 shows an example of using the EOF property to determine the bounds of a recordset.

LISTING 12.11 DETERMINING THE BOUNDS OF A RECORDSET

```
Sub DetermineLimits()
    Dim rst As ADODB.Recordset

    Set rst = New ADODB.Recordset
    rst.ActiveConnection = CurrentProject.Connection
```

continues

LISTING 12.11   CONTINUED

```
    rst.CursorType = adOpenStatic
    rst.Open "Select * from tblProjects"

    Do Until rst.EOF
        Debug.Print rst![ClientID]
        rst.MoveNext
    Loop

    rst.Close
    Set rst = Nothing
End Sub
```

In Listing 12.11, a recordset is opened based on tblProjects. The EOF property is evaluated. As long as the EOF property is equal to False, the contents of the ClientID field are printed and the record pointer is advanced to the next record in the recordset.

Counting the Number of Records in a Recordset

The RecordCount property returns the number of rows in the recordset. Not all types of recordsets and providers support the RecordCount property. If the RecordCount property is not supported, no error occurs. Instead, the RecordCount is –1. Listing 12.12 provides an example.

LISTING 12.12   A RECORDSET THAT DOES NOT SUPPORT THE RecordCount PROPERTY

```
Sub CountRecordsBad()
    Dim rst As ADODB.Recordset

    Set rst = New ADODB.Recordset
    rst.ActiveConnection = CurrentProject.Connection
    rst.Open "Select * from tblProjects"

    Debug.Print rst.RecordCount   'Prints -1
    rst.Close
    Set rst = Nothing
End Sub
```

Because the default CursorType is adOpenForwardOnly, and a forward-only cursor does not support the RecordCount property, –1 prints to the Immediate window. Listing 12.13 rectifies this problem.

LISTING 12.13 A RECORDSET THAT SUPPORTS THE RecordCount PROPERTY

```
Sub CountRecordsGood()
    Dim rst As ADODB.Recordset

    Set rst = New ADODB.Recordset
    rst.ActiveConnection = CurrentProject.Connection
    rst.CursorType = adOpenStatic
    rst.Open "Select * from tblProjects"

    Debug.Print rst.RecordCount  'Prints RecordCount
    rst.Close
    Set rst = Nothing

End Sub
```

Notice that the CursorType is set to adOpenStatic. Because the RecordCount property is supported with static cursors, the correct number of records is printed to the Immediate window.

> **NOTE**
>
> If you are accustomed to the DAO RecordCount property, you might be surprised by the ADO RecordCount property. The DAO RecordCount returns only the number of *visited* records in the recordset. This means that using DAO, you must move to the last record in the recordset to obtain an accurate record count. Although this step is unnecessary when using ADO, it is important to note that attempting to retrieve the RecordCount property might result in severe performance degradation. Whether or not obtaining the RecordCount degrades performance depends on the particular database provider.

One of the important uses of the RecordCount property is to determine if a recordset contains any rows. Listing 12.14 illustrates this important use of the RecordCount property.

LISTING 12.14 CHECKING TO SEE IF RECORDS ARE RETURNED IN A RECORDSET

```
Sub CheckARecordset()
    Dim rst As ADODB.Recordset

    Set rst = New ADODB.Recordset
    rst.ActiveConnection = CurrentProject.Connection
```

continues

12

WHAT ARE ADO
AND DAO?

LISTING 12.14   CONTINUED

```
    rst.CursorType = adOpenStatic
    rst.Open "Select * from tblEmpty"

    If Not AreThereRecords(rst) Then
      MsgBox "Recordset Empty...Unable to Proceed"
    End If

    rst.Close
    Set rst = Nothing
End Sub

Function AreThereRecords(rstAny As ADODB.Recordset) As Boolean
    AreThereRecords = rstAny.RecordCount
End Function
```

The CheckARecordset routine opens a recordset based on a table called tblEmpty. tblEmpty contains no data. The CheckARecordset routine calls the AreThereRecords function, passing a reference to the recordset. The AreThereRecords function evaluates the RecordCount property of the recordset that it is passed. It returns False if the RecordCount is zero and True if the RecordCount is non-zero.

Sorting, Filtering, and Finding Records

Sometimes it is necessary to sort, filter, or find data within an existing recordset. The Sort property, Filter property, and Find method of the Recordset object allow you to accomplish these tasks. These methods are covered in the sections that follow.

Sorting a Recordset

The Sort property of the Recordset object allows you to Sort data in an existing recordset. Its use is illustrated in Listing 12.15.

LISTING 12.15   THE Sort PROPERTY OF THE Recordset OBJECT

```
Sub SortRecordset()
    Dim rst As ADODB.Recordset
    Dim intCounter As Integer

    Set rst = New ADODB.Recordset
    rst.ActiveConnection = CurrentProject.Connection
```

```
    rst.CursorLocation = adUseClient
    rst.Open "Select * from tblTimeCardHours"

    Debug.Print "NOT Sorted!!!"
    Do Until rst.EOF
        Debug.Print rst![DateWorked]
        rst.MoveNext
    Loop

    Debug.Print "Now Sorted!!!"
    rst.Sort = "[DateWorked]"
    Do Until rst.EOF
        Debug.Print rst![DateWorked]
        rst.MoveNext
    Loop

    rst.Close
    Set rst = Nothing
End Sub
```

The code begins by opening a recordset based on the tblTimeCardHours tables. The records in the recordset are printed in their "natural" order. Next, the Sort property of the Recordset object is used to sort the data by the DateWorked field. Notice that the Sort property is set equal to a field. If you want to sort by more than one field, the field names must be separated with commas. When the records are once again printed, they appear in order by the DateWorked field.

NOTE

To sort in descending order, the field name must be followed by a space and then the keyword DESC.

Filtering a Recordset

Sometimes you might want to select a subset of the data returned in a recordset. The Filter property helps you to accomplish this task. Its use is illustrated in Listing 12.16.

LISTING 12.16 THE Filter PROPERTY OF THE Recordset OBJECT

```
Sub FilterRecordSet()
    Dim rst As ADODB.Recordset

    Set rst = New ADODB.Recordset
    rst.ActiveConnection = CurrentProject.Connection
    rst.CursorType = adOpenKeyset
    rst.LockType = adLockOptimistic
    rst.Open "Select * from tblTimeCardhours"

    Debug.Print "Without Filter"
    Do Until rst.EOF
        Debug.Print rst![DateWorked]
        rst.MoveNext
    Loop

    rst.Filter = "DateWorked >= #1/1/1995# and DateWorked <= #1/5/1995#"
    Debug.Print "With Filter"
    Do Until rst.EOF
        Debug.Print rst![DateWorked]
        rst.MoveNext
    Loop

    rst.Close
    Set rst = Nothing
End Sub
```

In the example, a recordset is opened based on tblTimeCardHours. The records are printed without a filter applied. The Filter property is then set to limit the data to only records with the DateWorked between 1/1/1995 and 1/5/1995. The records in the recordset are printed again.

> **NOTE**
>
> It is inefficient to build a large recordset and then filter to only those records you need. If you know that you need only records meeting specific criteria, you should build a recordset using that criteria. The difference in performance can be profound, particularly when dealing with client/server data. In summary, you should use the Filter property only when you are initially dealing with a larger set of records and then need to perform an operation on a subset of the records.

TIP

To return to the complete recordset after a filter has been applied, set the Filter property to a zero-length string ("").

Finding a Specific Record in a Recordset

The Find method allows you to locate a particular record in the recordset. It is different from the Filter property in that all records in the recordset remain available. Listing 12.17 illustrates the use of the Find method.

LISTING 12.17   THE Find METHOD OF A Recordset OBJECT

```
Sub FindProject(lngValue As Long)
    Dim rst As ADODB.Recordset
    Dim strSQL As String

    Set rst = New ADODB.Recordset
    rst.ActiveConnection = CurrentProject.Connection
    rst.CursorType = adOpenStatic
    rst.Open "Select * from tblProjects"
    strSQL = "[ProjectID] = " & lngValue

    rst.Find strSQL

    If rst.EOF Then
        MsgBox lngValue & " Not Found"
    Else
        MsgBox lngValue & " Found"
    End If

    rst.Close
    Set rst = Nothing
End Sub
```

TIP

Because the FindProject routine is found in more than one module, the routine must be executed as follows:

```
Call basADORecordsets.FindProject(1)
```

Preceding the name of the routine with the name of the module removes the ambiguity as to which FindProject routine to execute.

In the example, a recordset is opened based on all the records in the tblProjects table. The `Find` method is used to locate the first record where the ProjectID is equal to a specific value. If the record is not found, the EOF property of the `Recordset` object is `True`.

> **NOTE**
>
> Unlike its DAO counterpart, ADO does not support the `FindFirst`, `FindNext`, `FindPrevious`, and `FindLast` properties. The default use of the `Find` method locates the *next* record that meets the specified criteria. This means that if the record pointer is not at the top of the recordset, records meeting the specified criteria might not be located. The `SkipRows`, `SearchDirection`, and `Start` parameters of the `Find` method modify this default behavior. The `SkipRows` parameter allows you to specify the offset from the current row where the search begins. The `SearchDirection` parameter allows you to designate whether you want the search to proceed forward or backward from the current row. Finally, the `Start` parameter determines the starting position for the search.

Using the `AbsolutePosition` Property

The `AbsolutePosition` property of the `Recordset` object sets or returns the ordinal position of the current row in the recordset. Its use is illustrated in Listing 12.18.

LISTING 12.18   THE `AbsolutePosition` PROPERTY OF A Recordset OBJECT

```
Sub FindPosition(lngValue As Long)
    Dim rst As ADODB.Recordset
    Dim strSQL As String

    Set rst = New ADODB.Recordset
    rst.ActiveConnection = CurrentProject.Connection
    rst.CursorType = adOpenStatic
    rst.Open "Select * from tblProjects"
    strSQL = "[ProjectID] = " & lngValue

    rst.Find strSQL

    If rst.EOF Then
        MsgBox lngValue & " Not Found"
    Else
        Debug.Print rst.AbsolutePosition
    End If
```

```
        rst.Close
        Set rst = Nothing

End Sub
```

In the example, the `Find` method is used to locate a project with a specific ProjectID. If the project is found, the ordinal position of the record that is located is printed to the Immediate window.

Using the `Bookmark` Property

The `Bookmark` property of a `Recordset` object returns a variant variable that acts as a unique identifier for that particular record in the recordset. The `Bookmark` property is used to save the current position and then quickly and easily return to it at any time. This is illustrated by Listing 12.19.

LISTING 12.19   THE `Bookmark` PROPERTY OF A Recordset OBJECT

```
Sub UseBookMark()
    Dim rst As ADODB.Recordset
    Dim strSQL As String
    Dim vntPosition As Variant

    Set rst = New ADODB.Recordset
    rst.ActiveConnection = CurrentProject.Connection
    rst.CursorType = adOpenStatic
    rst.Open "Select * from tblProjects"

    vntPosition = rst.Bookmark

    Do Until rst.EOF
        Debug.Print rst!ProjectID
        rst.MoveNext
    Loop

    rst.Bookmark = vntPosition
    Debug.Print rst!ProjectID

    rst.Close
    Set rst = Nothing

End Sub
```

In the example, a unique identifier to the current record is stored into a variant variable. The code then loops through the remainder of the records in the recordset. When it is done, the `Bookmark` property of the `Recordset` object is set equal to the unique identifier stored in the variant variable.

> **CAUTION**
>
> Not all recordsets support bookmarks. Whether a recordset supports bookmarks depends on the provider as well as the type of recordset created.

Running Parameter Queries

You will not always know the criteria for a recordset at design time. Fortunately, ADO allows you to supply parameters to the `CommandText` property of the `Command` object. Listing 12.20 provides an example.

LISTING 12.20   RUNNING A PARAMETER QUERY

```
Sub RunParameterQuery(datStart As Date, datEnd As Date)
    Dim cmd As ADODB.Command
    Dim rst As ADODB.Recordset

    Set cmd = New ADODB.Command

    cmd.ActiveConnection = CurrentProject.Connection
    cmd.CommandText = "Select * from tblTimeCardHours " & _
        "Where DateWorked Between ? and ?"
    cmd.CommandType = adCmdText

    Set rst = cmd.Execute(Parameters:=Array(datStart, datEnd))

    Do Until rst.EOF
        Debug.Print rst![TimeCardID], rst![DateWorked]
        rst.MoveNext
    Loop

    rst.Close
    Set rst = Nothing
    Set cmd = Nothing

End Sub
```

Notice that in the example, the `CommandText` property contains two question marks. Each of these is considered a parameter. The parameters are supplied when the `Execute` method of the

Command object is used. Notice that the Parameters argument of the `Execute` method receives an array containing the parameter values.

MODIFYING TABLE DATA USING ADO CODE

So far, this chapter has only covered the process of retrieving data from a recordset. It is common that you might need to update the data in a recordset. The sections that follow show you how to change data one record at a time, update a batch of records, delete records, and add records.

Changing Record Data One Record at a Time

It is possible to loop through a recordset, modifying all the records in the recordset. This technique is shown in Listing 12.21.

LISTING 12.21   MODIFYING ONE RECORD AT A TIME

```
Sub IncreaseEstimate()

    Dim rst As ADODB.Recordset
    Set rst = New ADODB.Recordset
    Dim strSQL As String
    Dim intUpdated As Integer

    rst.ActiveConnection = CurrentProject.Connection
    rst.CursorType = adOpenDynamic
    rst.LockType = adLockOptimistic
    rst.Open ("Select * from tblProjectsChange")

    strSQL = "ProjectTotalEstimate < 30000"
    intUpdated = 0

    rst.Find strSQL

    Do Until rst.EOF
        intUpdated = intUpdated + 1
        rst!ProjectTotalEstimate = rst!ProjectTotalEstimate * 1.1
        rst.Update
        rst.Find strSQL, 1, adSearchForward
    Loop
    Debug.Print intUpdated & " Records Updated"

    rst.Close
    Set rst = Nothing

End Sub
```

In the example, a recordset is opened based on all the records in the tblProjectsChange table. The first record where the ProjectTotalEstimate is less than 30,000 is located. The ProjectTotalEstimate is increased by ten percent and the record is updated. The next record that meets the specified criteria is located. The process is continued until all records meeting the specified criteria are located.

This code is very inefficient from several standpoints. The first problem is that a recordset is opened based on all the records in the tblProjectsChange table when only those with a ProjectTotalEstimate less than 30,000 needed to be updated. A more efficient approach is to open a recordset containing only those records that need to be updated. Furthermore, it would be more efficient to simply execute an action query that performs the update. This is covered in the section that follows.

CAUTION

If you're accustomed to DAO, you might be quite surprised by the behavior of ADO. First, whereas DAO requires that the Edit method be used before field values are assigned, no Edit method is used with ADO. Furthermore, if you forget to issue the Update method on a DAO recordset, the record is not updated. On the other hand, with ADO the Update method is implied. The update occurs automatically as soon as the record pointer is moved. These behavior differences can lead to big surprises!

Making Bulk Changes

As mentioned in the previous section, it is inefficient to open a recordset and then update each record individually. It is much more efficient to execute an action query. Listing 12.22 illustrates this process.

LISTING 12.22   MAKING BULK CHANGES TO THE RECORDS IN A RECORDSET

```
Sub RunUpdateQuery()
    Dim cnn As ADODB.Connection
    Set cnn = New ADODB.Connection

    cnn.Open CurrentProject.Connection
    cnn.Execute "qryIncreaseTotalEstimate"
    cnn.Close

End Sub
```

In the example, the Execute method of the Connection object is used to execute a stored query called qryIncreaseTotalEstimate. Any criteria contained within the query is applied.

Deleting an Existing Record

You can use ADO code to delete a record in a recordset. The code appears in Listing 12.23.

LISTING 12.23   DELETING AN EXISTING RECORD

```
Sub DeleteCusts(lngProjEst As Long)
    Dim rst As ADODB.Recordset
    Dim intCounter As Integer

    Set rst = New ADODB.Recordset
    rst.ActiveConnection = CurrentProject.Connection
    rst.CursorType = adOpenDynamic
    rst.LockType = adLockOptimistic
    rst.Open "Select * from tblProjectsChange"

    intCounter = 0
    Do Until rst.EOF
        If rst!ProjectTotalEstimate < lngProjEst Then
            rst.Delete
            intCounter = intCounter + 1
        End If
        If Not rst.EOF Then
            rst.MoveNext
        End If
    Loop
    Debug.Print intCounter & " Customers Deleted"

    rst.Close
    Set rst = Nothing
End Sub
```

In the example, a recordset is opened, based on all the records in the tblProjectsChange table. The code loops through all the records in the recordset. If the ProjectTotalEstimate is less than the value passed as a parameter to the routine, the Delete method of the Recordset object is used to remove the record from the recordset.

As was discussed Listing 12.21, this example is very inefficient. You should either build a recordset containing only the records you want to delete, or use an action query to accomplish the task.

> **TIP**
>
> If you are using a provider that supports stored procedures, it is most efficient to add, edit, and delete data using a stored procedure. This is because stored procedures execute on the server, sending no data over the network wire.

Adding a New Record

Not only can you edit and delete data using ADO, but you can also add records as well. Listing 12.24 illustrates this process.

LISTING 12.24   ADDING A NEW RECORD TO A RECORDSET

```
Private Sub cmdAddADO_Click()
    Dim rst As ADODB.Recordset

    If IsNull(Me.txtProjectName) Or _
        IsNull(Me.cboClientID) Then

        MsgBox "The Project Name and Client Must Be Filled In"

    Else

        Set rst = New ADODB.Recordset

        With rst
            .ActiveConnection = CurrentProject.Connection
            .CursorType = adOpenKeyset
            .LockType = adLockOptimistic
            .Open "Select * from tblProjectsChange Where ProjectID = 0"
            .AddNew
                !ProjectName = Me.txtProjectName
                !ProjectDescription = Me.txtProjectDescription
                !ClientID = Me.cboClientID
            .Update
            Me.txtProjectID = !ProjectID
        End With

    End If

End Sub
```

This code, an event procedure for a command button on frmUnbound, begins by setting the CursorType property of the recordset to adOpenKeyset and the LockType property to adLockOptimistic. The AddNew method is used to create a buffer for a new record. All the field values are assigned, based on values in the text boxes on the form. The Update method writes the data to disk. Because the ProjectID field is an Autonumber field, the txtProjectID text box must be updated to reflect the Autonumber value that was assigned.

12

WHAT ARE ADO
AND DAO?

> **CAUTION**
>
> With DAO, you are not placed on the new record after it is added. With ADO, you are moved to the new record when the Update method is issued.

CREATING AND MODIFYING DATABASE OBJECTS USING ADO CODE

Although most of the time you will design your database structure before you deploy your application, there might be times when you will need to design or modify database objects at runtime. Fortunately, you can accomplish these tasks using ADO code. The following sections cover adding and removing tables, modifying relationships, and building queries, all using ADO code. These are only a few of the tasks that you can accomplish.

Adding a Table Using Code

It is relatively easy to add a table using ADO code. Listing 12.25 provides an example.

LISTING 12.25   ADDING A TABLE

```
Sub CreateTable()
    Dim cat As ADOX.Catalog
    Dim tbl As ADOX.Table
    Dim idx As ADOX.Index

    Set cat = New ADOX.Catalog
    cat.ActiveConnection = CurrentProject.Connection

    ' Create new Table
    Set tbl = New ADOX.Table
    ' Add field to Table Definition

    With tbl
        .Name = "tblFoods"
```

continues

LISTING 12.25 CONTINUED

```
       Set .ParentCatalog = cat
       .Columns.Append "FoodID", adInteger
       .Columns("FoodID").Properties("AutoIncrement") = True
       .Columns.Append "Description", adWChar
       .Columns.Append "Calories", adInteger
   End With

   cat.Tables.Append tbl

   Set idx = New ADOX.Index
   idx.Name = "PrimaryKey"
   idx.Columns.Append "FoodID"
   idx.PrimaryKey = True
   idx.Unique = True
   tbl.Indexes.Append idx

   Set idx = Nothing
   Set cat = Nothing

End Sub
```

The code begins by instantiating an ADOX table object. It sets the `Name` and `ParentCatalog` properties of the `Table` object. Then it uses the `Append` method of the Columns collection of the table to append each field to the table. When all the columns have been appended, it uses the `Append` method of the Tables collection of the `Catalog` object to append the `Table` object to the database.

When the table is appended to the `Catalog`, indexes can be added to the table. An `Index` object is instantiated. The `Name` property of the index is set. Next the `Append` method of the `Columns` object of the `Index` is used to add a column to the `Index`. The `PrimaryKey` property of the index is set to `True` and the `Unique` property of the index is set to `True`. Finally, the `Index` object is appended to the Indexes collection of the `Table` object.

CAUTION

When running code that appends an object, an error occurs if the object already exists. You must either include error handling in your routine to handle this eventuality or delete the existing instance of the object before appending the new object.

Removing a Table Using Code

Sometimes it is necessary to remove a table from a database. Fortunately, this is very easily accomplished using ADO code. Listing 12.26 illustrates the process.

LISTING 12.26   REMOVING A TABLE

```
Sub DeleteTable()
    Dim cat As ADOX.Catalog

    Set cat = New ADOX.Catalog
    cat.ActiveConnection = CurrentProject.Connection

    cat.Tables.Delete "tblFoods"

End Sub
```

First a `Catalog` object is declared and instantiated. Then the `Delete` method of the Tables collection of the `Catalog` object is used to remove the table from the database.

Establishing Relationships Using Code

If your application adds new tables to a database, it might be necessary to establish relationships between those tables. Listing 12.27 shows how to create a relationship between two tables in the database.

LISTING 12.27   ESTABLISHING A RELATIONSHIP

```
Sub CreateRelation()
    Dim cat As ADOX.Catalog
    Dim tbl As ADOX.Table
    Dim fk As ADOX.Key

    Set cat = New ADOX.Catalog
    cat.ActiveConnection = CurrentProject.Connection

    Set tbl = cat.Tables("tblPeople")

    Set fk = New ADOX.Key
    fk.Name = "PeopleFood"
```

continues

LISTING **12.27** CONTINUED

```
    fk.Type = adKeyForeign
    fk.RelatedTable = "tblFoods"

    fk.Columns.Append "FoodId"
    fk.Columns("FoodID").RelatedColumn = "FoodID"
    tbl.Keys.Append fk

    Set cat = Nothing
    Set tbl = Nothing
    Set fk = Nothing
End Sub
```

The code begins by pointing a Table object at the foreign key table in the relationship. A Key object is instantiated. The Name property of the Key object is set. Next the Type property of the Key object is established. The RelatedTable property is set equal to the name of the primary key table that is involved in the relationship. The Append method of the Columns collection of the Key object is used to append the foreign key field to the Key object. Then the RelatedColumn property of the column is set equal to the name of the primary key field. Finally, the Key object is appended to the Keys collection of the Table object.

Creating a Query Using Code

At times you will want to build a query on-the-fly and permanently store it in a part of the database. Listing 12.28 illustrates this process.

LISTING **12.28** CREATING A QUERY

```
Sub CreateQuery()
    Dim cat As ADOX.Catalog
    Dim cmd As ADODB.Command
    Dim strSQL As String

    Set cat = New ADOX.Catalog
    cat.ActiveConnection = CurrentProject.Connection

    Set cmd = New ADODB.Command
    cmd.CommandText = "Select * From tblClients Where State='CA'"
    cat.Views.Append "qryCAClients", cmd
    cat.Views.Refresh

    Set cat = Nothing
    Set cmd = Nothing

End Sub
```

The code begins by creating and instantiating a `Catalog` object and a `Command` object. The `CommandText` property of the `Command` object is set equal to the SQL statement that underlies the query. The `Append` method of the Views collection of the `Catalog` object is used to append the `Command` object to a query with the specified name. The View collection of the `Catalog` object is then refreshed.

EXAMINING THE DATA ACCESS OBJECT MODEL

Figure 12.2 shows an overview of the Data Access Object model for the Jet 4.0 Database Engine. At the top of the hierarchy is the Microsoft Jet Database Engine, referred to as the `DBEngine` object. The `DBEngine` object contains all the other objects that are part of the hierarchy. It is the only object that does not have an associated collection.

Each object within the Data Access Object model is important because you will manipulate the various objects at runtime using code to accomplish the tasks required by your application. The following sections describe each major object and how it affects your programming endeavors.

Workspaces

The Workspaces collection contains `Workspace` objects. Each `Workspace` object defines the area in which a particular user operates. All security and transaction processing for a given user takes place within a particular workspace. You can programmatically create multiple workspaces. This is of great value because, by using this technique, you can log in as another user behind the scenes and accomplish tasks not allowed by the security level of the current user. You can log in as a member of the Admins group, for example, change the structure of a table that the current user does not have rights to, and log back out without the user of the system ever knowing that anything happened.

Users

The Users collection contains the `User` objects for a particular workspace. Each `User` object is a user account defined by a workgroup database. Because each user is a member of one or more groups, each `User` object contains a Groups collection that consists of each group of which a particular user is a member. `User` objects easily can be added and manipulated at runtime.

Groups

The Groups collection contains all `Group` objects for a particular workspace. Each `Group` object is a group defined by a workgroup database. Because each group contains users, the `Group` object contains a Users collection that consists of each user who is a member of the group. Like `User` objects, `Group` objects can be added and manipulated at runtime.

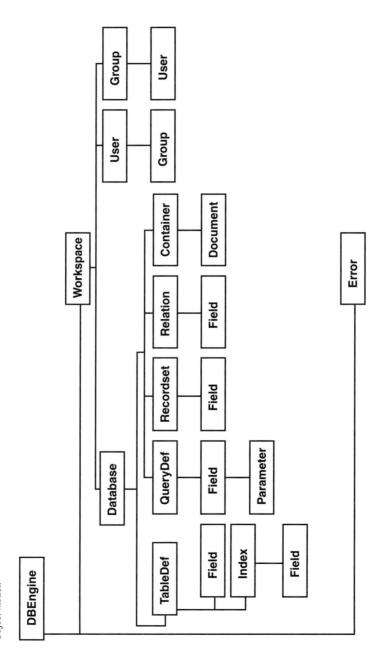

FIGURE 12.2
The Data Access Object model.

Databases

The Databases collection contains all the databases that are currently open within a particular workspace. You can open multiple databases at a time. These open databases can be Jet databases or external databases. A Database object refers to a particular database within the Databases collection. It is easy to loop through the Databases collection, printing the name of each Database object contained in the collection, as shown in Listing 12.29.

LISTING 12.29   PRINTING THE NAME OF EACH DATABASE IN A WORKSPACE

```
Sub EnumerateDBs()
    Dim ws As Workspace
    Dim db As DATABASE
    Dim db1 As DATABASE
    Dim db2 As DATABASE

    Set ws = DBEngine(0)
    Set db1 = CurrentDb
    Set db2 = ws.OpenDatabase("Chap9.MDB")

    For Each db In ws.Databases
        Debug.Print db.Name
    Next db
End Sub
```

This code loops through the open databases in the current workspace. It prints the name of each open database. It also is easy to perform all the other tasks required to build, modify, and manipulate database objects at runtime.

TableDefs

The TableDefs collection contains all the tables contained in a particular database—whether or not they are open. The TableDefs collection also includes linked tables. It contains detailed information about each table. It is easy to loop through the TableDefs collection, printing various properties (for example, the name) of each Table object contained within the collection. Listing 12.30 shows an example of using the TableDefs collection to print the properties of each Table object, in addition to printing the properties of each index on the table.

Indexes

Each TableDef object contains an Indexes collection, which enumerates all the indexes on the table. Each index contains a Fields collection to describe the fields in the index.

LISTING 12.30   USING THE TABLEDEFS AND INDEXES COLLECTIONS

```
Sub EnumerateTablesAndIndexes()
   Dim db As DATABASE
   Dim tbl As dao.TableDef
   Dim idx as dao.Index
   Dim fld as dao.Field

   Set db = CurrentDb

   For Each tbl In db.TableDefs
      Debug.Print "Table: "; tbl.Name
      For Each idx in tbl.Indexes
       Debug.Print "   Index: "; idx.Name
       Debug.Print "       Primary="; idx.Primary; ", Unique="; idx.Unique
       For Each fld in idx.Fields
           Debug.Print  "        Field:" ; fld.Name
       Next fld
    Next idx
   Next tbl
End Sub
```

This code loops through the TableDefs in the current database and prints the name of each table in the database. It then prints the name of every index on the table and every field in the index. It is easy to write code that adds, deletes, modifies, and otherwise manipulates tables and indexes at runtime.

QueryDefs

The QueryDefs collection includes all the queries contained within a particular database. It contains information about each query. It is easy to loop through the QueryDefs collection, printing various pieces of information about each query, as Listing 12.31 shows.

LISTING 12.31   PRINTING INFORMATION ABOUT EACH QUERY USING THE QUERYDEFS COLLECTION

```
Sub EnumerateQueries()
   Dim db As DATABASE
   Dim qry As QueryDef

   Set db = CurrentDb

   For Each qry In db.QueryDefs
      Debug.Print qry.Name
```

```
    Debug.Print qry.SQL
  Next qry
End Sub
```

This code loops through the QueryDefs in the current database and prints the name and SQL statement associated with each QueryDef. It is easy to write code that adds, deletes, modifies, and otherwise manipulates queries at runtime.

Fields

Fields collections are contained within the `TableDef`, `QueryDef`, `Index`, `Relation`, and `Recordset` objects. The Fields collection of an object is the collection of `Field` objects within the parent object. A `TableDef` object contains `Field` objects that are contained in the specific table, for example. Using the parent object, you can get information about its Fields collection, as shown in Listing 12.32.

LISTING 12.32   GETTING INFORMATION FROM THE FIELDS COLLECTION

```
Sub EnumerateFields()
    Dim db As DATABASE
    Dim tbl As TableDef
    Dim fld As Field

    Set db = CurrentDb

    For Each tbl In db.TableDefs
        For Each fld In tbl.Fields
            Debug.Print fld.Name
            Debug.Print fld.Type
        Next fld
    Next tbl
End Sub
```

This code loops through the TableDefs in the current database. As it loops through each TableDef, it prints the name and type of each field contained within the Fields collection of the TableDef. Code also can be used to add, delete, or change the attributes of fields at runtime. With a large database, this code is likely to output more information than can be contained in the Immediate window buffer. You might want to pause the code at some point to view the contents of the Immediate window.

NOTE

Notice that the `Type` property is an integer value. Each integer returned from this property represents a different field type. You might want to write a case statement that converts the integer value to a more meaningful text string.

Parameters

Access queries can contain parameters. These parameters are created so that the user can supply information required by the query at runtime. Each `QueryDef` object has a Parameters collection, which consists of `Parameter` objects. You can write code to manipulate these parameters at runtime, as Listing 12.33 shows.

LISTING 12.33 LISTING THE PARAMETERS OF EVERY QUERY

```
Sub EnumerateParameters()
    Dim db As DATABASE
    Dim qry As QueryDef
    Dim prm As Parameter

    Set db = CurrentDb

    For Each qry In db.QueryDefs
        Debug.Print "*****" & qry.Name & "*****"
        For Each prm In qry.PARAMETERS
            Debug.Print prm.Name
        Next prm
    Next qry
End Sub
```

This code loops through the `QueryDefs` object within the current database. It prints the name of the `QueryDef` object and then loops through its Parameters collection, printing the name of each parameter. `Parameter` objects can be added, deleted, and manipulated through code at runtime.

Recordsets

`Recordset` objects exist only at runtime. A `Recordset` object is used to reference a set of records coming from one or more tables. The Recordsets collection contains all the `Recordset` objects that are currently open within the current `Database` object. `Recordset` objects are covered extensively in "Understanding DAO Recordset Types," later in this chapter.

Relations

The Relations collection contains all the Relation objects that describe the relationships established within a Database object. The code in Listing 12.34 loops through the current database, printing the Table and ForeignTable of each Relation object.

LISTING 12.34 USING THE RELATIONS COLLECTION

```
Sub EnumerateRelations()
    Dim db As DATABASE
    Dim rel As Relation

    Set db = CurrentDb

    For Each rel In db.Relations
        Debug.Print rel.TABLE & " Related To: " & rel.ForeignTable
    Next rel
End Sub
```

Relationships can be created, deleted, and modified at runtime using VBA code.

Containers

The Containers collection contains information about each saved Database object. Using the Containers collection, you can view and modify all the objects contained within the current database, as demonstrated in Listing 12.35.

LISTING 12.35 LISTING EVERY CONTAINER IN A DATABASE

```
Sub EnumerateContainers()
    Dim db As DATABASE
    Dim cnt As Container

    Set db = CurrentDb

    For Each cnt In db.Containers
        Debug.Print cnt.Name
    Next cnt
End Sub
```

This code loops through the Containers collection, printing the name of each Container object. The results are DataAccessPages, Databases, Forms, Modules, Relationships, Reports, Scripts, SysRel, and Tables objects.

Documents

A `Document` object represents a specific object in the Documents collection. You can loop through the Documents collection of a `Container` object, as shown in Listing 12.36.

LISTING 12.36   PRINTING THE NAMES OF DOCUMENT OBJECTS

```
Sub EnumerateForms()
    Dim db As DATABASE
    Dim cnt As Container
    Dim doc As Document

    Set db = CurrentDb
    Set cnt = db.Containers!Forms

    For Each doc In cnt.Documents
        Debug.Print doc.Name
    Next doc

End Sub
```

This code points a `Container` object to the forms in the current database. It then loops through each document in the `Container` object, printing the name of each `Document` object (in this case, the name of each form).

> **NOTE**
>
> It is important to understand the difference between the Forms container and the Forms collection. The *Forms container* is part of the Containers collection; it contains all the forms that are part of the database. The *Forms collection* contains all the forms open at runtime. The properties of each form in the Forms container differ from the properties of a form in the Forms collection.

Properties

Each Data Access Object has a Properties collection. The Properties collection of an object is a list of properties associated with that particular object. This gives you a generic way to view and modify the properties of any object, as shown in Listing 12.37.

You can use this collection to create generic routines to handle common tasks. You could write a routine to set the font size of any control to 8 points, for example. Your routine could use the

Properties collection to verify that the control has a Font property before attempting to set the size.

LISTING 12.37   PRINTING EVERY PROPERTY OF Document OBJECTS

```
Sub EnumerateProperties()
    Dim db As DATABASE
    Dim cnt As Container
    Dim doc As Document
    Dim prp As Property

    Set db = CurrentDb
    Set cnt = db.Containers!Forms

    For Each doc In cnt.Documents
        Debug.Print doc.Name
        For Each prp In doc.Properties
            Debug.Print prp.Name & " = " & prp.Value
        Next prp
    Next doc
End Sub
```

This code loops through each form in the current database, printing all the properties of each Form object.

Errors

The Errors collection consists of Error objects. An Error object contains information about the most recent error that occurred. Each time an operation generates an error, the Errors collection is cleared of any previous errors. Sometimes a single operation can cause more than one error, so one or more Error objects might be added to the Errors collection when a single data access error occurs.

GETTING TO KNOW DBEngine

As mentioned, the DBEngine object refers to the Jet Database Engine, which is at the top of the Data Access Object hierarchy. The DBEngine object contains only two collections: Workspaces and Errors. When referring to the current database, you can use the CurrentDB() function discussed in the next section. When referring to any database other than the current database, you must refer to the DBEngine object, as in Listing 12.38.

LISTING 12.38   ACCESSING THE PROPERTIES OF THE DBEngine OBJECT

```
Sub ReferToCurrentDB()
    Dim ws As Workspace
    Dim db As DATABASE
    Dim err as Error

    Set ws = DBEngine(0)
    Set db = ws.OpenDatabase("Chap11")
    Debug.Print db.Version
End Sub
```

This code creates a `Workspace` object variable that points at the current workspace. The `OpenDatabase` method of the `Workspace` object then is used to open another database. The version of the database is printed by the routine.

USING `CurrentDB()`

Microsoft offers a shortcut you can use when creating an object variable that points to the current database. Using the `CurrentDB()` function, you do not need to first point at the workspace; nor do you need to issue the `OpenDatabase` method. Instead, you set the `Database` object variable equal to the result from the `CurrentDB()` function, as shown in Listing 12.39.

LISTING 12.39   LISTING THE ERRORS IN THE CURRENT DATABASE

```
Sub UseCurrentDBFunc()
    Dim db As DATABASE

    Set db = CurrentDB()
    Debug.Print db.Version
End Sub
```

This code sets the `Database` object variable so that it points at the current database object. It then prints the version of the database engine and each of the errors in the Errors collection.

The `CurrentDB()` function cannot be used to refer to objects that are not part of the current database. As with all VBA functions that do not require arguments, the parentheses after `CurrentDB` are optional.

UNDERSTANDING DAO RECORDSET TYPES

A `Recordset` object represents the records in a table or the records returned by a query. A `Recordset` object can be a direct link to the table, a dynamic set of records, or a snapshot of the data at a certain time. `Recordset` objects are used to directly manipulate data in a database. They enable you to add, edit, delete, and move through data as required by your application. DAO supports three types of `Recordset` objects: dynasets, snapshots, and tables.

Dynasets

You can use a `Recordset` object of the dynaset type to manipulate local or linked tables or the results of queries. A *dynaset* is actually a set of references to table data. Using a dynaset, you can extract and update data from multiple tables—even tables from other databases. In fact, the tables containing the data included in a dynaset can even come from databases that are not of the same type (for example, Microsoft SQL Server, Paradox, and dBase).

True to its name, a dynaset is a dynamic set of records. This means that changes made to the dynaset are reflected in the underlying tables, and changes made to the underlying tables by other users of the system are reflected in the dynaset. Although a dynaset is not the fastest type of `Recordset` object, it is definitely the most flexible.

Snapshots

A `Recordset` object of the snapshot type is similar to a dynaset. The major difference is that the data included in the snapshot is fixed at the time it is created. The data within the snapshot, therefore, cannot be modified and is not updated when other users make changes to the underlying tables. This trait can be an advantage or a disadvantage. It is a disadvantage, of course, if it is necessary for the data in the recordset to be updateable. It is an advantage if you are running a report and want to ensure that the data does not change during the time in which the report is being run. You therefore can create a snapshot and build the report from the `Snapshot` object.

> **NOTE**
>
> With small resultsets, snapshots are more efficient than dynasets because a `Snapshot` object creates less processing overhead. Regardless of their reduced overhead, snapshots actually are less efficient than dynasets when returning a resultset with a large volume of data (generally more than 500 records). This is because when you create a `Snapshot` object, all fields are returned to the user as each record is accessed. On the other hand, a `Dynaset` object contains a set of primary keys for the records in the resultset. The other fields are returned to the user only when they are required for editing or display.

Tables

A `Recordset` object of the table type often is used to manipulate local or linked tables created using Microsoft Access or the Jet Database Engine. When you open a table-type recordset, all operations are performed directly on the table.

Certain operations, such as a `Seek`, can be performed only on a table-type recordset. You get the best performance for sorting and filtering records when using a table type of recordset.

The downside of a table-type recordset is that it can contain the data from only one table. It cannot be opened using a join or union query. It also cannot be used with tables created using engines other than Jet (for example, ODBC and other ISAM data sources).

SELECTING AMONG THE TYPES OF DAO RECORDSET OBJECTS AVAILABLE

Deciding which type of recordset to use involves looking at the task to determine which type is most appropriate. When fast searching is most important and it is not a problem to retrieve all the records, a table is the best choice. If you must retrieve the results of a query and your resultset needs to be editable, a dynaset is the best choice. If there is no need for the results to be updated but the results must consist of a relatively small subset of the data, a snapshot is most appropriate.

WORKING WITH DAO `Recordset` PROPERTIES AND METHODS

Like other objects, `Recordset` objects have properties and methods. The properties are the attributes of the `Recordset` objects, and the methods are the actions you can take on the `Recordset` objects. Some properties are read-only at runtime; others can be read from and written to at runtime.

Creating a `Recordset` Variable

When working with a recordset, you first must create a `Recordset` variable. You use the `OpenRecordSet` method to create a `Recordset` object variable. You first must declare a generic `Recordset` variable and then point a specific recordset at the variable using a `Set` statement, as shown in the example in Listing 12.40.

LISTING 12.40   OPENING A RECORDSET

```
Sub OpenTable()
    Dim dbInfo As DATABASE
    Dim rstClients As Recordset

    Set dbInfo = CurrentDb()
    Set rstClients = dbInfo.OpenRecordset("tblClients")

    Debug.Print rstClients.Updatable
End Sub
```

This code creates a `Database` object variable and a `Recordset` object variable. It then uses the `CurrentDB` function to point the `Database` object variable to the current database. Next, it uses the `OpenRecordSet` method to assign the recordset based on `tblClients` to the object variable `rstClients`.

The type of recordset that is created is determined by the default type for the object or by a second parameter of the `OpenRecordSet` method. If the `OpenRecordSet` method is executed on a table and no second parameter is specified, the recordset is opened as the table type. If the `OpenRecordSet` method is performed on a query and no second parameter is specified, the recordset is opened as the dynaset type. You can override this default behavior by passing a second parameter to the `OpenRecordSet` method, as Listing 12.41 shows.

LISTING 12.41   OPENING A DYNASET-TYPE RECORDSET ON A TABLE

```
Sub OpenDynaSet()
    Dim dbInfo As DATABASE
    Dim rstClients As Recordset

    Set dbInfo = CurrentDb()
    Set rstClients = dbInfo.OpenRecordset("tblClients", dbOpenDynaset)

    Debug.Print rstClients.Updatable
End Sub
```

This code opens the recordset as a dynaset. `dbOpenTable`, `dbOpenDynaset`, and `dbOpenSnapshot` are all intrinsic constants that can be used to open a `Recordset` object. A query can be opened only as a dynaset or snapshot `Recordset` object. Listing 12.42 shows the code to open a recordset based on a query.

12

WHAT ARE ADO AND DAO?

LISTING 12.42   OPENING A RECORDSET BASED ON A QUERY

```
Sub OpenQuery()
    Dim dbInfo As DATABASE
    Dim rstClients As Recordset

    Set dbInfo = CurrentDb()
    Set rstClients = dbInfo.OpenRecordset("qryHoursByProject", _
    dbOpenSnapshot)

    Debug.Print rstClients.Updatable
End Sub
```

> **NOTE**
>
> As was the case with Access 95, the proper method to create a `Recordset` object in Access 97 and Access 2000 differs from that of earlier versions of Access. In earlier versions, it was appropriate to dimension a dynaset, snapshot, or table type of object variable and then use the `CreateDynaset`, `CreateSnapshot`, and `OpenTable` methods of the `Database` object to create the appropriate type of recordset. This method for creating recordsets is included in Access 97 and Access 2000 for backward compatibility only. It should be avoided and replaced with the code included in this section.

Using Arguments to Open a Recordset

Microsoft provides several arguments that control the way in which a recordset is opened. The arguments and their uses follow:

- `dbAppendOnly`—When this option is used, records can be added to the recordset only. Existing data cannot be displayed or modified. This option is useful when you want to ensure that existing data is not affected by the processing. This option applies to dynasets only.

- `dbConsistent`—This argument applies to dynasets. It allows consistent updates only. This means that in a one-to-many join, you can update only those fields that are not duplicated in other records in the dynaset. This is the default argument for dynasets.

- `dbDenyRead`—This argument prevents other users from even reading the data contained within the recordset as long as the recordset remains open. You can use this option only on table recordsets.

- `dbDenyWrite`—When creating a dynaset or snapshot, this option prevents all other users from modifying the records contained in the recordset until the recordset is closed. Other users still are able to view the data contained within the recordset. When this option is applied to a table type of recordset, other users are prevented from opening the underlying table.

- `dbForwardOnly`—This argument creates a forward-scrolling snapshot. This type of recordset is fast but limited because you can use only the `Move` and `MoveNext` methods to move directly through the snapshot.

- `dbInconsistent`—This argument allows for inconsistent updates. This means that in a one-to-many join, you can update all columns in the recordset.

- `dbReadOnly`—This option prevents your recordset from modifying data. If you don't want the data within the recordset to be updateable, but you expect a large number of records to be returned and you want to take advantage of the record paging offered by dynasets, you might want to open the recordset as a dynaset.

- `dbSeeChanges`—This option ensures that a user receives an error if the code issues an `Edit` method and another user modifies the data before an `Update` method is used. This option is useful in a high-traffic environment when it is likely that two users will modify the same record at the same time. This option applies to dynaset and table recordsets only.

- `dbSQLPassThrough`—When the source of the recordset is a SQL statement, this argument passes the SQL statement to an ODBC database for processing. This option does not completely eliminate Jet; it simply prevents Jet from making any changes to the SQL statement before passing it to the ODBC Drive Manager. You can use the `dbSQLPassThrough` argument only with snapshots and read-only dynasets.

The arguments described can be used in combination to accomplish the desired objectives. Listing 12.43 shows the use of an `OpenRecordSet` argument.

LISTING 12.43 USING AN `OpenRecordset` ARGUMENT

```
Sub OpenRecordsetArgs()
    Dim db As DATABASE
    Dim rst As Recordset

    Set db = CurrentDb
    Set rst = db.OpenRecordset("tblProjects", dbOpenDynaset, dbReadOnly)

    Debug.Print rst.Updatable
End Sub
```

This code opens a recordset as read-only.

Examining Record-Movement Methods

When you have a `Recordset` object variable set, you probably want to manipulate the data in the recordset. Table 12.3 shows several methods you can use to traverse through the records in a recordset.

TABLE 12.3 METHODS FOR MOVING THROUGH THE RECORDS IN A RECORDSET

Method	Moves
MoveFirst	To the first record in a recordset
MoveLast	To the last record in a recordset
MovePrevious	To the previous record in a recordset
MoveNext	To the next record in a recordset
Move[0]	Forward or backward a specified number of records

Listing 12.44 shows an example of using the record-movement methods on a dynaset.

LISTING 12.44 USING THE Move METHODS

```
Sub RecordsetMovements()
    Dim db As DATABASE
    Dim rst As Recordset

    Set db = CurrentDb
    Set rst = db.OpenRecordset("tblProjects", dbOpenDynaset)

    Debug.Print rst!ProjectID
    rst.MoveNext
    Debug.Print rst!ProjectID
    rst.MoveLast
    Debug.Print rst!ProjectID
    rst.MovePrevious
    Debug.Print rst!ProjectID
    rst.MoveFirst
    Debug.Print rst!ProjectID
    rst.Close
End Sub
```

This code opens a dynaset. The record pointer automatically is placed on the first record of the dynaset when the recordset is opened. The routine prints the contents of the ProjectID field and then moves to the next record, printing its ProjectID. It then moves to the last record of the dynaset, printing its ProjectID; moves to the previous record, printing its ProjectID; and moves to the first record, printing its ProjectID. The Close method is applied to the Recordset object. It is a good idea to always close an open recordset before exiting a routine. After changes are made to the recordset, the Close method properly closes the recordset, ensuring that all changes are written to disk.

Detecting the Limits of a Recordset

All the information discussed in the section about determining the limits of an ADO recordset apply when dealing with a DAO recordset. Listing 12.45 shows a DAO code sample that uses the EOF property with the MoveNext method.

LISTING 12.45   USING THE EOF PROPERTY WITH MoveNext

```
Sub DetermineLimits()
    Dim db As DATABASE
    Dim rstClients As Recordset

    Set db = CurrentDb()
    Set rstClients = db.OpenRecordset("tblClients", dbOpenSnapshot)
    Do While Not rstClients.EOF
        Debug.Print rstClients![ClientID]
        rstClients.MoveNext
    Loop
    rstClients.Close
End Sub
```

This code traverses through a snapshot recordset, printing the value of the ClientID field for each record until it reaches the position after the last record in the recordset. It then exits the loop and closes the recordset.

Counting the Number of Records in a Recordset

The RecordCount property of a recordset returns the number of records in a recordset that have been accessed. The problem with this is evident if you open a recordset and view the RecordCount property. You will discover that the count is equal to 0 if no records exist in the recordset or equal to 1 if there are records in the recordset. The record count is accurate only if you visit all the records in the recordset, which you can do by using the MoveLast method, as Listing 12.46 shows.

LISTING 12.46   DEMONSTRATING THE LIMITATIONS OF RecordCount

```
Sub CountRecords()
    Dim db As DATABASE
    Dim rstProjects As Recordset

    Set db = CurrentDb()
    Set rstProjects = db.OpenRecordset("tblProjects", dbOpenSnapshot)
    Debug.Print rstProjects.RecordCount   'Prints 0 Or 1
    rstProjects.MoveLast
    Debug.Print rstProjects.RecordCount 'Prints an accurate record Count
    rstProjects.Close
End Sub
```

The MoveLast method has its problems, though. It is slow and inefficient, especially in a client/server environment. Furthermore, in a multiuser environment, the RecordCount property becomes inaccurate as other people add and remove records from the table. This means that if determining the record count is not absolutely necessary, you should avoid it.

The RecordCount property has one good use, though: You can use it to see whether there are any records in a recordset. If you are performing an operation that might return an empty recordset, you easily can use the RecordCount property to determine whether records were returned, as Listing 12.47 shows.

LISTING 12.47   CHECKING FOR AN EMPTY RECORDSET USING RecordCount

```
Sub CheckARecordset()
    Dim db As Database
    Dim rstProjects As Recordset

    Set db = CurrentDb()
    Set rstProjects = db.OpenRecordset("tblEmpty", dbOpenSnapshot)
    If Not AreThereRecords(rstProjects) Then
      MsgBox "Recordset Empty...Unable to Proceed"
    End If
End Sub

Function AreThereRecords(rstAny As Recordset) As Boolean
    AreThereRecords = rstAny.RecordCount
End Function
```

The CheckARecordset procedure opens a recordset based on the tblEmpty table. It then calls the AreThereRecords function to determine whether any records are found in the recordset. If the AreThereRecords function returns False, an error message is displayed to the user.

Sorting, Filtering, and Finding Records

Sometimes you might need to sort or filter an existing recordset. You also might want to locate each record in the recordset that meets some specified criteria. The following techniques enable you to sort, filter, and find records within a Recordset object.

Sorting a Recordset

You can't actually change the sort order of an existing dynaset or snapshot. Instead, you create a second recordset based on the first recordset. The second recordset is sorted in the desired order. Listing 12.48 shows how this process works.

LISTING 12.48   SORTING AN EXISTING RECORDSET

```
Sub SortRecordset()
    Dim db As DATABASE
    Dim rstTimeCardHours As Recordset
    Set db = CurrentDb
    Set rstTimeCardHours = db.OpenRecordset("tblTimeCardHours", _
        dbOpenDynaset)
    Debug.Print "NOT Sorted!!!"
    Do While Not rstTimeCardHours.EOF
        Debug.Print rstTimeCardHours![DateWorked]
        rstTimeCardHours.MoveNext
    Loop
    Debug.Print "Now Sorted!!!"
    rstTimeCardHours.Sort = "[DateWorked]"
    Set rstTimeCardHours = rstTimeCardHours.OpenRecordset
    Do While Not rstTimeCardHours.EOF
        Debug.Print rstTimeCardHours![DateWorked]
        rstTimeCardHours.MoveNext
    Loop
End Sub
```

In this case, you are sorting a dynaset based on the tblTimeCardHours table. The first time you loop through the recordset and print each date worked, the dates are in the default order (usually the primary key order). After using the Sort method to sort the recordset, the records appear in order by the date worked.

Filtering a Recordset

Filtering a recordset is a useful technique when you want to select a subset of the records in your recordset. This is especially useful for allowing users to drill-down on a set of records to find the subset they need.

The process of filtering an existing recordset is similar to sorting one. Listing 12.49 is a variation of the example in Listing 12.48. Instead of sorting an existing recordset, it filters an existing recordset.

LISTING 12.49   FILTERING AN EXISTING RECORDSET

```
Sub FilterRecordSet()
    Dim db As DATABASE
    Dim rstTimeCardHours As Recordset
    Set db = CurrentDb
    Set rstTimeCardHours = db.OpenRecordset("tblTimeCardHours", _
      dbOpenDynaset)
    Debug.Print "Without Filter"
    Do While Not rstTimeCardHours.EOF
        Debug.Print rstTimeCardHours![DateWorked]
        rstTimeCardHours.MoveNext
    Loop
    rstTimeCardHours.Filter = "[DateWorked] Between #1/1/95# and #1/5/95#"
    Debug.Print "With Filter"
    Set rstTimeCardHours = rstTimeCardHours.OpenRecordset
    Do While Not rstTimeCardHours.EOF
        Debug.Print rstTimeCardHours![DateWorked]
        rstTimeCardHours.MoveNext
    Loop
End Sub
```

The first time the code loops through the recordset, no filter is set. The filter is set and the code loops through the recordset again. The second time, only the records meeting the filter criteria are displayed.

Finding a Specific Record Within a Recordset

The Seek methodenables you to find records in a table recordset. It is usually the quickest method of locating data because it uses the current index to locate the requested data. Listing 12.50 shows how the Seek method works.

LISTING 12.50   USING THE Seek METHOD

```
Sub SeekProject(lngProjectID As Long)
    Dim db As DATABASE
    Dim rstProjects As Recordset

    Set db = CurrentDb()
    Set rstProjects = db.OpenRecordset("tblProjects", dbOpenTable)
```

```
    rstProjects.INDEX = "PrimaryKey"
    rstProjects.Seek "=", lngProjectID

    If rstProjects.NoMatch Then
        MsgBox lngProjectID & " Not Found"
    Else
        MsgBox lngProjectID & " Found"
    End If
End Sub
```

This code uses the primary key index to locate the first project with the project number that was passed to the function. It then displays a message box to indicate whether the value was found.

You cannot use the Seek method to locate data in a dynaset or snapshot. Furthermore, you cannot use Seek to search for records in a linked table, regardless of whether the linked table is an Access table or a client/server table. In this case, you must use the FindFirst, FindLast, FindNext, and FindPrevious methods. The FindFirst method finds the first occurrence of data that meets the criteria, and FindLast finds the last occurrence of such data. The FindNext and FindPrevious methods enable you to find additional occurrences of the data.

The code in Listing 12.51 uses the FindFirst method to find the first occurrence of the parameter that was passed in. Again, it displays an appropriate message box.

LISTING 12.51 USING THE FindFirst METHOD

```
Sub FindProject(lngValue As Long)
    Dim db As DATABASE
    Dim rstProjects As Recordset
    Dim sSQL As String

    Set db = CurrentDb()
    Set rstProjects = db.OpenRecordset("tblProjects", dbOpenDynaset)
    sSQL = "[ProjectID] = " & lngValue

    rstProjects.FindFirst sSQL

    If rstProjects.NoMatch Then
        MsgBox lngValue & " Not Found"
    Else
        MsgBox lngValue & " Found"
    End If
End Sub
```

TIP

You can use another trick to search a linked table. You can open the database that contains the linked table and seek directly on the table data. This works only if the linked table is in another Access database.

Using the `AbsolutePosition` Property

The `AbsolutePosition` property returns the position of the current record. It is a zero-based value. You can use it to specify where in a recordset a specific record was found, as shown in Listing 12.52.

LISTING 12.52 SPECIFYING WHERE A RECORD WAS FOUND

```
Sub FindPosition(lngValue As Long)
    Dim db As DATABASE
    Dim rstProjects As Recordset
    Dim sSQL As String

    Set db = CurrentDb()
    Set rstProjects = db.OpenRecordset("tblProjects", dbOpenDynaset)
    sSQL = "[ProjectID] = " & lngValue

    rstProjects.FindFirst sSQL

    If rstProjects.NoMatch Then
        MsgBox lngValue & " Not Found"
    Else
        Debug.Print rstProjects.AbsolutePosition
    End If
End Sub
```

This code finds the first record with a ProjectID equal to the long integer received as a parameter. If the ProjectID is found, the value in the `AbsolutePosition` property of the record is printed.

CAUTION

Do not assume that the `AbsolutePosition` property of a particular record will stay the same. The `AbsolutePosition` property of a record changes as records are added or deleted or their order is changed as the records are modified.

Using the Bookmark Property

A *bookmark* is a system-generated byte array that uniquely identifies each record in a record-set. The Bookmark property of a recordset changes as you move to each record in the recordset. It often is used if you need to store the current position in the recordset so that you can perform some operation and then return to the position after the operation is completed. Three steps are involved in this process:

1. Storing the current bookmark of the recordset to a Variant variable.

2. Performing the desired operation.

3. Setting the Bookmark property of the recordset to the value contained within the Variant variable.

Listing 12.53 shows an example of using a bookmark.

LISTING 12.53   USING A BOOKMARK

```
Sub UseBookMark()
    Dim db As DATABASE
    Dim rstProjects As Recordset
    Dim sSQL As String
    Dim vntPosition As Variant

    Set db = CurrentDb()
    Set rstProjects = db.OpenRecordset("tblProjects", dbOpenDynaset)

    vntPosition = rstProjects.Bookmark

    Do Until rstProjects.EOF
        Debug.Print rstProjects!ProjectID
        rstProjects.MoveNext
    Loop

    rstProjects.Bookmark = vntPosition
    Debug.Print rstProjects!ProjectID
End Sub
```

This code begins by opening a recordset and storing the bookmark of the first record into a Variant variable. It then loops through each record in the recordset, printing the value in the ProjectID. After the loop completes, the Bookmark property of the recordset is set equal to the Variant variable, setting the current position of the recordset back to where it was before the loop began processing.

12

WHAT ARE ADO
AND DAO?

Using the `RecordsetClone` Property

You use the `RecordsetClone` property of a form to refer to the recordset underlying the form. This property often is used when you want to perform an operation and then synchronize the form with its underlying recordset. Listing 12.54 shows an example of using the `RecordsetClone` property.

LISTING 12.54 USING THE `RecordsetClone` PROPERTY

```
Private Sub cmdFindClient_Click()
    'This code is not found in the sample database
    Me.RecordsetClone.FindFirst "ClientID = " & Me!txtClientID
    If Me.RecordsetClone.NoMatch Then
        MsgBox Me!txtClientID & " Not Found"
    Else
        Me.Bookmark = Me.RecordsetClone.Bookmark
    End If
End Sub
```

This routine performs the `FindFirst` method on the `RecordsetClone` property of the current form. If the record is found, the `Bookmark` property of the form is set equal to the bookmark of the recordset. This matches the form's position to the underlying recordset's position.

Running Parameter Queries

Access parameter queries are very powerful. They enable the user to specify criteria at runtime. This capability often is helpful if your user wants to fill out a form at runtime and have the values on that form fed to the query. This also can be a useful way to protect your code from changes in the database schema. Creating a parameterized query is like writing a subroutine, where the details of implementing that routine are hidden from the caller. This programming technique is called *encapsulation*. Listing 12.55 shows an example of using parameter queries.

LISTING 12.55 USING PARAMETER QUERIES

```
Sub RunParameterQuery(datStart As Date, datEnd As Date)
    Dim db As DATABASE
    Dim qd As QueryDef
    Dim rs As Recordset

    Set db = CurrentDb
    Set qd = db.QueryDefs("qryBillAmountByClient")
    qd.PARAMETERS("Please Enter Start Date") = datStart
    qd.PARAMETERS("Please Enter End Date") = datEnd
    Set rs = qd.OpenRecordset
```

```
    Do While Not rs.EOF
        Debug.Print rs![CompanyName], rs![BillAmount]
        rs.MoveNext
    Loop
End Sub
```

This subroutine receives two date variables as parameters. It just as easily could receive form controls as parameters. It opens a query definition called qryBillAmountByClient. It then sets the values of the parameters called `Please Enter Start Date` and `Please Enter End Date` to the date variables passed into the subroutine as parameters. The query then is executed by issuing the `OpenRecordset` method on the `Recordset` object.

MODIFYING TABLE DATA USING DAO CODE

So far, you have learned how to loop through and work with `Recordset` objects. Now you will learn how to change the data contained in a recordset.

Changing Record Data One Record at a Time

Often, you want to loop through a recordset, modifying all the records that meet a specific set of criteria. Listing 12.56 shows the code required to accomplish this task.

LISTING 12.56 UPDATING RECORDS THAT MEET A SET OF CRITERIA

```
Sub IncreaseEstimate()
    Dim db As DATABASE
    Dim rstProjectst As Recordset
    Dim sSQL As String
    Dim intUpdated As Integer

    Set db = CurrentDb()
    Set rstProjectst = db.OpenRecordset("tblProjectsChange", _
        dbOpenDynaset)
    sSQL = "ProjectTotalEstimate < 30000"
    intUpdated = 0

    rstProjectst.FindFirst sSQL

    Do While Not rstProjectst.NoMatch
        intUpdated = intUpdated + 1
        rstProjectst.Edit
        rstProjectst!ProjectTotalEstimate = _
        rstProjectst!ProjectTotalEstimate * 1.1
```

continues

LISTING 12.56   CONTINUED

```
        rstProjectst.UPDATE
        rstProjectst.FindNext sSQL
    Loop
    Debug.Print intUpdated & " Records Updated"
    rstProjectst.Close
End Sub
```

This code finds the first record with a ProjectTotalEstimate less than 30,000. It uses the `Edit` method to prepare the current record in the dynaset for editing. It replaces the ProjectTotalEstimate with the ProjectTotalEstimate multiplied by 1.1. It then issues the `Update` method to write the changes to disk. Finally, it uses the `FindNext` method to locate the next occurrence of the criteria.

Making Bulk Changes

Many of the tasks that you can perform by looping through a recordset also be can accomplished with an Update query. Executing an Update query often is more efficient than the process of looping through a recordset. If nothing else, it takes much less code. Therefore, it is important to understand how to execute an Update query through code.

Suppose that you have a query called qryChangeTotalEstimate that increases the ProjectTotalEstimate for all projects where the ProjectTotalEstimate is less than 30,000. The query is an Update query. The code in Listing 12.57 executes the stored query definition.

LISTING 12.57   MAKING BULK CHANGES USING A PREDEFINED ACTION QUERY

```
Sub RunUpdateQuery()
    Dim db As DATABASE
    Dim qd As QueryDef
    Set db = CurrentDb
    Set qd = db.QueryDefs("qryIncreaseTotalEstimate")
    qd.Execute
End Sub
```

Notice that the `Execute` method operates on the query definition, executing the Action query.

Deleting an Existing Record

The `Delete` method enables you to programmatically delete records from a recordset, as shown in Listing 12.58.

LISTING 12.58 DELETING RECORDS WITH THE Delete METHOD

```
Sub DeleteCusts(lngProjEst As Long)
    Dim db As DATABASE
    Dim rstProjects As Recordset
    Dim intCounter As Integer
    Set db = CurrentDb
    Set rstProjects = db.OpenRecordset("tblProjectsChange", _
      dbOpenDynaset)
    intCounter = 0
    Do While Not rstProjects.EOF
        If rstProjects!ProjectTotalEstimate < lngProjEst Then
            rstProjects.Delete
            intCounter = intCounter + 1
        End If
        rstProjects.MoveNext
    Loop
    Debug.Print intCounter & " Customers Deleted"
End Sub
```

This code loops through the rstProjects recordset. If the ProjectTotalEstimate amount is less than the value passed in as a parameter, the record is deleted. This task also can be accomplished with a Delete query.

Adding a New Record

The AddNew method enables you to programmatically add records to a recordset, as shown in Listing 12.59.

LISTING 12.59 ADDING RECORDS TO A RECORDSET

```
Private Sub cmdAddDAO_Click()
    Dim db As DATABASE
    Dim rstProject As Recordset

    If IsNull(Me.txtProjectName) or _
        IsNull(Me.cboClientID) Then

        MsgBox "The Project Name and Client Must be Entered"

    Else

        Set db = CurrentDb()
        Set rstProject = db.OpenRecordset("tblProjectsChange", _
          dbOpenDynaset)
```

continues

Listing 12.59 CONTINUED

```
        With rstProject
            .AddNew
            !ProjectName = Me!txtProjectName
            !ProjectDescription = Me!txtProjectDescription
            ![ClientID] = Me!cboClientID
            .Update
        End With
        Me!txtProjectID = rstProject!ProjectID

    End If
End Sub
```

This code is used on an Unbound form called frmUnbound. The code issues an AddNew method, which creates a buffer ready to accept data. Each field in the recordset then is populated with the values from the controls on the form. The Update method writes the data to disk. If you forget to include the Update method, the record is never written to disk.

The last line of code does not work. The ProjectID field is an AutoNumber field, so Access will assign its value during the update. The offending line is supposed to copy the newly created ProjectID value into a text field on the form. The line is there to illustrate a problem: When an AddNew method is issued, the record pointer is not moved within the dynaset. Even after the Update method is issued, the record pointer remains at the record it was on prior to the AddNew method.

Therefore, this code will add a record, but it will place the ProjectID value of the previously existing record into the txtProjectId text box on the form. To get around this, you must explicitly move to the new record before populating the text box. This can be accomplished easily by using the LastModified property.

Using the LastModified Property

The LastModified property contains a bookmark of the most recently added or modified record. By setting the bookmark of the recordset to the LastModified property, the record pointer is moved to the most recently added record. Listing 12.60 is a modified version of Listing 12.59, using the LastModified property to fix the problem described previously.

LISTING 12.60 USING THE LastModified PROPERTY AFTER AddNew

```
Private Sub cmdLastModified_Click()
    Dim db As Database
    Dim rstProject As Recordset

    Set db = CurrentDb()
    Set rstProject = db.OpenRecordset("tblProjectsChange", _
      dbOpenDynaset)
    With rstProject
        .AddNew
        !ProjectName = Me!txtProjectName
        !ProjectDescription = Me!txtProjectDescription
        ![ClientID] = Me!cboClientID
        .Update
        .Bookmark = rstProject.LastModified
    End With
    Me!txtProjectID = rstProject!ProjectID
End Sub
```

12

WHAT ARE ADO
AND DAO?

Notice that the bookmark of the recordset is set to the LastModified property of the recordset.

CREATING AND MODIFYING DATABASE OBJECTS USING DAO CODE

When developing an Access application, it might be useful to add tables or queries, define or modify relationships, change security, or perform other data-definition techniques at runtime. You can accomplish all this by manipulating the various Data Access Objects.

Adding a Table Using Code

Many properties and methods are available for adding and modifying Jet Engine objects. The code in Listing 12.61 creates a table, adds some fields, and then adds a primary key index.

LISTING 12.61 CREATING A TABLE, ADDING FIELDS, AND ADDING A PRIMARY KEY INDEX

```
Sub CreateTable()
    Dim db As Database
    Dim tdf As TableDef
```

continues

Listing 12.61 CONTINUED

```
Dim fld As Field
Dim idx As Index

Set db = CurrentDb()
' Create new TableDef.
Set tdf = db.CreateTableDef("tblFoods")
' Add field to Table Definition
Set fld = tdf.CreateField("FoodID", dbText, 5)
tdf.Fields.Append fld
Set fld = tdf.CreateField("Description", dbText, 25)
tdf.Fields.Append fld
Set fld = tdf.CreateField("Calories", dbInteger)
tdf.Fields.Append fld
db.TableDefs.Append td
'Designate the FoodID field as the Primary Key Index
Set idx = tdf.CreateIndex("PrimaryKey")
Set fld = idx.CreateField("FoodID")
idx.Primary = True
idx.Unique = True
idx.Fields.Append fld
'Add the index to the Indexes collection
tdf.Indexes.Append idx
End Sub
```

This code first creates a table definition called tblFoods. Before it can add the table definition to the TableDefs collection, it must add fields to the table. Three fields are added to the table. Notice that the field name, type, and length are specified. After the table definition is added to the database, indexes can be added to the table. The index added in Listing 12.61 is a primary key index.

> **Caution**
>
> When running code that appends an object, an error occurs if the object already exists. You must either include error handling in your routine to handle this or delete the existing instance of the object before appending the new object.

Removing a Table Using Code

Just as you can add a table using code, you can remove a table using code, as shown in Listing 12.62

LISTING 12.62   REMOVING A TABLE

```
Sub DeleteTable()
    Dim db As DATABASE

    Set db = CurrentDb
    db.TableDefs.Delete "tblFoods"
End Sub
```

The Delete method is issued on the TableDefs collection. The table you want to delete is passed to the Delete method as an argument.

> **NOTE**
>
> If a relationship exists between the table that you are deleting and other tables in the database, an error occurs. You must therefore delete any relationships a table is involved in before deleting a table.

Establishing Relationships Using Code

When you create tables using the Access environment, you normally create relationships between the tables at the same time. If you are creating tables using code, you probably want to establish relationships between those tables using code as well. Listing 12.63 shows an example.

LISTING 12.63   ESTABLISHING RELATIONSHIPS BETWEEN DATABASE OBJECTS

```
Sub CreateRelation()
    Dim db As DATABASE
    Dim rel As Relation
    Dim fld As Field

    Set db = CurrentDb
    Set rel = db.CreateRelation()

    With rel
        .Name = "PeopleFood"
        .TABLE = "tblFoods"
```

continues

LISTING 12.63   CONTINUED

```
            .ForeignTable = "tblPeople"
            .Attributes = dbRelationDeleteCascade
        End With

        Set fld = rel.CreateField("FoodID")
        fld.ForeignName = "FoodID"
        rel.Fields.Append fld
        db.Relations.Append rel
End Sub
```

This code begins by creating a new `Relation` object. It then populates the `Name`, `Table`, `Foreign Table`, and `Attributes` properties of the relationship. After the properties of the relationship are set, the field is added to the `Relation` object. Finally, the `Relation` object is appended to the Relations collection.

Creating a Query Using Code

If you are running your application from the Access runtime, your users won't be able to design their own queries unless they have their own full copies of Access. You might want to build your own query designer into your application and then allow the users to save the queries they build. This requires that you build the queries yourself, using code, after the user designs them. Listing 12.64 shows the code needed to build a query.

LISTING 12.64   BUILDING A QUERY

```
Sub CreateQuery()
    Dim db As DATABASE
    Dim qdf As QueryDef
    Dim strSQL As String

    Set db = CurrentDb
    Set qdf = db.CreateQueryDef("qryBigProjects")
    strSQL = "Select ProjectID, ProjectName, ProjectTotalEstimate " _
        & "From tblProjects " _
        & "Where ProjectTotalEstimate >= 30000"
    qdf.SQL = strSQL
End Sub
```

This code uses the `CreateQueryDef` method of the `Database` object to create a new query definition. It then sets the SQL statement associated with the query definition. This serves to build and store the query.

> **NOTE**
>
> It is important to understand that the `CreateTableDef` method does not immediately add the table definition to the database, unlike the `CreateQueryDef` method of the database object, which immediately adds the query definition to the database. You must use the `Append` method of the TableDefs collection to actually add the table definition to the database.

> **TIP**
>
> You can create a temporary query definition by using a zero-length string for the name argument of the `CreateQueryDef` method.

USING THE DAO CONTAINERS COLLECTION

A `Container` object maintains information about saved `Database` objects. The types of objects in the Containers collection are data access pages, databases, tables (including queries), relationships, system relationships, forms, reports, scripts (Macros), and modules. The `Container` object is responsible for letting Jet know about the user interface objects. Databases, tables, relationships, and system relationships have Jet as their parent object. Forms, reports, scripts, and modules have the Access application as their parent object.

Each `Container` object possesses a collection of `Document` objects. These are the actual forms, reports, and other objects that are part of your database. The `Document` objects contain only summary information about each object (date created, owner, and so on); they do not contain the actual data of the objects. To refer to a particular document within a container, you must use one of two techniques:

```
Containers("Name")
```

or

```
Containers!Name
```

To list each `Container` object and its associated `Document` objects, you need to use the code shown in Listing 12.65.

LISTING 12.65   LISTING EACH Container OBJECT AND ITS ASSOCIATED Document OBJECTS

```
Sub ListAllDBObjects()
    Dim db As DATABASE
    Dim con As Container
    Dim doc As Document

    Set db = CurrentDb
    For Each con In db.Containers
        Debug.Print "*** " & con.Name & " ***"
        For Each doc In con.Documents
            Debug.Print doc.Name
        Next doc
    Next con
End Sub
```

This code loops through all the documents in all the containers, listing each one.

PRACTICAL EXAMPLES

Applying These Techniques to Your Application

The potential applications for the methodologies learned in this chapter are endless. This section explores just a few of the ways you can apply these techniques. The examples here are located in CHAP12.MDB.

Using Recordset Methods on a Data-Entry Form

At times, you might want to disable the default record movement and add, edit, or delete functionality from a form and code all the functionality yourself. You might want to perform these actions if you are going against client/server data and want to execute additional control over the data-entry environment. You also might want to use these techniques when you are developing applications for both the Access and Visual Basic environments and are striving for maximum code compatibility. Regardless of your reasons for using the following techniques, it is a good idea to know how to assign a Recordset object to a form and then use the form's underlying recordset to display and modify data.

Figure 12.3 shows a form in which the navigation buttons and record selectors have been removed. The form contains six command buttons: Move Previous (<), Move Next (>), Add, Delete, Find, and Exit. All the buttons use the recordset underlying the form to move from record to record in the form and modify the data contained within the form.

FIGURE 12.3

The frmRecordsets dialog box.

The RecordSource property of the form is not set. The Load event of the form is responsible for assigning a Recordset object to the form. Listing 12.66 shows the Load event of the form.

LISTING 12.66   THE Load EVENT IS USED TO ASSIGN A Recordset OBJECT TO THE FORM

```
Private Sub Form_Load()
    Dim rst As ADODB.Recordset
    Set rst = New ADODB.Recordset

    rst.ActiveConnection = CurrentProject.Connection
    rst.CursorType = adOpenKeyset
    rst.LockType = adLockOptimistic
    rst.Open "Select * from tblClients", Options:=adCmdText
    Set Me.Recordset = rst
End Sub
```

The code begins by declaring and instantiating an ADODB Recordset object. It then sets three properties of the Recordset object: the ActiveConnection, the CursorType, and the LockType. The Open method is used to open a recordset, based on the tblClients table. Finally, a Set statement is used to assign the recordset to the recordset underlying the form.

NOTE

When an ADO recordset is assigned to a form, and the form is based on Jet data, the form is rendered read-only. If an ADO recordset is assigned to a form based on SQL data, the form is rendered read/write.

Listing 12.67 shows the code for the Move Previous button.

LISTING 12.67   CODE FOR THE MOVE PREVIOUS BUTTON

```
Private Sub cmdPrevious_Click()
   Me.Recordset.MovePrevious
   If Me.Recordset.BOF Then
      Me.Recordset.MoveNext
      MsgBox "Already at First Record!!"
   End If
   Me.Bookmark = Me.Recordset.Bookmark
End Sub
```

This routine performs the MovePrevious method on the Recordset property of the form. If the BOF property becomes True, indicating that the record pointer is before the first valid record, the MoveNext method is performed on the Recordset property of the form to return the record pointer to the first record in the recordset. Finally, the bookmark of the form is synchronized with the bookmark of the Recordset property. Listing 12.68 shows the code for the Move Next button.

LISTING 12.68   CODE FOR THE MOVE NEXT BUTTON

```
Private Sub cmdNext_Click()
   Me.Recordset.MoveNext
   If Me.Recordset.EOF Then
      Me.Recordset.MovePrevious
      MsgBox "Already at Last Record!!"
   End If
   Me.Bookmark = Me.Recordset.Bookmark
End Sub
```

The code for the Add button is a little tricky, as Listing 12.69 shows.

LISTING 12.69   CODE FOR THE ADD BUTTON

```
Private Sub cmdAdd_Click()
   Me.Recordset.AddNew
   Me.Recordset!CompanyName = "New Company"
   Me.Recordset.Update
   Me.Bookmark = Me.Recordset.Bookmark
End Sub
```

The AddNew method is performed on the Recordset property of the form. This method creates a buffer in memory that is ready to accept the new data. When the Update method is issued, the record pointer is moved to the new record. Because the CompanyName field is a required field, you must populate it with data before issuing the Update method on the Recordset property.

By setting the bookmark of the form to the Bookmark property of the recordset, you synchronize the form with the new record. In a production environment, you would want to clear out all the text boxes and force the user to save or cancel before the AddNew or Update methods are issued.

The process of deleting a record is quite simple, as Listing 12.70 shows.

LISTING 12.70   DELETING A RECORD

```
Private Sub cmdDelete_Click()
   Dim intAnswer As Integer
   intAnswer = MsgBox("Are You Sure???", vbYesNo + vbQuestion, _
    "Delete Current Record?")
   If intAnswer = vbYes Then
      Me.Recordset.Delete
      Call cmdNext_Click
      Me.Refresh
   End If
End Sub
```

This code verifies that the user actually wants to delete the record and then issues the Delete method on the Recordset property of the form. Because the current record no longer is valid, the code calls the Click event of the cmdNext button.

The last piece of code involved in the form is the code for the Find button, as shown in Listing 12.71.

LISTING 12.71   CODE FOR THE FIND BUTTON

```
Private Sub cmdFind_Click()
   Dim strClientID As String
   Dim varBookmark As Variant
   varBookmark = Me.Recordset.Bookmark
   strClientID = InputBox("Enter Client ID of Client You Want to Locate")
```

continues

LISTING 12.71 CONTINUED

```
   Me.Recordset.Find "ClientID = " & strClientID, Start:=1
   If Me.Recordset.EOF Then
      MsgBox "Client ID " & strClientID & " Not Found!!"
      Me.Recordset.Bookmark = varBookmark
   Else
      Me.Bookmark = Me.Recordset.Bookmark
   End If
End Sub
```

This routine begins by storing the bookmark of the current record to a Variant variable. Users are prompted for the client ID they want to locate, and then the Find method is issued on the Recordset property of the form. If the EOF property is True, the user is warned and the bookmark of the recordset is set to the value within the Variant variable, returning the record pointer to the position it was in prior to the search. If the client ID is found, the bookmark of the form is synchronized with the bookmark of the Recordset property.

SUMMARY

In this chapter, you learned how to manipulate recordsets via code. The chapter begins by contrasting ActiveX Data Objects with Data Access Objects. It continues by introducing you to the ActiveX Data Object model. It explores the different types of ADO recordsets available, highlighting why you would want to use each type.

Next, you learned how to manipulate recordsets using code. The capability to manipulate recordsets behind the scenes is an important aspect of the VBA language. It frees you from the user interface and enables you to control what is going on programmatically. Finally, you learned how to create and modify database objects using code. This is important if the application you are creating requires you to create or modify tables, queries, or other objects at runtime. The techniques required for ActiveX Data Objects are covered as well as the different coding techniques that are needed for Data Access Objects.

WHAT TO DO WHEN THINGS DON'T GO AS PLANNED

PART
II

IN THIS PART

DEBUGGING: YOUR KEY TO SUCCESSFUL DEVELOPMENT

IN THIS CHAPTER

A good programmer is not necessarily one who can get things right the first time. To be fully effective as a VBA programmer, you need to master the art of debugging—the process of troubleshooting your application. Debugging involves locating and identifying problem areas within your code and is a mandatory step in the application-development process. Fortunately, the Access 2000 Visual Basic Editor provides excellent tools to help you with the debugging process. Using the Access 2000 debugging tools, you can step through your code, setting watchpoints and breakpoints as needed.

Using the VBA debugging tools is significantly more efficient than taking random stabs at fixes to your application. A strong command of the Access 2000 debugging tools can save you hours of trial and error. In fact, it can be the difference between a successfully completed application-development process and one that continues indefinitely with problems left unsolved.

AVOIDING BUGS

The best way to deal with bugs is to avoid them in the first place. Proper coding techniques can really aid you in this process. Using `Option Explicit`, strong typing, naming standards, and tight scoping can help you eliminate bugs in your code.

Option Explicit

`Option Explicit` requires that all your variables be declared before they are used. Including `Option Explicit` in each form, code, and report module helps the VBA compiler find typos in the names of variables.

As discussed in detail in Chapter 7, "VBA: An Introduction," the `Option Explicit` statement is a command that can be placed in the General Declarations section of any code, form, or report module. The `Option Explicit` command can be inserted manually into each program. If you prefer it can be inserted automatically by selecting Require Variable Declaration from the Editor tab after choosing Tools | Options from within the Visual Basic Editor (VBE.)

Strong Typing

Strong typing your variables is discussed in Chapter 7. *Strong typing* a variable means indicating what type of data is stored in a variable at the time it is declared. For example, `Dim intCounter As Integer` initializes a variable that contains integers. If elsewhere in your code you assign a character string to `intCounter`, the compiler will catch the error.

Naming Standards

Naming standards can also go a long way toward helping you eliminate errors. The careful naming of variables makes your code easier to read and makes the intended use of the variable more obvious. Problem code tends to stand out when naming conventions have been followed judiciously. Naming standards are covered in Chapter 1, "Access as a Development Tool," and are outlined in detail in Appendix B, "Naming Conventions."

Variable Scoping

Finally, giving your variables the narrowest scope possible reduces the chances of one piece of code accidentally overwriting a variable within another piece of code. You should use local variables whenever possible. Use module-level and global variables only when it is necessary to see the value of a variable from multiple subroutines or multiple modules. For more information about the issues surrounding variable scoping, see Chapter 7.

Bugs Happen!

Unfortunately, no matter what you do to prevent problems and errors, they still creep into your code. Probably the most insidious type of error is a logic error. A *logic error* is sneaky because it escapes the compiler; your code compiles but simply does not execute as planned. This type of error might become apparent when you receive a runtime error or when you don't get the results you expected. This is where the debugger comes to the rescue.

HARNESSING THE POWER OF THE IMMEDIATE WINDOW

The Immediate window serves several purposes. It provides you with a great way to test VBA and user-defined functions, it enables you to inquire about and change the value of variables while your code is running, and it enables you to view the results of `Debug.Print` statements. To open the Immediate window while in the Visual Basic Editor, do one of three things:

- Click the Immediate Window tool on the Debug toolbar.
- Choose View | Immediate window.
- Press Ctrl+G. The Immediate window is shown in Figure 13.1.

13

DEBUGGING

NOTE

The Debug tools are available on a separate toolbar called the Debug toolbar. To show the Debug toolbar, right-click any toolbar or menu bar and select Debug from the list of available toolbars.

Testing Values of Variables and Properties

The Immediate window enables you to test the values of variables and properties as your code executes. This can be quite enlightening as to what is actually happening within your code.

To practice with the Immediate window, you do not even need to be executing code. While in a form, report, or module, all you need to do is press Ctrl+G to invoke the Immediate window. To see how this works, follow these steps:

1. Run the frmClients form from the CHAP13EX.MDB database on the accompanying CD-ROM.

2. Press Ctrl+G to open and activate the Immediate window. You are placed in the Visual Basic Editor (VBE) within the Immediate window.

3. Type `?Forms!frmClients.txtClientID.Value` and press Enter. The client ID of the current client appears on the next line.

4. Type `?Forms!frmClients.txtCompanyName.Visible` and press Enter. The word `True` appears on the next line, indicating that the control is visible.

5. Type `?Forms!frmClients.txtAddress.BackColor` and press Enter. The number -2147483643 appears on the next line, specifying the background color of the address control.

Your screen should look like the one shown in Figure 13.2. You can continue to request the values of properties or variables within your VBA code.

FIGURE 13.2

Using the Immediate window to test the values of properties.

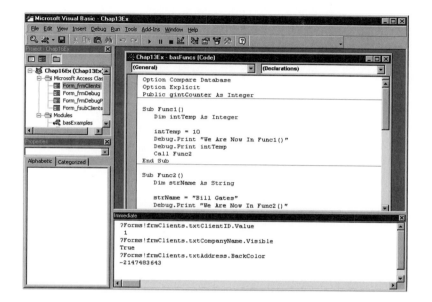

Setting Values of Variables and Properties

NOTE

You can invoke the Immediate window in three ways. You can click the Immediate Window button on the Debug toolbar, press Ctrl+G, or choose View | Immediate Window. An advantage of pressing Ctrl+G is that it invokes the Immediate window without a Code window being active. You can click the Immediate Window toolbar button or choose View | Immediate Window only from within the VBE.

Not only can you display things in the Immediate window—you can use the Immediate window to modify the values of variables and controls as your code executes. This feature becomes even more valuable when you realize that you can re-execute code within a procedure after changing the value of a variable. Here's how this process works:

1. Invoke the Immediate window if necessary. Remember that you can do this by pressing Ctrl+G.

2. Type `Forms!frmClients.txtContactTitle.Value = "Hello"` in the immediate pane. Press Enter. The contact title of the current record changes to `Hello`.

13

DEBUGGING

3. Type `Forms!frmClients.txtCompanyName.Visible = False`. Press Enter. The `txtCompanyName` control on the `frmClients` form becomes hidden.

4. Type `Forms!frmClients.txtAddress.BackColor = 123456`. Press Enter. The background color of the `txtAddress` control on the `frmClients` forms turns green. The Immediate window and your form now look like those shown in Figure 13.3.

FIGURE 13.3

Setting the values of properties using the Immediate window.

The Immediate window is an extremely valuable testing and debugging tool. The examples here barely begin to illustrate its power and flexibility.

CAUTION

Changes you make to data while working in the Immediate window are permanent. On the other hand, changes you make to the properties of controls or the values of variables are not saved with the form or report.

Clearing the Immediate Window

The Immediate window displays the last 200 lines of output. As additional lines of code are added to the Immediate window, older lines disappear. When you exit completely from Access and return to the Immediate window, it is cleared. If you want to clear the Immediate window at any other time, follow these three steps:

1. With the Immediate window active, press Ctrl+Home to go to the top of the Immediate window.

2. Hold down your Shift key and press Ctrl+End to go to the last statement in the Immediate window.

3. Press Delete.

Practicing with the Built-In Functions

In addition to being able to test and set the values of properties and variables using the Immediate window, you can test any VBA function. To test a VBA function, type the function and its arguments in the Immediate window, preceded by a question mark. This code returns the month of the current date, for example:

```
?datepart("m",date)
```

This tells you the date one month after today's date:

```
?dateadd("m",1,date)
```

This tells you how many days exist between the current date and the end of the millennium:

```
?datediff("d",date(),#12/31/9999#)
```

Executing Subroutines, Functions, and Methods

In addition to enabling you to test any VBA function, the Immediate window enables you to test any user-defined subroutine, function, or method. This is a great way to debug your user-defined procedures. To see how this works, follow these steps:

1. Open the basExamples module found in the CHAP13EX.MDB database on the accompanying CD-ROM.

2. Invoke the Immediate window if it is not already visible.

3. Type `?ReturnInitsFunc("Bill","Gates")`. This calls the user-defined function `ReturnInitsFunc`, sending `"Bill"` as the first parameter and `"Gates"` as the second parameter. The value `B.G.` appears in the Immediate window. This is the return value from the function.

4. Type `Call ReturnInitsSub("Bill","Gates")`. This calls the user-defined subroutine `ReturnInitsSub`, sending `"Bill"` as the first parameter and `"Gates"` as the second parameter. The value `B.G.` appears in a message box.

Notice the difference between how you call a function and how you call a subroutine. Because the function returns a value, you must call it using a question mark. On the other hand, when calling a subroutine, you use the `Call` keyword.

> **NOTE**
>
> You also can call a subroutine from the Immediate window using this syntax:
>
> `RoutineName Parameter1, Parameter2, ....`
>
> Notice that when you omit the `Call` keyword, the parameters do not need to be enclosed in parentheses.

Printing to the Immediate Window at Runtime

The capability to print to the Immediate window is useful because you can test what is happening as your code executes without having to suspend code execution. It also is valuable to be able to print something to a window when you are testing, without interfering with the user-interface aspect of your code. You can test a form without being interrupted and then go back and view the values of variables and so on. Here's how the process works:

1. Type `Call LoopThroughCollection`. This calls the user-defined subroutine `LoopThroughCollection`. The values `Skating`, `Basketball`, `Hockey`, and `Skiing` appear. These values are printed to the Immediate window by the routine.

2. Open the form frmDebugPrint in Form view.

3. Press Tab to move from the First Name field to the Last Name field.

4. Press Tab to move back to the First Name field.

5. Type your first name.

6. Open the Immediate window. Notice all the statements are printed to the Immediate window. (See Figure 13.4.) These `Debug.Print` statements are coded in all the appropriate form and control events.

FIGURE 13.4

Using Debug.Print *statements to print values to the Immediate window.*

INVOKING THE DEBUGGER

You can invoke the Access debugger in several ways:

- Place a breakpoint in your code.
- Place a watch in your code.
- Press Ctrl+Break while the code is running.
- Insert a Stop statement in your code.

A *breakpoint* is an unconditional point at which you want to suspend code execution. It is temporary because it is in effect only while the database is open. In other words, breakpoints are not saved with the database.

A *watch* is a condition under which you want to suspend code execution. You might want to suspend code execution when a counter variable reaches a specific value, for example. A watch also is temporary; it is removed after you close the database.

A Stop statement is permanent. In fact, if you forget to remove Stop statements from your code, your application stops execution while the user is running it.

USING BREAKPOINTS TO TROUBLESHOOT

As mentioned, a breakpoint is a point at which execution of code will be unconditionally halted. You can set multiple breakpoints in your code. You can add and remove breakpoints as your code executes.

A breakpoint enables you to halt your code execution at a suspicious area of code. This enables you to examine everything that is going on at that point in your code execution. By strategically placing breakpoints in your code, you quickly can execute sections of code that already are debugged, stopping only at problem areas.

To set a breakpoint, follow these steps:

1. Place your cursor on the line of code where you want to invoke the debugger.
2. You can insert a breakpoint in one of four ways:
   - Press your F9 function key.
   - Click in the gray margin area to the left of the line of the code that will contain the breakpoint.
   - Click the Toggle Breakpoint button on the Debug toolbar.
   - Choose Debug | Toggle Breakpoint.

     The line of code containing the breakpoint appears in a different color and a dot appears, indicating the breakpoint.
3. Run the form, report, or module containing the breakpoint. VBA suspends execution just before executing the line of code where you placed the breakpoint. The statement that is about to execute appears in a contrasting color (the default is yellow).

Now that your code is suspended, you can step through it one line at a time, change the value of variables, and view your call stack, among other things.

Keep in mind that a breakpoint is actually a toggle. If you want to remove a breakpoint, click in the gray margin area, press F9, or click Toggle Breakpoint on the Debug toolbar. Breakpoints are removed when the database is closed, when another database is opened, or when you exit Access.

It is easiest to get to know the debugger by actually using it. The following example gives you hands-on experience in setting and stopping code execution at a breakpoint. The example is developed further later in the chapter.

TRY IT Start by creating a form called frmDebug that contains a command button called cmdDebug. Give the button the caption `Start Debug Process`. Place the following code in the `Click` event of the command button:

```
Sub cmdDebug_Click ()
    Call Func1
End Sub
```

Create a module called basFuncs. Enter three functions into the module:

```
Sub Func1 ()
   Dim intTemp As Integer

   intTemp = 10
   Debug.Print "We Are Now In Func1()"
   Debug.Print intTemp
   Call Func2
End Sub

Sub Func2 ()
   Dim strName As String

   strName = "Bill Gates"
   Debug.Print "We Are Now In Func2()"
   Debug.Print strName
   Call Func3

End Sub

Sub Func3 ()
   Debug.Print "We Are Now In Func3()"
   MsgBox "Hi There From The Func3() Sub Procedure"
End Sub
```

Now you should debug. Start by placing a breakpoint within the `Click` event of cmdDebug on the line called `Call Func1`. Here are the steps:

1. Click anywhere on the line of code that says `Call Func1`.

2. Click in the gray margin area, press the F9 function key, click the Toggle Breakpoint button on the Debug toolbar, or choose Debug, Toggle Breakpoint. The line with the breakpoint turns a different color (red by default).

3. Go into Form view and click the Start Debug Process button. Access suspends execution just before executing the line where you placed the breakpoint. VBA displays the line that reads `Call Func1` in a different color (by default yellow), indicating that it is about to execute that line. (See Figure 13.5.)

FIGURE 13.5

*Code execution
halted at a break-
point.*

STEPPING THROUGH CODE

Access 2000 gives you three main options for stepping through your code. Each one is slightly different. The Step Into option enables you to step through each line of code within a subroutine or function, whereas the Step Over option executes a procedure without stepping through each line of code within it. The Step Out option runs all code in nested procedures and then returns you to the procedure that called the line of code that you are on. Knowing the right option to use to solve a particular problem is an acquired skill that comes with continued development experience.

Using Step Into

When you reach a breakpoint, you can continue executing your code one line at a time or continue execution until another breakpoint is reached. To step through your code one line at a time, click Step Into on the Debug toolbar, press F8, or choose Debug | Step Into.

The following example illustrates the process of stepping through your code, printing the values of variables to the Immediate window, and modifying the values of variables using the Immediate window.

TRY IT You can continue the debug process from the breakpoint you set in the previous example. Step two times (press F8). You should find yourself within `Func1`, about to execute the line of code `intTemp = 10`. (See Figure 13.6.) Notice that VBA did not stop on the line `Dim intTemp As Integer`. The debugger does not stop on variable declarations.

The `Debug` statements are about to print to the Immediate window. Take a look by opening the Immediate window. None of your code has printed anything to the Immediate window yet. Press F8 (step) three more times until you have executed the line `Debug.Print intTemp`. Your screen should look like Figure 13.7. Notice the results of the `Debug.Print` statements.

FIGURE 13.6

The Immediate window halted within Func1.

13

DEBUGGING

Now that you have seen how you can display variables and the results of expressions to the Immediate window, take a look at how you can use the Immediate window to modify values of variables and controls. Start by changing the value of `intTemp`. Click the Immediate window and type `intTemp = 50`. When you press Enter, you actually modify the value of `intTemp`. Type `?intTemp`, and you'll see that Access echoes back the value of 50. You also can see the value of `intTemp` in the Locals window. Notice in Figure 13.8 that the `intTemp` variable appears along with its value and type.

FIGURE 13.7

The Immediate window with entries generated by Debug.Print *statements.*

FIGURE 13.8

The Immediate and Locals windows after modifying the value of intTemp.

Executing Until the Next Breakpoint Is Reached

Suppose you have reached a breakpoint but you realize that your problem is farther down in the code execution. In fact, the problem is actually in a different function. You might not want to continue to move one step at a time down to the offending function. Use the Procedure drop-down menu to locate the questionable function, and then set a breakpoint on the line where you want to continue stepping. You now are ready to continue code execution until Access reaches this line. To do this, click Continue on the Debug toolbar, press F5, or choose Run | Continue. Your code continues to execute, stopping at the next breakpoint. To see how this works, continue the Debug process with the next example.

> **NOTE**
>
> You also can opt to resume code execution to the point at which your cursor is located. To do this, select Run to Cursor from the Debug menu, or press the Ctrl+F8 keystroke combination.

TRY IT Suppose that you realize your problem might be in Func3. You do not want to continue to move one step at a time down to Func3. No problem. Use the Procedure drop-down menu to view Func3, as shown in Figure 13.9. Set a breakpoint on the line that reads Debug.Print "We Are Now In Func3()". You now are ready to continue code execution until Access reaches this line. To continue execution, click Continue on the Debug toolbar, press F5, or choose Run | Continue. Your code continues to execute, stopping on the breakpoint you just set. Press F5 again. The code finishes executing. Return to the Form View window.

Using Step Over

Sometimes you already have a subroutine fully tested and debugged. You want to continue stepping through the routine that you are in, but you don't want to watch the execution of subroutines. In this case, you use Step Over. To step over a subroutine or function, click Step Over on the Debug toolbar, press Shift+F8, or choose Debug | Step Over. The code within the subroutine or function you are stepping over executes, but you do not step through it. To experiment with the Step Over feature, follow the next example.

FIGURE **13.9**

*Using the
Procedure drop-
down menu to
view another
function.*

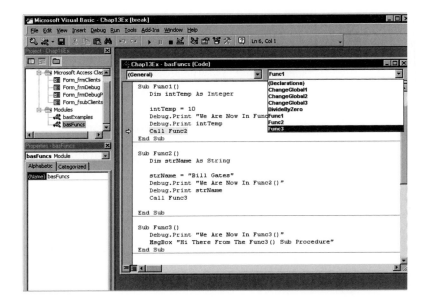

TRY	IT	Click back on the open form and click one more time on the Start Debug Process

button. Because your breakpoints are still set, you are placed on the line of code
that reads Call Func1. Select Clear All Breakpoints from the Debug menu, or use the
Ctrl+Shift+F9 keystroke combination to remove all breakpoints. Step (press F8) five times
until you are about to execute the line Call Func2. Suppose that you have tested Func2 and
Func3 and know that they are not the cause of the problems in your code. With Func2 highlighted as the next line to be executed, click Step Over on the toolbar. Notice that Func2 and
Func3 are both executed but that you now are ready to continue stepping in Func1. In this case,
you are placed on the End Sub line immediately following the call to Func2.

Using Step Out

TRY	IT	The Step Out feature is used to step out of the procedure you are in and to return to

the procedure that called the line of code you are on. You use this feature when you
have accidentally stepped into a procedure that you realize is fully tested. You want to execute
all the code called by the procedure you are in and then step out to the calling procedure so
that you can continue with the debugging process. To test how this works, follow this example.

1. Place a breakpoint on the call to Func2.

2. Click the Reset button on the toolbar to halt code execution.

3. Activate the frmDebug form and click the Start Debug Process command button.

4. Step once to place yourself in the first line of Func2.

5. Suppose that you realize you just stepped one step too far. You really intended to step over Func2 and all the procedures it calls. No problem! Click the Step Out button to step out of Func2 and return to the line following the line of code that called Func2. In this case, you should find yourself on the End Sub statement of Func1.

SETTING THE NEXT STATEMENT TO EXECUTE

After you have stepped through your code, watched the logical flow, and modified some variables, you might want to re-execute the code beginning at a prior statement. The easiest way to do this is to click and drag the yellow arrow in the margin to the statement on which you want to continue execution. If you prefer, you can click anywhere in the line of code where you want to commence execution and then choose Debug | Set Next Statement. Regardless of the method you chose, notice the contrasting color (usually yellow) indicating that the next line of code to be executed now is placed over that statement. You then can step through the code by pressing F8, or you can continue normal code execution by pressing F5. Access enables you to set the next line to be executed within a procedure only. This feature can be used to re-execute lines of code or to skip over a problem line of code.

The following example walks you through the process of changing the value of a variable and then re-executing code after the value is changed.

TRY IT | The preceding example left you at the last line of code (the End Sub statement) within Func1. You want to change the value of intTemp and re-execute everything.

1. Go to the Immediate window and type intTemp = 100.

2. You need to set the next statement to print on the line that reads Debug.Print "We Are Now in Func1()". To do this, click and drag the yellow arrow from the End Sub statement to the line of code that says Debug.Print "We Are Now In Func1()". Notice the contrasting color (yellow), indicating that the next line of code to be executed is now over that statement.

3. Press F8 (step) two times. The code now executes with intTemp set to 100. Observe the Immediate window again. Notice how the results have changed.

USING THE CALLS WINDOW

You have learned how to set breakpoints, step through and over code, use the Immediate window, set the next line to be executed, and continue to run until the next breakpoint is reached. When you reach a breakpoint, it often is important to see which functions were called to bring you to this point. This is where the Calls feature can help.

TRY IT To bring up the Call Stack window, click the Call Stack button on the toolbar or choose View | Call Stack. The window in Figure 13.10 appears. If you want to see the line of code that called a particular function or subroutine, double-click that particular function or click the function and then click Show. Although your execution point is not moved to the calling function or subroutine, you are able to view the code within the procedure. If you want to continue your code execution, press F8. You move back to the procedure through which you were stepping, and the next line of code executes. If you press F5, your code executes until another breakpoint or watch is reached. If you want to return to where you were without executing additional lines of code, choose Debug | Show Next Statement. To test this process, perform the next example.

FIGURE 13.10

Viewing the stack with the Call Stack window.

1. Click the Reset button to stop your code execution if you are still in Break mode.

2. Remove the breakpoint on the call to Func2.

3. Move to the procedure called Func3 in basFuncs. Set a breakpoint on the line Debug.Print "We Are Now in Func3()".

4. Run the frmDebug form and click the command button. You are placed in Func3 on the line where the breakpoint is set.

5. Bring up the Call Stack window by clicking the Call Stack button on the toolbar. If you want to see the line of code that called Func2 from Func1, double-click Func1. Although your execution point is not moved to Func1, you are able to view the code within the procedure. To return to the next line of code to execute, choose Debug | Show Next Statement.

6. Press F5, and the rest of your code executes.

WORKING WITH THE LOCALS WINDOW

The Locals window enables you to see all the variables on the current stack frame and to view and modify their values. To access the Locals pane, click Locals Window on the toolbar, or select Locals Window from the View menu. Three columns appear: Expression, Value, and Type. The Expression column shows you the variables, user-defined types, arrays, and other objects visible within the current procedure. The Value column displays the current value of the variable or expression. The Type column tells you what type of data the variable contains. Variables that contain hierarchical information—arrays, for example—are displayed with an Expand/Collapse button.

The information contained within the Locals window is dynamic. It is updated automatically as the code executes and as you move from routine to routine. Figure 13.11 illustrates how you can use the Locals window to view the variables available with the Func2 subroutine. To try this example yourself, remove all existing breakpoints. Place a breakpoint in Func2 on the line of code that reads Debug.Print strName. Click Reset if code is still executing, and click the Start Debug Process command button to execute code until the breakpoint. Click the Locals Window button on the toolbar. Click the plus sign to view the contents of the public variable gintCounter.

13

DEBUGGING

FIGURE 13.11

Viewing the Locals window.

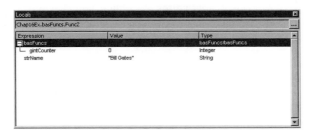

> **NOTE**
>
> You can change the value of a variable in the Locals window, but you cannot change its name or type.

WORKING WITH WATCH EXPRESSIONS

Sometimes it is not enough to use the Immediate window to test the value of an expression or variable. You might want to keep a constant eye on the expression's value. A feature introduced in Access 95 was the capability to set watches. You can set a watch before running a procedure or while code execution is suspended. After a `Watch` expression is added, it appears in the Watch window. As you'll see, you can create several types of watches.

Using Auto Data Tips

The quickest and easiest way to view the value contained within a variable is to use Auto Data Tips, which is an available option for working with modules. This feature is available only when your code is in Break mode. While in Break mode, simply move your mouse over the variable or expression whose value you want to check. A tip appears with the current value. To set the Auto Data Tips option, from the Visual Basic Editor (VBE) choose Tools|Options, click the Editor tab, and check the option for Auto Data Tips, which is under the Code Settings options.

Using Quick Watch

A *quick watch* is the most basic type of watch. To add a quick watch, highlight the name of the variable or expression you want to watch and click the Quick Watch button on the toolbar. The Quick Watch dialog box, shown in Figure 13.12, appears. You can click Add to add the expression as a permanent watch or choose Cancel to view the current value without adding it as a watch. If you click Add, the Watches window looks like the one in Figure 13.13. This window is discussed in more detail in the next section.

FIGURE 13.12

The Quick Watch dialog box enables you to quickly view the value of a variable or add an expression as a permanent watch.

FIGURE 13.13

The Watches window with a Watch *expression.*

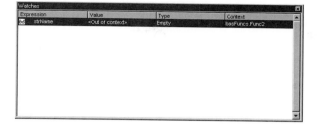

Adding a Watch Expression

As you saw, you can add a Watch expression using the quick watch. Adding a watch this way does not give you full control over the nature of the watch, however. If you need more control over the watch, you must choose Debug | Add Watch. The Add Watch dialog box appears, as shown in Figure 13.14.

> **TIP**
>
> If you add a quick watch or you add a watch by choosing Debug | Add Watch, you easily can customize the specifics of the watch by clicking with the right mouse button over the watch in the Watches window. Then select Edit Watch.

FIGURE 13.14

The Add Watch dialog box enables you to easily designate all the specifics of a Watch *expression.*

You use the Expression text box to enter a variable, property, function call, or any other valid expression. It is important to select the procedure and module in which you want the expression to be watched. Next, indicate whether you want to simply watch the value of the expression in the Immediate window, break when the expression becomes True, or break whenever the value of the expression changes. The two latter options are covered in detail in the following sections.

TRY IT The next example walks you through the process of adding a watch and viewing the `Watch` variable as you step through your code. It illustrates how a variable goes in and out of scope, as well as changes value, during code execution.

1. To begin, stop code execution if your code is running, and remove any breakpoints you have set.

2. Click within the `strName` variable in `Func2`.

3. Right-click and choose Add Watch.

4. Click OK to accept the `Func2` procedure as the context for the variable and basFuncs as the module for the variable.

5. Set a breakpoint on the line `strName = "Bill Gates"`.

6. Run the frmDebug form and click the command button. View the Watches window and notice that `strName` has the value of a zero-length string.

7. Step one time and notice that `strName` is equal to `Bill Gates`.

8. Step three more times. Notice that, although you are in the `Func3` routine, `strName` still has the value `Bill Gates`. This is because the variable is still in memory in the context of `basFuncs.Func2`.

9. Step four more times until you are back on the `End Sub` statement of `Func2`. The `strName` variable is still in context.

10. Step one more time. The `strName` variable is finally out of context because `Func2` has been executed.

Editing a `Watch` Expression

After you add a watch, you might want to edit the nature of the watch or remove it entirely. You use the Edit Watch dialog box to edit or delete a `Watch` expression. Follow these steps:

1. Activate the Watches window.

2. Select the expression you want to edit.

3. Choose Debug | Edit Watch or right-click and choose Edit Watch. The dialog box in Figure 13.15 appears.

4. Make changes to the watch or click Delete to remove it.

FIGURE 13.15

You can use the Edit Watch dialog box to modify the specifics of a watch after you add it.

Breaking When an Expression Is True

A powerful aspect of a Watch expression is that you can break whenever an expression becomes True. You can break whenever a Public variable reaches a specific value, for example. You might want to do this when a Public or Private variable somehow is being changed and you want to find out where. Consider the following code, located in the basFuncs module of CHAP13EX.MDB:

```
Sub ChangeGlobal1()
   gintCounter = 50
   Call ChangeGlobal2
End Sub

Sub ChangeGlobal2()
   gintCounter = gintCounter + 10
   Call ChangeGlobal3
End Sub

Sub ChangeGlobal3()
   Dim intCounter As Integer
   For intCounter = 1 To 10
      gintCounter = gintCounter + intCounter
   Next intCounter
End Sub
```

You might find that gintCounter somehow is reaching a number greater than 100 and you are not sure how. To solve the problem, add the watch shown in Figure 13.16. Notice that the expression you are testing for is gintCounter > 100. You have set the breakpoint to break the code whenever the expression becomes True. To test the code, type ChangeGlobal1 in the Immediate window and press Enter. The code should break in the ChangeGlobal3 routine, indicating that this routine is the culprit.

13

DEBUGGING

FIGURE **13.16**

*Defining a watch
that will cause the
code execution to
break whenever
the expression is
True.*

Breaking When an Expression Changes

Instead of breaking when an expression becomes True, you might want to break whenever the value of the expression changes. This is a great way to identify the place where the value of a variable is mysteriously altered. Like Break When Expression Is True, the Break When Expression Has Changed option is great for tracking down problems with Public and Private variables. Notice the watch being set in Figure 13.17. It is in the context of all procedures within all modules. It is set to break whenever the value of gintCounter changes. If you execute the ChangeGlobal1 routine, you'll find that the code halts execution within ChangeGlobal1 immediately after the value of gintCounter is set to 50. If you press F5 to continue execution, the code halts within ChangeGlobal2 immediately after gintCounter is incremented by 10. In other words, every time the value of gintCounter is modified, the code execution breaks.

FIGURE **13.17**

*Creating a watch
that will cause
code execution to
break whenever
the value of an
expression
changes.*

CONTINUING EXECUTION AFTER A RUNTIME ERROR

As you are testing, you often discover runtime errors that are quite easy to fix. When a runtime error occurs, a dialog box similar to the one shown in Figure 13.18 appears.

If you click Debug, you are placed in the Code window on the line that generated the error. After rectifying the problem, click the Continue button on the toolbar or choose Run | Continue.

FIGURE 13.18

*The Runtime
Error dialog box.*

Figure 13.19 shows a divide-by-zero error, for example, after Debug was clicked from the Runtime Error dialog box. The value of int2 was set to 20. Code execution now can continue without error.

FIGURE 13.19

*Debug mode after
a divide-by-zero
error.*

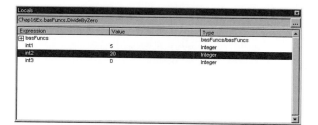

Often, after an error occurs, VBA displays a message giving you the option of resetting your code. If you opt to reset your code, all variables (including Publics and Statics) lose their values. You also can click Reset on the toolbar. You must decide whether it is better to proceed with your variables already set or to reset the variables and then proceed.

LOOKING AT GOTCHAS WITH THE IMMEDIATE WINDOW

Although the Access debugger is excellent, the debugging process itself is wrought with an array of potential problems, as follows:

- The debugging process can interrupt code execution, especially when forms are involved. When this occurs, the best bet is to place Debug.Print statements in your code and examine what happens after the code executes.

- Along the lines of the previous problem, it is difficult to debug code where GotFocus and LostFocus events are coded. Moving to the VBE (Visual Basic Editor) triggers the LostFocus event of the control. Returning to the form causes the GotFocus event of the control to be triggered. Once again, a great solution is Debug.Print. You also might consider writing information to an error log for perusal after the code executes.

13

DEBUGGING

- Code that uses `Screen.ActiveForm` and `Screen.ActiveControl` wreaks havoc on the debugging process. When the IDE is active, there is no active form and no active control. Avoiding these lines in your code wherever possible alleviates this problem.

- Finally, be aware that resetting code can cause problems. If you are modifying environmental settings, you are left with whatever environmental settings your application code changed. If you continue execution after the error without resetting, all sorts of other problems can occur. It is a good idea to code a special utility routine that resets your environment.

PRACTICAL EXAMPLES

Debugging Real Applications

As you develop the Time and Billing application, use the techniques you learned to help solve any problems you encounter. For now, use the debugger to step through and learn more about the debugging process with one of the routines found in the Time and Billing application.

Open the frmClients form in CHAP13.MDB in Design view. Place a breakpoint on the line of code `If IsNull(Me![ClientID]) Then` found in the View Project's button `Click` event. (See Figure 13.20.) Run the form and click the View Projects command button. Step through the code and watch it execute.

FIGURE 13.20

Setting a breakpoint in frmClients.

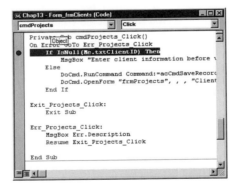

SUMMARY

If programming were a perfect science, there would be no reason to use a debugger. Given the reality of the challenges of programming, a thorough understanding of the use of the debugger is imperative. Fortunately, the Access 2000 IDE provides an excellent tool to assist in the debugging process.

This chapter begins by showing you how you can reduce the chance of bugs within your application in the first place. It then taught you how to use the Immediate window to test and change the values of variables and properties. You learned how to use watches and breakpoints, as well as how to view the call stack. All these techniques help make the process of testing and debugging your application a pleasant experience.

13

ERROR HANDLING: PREPARING FOR THE INEVITABLE

IN THIS CHAPTER

WHY THIS CHAPTER IS IMPORTANT

Errors happen, even in the absence of programmer error. You need to protect your programs and your data from the adverse effects of errors by practicing error handling.

Error handling is also known as error trapping. *Error handling* is the process of intercepting Jet's or VBA's response to an error. It enables the developer to determine the severity of an error and to take the appropriate action in response to the error. This chapter shows you the techniques required to successfully implement error handling within your applications.

IMPLEMENTING ERROR HANDLING

Without error handling, the user of your application is forced to exit abruptly from your application code. Consider the example in Listing 14.1.

LISTING 14.1   AN EXAMPLE OF CODE WITHOUT ERROR HANDLING

```
Private Sub cmdCauseError_Click()
    Call TestError1(txtValue1, txtValue2)
End Sub

Sub TestError1(Numerator As Integer, Denominator As Integer)
    Debug.Print Numerator / Denominator
    MsgBox "I am in Test Error"
End Sub
```

The click event behind the command button calls the routine TestError1, passing it the values from two text boxes. TestError1 accepts those parameters and attempts to divide the first parameter by the second parameter. If the second parameter is equal to 0, a runtime error occurs. Because no error handling is in effect, the program terminates.

Figure 14.1 shows the error message the user receives. As you can see, the choices are Continue, End, Debug, and Help. If users choose Debug, the module window appears and they are placed in Debug mode on the line of code causing the error. Choosing Continue (this is not always available), tells Access to ignore the error and continue with the execution of the program. End terminates execution of the programming code. If the application is running with the runtime version of Access, it shuts down and users are returned to Windows. With error handling in effect, you can attempt to handle the error in a more appropriate way whenever possible.

FIGURE 14.1

The default error handling message.

You can add error-handling code to the error event procedure of a form or report. You also can add it to any VBA subroutine, function, or event routine. You easily can modify the code in Listing 14.1 to handle the error gracefully. The code in Listing 14.2 shows a simple error-handling routine.

LISTING 14.2 A SIMPLE ERROR-HANDLING ROUTINE

```
Sub TestError2(Numerator As Integer, Denominator As Integer)
On Error GoTo TestError2_Err
    Debug.Print Numerator / Denominator
    MsgBox "I am in Test Error"

    Exit Sub

TestError2_Err:
    If Err = 11 Then
        MsgBox "Variable 2 Cannot Be a Zero", , "Custom Error Handler"
    End If
    Exit Sub

End Sub
```

 This code is located in the basError module, which is in the CHAP14EX.MDB database on the accompanying CD-ROM.

The routine now invokes error handling. If a divide-by-zero error occurs, a message box alerts the user to the problem, as Figure 14.2 shows.

FIGURE 14.2

A custom error handler message.

WORKING WITH ERROR EVENTS

Every form and report contains an error event procedure. This event is triggered by any interface or Jet Database Engine error. It is not triggered by a programming error made by the Access developer.

Errors often occur in the interface of a form or report, as well as in the Jet Database Engine. A user might try to enter an order for a customer who doesn't exist, for example. Instead of displaying Access's default error message, you might want to intercept and handle the error in a particular way.

After an error occurs within a form, its error event is triggered. In Listing 14.3, you can see Sub Form_Error. It contains two parameters. The first parameter is the number of the error. The second parameter is the way you want to respond to the error. The error number is an Access-generated number.

This code, which is located in the frmOrders form in the CHAP14EX.MDB database, tests to see whether a referential integrity error has occurred. If it has, a message box asks whether the user wants to add the customer. If the user answers Yes, the customer form is displayed.

LISTING 14.3   VIEWING Sub Form_Error FROM THE FORM FRMORDERS

```
Private Sub Form_Error(DataErr As Integer, Response As Integer)
    Dim intAnswer As Integer
    If DataErr = 3201 Then  'Referential Integrity Error
        intAnswer = MsgBox("Customer Does Not Exist... _
                Would You Like to Add Them Now", vbYesNo)
        If intAnswer = vbYes Then
            DoCmd.OpenForm "frmCustomer", , , , acAdd, acDialog
        End If
    End If
    Response = acDataErrContinue
End Sub
```

CAUTION
Be aware that the sample in Listing 14.3 only traps referential integrity errors. It does not handle any other error.

The `Response = acDataErrContinue` line is very important. It instructs Access to continue the code execution without displaying the standard error message. The other option for `Response` is `AcDataErrDisplay`. It tells Access to display the default error message.

NOTE

If you want to get a list of all the errors that can occur in your VBA code, as well as a description of what each error number means, select Help | Microsoft Visual Basic Help from the VBE. Click the Index tab and type `Error` as the keyword. Click Search. Select Determine the Error Codes Reserved by Visual Basic from the Choose a Topic list box. The code required to build a table of VBA error numbers and descriptions appears in the right pane of the help window. You can copy this code into any module and run it. A table of error numbers and descriptions is created.

USING On Error STATEMENTS

`On Error` statements activate error handling. Each routine must contain its own `On Error` statement if you want that routine to do its own error handling. Otherwise, error handling is cascaded up the call stack. If no `On Error` statements are found in the call stack, VBA's own error handling is invoked.

Suppose that `Func1` calls `Func2`, and `Func2` calls `Func3`. Only `Func1` contains error handling. An error occurs in `Func3`. `Func3` passes control up to `Func2`. `Func2` has no error handling, so it passes control up to `Func1`. `Func1` handles the error. Needless to say, the error handler found in `Func1` is not necessarily appropriate to handle the error that occurred in `Func3`.

Using an `On Error` statement, you can cause the application to branch to error-handling code, resume on the line immediately following the error, or attempt to re-execute the problem line of code.

You must decide the most appropriate response to a particular error. Sometimes it is most appropriate for your application to halt in response to an error. At other times, it is best if the routine skips the offending line entirely. By combining the use of `On Error Goto`, `On Error Resume Next`, and the `Resume` statement, you can handle each error appropriately.

Using On Error Goto

The statement `On Error Goto <label>` tells VBA that, from this point forward in the subroutine or function, if an error occurs, it should jump to the label specified in the statement. This is the most common form of error handling.

The label specified in the On Error statement must be located in the current procedure, and it must be unique within a module. Listing 14.4 shows a simple example of error handling.

LISTING 14.4 AN EXAMPLE OF ERROR HANDLING USING THE On Error GoTo STATEMENT

```
Sub SimpleErrorHandler(iVar1 As Integer, iVar2 As Integer)
    On Error GoTo SimpleErrorHandler_Err

    Dim sngResult As String
    sngResult = iVar1 / iVar2

    Exit Sub

SimpleErrorHandler_Err:
    MsgBox "Oops!"
    Exit Sub

End Sub
```

You can learn some important things from this simple routine. The routine receives two integer values. It then invokes the error handler. When an error occurs, execution continues at the label. Notice that this routine contains two Exit Sub statements. If you remove the first Exit Sub statement, the code falls through to the label regardless of whether an error occurred. The Exit Sub statement at the bottom gracefully exits the procedure, setting the error code back to 0.

Including the Error Number and Description in the Error Handler

The error-handling code in Listing 14.4 did not give a very descriptive message to users. The Description and Number properties of the Err object give users more meaningful error messages. The Err object is covered in detail later in this chapter in the section "Using the Err Object." For now, take a look at the Description and Number properties to see how you can use them to enhance an error-handling routine. To display the error number and description, you must modify the error-handling code to look like this:

```
SimpleErrorHandler_Err:
    MsgBox "Error #" & Err.Number & ": " & Err.Description
    Exit Sub
```

This time, instead of hard-coding the error message, you display the error number and VBA's internal error string. Figure 14.3 shows the resulting error message. The SimpleErrorHandler routine and all the following examples are located in the basError module of the CHAP14EX.MDB database.

FIGURE 14.3

An error message with an error number and error string.

Using On Error Goto 0

You use On Error Goto 0 for two purposes:

- When you want Access to return to its default error handler
- To have Access return to the error handler of a routine above the current routine

Generally, you don't want Access to return to its default error handler. You might do this only if you are unable to handle the error or if you are in the testing phase and not yet ready to implement your own error handler.

The reason why you want Access to return the error to a higher-level routine is much clearer. You do this if you want to *centralize* the error handling, meaning that one routine might call several others. Instead of placing error-handling code in each routine that is called, it is appropriate in certain situations to place the error handling in the calling routine.

Using On Error Resume Next

On Error Resume Next continues program execution on the line immediately following the error. This construct generally is used when it is acceptable to ignore an error and continue code execution. Listing 14.5 shows an example of such a situation.

LISTING 14.5   IGNORING AN ERROR AND CONTINUING EXECUTION

```
Sub TestResumeNext()
    On Error Resume Next
    Kill "AnyFile"
    MsgBox "We Didn't Die, But the Error Was: " & Err.Description
End Sub
```

You use the Kill statement to delete a file from disk. If the specified file is not found, an error results. You delete the file only if it exists, so you are not concerned about an error. On Error Resume Next is very appropriate in this situation because no harm is done by resuming execution after the offending line of code.

USING Resume STATEMENTS

While you are in your error-handling code, you can use the Resume, Resume Next, and Resume *<LineLabel>* statements to specify how you want VBA to respond to the error. Resume attempts to re-execute the offending line of code, Resume Next resumes execution after the offending line of code, and Resume *<LineLabel>* continues execution at a specified line label. The following sections cover these statements in detail.

The Resume Statement

The Resume statement resumes code execution on the line of code that caused the error. You must use this statement with extreme care because it can throw the code into an unrecoverable endless loop. Listing 14.6 shows an example of an inappropriate use of the Resume statement.

LISTING 14.6   USING Resume INAPPROPRIATELY

```
Function BadResume(strFileName As String)
    On Error GoTo BadResume_Err
    Dim strFile As String
    strFile = Dir(strFileName)
    If strFile = "" Then
      BadResume = False
    Else
      BadResume = True
    End If
    Exit Function

BadResume_Err:
    MsgBox Error
    Resume
End Function
```

This function is passed a filename. The Dir function searches for the filename and returns True or False, depending on whether the specified filename is found. The problem occurs when the drive requested is not available or does not exist. This code throws the computer into an endless loop. To remedy the problem, you should modify your code to look like the code in Listing 14.7.

LISTING 14.7 USING Resume CONDITIONALLY BASED ON USER FEEDBACK

```
Function GoodResume(strFileName As String)
    On Error GoTo GoodResume_Err
    Dim strFile As String
    strFile = Dir(strFileName)
    If strFile = "" Then
      GoodResume = False
    Else
      GoodResume = True
    End If
    Exit Function

GoodResume_Err:
    Dim intAnswer As Integer
    intAnswer = MsgBox(Error & ", Would You Like to Try Again?", vbYesNo)
    If intAnswer = vbYes Then
        Resume
    Else
        Exit Function
    End If
End Function
```

In this example, the error handler enables the user to decide whether to try again. The Resume occurs only if the user's response is affirmative.

The Resume Next Statement

Just as you can invoke error handling using an On Error Resume Next statement, you can place a Resume Next statement in your error handler, as Listing 14.8 shows.

LISTING 14.8 PLACING A Resume Next STATEMENT IN YOUR ERROR HANDLER

```
Sub TestResumeNextInError()
    On Error GoTo TestResumeNextInError_Err
    Kill "AnyFile"
    MsgBox "We Didn't Die!"
    Exit Sub

TestResumeNextInError_Err:
    Resume Next
End Sub
```

In this example, the code is instructed to go to the label called `TestResumeNextInError_Err` when an error occurs. The `TestResumeNextInError_Err` label issues a `Resume Next` statement. This clears the error and causes execution to continue on the line after the line on which the error occurred.

The Resume *<LineLabel>* Statement

The `Resume` *<LineLabel>* statement enables you to specify a line of code where you want code execution to continue after an error occurs. This is a great way to eliminate the two `Exit Sub` or `Exit Function` statements required by the error-handling routines you have looked at so far. Listing 14.9 shows an example.

LISTING 14.9   USING THE `Resume` <LineLabel> STATEMENT TO SPECIFY WHERE EXECUTION CONTINUES AFTER AN ERROR OCCURS

```
Sub TestResumeLineLabel(intVar1 As Integer, intVar2 As Integer)
    On Error GoTo TestResumeLineLabel_Err

    Dim sngResult As String
    sngResult = intVar1 / intVar2

TestResumeLineLabel_Exit:
    Exit Sub

TestResumeLineLabel_Err:
    MsgBox "Error #" & Err.Number & ": " & Err.Description
    Resume TestResumeLineLabel_Exit

End Sub
```

Notice that this routine contains only one `Exit Sub` statement. If no error occurs, Access drops through the `TestResumeLineLabel_Exit` label to the `Exit Sub` statement. If an error *does* occur, the code in the `TestResumeLineLabel_Err` label executes. Notice that the last line of the error label resumes execution at the `TestResumeLineLabel_Exit` label.

This method of resolving an error is useful because any code required to execute as the routine is exited can be written in one place. Object variables might need to be set equal to `Nothing` as the routine is exited, for example. You can place these lines of code in the exit routine.

CLEARING AN ERROR

When an error occurs, the `Err` object remains set with the error information until one of the following clears the error:

- Resume, Resume Next, or Resume `<LineLabel>`
- Exit Sub, Exit Function, or Exit Property
- Any Goto statement
- Explicitly using the Clear method on the Err object

Until the error is cleared somehow, all the information remains set in the Err object. After the error is cleared, no information is found in the Err object.

EXAMINING THE CASCADING ERROR EFFECT

As mentioned earlier in the section "Using On Error Statements," if Access does not find any error handling in a particular subroutine or function, it looks up the call stack for a previous error handler. Listing 14.10 shows an example of this process.

LISTING 14.10 LOOKING UP THE CALL STACK FOR A PREVIOUS ERROR HANDLER

```
Sub Func1()
    On Error GoTo Func1_Err
    Debug.Print "I am in Function 1"
    Call Func2
    Debug.Print "I am back in Function 1"
    Exit Sub

Func1_Err:
    MsgBox "Error in Func1"
    Resume Next
End Sub

Sub Func2()
    Debug.Print "I am in Func 2"
    Call Func3
    Debug.Print "I am still in Func2"
End Sub

Sub Func3()
    Dim sngAnswer As Single
    Debug.Print "I am in Func 3"
    sngAnswer = 5 / 0
    Debug.Print "I am still in Func3"
End Sub
```

In this situation, the error occurs in Func3. Because Func3 does not have its own error handling, it refers back to Func2. Func2 does not have any error handling either, so Func2 relinquishes control to Func1. VBA executes the error code in Func1. The real problem occurs because of the Resume Next statement. The application continues executing within Func1 on the Debug.Print "I am back in Function 1" statement. This type of error handling is dangerous and confusing. Therefore, it is best to develop a generic error-handling routine that is accessed throughout your application. The creation of a generic error handler is discussed in the section "Creating a Generic Error Handler."

USING THE Err OBJECT

The Err object contains information about the most recent error that occurred. As with all Access objects, it has its own built-in properties and methods. Table 14.1 lists the properties of the Err object.

TABLE 14.1 PROPERTIES OF THE Err OBJECT

Property	Description
Description	Description of the error that occurred
HelpContext	Context ID for the Help file
HelpFile	Path and filename of the Help file
LastDLLError	Last error that occurred in a 32-bit DLL
Number	Number of the error that was set
Source	System in which the error occurred (which is extremely useful when you are using OLE automation to control another application, such as Excel)

The Err object has only two methods: Clear and Raise. The Clear method enables you to clear an error condition explicitly. This is used primarily when you write code that uses the On Error Resume Next statement. This statement does not clear the error condition. Remember that there is no reason to issue the Clear method explicitly with any type of Resume, Exit Sub, Exit Function, Exit Property, or On Error Goto statement. The Clear method is implicitly issued when these constructs are used. The Raise method of the Err object is covered in the next section.

RAISING AN ERROR

You use the Raise method of the error object in these situations:

- When you want to generate an error on purpose (for example, in testing)

- When you want to generate a user-defined error
- When no code in the error routine handles the current error and you want to allow other parts of the call stack to attempt to handle the error
- When you want to nest an error handler

Using the `Raise` method to generate an error on purpose and creating a user-defined error are covered in the following sections.

Generating an Error on Purpose

Many times, you want to generate an error when testing so that you can test out your own error handling. Instead of figuring out how to cause the error condition, you can use the `Raise` method of the `Err` object to accomplish this task, as Listing 14.11 shows.

LISTING 14.11   RAISING AN ERROR

```
Sub TestRaiseError()
    On Error GoTo TestRaiseError_Err

    Dim sngResult As String
    Err.Raise 11

    Exit Sub

TestRaiseError_Err:
    MsgBox "Error #" & Err.Number & ": " & Err.Description
    Exit Sub

End Sub
```

This code invokes an error 11 (divide by 0). By generating the error, you can test the effectiveness of your error-handling routine.

Creating User-Defined Errors

Another important use of the `Raise` method of the `Err` object is the generation of a custom error condition. This is useful when you want to have something, which does not generate an Access error, generate a user-defined error that you send through the normal error-handling process. Because the `Raise` method enables you to set all the properties of the `Err` object, you can create a user-defined error complete with a number, description, source, and so on, as shown in Listing 14.12.

LISTING 14.12 CREATING A USER-DEFINED ERROR

```
Sub TestCustomError()
   On Error GoTo TestCustomError_Err
   Dim strName As String
   strName = InputBox("Please Enter Your Name")
   If Len(strName) < 5 Then
      Err.Raise Number:=11111, _
               Description:="Length of Name is Too Short"
   Else
      MsgBox "You Entered " & strName
   End If
   Exit Sub

TestCustomError_Err:
   MsgBox "Error # " & Err.Number & _
          " - " & Err.Description
   Exit Sub
End Sub
```

Although it is very simple, this example illustrates an important use of generating user-defined errors. The code tests to see whether the value entered has less than five characters. If it does, a user-defined error (number 11111) is generated. The routine drops into the normal error-handling routine. The section, "Creating a Generic Error Handler," later in this chapter, explores how to put together a generic error handler. By passing user-defined errors through your generic error handler, all errors—user-defined or not—are handled in the same way.

USING THE ERRORS COLLECTION

The Errors collection is part of Access's Jet Engine. It stores the most recent set of DAO errors that have occurred. This is important when dealing with DAO and ODBC, when one operation can result in multiple errors. If you are concerned with each error that was generated by one operation, you need to look at the Errors collection. The Errors collection has the same properties as the Err object. If you want to view the errors stored in the Errors collection, you must loop through it, viewing the properties of each Err object. Listing 14.13 shows the code you can use to accomplish this.

LISTING 14.13   VIEWING THE ERRORS STORED IN THE ERRORS COLLECTION

```
Sub TestErrorsCollection()
    On Error GoTo TestErrorsCollection_Err
    Dim db As DAO.Database
    Set db = CurrentDb
    db.Execute ("qryNonExistent")
    Exit Sub

TestErrorsCollection_Err:
    Dim ErrorDescrip As Error
    For Each ErrorDescrip In Errors
        Debug.Print ErrorDescrip.Description
    Next ErrorDescrip
    Exit Sub
End Sub
```

This routine loops through each `Error` object in the Errors collection, printing the description of each error contained in the collection.

CREATING A GENERIC ERROR HANDLER

A *generic* error handler is an error handler that can be called from anywhere in your application. It is capable of responding to any type of error.

A generic error handler prevents you from having to write specific error handling in each of your subroutines and functions. This enables you to invoke error handling throughout your application in the most efficient manner possible.

You can take many approaches to create a generic error handler. A generic error handler should give users information about the error, enable users to print this information, and log the information to a file. A generic error handler should be able to be called from every procedure within your application.

The `On Error` routine (in this case, the label `AnySub_Err`) of every procedure that performs error handling should look like the error-handling routine contained in the subroutine in Listing 14.14.

LISTING 14.14 A GENERIC ERROR HANDLER FOR ALL YOUR FUNCTIONS AND SUBROUTINES

```
Sub AnySub()
    Const SUBNAME = "ANYSUB"
    On Error GoTo AnySub_Err

    MsgBox "This is the rest of your code...."
    Err.Raise 11
    MsgBox "We are Past the Error!!"

    Exit Sub


AnySub_Err:
    Dim intAction As Integer
    intAction = ErrorHandler(intErrorNum:=Err.Number, _
                strErrorDescription:=Err.Description, _
                strModuleName:=MODULENAME, _
                strRoutineName:=SUBNAME)


    Select Case intAction
        Case ERR_CONTINUE
            Resume Next
        Case ERR_RETRY
            Resume
        Case ERR_EXIT
            Exit Sub
        Case ERR_QUIT
            Quit
    End Select
End Sub
```

This error-handling routine in AnySub creates an Integer variable that holds the return value from the error system. The intAction variable holds an appropriate response to the error that occurred. The error routine calls the generic error-handling function ErrorHandler, passing it the error number (Err.Number), a description of the error (Err.Description), the name of the module containing the error, and the name of the subroutine or function containing the error. The name of the module is stored in a Private constant called MODULENAME. The Private constant is declared in the General section of the module and needs to be created for every module you make. The name of the subroutine or function is stored in a local constant called SUBNAME. With this approach, you create a local constant and assign it the name of the sub at the beginning of each procedure. This requires upkeep because procedure names can change and you need to remember to change your string. Unfortunately, because the VBA environment does not expose the subroutine and module names to you when an error occurs, this sort of brute force is necessary if you want your error handler to track the subroutine and module. When the code returns from the `ErrorHandler` function, a return value is placed in the `intAction` variable. This return value is used to determine the fate of the routine.

Now that you have seen how to implement error handling in your procedures, take a look at the function that is called when an error occurs, as shown in Listing 14.15.

LISTING 14.15 A Type Structure Declaration to be Used for Generic Error Handling

```
Type typErrors
    intErrorNum As Integer
    strMessage As String
    strModule As String
    strRoutine As String
    strUserName As String
    datDateTime As Variant
End Type

Public gtypError As typErrors

Public Const ERR_CONTINUE = 0   'Resume Next
Public Const ERR_RETRY = 1 'Resume
Public Const ERR_QUIT = 2   'End
Public Const ERR_EXIT = 3   'Exit Sub or Func
```

This code is placed in the General section of `basHandleErrors`. The type structure declared holds all the pertinent information about the error. Type structures are covered in Chapter 24, "Advanced VBA Techniques." For now, it is sufficient to understand that a type structure is a special kind of variable that is comprised of various parts. Each part stores a different piece of information. The public variable `gtypError` holds all the information from the type structure. The constants are used to help determine the fate of the application after an error occurs. Listing 14.16 shows the `ErrorHandler` function.

LISTING 14.16 Using the `ErrorHandler` Function

```
Function ErrorHandler(intErrorNum As Integer, _
                strErrorDescription As String, _
                strModuleName As String, _
                strRoutineName As String) As Integer
    gtypError.intErrorNum = intErrorNum
    gtypError.strMessage = strErrorDescription
    gtypError.strModule = strModuleName
    gtypError.strRoutine = strRoutineName
    gtypError.strUserName = CurrentUser()
    gtypError.datDateTime = Now
```

continues

LISTING 14.16 CONTINUED

```
Call LogError

Dim rst As ADODB.Recordset
Set rst = New ADODB.Recordset
rst.Open "Select Response from tblErrors Where ErrorNum = " _
 & intErrorNum,
    CurrentProject.Connection, adOpenStatic
If rst.EOF Then
    DoCmd.OpenForm "frmError", WindowMode:=acDialog, _
        OpenArgs:="ErrorHandler"
    ErrorHandler = ERR_QUIT
Else
    Select Case rst!Response
        Case ERR_QUIT
            DoCmd.OpenForm "frmError", WindowMode:=acDialog, _
                OpenArgs:="Critical Error:  _
                Application will Terminate"
            ErrorHandler = ERR_QUIT
        Case ERR_RETRY
            ErrorHandler = ERR_RETRY
        Case ERR_EXIT
            DoCmd.OpenForm "frmError", WindowMode:=acDialog, _
                OpenArgs:="Severe Error:  Processing Did Not Complete"
            ErrorHandler = ERR_EXIT
        Case ERR_CONTINUE
            ErrorHandler = ERR_CONTINUE
    End Select
End If

End Function
```

The ErrorHandler function receives the error number, error description, module name, and subroutine or function name as parameters. It then fills in the gtypError type structure with the information that it was passed, as well as the current user and date. Next, it calls a routine that logs the error into an Access table. The routine looks up the severity of the error code in an Access table called tblErrors to decide the most appropriate way to handle the error. If the error code is not found in the error table, an error form is displayed and a return value is sent to the calling function, indicating that application execution is to be terminated. If the error code is found in the tblErrors table and determined to be critical or severe, an error form appears before control is returned to the calling routine. In any case, a severity code for the error is returned to the calling function. The following section discusses the details involved in each step of the process.

Logging the Error

The LogError routine is responsible for logging all the error information into an Access table. Because users often decide not to print the error form or provide you with inaccurate information about what was happening when the error occurred (or neglect to tell you about the error), it is important that you log each error so that you can review the error log at any time. Errors can be logged to a text file or a data table. This section shows you both methods of logging your error. Start with logging your errors to a table. Listing 14.17 shows the LogError routine.

LISTING 14.17   USING THE LogError ROUTINE

```
Sub LogError()
    Dim cnn As ADODB.Connection
    Dim strSQL As String
    Set cnn = CurrentProject.Connection
    strSQL = "INSERT INTO tblErrorLog ( ErrorDate, ErrorTime, " _
    "UserName, ErrorNum, ErrorString, ModuleName, RoutineName) "
    strSQL = strSQL & "Select #" & gtypError.datDateTime & "#, #" _
                            & gtypError.datDateTime & "#, '" _
                            & gtypError.strUserName & "', " _
                            & gtypError.intErrorNum & ", '" _
                            & gtypError.strMessage & "', '" _
                            & gtypError.strModule & "', '" _
                            & gtypError.strRoutine & "'"

    cnn.Execute strSQL, , adExecuteNoRecords

End Sub
```

This routine uses the Execute method of the ADO Connection object to add a record to your error table. The record contains all the information from the structure called gtypError. The information is logged to a table called tblErrorLog. Figure 14.4 shows the structure of this table.

14

ERROR HANDLING:
PREPARING FOR
THE INEVITABLE

FIGURE 14.4

The structure of the tblErrorLog table.

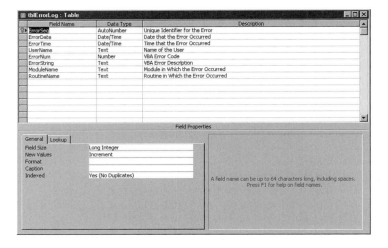

The alternative is to write the information to a textual error log file, as shown in Listing 14.18.

LISTING 14.18   WRITING INFORMATION TO A TEXTUAL ERROR LOG FILE

```
Sub LogErrorText()
    Dim intFile As Integer
    intFile = FreeFile
    Open CurDir & "\ErrorLog.Txt" For Append Shared As intFile
    Write #intFile, "LogErrorDemo", Now, Err, Error, CurrentUser()
    Close intFile
End Sub
```

This code uses the low-level file functions `Open` and `Write` to open and write to an ASCII text file. All the pertinent information about the error is written to this text file. The routine then uses the `Close` command to close the text file. The potential advantage of this routine is that, if the problem is with the database (for example, the network is down), the error logging process still succeeds.

Determining the Appropriate Response to an Error

After the error is logged, you are ready to determine the best way to respond to the error. By making your error system data driven, you can handle each error a little differently. Figure 14.5 shows the structure of the tblErrors table. This table should contain a list of all the error numbers that you want to trap. It contains three fields: ErrorNum, ErrorDescription, and Response. When an error occurs, the `ErrorHandler` function searches for a record with a value in the ErrorNum field that matches the number of the error that occurred. The `ErrorHandler` function, as shown in Listing 14.16, uses the code in Listing 14.19 to locate the error code in the tblErrors table.

LISTING 14.19 LOCATING THE ERROR CODE IN THE TBLERRORS TABLE

```
Dim rst As ADODB.Recordset
Set rst = New ADODB.Recordset
rst.Open "Select Response from tblErrors Where ErrorNum = "
  _& intErrorNum, CurrentProject.Connection, adOpenStatic
If rst.EOF Then
    DoCmd.OpenForm "frmError", WindowMode:=acDialog, _
        OpenArgs:="ErrorHandler"
    ErrorHandler = ERR_QUIT
Else
    Select Case rst!Response
        Case ERR_QUIT
            DoCmd.OpenForm "frmError", WindowMode:=acDialog, _
                OpenArgs:="Critical Error:  Application will Terminate"
            ErrorHandler = ERR_QUIT
        Case ERR_RETRY
            ErrorHandler = ERR_RETRY
        Case ERR_EXIT
            DoCmd.OpenForm "frmError", WindowMode:=acDialog, _
                OpenArgs:="Severe Error:  Processing Did Not Complete"
            ErrorHandler = ERR_EXIT
        Case ERR_CONTINUE
            ErrorHandler = ERR_CONTINUE
    End Select
End If
```

FIGURE 14.5

The structure of the tblErrors table.

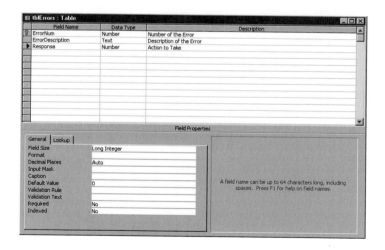

This part of the ErrorHandler function creates an ADO Recordset object variable. It opens a recordset using a Select statement. The Select statement searches a table called tblErrors. If a match is found, the Response column is used to determine the response to the error. Notice in Listing 14.19 that, if the error number is not found in tblErrors, default error handling occurs, which means that the code handles all other errors as a group. (This is my default error handling, not Access's.) If the error number is found, the Response field is evaluated and the appropriate action is taken (via the case statement). If it is not found, the frmError form is opened and the ERR_QUIT constant value is returned from the ErrorHandler function. By using this method, you need to add to the table only specific errors that you want to trap.

If no records are found in tblErrors that match the SQL statement, the frmError form is opened, and the return value for the function is set equal to the constant value ERR_QUIT. If the error number is found in tblErrors, the Response field from the recordset is evaluated. If the Response field contains the constant value ERR_QUIT or ERR_EXIT, the frmError form appears before the constant value is returned to the offending function or subroutine. If the Response field contains the constant value for ERR_RETRY or ERR_CONTINUE, the constant value is returned without displaying the frmError form.

> **NOTE**
>
> The tblErrors table is included in CHAP14EX.MDB on the sample code CD-ROM. To take full advantage of this table, you must add all errors that you want to trap for along with the actions that you want the error handler to take when that error occurs.

The return value from the ErrorHandler function is used as shown in Listing 14.20.

LISTING 14.20   USING THE RETURN VALUE FROM THE ErrorHandler FUNCTION

```
Sub AnySub()

    CONST SUBNAME as String = "AnySub"
    On Error GoTo AnySub_Err

    MsgBox "This is the rest of your code...."
    Err.Raise 11
    MsgBox "We are Past the Error!!"

    Exit Sub

AnySub_Exit:
```

```
      Exit Sub

AnySub_Err:
    Dim intAction As Integer
    intAction = ErrorHandler(intErrorNum:=Err.Number, _
                strErrorDescription:=Err.Description, _
                strModuleName:=MODULENAME, _
                strRoutineName:=SUBNAME)

    Select Case intAction
        Case ERR_CONTINUE
            Resume Next
        Case ERR_RETRY
            Resume
        Case ERR_EXIT
            Resume AnySub_Exit
        Case ERR_QUIT
            Quit
    End Select
End Sub
```

In this example, the AnySub routine generates an error 11 (divide by 0). Because tblErrors contains the number 3 in the Response column and the ERR_CONTINUE constant is equal to 3, the error form is displayed and the AnySub routine is exited with an Exit Sub statement.

NOTE

To test what happens when the error code is not found in the tblErrors table, run the SubWithUnknownError routine found in basError. To test what happens when the ERR_CONTINUE code is returned, execute the SubWithContinue routine.

Creating an Error Form

The code in the error form's load event calls two subroutines: GetSystemInfo and GetErrorInfo, as shown here:

```
Private Sub Form_Load()
    Call GetSysInfo(Me)
    Call GetErrorInfo(Me)
    Me!lblAction.Caption = Me.OpenArgs
End Sub
```

14

ERROR HANDLING:
PREPARING FOR
THE INEVITABLE

The first subroutine is called `GetSystemInfo`. It performs several Windows API calls to fill in the system information on your form. The code is shown in Listing 14.21, and it is discussed in Chapter 27, "Exploiting the Power of the Windows API."

LISTING 14.21 GETTING SYSTEM INFORMATION THROUGH CODE

```
Sub GetSysInfo (frmAny As Form)
'Get Free Memory
    Dim MS As MEMORYSTATUS
    MS.dwLength = Len(MS)
    GlobalMemoryStatus MS

    frmAny!lblMemoryTotal.Caption = Format(MS.dwTotalPhys, "Standard")
    frmAny!lblMemoryAvail.Caption = Format(MS.dwAvailPhys, "Standard")

    'Get Version Information
    Dim OSInfo As OSVERSIONINFO
    OSInfo.dwOSVersionInfoSize = Len(OSInfo)
    If GetVersionEx(OSInfo) Then
        frmAny!lblOSVersion.Caption = OSInfo.dwMajorVersion & "." _
            & OSInfo.dwMinorVersion
        frmAny!lblBuild.Caption = OSInfo.dwBuildNumber And &HFFFF&
        If OSInfo.dwPlatformId = 0 Then
            frmAny!lblPlatform.Caption = "Windows 95"
        Else
            frmAny!lblPlatform.Caption = "Windows NT"
        End If
    End If

    'Get System Information
    Dim SI As SYSTEM_INFO
     GetSystemInfo SI
    frmAny!lblProcessor.Caption = SI.dwProcessorType
End Sub
```

These API calls require the `Declare` statements and constants shown in Listing 14.22. They are placed in a module called basAPI.

LISTING 14.22   DECLARING WINDOWS API CALLS

```
Option Compare Database
Option Explicit

Private Declare Sub GlobalMemoryStatus Lib "Kernel32"_
(lpBuffer As MEMORYSTATUS)

Private Type MEMORYSTATUS
    dwLength As Long
    dwMemoryLoad As Long
    dwTotalPhys As Long
    dwAvailPhys As Long
    dwTotalPageFile As Long
    dwAvailPageFile As Long
    dwTotalVirtual As Long
    dwAvailVirtual As Long
End Type

Private Declare Function GetVersionEx Lib "Kernel32" _
  Alias "GetVersionExA" (lpOSInfo As OSVERSIONINFO) As Boolean

Type OSVERSIONINFO
    dwOSVersionInfoSize As Long
    dwMajorVersion As Long
    dwMinorVersion As Long
    dwBuildNumber As Long
    dwPlatformId As Long
    strReserved As String * 128
End Type

Private Declare Sub GetSystemInfo Lib "Kernel32"_
  (lpSystemInfo As SYSTEM_INFO)

Private Type SYSTEM_INFO
    dwOemID As Long
    dwPageSize As Long
    lpMinimumApplicationAddress As Long
    lpMaximumApplicationAddress As Long
    dwActiveProcessorMask As Long
    dwNumberOrfProcessors As Long
    dwProcessorType As Long
    dwAllocationGranularity As Long
    dwReserved As Long
End Type
```

The second subroutine, GetErrorInfo, fills in the labels on the error form with all the information from your structure, as shown in Listing 14.23.

LISTING 14.23 USING THE GetErrorInfo SUBROUTINE

```
Sub GetErrorInfo(frmAny As Form)
    frmAny!lblErrorNumber.Caption = gtypError.intErrorNum
    frmAny!lblErrorString.Caption = gtypError.strMessage
    frmAny!lblUserName.Caption = gtypError.strUserName
    frmAny!lblDateTime.Caption = Format(gtypError.datDateTime, "c")
    frmAny!lblModuleName.Caption = gtypError.strModule
    frmAny!lblRoutineName.Caption = gtypError.strRoutine
End Sub
```

Finally, the disposition of the error, sent as an OpenArg from the ErrorHandler function, is displayed in a label on the form. Figure 14.6 shows the error form.

FIGURE 14.6

The frmErrors form displays important information about the error that occurred.

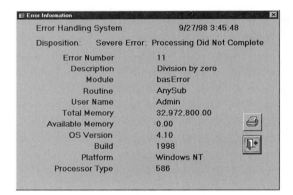

Printing the Error Form

Users often are not very accurate in describing an error and corresponding error message. It therefore is important to give them the capability to print their error message. The code in Listing 14.24 prints your error form. It is found behind the click event of the Print button on the error form.

LISTING 14.24   PRINTING YOUR ERROR FORM

```
Sub cmdPrint_Click()
On Error GoTo Err_cmdPrint_Click


    DoCmd.PrintOut

Exit_cmdPrint_Click:
    Exit Sub

Err_cmdPrint_Click:
    MsgBox Err.Description
    Resume Exit_cmdPrint_Click

End Sub
```

PREVENTING YOUR OWN ERROR HANDLING FROM BEING INVOKED

When you are testing your application, you do not want your own error handling to be triggered. Instead, you want VBA's error handling to be activated. The trick is in the Options dialog box of the VBE. Choose Tools | Options and click the General tab. Enable the option Break on All Errors located in the Error Trapping section. As long as this option is set, your error handling is ignored and Access's default error handling is invoked. Using this setting, you can turn error handling on and off from one central location.

PRACTICAL EXAMPLES

Incorporating Error Handling

Error-handling code should be added throughout the Time and Billing application. The following example shows you how to incorporate the generic error handler into the Time and Billing application.

The Time and Billing application contains a routine called GetCompanyInfo. This routine reads all the company information from the tblCompanyInfo table. The information is read from the type structure, as needed, while the application is running. This routine, like any routine, has the potential for error. The original routine has been modified to incorporate the generic error handler, as shown in Listing 14.25.

LISTING 14.25   INCORPORATING THE GENERIC ERROR HANDLER INTO YOUR CODE

```
Sub GetCompanyInfo()
    On Error GoTo GetCompanyInfo_Err
    Dim strSubName As String
    Dim db As DATABASE
    Dim rs As Recordset
    strSubName = "GetCompanyInfo"
    Set db = CurrentDb
    Set rs = db.OpenRecordset("tblCompanyInfo", dbOpenSnapshot)
    gtypCompanyInfo.SetUpID = rs!SetUpID
    gtypCompanyInfo.CompanyName = rs!CompanyName
    gtypCompanyInfo.Address = rs!Address
    gtypCompanyInfo.City = rs!City
    gtypCompanyInfo.StateProvince = rs!StateProvince
    gtypCompanyInfo.PostalCode = rs!PostalCode
    gtypCompanyInfo.Country = rs!Country
    gtypCompanyInfo.PhoneNumber = rs!PhoneNumber
    gtypCompanyInfo.FaxNumber = rs!PhoneNumber
    rs.Close
    db.Close
    Exit Sub

GetCompanyInfo_Err:
    Dim intAction As Integer
    intAction = ErrorHandler(intErrorNum:=Err.Number, _
                strErrorDescription:=Err.Description, _
                strModuleName:=mstrModuleName, _
                strRoutineName:=strSubName)

    Select Case intAction
        Case ERR_CONTINUE
            Resume Next
        Case ERR_RETRY
            Resume
        Case ERR_EXIT
            Exit Sub
        Case ERR_QUIT
            Quit
    End Select

End Sub
```

Notice the `On Error Goto` statement at the beginning of the routine and that the local variable `strSubName` has been declared and set equal to `GetCompanyInfo`. The generic error handler uses the local variable to display the routine within which the error occurred. The error handler `GetCompanyInfo_Err` calls the `ErrorHandler` function and then evaluates its return value.

SUMMARY

In this chapter, you learned the alternatives for handling errors in your Access applications. Regardless of the amount of testing done on an application, errors will occur. It is important that you properly trap for those errors.

This chapter covers how you can use the error event to trap for application and Jet Engine errors in forms and reports. You also learned how to use the `On Error` statement. Finally, you learned how to build a generic error system.

OPTIMIZING YOUR APPLICATION

IN THIS CHAPTER

WHY THIS CHAPTER IS IMPORTANT

In a world where it is often difficult for hardware to keep up with software, it is important to do everything you can to improve the performance of your application. This chapter helps you optimize your applications for speed and reduce the memory and hard disk space required by your applications.

INTRODUCING OPTIMIZATION

Optimization is the process of reviewing your operating environment, VBA code, application objects, and data structures to ensure that they are providing optimum performance. In a nutshell, optimization is the process of making your application leaner and meaner.

Users become frustrated when an application runs slowly. In fact, if a user is not warned about a slow process, he often will reboot or shut down the power on the machine while a process is running. This can have dire results on the integrity of the data.

TIP

To help reduce the chance of users rebooting the computer during a lengthy process, it generally is a good idea to provide them with some sort of indication that a process will take a while. You can do this by using a message box that appears before processing begins, or by providing a status bar or progress meter that shows the progress of the task being completed.

You can do many things to optimize an application's performance, ranging from using a front-end tool such as the Performance Analyzer to fastidiously adhering to certain coding techniques. This chapter highlights the major things you can do to optimize the performance of your applications.

MODIFYING HARDWARE AND SOFTWARE CONFIGURATIONS

The Access *environment* refers to the combination of hardware and software configurations under which Microsoft Access is running. These environmental settings can greatly affect the performance of an Access application.

The easiest way to improve the performance of an Access application is to upgrade the hardware and software configuration under which it is running. This form of optimization requires no direct intervention from the developer. A side benefit of most of the environmental changes you can make is that any improvements made to the environment are beneficial to users in all their Windows applications.

Improving the environment involves more than just adding some RAM. It also can mean optimally configuring the operating system and the Access application.

Hardware, Hardware, More Hardware Please!

The bottom line is that Windows 95, Windows 98, Windows NT, and Access 2000 all crave hardware—the more, the better. The faster your users' machines are, and the more memory they have, the better. Additional hardware might not be the least expensive solution, but it certainly is the quickest and easiest thing you can do to improve the performance of your application.

RAM, RAM, That's All I Need!

Memory is what Access craves most, whether you are running under the full version of Microsoft Access or using the runtime version of the product. Microsoft Access requires 12MB of RAM just to run under Windows 95 and Windows 98, its standard operating environments. Although 12MB of RAM is required, 16MB of RAM is recommended by Microsoft. Under Windows NT, Access requires a minimum of 16MB. Both requirements can climb dramatically if your user is running other applications or if your application uses OLE automation to communicate with other applications. Put in a very straightforward way, the more RAM you and the users of your application have, the better. 64MB is a great environment for Access 2000. In fact, if every one of your users has at least 64MB of RAM, you can stop reading this chapter because everything else covered here is going to provide you with minor benefits compared to adding more RAM. If you are like most of us, though, where not every one of your users has a Pentium II 450mhz with 64MB of RAM, read on.

> **NOTE**
>
> Developers should have a bare minimum of 64MB of RAM installed on their machines. Remember that this is a minimum! Most developers agree that 128MB of RAM is ideal if you intend to do any serious development work, especially if you plan to develop client/server or Internet/intranet applications.

Defragment Your User's Hard Disk

As your computer writes information to disk, it attempts to find contiguous space on which to place data files. As the hard disk fills up, files are placed in fragmented pieces on the hard disk. Each time your application attempts to read data and programs, it must locate the information scattered over the disk. This is a very time-consuming process. It therefore is helpful to defragment the hard disk on which the application and data tables are stored, using a utility such as the Disk Defragmenter that ships with Windows 95, 98, and Windows NT 5.0.

TIP

The process of defragmenting a hard disk easily can be automated by using the System Agent, which is included as part of the Microsoft Plus! Pack. The Microsoft Plus! package is sold as an add-on to Windows 95. The System Agent is a useful tool that enables you to schedule when and how often the defragmentation process occurs. Windows 98 ships with the Maintenance Wizard that is used to schedule various system tasks to run automatically such as the Disk Deframenter and the Scandisk utility.

Compact Your Database

Just as the operating system fragments your files over time, Access itself introduces its own form of fragmentation. Each time you add and modify data, your database grows. The problem is that when you delete data or objects within your database, it does not shrink. Instead, Access leaves empty pages available in which new data will be placed. The problem is that these empty pages are not necessarily filled with data. The empty space can be freed using the Compact utility, which is part of the Microsoft Access software. The Compact utility frees excess space and attempts to make all data pages contiguous. You should compact your database frequently, especially if records or database objects (for example, forms and reports) are regularly added and deleted. The Compact utility can be accessed only when no database is open. To access the Compact utility, choose Tools|Database Utilities. Then choose the Compact and Repair Database option.

NOTE

It is worth noting that if you plan to distribute an Access application to other users, possibly via the runtime module, it is a good idea to include some means of compacting the database. Often, the runtime module does not allow access to the Compact menu item. The `CompactDatabase` method enables you to compact a database from within an Access database, but you cannot call this command from within the current application. A second application must be created to use the `CompactDatabase` method on the original application.

Don't Use Compressed Drives

Regardless of the compression utility you are using, disk compression will significantly degrade performance with Access 2000. This fact is documented in the README file.

Tune Virtual Memory: Tweak the Swap File

Although Windows 95 and Windows 98 attempt to manage virtual memory on their own, you might find it useful to provide them with some additional advice. To modify the physical location of the swap file, right-click My Computer. Choose Properties and then select the Performance tab. Click the Virtual Memory button. It might be useful to move the swap file to a faster disk drive or a drive connected to a separate controller card. Any changes you make might adversely affect performance. It is important that you evaluate whether any changes you make will help the situation—or, perhaps, make things worse! In general, it is advisable to let Windows dynamically manage the size of the swap file unless the system is running very low on disk space.

> **TIP**
>
> If Access 2000 or Windows is running on a compressed drive, you can improve performance by moving the swap file to an uncompressed drive. If possible, the swap file should be located on a drive or partition solely dedicated to the swap file, or a drive or partition that is accessed rarely by other applications. This helps to ensure that the swap file remains in a contiguous location on disk.

Run Access and Your Application Locally

In Chapter 17, "Developing Multiuser Applications," you will learn that it is best to install both the Access software and your application objects on each user's local machine. Only the data tables should be stored on a network file server. Otherwise, you will be sending DLLs, OLE objects, help files, type libraries, executables, and database objects all over the network wire. If you want to get the worst possible performance out of an Access application, install it on a diskless workstation with 16MB of RAM!

Do Everything You Can to Make Windows Itself Faster

It always amuses me that the users with the slowest machines and the least memory have the most accessories running. These accessories include multimedia, fancy wallpapers, and other nifty utilities. If performance is a problem, you might try to see whether eliminating some of the frivolous niceties improves the performance of your application. If it does, encourage the user to eliminate the frills, get more memory, or accept your application's performance. Furthermore, if you are finished using other applications, such as Microsoft Excel, close them. This frees up system memory for Access.

Another tip to make Windows 95 and Windows 98 run faster is to shut down and restart on a regular basis. Memory tends to get fragmented, and applications run more slowly. Whereas I can go weeks or months in Windows NT without rebooting, I find it beneficial to reboot my Windows 95 and Windows 98 machines a couple of times a day.

Change Access's Software Settings

In addition to the more obvious measures just outlined, some minor software tweaking can go a long way toward improving performance. Adjusting several settings in the Windows registry can dramatically improve performance. These changes all involve the registry's ISAM section. The properties you might want to change include `MaxBufferSize` and `ReadAheadPages`. Both these settings determine how the Jet Engine uses memory.

`MaxBufferSize` controls the maximum size of the Jet Engine's internal cache. By default, it is set to optimize performance on most machines. It does this by reading data in 2KB pages, placing the data in a memory cache. The data in the cache is readily available to forms, reports, tables, and queries. Lowering the value for `MaxBufferSize` frees memory for other tasks. This might be helpful on a machine with a minimum memory configuration.

`ReadAheadPages` controls the number of 2KB data pages that the Jet Engine reads ahead when performing sequential page reads. This number can range from 0–31, with the default at 16. The higher the number, the more efficient Access is at reading ahead so that data is available when you need it. The lower this number, the more memory is freed up for other tasks.

As you configure any of these settings, remember that what is good for one machine is not necessarily good for the next. The settings for each machine must be optimized with its unique hardware configuration in mind.

UNDERSTANDING WHAT JET 4.0 DOES TO IMPROVE PERFORMANCE

Improvements have been made to the Jet 4.0 Engine to dramatically improve performance over its predecessors. Some of these improvements appeared with the Jet 3.0 Engine that shipped with Access 95 or the Jet 3.5 Engine that shipped with Access 97, but many are new to Jet 4.0. The Jet 4.0 Engine is thoroughly 32-bit. It takes advantage of multiple execution threads, providing significant performance benefits.

Specific improvements that appeared with Jet 3.5 (Access 97) include the following:

- Faster delete operations. Portions of a page can be removed at once, instead of removing data row by row.

- Better multiuser concurrency on indexed columns. More users can read and update indexed columns without experiencing locking conflicts; indexed columns no longer contain read locks.

- Implicit transaction processing. Whereas many people wrapped processing loops in the `BeginTrans...CommitTrans` construct in earlier versions of Access to limit the number of disk writes, the Jet 3.5 Engine handled this quite well on its own.

- Large queries run faster. This is because of improvements in the transactional behavior for SQL data manipulation language (DML) statements as well as new registry settings that force transactions to commit when a certain lock threshold is reached.

- Queries containing the inequality operator (<>) run faster.

- Sequential reads are faster. Up to 64KB of disk space can be allocated at a time.

- Temporary queries run faster.

- Deleting a table is faster when you use `SQL DROP` or `SQL DELETE`.

- The amount of space occupied by indexes is reduced.

- When you compact a database, all indexes are optimized for performance.

- Improved page allocation mechanism. This better ensures that data from a table is stored on adjacent pages and improves the read-ahead capability.

- Dynamically configured cache. The cache is configured at startup based on the amount of system memory available and contains the most recently used data, thereby enhancing performance.

- ISAM support for HTML files.

- The MaxLocksPerFile registry setting enables you to force records to commit when a certain lock threshold is hit. This speeds up the completion of large queries when data is stored on NetWare and Windows NT-based servers.

The following are new improvements to Jet 4.0:

- Data page size is now 4KB instead of 2KB. This increases the maximum database size from 1.07GB to 2.14GB, and provides better performance for many operations because of a decrease in I/O.

- The native OLEDB Provider offers superior performance to ODBC data.

- The first 255 characters of memo fields can be indexed. This significantly improves performance when searching and sorting memo fields.

15

OPTIMIZING YOUR APPLICATION

LETTING THE PERFORMANCE ANALYZER DETERMINE PROBLEM AREAS

You can do many things to improve the performance of an application. Most of them require significant attention and expertise on your part. The Performance Analyzer is a tool that does some of the work for you. This tool analyzes the design of an Access application. It suggests techniques you can use to improve the application's performance. Many of the techniques the Performance Analyzer suggests can be implemented automatically.

To use the Performance Analyzer, choose Tools | Analyze | Performance. The dialog box in Figure 15.1 appears.

FIGURE 15.1

The Performance Analyzer dialog box.

Select the individual tables, queries, forms, reports, macros, modules, and relationships you want the Performance Analyzer to scrutinize. If you want Access to analyze the relationships, you must click the Current Database tab and then select Relationships. After you make all your selections and click OK, the Performance Analyzer analyzes the selected objects. When it completes the analysis process, the Performance Analyzer dialog box appears, as shown in Figure 15.2. The Performance Analyzer dialog box provides you with a list of suggested improvements to the selected objects. The suggested improvements are broken down into recommendations, suggestions, ideas, and items that were automatically fixed. Suggested improvements will include things such as the addition of an index or conversion of an OLE object. After analyzing the Northwind database that ships with Access, for example, the Performance Analyzer suggested that fewer controls should be placed on the Employees form.

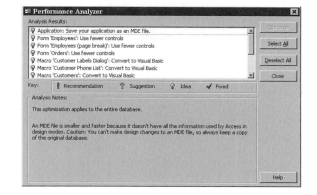

FIGURE 15.2

The second part of the Performance Analyzer dialog box.

DESIGNING TABLES TO OPTIMIZE PERFORMANCE

Now that you have seen the changes you can make to your environment to improve performance, take a look at the changes you can make to your data structures to optimize performance. Such changes include eliminating redundant data, using indexes, selecting appropriate field data types, and using various query techniques.

Optimizing performance by tweaking the data structure is imperative for good performance. No matter what else you do to improve performance, poor data design can dramatically degrade the performance of your application. All other optimization attempts are futile without proper attention to this area.

Days and days can be spent optimizing your data. These changes must be well thought out and carefully analyzed. Changes often are made over time as problems are identified. Such changes can include those in the following sections.

Why Be Normal?

In essence, this means normalize your tables. Data that appears in multiple places can significantly slow down your application. This is due to both the volume of data that is generated, as well as the need to update all copies of the data whenever the data changes. Suppose a company address appears in both the Customer table and the Orders table. If the company address changes, it must be changed in both the Customer table and in the Orders table. This information should be included only in the Customer table. Queries should be used to combine the address and order data when needed.

15

OPTIMIZING YOUR
APPLICATION

I Thought You Just Told Me to Normalize

When it comes to performance, unfortunately, there are no hard-and-fast rules. Although, most of the time, you gain performance by normalizing your data structure, denormalizing your structure can help at times. This generally is the case when you find yourself creating a particular join over and over again. Another example is an accounting application where you need to be able to readily see the total amount that a customer owes. Rather than evaluating all the open invoices each time you move to a customer record, you can store the total amount that the customer owes on the customer record. Of course, this requires that you update the summarized figure whenever the customer is billed or makes a payment. In summary, you can try denormalizing the data to see whether dramatic performance improvements result. Remember that denormalization has definite downsides regarding data integrity and maintenance.

Index, Index, Index!

It is amazing how far an index can go in improving performance. Any fields or combination of fields on which you search should be included in an index. You should create indexes for all columns used in query joins, searches, and sorts. You should create primary key indexes rather than unique indexes, and unique indexes rather than non-unique indexes. It is not necessary to create an index for the foreign key field in a one-to-many relationship. The index is created automatically by Access when the relationship is established. Furthermore, there is no benefit to creating an index on a field containing highly repetitive data. An example is a state field in a customer table where all the customers are located in one of two states. Although indexes can be overused, when used properly, the performance improvements rendered by indexes are profound.

CAUTION

Although indexes can dramatically improve performance, you should not create an index for every field in a table. Indexes do have their downside. Besides taking up disk space, they also slow down the process of adding, editing, and deleting data.

TIP

In a multiple-field index, index on as few fields as possible. Multiple-field indexes can dramatically degrade performance.

NOTE

Client/server optimization strategies are covered in Chapter 20, "Client/Server Strategies."

Select the Correct Data Type

When defining a field, select the shortest data type available for the storage of the data. If you will be storing a code between 1 and 10 within the field, for example, there is no reason to select Double for a numeric field.

DESIGNING QUERIES TO OPTIMIZE PERFORMANCE

Optimizing your queries requires a great deal of practice and experimentation. Some queries involving a one-to-many relationship run more efficiently if the criteria is placed on the one side of the relationship, for example. Others run more efficiently if the criteria is placed on the many side. Understanding some basics can go a long way toward improving the performance of your queries and your application as a whole, as listed in the following:

- Include as few columns in the resultset as possible.
- Try to reduce the number of complex expressions contained in the query. Although including a complex expression in a query eliminates the need to build the expression into each form and report, the performance benefits gained sometimes are worth the trouble.
- Use the Between operator rather than greater than (>) and less than (<).
- Use Count(*) rather than Count([column]).
- Group Totals queries by the field that is in the same table you are totaling. In other words, if you are totaling cost multiplied by price for each order in the Order Detail table, group by the order ID within the Order Detail table, not the order ID within the Orders table.

Now that you have seen what you can do with the design of your queries to improve performance, take a look at a couple of simple techniques you can use to improve the performance of your queries.

A simple but often neglected method of optimizing queries is to deliver your queries compiled. A query compiles when you open it in Datasheet view and then simply close it. If you modify a query and then save it, it is not compiled until the query runs. All queries are compiled when you compact a database. Delivering precompiled queries ensures that they run as quickly as possible. It is therefore a good idea to compact a database before you distribute it to your users.

Finally, it is important that you compile your queries using the same amount of data your application will contain. This is because Jet's Query Optimizer optimizes the query differently, depending on the amount of data it finds. If you build a query using 100 records that will run on a live table containing 100,000 records, the query will not be optimized properly. You must rerun and resave your query using the correct quantity of data if you want the query to be optimized properly, or compact the database after the live data has been entered.

MAKING CODING CHANGES TO IMPROVE PERFORMANCE

No matter what you do to optimize the operating system environment and improve your data design, poor code can continue to bog you down. A properly optimized application is optimized in terms of the environment, data design, and code. Just as poor table design can degrade performance, poor coding techniques also can have a dramatic negative effect on performance. Changes to your code include eliminating variants and dead code, using built-in collections, and using specific object types. An important code-related optimization is to deliver your modules precompiled.

The following changes and techniques can aid in the improvement of performance. It is important to recognize that any one change won't make much of a difference. However, an accumulation of all the changes, especially where code is being re-executed in a loop, can make a significant impact on your application's performance.

Eliminate Variants and Use the Smallest Data Type Possible

Variant variables are the slowest; they carry a lot of overhead because they are resolved at runtime. Remember that this statement declares a variant type of variable:

```
Dim intCounter
```

To strong type this variable as an integer, for example, your code must be modified to look like this:

```
Dim intCounter As Integer
```

Not only should you strong type your variables, but you also should use the smallest data type possible. Remember that data types such as Boolean, Byte, Integer, and Long are the smallest and therefore the fastest. These are followed by Single, Double, Currency, and (finally) Variant. Of course, if you must store very large numbers with decimal points into a variable, you cannot pick Single. Just keep in mind that it is wise to select the smallest data type appropriate for the use of the variable.

Use Specific Object Types

Just as the General variant data type is inefficient, generic object variables also are inefficient. The `MakeItBold` subroutine uses a generic object variable, as shown in Listing 15.1.

LISTING 15.1   THE `MakeItBold` SUBROUTINE

```
Private Sub cmdMakeBold_Click()
    Call MakeItBold(Screen.PreviousControl)
End Sub

Sub MakeItBold(ctlAny As Control)
    ctlAny.FontBold = True
End Sub
```

On the other hand, the `SpecificBold` subroutine uses a specific object variable, as Listing 15.2 shows.

LISTING 15.2   THE `SpecificBold` SUBROUTINE

```
Private Sub cmdSpecificBold_Click()
    Call SpecificBold(Screen.PreviousControl)
End Sub

Sub SpecificBold(txtAny As TextBox)
    txtAny.FontBold = True
End Sub
```

The difference is that the `SpecificBold` routine expects to receive only text boxes. It does not need to resolve the type of object it receives and therefore is more efficient.

This code is contained in the CHAP15EX.MDB database on the accompanying CD-ROM. You can find the example in frmObjVar.

15

Use Inline Code

There is a tendency to call out to procedures for everything. This is good from a maintenance standpoint but not from an efficiency standpoint. Each time VBA calls out to a procedure, additional time is taken to locate and execute the procedure. This is particularly evident when the procedure is called numerous times. The alternative is to use inline code. Executing inline code is more efficient than calling out to procedures because Access does not need to locate the code. The downside of inline code is that it is more difficult to maintain. You must decide how important maintainability is compared to speed.

Toggle Booleans Using Not

This code is very inefficient:

```
If bFlag = True Then
  bFlag = False
Else
   bFlag = True
End If
```

It should be modified to look like this:

```
bFlag = Not bFlag
```

Besides requiring fewer lines of code, this expression evaluates much more quickly at runtime.

Use the Built-In Collections

The built-in collections are there whether or not you use them. By using For Each...Next and a collection of objects, you can write very efficient code, as shown in Listing 15.3.

LISTING 15.3   USING For Each...Next

```
Sub FormCaption()
   Dim frm As Form
   For Each frm In Forms
      frm.Caption = frm.Caption & " - " & CurrentUser()
   Next
End Sub
```

In this example, you use the Forms collection to quickly and efficiently loop through each form, changing the caption on its title bar.

Use the Length Function

Using the Len function (as shown in Listing 15.4) is more efficient than testing for a zero-length string (as shown in Listing 15.5).

LISTING 15.4   USING THE Len FUNCTION

```
Sub SayNameLen(strName As String)
   If Len(strName) Then
      MsgBox strName
   End If
End Sub
```

LISTING 15.5   TESTING FOR A ZERO-LENGTH STRING

```
Sub SayNameZero(strName As String)
   If strName <> "" Then
      MsgBox strName
   End If
End Sub
```

Listing 15.4 is easier for VBA to evaluate and therefore runs more quickly and efficiently.

Use True and False Instead of 0

This example is similar to the preceding one. It is better to evaluate for True and False (as shown in Listing 15.6) instead of 0 (as shown in Listing 15.7).

LISTING 15.6   EVALUATING FOR True AND False

```
Sub SaySalaryTrue(lngSalary As Long)
   If lngSalary Then
      MsgBox "Salary is " & lngSalary
   End If
End Sub
```

LISTING 15.7   EVALUATING FOR 0

```
Sub SaySalaryZero(lngSalary As Long)
   If lngSalary <> 0 Then
      MsgBox "Salary is " & lngSalary
   End If
End Sub
```

The code in Listing 15.6 runs more efficiently.

Use Transactions... Sometimes?

In versions of Access prior to Access 95, transactions dramatically improved performance. Using explicit transactions, the data is written to disk only once, after the `CommitTrans`. All changes between a `BeginTrans` and a `CommitTrans` are buffered in memory. Because disk access has the slowest throughput on a computer, this technique offered you major performance benefits in versions of Access prior to Access 95. The difference with Access 95 and Access 2000 is that the Jet 3.0, 3.5, 3.6 and 4.0 engines implicitly buffer transactions. Most of the time, Jet's own transaction-handling offers better performance than your own. At other times, you can improve on what Jet does on its own. The only way you will know for sure is to do your own benchmarking. Each situation is different.

Eliminate Unused `Dim` and `Declare` Statements

As you modify your subroutines and functions, you often declare a variable and then never use it. Each `Dim` statement takes up memory, whether or not you are using it. Furthermore, `Declare` statements, which are used to call external library functions, also take up memory and resources. You should remove these statements if they are not being used.

Eliminate Unused Code

Most programmers experiment with various alternatives for accomplishing a task. This often involves creating numerous test subroutines and functions. The problem is that most people do not remove this code when they are done with it. This dead code is loaded with your application and therefore takes up memory and resources. Several third-party tools are available that can help you find both dead code and variable declarations. One tool that many people use is called Total Access Analyzer, by FMS, Inc.

Use Variables to Refer to Properties, Controls, and Data Access Objects

If you are going to repeatedly refer to an object, you should declare an object and refer to the object variable rather than the actual control, as shown in Listing 15.8.

LISTING 15.8   DECLARING AN OBJECT AND REFERRING TO THE OBJECT VARIABLE

```
Forms!frmAny.txtHello.FontBold = True
Forms!frmAny.txtHello.Enabled = True
Forms!frmAny.txtHello.Left = 1
Forms!frmAny.txtHello.Top = 1
```

This is a very scaled-down example, but if numerous properties are being changed, or if this code is being called recursively, an object variable can be used to make the code more efficient, as Listing 15.9 shows.

LISTING 15.9. USING AN OBJECT VARIABLE TO MAKE YOUR CODE MORE EFFICIENT

```
Private Sub cmdChangeObject_Click()
    Dim txt As TextBox
    Set txt = Forms!frmHello.txtHello1
    txt.FontBold = True
    txt.Enabled = True
    txt.Left = 100
    txt.Top = 100
End Sub
```

Use `With...End With`

Another way to optimize the code in the preceding example is to use a `With...End With` construct, as shown in Listing 15.10.

LISTING 15.10 USING `With...End With`

```
Private Sub cmdChangeObjectWith_Click()
    With Forms!frmHello.txtHello2
        .FontBold = True
        .Enabled = True
        .Left = 100
        .Top = 100
    End With
End Sub
```

Use the `Me` Keyword

In the preceding example, you used `Forms!frmHello.txtHello` to refer to a control on the current form. It is more efficient to refer to the control as `Me.txtHello`. This is because VBA searches only in the local name space. Although this makes your code more efficient, the downside is that the `Me` keyword only works within form, report, and class modules. It won't work within standard code modules. This means that you cannot include the `Me` keyword in generic functions that are accessed by all your forms.

Use String Functions When Possible

Many of the functions come in two forms: one with a dollar sign ($) and one without. An example is Left(sName) versus Left$(sName). It is more efficient to use the version with the dollar sign whenever possible. The functions with the dollar sign return strings rather than variants. When a string variable is returned, VBA doesn't need to perform type conversions.

Use Dynamic Arrays

Array elements take up memory, whether or not they are being used. It therefore is sometimes preferable to use dynamic arrays. You can increase the size of a dynamic array as necessary. If you want to reclaim the space used by all the elements of the array, you can use the Erase keyword, as in this example:

```
Erase aNames
```

If you want to reclaim some of the space being used by the array without destroying data in the elements you want to retain, use Redim Preserve:

```
Redim Preserve aNames(5)
```

This statement sizes the array to six elements. (It is zero-based.) Data within those six elements is retained.

CAUTION

You must be careful when using dynamic arrays with Redim Preserve. When you resize an array using Redim Preserve, the entire array is copied in memory. If you are running in a low-memory environment, this can mean that virtual disk space is used, which slows performance—or worse than that, the application can fail if both physical and virtual memory are exhausted.

Use Constants When Possible

Constants improve both readability and performance. A constant's value is resolved after compilation. The value the constant represents is written to code. A normal variable has to be resolved as the code is running because VBA needs to obtain the current value of the variable.

Use Bookmarks

A bookmark provides you with the most rapid access to a record. If you are planning to return to a record, set a variable equal to that record's bookmark. It is very easy to return to that record at any time. Listing 15.11 shows an example that uses a bookmark.

LISTING 15.11 USING A BOOKMARK

```
Sub BookMarkIt()
    Dim rst As ADODB.Recordset
    Set rst = New ADODB.Recordset

    Dim varBM As Variant

    rst.Open "tblProjects", CurrentProject.Connection, adOpenStatic
    varBM = rst.Bookmark
    Do Until rst.EOF
        Debug.Print rst!ProjectID
        rst.MoveNext
    Loop
    rst.Bookmark = varBM
    Debug.Print rst!ProjectID
End Sub
```

 You can find this code in basOptimize of CHAP15EX.MDB. The bookmark is stored in a variable before the Do Until loop executes. After the Do Until loop executes, the recordset's bookmark is set equal to the value contained within the variable.

Set Object Variables Equal to Nothing

Object variables take up memory and associated resources. Their value should be set equal to Nothing when you are finished using them. This conserves memory and resources. For example,

```
Set oObj = Nothing
```

Use Action Queries Instead of Looping Through Recordsets

Besides being easier to code, it is much more efficient to execute a stored query than to loop through a recordset, performing some action on each record. Listing 15.12 shows an example that loops through a recordset.

LISTING 15.12 LOOPING THROUGH A RECORDSET

```
Sub LoopThrough()
    Dim rst As ADODB.Recordset
    Set rst = New ADODB.Recordset

    rst.Open "tblProjects", CurrentProject.Connection, adOpenDynamic, _
    adLockOptimistic
    Do Until rst.EOF
        rst!ProjectTotalEstimate = rst!ProjectTotalEstimate + 1
        rst.UPDATE
        rst.MoveNext
    Loop
End Sub
```

 This code, which is located in basOptimize of CHAP15EX.MDB, loops through a recordset, adding one to each project total estimate. Contrast this with the code in Listing 15.13.

LISTING 15.13 EXECUTING A STORED QUERY

```
Sub ExecuteQuery()
    Dim adoCat As ADOX.Catalog
    Dim cmd As ADODB.Command
    Set adoCat = New ADOX.Catalog
    Set cmd = New ADODB.Command

    Set adoCat.ActiveConnection = CurrentProject.Connection
    Set cmd = adoCat.Procedures("qupdLowerEstimate").Command
    cmd.Execute

End Sub
```

This code uses a command object to execute a stored query called qupdLowerEstimate. The query runs much more efficiently than the Do Until loop shown in Listing 15.12.

Deliver Your Application with the Modules Compiled

Applications run slower when they are not compiled. Forms and reports load slower, and the application requires more memory. If you deliver your application with all the modules compiled, they do not need to be compiled on the user's machine before they are run.

To easily recompile all modules, choose Debug | Compile with the Visual Basic Editor (VBE) active. This command opens and compiles all code in the application, including the code behind forms and reports. It then saves the modules in the compiled state. This preserves the compiled state of the application.

Retaining the Compiled State

Don't bother choosing the Debug | Compile command if you plan to make additional changes to the application. An application becomes decompiled whenever the application's controls, forms, reports, or modules are modified. Even something as simple as adding a single control to a form causes the application to lose its compiled state. It therefore is important to choose the Debug | Compile command immediately before you distribute the application.

> **CAUTION**
>
> Renaming a database file causes the code contained in the database to decompile. It therefore is important to always choose the Compile and Save All Modules command after renaming a database.

Distribute Your Application as an MDE

The process of creating an MDE file compiles all modules, removes editable source code, and compacts the destination database. All Visual Basic code will run, but cannot be viewed or edited. This improves performance, reduces the size of the database, and protects your intellectual property. Memory use also is improved. The process of saving an application as an MDE, and the implications of doing so, are covered in Chapter 39, "Distributing Your Application."

Organize Your Modules

VBA code theoretically can be placed in any module within your application. The problem is that a module is not loaded until a function within it is called. After a single procedure in a module is called, the entire module is loaded into memory. Furthermore, if a single variable within a module is used, the entire module is loaded into memory. As you might imagine, if you design your application without much thought, every module in your application will be loaded.

If you place similar routines all in one module, that module will be loaded and others will not. This means that if people are using only part of the functionality of your application, they will never be loading other code modules. This conserves memory and therefore optimizes your application.

DESIGNING FORMS AND REPORTS TO IMPROVE PERFORMANCE

You can do several things to forms and reports to improve your application's performance. These include techniques to quickly load the forms and reports, tips and tricks regarding OLE objects, and special coding techniques that apply only to forms and reports.

Designing Forms

Because forms are your main interface to your user, making them as efficient as possible can go a long way toward improving the user's perception of performance within your application. Additionally, many of the form techniques are extremely easy to implement.

Form-optimization techniques can be categorized in two ways: those that make the forms load more quickly, and those that enable you to more efficiently manipulate objects within the form.

The larger a form and the more controls and objects you have placed on it, the less efficient that form is. Make sure that controls on the form do not overlap. It also is extremely beneficial to group form data onto logical pages. This is especially important if your users have insufficient video RAM. Objects on subsequent pages should not be populated until the user moves to that page.

Forms and their controls should be based on saved queries or embedded SQL statements. Include only fields required by the form in the form's underlying query. Avoid using `Select *` queries. Because Access is so efficient at internally optimizing the manipulation of query results, this improves the performance of your forms. To further take advantage of the power of queries, reduce the number of records that the query returns, loading only the records you need to at a particular time.

If you will use a form solely to add new records, set the `DataEntry` property of the form to `Yes` so that it opens to a blank record. This is necessary because otherwise Access must read all records in order to display the blank record at the end of the recordset.

Avoid bitmaps and other graphic objects if possible. If you must display an image, it is important to remember that OLE objects take far more resources than images. If an OLE bitmapped object does not need to be changed, convert it to an image. To accomplish this, right-click the object and choose Change To|Image.

Avoid the use of subforms whenever possible. Access treats a subform as a separate form. It therefore takes up significant memory. Make sure that all fields in a subform that are either linked to the main form or used for criteria are indexed. Make sure that only necessary fields are included in the record source of the subform. If the data in the subform does not need to be edited, set its `AllowEdits`, `AllowAdditions`, and `AllowDeletions` properties to `No`, or set its `RecordsetType` property to `Snapshot`.

Make sure that the `RowSource` for a combo box includes only the columns needed for the combo box. Index on the first field that appears in the combo box. This has a dramatic effect on the speed at which a user can move to an element of the combo box. Also, whenever possible, make the first visible field of a combo box a text field. Access converts numeric fields to text as it searches through the combo box to find a matching value. Finally, don't base list boxes or combo boxes on linked data if that data rarely, if ever, changes. Instead, make the static table local, updating it whenever necessary.

A general rule regarding the performance of forms is to place all database objects, except data, on each user's machine. This eliminates the need for Access to constantly pull object definitions over the network.

Close forms that no longer are being used. Open forms take up memory and resources, degrading performance.

Another tip that can help you dramatically improve the performance of your forms is to use the default formatting and properties for as many controls as possible. This significantly improves performance, because only the form and control properties that differ from the default properties are saved with the form.

> **TIP**
>
> If most controls have a set of properties that are different from the default control for the form, you should change the default control for the form and then add controls based on the default. Access saves only the properties of the default control and does not need to store the properties for each control placed on the form. This can result in dramatic performance improvements. Changing the default control is covered in Chapter 5, "What Every Developer Needs to Know About Forms."

Finally, eliminate the code module from forms that don't need it. A form without a form module loads more quickly and occupies less disk space. You still can call function procedures from an event property using an expression, or you can navigate about your application from the form using hyperlinks. You can remove the module associated with a form by setting the `HasModule` property to `No`.

Designing Reports

Many of the report-optimization techniques are the same as the form-optimization techniques. Reducing the number of controls, avoiding overlapping controls, basing reports on queries, avoiding OLE objects, and converting unbound object frames that display graphics to image controls are all techniques that improve the performance of reports as well as forms.

You can use a few additional techniques to specifically improve the performance of reports. Eliminate any unnecessary sorting and grouping expressions, and index all fields on which you sort or group. Base subreports on queries rather than on tables, and include only necessary fields in the queries. Make sure that the queries underlying the report are optimized and that you index all fields in the subreport that are linked to the main report.

A special technique that you can use to improve the performance of reports was introduced with Access 95. It involves the No Data event and the HasData property. The No Data event is fired when a report is opened, and no data is returned by the record source of the report. The HasData property is used to determine whether a report is bound to an empty recordset. If the HasData property of a subreport is False, you can hide the subreport, thereby improving performance.

PRACTICAL EXAMPLES

Improving the Performance of the Time and Billing Application

To ensure that the Time and Billing Application is optimized, you can do several things:

- Make sure that the database is compacted.
- Use the Performance Analyzer to analyze the application and make recommendations for improvement.
- Choose Debug | Compile from the VBE before distributing the application.

SUMMARY

The most attractive application can be extremely frustrating to use if its performance is less than acceptable. Because Access itself requires significant resources, you must take the responsibility of making your code as lean and efficient as possible.

This chapter focuses on several techniques for improving performance. Probably one of the easiest ways to improve performance is by modifying the hardware and software environment within which Access operates. You learned about adding RAM, defragmenting a hard disk, and tuning virtual memory and other settings to dramatically improve the performance of your applications. You also looked at using the Performance Analyzer to quickly and easily identify problem areas in your application. Finally, the chapter focuses on data-design fundamentals, coding techniques, and form- and report-optimization techniques.

By following the guidelines covered in this chapter, you can help ensure that you are not inadvertently introducing bottlenecks into your application. Although any one of the suggestions included in this chapter might not make a difference by itself, the combined effect of these performance enhancements can be quite dramatic.

DEVELOPING MULTIUSER AND ENTERPRISE APPLICATIONS

PART III

A STRATEGY TO DEVELOPING ACCESS APPLICATIONS

IN THIS CHAPTER

WHY THIS CHAPTER IS IMPORTANT

You should know about several tricks of the trade that can save you a lot of time in the development process and help ensure that your applications are as optimized as possible for performance. This chapter addresses these strategies and also explains several commonly misunderstood aspects of the Jet Engine, Access Runtime Engine, and security. All the topics covered in this chapter should be kept in mind when developing your Access applications. When reading this chapter, think of the general strategy outlined rather than the details of each topic. Each topic is covered in depth in other chapters of the book.

SPLITTING DATABASES INTO TABLES AND OTHER OBJECTS

In earlier versions of Access it was almost imperative in a multiuser environment that the tables that made up your system be placed in one database and the rest of the system objects in another database. With Access 95 and the advent of replication, you could either split the tables from the other objects or utilize replication to deploy design changes without comprising live data. Access 2000 takes this a step further with the Access Data Project (ADP), where tables, views, stored procedures, and data diagrams are stored in a SQL Server database or by the Microsoft Data Engine (MSDE), and the other system objects are stored in the ADP file.

As mentioned earlier, splitting tables from other system objects is still a very viable solution. For simplicity, I'll refer to the database containing the tables as the Table database and the database with the other objects as the Application database. The two databases are connected by linking from the Application database to the Table database. Here are the reasons for this strategy:

- Maintainability
- Performance
- Scalability

Assume for a moment that you distribute your application as one MDB file. Your users work with your application for a week or two, writing down all problems and changes. It's time for you to make modifications to your application. Meanwhile, live data has been entered into the application for two weeks. You make a copy of the database (which includes the live data) and

A Strategy to Developing Access Applications
CHAPTER 16

585

16

DEVELOPING
ACCESS
APPLICATIONS

make all the fixes and changes. This process takes a week. You're ready to install your copy of the database on the network. Now what? The users of the application have been adding, editing, and deleting records all week. Data replication, covered in Chapter 23, "Replication Made Easy," could help you with this problem, but it isn't always feasible.

The simplest solution is to split the database objects so that the tables (your data) are in one MDB file, and the rest of your database objects (your application) are in a second MDB file. When you're ready to install the changes, all you need to do is copy the Application database to the file server. The new Application database can then be installed on each client machine from the file server. In this way, users can run new copies of the application from their machines. The database containing your data tables remains intact and is unaffected by the process. (Of course, this is possible only if you finalize your table structure before splitting the database.)

The second benefit of splitting the database objects has to do with performance. Your Table database obviously needs to reside on the network file server, so the data can be shared among the system's users; however, there's no good reason why the other database components need to be shared. Access gives you optimal performance if the Application database is stored on each local machine. This method not only improves performance, but significantly reduces network traffic. If the Application database is stored on the file server, the application objects and code will need to be sent over the network each time an object in the database is opened. If the Application database is stored on each local machine, only the data will need to be sent over the network. The only complication of this scenario is that each time the Application is updated, it will need to be redistributed to the users. On an already overtaxed network, this is a small inconvenience compared to the performance benefits gained from this structural split.

The third benefit of splitting tables from the other database objects has to do with scalability. Because the tables are already linked, it's easy to change from a link to a table stored in Access's own proprietary format to any ODBC database, such as Microsoft SQL Server. This capability gives you quick-and-dirty access to client/server databases. If you have already thought through your system's design with linked tables in mind, the transition will be that much easier. Don't be fooled, though, by how easy this sounds. There are many issues associated with using Access as a front end to client/server data that go far beyond a matter of simply linking to the external tables. Some of these issues are covered in this chapter, and others are covered in Chapter 19, "Client/Server Techniques."

> **TIP**
>
> A few special types of tables should be stored in the Application database rather than the Table database. Tables that rarely change should be stored in the Application database on each user's local machine. For example, a State table rarely, if ever, changes, but it's continually accessed to populate combo boxes, participate in queries, and so on. Placing the State table on each local machine, therefore, improves performance and reduces network traffic. Lookup tables containing localized information such as department codes should also be placed in the Application database.
>
> Temporary tables should also be placed on each local machine—this is more a necessity than an option. If two users are running the same process at the same time and that process uses temporary tables, a conflict occurs when one user overwrites the other's temporary tables. Placing temporary tables on each local machine improves performance and eliminates the chance of potentially disastrous conflicts.

If you have already designed your application and included all the tables in the same database as the rest of your database objects, don't despair; Access 2000 includes a Database Splitter Wizard. You can find this valuable tool by choosing Tools | Database Utilities | Database Splitter. The Database Splitter, as well as linked tables, is covered in Chapter 18, "Using External Data."

> **NOTE**
>
> I split all the applications I build into two databases. However, you might notice when looking at the sample databases that none of them are split in the manner I recommend until Chapter 18. This is because until you learn all you need to know about splitting database objects, I don't think it's helpful to split the sample databases. Each chapter, from Chapter 19 on, uses the strategy recommended in this chapter.

BASING FORMS AND REPORTS ON QUERIES OR EMBEDDED SQL STATEMENTS

The record source for a form or report can be based on a table object, a query object, or a SQL statement. By basing forms and reports on stored queries or embedded SQL statements, you

A Strategy to Developing Access Applications

CHAPTER 16

587

16

DEVELOPING
ACCESS
APPLICATIONS

can improve the performance and flexibility of your applications. In most cases, you don't need to display all fields and all records on a form or report. By basing a form or report on a query or embedded SQL statement, you can better limit the data transferred over the network. These benefits are most pronounced in a client/server environment. When you base a form or report on a table object, Access sends a SQL statement that retrieves all fields and all records from the database server. On the other hand, if the record source for the form or report is a query or embedded SQL statement, just the fields and records specified within the query are returned to the workstation.

In Access 2.0, a form or report based on a stored query was more efficient than a form or report based on a SQL statement. This was the case because when you save a query, the Access database Jet Engine creates a Query Plan, which contains information on the most efficient method of executing the query. When the query is saved, the Jet Engine looks at the volume of data as well as available indexes, determines the optimal method of executing the query, and stores the method as the Query Plan. This plan is used whenever a form or report based on that query is executed. With Access 2.0, when a form or report was based on a SQL statement, the optimization process happened when the form or report was opened, and the Query Plan was executed on-the-fly. With Access 97 and Access 2000, an embedded SQL statement is optimized just like a stored query. It is therefore up to you whether you prefer to use a stored query or an embedded SQL statement as the foundation for your forms and reports.

On the other hand, when basing a form on table data, you can't control the order of the records in the form, nor can you base the form on more than one table. You can't limit the records displayed on the form until after the form is opened, unless you are using Access's OpenForm method with a Where argument. By basing a form on a query or embedded SQL statement, you can control the criteria for the form as well as the default order in which the records are displayed. Everything just mentioned applies to reports as well, except the order of the records, which is determined by the sorting and grouping of the report itself.

TIP

Many other techniques are available to you when displaying a form based on a large recordset. My favorite involves basing the form on only a single record at a time and changing the form's RecordSource property each time the user wants to view a different record. This technique, and others, are covered in detail in Chapter 9, "Advanced Form Techniques," And Chapter 20, "Client/Server Strategies."

UNDERSTANDING THE ACCESS RUNTIME ENGINE

Many developers misunderstand what Access has to offer out of the box and what the Microsoft Office Developer (MOD) tools can add to the picture. They often tell me "I can't develop applications in Access because my company refuses to buy each user a copy of Access," or "I'm going to buy the MOD so that I can compile my applications with the MOD tools." These are just two of the many misconceptions about exactly what the MOD tools do and don't have to offer.

Features of the MOD

You no longer need to buy a separate product to create runtime versions of your Access applications. As a developer, you will likely buy the MOD, which includes Office Premium plus all the features from the old Office Developer Environment (ODE), plus many new components. An important feature of the MOD is a royalty-free distribution license that allows you to distribute unlimited copies of your Access application without your users having to own separate licensed copies of Access. This means that by using the MOD tools, you can create applications you distribute to your users, who can run the application with the runtime engine you distribute to them. The MOD tools also include the following:

- *The Microsoft Office Object Model Guide* and the *Office Programmer's Guide*. In addition, numerous code samples are provided on CD-ROM.

- A Package and Deployment Wizard that helps you to create disks containing compressed files with everything you need to install and run your application. The Package and Deployment Wizard is covered in Chapter 39, "Distributing Your Application," and is pictured in Figure 16.1.

Figure 16.1

The Package and Deployment Wizard used for application distribution.

A Strategy to Developing Access Applications

CHAPTER 16

589

16

DEVELOPING
ACCESS
APPLICATIONS

- A host of data-bound ActiveX custom controls that can be used to enhance your application's functionality and distributed to your users as part of your MOD license. These controls include the Enhanced FlexGrid and the Data Repeater controls. ActiveX custom controls are covered in Chapter 25, "Using ActiveX Controls."

- The Microsoft Data Engine (MSDE) is an alternative to the Jet Engine. It provides local data storage compatible with and easily upgradable to SQL Server. The MSDE is not automatically installed with Microsoft Access. To install it, run \Sql\x86\Setup\Setupsql.exe, located on the Office 2000 CD-ROM #1.

- The Microsoft Replication Manager helps you with the replication process by letting you schedule updates between replicas, determine which objects in the database are replicated, display all the replicas in a replica set, and manage multiple replica sets. The Replication Manager is covered in Chapter 23, "Replication Made Easy."

- The COM Add-in Designer allows you to create and debug standalone COM add-ins. COM add-ins are DLLs that can be used from multiple Office applications.

- The Code Librarian provides a reusable centralized database of pre-written standard routines. This database can be easily shared across development teams.

- The Data Environment Designer allows developers to easily connect VBA code to external data sources. Using the Data Environment Designer, you can create hierarchical recordset command objects without writing any code.

- Visual Source Safe and VSS Integration provide both versioning and team management for your Access applications. After integrating Visual Source Safe into your applications, team members can check objects in and out, view the differences between versions, view the history of an object, and more.

- The String Editor is a WYSIWYG interface that allows you to quickly and easily build SQL statements. It facilitates the process of embedding SQL statements in VBA code.

- The Code Commenter automatically adds comments and headers to procedures. This is accomplished using customizable templates.

- The Error Handler is used to easily create a standard error handler for your application. It enables you to insert error handling code into your routines, using a customizable template.

- The Multi-Code Import/Export tool allows you to transfer multiple code modules in and out of an application. This makes it easy for you to share code libraries.

- The Data Report Designer provides a drag-and-drop interface to report creation. This interface is available throughout the Office suite.

- The Windows API Viewer has all the declarations, constants, and type structures used with the 32-bit Windows application programming interface (API). It allows you to easily copy the function, constant, and type declarations into your code modules.

Differences Between the Standard and Runtime Versions of Access

It's important to understand the differences between the standard and runtime versions of Access. The following differences have definite implications for the way you develop any applications you expect to run from the runtime version:

- The Database, Macro, and Module windows aren't available in the runtime environment.
- No Design views are available in the runtime environment.
- No built-in toolbars are available in the runtime environment.
- Many windows, menus, and commands are invisible in the runtime environment. For example, the Window | Hide and Window | Unhide commands are invisible. Although these and other commands aren't visible, their functions are generally accessible by using code.
- You must build error handling into your runtime applications. If you don't, when an error occurs the application displays a standard Access dialog box indicating an irrecoverable error and then exits to the desktop.
- You must build your own custom help files for each runtime application.
- Some keystrokes aren't available in the runtime application.

Some of the disabled features protect your applications. For example, the absence of the Database and Design windows means that your users can't modify your application while running it under Access's runtime version. Other disabled features translate into additional coding chores for you, such as the absence of command bars. If you want your application to offer toolbars, you have to build your own and then assign them to the forms and reports in your database.

Steps for Preparing an Application for Distribution

With all the features absent from the runtime version of Access, it's not surprising you must take some special steps to prepare your application for distribution. Some of the steps are specific to running from the runtime version, but most are steps you'll probably want to take so your application seems professional to the user. These are the steps to prepare your application for distribution with the runtime version of Access:

- Basing your application around forms
- Adding startup options to your database
- Securing the objects in your application
- Building error handling into your application

- Adding some level of custom help to your application
- Building custom command bars to be associated with your application's forms and reports

Basing Your Application Around Forms

Your application should be based on and controlled through forms. It should generally begin with a main switchboard that lets the user get to the other components of your application; or, it can start with a core data-entry form around which the rest of the application is based. If you opt to go with an application switchboard, the main switchboard can bring the user to additional switchboards, such as a data-entry switchboard, a report switchboard, or a maintenance switchboard. You can build switchboards by using an add-in called the Switchboard Manager or by designing them as custom dialog boxes. Building a switchboard as a custom dialog box is covered in Chapter 9, "Advanced Form Techniques", and using the Switchboard Manager to create switchboards is covered in Chapter 39, " Distributing Your Application." The main advantage of using the Switchboard Manager is that it lets you quickly and easily create a polished application interface. The primary advantage of custom switchboards is the flexibility and freedom they offer. An alternative to the switchboard approach is to build the application around a core data-entry form. An example is a contact management application that is based around the contacts form. All other forms and reports that make up the application are then accessed via the contacts form. This is accomplished using custom menu bars and toolbars.

Adding Start-Up Options to Your Database

Regardless of the approach that you take, you set a form as the starting point for your application by modifying the startup options for your database. Set these options by choosing Tools | Startup to open the Startup dialog box. (See Figure 16.2.) In this dialog box, you can set startup options, such as a startup form, an application title, and an icon that appears when your application is minimized. These options are covered in detail in Chapter 39.

FIGURE 16.2

The Startup dialog box lets you control many aspects of your application environment.

Securing Your Application

As you will learn in the next section, a database isn't secure just because you're running it from a runtime version of Access. Without security, your application can be modified by anyone with a full copy of Access, so securing your database objects is an important step in preparing your application for distribution. Security is covered in Chapters 33, "Database Security Made Easy," and 34, "Advanced Security Techniques."

In addition to security, Access 2000 offers you the ability to remove the source code from your applications. This protects your intellectual property and improves the performance of your application. The resulting database is called an MDE (covered in Chapter 39).

Building Error Handling Into Your Applications

If error handling isn't built into your application and an error occurs while your user is running your application from Access's runtime version, the user will be rudely exited out of the program. She won't get an appropriate error message and will be left wondering what happened, so it's essential that you add error handling to your application's procedures. Error handling is covered in Chapter 14, "Error Handling: Preparing for the Inevitable." The VBA Error Handler, included with the Microsoft Office Developer (MOD), can also assist with the process of building error handling into your application.

Adding Custom Help

In most cases, you want your users to have at least some level of custom help specific to your application. You can use the `ControlTip` Text property of controls and the `Description` property of fields to add the most basic level of help to your application. The `ControlTip` Text property of controls is used to provide the user with a description of a control when he hovers his mouse pointer over the control. The `Description` property of a field, when entered, appears on the status bar when a control based on that field has the focus. If you are more ambitious, and if the scope and budget for the application warrant it, you can build a custom help file for your application. To add custom help to your application, you must build a help file; then attach parts of it to forms and controls in your application. The HTML Help Workshop, included with the Microsoft Office Developer (MOD), can assist with the process of including custom help with your application.

Building Custom Command Bars

Finally, because built-in toolbars aren't available in the runtime version and most of the features on the standard built-in menus are disabled, you should build your own command bars associated with specific forms and reports. Creating custom command bars adds both polish and functionality to your application.

A Strategy to Developing Access Applications

CHAPTER 16

593

16

DEVELOPING
ACCESS
APPLICATIONS

After you complete these steps, you'll be ready for the final phase of preparing your application for distribution, which includes the following:

- Test your application by using the /Runtime switch (covered in Chapter 39)
- Create setup disks or perform a network install with the Package and Deployment Wizard.
- Install your application on a machine that has never run a copy of either the standard or runtime version of Access.
- Test your application on the machine; make sure it runs as expected.

Before you bother running the Package and Deployment Wizard (a somewhat lengthy process), it's best that you run your application using the /Runtime switch. This switch simulates the runtime environment, allowing you to simulate user actions under the runtime version of Access. Taking this step saves you a lot of time and energy. It will find most, if not all, of the problems associated with running under the runtime version.

After you test your application with the /Runtime switch, you're ready to run the Package and Deployment Wizard (covered in Chapter 39) which lets you create setup disks or perform a network install. When your users are ready to install your application, they run the installation program by using A:Setup (or the appropriate network drive and path) to get a professional-looking, familiar setup program similar to those included with most Microsoft products.

After you run the Package and Deployment Wizard, you must test your application by running the install on a machine that has never had a copy of either the standard or runtime version of Access. I suggest you use a compression utility such as WinZip to zip all the files in the test machine's Windows System directory or back up the entire Windows directory to another directory. Install and fully test your application; make sure you experiment with every feature. When you're done testing, delete everything but the zip file, and then unzip the zip file into the Windows System directory (so that it holds all the files it contained before your program's installation). The whole idea is to test your application on a machine containing no Access-related files. This ensures that all the required files are included on your setup disks. After you test your application, restore the machine to its original state so that you can use it to test your next installation.

CAUTION

Although this process cleans up much of what was changed as a result of installing the application, it doesn't fully restore the machine to its original state. This is because the registry is modified during the install process. If you want to fully restore the machine to its original state, you must back up the registry before the install and restore it once you're done testing the application.

> **TIP**
>
> WinZip, a Windows zip utility, can be downloaded from http://www.winzip.com.

The Access Runtime Engine: Summing It Up

You have just read an overview of the differences between the full and runtime versions of Access. The process of preparing an application for distribution with the runtime version of Access is covered in detail in Chapter 39. If you plan to distribute an application with the runtime version of Access, remember which features will be available to your users; otherwise, you and your users will be in for some big surprises.

USING AN EXE VERSUS ACCESS DATABASE: WHAT IT MEANS TO YOU

Many developers mistakenly think that distributing an application with the runtime version of Access is equivalent to distributing an EXE. An unsecured database distributed with the runtime version of Access can be modified just like any other database.

Users can run your application using Access's runtime version, and all the rules of running an application under the runtime version apply. This means that while running under the runtime version of Access, users can't go into Design view, can't create their own objects, don't have access to the built-in toolbars, and so on.

These same users can install their own copies of the standard Access product. Using the standard version of Access, they can open the same database. If the objects in the database haven't been secured, users can modify the application at will.

In short, a database prepared with the Package and Deployment Wizard is no different from any other database. The Package and Deployment Wizard doesn't modify an MDB file in any way. It simply compresses all the files needed to run your application, including the database and runtime engine, and creates a network install folder or distribution disks containing the compressed files. Two ways to protect the design of your application are to set up security and to distribute your application as an MDE file.

UNDERSTANDING THE IMPORTANCE OF SECURING YOUR DATABASE

By now, you should understand the importance of securing your application. Setting up security is a complex but worthwhile process that can be done at either a group or user level. You can assign rights to objects, and those rights can be assigned to either individual users or a group of users. Figure 16.3 shows the User and Group Permissions dialog box. As you can see, rights can be assigned for each object. For a table, the user or group can be assigned rights to read, insert, update, and delete data as well as read, modify, or administer the table's design. Different groups of users can be assigned different rights to an object. For example, one group can be assigned rights to add, edit, and delete data. Another group can be assigned rights to edit only, another group to view only, and another can be denied the right to even view the data.

FIGURE 16.3

The User and Group Permissions dialog box lets you assign user and group rights to each database object.

Available rights differ for tables, queries, forms, reports, macros, and modules. The types of rights that can be assigned are appropriate to each particular type of object. When security has been properly invoked, it can't be violated, no matter how someone tries to access the database objects (including using the runtime version of Access, a standard copy of Access, programming code, or even a Visual Basic application). If properly secured, the database is as difficult to illegally access as an executable file.

USING ACCESS AS A FRONT END

If you're planning to use Access as a front end to other databases, you need to consider a few issues. In fact, the whole design methodology of your system will differ depending on whether you plan to store your data in an Access database or on a back-end database server.

In a system where your data is stored solely in Access tables, the Jet Engine part of Access supplies all data retrieval and management functions. The Jet Engine also handles security, data validation, and enforcing referential integrity.

In a system where Access acts as a front end to client/server data, the server handles the data management functions. It's responsible for retrieving, protecting, and updating data on the back-end database server. When Access acts as a front end, the local copy of Access is responsible only for sending requests and getting either data or pointers to data back from the database server. If you're creating an application in which Access acts as a front end, capitalizing on the strengths of both Access and the server can be a challenging endeavor.

Things You Need to Worry About in Converting to Client/Server

The transition to client/server isn't always a smooth one. You need to consider several factors if you're developing a client/server application or planning to eventually move your application from an Access database to a back-end structured query language (SQL) database server:

- Not all field types supported in Access are supported in every back-end database.
- Any security you set up in Access won't be converted to your back-end database.
- Validation rules you set up in Access need to be re-established on the back end.
- Referential integrity isn't supported on all back ends. If it is on yours, it won't automatically be carried over from Access.
- Queries involving joins that could be updated in Access can't be updated on the back-end server.

This list is just an overview of what you need to think about when moving an application from an Access database with linked tables to a back-end server or when developing an application specifically for a back end. Many of these issues have far-reaching implications. For example, if you set up validation rules and validation text in your application, the rules will need to be rewritten as triggers on the back end, but that isn't your only problem. If a validation rule is violated on the back end, you will get a returnable error code. You have to handle this returnable error code by using error handling in your application, displaying the appropriate message to your user. The Validation Text property can't be used.

TIP

Some of the issues covered in this chapter can be handled by the Upsizing Wizard. This tool, included as part of Access 2000, automates the migration of data from the native Access data format to Microsoft SQL Server. The Upsizing Wizard is covered in Chapter 19.

Benefits and Costs of Client/Server Technology

With all the issues discussed in the previous section, you might ask "Why bother with client/server?" Client/server technology offers important benefits but requires high costs in time and money if it's to be used properly. In each case, you need to evaluate whether the benefits of client/server technology outweigh the costs. The major benefits include the following:

- Greater control over data integrity
- Increased control over data security
- Increased fault tolerance
- Reduced network traffic
- Improved performance
- Centralized control and management of data

These are some of the major costs:

- Increased development costs
- Hardware costs for the server machine
- Setup costs for the server database
- Full- or part-time database administrator (DBA)

These lists summarize the major costs and benefits of client/server technology; they are meant only to alert you to what you need to think about when evaluating your data's movement to a back-end database server. These and other issues are covered in more detail in Chapter 19.

Your Options When Using Access as a Front End

Client/server is not an all-or-none proposition, nor is there only one way to implement it using Access as a front end. One option is to use Access as a true front end, which means all data is stored on the server and all queries are processed on the server. This is done by using pass-through queries rather than stored Access queries. With pass-through queries (covered in Chapter 20, "Client/Server Strategies"), a back-end–specific SQL statement is passed to the back end instead of being processed by Access. To make Access a true front end, you must also disable its natural ability to bind data to forms and reports. After you've done all this, though, you have eliminated all the features that make Access a strong product in the first place. Unfortunately, you haven't eliminated all the overhead associated with the functionality you removed. If you want to use this approach, you're better off developing the entire application in a lower-overhead environment, such as Visual Basic.

Another approach is a hybrid method in which you use a combination of linked tables, SQL pass-through queries, and local Access tables. The idea is that you take advantage of Access's features and strong points whenever possible. Pass-through queries are used to perform functions that are done more efficiently by communicating directly to the back end or that aren't available at all with Access SQL. To further improve performance, many tasks can be performed locally and then communicated to the server as one transaction, after any initial validation has been done. A new type of file, called a Project file, allows you to communicate with the back-end database without loading the Microsoft Jet Engine. With Access Projects, commonly referred to as ADP files, you can improve both the performance and functionality of a client/server application. ADP files are covered extensively in Chapter 19. In addition to the solutions just discussed, data can also be downloaded to Access in bulk so that additional processing is done locally. Many possibilities exist, and each is appropriate in different situations. It takes experience and experimentation to determine the combination of methods that will optimize performance in a given situation.

What Are the Considerations for Migrating to a Client/Server Environment?

The preceding sections have given you an overview of the issues you need to consider when building an application for client/server or considering moving it to client/server in the future. More detailed information is given in Chapters 19 and 20. The issues behind developing client/server applications are highlighted here to reduce the chances of unexpected grief in the future. If you proceed through this book with these issues in mind, you will be a much happier developer. If you're using Access as a front end, make sure as you read through this book, particularly the more advanced chapters, that you take special note of any cautions about developing client/server applications.

PRACTICAL EXAMPLES

Applying the Strategy to the Computer Consulting Firm Application

When it's finished, the Time and Billing application for the computer consulting firm introduced in Chapter 1, "Access as a Development Tool," will be made up of two databases: one containing the majority of the tables, and the other with the remainder of the database objects, including static and temporary tables. The application will be developed with the idea that the data might eventually be moved to a back-end database server and designed so that the transition to client/server will be as smooth as possible. The forms and reports that make up the

A Strategy to Developing Access Applications

CHAPTER 16

599

16

DEVELOPING
ACCESS
APPLICATIONS

application will be based on stored queries or embedded SQL statements to maximize their flexibility and efficiency. Finally, the application will be designed so that it can easily run from Access's runtime version and will be secured so that its data and other objects can't be accessed by unauthorized users. As you move through the chapters in the book, each of these design strategies will be carried out.

SUMMARY

It's important that you have a strategy before you begin the application development process. This chapter introduces many strategic issues, such as splitting a database into tables and other objects and using Access as a front end. It also covers converting to client/server, the benefits and costs of client/server technology, and the different options available to you. These concepts have then been tied together by the explanation of what you can do to prepare your applications for future growth.

Many people don't fully understand the Access runtime engine, so this chapter explains what it is and what it isn't. It also explains what you need to be concerned about in preparing an application for distribution, including the importance of properly securing your databases.

600

DEVELOPING MULTIUSER APPLICATIONS

IN THIS CHAPTER

DESIGNING YOUR APPLICATION WITH MULTIUSER ISSUES IN MIND

When you develop applications that will be accessed over the network by multiple users, you must make sure they effectively handle sharing data and other application objects. Many options are available for developers when they design multiuser applications, and this chapter covers the pros and cons of these options.

Multiuser issues revolve around locking data; they include deciding where to store database objects, when to lock data, and how much data to lock. In a multiuser environment, having several users simultaneously trying to modify the same data can cause conflicts. As a developer, you need to handle these conflicts. Otherwise, your users will experience unexplainable errors.

Multiuser Design Strategies

There are many methods for handling concurrent access to data and other application objects by multiple users; each one offers both solutions and limitations. It's important to select the best solution for your particular environment.

Strategies for Installing Access

There are two strategies for installing Access:

- Running Access from a file server across a network
- Running a separate copy of Access on each workstation

Each of these strategies has associated pros and cons. The advantages of running Access from a file server are as follows:

- Allows for central administration of the Access software.
- Potentially reduces the licensing requirements. This is true because when Access is installed on a file server, the licensing requirements deal with concurrent users. When Access is installed locally, each user must have her own license, even if she rarely uses any Access applications. If all users won't be working with Access applications at the same time, it might be more cost-effective to buy a LAN license and install Access on the file server.
- Reduces hard disk requirements. The Access software takes up a significant amount of disk space. Although disk space requirements can be reduced by using the Access run-time engine, local hard-disk space can definitely be a problem. Installing Access on the file server at least partially eliminates this problem. It can totally eliminate the problem if dynamic link libraries (DLLs) are also installed on the file server.
- Access applications can be installed on diskless workstations.

Although the advantages of installing Access on a file server might seem compelling, there are serious drawbacks to a file server installation, including the following:

- Every time the user launches an Access application, the Access EXE, DLLs, and any other files required to run Access are *all* sent over the network wire to the local machine. Obviously, this generates a significant volume of network traffic.

- Performance is generally degraded to unacceptable levels.

Because the disadvantages of running Access from a file server are so pronounced, I strongly recommend that Access, or at least the runtime engine, be installed on each user's machine.

Strategies for Installing Your Application

Just as there are different strategies for installing Access, there are also various strategies for installing your application, such as the following:

- Install both the application and data on a file server.
- Install the data on the file server and the application on each workstation.

In other words, after you have created an application, you can place the entire application on the network, which means that all the tables, queries, forms, reports, macros, and modules that make up the system reside on the file server. Although this method of shared access keeps everything in the same place, you will see many advantages to placing only the database's data tables on the file server. The remainder of the objects are placed in a database on each user's machine, and each local application database is linked to the tables on the network. In this way, users share data but not the rest of the application objects.

The advantages of installing one database with data tables on the file server and installing another database with the other application objects locally are as follows:

- Because each user has a copy of the local database objects (queries, forms, reports, macros, and modules), load time and network traffic are both reduced.

- It's very easy to back up data without having to back up the rest of the application objects.

- When redistributing new versions of the application, you don't need to worry about overwriting the application's data.

- Multiple applications can all be designed to use the same centrally located data.

- Users can add their own objects (such as their own queries) to their local copies of the database.

In addition to storing the queries, forms, reports, macros, and modules that make up the application in a local database, I also recommend that you store the following objects in each local database:

- Temporary tables
- Static tables
- Semistatic tables

Temporary tables should be stored in the database that's on each workstation because if two users are performing operations that build the same temporary tables, you don't want one user's process to interfere with the other user's process. The potential conflict of one user's temporary tables overwriting the other's can be eliminated by storing all temporary tables in each user's local copy of the database.

You should also place static lookup tables, such as state tables, on each workstation. Because the data doesn't change, maintenance isn't an issue. The benefit is that Access doesn't need to pull that data over the network each time it's needed.

Semistatic tables—tables that are rarely updated—can also be placed on the local machine. As with static tables, the major benefit of having these tables in a local database is that reduced network traffic means better performance, not only for the user needing the data, but also to anyone sharing the same network wire. Changes made to the semistatic tables can be transported to each workstation by using replication (covered in Chapter 23, "Replication Made Easy").

The configuration described throughout this section is shown in Figure 17.1.

FIGURE 17.1

An example of a configuration with database objects split, storing temporary and static tables locally and shared tables remotely (on the file server).

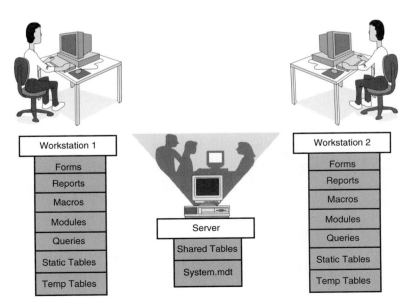

The Basics of Linking to External Data

Linking to external data, including data not stored in another Access database, is covered extensively in Chapter 18, "Using External Data." Three options are available to you:

- Design the databases separately from the start.
- Include all objects in one database; then split them manually when you're ready to distribute your application.
- Include all objects in one database; then split them by using the Database Splitter Wizard.

The first two options are covered in Chapter 18. The last option, the Database Splitter Wizard, is covered here. To split the objects in a database into two separate .MDB files, follow these steps:

1. Open the database whose objects you want to split.
2. Choose Tools | Database Utilities | Database Splitter to open the Database Splitter dialog box, shown in Figure 17.2.

FIGURE 17.2

The Database Splitter Wizard helps you split the data tables that should reside on the server.

3. Click Split Database; this opens the Create Back-end Database dialog box. (See Figure 17.3.)
4. Enter the name for the database that will contain all the tables. Click Split. The Database Splitter Wizard creates a new database holding all the tables, and links are created between the current database and the database containing the tables. (See Figure 17.4.)

FIGURE 17.3

Entering a name for the new shared database.

FIGURE 17.4

The database that has been split.

CAUTION

Be aware that when you're distributing an application using linked tables, you must write code to make sure the data tables can be located from each application database on the network. If each user has the same path to the file server, this isn't a problem. However, if the path to the file server varies, you need to write a routine that makes sure the tables can be located. If they can't, the routine prompts the user for the data's location. This routine is covered in Chapter 18.

UNDERSTANDING ACCESS'S LOCKING MECHANISMS

Although the preceding tips for designing network applications reduce network traffic, they in no way reduce locking conflicts. To protect shared data, Access locks either a record or a page of data as the user edits a record. In this way, multiple users can read the data, but only one user can make changes to it. Data can be locked through a form and also through a recordset that isn't bound to a form.

Here are the methods of locking for an Access application:

- Record locking
- Page locking
- Table and Recordset locking
- Opening an entire database with Exclusive Access

With Record locking, only the record the user is editing is locked. With Page locking, the 4K page with the record being edited is locked. On the other hand, in Table and Recordset locking, the entire table or recordset with the record being edited is locked. With Database locking, the entire database is locked, unless the user opening the database has opened it for read-only access. If the user opens the database for read-only access, other users can also open the database for read-only access. The ability to get exclusive use of a database can be restricted through security.

It's important to note that the locking scheme you adhere to depends on the source providing the data. If you're using client/server data, you inherit the locking scheme of the particular back end you're using. If you're manipulating ISAM data over a network, you get any record locking that the particular ISAM database supports. For example, if you're working with a FoxPro database, you can use record locking or any other locking scheme that FoxPro supports.

LOCKING AND REFRESHING STRATEGIES

Access has several tools for controlling locking methods in datasheets, forms, and reports. To configure the global multiuser settings, choose Tools | Options, and then click the Advanced tab. The dialog box shown in Figure 17.5 appears.

FIGURE 17.5
The Advanced Options dialog box.

The following multiuser settings can be configured from this dialog box:

- Default Record Locking
- Record-level Locking
- Default Open Mode
- Number of Update Retries
- ODBC Refresh Interval
- Refresh Interval
- Update Retry Interval

Default Record Locking

The Default Record Locking option lets you specify the default record locking as No Locks (optimistic), All Records (locks entire table or dynaset), or Edited Record (pessimistic). This dialog is where you can affect settings for all the objects in your database. Modifying this option doesn't affect any existing queries, forms, and reports, but it does affect any new queries, forms, and reports. The record-locking options are discussed later in this chapter because they apply to forms and recordsets.

Determining the Locking Mechanism for a Query

If you want to determine the locking method for a particular query, you can do this by modifying the Record Locks query property. Once again, the options are No Locks, All Records, and Edited Record. Query Properties can be viewed and modified by clicking a blank area of the Query design window with the Properties window open. The Query Properties window can be seen in Figure 17.6.

FIGURE 17.6

Setting the locking method for a query.

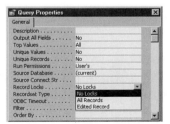

Determining the Locking Mechanism for a Form or Report

Just as you can configure the locking mechanism for a query, you can also configure the locking mechanism for each form and report. Forms and reports have Record Locks properties. (See Figure 17.7.) Changing these properties modifies the locking mechanism for that particular form or report.

FIGURE 17.7

Setting the locking method for a form.

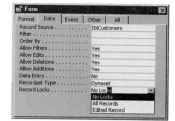

NOTE

Reports don't offer the choices for locking because report data can't be modified.

Record-Level Locking

Regardless of the default record locking that you have chosen, the Open Databases Using Record-Level Locking check box allows you to designate whether only one record is locked, or a page of records is locked. For example, if you select the No Locks option, the optimistic locking is used, but the locking occurs at the record level, rather than at the page level.

Default Open Mode

The Default Open Mode option allows you to configure the default open mode for databases. By encouraging users to set this option in their own copies of Access, you prevent people from inadvertently opening up a database exclusively. Take a good look at the options available under the Open command button within the Access File Open dialog box, shown in Figure 17.8. This is where you can override the default open mode and open a database with the locking method you desire.

Number of Update Retries

The number of update retries specifies how many times Access will try to save data to a locked record. The higher this number is, the greater the chance that the update will succeed. The downside is that the user has to wait while Access continues trying to update the data, even when there's no hope that the update will be successful. The default for this setting is 2; the value can range from 0 to 10.

FIGURE 17.8

The Open command button in the File Open dialog box allows you to specify the open mode for a database.

ODBC Refresh Interval

The ODBC Refresh Interval determines how often your form or datasheet is updated with changes made to data stored in ODBC data sources. For example, assume that two users are viewing the same data stored in a back-end Microsoft SQL Server database. User 1 makes a change to the data, and the ODBC Refresh Interval determines how long it is before User 2 sees the change. The higher this number is, the less likely it is that User 2 will see the current data. The lower this number is, the more network traffic will be generated. The default for this setting is 1500 seconds (just over twenty-five minutes), and the value can range from 1 to 32,766 seconds.

Refresh Interval

The Refresh Interval specifies how long it takes for a form or datasheet to be updated with changed data from an Access database. This is very similar to the ODBC Refresh Interval, but the ODBC Refresh Interval applies only to ODBC data sources, and the Refresh Interval applies only to Access data sources. As with the ODBC Refresh Interval, the higher this number is, the lower the chance that the data seen by the user is current. The lower this number is, the more network traffic is generated. The default for this setting is 60 seconds; the value can range from 1 to 32,766 seconds.

> **NOTE**
>
> Access automatically refreshes the data in a record whenever the user tries to edit the record. The benefit of a shorter Refresh Interval is that the user sees the record has been changed or locked by another user before he tries to edit it.

Update Retry Interval

The Update Retry Interval determines how many seconds Access waits before once again trying to update a locked record. The default for this setting is 250 milliseconds, and the value can range from 0 to 1,000 milliseconds (one second).

Refreshing Versus Requerying Data

It's important to understand the difference between refreshing and requerying a recordset. *Refreshing* a recordset updates changed data and indicates any deleted records. It doesn't try to bring a new recordset over the network wire; instead, it *refreshes* the data in the existing recordset. This means that records aren't reordered, new records don't appear, and deleted records aren't removed from the display. The record pointer remains on the same record. Not all recordset types can be refreshed.

Requerying, on the other hand, gets a new set of records. This means that the query is run again, and all the resulting data is sent over the network wire. The data is reordered, new records appear, and deleted records are no longer displayed. The record pointer is moved to the first record in the recordset.

FORM LOCKING STRATEGIES

Earlier in the chapter, you learned about the locking strategies for forms: No Locks, All Records, and Edited Record. Using the three locking strategies as appropriate, you can develop a multiuser application with little to no multiuser programming. You won't gain the same power, flexibility, and control that you get out of recordsets, but you can quickly and easily implement multiuser techniques. In this section, you will see how all three of these strategies affect the bound forms in your application.

No Locks

The No Locks option means that the page of data with the edited record won't be locked until Access tries to write the changed data to disk. This happens when there's movement to a different record or the data in the record is explicitly saved. If page locking is in place, the No Locks option is the least restrictive locking option for forms.

Several users can be editing data in the same 4K page of data at the same time, but the conflict occurs when two users try to modify the same record. Say, for example, that User 1 tries to modify data in the record for customer ABCDE, and User 2 tries to modify the *same* record. No error occurs because the No Locks option is specified for the form both users are accessing. Next, User 1 makes a change to the address, and User 2 makes a change to the Contact Title. User 1 moves off the record, saving her changes. No error occurs because Access has no way of knowing that User 2 is modifying the record. Now User 2 tries to move off the record, and the Write Conflict dialog box, shown in Figure 17.9, appears. User 2 has the choice of saving her changes, thereby overwriting the changes that User 1 made; copying User 1's changes to the Clipboard so she can make an educated decision as to what to do; or dropping her own changes and accepting the changes User 1 made.

FIGURE 17.9

The Write Conflict dialog box appears when two users edit the same record.

All Records

The All Records locking option is the most restrictive. When All Records is in effect, other users can only view the data in the tables underlying the form. They can't make any changes to the data, regardless of their own locking options. When they open the form, they see a quick status bar message that the data can't be updated. If they try to modify data in the form, the computer beeps and a message is displayed in the status bar.

Edited Record

The Edited Record option is used when you want to prevent the conflicts that happen when the No Locks option is in place. With page-level locking, instead of getting potential conflicts for changed data, users are much more likely to experience locking conflicts, because every time a user begins editing a record, the entire 4K page of data surrounding the record is locked. If row-level locking is used, this is not an issue because only the record actually being edited is locked.

Consider this scenario with page-level locking. User 1 begins editing a record, and User 2 tries to modify the same record. The computer beeps and a lock symbol appears in the form's record selector. (See Figure 17.10.) Now User 2 moves to another record. If the other record is in the same 4K page as the record User 1 has locked, the locking symbol appears and User 2 can't edit that record either until User 1 has saved the record she was working on, thereby releasing the lock.

FIGURE 17.10

The lock symbol on an edited record.

> **NOTE**
>
> If you want to override any of the default locking error dialogs that appear when you're in a form, you must code the form's Error event. Although you can use this method to replace any error message that appears, you can't trap for the situation with pessimistic locking when another user has the record locked. Users are cued that the record is locked only by viewing the locking symbol and hearing the beep when they try to edit the record. If you want to inform users that the record is locked before they try to edit it, you need to place code in the form's Timer event that checks whether the record is locked. This technique is covered in the "Testing a Record for Locking Status" section of this chapter.

RECORDSET LOCKING

Recordset locking locks pages of data found in a recordset. By using recordset locking, you can control when and for how long the data is locked. This is different from locking data through bound forms, which gives you little control over the specifics of the locking process.

When you're traversing through a recordset, editing and updating data, locking occurs regardless of whether you intervene, so you must understand when the locking occurs and whether you need to step in to intercept the default behavior. If you do nothing, a record, or possibly an entire page of records, will be locked each time you begin editing data from your VBA code. This record page is 4096 bytes (4K) and surrounds the record being edited. If an OLE object is found in the record being edited, it isn't locked with the record because it occupies its own space.

Pessimistic Locking

VBA lets you determine when and for how long a page is locked. The default behavior is called *pessimistic locking*, which means that the record or page is locked when the first field is updated. Listing 17.1 illustrates this process.

LISTING 17.1   UTILIZING PESSIMISTIC LOCKING

```
Sub PessimisticLock(strAuthorID As String)
    Dim cnn As ADODB.Connection
    Dim rst As ADODB.Recordset
    Dim strCriteria As String

    Set cnn = New ADODB.Connection
    cnn.ConnectionString = " Provider=sqloledb;" & _
        "Data Source=(local);Initial Catalog=pubs;uid=sa;pwd="
    cnn.Open

    Set rst = New ADODB.Recordset
    rst.ActiveConnection = cnn
    rst.CursorType = adOpenKeyset
    rst.LockType = adLockPessimistic 'Invoke Pessimistic Locking
    rst.CursorLocation = adUseServer
    rst.Open "Select * from Authors Where Au_ID ='" _
        & strAuthorID & "'", _
        Options:=adCmdText

    rst!City = "Thousand Oaks" 'Lock occurs here
    rst.Update 'Lock Released Here
End Sub
```

NOTE

This code, and the rest of the code in this chapter, can be found in CHAP17EX.MDB on this book's CD-ROM.

> **NOTE**
>
> Not all database providers support all lock types. To determine the functionality available for a particular Recordset object, use the Supports method with adUpdate and adUpdateBatch. Furthermore, the adLockPessimistic setting is not supported when the CursorLocation property is set to adUseClient. Whether the provider does not support the locking type, or the cursor location does not support the locking type, no error results. Instead, the closest available locking type is used.

In this scenario, although the lock occurs for a very short period of time, it's actually being issued when the data is first edited; then released at the update.

The advantage of this method of locking is that you can make sure no changes are made to the data between the time the edit process begins and the time the Update method is issued. Furthermore, when the edit process begins successfully, you are ensured write access to the record. The disadvantage is that the time between the edit and the update might force the lock to persist for a significant period of time, locking other users out of not only that record, but if page locking is used, the entire page of records the edited record is in.

This phenomenon is exacerbated when transaction processing (covered in Chapter 22, "Transaction Processing") is invoked. Basically, transaction processing ensures that when you make multiple changes to data, all changes are made successfully or no changes occur. Listing 17.2 illustrates how pessimistic record locking affects transaction processing:

LISTING 17.2 PESSIMISTIC RECORD LOCKING AND ITS EFFECT ON TRANSACTION PROCESSING

```
Sub PessimisticTrans(strOldCity As String, strNewCity As String)
    Dim cnn As ADODB.Connection
    Dim rst As ADODB.Recordset
    Dim strCriteria As String

    Set cnn = New ADODB.Connection
    cnn.ConnectionString = " Provider=sqloledb;" & _
        "Data Source=(local);Initial Catalog=pubs;uid=sa;pwd="
    cnn.Open

    Set rst = New ADODB.Recordset
    rst.ActiveConnection = cnn
    rst.CursorType = adOpenKeyset
    rst.LockType = adLockPessimistic 'Invoke Pessimistic Locking
```

continues

LISTING 17.2   CONTINUED

```
    rst.CursorLocation = adUseServer
    rst.Open "SELECT * FROM Authors WHERE City = '" & strOldCity & "'", _
        Options:=adCmdText

    cnn.BeginTrans
    Do Until rst.EOF
        rst!City = strNewCity 'Lock occurs here
        rst.Update
        rst.MoveNext
    Loop
    cnn.CommitTrans   'Lock released here
End Sub
```

Here you can see that the lock is in place from when the city of the very first record is edited until the `CommitTrans` is issued. This means that no one can update any records, or possibly pages of data, involving the edited records until the `CommitTrans` is issued. This can take a prohibitive amount of time during a long process.

Optimistic Locking

Optimistic locking delays the time at which the record is locked. The lock is issued upon update rather than when the first field is edited. The code is shown in Listing 17.3.

LISTING 17.3   UTILIZING OPTIMISTIC LOCKING

```
Sub OptimisticLock(strAuthorID As String)
    Dim cnn As ADODB.Connection
    Dim rst As ADODB.Recordset
    Dim strCriteria As String

    Set cnn = New ADODB.Connection
    cnn.ConnectionString = " Provider=sqloledb;" & _
        "Data Source=(local);Initial Catalog=pubs;uid=sa;pwd="
    cnn.Open

    Set rst = New ADODB.Recordset
    rst.ActiveConnection = cnn
    rst.CursorType = adOpenKeyset
    rst.LockType = adLockOptimistic 'Invoke Optimistic Locking
    rst.CursorLocation = adUseServer
    rst.Open "Select * from Authors Where Au_ID = '" & _
```

```
            strAuthorID & "'", _
            Options:=adCmdText

    rst!City = "Thousand Oaks"
    rst.Update 'Lock occurs and is Released Here
End Sub
```

As you can see, the lock doesn't happen until the `Update` method is issued. The advantage of this method is that the page, or record, is locked very briefly. However, the disadvantage occurs when two users grab the record for editing at the same time. When one user tries to update, no error occurs. When the other user tries to update, she gets an error indicating that the data has changed since her edit was first issued. Handling this error message is covered in "Coding Around Optimistic Locking Conflicts," later in this chapter.

Optimistic locking with transaction handling isn't much different from pessimistic locking. As the code reaches the `Update` method for each record, the page containing that record is locked, and it remains locked until the transaction is committed. The code appears in Listing 17.4.

LISTING 17.4 OPTIMISTIC RECORD LOCKING AND ITS EFFECT ON TRANSACTION PROCESSING

```
Sub OptimisticTrans(strOldCity As String, strNewCity As String)
    Dim cnn As ADODB.Connection
    Dim rst As ADODB.Recordset
    Dim strCriteria As String

    Set cnn = New ADODB.Connection
    cnn.ConnectionString = " Provider=sqloledb;" & _
        "Data Source=(local);Initial Catalog=pubs;uid=sa;pwd="
    cnn.Open

    Set rst = New ADODB.Recordset
    rst.ActiveConnection = cnn
    rst.CursorType = adOpenKeyset
    rst.LockType = adLockOptimistic 'Invoke Optimistic Batch Locking
    rst.CursorLocation = adUseServer
    rst.Open "SELECT * FROM Authors WHERE City = '" & strOldCity & "'", _
        Options:=adCmdText

    cnn.BeginTrans
    Do Until rst.EOF
        rst!City = strNewCity
        rst.Update 'Lock occurs here
        rst.MoveNext
    Loop
    cnn.CommitTrans   'Lock released here
End Sub
```

> **NOTE**
>
> The constant `adLockBatchOptimistic` is used when batch updates, rather than immediate updates, are desired. The updates do not occur until the `UpdateBatch` method of the `Recordset` object is used. In the case of batch optimistic locking, the records are not locked until the `UpdateBatch` method is issued.

EFFECTIVELY HANDLING LOCKING CONFLICTS

If a user has a page or record locked and another user tries to view data in the record, or on that page, no conflict occurs. On the other hand, if other users try to edit data on that same page, they get an error.

You won't always want Access's own error handling to take over when a locking conflict occurs. For example, rather than having Access display its generic error message indicating that a record is locked, you might want to display your own message and then try to lock the record a couple of additional times. To do something like this, you must learn to interpret each locking error generated by VBA, so you can make a decision about how to respond.

Locking conflicts happen in the following situations:

- A user tries to edit a record that's already locked.
- A record has changed or been deleted since the user first started to edit it.

These errors can occur whether you're editing bound data through a form or accessing the records through VBA code.

Errors with Pessimistic Locking

To begin the discussion of locking conflicts, take a look at the types of errors that occur when pessimistic locking is in place. With pessimistic locking, you generally need to code for the following errors:

- The current record is locked by another user. Usually, you can just wait a short period of time and then try the lock again.
- The record has been deleted since the recordset was retrieved. In this case, it's best to refresh the data.

> **NOTE**
>
> The error numbers that occur differ based on the provider that is being used. The examples in this chapter therefore use sample error numbers. Refer to online help for trappable Microsoft Jet errors, ADO error codes, and ADO provider errors. As an alternative to the VBA error code, you can use the Errors collection of the Connection object to view properties of the error that occurred.

Coding Around Pessimistic Locking Conflicts

It's fairly simple to write code to handle pessimistic locking conflicts. Your code should look like Listing 17.5.

LISTING 17.5   HANDLING PESSIMISTIC LOCKING ERRORS

```
Sub PessimisticRS(strAuthorID As String)
    On Error GoTo PessimisticRS_Err
    Dim cnn As ADODB.Connection
    Dim rst As ADODB.Recordset
    Dim strCriteria As String
    Dim intChoice As Integer

    Set cnn = New ADODB.Connection
    cnn.ConnectionString = "Provider=sqloledb;" & _
        "Data Source=(local);Initial Catalog=pubs;uid=sa;pwd="
    cnn.Open

    Set rst = New ADODB.Recordset
    rst.ActiveConnection = cnn
    rst.CursorType = adOpenKeyset
    rst.LockType = adLockPessimistic 'Invoke Pessimistic Locking
    rst.CursorLocation = adUseServer
    rst.Open "Select * from Authors Where Au_ID = '" & _
        strAuthorID & "'", _
        Options:=adCmdText

    rst!City = "Thousand Oaks" 'Lock occurs here
    rst.Update 'Lock Released Here
    Exit Sub

PessimisticRS_Err:
    Select Case Err.Number
```

continues

LISTING 17.5 CONTINUED

```
        Case 3197
            rst.Move 0
            Resume
        Case -2147217887
          intChoice = MsgBox(Err.Description, vbRetryCancel + vbCritical)
          Select Case intChoice
              Case vbRetry
                  Resume
              Case Else
                  MsgBox "Couldn't Lock"
          End Select
        Case 3021
            MsgBox "Record Has Been Deleted"
        Case Else
            MsgBox Err.Number & ": " & Err.Decription
        End Select

End Sub
```

The error-handling code for this routine handles the errors that can happen with pessimistic locking. If a -2147217887 Record Is Locked error occurs, the user is asked whether she wants to try again. If she responds affirmatively, the edit process resumes; otherwise, the user is informed that the lock failed. If the record being edited has been deleted, an error 3021 occurs, and the user is informed that the record has been deleted. The situation looks like Listing 17.6 when transaction processing is involved.

LISTING 17.6 HANDLING PESSIMISTIC LOCKING ERRORS IN TRANSACTIONS

```
Sub PessimisticRSTrans()
    On Error GoTo PessimisticRSTrans_Err
    Dim cnn As ADODB.Connection
    Dim rst As ADODB.Recordset
    Dim strCriteria As String
    Dim intCounter As Integer
    Dim intTry As Integer
    Dim intChoice As Integer

    Set cnn = CurrentProject.Connection
    Set rst = New ADODB.Recordset

    rst.ActiveConnection = cnn
    rst.CursorType = adOpenKeyset
```

```
    rst.CursorLocation = adUseServer
    rst.LockType = adLockPessimistic 'Invoke Pessimistic Locking
    rst.Open "tblCustomers", _
        Options:=adCmdTable
    cnn.BeginTrans
    Do Until rst.EOF
        rst!CompanyName = rst!CompanyName & 1 'Lock occurs here
        rst.Update
        rst.MoveNext
    Loop
    cnn.CommitTrans  'Lock released here

PessimisticRSTrans_Exit:
    Exit Sub

PessimisticRSTrans_Err:
    Select Case Err.Number
        Case 3197
            rst.Move 0
            Resume
        Case -2147217887
            intCounter = intCounter + 1
            If intCounter > 2 Then
                intChoice = MsgBox(Err.Description, _
                  vbRetryCancel + vbCritical)
                Select Case intChoice
                    Case vbRetry
                        intCounter = 1
                    Case vbCancel
                        Resume CantLock
                End Select
            End If
            DoEvents
            For intTry = 1 To 100: Next intTry
            Resume
        Case Else
            MsgBox "Error: " & Err.Number & ": " & Err.Description
    End Select

CantLock:
    cnn.RollbackTrans
    Exit Sub
End Sub
```

17

DEVELOPING
MULTIUSER
APPLICATIONS

This code tries to lock the record. If it's unsuccessful (that is, an error -2147217887 is generated), it tries three times; then prompts the user for a response. If the user selects Retry, the process repeats. Otherwise, a rollback occurs and the subroutine is exited. If any other error occurs, the rollback is issued and none of the updates are accepted.

> **NOTE**
>
> Listing 17.6 opens the tblCustomers table directly. This is for the example only. You should never open a base table directly because this downloads all the rows and their column properties from the server. Instead, you should limit the rows returned to only those rows you need to work with. Finally, when using a database server such as Microsoft SQL Server, the task of updating records is accomplished much more effectively using a stored procedure.

Errors with Optimistic Locking

Now that you have seen what happens when a conflict occurs with pessimistic locking, see what happens when optimistic locking is in place. These are the two most common error codes generated by locking conflicts when optimistic locking is in place:

- An error occurs when the Update method is used to save a locked record or a record on a locked page. This error can occur when optimistic locking is used and a user tries to update a record on the same page as a record that's locked by another machine. You can usually just wait a short period of time and then try the lock again.

- An error occurs with optimistic locking when someone else has updated a record in the time since you first started viewing it.

Coding Around Optimistic Locking Conflicts

Remember that with optimistic locking, VBA tries to lock the page when the Update method is issued. There's a chance that a Data Has Changed error could occur. This needs to be handled in your code, so modify the preceding subroutine for optimistic locking with the code in Listing 17.7.

LISTING 17.7   HANDLING OPTIMISTIC LOCKING ERRORS

```
Sub OptimisticRS(strAuthorID)
    On Error GoTo OptimisticRS_Err
    Dim cnn As ADODB.Connection
```

```
    Dim rst As ADODB.Recordset
    Dim strCriteria As String
    Dim intChoice As Integer

    Set cnn = New ADODB.Connection
    cnn.ConnectionString = " Provider=sqloledb;" & _
        "Data Source=(local);Initial Catalog=pubs;uid=sa;pwd="
    cnn.Open

    Set rst = New ADODB.Recordset
    rst.ActiveConnection = cnn
    rst.CursorType = adOpenKeyset
    rst.LockType = adLockOptimistic 'Invoke Optimistic Locking
    rst.CursorLocation = adUseServer
    rst.Open "Select * From Authors Where Au_ID = '" & _
        strAuthorID & "'", _
        Options:=adCmdText

    rst!City = "Thousand Oaks"
    rst.Update 'Lock occurs and is Released Here

OptimisticRS_Exit:
    Exit Sub

OptimisticRS_Err:
    Select Case Err.Number
     Case -2147217885
        If rst.EditMode = adEditInProgress Then   'Data has Changed
            MsgBox "Another User has Edited Record Since You Began " & _
                "Modifying It"
        End If
     Case -2147217871    'Locked or ODBC Timeout
        intChoice = MsgBox(Err.Description, vbRetryCancel + vbCritical)
            Select Case intChoice
                Case vbRetry
                    Resume
                Case vbCancel
                    MsgBox "Update Cancelled"
            End Select
     Case Else
        MsgBox "Error: " & Err.Number & ": " & Err.Description
    End Select
    Resume OptimisticRS_Exit
End Sub
```

As with pessimistic error handling, this routine traps for all potential errors that can occur with optimistic locking. In the case of a `Data Has Changed` conflict, the user is warned of the problem. In the case of a locking conflict, the user is asked whether she wants to try again. Listing 17.8 shows what it looks like with transaction processing involved.

LISTING 17.8   HANDLING OPTIMISTIC LOCKING ERRORS IN TRANSACTIONS

```
Sub OptimisticRSTrans()
    On Error GoTo OptimisticRSTrans_Err
    Dim cnn As ADODB.Connection
    Dim rst As ADODB.Recordset
    Dim strCriteria As String
    Dim intChoice As Integer
    Dim boolInTrans As Boolean

    Set cnn = New ADODB.Connection
    cnn.ConnectionString = " Provider=sqloledb;" & _
        "Data Source=(local);Initial Catalog=pubs;uid=sa;pwd="
    cnn.Open

    Set rst = New ADODB.Recordset
    rst.ActiveConnection = cnn
    rst.CursorType = adOpenKeyset
    rst.LockType = adLockOptimistic 'Invoke Optimistic Locking
    rst.CursorLocation = adUseServer
    rst.Open "tblCustomers", _
        Options:=adCmdTable

    cnn.BeginTrans
    boolInTrans = True
    Do Until rst.EOF
        rst!CompanyName = rst!CompanyName & 1 'Lock occurs here
        rst.Update
        rst.MoveNext
    Loop
    cnn.CommitTrans   'Lock released here
    Exit Sub

OptimisticRSTrans_Err:
    Select Case Err.Number
        Case -2147217885 'Data has Changed
            If rst.EditMode = adEditInProgress Then
                MsgBox "Another User has Edited Record" & _
                " Since You Began " & _
                 "Modifying It"
            End If
```

```
            Case -2147217871    'Locked or ODBC Timeout
                intChoice = MsgBox(Err.Description, _
                    vbRetryCancel + vbCritical)
                    Select Case intChoice
                        Case vbRetry
                            Resume
                        Case vbCancel
                            MsgBox "Update Cancelled"
                    End Select
        Case Else
            MsgBox "Error: " & Err.Number & ": " & Err.Description
    End Select

    If boolInTrans Then
        cnn.RollbackTrans
    End If

    Exit Sub
End Sub
```

If a `Data Has Changed` conflict occurs, the entire processing loop is canceled (a rollback occurs). If a locking error occurs, the lock is retried several times. If it's still unsuccessful, the entire transaction is rolled back.

TESTING A RECORD FOR LOCKING STATUS

Often, you want to determine the locking status of a record *before* you attempt an operation with it. By utilizing pessimistic locking and trying to modify the record, you can determine whether the current row is locked. The code looks like Listing 17.9.

LISTING 17.9   DETERMINING WHETHER A RECORD IS LOCKED BEFORE EDITING IT

```
Sub TestLocking()

    Dim cnn As ADODB.Connection
    Dim rst As ADODB.Recordset
    Dim boolLocked As Boolean

    Set cnn = New ADODB.Connection
    cnn.ConnectionString = " Provider=sqloledb;" & _
```

continues

LISTING **17.9**   CONTINUED

```
        "Data Source=(local);Initial Catalog=pubs;uid=sa;pwd="
    cnn.Open

    Set rst = New ADODB.Recordset
    rst.ActiveConnection = cnn
    rst.CursorType = adOpenKeyset
    rst.LockType = adLockPessimistic 'Invoke Pessimistic Locking
    rst.CursorLocation = adUseServer
    rst.Open "Authors", Options:=adCmdTable

    boolLocked = IsItLocked(rst)
    MsgBox boolLocked

End Sub

Function IsItLocked(rstAny As ADODB.Recordset) As Boolean
    On Error GoTo IsItLocked_Err
    IsItLocked = False

    With rstAny
        .Update
    End With
    Exit Function

IsItLocked_Err:
    If Err = -2147467259 Then
        IsItLocked = True
        Exit Function
    End If
End Function
```

The TestLocking routine sends its recordset to the IsItLocked() function, which receives the recordset as a parameter. It then issues an Update method on the recordset. If an error occurs, the record is locked. The error handler sets the return value for the function to True.

USING CODE TO REFRESH OR REQUERY

In this section, you'll see how to requery by using code. The Requery method makes sure the user gets to see any changes to existing records, as well as any records that have been added. It also ensures that deleted records are removed from the recordset. It's easiest to understand the `Requery` method by looking at the data underlying a form:

```
Private Sub cmdRequery_Click()
    If Me.RecordsetClone.Restartable Then
        Me.RecordsetClone.Requery
    Else
        MsgBox "Requery Method Not Supported on this Recordset"
    End If
End Sub
```

This code first tests the `Restartable` property of the recordset underlying the form. If the `Restartable` property is `True`, the recordset supports the `Requery` method that's performed on the form's recordset. Of course, the `Restartable` property and `Requery` method work on any recordset, not just the recordset underlying a form. The only reason a recordset might not be restartable is because some back-end queries can't be restarted.

Before running this code, new records don't appear in the recordset and deleted records appear with `#Deleted`. (See Figure 17.11.) After the `Requery` method is issued, all new records appear, and deleted records are removed.

FIGURE 17.11

A recordset that hasn't been requeried yet.

UNDERSTANDING THE .LDB FILE

Every database opened for shared use has a corresponding .LDB file, a locking file created to store computer and security names and to place byte range locks on the recordset. The .LDB file always has the same name and location as the databases whose locks it's tracking, and it's automatically deleted when the last user exits the database file. There are two times when the .LDB file is *not* deleted:

- The database is marked as damaged (politically correct term).
- The last user out doesn't have delete rights in the folder with the database and .LDB files.

The Jet Engine writes an entry to the .LDB file for every user who opens the database. The entry is 64 bytes; the first 32 bytes contain the user's computer name, and the last 32 bytes contain his security name. Because the maximum number of users for an Access database is 255, the .LDB file can't get larger than 16K. The .LDB file information prevents users from writing data to records or pages that other users have locked and determines who has the records or pages locked.

THE USER ROSTER

New to Access 2000 is the user roster. The user roster allows you to programmatically determine who is logged onto a database. This information is provided via the OpenSchema method of the Connection object.

The OpenSchema method receives three parameters. They include the Query Type, Restrictions, and a Schema ID. Listing 17.10 illustrates the use of the OpenSchema method to identify the user roster.

LISTING 17.10   DETERMINING WHO IS USING A DATABASE

```
Public Const JET_SCHEMA_USERROSTER = _
    "{947bb102-5d43-11d1-bdbf-00c04fb92675}"


Sub UserRoster()
    Dim cnn As ADODB.Connection
    Dim rst As ADODB.Recordset

    Set cnn = New ADODB.Connection
    cnn.ConnectionString = "Provider=Microsoft.Jet.OLEDB.4.0;" & _
    "Data Source=C:\My Documents\Test.mdb"
    cnn.Open

    Set rst = cnn.OpenSchema(adSchemaProviderSpecific, _
        , JET_SCHEMA_USERROSTER)
    Debug.Print rst.GetString
End Sub
```

The code begins by declaring and instantiating a Connection object. The connection is opened, using a connection string to the database for which you want to obtain the user roster. The OpenSchema method is executed on the Connection object. The parameters passed to the OpenSchema method designate that you want to return a user roster. The roster is returned into the Recordset object.

CREATING CUSTOM COUNTERS

Access offers an AutoNumber field type that can be set to automatically generate sequential or random values. Although the AutoNumber field type is adequate for most situations, you might want to home-grow your own AutoNumber fields for any of the following reasons:

- You don't like the AutoNumber field discarding values from canceled records.
- The primary key value needs to be some algorithm of the other fields in the table (the first few characters from a couple of fields, for example).
- The primary key value needs to contain an alphanumeric string.

To generate your own automatically numbered sequential value, you should probably build a system table that holds the next available value for your custom AutoNumber field. You must lock this table while a user is grabbing the next available sequential value, or else two users might be assigned the same value.

USING UNBOUND FORMS

One solution to locking conflicts is to use unbound forms. By doing this, you can greatly limit the amount of time a record is locked and fully control when Access tries to secure the lock. Unbound forms require significantly more coding than bound forms, so you should make sure the benefits you get from using unbound forms outweigh the coding and maintenance involved. With improvements to both forms and the Jet Engine in Access 2000, the reasons to use unbound forms with Access data are less compelling. Unbound forms are covered in more detail in Chapter 19, "Client/Server Techniques."

USING REPLICATION TO IMPROVE PERFORMANCE

Replication, covered in Chapter 23, can be used to improve performance in a multiuser application. Using replication, you can place multiple copies of the database containing the tables out on the network, each on a different file server. Different users can be set up to access data from the different file servers, thereby better distributing network traffic. Using the Replication Manager, which ships with the Microsoft Office Developer Edition (ODE), the databases can be synchronized at regular intervals. Although this isn't a viable solution when the data users are viewing needs to be fully current, there are many situations in which this type of solution might be adequate. It's often the only solution when limited resources don't allow migrating an application's data to a client/server database.

> **NOTE**
>
> The Replication Manager comes only with Office 2000 Developer.

PRACTICAL EXAMPLES

Making an Application Multiuser Ready

The Time and Billing application is built mostly around forms. Because it's unlikely that two users will update the data in the same record at the same time, you can opt for optimistic locking. This reduces the chance of a page of records inadvertently being locked for a long period of time. Alternatively, you can employ row-level locking. The example in Listing 17.11 illustrates how you can use the form's Error event to override the default locking error messages when optimistic locking is in place.

LISTING 17.11 OVERRIDING DEFAULT ERROR HANDLING UNDER A FORM

```
Private Sub Form_Error(DataErr As Integer, Response As Integer)
    On Error GoTo Form_Error_Err:
    Dim intAnswer As Integer
    If DataErr = 7787 Then  'Data Has Changed Error
        intAnswer = MsgBox("Another User Has Modified This Record " _
            & vbCrLf & _
            "Since You Began Editing It. " & vbCrLf & vbCrLf & _
            "Click OK to Cancel Your Changes", _
            vbOK, "Locking Conflict")
    End If
    Response = acDataErrContinue
    Exit Sub

Form_Error_Err:
    MsgBox "Error # " & Err.Number & ": " & Err.Description
    Exit Sub
End Sub
```

This code is placed in the Error event of the frmClients form in the CHAP17.MDB database. It begins by checking to see whether the DataErr is equal to 7787. This is the error code for DataErr when a Data Has Changed error has occurred in a form. If a 7787 has occurred, the user sees a message box notifying her of the conflict. The Response is set equal to acDataErrContinue so that the normal error message is suppressed.

SUMMARY

VBA offers several alternative locking strategies for the developer, ranging from locking the entire database to locking one record at a time. In addition, VBA lets you control how long data will be locked. You use this feature through the techniques of optimistic and pessimistic locking, as well as deciding on page locking versus record locking. The developer must select which combination of strategies should be used in each particular application. The decision about which method to use is influenced by many factors, including the volume of traffic on the network and the importance of making sure collisions never happen.

USING EXTERNAL DATA

IN THIS CHAPTER

WHY THIS CHAPTER IS IMPORTANT

Microsoft Access is very capable of interfacing with data from other sources. It can use data from any ODBC data source, as well as data from FoxPro, dBase, Paradox, Lotus, Excel, and many other sources. In this chapter, you will learn how to interface with external data sources, with the user interface, and by using code.

External data is data stored outside the current database. It can refer to data stored in another Microsoft Access database, as well as data stored in a multitude of other file formats—including ISAM, spreadsheet, ASCII, and more. This chapter focuses on accessing data sources other than ODBC data sources. ODBC data sources are covered extensively in Chapter 19, "Client/Server Techniques," Chapter 20, "Client/Server Strategies," and Chapter 21, "A Client/Server Application in Action."

Access is an excellent *front-end* product, which means that it provides a powerful and effective means of presenting data—even data from external sources. Data is stored in places other than Access for many reasons. Large databases, for example, can be managed more effectively on a back-end database server such as Microsoft SQL Server. Data often is stored in a FoxPro, dBase, or Paradox file format because the data is being used by a legacy application written in one of those environments. Text data often has been downloaded from a mainframe. Regardless of the reason why data is stored in another format, it is necessary that you understand how to manipulate this external data in your VBA modules. With the capability to access data from other sources, you can create queries, forms, and reports.

When accessing external data, you have three choices. You can import the data into an Access database, access the data by linking to it from your Access database, or open a data source directly. Importing the data is the optimum route (except with ODBC data sources) but not always possible. If you can't import external data, you should link to external files because Microsoft Access maintains a lot of information about these linked files. This optimizes performance when manipulating the external files. Sometimes a particular situation warrants accessing the data directly. You therefore should know how to work with linked files, as well as how to open and manipulate files directly.

IMPORTING, LINKING, AND OPENING: WHEN AND WHY

When you import data into an Access table, a copy is made of the data and is placed in an Access table. After data is imported, it is treated like any other native Access table. In fact, neither you nor Access has any way of knowing from where the data came. As a result, imported data offers the same performance and flexibility as any other Access table.

Linking to external data is quite different from importing data. Linked data remains in its native format. By establishing a link to the external data, you can build queries, forms, and reports that present the data. After you create a link to external data, the link remains permanently established unless you explicitly remove it. The linked table appears in the database window just like any other Access table, except that its icon is different. The other difference is that you cannot modify its structure from within Access. In fact, if the data source permits multiuser access, the users of your application can modify the data along with users of the applications written in the data source's native database format (such as FoxPro, dBase, or Paradox).

Opening an external table is similar to linking to the table, except that a permanent relationship is not created. When you *link* to an external table, connection information is maintained from session to session. When you *open* a table, you create a recordset from the table, and no permanent link is established.

Selecting an Option

It is important that you understand when to import external data, when to link to external data, and when to open an external table directly. You should import external data in either of these circumstances:

- You are migrating an existing system into Access.
- You want to use external data to run a large volume of queries and reports, and you will not update the data. You want the added performance that native Access data provides.

When you are migrating an existing system to Access and you are ready to permanently migrate test or production data into your application, you import the tables into Access. Another good reason to import external data is if the data is downloaded from a mainframe into ASCII format on a regular basis, and you want to use the data for reports. Instead of attempting to link to the data and suffering the performance hits associated with such a link, you can import the data each time it is downloaded from the mainframe.

You should link to external data in any of the following circumstances:

- The data is used by a legacy application requiring the native file format.
- The data resides on an ODBC-compliant database server.
- You will access the data on a regular basis (making it prohibitive to keep the data up-to-date if it is not linked).

Often, you won't have the time or resources to rewrite an application written in FoxPro, Paradox, or some other language. You might be developing additional applications that will share data with the legacy application, or you might want to use the strong querying and reporting capabilities of Access instead of developing queries and reports in the native environment.

By linking to the external data, users of existing applications can continue to work with the applications and their data. Your Access applications can retrieve and modify data without concern for corrupting, or in any other way harming, the data.

If the data resides in an ODBC database such as Microsoft SQL Server, you want to reap the data-retrieval benefits provided by a database server. By linking to the ODBC data source, you can take advantage of Access's ease of use as a front-end tool, while taking advantage of client/server technology at the same time.

Finally, if you intend to access data on a regular basis, linking to the external table instead of temporarily opening the table directly provides you with ease of use and performance benefits. After you create the link, in most cases Access treats the table just like any other Access table.

You should open an external table directly in either of these circumstances:

- You rarely need to establish a connection to the external data source.
- You have determined that performance actually improves by opening the data source directly.

If you rarely need to access the external data, it might be appropriate to open it directly. Links increase the size of your MDB file. This size increase is not necessary if you rarely will access the data. Furthermore, in certain situations, when accessing ISAM (inde XE d sequential access method) data, you might find that opening the table directly provides better performance than linking to it.

Although this chapter covers the process of importing external data, this is essentially a one-time process and doesn't require a lot of discussion. It is important to note, however, that after data is imported into an Access table, it no longer is accessed by the application in its native format. The majority of this chapter focuses on linking to or directly opening external data tables.

Looking at Supported File Formats

Microsoft Access enables you to import, link to, and open files in these formats:

- Microsoft Jet databases (including previous versions of Jet)
- ODBC databases
- HTML documents
- Microsoft Exchange/Outlook
- dBase III, dBase IV, and dBase 5.0

- Paradox 3.*x*, 4.*x*, and 5.*x*
- Microsoft Excel spreadsheets, versions 3.0, 4.0, 5.0, and 8.0
- Lotus WKS, WK1, WK3, and WK4 spreadsheets
- ASCII text files stored in a tabular format

IMPORTING EXTERNAL DATA

The process of importing external data is quite simple. You can import external data by using the user interface or by using VBA code. If you are planning to import the data only once or twice, you should use the user interface. If you are importing data on a regular basis (for example, from a downloaded mainframe file), you should write code that accomplishes the task transparently to the user.

Using the User Interface

To import an external data file using the user interface, follow these steps:

1. Right-click anywhere within the database window.
2. Choose Import (or choose File | Get External Data | Import). The Import dialog box appears, as shown in Figure 18.1.

FIGURE 18.1

The Import dialog box.

3. From the Files of Type drop-down list, select the type of file you are importing.
4. Select the file you want to import and click Import.
5. Depending on the type of file you select, the import process finishes or you see additional dialog boxes. If you select Excel Spreadsheet for example, the Import Spreadsheet Wizard appears, as shown in Figure 18.2. This wizard walks you through the process of importing spreadsheet data.

FIGURE 18.2

*The Import
Spreadsheet
Wizard.*

CAUTION

If you find that you can't bring a text file directly into a large (4M–5M) Access database, change the text file into an Excel spreadsheet first and then import that file.

Using Code

The DoCmd object has three methods that assist you with importing external data. They are TransferDatabase, TransferText, and TransferSpreadsheet, each of which is covered in this section.

Importing Database Data Using Code

You use the TransferDatabase method of the DoCmd object to import data from a database such as FoxPro, dBase, Paradox, or another Access database. A public constant called APPPATH has been declared in the General Declarations section of basImport. You need to change the value of this constant if you run the sample code from this chapter in a different directory. Listing 18.1, included in basImport, shows an example that uses the TransferDatabase method.

LISTING 18.1   USING THE TransferDatabase METHOD

```
Sub ImportDatabase()
  DoCmd.TransferDatabase _
    TransferType:=acImport, _
    DatabaseType:="dBase III", _
    DatabaseName:=APPPATH, _
    ObjectType:=acTable, _
```

```
    Source:="Customer", _
    Destination:="tblCustomers", _
    StructureOnly:=False
End Sub
```

NOTE

 This code and all the code in this chapter are located in the CHAP18EX.MDB file on the sample code CD-ROM.

Table 18.1 lists the arguments for the TransferDatabase method.

TABLE 18.1   TransferDatabasE ARGUMENTS

Argument	Specifies
TransferType	Type of transfer being performed.
DatabaseType	Type of database being imported.
DatabaseName	Name of the database. If the table is a separate file (as is the case with dBase, Paradox, and earlier versions of FoxPro), the database name is the name of the directory that contains the table file. Do *not* include a backslash after the name of the directory.
ObjectType	Type of object you want to import. This argument is ignored for all but Access objects.
Source	Name of the object you are importing. Do *not* include the file extension.
Destination	Name of the imported object.
StructureOnly	Whether you want the structure of the table only or the structure and data.
SaveLoginID	Whether you want to save the login ID and password for an ODBC database in the connection string for linked tables.

Importing Text Data Using Code

You use the TransferText method of the DoCmd object to import text from a text file. Listing 18.2 shows an example of this method.

Listing 18.2   Using the TransferText Method

```
Sub ImportText()
  DoCmd.TransferText _
    TransferType:=acImportDelim, _
    TableName:="tblCustomerText", _
    FileName:=APPPATH & "\Customer.Txt"
End Sub
```

Table 18.2 lists the arguments for the `TransferText` method.

Table 18.2   TransferText Arguments

Argument	Specifies
TransferType	Type of transfer you want to make.
SpecificationName	Name for the set of options that determines how the file is imported.
TableName	Name of the Access table that will receive the imported data.
FileName	Name of the text file to import from.
HasFieldHeadings	Whether the first row of the text file contains field headings.

Importing Spreadsheet Data Using Code

You use the `TransferSpreadsheet` method of the `DoCmd` object to import data from a spreadsheet file. Listing 18.3 shows an example that uses the `TransferSpreadsheet` method.

Listing 18.3   Using the TransferSpreadsheet Method

```
Sub ImportSpreadsheet()
  DoCmd.TransferSpreadsheet _
    TransferType:=acImport, _
    SpreadsheetType:=acSpreadsheetTypeExcel9, _
    TableName:="tblCustomerSpread", _
    FileName:=APPPATH & "\Customer.Xls", _
    HasFieldNames:=True
End Sub
```

Table 18.3 lists the arguments for the `TransferSpreadsheet` method.

TABLE 18.3 TransferSpreadsheet ARGUMENTS

Argument	Specifies
TransferType	Type of transfer you want to make.
SpreadsheetType	Type of spreadsheet to import from. The default is Excel 3.0.
TableName	Name of the Access table that will receive the imported data.
FileName	Name of the spreadsheet file to import from.
HasFieldNames	Whether the first row of the spreadsheet contains field headings.
Range	Range of cells to import.

CREATING A LINK TO EXTERNAL DATA

If you need to keep the data in its original format but want to treat the data just like any other Access table, linking is the best solution. All the information required to establish and maintain the connection to the remote data source is stored within the linked table definition. You can create links through the user interface and by using code. This section covers both alternatives.

One of the most common types of links is a link to another Access table. This type of link is created so that the application objects (queries, forms, reports, macros, and modules) can be placed in a local database and the tables can be stored in another database on a file server. Numerous benefits are associated with such a configuration. Chapter 17, "Developing Multiuser Applications," discusses these benefits in detail.

Using the User Interface

It is very common to create a link using the user interface. If you know what links you want to establish at design time, this is probably the easiest way to establish links to external data. You can establish links using the Database Splitter or by doing it manually.

Using the Database Splitter to Create Links

The Database Splitter was designed to split databases that already have been built with the tables and other database objects all in one physical MDB database file. It automates the process of moving the data tables to another database. The Database Splitter is covered in detail in Chapter 17.

> **NOTE**
>
> You can create links to tables only from an Access database, not from an Access project.

Creating Links to Access Tables

To create a link to an Access table, follow these steps:

1. Right-click anywhere within the Database window.

2. Choose Link Tables. The Link dialog box appears, as shown in Figure 18.3.

FIGURE 18.3
The Link dialog box.

3. Select the name of the database containing the table to which you want to link.

4. Click the Link button. The Link Tables dialog box appears, as shown in Figure 18.4.

FIGURE 18.4
The Link Tables dialog box.

5. Select the tables to which you want to establish a link.

6. Click OK. The link process finishes. Notice the arrows in Figure 18.5, which indicate that the tblCustomer, tblOrders, and tblOrderDetails tables are linked tables instead of tables stored in the current database.

FIGURE 18.5

Linked tables in the Database window.

Creating Links to Other Types of Tables

The process of creating links to other types of database files is a little different. It works like this:

1. Right-click anywhere within the Database window.

2. Choose Link Tables. The Link dialog box appears.

3. In the Files of Type drop-down list, select the type of table to which you are linking.

4. Select the external file containing the data to which you will be linking.

5. Click the Link button. The next dialog box varies, depending on the type of table to which you want to link. With a dBase file, for example, the Select Index Files dialog box appears, as shown in Figure 18.6. It is important that you select any index files associated with the data file. These indexes are updated automatically by Access as you add, change, and delete table data from within Access.

6. You receive a message indicating that the index was added successfully and that you can add other indexes if you choose. Click OK.

7. Add any additional indexes and click Close.

8. The Select Unique Record Identifier dialog box appears, as shown in Figure 18.7. This dialog box enables you to select a unique identifier for each record in the table. Select a unique field and click OK.

FIGURE 18.6
The Select Index Files dialog box.

FIGURE 18.7
The Select Unique Record Identifier dialog box.

Notice the icon indicating the type of file you linked to, as shown in Figure 18.8.

FIGURE 18.8
An icon indicating that the file database is linked to a dBase database file.

> **NOTE**
>
> Earlier versions of Access supported links to FoxPro files using the FoxPro ISAM driver. With Access 2000 and Jet 4.0, you must link to FoxPro tables using the Visual FoxPro ODBC Driver.

Using Code

Creating a link to an external table using code is a six-step process. Here are the steps involved in establishing the link:

1. Create a reference to the Microsoft ADO Extension 2.1 for DDL and Security (ADOX) library.
2. Create a Catalog object.
3. Set the Connection property of the Catalog object to the database that will contain the linked table.
4. Create a new Table object.
5. Set properties of the Table object.
6. Append the Table object to the Catalog.

Listing 18.4 shows the code for linking to an external table, which in this case exists in another Microsoft Access database.

LISTING 18.4   LINKING TO AN EXTERNAL TABLE

```
Sub LinkToAccessTableProps()
    Dim cat As ADOX.Catalog
    Dim tbl As ADOX.Table

    Set cat = New ADOX.Catalog
    cat.ActiveConnection = CurrentProject.Connection

    Set tbl = New ADOX.Table
    tbl.Name = "tblLinkedTable"
    Set tbl.ParentCatalog = cat

    tbl.Properties("Jet OLEDB:Create Link") = True
    tbl.Properties("Jet OLEDB:Link Provider String") = ";pwd=password"
    tbl.Properties("Jet OLEDB:Remote Table Name") = "tblClients"
    tbl.Properties("Jet OLEDB:Link Datasource") = APPPATH & _
        "\Chap18Data.mdb"

    cat.Tables.Append tbl
End Sub
```

In Listing 18.4, a Catalog object is created. The ActiveConnection property of the Catalog object is pointed at the connection associated with the current database. Next a Table object is created. The Name property of the Table object is set equal to tblLinkedTable. The

18

USING EXTERNAL DATA

`ParentCatalog` property of the Table object is set to point at the Catalog object. Four properties in the properties collection of the Table object are set to the appropriate values, and the Table object is appended to the Catalog object. This process is discussed in further detail in the following sections.

Providing Connection Information

When you link to an external table, you must provide information about the type, name, and location of the external database. This is accomplished by setting the following properties in the Properties collection of the Table object:

- Jet OLEDB:Link Provider String
- Jet OLEDB:Remote Table Name
- Jet OLEDB:Link Datasource

The process of setting the provider string, name, and location of the source table is illustrated by these three lines of code:

```
tbl.Properties("Jet OLEDB:Link Provider String") = ";pwd=password"
tbl.Properties("Jet OLEDB:Remote Table Name") = "tblClients"
tbl.Properties("Jet OLEDB:Link Datasource") = APPPATH & "\Chap18Data.mdb"
```

The Jet OLEDB:Link Provider is the ISAM format that will be used for the link. Each source database type is a different folder in the Windows Registry. The folders are located in the HKEY_LOCAL_MACHINE\SOFTWARE\Microsoft\Jet\4.0\ISAM Formats section of the Registry. Valid source database types are as follows:

dBase	dBase III, dBase IV, and dBase 5.0
Excel	Excel 3.0, Excel 4.0, Excel 5.0, and Excel 8.0
HTML	HTML Export and HTML Import
Jet	Jet 2.x, Jet 3.x
Lotus	Lotus WK1, Lotus WK3, Lotus WK4, Lotus WJ2, and Lotus WJ3
Exchange	Exchange 4.0
Outlook	Outlook 9.0
Paradox	Paradox 3.x, Paradox 4.x, Paradox 5.x, and Paradox 7.x
Text	

The Jet OLEDB:Link Datasource must include a fully qualified path to the file. You can specify the path with a drive letter and directory path or by using *universal naming conventions* (UNCs). For a local database, you must specify the path like this:

```
tbl.Properties("Jet OLEDB:Link Datasource") = "c:\Databases\Chap18Data"
```

For a file server, you can specify the UNC path or the drive letter path. The UNC path looks like this:

```
tbl.Properties("Jet OLEDB:Link Datasource") = _
    "\\FILESERVERNAME\Databases\Chap18Data"
```

In this case, the database called Chap18Data is stored on the databases share of a particular file server.

Creating the Link

Listing 18.5 shows how you put all the connection information together to establish a link to an external table.

LISTING 18.5   ESTABLISHING A LINK TO AN EXTERNAL TABLE

```
Sub LinkToDBase(strDirName As String, strTableName As String, _
    strAccessTable)
    Dim cat As ADOX.Catalog
    Dim tbl As ADOX.Table

    Set cat = New ADOX.Catalog
    cat.ActiveConnection = CurrentProject.Connection

    Set tbl = New ADOX.Table
    tbl.Name = strAccessTable
    Set tbl.ParentCatalog = cat

    tbl.Properties("Jet OLEDB:Create Link") = True
    tbl.Properties("Jet OLEDB:Link Datasource") = strDirName
    tbl.Properties("Jet OLEDB:Link Provider String") = _
        "dBase III;HDR=NO;IMEX=2;"
    tbl.Properties("Jet OLEDB:Remote Table Name") = strTableName

    cat.Tables.Append tbl
End Sub
```

Here is an example of how this subroutine is called:

```
Call LinkToDBase("c:\customer\data","customer","tblCustomers")
```

The LinkToDBase subroutine receives three parameters:

- The name of the directory in which the dBase file is stored.
- The name of the file (the name of the table, without the DBF extension) to which you want to connect.
- The name of the Access table that you are creating.

The subroutine creates two object variables: a Catalog object variable and a Table object variable. It points the `ActiveConnection` property of the Catalog object variable at the connection associated with the current database. Next, it establishes properties of the Table object. The Link Datasource is the name of the directory within which the dBase file is stored. The Link Provider String specifies that the type of table you are linking to is a dBase III file. The Remote Table Name is the name of the dBase file you are linking to. After setting these properties, you are ready to append the table definition to the database.

You have seen how you can link to a dBase table. Listing 18.6 puts together everything you have learned in this chapter by creating a link to an Access table stored in another database.

LISTING 18.6   CREATING A LINK TO AN ACCESS TABLE STORED IN ANOTHER DATABASE

```
Sub LinkToAccess(strDBName As String, strTableName As String, _
   strAccessTable)
   Dim cat As ADOX.Catalog
   Dim tbl As ADOX.Table

   Set cat = New ADOX.Catalog
   cat.ActiveConnection = CurrentProject.Connection

   Set tbl = New ADOX.Table
   tbl.Name = strAccessTable
   Set tbl.ParentCatalog = cat

   tbl.Properties("Jet OLEDB:Create Link") = True
   tbl.Properties("Jet OLEDB:Link Datasource") = strDBName
   tbl.Properties("Jet OLEDB:Link Provider String") = ";pwd=password"
   tbl.Properties("Jet OLEDB:Remote Table Name") = strTableName

   cat.Tables.Append tbl
End Sub
```

Notice that the Jet OLEDB Link Provider string no longer specifies the type of database to which you are connecting. Everything else in this routine is the same as the routine that connected to dBase. Also notice that the parameters passed to this routine:

```
Call LinkToAccess("C:\databases\northwind","Customers","tblCustomers")
```

The database passed to the routine is an actual Access database (as opposed to a directory), and the table name is the name of the Access table in the other database (instead of the DBF filename).

> **NOTE**
>
> Whether you link to an external database using the user interface or code, you should always use the UNC path, rather than a drive letter. This ensures that all users with access to the network share are able to see the data, regardless of their drive letter mappings.

OPENING AN EXTERNAL TABLE

It generally is preferable to link to, rather than open, an external table. Linking provides additional performance and ease of use when dealing with an external table. After you link to a table, it is treated just like any other Access table. Occasionally, though, it is necessary to open an external table without creating a link to it. Opening an external table is a two-step process:

1. Establish a connection to the external data source.
2. Point a recordset object at the result of executing a SQL statement against the Connection object.

Providing Connection Information

The connection information you provide when you open an external table is similar to the information you provide when you link to the table. The connection information is provided as the ConnectionString argument of the Open method or the Connection object. Here's an example:

```
cnn.Open "Provider=Microsoft.Jet.OLEDB.4.0;Data Source=" & _
         "c:\my documents\tblCustomers.xls;" & _ _
         "Extended Properties=Excel 8.0;"
```

Here, the connection string is to the c:\my documents\tblCustomers.xls spreadsheet using the 8.0 ISAM.

Opening the Table

The Recordset object is pointed at the result of executing a Select statement against the Connection object:

```
Set rst = cnn.E XE cute("Select * from tblCustomers")
```

Listing 18.7 shows what the entire process looks like in code.

LISTING 18.7   USING THE OpenDatabase METHOD

```
Sub OpenExternalExcel(strDBName As String, strTableName As String)
    Dim cnn As ADODB.Connection
    Dim rst As ADODB.Recordset

    Set cnn = New ADODB.Connection
    Set rst = New ADODB.Recordset
    cnn.Open "Provider=Microsoft.Jet.OLEDB.4.0;Data Source=" & _
        strDBName & "\" & strTableName & _
        ";Extended Properties=Excel 8.0;"
    Set rst = cnn.E XE cute("Select * from tblCustomers")

    Do Until rst.EOF
        Debug.Print rst.Fields(0).Value
        rst.MoveNext
    Loop

    cnn.Close
End Sub
```

Listing 18.7 is called with this code:

```
Call OpenExternalExcel("c:\my documents","tblCustomers.xls")
```

Notice that you are not appending a table definition here. Instead, you are creating a temporary recordset that refers to the external data. After the external table is opened as a recordset, the code traverses through each record of the table, printing the value of the first field. Of course, after the recordset is opened, you can manipulate it in any way you want. The table does not show up as a linked table in the database window. In fact, when the routine completes and the local variable goes out of scope, the recordset no longer exists.

Now that you have seen how you can link to external tables as well as open them, you are ready to take a look at how you can refine both these processes. This involves learning the Windows Registry settings that affect the linking process, learning more about the parameters that are available to you when specifying connection information, learning how to specify passwords, learning how to refresh and remove links, and learning how to create an external table using VBA code.

UNDERSTANDING WINDOWS REGISTRY SETTINGS

Each ISAM driver has a separate key in the Windows Registry. These keys are located in the appropriate ISAM driver in the HKEY_LOCAL_MACHINE\SOFTWARE\Microsoft\ Jet\4.0\ISAM Formats section of the Registry. These keys are used to configure the driver after initialization. As you can see in Figure 18.9, the setup program has created keys for several data sources. If you look at a specific data source (in this case, dBase III), you can see all the settings that exist for the dBase driver. The `IndexFilter` is set to `dBase Index(*.ndx)`, for example. At times, you will need to modify one of the Registry settings to customize the behavior of the ISAM driver; this is covered later in this chapter in the section "Looking at Special Considerations."

FIGURE 18.9

The Windows Registry with keys for ISAM drivers.

USING THE JET OLEDB:LINK PROVIDER STRING

The Jet OLEDB:Link Provider String includes the source database type, user ID, and password. Each part of the connection string must be separated by a semicolon.

Each source database type has a valid name. This is the name that must be used when accessing that type of data. These database types are the types found in the Windows Registry under HKEY_LOCAL_MACHINE\Software\Microsoft\Jet\4.0\ISAM Formats. You must accurately specify the source database type, or you will be unable to access the external data.

The user ID is used whenever a username must be specified in order to successfully log on to the data source. This is most common when dealing with back-end databases such as Oracle, Sybase, or Microsoft SQL Server. This part of the provider string can be required to log the user on to the system where the source data resides. The `UID` keyword is used to refer to the user ID.

As with the user ID, the password most often is included when dealing with back-end data. It also can be used on other database types that support passwords, such as Paradox, or when linking to an external Access table. The PWD keyword is used when specifying the password.

Finally, the dataset name is used to refer to a defined ODBC data source. Communicating with an ODBC data source is covered in detail in Chapter 19, "Client/Server Techniques." The DSN keyword is used when referring to the dataset name in the connection string. The following is an example of a Jet OLEDB Link Provider String:

```
tbl.Properties("Jet OLEDB:Link Provider String") = "ODBC" & _
    ";DATABASE=Pubs" & _
    ";UID=Alison" & _
    ";PWD=MyPass" & _
    ";DSN=PublisherData"
```

In the example, the SQL Server database being accessed is Pubs, the user id is Alison, the Password is MyPass, and the data source name is PublisherData.

WORKING WITH PASSWORDS

In working with passwords, you probably won't want to hard-code the password into your application because it defeats the purpose of placing a password on your database. In Listing 18.8, the database's password is included in the code, allowing the link to be made to the secured table without any password validation.

LISTING 18.8   EMBEDDING A DATABASE PASSWORD IN CODE

```
Sub LinkToSecured()
    Dim cat As ADOX.Catalog
    Dim tbl As ADOX.Table

    Set cat = New ADOX.Catalog
    cat.ActiveConnection = CurrentProject.Connection

    Set tbl = New ADOX.Table
    tbl.Name = "tblLinkedTable"
    Set tbl.ParentCatalog = cat

    tbl.Properties("Jet OLEDB:Create Link") = True
    tbl.Properties("Jet OLEDB:Link Provider String") = "ODBC" & _
        ";DATABASE=Pubs" & _
        ";UID=Alison" & _
        ";PWD=MyPass" & _
```

```
            ";DSN=PublisherData"
        tbl.Properties("Jet OLEDB:Remote Table Name") = "Authors"

        cat.Tables.Append tbl
End Sub
```

An invalid password results in a message appearing, requiring the user to log on. Unless you are using integrated Windows NT security to log on to your database server, it is best to require the user to supply the password at runtime. In Listing 18.9, the password argument is left blank, which causes the user to be prompted for a password.

LISTING 18.9   REQUIRING PASSWORD VALIDATION

```
Sub ReallySecure()
    Dim cat As ADOX.Catalog
    Dim tbl As ADOX.Table
    Dim strPassword As String

    Set cat = New ADOX.Catalog
    cat.ActiveConnection = CurrentProject.Connection

    Set tbl = New ADOX.Table
    tbl.Name = "tblLinkedTable"
    Set tbl.ParentCatalog = cat

    strPassword = InputBox("Please Enter Your Password", _
        "Database Security!!!")

    tbl.Properties("Jet OLEDB:Create Link") = True
    tbl.Properties("Jet OLEDB:Link Provider String") = "ODBC" & _
        ";DATABASE=Pubs" & _
        ";UID=SA" & _
        ";PWD=" & strPassword & _
        ";DSN=PubsData"
    tbl.Properties("Jet OLEDB:Remote Table Name") = "Authors"

    cat.Tables.Append tbl
End Sub
```

The password is retrieved from the user and stored in a variable called strPassword. This strPassword variable is included in the connection string at runtime.

REFRESHING AND REMOVING LINKS

Refreshing links refers to updating the link to an external table. It is done when the location of an external table has changed. *Removing links* refers to the process of permanently removing a link to an external table.

Access cannot find external tables if their locations have moved. You need to accommodate for this in your VBA code. Furthermore, there might be times when you want to remove a link to external data—when it is no longer necessary to use the data, or when the data has been imported permanently into Access.

Updating Links That Have Moved

To refresh a link using VBA code, simply redefine the Jet OLEDB:Link Datasource. Listing 18.10 shows the code to refresh a link.

LISTING 18.10 REFRESHING A LINK

```
Sub RefreshLink()
    Dim cat As ADOX.Catalog
    Dim tdf As ADOX.Table

    Set cat = New ADOX.Catalog
    Set cat.ActiveConnection = CurrentProject.Connection
    tdf.Properties("Jet OLEDB:Link Datasource") = _
        strNewLocation
End Sub
```

You can modify this routine to prompt the user for the directory containing the data tables, as Listing 18.11 shows.

LISTING 18.11 PROMPTING THE USER FOR THE DATABASE PATH AND NAME

```
Sub RefreshLink()
    On Error GoTo RefreshLink_Err
    Dim cat As ADOX.Catalog
    Dim tdf As ADOX.Table
    Dim strNewLocation As String
    Dim strTemp As String

    Set cat = New ADOX.Catalog
    Set cat.ActiveConnection = CurrentProject.Connection
    Set tdf = cat.Tables("tblClients")
```

```
    strTemp = tdf.Columns(0).Name
    Exit Sub

RefreshLink_Err:
    strNewLocation = InputBox("Please Enter Database Path and Name")
    tdf.Properties("Jet OLEDB:Link Datasource") = _
        strNewLocation
    Set cat.ActiveConnection = CurrentProject.Connection
    Set tdf = cat.Tables("tblClients")
    Resume
End Sub
```

This routine points a `Table` object to the tblClients table. It then attempts to access the name of the first column in the table. If an error occurs, an input box prompts the user for the new location of the database. The `Jet OLEDB:Link Datasource` property for the database is modified to incorporate the new location. The code then resumes on the offending line of code. You should modify this routine to give the user a way out. `Resume` throws the user into an endless loop if the database is not available. An enhanced routine (Listing 18.13) is presented later in the "Practical Examples" section of this chapter.

Deleting Links

To remove a link using VBA code, simply execute a Delete method of the Tables collection of a Catalog object connected to the database, as shown in Listing 18.12.

LISTING 18.12   REMOVING A LINK

```
Sub RemoveLink()
    Dim cat As Catalog

    Set cat = New ADOX.Catalog
    cat.ActiveConnection = CurrentProject.Connection

    cat.Tables.Delete ("tblClients")

End Sub
```

LOOKING AT SPECIAL CONSIDERATIONS

When dealing with different types of external files, various problems and issues arise. If you understand these stumbling blocks before they affect you, you will get a great head start in dealing with these potential obstacles.

18

USING EXTERNAL
DATA

dBase

The major concerns you will have when dealing with dBase files surround deleted records, indexes, data types, and memo fields. When you delete a record from a dBase table, it is not actually removed from the table. Instead, it is just marked for deletion. A Pack process must be completed in order for the records to actually be removed from the table. If records are deleted from a dBase table using an Access application, the records are not removed. Because you cannot pack a dBase database from within an Access application, the records still remain in the table. In fact, they are not automatically filtered from the Access table. In order to filter deleted records so that they cannot be seen within the Access application, the `Deleted` value in the \HKEY_LOCAL_MACHINE\SOFTWARE\Microsoft\Jet\4.0\Engines\Xbase section of the registry must be set to `01` (True).

Access can use the dBase indexes to improve performance. After you link to a dBase table and select an index, an INF file is created. This file has the same name as your dBase database with an INF extension. It contains information about all the indexes being used. Here's an example of an INF:

```
[dBase III]
NDX1=CUSTID.NDX
UNDX1=CUSTID.NDX
```

`dBase III` is the database type identifier. `NDX1` is an index number for the first index. The `UNDX1` entry specifies a unique index.

The data types available in dBase files are different from those available in Access files. It is important to understand how the field types are mapped. Table 18.4 shows how each dBase data type is mapped to a Jet data type.

TABLE 18.4 MAPPING OF dBASE DATA TYPES

dBase Data Type	Jet Data Type
Character	Text
Numeric, Float	Double
Logical	Boolean
Date	Date/Time
Memo	Memo
OLE	OLE Object

Finally, it is important to ensure that the dBase memo files are stored in the same directory as the table. Otherwise, Access is unable to read the data in the memo file.

Text Data

When linking to an ASCII text file, Jet can determine the format of the file directly, or it can use a schema information file, which resides in the same directory as the text file. It always is named SCHEMA.INI, and it contains information about the format of the file, the column names, and the data types. The schema information file is optional for delimited files, but it is required for fi XE d length files. It is important to understand that ASCII files can never be opened for shared use.

TROUBLESHOOTING

Unfortunately, working with external data is not always a smooth process. Many things can go wrong, including connection problems and a lack of temporary disk space.

Connection Problems

Difficulties with accessing external data can be caused by any of the following circumstances:

- The server on which the external data is stored is down.
- The user does not have rights to the directory in which the external data is stored.
- The user does not have rights to the external data source.
- The external data source was moved.
- The UNC path or network share name was modified.
- The connection string is incorrect.
- The installable ISAM driver has not been installed.

Temp Space

Access requires a significant amount of disk space in order to run complex queries on large tables. This disk space is required whether the tables are linked tables stored remotely in another format, or they reside on the local machine. If not enough disk space is available to run a query, the application behaves unpredictably. It therefore is necessary to ensure that all users have enough disk space to meet the requirements of the queries that are run.

LOOKING AT PERFORMANCE CONSIDERATIONS AND LINKS

Because your application has to go through an extra translation layer, the installable ISAM, performance is not nearly as good with ISAM files as it is with native Jet data. It always is best to import ISAM data whenever possible. If it is not possible to import the data, you need to accept the performance that linking offers or consider linking the best solution to an otherwise unsolvable problem.

WORKING WITH HTML DOCUMENTS

Access 2000 enables you to import, export, and link to HTML documents. Although working with HTML documents is similar to working with other files types, HTML documents deserve special mention. To import an HTML document, follow these steps:

1. Right-click anywhere within the Database window and choose Import.

2. From the Files of Type drop-down list, select HTML Documents.

3. Select the document you want to import and click Import. The Import HTML Wizard appears, as shown in Figure 18.10.

FIGURE 18.10

The first step of the Import HTML Wizard.

4. The first step of the wizard attempts to parse the HTML document into fields. You can accept what the wizard has done or click Advanced. The Import Specification dialog box that appears enables you to designate field names, data types, and indexes for each field; and to select any fields you want to eliminate from the imported file. (See Figure 18.11.) This dialog box also enables you to modify the date order, date delimiter, and more.

5. After you make any required changes to the import specifications, click OK to return to the Import HTML Wizard. Click Next to advance to the next step of the wizard, which enables you to select whether the imported data is stored in a new table or in an existing table. Make your selection and then click Next.

6. The third step of the wizard enables you to designate a field name, data type, and index for each field, as shown in Figure 18.12. Make any desired changes here and click Next.

FIGURE **18.11**

The Import Specification dialog box enables you to designate the specifics of the import.

FIGURE **18.12**

Customizing the properties of each imported field.

7. The fourth step of the wizard enables you to indicate that you want Access to add a primary key to the table, that you want to select your own primary key, or that you don't want the imported table to have a primary key. Make your selection and click Next.

8. The final step of the wizard enables you to assign a name to the table. You even can have the wizard analyze the table after importing it. Click Finish after you make your selection.

Not only can you import an HTML document, but you also can link to one. To link to an HTML document, follow these steps:

1. Right-click anywhere within the Database window and choose Link Tables.

2. From the Files of Type drop-down list, select HTML Documents.

3. Select the table you want to link to and click Link. The Link HTML Wizard appears.

4. Click the Advanced button to modify any link specifications and return to the first step of the wizard. Click Next to move to the second step of the wizard.

5. The second step of the Link HTML Wizard enables you to specify information about each field you are linking to. Make any required changes and click Next.

6. Supply a name for the linked table and click Finish.

Whereas an imported HTML document acts like any other Access table, the data in a linked HTML document is not modifiable from within Access. You can use the linked document to create queries, reports, and forms.

PRACTICAL EXAMPLES

Working with External Data from within Your Application

It's time to split the data tables from the remainder of the application objects. You easily can accomplish this using the Database Splitter. After you split the tables from the rest of the database objects, you need to write code to refresh links. Both these topics are covered in this section.

Splitting the Database Using the Database Splitter

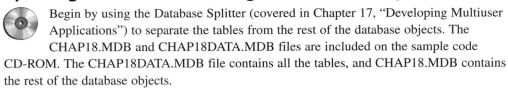 Begin by using the Database Splitter (covered in Chapter 17, "Developing Multiuser Applications") to separate the tables from the rest of the database objects. The CHAP18.MDB and CHAP18DATA.MDB files are included on the sample code CD-ROM. The CHAP18DATA.MDB file contains all the tables, and CHAP18.MDB contains the rest of the database objects.

Refreshing Links

If you distributed the Time and Billing application and all users did not have the same path to the CHAP18DATA.MDB file, the application would not load successfully. The LinkTables routine, located in the Switchboard startup form, ensures that the tables are successfully linked, as Listing 18.13 shows.

LISTING 18.13   LOADING THE APPLICATION AND CHECKING TABLE ATTACHMENTS

```
Sub LinkTables()
    On Error GoTo LinkTables_Err:

    DoCmd.Hourglass True

    If Not VerifyLink Then
        If Not ReLink(CurrentProject.FullName, True) Then
```

```
            Me.dlgCommon.ShowOpen
            If Not ReLink(Me.dlgCommon.FileName, False) Then
                MsgBox "You Cannot Run This App Without " & _
                    "Locating Data Tables"
                DoCmd.Close acForm, "frmSplash"
                DoCmd.Quit
            End If
        End If
    End If

    Call GetCompanyInfo
    DoCmd.Hourglass False
    Exit Sub

LinkTables_Err:
    DoCmd.Hourglass False
    MsgBox "Error # " & Err.Number & ": " & Err.Description
    Exit Sub

End Sub
```

Notice that the `VerifyLink` routine is called from the LinkTables routine. The `VerifyLink` routine appears in Listing 18.14.

LISTING 18.14 THE `VerifyLink` ROUTINE TESTS TO SEE WHETHER ANY TABLE LINKS ARE BROKEN

```
Function VerifyLink() As Boolean
    'Verify connection information in linked tables.

    'Declare Required Variables
    Dim cat As ADOX.Catalog
    Dim tdf As ADOX.Table
    Dim strTemp As String

    'Point Database object variable at the current database
    Set cat = New ADOX.Catalog

    With cat
        Set .ActiveConnection = CurrentProject.Connection

        'Continue if links are broken.
        On Error Resume Next
```

continues

LISTING 18.14   CONTINUED

```
        'Open one linked table to see if connection
        'information is correct.
        For Each tdf In .Tables
            If tdf.Type = "LINK" Then
                strTemp = tdf.Columns(0).Name
                If Err.Number Then
                    Exit For
                End If
            End If

        Next tdf
    End With

    VerifyLink = (Err.Number = 0)

End Function
```

The routine begins by pointing the `ActiveConnection` property of the Catalog object to the connection associated with the current database. It then loops through each table in the Tables collection of the Catalog object. If the table is a linked table, it attempts to access the name of the first column in the table. If any of the links are broken, an error occurs, and the `For...Each` loop is exited. If no error occurs, the function returns `True`; otherwise the function returns `False`.

If the `VerifyLink` routine returns `False`, the `ReLink` routine is called. Listing 18.15 shows the `ReLink` routine.

LISTING 18.15   THE ReLink ROUTINE ATTEMPTS TO RE-ESTABLISH THE BROKEN LINKS

```
Function ReLink(strDir As String, DefaultData As Boolean) _
    As Boolean

    ' Relink a broken linked Access table.

    Dim cat As ADOX.Catalog
    Dim tdfReLink As ADOX.Table
    Dim oDBInfo As DBInfo
    Dim strPath As String
    Dim strName As String
    Dim intCounter As Integer
    Dim vntStatus As Variant
```

```
        vntStatus = SysCmd(acSysCmdSetStatus, "Updating Links")

        Set cat = New ADOX.Catalog
        Set oDBInfo = New DBInfo

        With cat
            .ActiveConnection = CurrentProject.Connection
            oDBInfo.FullName = strDir
            strPath = oDBInfo.FilePathOnly
            strName = Left(oDBInfo.FileName, InStr(oDBInfo.FileName, ".") - 1)

            On Error Resume Next
            Call SysCmd(acSysCmdInitMeter, "Linking Data Tables", .Tables.Count)

            For Each tdfReLink In .Tables
                intCounter = intCounter + 1
                Call SysCmd(acSysCmdUpdateMeter, intCounter)
                If .Tables(tdfReLink.Name).Type = "LINK" Then
                    tdfReLink.Properties("Jet OLEDB:Link Datasource") _
    = strPath & strName & IIf(DefaultData, "Data.Mdb", ".mdb")
                End If
                If Err.Number Then
                    Exit For
                End If
            Next tdfReLink
        End With

        Call SysCmd(acSysCmdRemoveMeter)

        vntStatus = SysCmd(acSysCmdClearStatus)

        ReLink = (Err = 0)

End Function
```

The ReLink function receives two parameters. The first parameter is the name of the database the function will attempt to link to. The second parameter is a Boolean variable that is used to designate whether the database is considered the default database.

The function begins by modifying the status bar. It then creates a Catalog object and an instance of a custom class called DBInfo. This custom class is covered in further detail in Chapter 39, "Distributing Your Application." Class modules are covered in Chapter 28, "Exploiting the Power of Class Modules." The ActiveConnection property of the catalog object is set equal to the Connection property of the current project. Next, the FullName property of the DBInfo class is set equal to the name of the file that is passed as a parameter to the function. The DBInfo class extracts the path and the filename from the full filename. Just as with the VerifyLink function, the ReLink function uses a For...Next loop to loop through all the tables in the database. As it loops through each table, it attempts to establish a link to a database with the name passed as parameter to the ReLink function.

This ReLink function is called twice from the LinkTables routine, shown in Listing 18.13. The first time it is passed, the FullName property of the CurrentProject object and the boolean are True, indicating that it will try to locate the table in a database with the same location as the application database. If that attempt is not successful, the LinkTables routine displays the File Open common dialog, allowing the user to attempt to locate the database. The ReLink function is called again, searching for the table in the database selected by the user. If it is still unsuccessful, the routine quits the application.

SUMMARY

The capability to link to external data is one of Access 2000's strongest attributes. It is important that you understand how to link to external data via the user interface and by using VBA code. This chapter taught you how to link to external tables, open external data sources directly, refresh and remove links, and create external tables using VBA code. Many of the techniques covered in this chapter are explored further in Chapter 19.

CLIENT/SERVER TECHNIQUES

IN THIS CHAPTER

UNDERSTANDING THE CLIENT/SERVER MODEL

Client/server is one of the hot computing terms of the 90s. It refers to distributed processing of information. It involves the storage of data on database servers dedicated to the tasks of processing data and storing it. These database servers are referred to as *back ends*. A front-end tool such as Microsoft Access accomplishes the presentation of the data. Microsoft Access, with its tools that assist in the rapid development of queries, forms, and reports, provides an excellent front end for the presentation of back-end data. As more and more applications are downsized from mainframes and upsized from personal computers, more users need to understand the details of client/server technology.

For years, most information professionals have worked with traditional programming languages. These languages are responsible for both processing and maintaining data integrity in the application. This means that data validation rules must be embedded in the programming code. Furthermore, these types of applications are record oriented. All records are read into memory and processed. This scenario has several drawbacks:

- If the underlying data structure changes, every application that uses the data structure must be changed.
- Data validation rules must be placed in *every* application that accesses a data table.
- Presentation, processing, and storage are handled by one program.
- Record-oriented processing results in an extraordinary amount of unnecessary network traffic.

The client/server model introduces a separation of functionality. The *client*, or front end, is responsible for presenting the data and doing some processing. The *server*, or back end, is responsible for storing, protecting, and performing the bulk of the data processing.

DECIDING WHETHER TO USE THE CLIENT/SERVER MODEL

Client/server technology was not as necessary when there was a clear delineation between mainframe applications and personal computer applications. Today, the line of demarcation has blurred. Personal computer applications are beginning to take over many applications that had been relegated to mainframe computers in the past. The problem is that users still are very limited by the bandwidth of network communications. This is one place where client/server technology can really help.

Many developers are confused about what client/server architecture really is. (In fact, I have participated in many debates in which other developers have insisted that Access itself is a database server application. Well, it's not.) Access is a front-end application that can process data stored on a back end. In this scenario, the Access application runs on the client machine accessing data stored on a database server running software such as Microsoft SQL Server. Access does an excellent job acting as the client-side, front-end software in this scenario. The confusion lies in Access's capability to act as a database server.

Many people mistakenly believe that an Access MDB database file stored on a file server acts as a database server. This is not the case. The difference is in the way data is retrieved when Access is acting as the front end to a database server versus when the data is stored in an Access MDB file. Suppose that you have a table with 500,000 records. A user runs a query based on the 500,000-record table stored in an Access database on a file server. The user wants to see a list of all the Californians who make more than $75,000 per year. With the data stored on the file server in the Access MDB file format, all records are sent over the network to the workstation, and the query is performed on the workstation. (See Figure 19.1.) This results in significant network traffic.

FIGURE 19.1

Access as a front end and a back end.

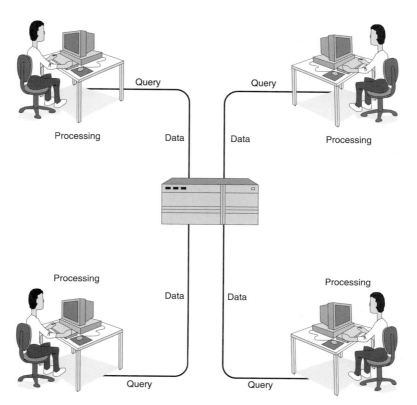

On the other hand, assume that these 500,000 records are stored on a database server such as Microsoft SQL Server. The user runs the same query. In this case, only the names of the Californians who make more than $75,000 per year are sent over the network. In fact, if you request only specific fields, only the fields you request are retrieved. (See Figure 19.2.)

FIGURE 19.2

Access as a front end using a true back end.

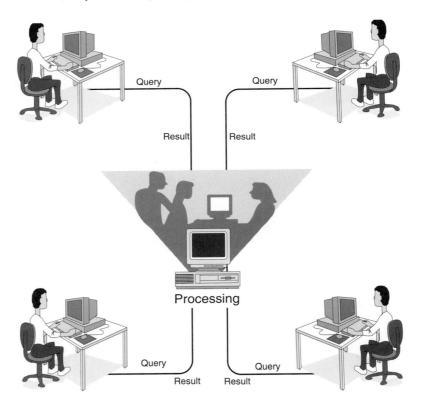

What does this mean to you? When should you become concerned with client/server technology and what it can offer you? The following sections present some guidelines for why you might want to upsize.

Dealing with a Large Volume of Data

As the volume of data in an Access database increases, you probably will notice a degradation in performance. Many people say that 100MB is the magical number for the maximum size of an Access database, but many back-end database servers can handle databases containing multiple gigabytes of data. Although a maximum size of 100MB for an Access database is a good general guideline, it is *not* a hard-and-fast rule. You might find that the need to upsize occurs when your database is significantly larger or smaller than 100MB. The magic number for you depends on all the factors discussed in the following sections, as well as on how many tables are included in the database. Generally, Access performs better with large volumes of data stored in a single table rather than in multiple tables.

Dealing with a Large Number of Concurrent Users

Just as a large volume of data can be a problem, so can a large number of concurrent users. In fact, more than 10 users concurrently accessing an Access database can degrade performance. As with the amount of data, this is not a magical number. I have seen applications with fewer than 10 users where performance is awful, and I have seen applications with significantly more than 10 users where performance is acceptable. It often depends on how the application is designed, as well as what tasks the users are performing.

Demanding Faster Performance

Certain applications demand better performance than other applications. An Online Transaction Processing system (OLTP) generally requires significantly better performance than a Decision Support System (DSS), for example. Suppose that 100 users are simultaneously taking phone orders. It would not be appropriate for the users of the system to ask their customers to wait 15 seconds between entering each item that is ordered. On the other hand, asking users to wait 60 seconds to process a management report that users run once each month is not a lot to ask (although many still will complain about the minute). Not only does the client/server architecture itself lead to better performance, but also most back-end database servers can use multithreaded operating systems with multiple processors; Access cannot.

Handling Increased Network Traffic

As a file server in an organization experiences increasing demands, the Access application simply might exacerbate an already growing problem. By moving the application data to a database server, the overall reduced demands on the network might provide all users on the network with better performance regardless of whether they are using the Access application.

Probably one of the most exaggerated situations I have seen is one in which all the workstations were diskless. Windows and all application software were installed on a file server. All the users were concurrently loading Microsoft Word, Microsoft Excel, and Microsoft PowerPoint over the network. In addition, they had large Access applications with many database objects and large volumes of data. All this was stored on the file server as well. Needless to say, performance was abysmal. You can't expect an already overloaded file server to handle sending large volumes of data over a small bandwidth. The benefits offered by client/server technology can help alleviate this problem.

Implementing Backup and Recovery

The backup and recovery options offered with an Access MDB database stored on a file server simply do not rival the options for backup and recovery on a database server. Any database server worth its salt sports very powerful uninterruptible power sources (UPSs). Many have hot-swappable disk drives with disk mirroring, disk duplexing, or disk striping with parity (RAID Level 5). With disk mirroring and duplexing, data can be written to multiple drives at one time, providing instantaneous backups. Furthermore, some database server tape backup software enables backups to be completed while users are accessing the system. Many offer automatic transaction logging. All these options mean less chance of data loss or downtime. With certain applications, this type of backup and recovery is overkill. With other applications, it is imperative. Although some of what back ends have to offer in backup and recovery can be mimicked by using code and replication, it is nearly impossible to get the same level of protection from an Access database stored on a file server that you can get from a database stored on a database server.

Focusing on Security

Access offers what can be considered the best security for a desktop database. Although this is the case, the security offered by an Access database cannot compare with that provided by most database servers. Database server security often works in conjunction with the network operating system. This is the case, for example, with Microsoft SQL Server and Windows NT Server. The user is given no direct rights to the physical database file. The physical database file can be accessed only via an ODBC data source or an ADO connection. Remember that no matter how much security you place on an Access database, this does not prevent a user from seeing or even deleting the entire MDB file from the network disk. It is very easy to offer protection from this potential problem, and others, on a database server. Furthermore, many back-end application database server products offer field-level security not offered within an Access MDB file. Finally, many back ends offer integrated security with one logon for both the network and the database.

Sharing Data Among Multiple Front-End Tools

The Access MDB file format is proprietary. Very few other products can read data stored in the Access database format. With a back-end database server that supports open database connectivity (ODBC), front-end applications can be written in a variety of front-end application software, all concurrently using the same back-end data.

Understanding What It All Means

You must evaluate the specific environment in which your application will run:

- How many users are there?
- How much data exists?
- What is the network traffic already like?
- What type of performance is required?
- How disastrous is downtime?
- How sensitive is the data?
- What other applications will use the data?

After you answer all these questions, as well as additional ones, you can begin to make decisions about whether the benefits of the client/server architecture outweigh the costs involved. The good news is that it is not an all-or-none decision. Various options are available for client/server applications using Access as a front end. Furthermore, if you design your application with upsizing in mind, moving to client/server technology will not require you to throw out what you have done and start again. In fact, Microsoft provides an upsizing wizard that makes upsizing to a SQL Server database a relatively painless process. How painless the process is depends on numerous factors, including how complex your queries are, whether your queries include VBA functions, and other factors that are covered in various sections later in this chapter.

THE ROLES ACCESS PLAYS IN THE APPLICATION DESIGN MODEL

Before you move on to learn more about client/server technology, take a look at the different roles Access can take in an application design. Several options are available, which are explored in this section.

The Front End and Back End as Access MDB Files

Earlier in this book, you learned about using Access as both the front end and the back end. The Access database is not acting as a true back end because it is not doing any processing. Figure 19.3 shows the architecture in this scenario. The Access application resides on the workstation. Access uses the Microsoft Jet Engine to communicate with data stored in an Access MDB database file stored on the file server.

FIGURE 19.3

Access as a front end using an MDB file for data storage.

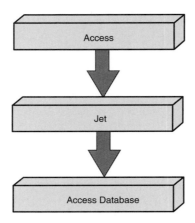

The Front End as an MDB File Using Links to Communicate to a Back End

In the second scenario, back-end tables can be linked to the front-end application database (.MDB). The process of linking to back-end tables is almost identical to that of linking to tables in other Access databases or to external tables stored in FoxPro, Paradox, or dBASE. After the back-end tables are linked to the front-end application database, they can be treated like any other linked tables. Access uses ODBC to communicate with the back-end tables. (See Figure 19.4.) Your application sends an Access SQL statement to the Access Jet Engine. Jet translates the Access SQL statement into ODBC SQL. The ODBC SQL statement then is sent to the ODBC Manager. The ODBC Manager locates the correct ODBC driver and passes it the ODBC SQL statement. The ODBC driver, supplied by the back-end vendor, translates the ODBC SQL statement into the back end's specific dialect. The back-end specific query is sent to the SQL server and to the appropriate database. As you might imagine, all this translation takes quite a bit of time. Furthermore, ODBC is becoming a technology of the past and is quickly being replaced by the ADO/OLEDB technology. That is why one of the two alternatives that follow might be a better solution.

FIGURE 19.4

Access as a front end using links to back-end tables.

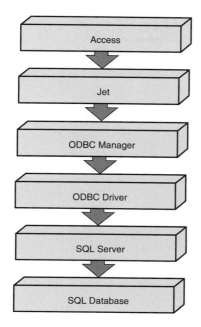

The Front End Using SQL Pass-Through to Communicate to a Back End

One of the bottlenecks of linked tables is the translation of the Access SQL statement by Jet to ODBC SQL, which then is translated by the ODBC driver to a generic SQL statement. Not only is the translation slow, but also there might be other reasons why you want to bypass the translation process:

- Access SQL might not support some operation that is supported by the native query language of the back end.

- Either the Jet Engine or the ODBC driver produces a SQL statement that is not optimized for the back end.

- You want a process performed in its entirety on the back end.

Pass-through queries are covered in more detail in the "Using Pass-Through Queries" section of this chapter. For now, look at what happens when a pass-through query is executed. The pass-through query is written in the syntax specific to the back-end database server. Although the query does pass through the Jet Engine, Jet does not perform any translation on the query. Neither does ODBC. The ODBC Manager sends the query to the ODBC driver. The ODBC driver passes the query to the back end without performing any translation. In other words, exactly what was sent from Access is what is received by the SQL database. Figure 19.5 illustrates this scenario. Notice that the Jet Engine, the ODBC Manager, and the ODBC driver are not eliminated entirely. They are still there, but they have much less impact on the process than they do with attached tables.

As you will see later in this chapter, pass-through queries are not a panacea, although they are very useful. The results of a pass-through query are not updatable, for example. Furthermore, because pass-through queries are written in the back end's specific SQL dialect, you must rewrite them if you swap out your back end. For these reasons and others, pass-through queries generally are used with other solutions.

FIGURE 19.5

Access sending a pass-through query to a back-end database.

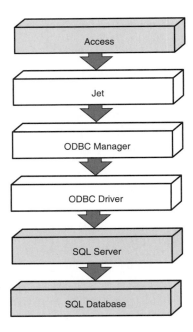

The Front End as a Microsoft Access Data Project Communicating Directly to a Back End

An additional, very viable solution is available when working with a back-end database server. This involves using a Microsoft Access Data Project (.adp), which now is available with Access 2000. By using a Microsoft Access Data Project (ADP), you bypass the Jet Engine entirely. An Access project contains only code-based objects such as forms, reports, data access pages, macros, and modules. All tables, views, database diagrams, and stored procedures are stored in a SQL Server database. After you have connected with a SQL Server database, you can easily view, create, modify, and delete SQL Server objects. Figure 19.6 illustrates this scenario. Notice that neither the Jet Engine nor ODBC is involved in the scenario.

FIGURE 19.6

Access using a Microsoft Access Data Project to communicate to a back end.

LEARNING THE CLIENT/SERVER BUZZWORDS

People who talk about client/server technology use many terms that are unfamiliar to the average database developer. To get a full appreciation of client/server technology and what it offers, you must have at least a general understanding of the terminology. Table 19.1 lists the most commonly used terms.

TABLE 19.1   CLIENT/SERVER TERMS

Term	Definition
Column	A field.
DDL	A data Definition Language used to define and describe the database structure.
Foreign key	A value in one table that must be looked up in another table for validation.
Jet	The native database engine used by Microsoft Access.

continues

TABLE 19.1   CONTINUED

Term	Definition
ODBC (Open Database Connectivity)	A standard proposed by Microsoft that provides access to a variety of back-end databases through a common interface. In essence, ODBC is a translator.
OLE DB	A new standard for connecting to relational and nonrelational data sources.
DAO	Data Access Objects (DAO) is a method of manipulating data. It is being replaced by ADO and was optimized for accessing Jet databases.
ADO	ActiveX Data Objects (ADO) is a COM-based object model that allows you to easily manipulate OLE DB data sources. It is the data access methodology that replaces DAO.
Primary key	A set of fields that uniquely identifies a row.
Row	A record.
Schema	A blueprint of the entire database. Includes table definitions, relationships, security, and other important information about the database.
SQL (Structured Query Language)	A type of data manipulation language commonly used to talk to tables residing on a server.
Stored procedures	Compiled SQL statements, such as queries, stored on the database server. Can be called by an application.
Transaction	A set of actions that must be performed on a database. If any one action fails, all the actions are discarded.
Triggers	Pieces of code that execute in response to an action occurring on a table (insert, edit, or delete).

Many books are devoted solely to client/server technology; one good book is *Visual Basic/SQL Server Primer* by Heng Tan. Most magazines targeted at developers contain numerous articles on client/server technology: *VB Programmer's Journal* always contains many excellent articles, and *Access/Office/VB Advisor* usually offers numerous articles. Many of the articles are specifically about client/server connectivity using Access as a front end. Another excellent source of information is the Microsoft Developer Network CD. Offered as a subscription by Microsoft, it includes numerous articles and white papers on client/server technology, ODBC, and using Access as a front end to a database server.

UPSIZING: WHAT TO WORRY ABOUT

Suppose your database is using Microsoft Access as both the front end and back end. Although an Access database on a file server might have been sufficient for a while, the need for better performance, enhanced security, or one of the other benefits that a back-end database provides compels your company (or your client's company) to upsize to a client/server architecture. The Access tables already have been created and even contain volumes of data. In this scenario, it might make sense to upsize.

Because all the tables have been designed as Access tables, they must be upsized to the back-end database server. Upsizing involves moving tables from a local Access database (or from any PC database) to a back-end database server that usually runs on UNIX, Windows NT Server, and OS/2 LAN Server or as a Novell NetWare NLM.

Another reason why tables are upsized from Access to a back-end server is that many developers prefer to design their tables from within the Access environment. Access offers a more user-friendly environment for table creation than most server applications.

Regardless of your reasons for upsizing, you need to understand several issues regarding the movement, or upsizing, of Access tables to a database server. Indeed, because of the many caveats involved when moving tables from Access to a back end, many people opt to design the tables directly on the back end. If you do design your tables in Access, you can export them to the back end and then link them to your local database, or you can use the Upsizing Wizard to greatly facilitate this process. Regardless of the method that you choose, as you export your tables to the database server, you need to be aware of the issues covered in the following sections.

NOTE

If you are updating to a SQL Server database, most of the concerns regarding upsizing are handled by the Upsizing Wizard included as part of Microsoft Access 2000.

Indexes

When exporting a table to a server, no indexes are created. All indexes need to be re-created on the back-end database server. If your database server is running Microsoft SQL Server, you can use the Access Upsizing Wizard for Access 2000. This tool creates indexes for server tables in the place where the indexes exist in your Access tables.

AutoNumber Fields

AutoNumber fields are exported as Long integers. Because some database servers do not support autonumbering, you have to create an insert trigger on the server that provides the next key value. You also can achieve autonumbering by using form-level events, but this is not desirable because the numbering will not be enforced if other applications access the data. If you are upsizing to Microsoft SQL Server, the Upsizing Wizard for Access 2000 converts all AutoNumber fields to Identity fields.

Default Values

Default values are not automatically moved to the server, even if the server supports them. You can set up default values directly on the server, but these values do *not* automatically appear when new records are added to the table unless the record is saved without data being added to the field containing the default value. As with autonumbering, default values can be implemented at the form level, with the same drawbacks. If the Upsizing Wizard for Access 2000 is used to move the data to Microsoft SQL Server, default values are exported to your server database.

Validation Rules

Validation rules are not exported to the server. They must be re-created using triggers on the server. No Access-defined error messages are displayed when a server validation rule is violated. Your application should be coded to provide the appropriate error messages. You also can perform validation rules at the form level, but they are not enforced if the data is accessed by other means. If the Upsizing Wizard for Access 2000 is used to move the data to Microsoft SQL Server, validation rules are exported to the server database.

Relationships

Relationships need to be enforced using server-based triggers. Access's default error messages do not appear when referential integrity is violated. You need to respond to, and code for, these error messages in your application. You can enforce relationships at the form level, but as with other form-level validations, this method of validation does not adequately protect your data. If the Upsizing Wizard for Access 2000 is used to move the data to Microsoft SQL Server, all relationships and referential integrity that you have set up in your Access database are set up within the server database.

Security

Security features that you have set up in Access do not carry forward to the server. You need to re-establish table security on the server. After security is set up on the server, Access is unaware that the security exists until the Access application attempts to violate the server's security. Then, error codes are returned to the application. You must handle these errors by using code and displaying the appropriate error message to users.

Table and Field Names

Servers often have much more stringent rules than Access does regarding the naming of fields. When you export a table, all characters that are not alphanumeric are converted to underscores. Most back ends do not allow spaces in field names. Furthermore, most back ends limit the length of object names to 30 characters or fewer. If you already have created queries, forms, reports, macros, and modules that use spaces and very long field and table names, these database objects might become unusable when you move your tables to a back-end database server.

Reserved Words

Most back ends have many reserved words. It is important to be aware of the reserved words of your specific back end. It is quite shocking when you upsize a table and find that field names you have been using are reserved words on your database server. If this is the case, you need to rename all the fields in which a conflict occurs. Once again, this means modifying all the queries, forms, reports, macros, and modules that reference the original field names.

Case Sensitivity

Many back-end databases are case sensitive. If this is the case with your back end, you might find that your queries and application code don't process as expected. Queries or code that refer to the field or table name by using the wrong case are not recognized by the back-end database and do not process correctly.

Properties

Most properties cannot be modified on remote tables. Any properties that can be modified are lost upon export, so you need to set them up again when the table is exported.

Visual Basic Code

Certain properties and methods that work on Access tables might not work on remote tables. This might necessitate some coding changes after you export your tables.

PROACTIVELY PREPARING FOR UPSIZING

If you set up your tables and code modules with upsizing in mind, you can eliminate many of the preceding pitfalls. Despite any of the problems that upsizing can bring, the scalability of Access is one of its stronger points. Sometimes resources are not available to implement

19

CLIENT/SERVER TECHNIQUES

client/server technology in the early stages of an application. If you think through the design of the project with the possibility of upsizing in mind, you will be pleased at how relatively easy it is to move to client/server technology when the time is right. With the Access 2000 Upsizing Wizard, which is designed to take an Access application and upsize it to Microsoft SQL Server, the process is relatively simple. The upsizing tool for Access 2000 performs a lot of the work involved in upsizing a database, with just the click of a few buttons.

USING THE UPSIZING WIZARD

As mentioned in the previous sections, the Upsizing Wizard, included with Access 2000, greatly facilitates the process of upsizing to a SQL Server database. To invoke the Upsizing Wizard, follow these steps:

1. Select Tools | Database Utilities | Upsizing Wizard. The Upsizing Wizard appears (see Figure 19.7). Here you can opt to upsize to an existing SQL Server database or to create a new database.

FIGURE 19.7

The first step of the Upsizing Wizard allows you to create a new SQL Server database or to use an existing database.

2. Make the appropriate selection and click next. If you opt to create a new database, the Upsizing Wizard appears as in Figure 19.8.

FIGURE 19.8

The second step of the Upsizing Wizard allows you to designate the server, a login ID, password, and other important information required when creating a new database.

3. Select the server where you want the database to reside.

4. Enter a login ID and password with privileges to create a database.

5. Enter a name for the new database. Click Next. The Upsizing Wizard appears as in Figure 19.9.

FIGURE 19.9

The third step of the Upsizing Wizard allows you to select the tables you want to upsize.

6. Select the tables that you want to export to SQL Server and click Next.

7. The next step of the Upsizing Wizard, shown in Figure 19.10, allows you to specify important information about what is included in the upsized tables. You can designate whether indexes, validation rules, defaults, and table relationships are upsized. You can also determine whether timestamps are added to the tables. Finally, you must designate whether table structures only or table structures and data are upsized. Make your selections and click Next.

FIGURE 19.10

The fourth step of the Upsizing Wizard allows you to designate whether indexes, validation rules, defaults, and table relationships are upsized.

8. In the next step of the Upsizing Wizard, pictured in Figure 19.11, you can opt for Access to modify your database to create links to the new tables. If you prefer, Access will create an ADP. Otherwise, you can opt for no application changes to be made. If you specify that you want access to create a new Access client/server application (ADP), you must specify the ADP filename. Click Next after making your selection.

Figure 19.11

In the fifth step of the Upsizing Wizard, you specify whether the Wizard establishes table links or creates an access data project file as part of the upsizing process.

9. Click Finish. The database is upsized. An Upsizing Wizard report is produced (see Figure 19.12). You should review this report because it contains important information about the status of the upsizing process. Figure 19.13 shows the result of upsizing the Chap18Data database.

Figure 19.12

The Upsizing Report provides important information about the upsizing process.

FIGURE 19.13

The Chap18DataSQL database after upsizing.

DEFINING AN ODBC DATA SOURCE

If you plan to link to ODBC tables, you must load the appropriate ODBC drivers. These drivers come with Access and are installed with the product. You also need to load drivers for the specific back-end database servers to which you want to connect. These drivers usually are purchased from the back-end database vendor and often come with a per-seat charge. This means that you must purchase a client license for each user who will connect to the remote data.

An ODBC *data source* is a user-defined name that points to a remote source of data. It contains all the properties of the data source that are necessary to communicate with data stored on a database server.

Before you can access a remote table from Access, you must define it by using the ODBC Data Source Administrator. If you do not define that data source, or if it is not defined correctly, you will be unable to access the data.

You set up ODBC data sources in the ODBC Data Source Administrator. (See Figure 19.14.) Depending on your installation, the ODBC Data Source Administrator could be a standalone application, or it could appear as a Control Panel icon. By default, this icon appears as ODBC

Data Sources. It enables you to create, modify, and delete data sources and to obtain information about existing drivers. Remember that a data source is simply a user-definable name that stores settings that can be used to access a back end located on a particular server using a specified driver.

FIGURE 19.14

The User Data Sources window in the ODBC Data Source Administrator.

The ODBC Data Source Administrator is a tabbed dialog box. Table 19.2 describes how you use these tabs.

TABLE 19.2   USING THE ODBC DATA SOURCE ADMINISTRATOR

Tab	Function
User DSN	Enables you to add, delete, and set up data sources that are local to a computer and can be used only by the current user.
System DSN	Enables you to add, delete, and set up data sources that are local to a computer but are not specific to a particular user.
File DSN	Enables you to add, delete, and set up data sources that are file-based and can be shared between all users who have the same drivers installed. File DSNs are not limited to a specific machine.
Drivers	Displays information about installed ODBC drivers.
Tracing	Enables you to specify how the ODBC Driver Manager traces calls to ODBC functions. The available options are when to trace, the log file path, and the custom trace DLL.
Connection Pooling	Allows you to designate settings that enable you to reuse open connection handles, saving round trips to the server.
About	Gives information about core components such as the location of files and version numbers.

After you enter the ODBC Data Source Administrator, you probably should set up a new data source. To define a new data source, click the Add button on the User DSN or System DSN tab, or click Add on the File DSN tab of the dialog box. The Create New Data Source dialog appears, from which you must select the name of the driver that the data source will use. (See Figure 19.15.)

FIGURE 19.15

The Create New Data Source dialog box.

The list of available drivers varies, depending on which client drivers have been installed on the machine. After you select a data source and click Finish, a wizard appears, which varies depending on which driver you selected. You use this wizard to define specific information about the data source you are creating. An example is the Create a New Data Source to SQL Server Wizard shown in Figure 19.16.

FIGURE 19.16

The first step of the Create a New Data Source to SQL Server Wizard allows you to specify the data source name, a description, and the name of the database server.

19

CLIENT/SERVER TECHNIQUES

1. The first step of this wizard (shown in Figure 19.16) allows you to specify the data source name, a description for the data source, and the name of the SQL server you want to connect to. Click Next when you are finished specifying the desired options.

2. The second step of the Create a New Data Source to SQL Server Wizard appears in Figure 19.17. It allows you to specify login information for the ODBC data source. Select the appropriate choices and click Next.

FIGURE 19.17

In the second step of the wizard, you specify login information for the ODBC data source.

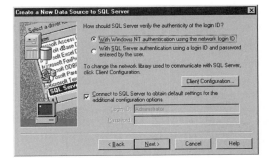

3. The third step of the wizard, pictured in Figure 19.18, allows you to specify information about the database that you are linking to. In Figure 19.18, the default database is designated as Northwind. Click Next when you are ready to continue.

FIGURE 19.18

The third step of the wizard allows you to specify information for the database you are linking to.

4. The fourth and final step of the Create a New Data Source to SQL Server Wizard allows you to further refine the connection to the SQL Server data source (see Figure 19.19). When you're finished specifying all options, click Finish.

FIGURE 19.19

In the fourth step of the wizard, you can specify additional attributes of the data source.

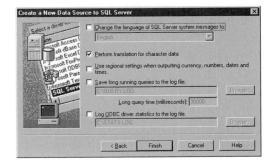

5. The ODBC Microsoft SQL Server Setup dialog appears (see Figure 19.20). This dialog provides you with information about the data source and allows you to test the data source. It is a good idea to test the data source to confirm that all the specified settings are valid. A successful test appears in Figure 19.21. Click OK when you're finished.

FIGURE 19.20

The ODBC Microsoft SQL Server Setup dialog provides you with information about the data source and allows you to test the data source.

FIGURE 19.21

An example of a successful test of an ODBC data source.

19

NOTE

You might be wondering how you can possibly go through the process of defining data sources on thousands of user machines in a large installation. Fortunately, you can automate the process of defining data sources by using DLL functions. It is a matter of using the ODBC Data Source Administrator DLL function calls to set up the data source by using code. The alternative is to set up file DSNs that are available to all your users.

CONNECTING TO A DATABASE SERVER

After you define a data source, you are ready to connect to it. You can use these methods to access server data:

- Link to tables residing on the server.
- Link to views residing on the server.
- Use pass-through queries to send SQL statements directly to the server.
- Use VBA code to open the server tables directly.
- Create an access data project (with this option, you do not define an ODBC data source).

WORKING WITH LINKED TABLES

The easiest method of accessing data on the server is to link to the external tables. These linked tables act almost exactly like native Access tables. When you link to remote tables, Access analyzes the fields and indexes contained in the tables so that it can achieve optimal performance. It is important to relink the tables if the structures of the remote tables change. This section discusses how you can link to remote tables through the user interface and by using code.

Linking to External Tables via the User Interface

To link to a remote table through the user interface, right-click within the Database window, and then select Link Tables. From the Files of Type drop-down list, select ODBC Databases. The Select Data Source dialog box shown in Figure 19.22 appears. This dialog box has two tabs: File Data Source and Machine Data Source. You use the File Data Source tab to select from the file DSNs that have been defined. These are the data sources available to all users on all machines. You use the Machine Data Source tab to select from the user and system data sources you have defined. These data sources are available to just one user and just one machine.

FIGURE 19.22

The Select Data Source dialog box.

You can select an existing data source or define a new data source directly from the Select Data Source dialog box. After you select a data source, you are prompted with a Login dialog box. You can't obtain access to the server data unless you have a valid login ID and password. Figure 19.23 shows the SQL Server Login dialog box.

FIGURE 19.23

The SQL Server Login dialog box.

If you successfully log on to the server, you are presented with a list of tables contained in the database that the data source is referencing. Here, you must select the table to which you want to link. Figure 19.24 shows the Link Tables dialog box.

FIGURE 19.24

The Link Tables dialog box.

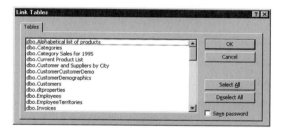

After you select one or more tables and click OK, you might be prompted with the Select Unique Record Identifier dialog box. Selecting a unique identifier for the table enables you to update records on the back-end data source. Select a unique identifier and click OK. The linked tables appear in the Database window, as shown in Figure 19.25. These tables can be treated like any other table (with a few exceptions that are covered later in this chapter).

19

CLIENT/SERVER
TECHNIQUES

FIGURE 19.25

The Database window with links to ODBC tables.

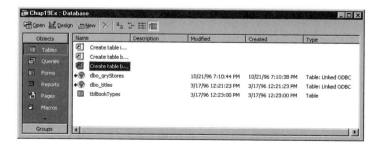

Linking to External Tables Using Code

You just learned how you can link to a remote table by using Access's user interface. Now take a look at how you can link to the same table by using code. The subroutine in Listing 19.1 accepts six parameters: the name for the Access table, the name of the server database, the name of the server table, the data source name, the user ID, and the password.

LISTING 19.1   VBA CODE FOR LINKING TO AN EXTERNAL TABLE

```
Sub LinkToSQL(strAccessTable, strDBName, strTableName, _
    strDataSourceName, strUserID, strPassWord)
    Dim cat As ADOX.Catalog
    Dim tbl As ADOX.Table

    Set cat = New ADOX.Catalog
    cat.ActiveConnection = CurrentProject.Connection

    Set tbl = New ADOX.Table
    tbl.Name = strAccessTable
    Set tbl.ParentCatalog = cat

    tbl.Properties("Jet OLEDB:Create Link") = True
    tbl.Properties("Jet OLEDB:Link Provider String") = "ODBC" & _
        ";DATABASE=" & strDBName & _
        ";UID=" & strUserID & _
        ";PWD=" & strPassWord & _
        ";DSN=" & strDataSourceName
    tbl.Properties("Jet OLEDB:Remote Table Name") = strTableName

    cat.Tables.Append tbl
End Sub
```

> **NOTE**
>
> This example requires that you reference the Microsoft ADO Ext. 2.1 for DDL and Security library.

Here is an example of how you call the subroutine. The Access table you are creating is named tblStores. The database name on the server is Pubs. The table to which you are linking is named Stores, and the data source name is PublisherData. You are logging in as SA (database system administrator) without a password. The user ID and password could have been supplied as the user logged on to your application and could have been stored in variables until needed for logging on to the server, as this code shows:

```
Call LinkToSQL("tblStores", "Pubs", " Stores", "PublisherData", "SA", "")
```

> **NOTE**
>
> This code, and most of the code found in this chapter, is located in the CHAP19EX.MDB database on the sample code CD-ROM.

Linking to Views Rather Than Tables

Views on a database server are similar to Access queries. Views provide a form of security by limiting which rows and columns a user can see. Access is given to the view rather than directly to the underlying table. By default, views are not updatable. You can make a view updatable by including all the fields that compose the primary key in the view and building a unique index on the primary key. You can create views in one of three ways:

- Using the SQL Server Enterprise Manager for SQL 6.5 or SQL 7.0 (or the equivalent option for your back-end database server)
- Using the `Create View` statement in Access
- Using the View tab of an ADP file

To create a remote view from a standard Access database (.MDB), follow these steps:

1. Create a new query.
2. When you are prompted with the Show Table dialog box, click Close *without* selecting a table.
3. Choose Query | SQL Specific | Pass-Through.
4. Type the `Create View` statement, as shown in Figure 19.26.

FIGURE 19.26

Creating a query for a remote view.

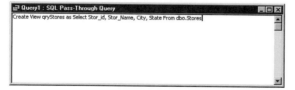

```
Query1 : SQL Pass-Through Query
Create View qryStores as Select Stor_Id, Stor_Name, City, State From dbo.Stores
```

5. Click Run.

6. Select a SQL data source and click OK.

7. Supply the login information and click OK. You might receive the message shown in Figure 19.27. This message, and how to avoid it, is explained in the section "Executing and Creating Stored Procedures" later in this chapter.

FIGURE 19.27

The error message received when creating a remote view.

After you create a remote view using this technique, you can link to it like any other table. If you link to the view, you are prompted with the Select Unique Record Identifier dialog box, as shown in Figure 19.28. It is very important to supply Access with a unique index. Otherwise, the results of the view will not be updatable. The view then can be treated as though it were a link to a table.

FIGURE 19.28

The Select Unique Record Identifier dialog box after selecting a view.

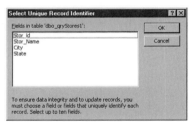

ADP are covered in detail in the section of this chapter titled "Using a Microsoft Access Data Project to Access Client/Server Data." To create a remote view from an Access Data Project file (.ADP), follow these steps:

1. Click Views in the list of objects in the Database window.

2. Double-click the Create View in Designer icon. A New View appears (see Figure 19.29).

FIGURE 19.29

An example of a new view.

3. Click the Show Table tool on the toolbar. The Show Table window appears. Use the plus (+) symbols to view the tables and views in the database associated with the Access Data Project file (see Figure 19.30).

FIGURE 19.30

The Show Tables window shows all the tables and views in the database associated with the Access Data Project.

4. Drag and drop the tables that you want included in the view to the View window. In the example shown in Figure 19.31, the tblClients and tblProjects tables have been added to the view.

5. Click the check boxes to the left of the field names to select the fields that you want to add to the view. If you prefer, you can drag and drop fields to the column list on the query grid. Figure 19.32 shows a view with the ClientID, CompanyName, ProjectName, ProjectDescription, and City fields included.

6. Specify any criteria that you want to apply to the view. To add criteria, enter the desired criteria in the Criteria column of the appropriate field on the query grid. Adding criteria limits the records returned when the view is run. Figure 19.32 shows criteria limiting the selected records to those in Boston and Los Angeles.

7. Test the view using the Run button. You are prompted to save changes to the view.

8. The view appears in the Database window and can be treated much like a table.

USING PASS-THROUGH QUERIES

Ordinarily, when you store and execute a query in Access, even if it is running on remote data, Access compiles and optimizes the query. In many cases, this is exactly what you want. On other occasions, however, it might be preferable for you to execute a pass-through query because these queries are not analyzed by Access's Jet Engine. These queries are passed directly to the server, and this reduces the time Jet needs to analyze the query and enables you to pass server-specific syntax to the back end. Furthermore, pass-through queries can log informational messages returned by the server. Finally, bulk update, delete, and append queries are faster using pass-through queries than they are using Access action queries based on remote tables.

Pass-through queries do have their downside. They always return a snapshot, rendering them not updatable. You also must know the exact syntax the server requires, and you must type the statement into the Query window instead of painting it graphically. Finally, you cannot parameterize a query so that it prompts the user for a value.

Creating a Pass-Through Query in an MDB File Using the User Interface

To create a pass-through query, you can build the query in the Access query builder. Choose Query|SQL Specific|Pass-Through. You are presented with a text-editing window where you can enter the query statement. The SQL statement you enter must be in the SQL flavor specific to your back end.

Executing a Pass-Through Query Using Code

You also can perform a pass-through query by using VBA code. In fact, you must create the pass-through query by using VBA code if you want the query to contain parameters that you will pass to the server. Here's one way you can create a pass-through query by using VBA code:

1. Create a connection to the SQL Server database.

2. Use the `Execute` method of the `Connection` object to execute the SQL statement on the back-end database server. As with a SQL statement created by choosing Query | SQL Specific | Pass-Through, the statement you create must be in the syntax specific to your particular back end.

Listing 19.2 shows the code for this procedure.

LISTING 19.2 EXECUTING A PASS-THROUGH QUERY USING CODE

```
Sub PassThroughQuery(strDBName As String, _
              strDataSourceName As String, _
              strUserID As String, _
              strPassWord As String)

    Dim cnn As ADODB.Connection
    Dim strConnectString As String

    strConnectString = "ODBC" & _
        ";DATABASE=" & strDBName & _
        ";UID=" & strUserID & _
        ";PWD=" & strPassWord & _
        ";DSN=" & strDataSourceName

    Set cnn = New ADODB.Connection
    cnn.ConnectionString = strConnectString
    cnn.Open

    cnn.Execute "Update dbo.Sales Set Qty = Qty + 1", _
        adCmdText
End Sub
```

The routine is called as shown in this code:

```
Call PassThroughQuery("Pubs", "PublisherData", "SA","" )
```

This subroutine uses a connect string that connects to a database named Pubs, with a data source named PublisherData, a user ID of SA, and no password. It then executes a pass-through query that updates the Qty field of each record to `Qty+1`.

As you saw, one method of executing a pass-through query is to create a connection to the database using the `Open` method of the `Connection` object and then execute the query using the

Execute method on the database object. The limitation of this method is that the Execute method does not enable you to execute queries that return data. You can use another method of executing a pass-through query when you want to return records. It involves returning the result of the pass-through query into a recordset object. This is illustrated in Listing 19.3.

LISTING 19.3 EXECUTING A PASS-THROUGH QUERY THAT RETURNS RECORDS

```
Sub PassThroughQueryResults(strDBName As String, _
            strDataSourceName As String, _
            strUserID As String, _
            strPassWord As String)

    Dim cnn As ADODB.Connection
    Dim rst As ADODB.Recordset
    Dim strConnectString As String

    strConnectString = "ODBC" & _
        ";DATABASE=" & strDBName & _
        ";UID=" & strUserID & _
        ";PWD=" & strPassWord & _
        ";DSN=" & strDataSourceName

    Set cnn = New ADODB.Connection
    cnn.ConnectionString = strConnectString
    cnn.Open

    Set rst = cnn.Execute("Select * from dbo.Sales Where Qty >5", _
        adCmdText)
    Do Until rst.EOF
        Debug.Print rst!Stor_id, rst!Qty
        rst.MoveNext
    Loop

End Sub
```

19

EXECUTING AND CREATING STORED PROCEDURES

You also can execute stored procedures on a back-end database server. A stored procedure is similar to a query or program stored on the back end, and it performs some action. An example is the SQL Server 7.0 stored procedure named sp_columns. This stored procedure returns information on the fields in a particular table. Figure 19.33 shows how you would execute the sp_columns stored procedure from the Query Design window. You simply type the name of the stored procedure and any parameters it must receive. Take a good look at the Query Properties window shown in Figure 19.33. If you enter a valid ODBC connect string, the user is not prompted to log on at runtime. The Return Records property is another important property. In this case, you want to set the value of the property to Yes so that you can see the results of the stored procedure. If the stored procedure does not return records, as is the case with the Create View pass-through query created in the "Linking to Views Rather Than Tables" section, it is important to set this property to No. Otherwise, you receive an error message indicating that no rows were returned. Figure 19.34 shows the results of running the stored procedure.

FIGURE 19.33

Executing a stored procedure from the Query Design window by typing the name of the stored procedure and any parameters it must receive.

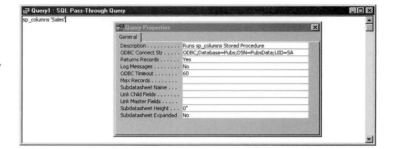

FIGURE 19.34

The result of running the sp_columns stored procedure.

Listing 19.4 shows the procedure that executes the sp_columns stored procedure using code.

LISTING 19.4   EXECUTING THE SP_COLUMNS STORED PROCEDURE

```
Sub StoredProcedure()
    Dim cnn As ADODB.Connection
    Dim rst As ADODB.Recordset
    Dim strConnectString As String

    strConnectString = "ODBC" & _
        ";DATABASE=Pubs" & _
        ";UID=SA" & _
```

```
        ";PWD=" & _
        ";DSN=PubsData"

    Set cnn = New ADODB.Connection
    cnn.ConnectionString = strConnectString
    cnn.Open

    Set rst = cnn.Execute("sp_columns('sales')", _
        Options:=adCmdStoredProc)

    Do While Not rst.EOF
        Debug.Print rst!Column_Name
        rst.MoveNext
    Loop
End Sub
```

Here's how it works. A Connection object is established and opened. A Recordset object is created to hold the results of executing the stored procedure. Notice that the sp_columns stored procedure receives a parameter. This parameter is passed within parentheses. The adCmdStoredProc constant, when passed as the Options parameter, tells ADO that the Command Text for the Execute statement is a stored procedure name.

Creating a Stored Procedure

If your application is an ADP file, you can create stored procedures directly from the Access environment. The following steps are required:

1. Select Stored Procedures in the Objects list of the Database window.

2. Double-click Create Stored Procedure in Designer. The Stored Procedure window appears (see Figure 19.35).

FIGURE 19.35

The Stored Procedure dialog allows you to build a stored procedure on a database server.

19

CLIENT/SERVER
TECHNIQUES

3. Enter the text for the stored procedure.

4. Click the Save tool on the toolbar. The Save As dialog appears.

5. Enter the name for the stored procedure and click OK. The stored procedure is added to the database associated with the Access Data Project. It appears in the list of stored procedures in the Database window and can be modified from within Access.

USING A MICROSOFT ACCESS DATA PROJECT TO ACCESS CLIENT/SERVER DATA

As mentioned earlier in this chapter, Access projects (ADP files) enable you to work with SQL Server databases without loading the Microsoft Jet Database Engine. Access projects have the following advantages over the other methods of accessing client/server data covered in this chapter:

- They provide you direct access to a Microsoft SQL Server database.
- You can easily create and modify SQL Server tables, views, database diagrams, and stored procedures, all from the Access development environment.
- You can build forms, reports, data access pages, and modules that access SQL Server data, without involving Jet.
- Fewer resources are required on the client side.
- The server is responsible for all query processing.
- You are able to access functionality not available when accessing ODBC via Jet.
- You can execute asynchronous queries. This means that you don't have to wait for a query to complete execution before you begin another operation.
- You can perform batch updates. This means that you can cache changes locally and then submit them to the server as a batch.
- You can run queries that return multiple resultsets.
- You easily can limit the number of records returned in a resultset.
- You easily can monitor messages and errors generated by the remote data source.

The disadvantages of Access Data Project files follow:

- You cannot create local tables.
- You cannot create local queries.
- The process of creating tables, views, database diagrams, and stored procedures involves a learning curve.

Creating an Access Data Project (ADP)

Access 2000 introduces Access Data Projects (ADP). Whereas an Access database uses the Jet Engine and ODBC to access client/server data, ADPs use OLE DB to access client/server data. This provides you with greatly enhanced functionality and performance when dealing with client/server data. The only caveat is that the client/server data must be stored in a Microsoft SQL Server 7.0 database, the MSDE file format, or a Microsoft SQL Server 6.5 database with Service Pack 5 installed.

> **NOTE**
>
> The MSDE is located on the Office 2000 CD-ROM in the folder \sql\x86\setup.

If you use an Access database to access client/server data, you must use linked tables, SQL pass-through queries, and ODBC direct to manipulate the data. If you want to modify the structures of the client/server tables, you must do so within the SQL Server environment. With an Access Data Project, you can create and modify tables, views, database diagrams, and stored procedures directly from the Access environment.

To create an Access Data Project:

1. Click the New button on the toolbar. The New dialog appears (see Figure 19.36).

FIGURE 19.36
The New dialog allows you to create an ADP based on a new or existing SQL Server database.

2. Two options allow you to build an ADP. The first allows you to create an ADP file using an existing SQL Server database. The second allows you to build an ADP file based on a new SQL Server database. If you double-click to create a project based on an existing database, the File New Database dialog appears. Enter the name and location of the ADP file and click Create. The Data Link Properties dialog appears (see Figure 19.37).

19

CLIENT/SERVER
TECHNIQUES

FIGURE **19.37**

*The Data Link
Properties dialog
allows you to
specify connection
information about
the SQL Server
database that the
ADP file is asso-
ciated with.*

3. Enter the server name, security information, and the name of the database you want to connect to.

4. Click the Advanced tab to enter advanced options or the All tab to view or modify any connection options.

5. When you're finished specifying all options, click the Connection tab and click Test Connection to ensure that all settings have been specified correctly.

6. Click OK to create the Access Data Project.

Figure 19.38 shows an ADP file based on the Time and Billing application. Notice that the tables appear as if they were contained within the ADP file. In fact, they are stored in the SQL Server database. The important point here is that the tables are not linked! Because they are not linked, they appear and can be manipulated as if they are part of the ADP.

FIGURE **19.38**

*The ADP file
shows you the
tables, views,
database dia-
grams, and stored
procedures con-
tained in the SQL
Server database.*

As you can see in Figure 19.38, the Database window is different for an ADP file than for an MDB file. The Objects list contains Tables, Views, Database Diagrams, and Stored Procedures, rather than Tables and Queries. In fact, no local tables or queries can be stored in an ADP file.

Working with SQL Server Tables

One of the major benefits of an ADP is that you can create, modify, rename, and delete SQL Server tables directly from the Access environment. It is important to remember that any changes from within Access are immediately reflected within the associated SQL Server database.

Creating a SQL Server Table

The SQL Server Table Designer allows you to create SQL Server tables from within Access. To create a table using the SQL Server Table Designer, do the following:

1. Select Tables from the Objects list.
2. Double-click Create Table in Design View. The Choose Name dialog appears.
3. Enter a name for the SQL Server table and click OK. You are taken to the SQL Server Table Designer, where you define the fields and their attributes (see Figure 19.39).

FIGURE 19.39

The SQL Server Designer allows you to enter the names of the columns and their attributes.

4. Enter the names of the columns and their attributes within the SQL Server Table Designer.
5. Close the window and save your changes when you are done.

Modifying a SQL Server Table

To modify the structure of an existing SQL Server table, do the following:

1. Select Tables from the Objects list.

2. Select the table whose structure you want to modify.

3. Click Design. The structure of the existing table appears. Figure 19.40 shows the tblClients table in Design view.

FIGURE 19.40

The tblClients table in Design view.

4. Modify the names and attributes of the desired columns.

5. Close the window and save your changes when you are done.

NOTE

Creating and working with SQL Server tables, views, database diagrams, and stored procedures is covered in detail in *Sams Teach Yourself Microsoft SQL Server 7.0 in 12 Days* or *Microsoft SQL Server 7.0 Unleashed*, both from Sams Publishing.

Deleting a SQL Server Table

Deleting a SQL Server table is very simple.

1. Select Tables from the Objects list.

2. Right-click the table you want to delete.

3. Select Delete from the pop-up menu

It is important to remember that deleting the table from the ADP removes it from the SQL Server database. The ease of deleting a SQL Server table via an ADP further necessitates that proper security be established on the SQL Server database!

Working with SQL Server Views

SQL Server views are analogous to Access select queries. The major difference is that SQL Server views do not support the use of parameters.

Creating a SQL Server View

1. Select Views from the Objects list.
2. Double-click Create View in Designer. The View window appears.
3. Define the columns, criteria, and other attributes of the view as covered in the section of this chapter titled "Linking to Views Rather Than Tables."

Modifying a SQL Server View

Modifying a view is similar to modifying a table.

1. Select Views from the Objects list.
2. Select the view whose attributes you want to modify.
3. Click Design. The design of the existing view appears.
4. Modify the attributes of the view.
5. Close the window and save your changes when you are done.

Deleting a SQL Server View

Deleting a SQL Server view is very simple.

1. Select Views from the Objects list.
2. Right-click the view you want to delete.
3. Select Delete from the pop-up menu

As with tables, it is important to remember that deleting a view from an ADP removes it from the SQL Server database. Once again, this highlights the need for establishment of proper security on the SQL Server database.

Working with Database Diagrams

Database diagrams provide you with a visual method of managing and designing your database tables. Using a database diagram, you can establish and modify table relationships and edit table structures.

Creating a Database Diagram

To create a database diagram, follow these steps:

1. Select Database Diagrams from the Objects list.

2. Double-click Create Database Diagram in Designer. A blank Diagram window appears.

3. Click the Show Table tool to show the tables included in the SQL Server database that is associated with the ADP (see Figure 19.41).

Figure 19.41

You add tables to the blank database diagram window to begin the process of creating a database diagram.

4. Click and drag the desired tables to the database diagram.

5. To modify the structure of a table, right-click the table within the designer and select Column Properties. Properties changed in the database designer are immediately modified in the SQL Server database.

6. To modify a relationship, right-click the relationship line and select Properties. The Properties dialog appears (see Figure 19.42). Here you can modify all the attributes of an existing relationship.

7. To add a relationship, click and drag the field selector from one table to another. The Create Relationship dialog appears (see Figure 19.43).

Figure 19.42

The Properties window allows you to modify the attributes of an existing relationship.

Figure 19.43

The Create Relationship dialog allows you to establish the properties of a new relationship.

Modifying a Database Diagram

To modify an existing database diagram, do the following:

1. Select Database Diagrams from the Objects list.
2. Select the database diagram whose attributes you want to modify. Figure 19.44 shows the database diagram associated with the NorthwindCS data project that ships with Microsoft Access.

FIGURE 19.44

The database diagram window allows you to establish table relationships and modify the structure of tables.

3. Click Design. The design of the database diagram appears.

4. Modify the attributes of the database diagram.

5. Close the window and save your changes when you are done.

Working with Stored Procedures

The process of creating and modifying stored procedures is covered in the section of this chapter titled "Executing and Creating Stored Procedures." It is important to note that although similar to views, stored procedures add two pieces of functionality unavailable within views. Stored procedures can include parameters. Therefore, a stored procedure can accept criteria at runtime. In addition, stored procedures can be designed to edit table data.

There is a major distinction between executing an Access action query against a linked table and executing a stored procedure. In the case of an action query, all the data affected by the action query must travel over the network wire to be updated by the action query at the workstation. On the other hand, a stored procedure updates data directly on the server, without requiring the data to travel over the network wire. This can result in major performance differences, especially when dealing with large volumes of data.

Creating and Working with Forms, Reports, Macros, and Modules

Creating and working with forms, reports, macros, and modules in an ADP file is very similar to working with like objects in an Access database. It is important to recognize that, whereas the tables, views, database diagrams, and stored procedures are stored on the server, the forms, reports, macros, and modules are stored as an OLE document chunk within the ADP file. ADP files are generally smaller than MDB files and are less susceptible to corruption!

Exploring Other Features Available with Access Data Projects

Besides providing you with the ability to maintain SQL Server tables, views, database diagrams, and stored procedures from within the Access environment, ADPs provide you with other benefits. From an ADP file, you can perform the following tasks:

- Backup of the SQL Server database
- Restore of the SQL Server database
- Replication of the SQL Server database, including the ability to create new SQL Server publications, synchronize replicas, and resolution of conflicts
- Maintenance of SQL Server security

SUMMARY

In this chapter, you learned to be concerned with client/server technology when dealing with large volumes of data, large numbers of concurrent users, a demand for faster performance, problems with increased network traffic, backup and recovery, security, and a need to share data among multiple front-end tools. You also learned the roles Access can play in the application design model. In particular, you learned about upsizing and the various ways you can interface with a client/server database, including using Access Data Projects (ADPs). ADP files are new to Access 2000. They allow you to connect directly to a Microsoft SQL Server database. Many client/server buzzwords and concepts are also introduced in the chapter.

19

CLIENT/SERVER
TECHNIQUES

CLIENT/SERVER STRATEGIES

IN THIS CHAPTER

WHY THIS CHAPTER IS IMPORTANT

As you saw in the previous chapter, it is very easy to implement client/server strategies ineffectively. This can result in worse performance rather than better performance. The developer's task is to intelligently apply appropriate techniques that deploy client/server systems effectively.

This chapter discusses strategies to help you develop smart client/server applications.

SELECTING THE BEST RECORDSET TYPE

The type of recordset that you select has a significant effect on performance. The `CursorType` and `Locktype` properties, as well as the `Options` parameter of the `Open` method of the `Recordset` object, all determine the type of recordset that is returned.

The `CursorType` Property

The `CursorType` property determines the type of cursor returned by the `Recordset` object. The following options are available for the `CursorType` property:

- adOpenForwardOnly
- adOpenStatic
- adOpenKeyset
- adOpenDynamic

Each of these cursor types offers different functionality, as well as different performance. In terms of performance, a forward-only cursor provides the best performance, followed by a static cursor, keyset, and then dynamic cursor. In terms of functionality, a forward-only cursor provides the least functionality, followed by a static cursor, a keyset, and finally a dynamic cursor.

As mentioned previously, a forward-only cursor offers the best performance but the least functionality. As its name implies, a forward-only cursor allows only forward movement through the records in the recordset. It is appropriate only in situations where it is adequate to make one pass through the records.

A static cursor allows both forward and backward movement through the records in the recordset. Its biggest limitation is that changes (including adds, edits, and deletes) made by other users on the network are not reflected in the recordset. Although a static cursor is not as efficient as a forward-only cursor, it is significantly more efficient than a keyset or dynamic cursor. This is because it does not need to worry about constantly refreshing data from the server.

A keyset cursor offers everything that a static cursor offers. In addition, data changes by other users are visible to the recordset. Records that other users add are not available to the recordset. Records that other users delete appear as "holes" in the recordset and are inaccessible to the recordset.

A dynamic cursor offers the most functionality but the worst performance. With a dynamic cursor, not only are changes that other users make to the data available to the recordset, but additions and deletions are also available.

There is a very simple rule to follow when selecting a cursor type. You should select the type of cursor with the best performance that provides the functionality that you need. You need to really consider how important it is to see changes that other users make, as well as whether it is necessary to be able to move both forward and backward through the recordset.

The `LockType` Property

The `Locktype` property can also affect performance. The `Locktype` property determines how and whether the data in the recordset will be updateable. The options for `Locktype` are

- `adLockReadOnly`
- `adLockPessimistic`
- `adLockOptimistic`
- `adLockBatchOptimistic`

The most important differentiation is between the read-only option and the other options. By default, a recordset is opened read-only. This affords the best performance because the updateability of the recordset is not an issue. The important thing to remember is that if the data in the recordset does not need to be updated, the read-only option should be selected.

The `Options` Parameter of the `Open` Method

The `Options` parameter of the `Open` method determines how the provider should evaluate the `Source` argument of the `Open` method of the `Recordset` object. The following choices are available for the `Options` parameter:

- `adCmdText`
- `adCmdTable`
- `adCmdTableDirect`
- `adCmdStoredProc`
- `adCmdUnknown`

20

- adCmdFile
- adAsyncExecute
- adAsyncFetch
- adAsyncFetchNonBlocking

It is first important to understand that merely supplying the `Options` parameter offers improvements in performance. This is because ADO does not need to determine what is contained within the Source argument.

In selecting a choice for the `Options` parameter, the values that most strongly impact performance are `adCmdTable`, `adCmdTableDirect`, `adCmdStoredProc`, `adAsyncExecute`, `adAsyncFetch`, and `adAsyncFetchNonBlocking`. The `adCmdTable` and `adCmdTableDirect` options negatively impact performance because both options return all rows from the table named in the `Source` argument. This can have dire consequences with large tables in a client/server environment. In fact, these choices basically undermine the reason why an application was placed in a client/server environment in the first place. The `adCmdStoredProc` option is an excellent choice simply because it dictates that the source is evaluated and executed as a stored procedure on the server. The `adAsyncExecute` option indicates that the Source is executed asynchronously. This means that other operations can proceed as the records are retrieved. Depending on the specific situation, the `adAsyncFetch` option can either improve or degrade performance. This option indicates that after the number of records specified in the Initial Fetch Size property are fetched, any remaining rows are fetched asynchronously. The problem is that if a requested row is unavailable, the main thread is blocked until the request row is fetched. Finally, the `adAsyncFetchNonBlocking` option ensures that the main thread is never blocked. If the requested row is unavailable, the current row moves to the end of the file.

USING PASS-THROUGH QUERIES AND STORED PROCEDURES

It is important to remember that executing pass-through queries and stored procedures is much more efficient than returning a recordset to be processed by Access. Pass-through queries and the details of how they are implemented are covered in Chapter 19, "Client/Server Techniques." The difference with pass-through queries lies in where the processing occurs. With pass-through queries and stored procedures, all the processing is completed on the server. When operations are performed using VBA code, all the records that will be affected by the process must be returned to the user's workstation, modified, and then returned to the server. This generates a significant amount of network traffic and slows down processing immensely.

USING ACCESS DATA PROJECTS

Access Data Projects (.ADP files) enable you to access Microsoft SQL Server data without loading the Microsoft Jet Database Engine. They provide dramatic increases in performance by eliminating the bottlenecks that the Jet Engine imposes. Requests for data are sent directly to Microsoft SQL Server instead of being parsed and translated by Jet. Access Data Projects are covered in detail in Chapter 19. The performance gained by Access Data Projects might be necessary for you to achieve satisfactory performance with an application that uses Microsoft SQL Server data. Furthermore, Access Data Projects enable you to easily manage the tables, views, database diagrams, and stored procedures associated with a Microsoft SQL Server database. The major drawback of Access Data Projects is that they can be used only to access Microsoft SQL Server databases.

OPTIMIZING DATA HANDLING

One of the best things you can do to optimize data handling—such as edits, inserts, and deletes—is to add a version field (timestamp) to each remote table. This version field is employed when users update the data on the remote table to avoid overwrite conflicts. If this field does not exist, the server compares every field to see whether it has changed since the user first began editing the record. This is quite inefficient and is much slower than evaluating a timestamp.

OPTIMIZING QUERIES AND FORMS

On the whole, the movement to client/server architecture improves performance. If you are not careful when designing your queries, forms, and reports, this movement actually can degrade performance. You can do several things to ensure that the movement to client/server applications is beneficial. These techniques are broken down into query techniques and form techniques.

Optimizing Queries

Servers cannot perform many of the functions offered by the Access query builder. The functions that cannot be processed on the server are performed on the workstation. This often results in a large amount of data being sent over the network wire. You can eliminate this extra traffic if you design your queries so that they can be processed solely by the server.

Examples of problem queries that cannot be performed on the server follow:

- Top N percent queries
- Queries containing user-defined or Access functions
- Queries that involve tables from two different data sources—for example, a query that joins tables from two servers or from an Access table and a server table

NOTE

Both Top N percent queries and heterogenous joins are supported in Microsoft SQL Server 7.0.

Optimizing Forms

You can use the techniques in this section to design forms that capitalize on the benefits of the client/server architecture. The idea is to design your forms so that they request the minimal amount of data from the server and obtain additional data only if requested by the user. This means that you request as few records and fields as possible from the server. You can accomplish this by basing forms on queries instead of directly on the tables. You can further refine this process by designing your forms specifically with data retrieval in mind. A form can be opened initially with no RecordSource, for example. The form can require that users limit the criteria before any records are displayed.

You should store static tables, such as a state table, locally. This practice reduces network traffic and requests to the server. Furthermore, you should not base combo boxes and list boxes on server data. Whenever possible, you should base the row source for combo boxes and list boxes on local static tables. If this is not possible, you can use a text box with a combo box. The row source of the combo box initially is left blank. The user must enter the first few characters in the text box. The row source of the combo box then is based on a Select statement using the characters entered in the text box.

Furthermore, OLE object and Memo fields are large and therefore significantly increase network traffic. It is best not to display the contents of these fields unless they are requested specifically by the user. You can do this by setting the Visible property of OLE and Memo fields to False, or by placing these fields on another page of the form. You can add a command button that enables users to display the additional data when required.

Figure 20.1 shows a form that illustrates the implementation of several of these methods. The detail section of the form initially is not visible. The form has no RecordSource, and the data that underlies the combo box that appears on the form is stored in a local table.

The After Update event of the combo box looks like this:

```
Private Sub cboBookType_AfterUpdate()
    Me.RecordSource = "Select * From dbo_titles Where Type Like '" & _
            cboBookType.Value & "*';"
    Me.Detail.Visible = True
End Sub
```

FIGURE 20.1

A form using the After Update *event of the combo box to populate the* RecordSource *and make detail visible.*

The Visible property of the detail section of the form initially is set to False. After the user selects an entry from the combo box, the RecordSource of the form is set equal to a Select statement, which selects specific titles from the dbo_titles table database. The detail section of the form then is made visible, as shown in Figure 20.2.

FIGURE 20.2

A form using the After Update *event of the combo box to populate the* RecordSource *with detail visible.*

Finally, you might want to use unbound forms. This involves creating a form and then removing its RecordSource. Users are provided with a combo box that enables them to select one record. A recordset is built from the client/server data with the row the user selected. When using this method of form design, everything must be coded. Your form needs to handle all adds, edits, and deletes. Figure 20.3 shows an example of such a form. None of the controls on the form has its control source filled in. The name of each control corresponds with a field in the database server table.

FIGURE 20.3

An unbound form.

The Open event of the form looks like this:

```
Private Sub Form_Open(Cancel As Integer)
    Set mrst = New ADODB.Recordset
    Me.txtTitle.SetFocus
End Sub
```

This code sets a module-level database variable to the current database and sets focus to the txtTitle text box. The After Update event of the text box looks like this:

```
Private Sub txtTitle_AfterUpdate()
  Me!cboTitle.RowSource = "SELECT DISTINCTROW [dbo_titles].[title_id] " _
    & "FROM [dbo_titles] " _
     & "WHERE [dbo_titles].[title_id] Like '" & Me!txtTitle.Text & "*';"
End Sub
```

This code sets the RowSource property of the combo box to a Select statement that selects all records from the titles table where the title_id field begins with the first few characters the user typed. In this way, the combo box is not populated with all the titles from the server. The After Update event of the combo box looks like this:

```
Private Sub cboTitle_AfterUpdate()
    Dim boolSuccess As Boolean
    mrst.ActiveConnection = CurrentProject.Connection
    mrst.Open "Select * From dbo_Titles " _
        & "Where Title_ID = '" & Me!cboTitle.Value & "';"
        boolSuccess = PopulateForm(Me, mrst)
    If Not boolSuccess Then
        MsgBox "Record Not Found"
    End If
End Sub
```

The Open method is used to open a recordset based on the linked table called dbo_Titles. Notice that only the records with the matching Title_ID are retrieved. Because the Title_ID is the primary key, only one record is returned. The PopulateForm function then is called, as shown here:

```
Function PopulateForm(frmAny As Form, rstAny As ADODB.Recordset)
    Dim fld As ADODB.Field

    If rstAny.EOF Then
        PopulateForm = False
    Else

    For Each fld In rstAny.Fields
        frmAny(fld.Name) = fld
    Next fld

    PopulateForm = True
    End If
End Function
```

The PopulateForm function checks to ensure that the recordset that was passed has records. It then loops through each field on the form, matching field names with controls on the form. It sets the value of each control on the form to the value of the field in the recordset with the same name as the control name.

Note that these changes to the data in the form do not update the data on the database server. Furthermore, the form does not provide for inserts or deletes. You need to write code to issue updates, inserts, and deletes, and you have to provide command buttons to give your users access to that functionality.

NOTE

Both of the preceding techniques can be used with both linked tables and with Access Data Projects. The benefits of the techniques will be most profound with Access Data Projects.

20

CLIENT/SERVER
STRATEGIES

Using Client/Server Strategies

Suppose that the Employees table is probably going to be moved to a database server in the near future because it contains sensitive data. You therefore must design the Employees form with client/server architecture in mind. The form limits the data displayed in the form. The form opens with only an option group containing the letters of the alphabet, as Figure 20.4 shows. After the user selects a letter, the detail section of the form is displayed and the RecordSource for the form is populated with a Select statement, as Figure 20.5 shows.

FIGURE 20.4

The Employees form with an option group to select the employee's last name.

FIGURE 20.5

The full view of the Employees form.

The Open event of the form looks like this:

```
Private Sub Form_Open(Cancel As Integer)
    Me.Detail.Visible = False
End Sub
```

The Visible property of the detail section of the form is set to False. The AfterUpdate event of the option group looks like this:

```
Private Sub optEmpName_AfterUpdate()
    Me.RecordSource = "Select * from tblEmployees Where LastName Like '" _
        & Chr$(Me![optEmpName].Value) & "*';"
```

```
    Me.NavigationButtons = True
    Me.Detail.Visible = True
    DoCmd.DoMenuItem acFormBar, 7, 6, , acMenuVer70
End Sub
```

This code populates the `RecordSource` of the form using a `Select` statement. It makes the navigation buttons and the detail section of the form visible. Finally, it resizes the window to the form.

SUMMARY

In this chapter, you learned client/server strategies and optimization techniques that will improve the performance and maintainability of your applications. You were instructed on methods for selecting the best recordset type. You learned how to use pass-through queries and stored procedures. Finally, you learned how to optimize data handling, queries, and forms.

A CLIENT/SERVER
APPLICATION IN ACTION

IN THIS CHAPTER

WHY THIS CHAPTER IS IMPORTANT

It is often difficult to tie together techniques covered in a book. This chapter shows you how to apply many of the client/server techniques and concepts covered in Chapter 19, "Client/Server Techniques," and Chapter 20, "Client/Server Strategies."

CREATING A CLIENT/SERVER APPLICATION USING LINKED TABLES

One option for building a client/server application is to use linked tables. If done properly, this can be a very viable solution. An overview of the steps required to build the client/server application using linked tables includes the following:

1. Link to the tables contained in the SQL Server database.
2. Build a tabbed form that will contain customer, order, and order detail tabs.
3. Add a combo box to the form that allows the user to locate data for a specific company.
4. Create a query that is used to populate the detail section of the form. The query retrieves data only for the selected customer.
5. Create a query that is used to populate the detail section of the orders subform.
6. Create a query that is used to populate the detail section of the order details subform.
7. Hide the order and order detail subforms until the appropriate tab is selected.
8. Specify blank record sources for the subforms.
9. Designate the record source for the subforms and make the subforms visible only when the appropriate tab is selected.

The following sections provide you with the details of each of the steps involved in creating the application.

Linking to Tables Contained in the SQL Server Database

Because this version of the application uses linked tables, the first step in the process is to link to the tables that are used by the application. The example will use the SQL Server version of the Northwind database. Follow these steps to link to tables in the Northwind database:

1. Right-click within the Database window and select Link Tables. The Link dialog appears.
2. Select ODBC databases in the Files of Type drop-down. The Select Data Source Dialog appears.
3. Click the Machine Data Source tab (see Figure 21.1).

A Client/Server Application in Action

CHAPTER 21

725

21

A CLIENT/SERVER
APPLICATION IN
ACTION

FIGURE 21.1

*The Machine
Data Source tab
allows you to set
up a machine data
source.*

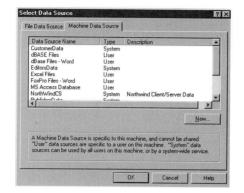

4. Click New to create a new data source. The Create New Data Source dialog appears (see Figure 21.2).

FIGURE 21.2

*The Create New
Data Source
Wizard walks you
through the steps
of creating a new
data source.*

5. Select System Data Source and click Next.

6. Select the SQL Server driver from the list of drivers (see Figure 21.3). Click Next.

FIGURE 21.3

*Select the SQL
Server driver from
the list of avail-
able drivers.*

7. Click Finish. The Create a New Data Source to SQL Server dialog appears (see Figure 21.4).

FIGURE 21.4

The Create a New Data Source to SQL Server dialog walks you through the steps of establishing the new SQL Server data source.

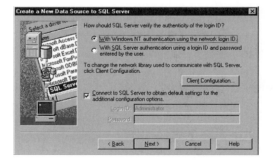

8. Enter a Name and optional Description for the data source.

9. Select the SQL Server you want to connect to. Click Next.

10. Select the appropriate security options and click Next (see Figure 21.5).

FIGURE 21.5

Enter the appropriate security options for the database.

11. Select the appropriate database options. These include how stored procedures are executed and how quotes and nulls are treated. Click Next (see Figure 21.6).

12. Modify any of the remaining options and click Finish.

13. A list of selected options appears (see Figure 21.7). Click Test Data Source to test the new data source. You should be notified that the test completed successfully.

14. Click OK to close the test dialog. Click OK again to close the ODBC Microsoft SQL Server Setup dialog. You are returned to the Select Data Source dialog.

15. Select the data source that you just created and click OK. You are prompted to log in to the SQL Server (see Figure 21.8). Enter a valid login ID and password and click OK. The Link Tables dialog appears (see Figure 21.9).

FIGURE 21.6

Select the appropriate database options.

FIGURE 21.7

Click Test Data Source to test the data source with all the listed options.

FIGURE 21.8

The SQL Server Login dialog allows you to log in to the SQL Server.

FIGURE 21.9

The Link Tables dialog allows you to designate the SQL Server tables you want to link to.

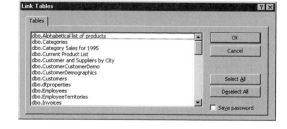

16. Click to select each table you want to link to. Click OK when you're finished. The Database window, with the links established, appears in Figure 21.10.

FIGURE 21.10

The Database window with links to the Northwind database.

Building the Customer Form

The form that you will build is pictured in Figure 21.11. Notice that initially no data appears. This form is designed to display only one customer record at a time. It accomplishes this because the form is based on a query that retrieves data only for the customer selected in the Select a Company combo box. Furthermore, the data for the Orders and Order Details tabs is not retrieved until the tabs are selected. This ensures that records on the many side of the one-to-many relationship are not retrieved unless they are needed.

FIGURE 21.11

The completed customer form initially appears without any data.

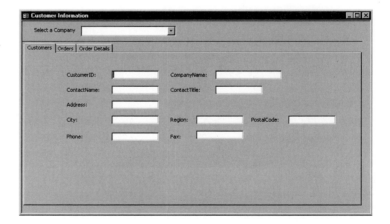

To begin the process of designing the frmCustomer form, follow these steps:

1. Select Forms in the Objects list of the Database window.

2. Double-click Create form in Design view.

3. Select View | Form Header/Footer to add a header and footer to the form.

A Client/Server Application in Action

CHAPTER 21

729

21

A CLIENT/SERVER
APPLICATION IN
ACTION

Adding a Locate Combo Box to the Form

The first step required to build the form is to add a combo box to the form that allows the user to select the company whose information he wants to view. The combo box is populated with the CustomerID and CompanyName of each company in the company table. When a company is selected in the combo box, the form is requeried to display data for the selected customer. Build the combo box using the combo box wizard. Take the following steps:

1. Make sure the Control Wizards tool in the toolbox is selected.

2. Click to select the Combo Box tool in the toolbox, and then click and drag to add the combo box to the header of the form. The Combo Box Wizard launches.

3. Select I Want the Combo Box to Look Up the Values in a Table or Query. Click Next.

4. Select dbo_Customers (the linked table) from the list of tables (see Figure 21.12). Click Next.

FIGURE 21.12

Select the dbo_Customers table from the list of available tables.

5. Select the CustomerID and CompanyName fields from the list of available fields (see Figure 21.13). Click Next.

FIGURE 21.13

Select the CustomerID and CompanyName fields as the fields to be included in the combo box.

6. Double-click the right side of the CompanyName column to size the column to the largest entry (see Figure 21.14). Leave the Hide Key Column option checked. Click Next.

FIGURE 21.14

Double-click the right side of the CompanyName column to size the column to the largest entry.

7. Enter Select a Company as the label for the combo box. Click Finish. The combo box is added to the form (see Figure 21.15).

FIGURE 21.15

The combo box is added to the form.

8. Click to select the combo box that you added.

9. Change the name of the combo box to cboSelectCompany.

10. Save the form as frmCustomer.

A Client/Server Application in Action

CHAPTER 21

731

21

A CLIENT/SERVER
APPLICATION IN
ACTION

11. Test the form to make sure that the combo box displays a list of all the customers (see Figure 21.16).

FIGURE 21.16

The completed combo box displays a list of customers.

FIGURE 21.16

The completed combo box displays a list of customers.

Building the Query for the Customer Form

The next step is to design the query that underlies the frmCustomer form. The query will reference the CustomerID of the customer that is selected in the cboSelectCompany combo box. Here are the steps involved:

1. Return to Design view, if necessary.

2. Select the Form.

3. Click the Data tab in the Properties window.

4. Click the Record Source property (see Figure 21.17).

5. Click Build. The Show Table dialog appears.

6. Select dbo_Customers from the list of tables (see Figure 21.18). Click Add.

7. Click Close.

8. Add the CustomerID, CompanyName, ContactName, ContactTitle, Address, City, Region, PostalCode, Phone, and Fax fields to the query (see Figure 21.19).

FIGURE 21.17

The Record Source property allows you to designate the record source for the form.

FIGURE 21.18

Select the dbo_Customers table from the Show Table dialog.

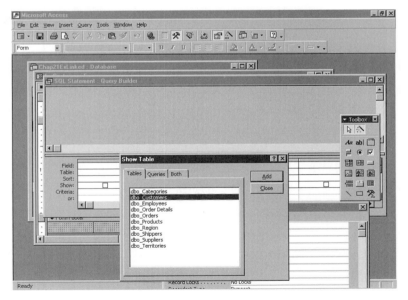

A Client/Server Application in Action

CHAPTER 21

733

21

A CLIENT/SERVER
APPLICATION IN
ACTION

FIGURE 21.19

Add the desired fields to the query grid.

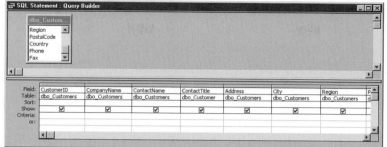

9. Enter `Forms!frmCustomer!cboSelectCompany` as the criteria for the CustomerID field (see Figure 21.20).

FIGURE 21.20

Selection criteria for the CustomerID field.

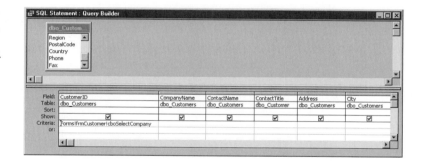

10. Close the SQL Statement Builder.

11. Click Yes that you want to save the changes made to the SQL statement and update the property.

Before you can add the fields to the form, you must design the tabs for the form. Take the following steps:

1. Select a tab control from the toolbox.

2. Click and drag to add it to the frmCustomer form.

3. Change the Caption property of the first tab to Customers.

4. Change the Name property of the first tab to pagCustomers.

5. Change the Caption property of the second tab to Orders.

6. Change the Name property of the second tab to pagOrders.

7. Right-click the page control and select Insert Page. A third page appears.

8. Change the Caption property of the third tab to Order Details.

9. Change the Name property of the third tab to pagOrderDetails.

10. Change the Name property of the tab control to tabDataEntry.

11. Add the fields to the Customers tab of the form as shown in Figure 21.21.

FIGURE 21.21

The Customers tab with the selected fields added.

Building the Query for the Orders Subform

The next step is to build the query that underlies the Orders subform. The query will select all orders where the CustomerID is that of the customer selected in the cboSelectCompany combo box. To create the query, follow these steps:

1. Select Queries from the list of objects in the Database window.

2. Double-click Create Query in Design view. The Show Tables dialog appears.

3. Select dbo_Orders from the list of tables and click Add.

4. Click Close.

5. Add the OrderID, CustomerID, EmployeeID, OrderDate, RequiredDate, ShippedDate, ShipVia, and Freight fields to the query.

6. Enter Forms!frmCustomer!cboSelectCompany as the criteria for the CustomerID.

7. Save the query as qryOrders. The completed query appears in Figure 21.22.

A Client/Server Application in Action

CHAPTER 21

735

21

A CLIENT/SERVER
APPLICATION IN
ACTION

FIGURE 21.22

*The completed
qryOrders query.*

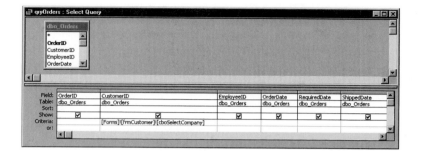

Building the Query for the Order Details Subform

The next step is to build the query that underlies the OrderDetails subform. The query will select all order detail items where the OrderID is that of the order selected in the fsubOrders subform. To create the query:

1. Select Queries from the list of objects in the Database window.
2. Double-click Create Query in Design view. The Show Tables dialog appears.
3. Select dbo_OrderDetails from the list of tables and click Add.
4. Click Close.
5. Add the OrderID, ProductID, UnitPrice, Quantity, and Discount fields to the query.
6. Enter `Forms!frmCustomer.Form!fsubOrders!OrderID` as the criteria for the OrderID.
7. Save the query as qryOrderDetails. The completed query appears in Figure 21.23.

FIGURE 21.23

*The completed
qryOrderDetails
query.*

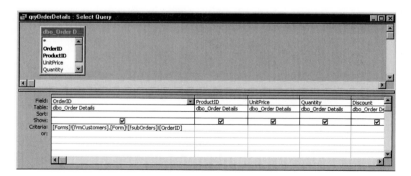

Creating the fsubOrder Subform

The fsubOrders subform will be used to display the orders associated with the selected customers. Take the following steps to create the fsubOrders subform and add it to the Orders page of the tab control:

1. Activate the frmCustomer form in Design view.

2. Click to select the Orders page of the tab control.

3. Make sure that the Control Wizards tool is selected.

4. Select the Subform/Subreport control.

5. Click and drag to add a subform control to the Orders tab. The SubForm Wizard appears (see Figure 21.24).

FIGURE 21.24

The Subform Wizard assists you with the process of adding the Orders subform to the Orders tab.

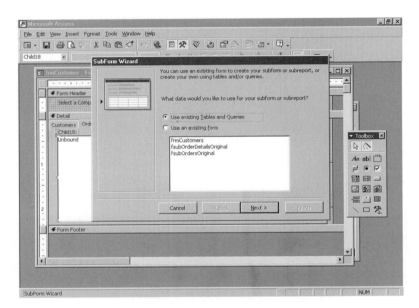

6. Select Use Existing Tables and Queries and click Next.

7. Select qryOrders from the Tables/Queries drop-down.

8. Add all fields in the query to the Selected Fields list (see Figure 21.25).

9. Click Next.

10. Select None as the link between the main form and the subform (see Figure 21.26) and click Next.

11. Enter fsubOrders as the name of the subform and click Finish.

12. Size the subform control so that it appears as in Figure 21.27.

A Client/Server Application in Action

CHAPTER 21

737

21

A CLIENT/SERVER
APPLICATION IN
ACTION

FIGURE 21.25
Add all fields from qryOrders to the list of selected fields.

FIGURE 21.26
Select None as the link between the parent form and the subform.

FIGURE 21.27
The fsubOrders subform after it has been added to the Orders tab.

Creating the fsubOrderDetail Subform

The fsubOrderDetails subform will be used to display the order detail items associated with the selected order. Take the following steps to create the fsubOrderDetails subform and add it to the Order Details page of the tab control:

1. Activate the frmCustomer form in Design view.

2. Click to select the Order Details page of the tab control.

3. Make sure that the Control Wizards tool is selected.

4. Select the Subform/Subreport control.

5. Click and drag to add a subform control to the Order Details tab. The SubForm Wizard appears.

6. Select Use Existing Tables and Queries and click Next.

7. Select qryOrderDetails from the Tables/Queries drop-down.

8. Add all fields in the query to the list of Selected Fields.

9. Click Next.

10. You are prompted to define links between the main form and the subform (see Figure 21.28). Click Next without defining any links.

FIGURE 21.28

No links are created between the main form and the subform.

11. Enter `fsubOrderDetails` as the name of the subform and click Finish.

12. Size the subform control so that it appears as in Figure 21.29.

A Client/Server Application in Action

CHAPTER 21

739

21

A CLIENT/SERVER
APPLICATION IN
ACTION

FIGURE 21.29

The fsubOrderDetails subform after it has been added to the Order Details tab.

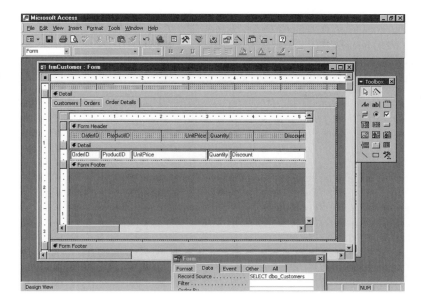

Hiding the Order and Order Details Subforms Until the Appropriate Tab Is Selected

Probably the largest goal in client/server development is to limit the data that is transferred from the database server to the workstation. Many times a user will need to view the main customer information without needing to see the Order or Order Detail information. It is therefore unnecessary to retrieve the Order and Order Detail information unless the user explicitly requests it by clicking to select the Order or Order Details tab. The code shown is Listing 21.1 handles the process of hiding and showing the appropriate subforms, as the user clicks the various tabs on the form. As the code shows the subforms, it populates the RecordSource property of the subforms to display the appropriate data.

LISTING 21.1 THE Change EVENT OF THE TABDATAENTRY CONTROL HANDLES THE PROCESS OF HIDING AND SHOWING THE APPROPRIATE SUBFORMS

```
Private Sub tabDataEntry_Change()
    Select Case Me.tabDataEntry.Pages. _
        Item(Me.tabDataEntry.Value).Name

        Case "pagCustomers"
            Me.fsubOrders.Visible = False
            Me.fsubOrderDetails.Visible = False
```

continues

LISTING 21.1   CONTINUED

```
        Case "pagOrders"
            Me.fsubOrders.Form.RecordSource = "qryOrders"
            Me.fsubOrders.Visible = True
            Me.fsubOrderDetails.Visible = False


        Case "pagOrderDetails"
            Me.fsubOrderDetails.Form.RecordSource = "qryOrderDetails"
            Me.fsubOrders.Visible = False
            Me.fsubOrderDetails.Visible = True


    End Select
End Sub
```

The code begins by evaluating which page is selected. If the pagCustomers page is selected, the Visible property of the fsubOrders and fsubOrderDetails subform controls are set to False.

If the pagOrders page is selected, the RecordSource property of the subform is set to the qryOrders query. The Visible property of the fsubOrders subform control is set to True and the Visible property of the fsubOrderDetails subform control is set to False.

If the pagOrderDetails page is selected, the RecordSource property of the subform is set to the qryOrderDetails query. The Visible property of the fsubOrders subform control is set to False and the Visible property of the fsubOrderDetails subform control is set to True.

Specifying Blank Record Sources for the Subforms

It all comes together when the user selects a company from the cboSelectCompany combo box. The AfterUpdate event of the combo box executes. It is found in Listing 21.2.

LISTING 21.2   THE AfterUpdate EVENT OF THE CBOSELECTCOMPANY COMBO BOX APPROPRIATELY SETS THE RecordSource OF THE SUBFORMS AND REQUERIES THE MAIN FORM

```
Private Sub cboSelectCompany_AfterUpdate()
    Select Case Me.tabDataEntry.Pages. _
        Item(Me.tabDataEntry.Value).Name

        Case "pagCustomers"
            Me.fsubOrders.Form.RecordSource = ""
            Me.fsubOrderDetails.Form.RecordSource = ""

        Case "pagOrders"
            Me.fsubOrderDetails.Form.RecordSource = ""
```

A Client/Server Application in Action

Chapter 21

741

21

A Client/Server
Application in
Action

```
        End Select

        Me.Requery
End Sub
```

It begins by evaluating the name of the page that is selected. If the name of the page is pagCustomers, the RecordSource property of both the fsubOrders subform and the fsubOrderDetails subform are set to a zero-length string. If the name of the selected page is pagOrders, the RecordSource property of the fsubOrderDetails page is set to a zero-length string. In essence, the code ensures that when a different customer is selected, their order and order detail records are not retrieved until the appropriate page is selected. This acts to eliminate a lot of unnecessary network traffic.

Designating the Record Source for the Subforms

Because the record source of the subforms are set to a zero-length string when a different customer is selected, it is necessary to repopulate the RecordSource property when the page is activated. The Change event of the tabDataEntry tab control, shown is Listing 21.3, handles this.

LISTING 21.3 THE Change EVENT OF THE tabDataEntry TAB CONTROL REPOPULATES THE RecordSource PROPERTY WHEN A PAGE IS ACTIVATED

```
Private Sub tabDataEntry_Change()
    Select Case Me.tabDataEntry.Pages. _
        Item(Me.tabDataEntry.Value).Name

        Case "pagCustomers"
            Me.fsubOrders.Visible = False
            Me.fsubOrderDetails.Visible = False

        Case "pagOrders"
            Me.fsubOrders.Form.RecordSource = "qryOrders"
            Me.fsubOrders.Visible = True
            Me.fsubOrderDetails.Visible = False


        Case "pagOrderDetails"
            Me.fsubOrderDetails.Form.RecordSource = "qryOrderDetails"
            Me.fsubOrders.Visible = False
            Me.fsubOrderDetails.Visible = True


    End Select
End Sub
```

Notice that the record source of the fsubOrders subform is established when the pagOrders page is selected, and the record source of the fsubOrderDetails subform is established when the pagOrderDetails page is selected.

CREATING A CLIENT/SERVER APPLICATION USING AN ACCESS DATA PROJECT

One alternative to our client/server solution is linked tables. The other alternative is to use an Access Data Project to solve the problem. Once again the application will be built around the Northwind client/server database.

To build the ADP file:

1. Click File | New.

2. Select Project (Existing Database) and Click OK.

3. Select a name and location for the Access Data Project (.ADP). Click Create. The Data Link Properties dialog appears.

4. In the Select or Enter a Server Name text box, enter the name of the server where the Northwind database resides.

5. Specify how you will log on to the server.

6. Select the Northwind database as the database on the server. The completed dialog should appear similar to Figure 21.30.

FIGURE 21.30

Use the Data Link Properties dialog to specify information about the location of the data.

A Client/Server Application in Action

CHAPTER 21

743

21

A CLIENT/SERVER
APPLICATION IN
ACTION

7. Click Test Connection to test the connection to the server and database. A dialog should appear, indicating the test connection succeeded. Click OK to continue.

8. Click OK to close the Data Link Properties dialog. The ADP file is built. The Database window should appear as in Figure 21.31.

FIGURE 21.31
The Database window after the ADP file is built.

Designing the Customer Form

The form that you will build is pictured in Figure 21.32. Follow these steps to begin the process of designing the frmCustomer form:

1. Click Forms in the Objects list

2. Double-click Create form in Design view.

3. Select View|Form Header/Footer to add a header and footer to the form.

FIGURE 21.32
The completed frmCustomer form.

Adding a Locate Combo Box to the Form

As with the linked table application, the first step is to add a combo box to the form that allows the user to select the company whose information she wants to view. The combo box is populated with the CustomerID and CompanyName of each company in the company table. Build the combo box using the Combo Box Wizard. The steps are as follows:

1. If necessary, click the Control Wizards tool in the toolbox to turn the Control Wizards on.

2. Select a combo box from the toolbox and click and drag to add it to the header of the form. The Combo Box Wizard appears (see Figure 21.33).

FIGURE 21.33

The Combo Box Wizard is used to add a combo box to the form.

3. Select I Want the Combo Box to Look Up the Values in a Table or View. Click Next.

4. Select the Customers table and click Next.

5. Select the CustomerID and CompanyName fields and click Next (see Figure 21.34).

6. Size the CompanyName column if necessary, and click Next.

7. Enter the label "Select a Company" and click Finish.

8. Name the combo box cboSelectCompany.

A Client/Server Application in Action
CHAPTER 21

745

21

A CLIENT/SERVER
APPLICATION IN
ACTION

FIGURE 21.34
*The CustomerID
and
CompanyName
fields are added
to the combo box.*

Adding Pages and Controls to the Form

Before you can add the fields to the form, you must design the tabs for the form. Take the
following steps:

1. Select a tab control from the toolbox.
2. Click and drag to add it to the frmCustomer form.
3. Change the Caption property of the first tab to Customers.
4. Change the Name property of the first tab to pagCustomers.
5. Change the Caption property of the second tab to Orders.
6. Change the Name property of the second tab to pagOrders.
7. Right-click the page control and select Insert Page. A third page appears.
8. Change the Caption property of the third tab to Order Details.
9. Change the Name property of the third tab to pagOrderDetails.
10. Change the Name property of the tab control tabDataEntry.
11. Temporarily set the RecordSource property of the form to the Customers table. This
    allows you to add controls to the form.
12. Add the fields to the Customers tab of the form as shown in Figure 21.35.

FIGURE 21.35

The Customers tab with the selected fields added.

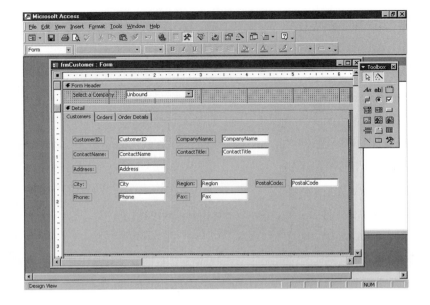

13. Remove the record source from the form.

Populating the Record Source of the Form

Next it is time to establish the record source for the form. This is initially handled within the Load event of the form. The code appears in Listing 21.4.

LISTING 21.4   THE FORM Load EVENT ESTABLISHES THE RECORD SOURCE FOR THE FORM

```
Private Sub Form_Load()
    Set mrstCustomers = New ADODB.Recordset
    With mrstCustomers
        .ActiveConnection = CurrentProject.Connection
        .CursorLocation = adUseClient
        .CursorType = adOpenDynamic
        .LockType = adLockOptimistic
        .Source = "Select * from Customers Where CustomerID = '" & _
        Me.cboSelectCompany & "'"
        .Open
    End With
    Set Me.Recordset = mrstCustomers
End Sub
```

A Client/Server Application in Action

Chapter 21

747

21

A CLIENT/SERVER
APPLICATION IN
ACTION

The code begins by instantiating an ADODB recordset declared as Private in the General Declarations section of the form. It then sets several properties of the recordset. Notice that the CursorType is adOpenDynamic and the LockType is adLockOptimistic. The combination of these properties renders the form updateable. The Source property of the recordset is set to a SQL select statement that is based on the customer selected in the cboSelectCompany combo box. The recordset is then opened. Finally, the recordset associated with the frmCustomer form is established based on the recordset containing the one customer record.

Handling the AfterUpdate Event of the cboSelectCompany Combo Box

When a different customer is selected in the cboSelectCompany combo box, the recordset underlying the form must be re-created with the selected customer's information. The AfterUpdate event of the combo box appears in Listing 21.5.

LISTING 21.5 THE AfterUpdate EVENT OF THE CBOSELECTCOMPANY COMBO BOX CREATES THE RECORDSET ASSOCIATED WITH THE FRMCUSTOMERS FORM

```
Private Sub cboSelectCompany_AfterUpdate()
    mrstCustomers.Close
    mrstCustomers.Source = "Select * from Customers Where _
        CustomerID = '" & Me.cboSelectCompany & "'"
    mrstCustomers.Open
    Set Me.Recordset = mrstCustomers

    Select Case Me.tabDataEntry.Pages. _
        Item(Me.tabDataEntry.Value).Name

        Case "pagCustomers"
            Set Me.fsubOrders.Form.Recordset = Nothing
            Set Me.fsubOrderDetails.Form.Recordset = Nothing

        Case "pagOrders"
            Set Me.fsubOrderDetails.Form.Recordset = Nothing
            Call CreateOrdersRecordset

        Case "pagOrderDetails"
            Call CreateOrdersRecordset
            Call CreateOrderDetailsRecordset

    End Select

End Sub
```

The code begins by closing the mrstCustomers recordset. This is necessary so that the properties of the recordset can be modified. The source of the recordset is modified so that it is based on the customer that was just selected in the combo box. The recordset is then opened and the recordset property of the form is pointed to the recordset that was just created.

The case statement evaluates which tab of the form is selected. If the Customers tab is selected, the recordsets associated with the Order and Order Detail subforms are destroyed. If the Orders tab is selected, the recordset associated with the Order Detail subform is destroyed, and the CreateOrdersRecordset routine is called. The CreateOrdersRecordset routine builds the recordset associated with the fsubOrders subform. If the Order Details tab is selected, the CreateOrdersRecordset routine is called and then the CreateOrderDetailsRecordset routine is called. The CreateOrderDetailsRecordset routine is responsible for building the recordset associated with the fsubOrderDetails subform. Both the CreateOrdersRecordset routine and the CreateOrderDetailsRecordset routine are covered later in this chapter.

Creating the fsubOrder Subform

The fsubOrders subform will be used to display the orders associated with the selected customers. Take the following steps to create the fsubOrders subform and add it to the Orders page of the tab control:

1. Activate the frmCustomer form in Design view.
2. Click to select the Orders page of the tab control.
3. Make sure that the Control Wizards tool is selected.
4. Select the Subform/Subreport control.
5. Click and drag to add a subform control to the Orders tab. The SubForm Wizard appears.
6. Select Use Existing Tables and Queries and click Next.
7. Select tblOrders from the Tables/Queries drop-down.
8. Add all fields in the query to the list of Selected Fields.
9. Click Next.
10. Enter fsubOrders as the name of the subform and click Finish.
11. Size the subform control as needed.
12. Open the fsubOrders form and delete its record source. The record source of the form will be handled programmatically.

Creating the fsubOrderDetail Subform

The fsubOrderDetails subform will be used to display the order detail items associated with the selected order. Take the following steps to create the fsubOrderDetails subform and add it to the Order Details page of the tab control:

1. Activate the frmCustomer form in Design view.

2. Click to select the Order Details page of the tab control.

3. Make sure that the Control Wizards tool is selected.

4. Select the Subform/Subreport control.

5. Click and drag to add a subform control to the Order Details tab. The SubForm Wizard appears.

6. Select Use Existing Tables and Queries and click Next.

7. Select qryOrderDetails from the Tables/Queries drop-down.

8. Add all fields in the query to the list of Selected Fields.

9. Click Next.

10. Enter `fsubOrderDetails` as the name of the subform and click Finish.

11. Size the subform control as needed.

12. Open the fsubOrderDetails form and delete its record source. The record source of the form will be handled programmatically.

Populating the Subforms with Data

 Because the `RecordSource` properties of the fsubOrders and fsubOrderDetails forms are blank, they must be populated programmatically. The code in Listing 21.6, located in the frmCustomers form, is responsible for populating the fsubOrders form with data.

LISTING 21.6 THE `CreateOrdersRecordset` ROUTINE BUILDS THE RECORDSET THAT IS USED TO POPULATE THE FSUBORDERS SUBFORM WITH DATA

```
Sub CreateOrdersRecordset()
    Set mrstOrders = New ADODB.Recordset
    With mrstOrders
        .ActiveConnection = CurrentProject.Connection
        .CursorLocation = adUseClient
        .CursorType = adOpenDynamic
        .LockType = adLockOptimistic
        .Source = "Select * from Orders Where CustomerID = '" & _
        Me.cboSelectCompany & "'"
        .Open
    End With
    Set Me.fsubOrders.Form.Recordset = mrstOrders
End Sub
```

A module-level recordset variable is instantiated. Its properties are then set. Notice that its `CursorType` property is set to dynamic and its `LockType` is set to optimistic. The combination of these two properties renders the resulting recordset updateable. The Source property of the recordset is based on a SQL statement that selects all records from the Orders table where the CustomerID field is equal to the CustomerID of the customer selected in the cboSelectCompany combo box. The recordset is then opened and is used to populate the recordset associated with the fsubOrders subform.

 The code in Listing 21.7, also located in the frmCustomers form, is responsible for populating the fsubOrderDetails form with data.

LISTING 21.7   THE CreateOrderDetailsRecordset ROUTINE BUILDS THE RECORDSET THAT IS USED TO POPULATE THE FSUBORDERDETAILS SUBFORM WITH DATA

```
Sub CreateOrderDetailsRecordset()
    Set mrstOrderDetails = New ADODB.Recordset
    With mrstOrderDetails
        .ActiveConnection = CurrentProject.Connection
        .CursorLocation = adUseClient
        .CursorType = adOpenDynamic
        .LockType = adLockOptimistic
        .Source = "Select * from [Order Details] Where OrderID = " & _
        Me.fsubOrders!OrderID
        .Open
    End With
    Set Me.fsubOrderDetails.Form.Recordset = mrstOrderDetails

End Sub
```

This routine is identical to the CreateOrdersRecordset routine except for the Source property. The Source property selects all records from the Order Details table where the OrderID field in the Order Details table is equal to the OrderID of the currently selected record in the fsubOrders subform. The resulting recordset is then used to populate the fsubOrderDetails subform.

Reacting to a User Clicking the Various Pages of the Form

The final piece of the puzzle is the code that reacts to the user selecting the various pages of the form. It appears in Listing 21.8.

LISTING 21.8   THE Change EVENT OF THE TABDATAENTRY TAB CONTROL REACTS TO THE USER SELECTING THE VARIOUS PAGES ON THE FORM

```
Private Sub tabDataEntry_Change()
    Select Case Me.tabDataEntry.Pages. _
```

```
        Item(Me.tabDataEntry.Value).Name

        Case "pagCustomers"
            Me.fsubOrders.SourceObject = ""
            Me.fsubOrderDetails.SourceObject = ""

        Case "pagOrders"
            Me.fsubOrders.SourceObject = "fsubOrders"
            Call CreateOrdersRecordset
            Me.fsubOrderDetails.SourceObject = ""


        Case "pagOrderDetails"
            Me.fsubOrderDetails.SourceObject = "fsubOrderDetails"
            Call CreateOrderDetailsRecordset

    End Select
End Sub
```

It begins by evaluating the selected page. If the Customers page is selected, the SourceObject property of both the fsubOrders and fsubOrderDetails subform controls is set to "".

If the Orders page is selected, the SourceObject property of the fsubOrders subform control is set to "fsubOrders". The CreateOrdersRecordset routine is called so that the fsubOrders form is populated with the appropriate data. The SourceObject property of the fsubOrderDetails subform control is set to "".

If the Order Details page is selected, the SourceObject property of the fsubOrderDetails subform control is set to "fsubOrderDetails". The CreateOrderDetailsRecordset routine is called so that the fsubOrderDetails subform is populated with the appropriate data.

SUMMARY

There are two techniques available for building client/server applications. The first employs the use of linked tables within a standard database file (.mdb). This method can be quite successful if the application is built so that a minimal amount of data travels over the network wire. The alternative to this technique is to use an Access data project. With an Access data project, a direct connection is established to the client/server database and no linked tables are involved. Regardless of the technique employed, the objective is to minimize the data that travels over the network wire. Traffic is reduced by ensuring that only the data the user specifically requests is returned. Techniques that achieve this goal include not requesting data until the user clicks the tab containing that data. This chapter shows you how to build forms that keep network traffic to a minimum.

TRANSACTION PROCESSING

IN THIS CHAPTER

WHY THIS CHAPTER IS IMPORTANT

Transaction processing refers to the grouping of a series of changes into a single batch. The entire batch of changes is either accepted or rejected as a group. One of the most common implementations of transaction processing is a bank automated teller machine (ATM) transaction. Imagine that you go to the ATM to deposit your paycheck. In the middle of processing, a power outage occurs. Unfortunately, the bank recorded the incoming funds prior to the outage, but the funds had not yet been credited to your account when the power outage occurred. You would not be very pleased with the outcome of this situation. Transaction processing would prevent this scenario from occurring. With transaction processing, the whole process succeeds or fails as a unit.

A group of operations is considered a transaction if it meets the following criteria:

- It is atomic—The group of operations should complete as a unit or not at all.
- It is consistent—The group of operations, when completed as a unit, retains the consistency of the application.
- It is isolated—The group of operations is independent of anything else going on in the system.
- It is durable—After the group of operations is committed, the changes persist, even if the system crashes.

If your application contains a group of operations that are atomic and isolated, and if, in order to maintain the consistency of your application, all changes must persist even if the system crashes, you should place the group of operations in a transaction loop. With Access 2000, the primary benefit of transaction processing is data integrity. As you will see in the next section, with versions prior to Access 95, transaction processing also provided performance benefits.

UNDERSTANDING THE BENEFITS

In Access 2.0, there were many marginal benefits of added transaction processing because Access 2.0 did no implicit transaction processing itself. Listing 22.1 shows code that, when run in Access 2.0, writes the data to disk each time the Update method occurs in the loop. These disk writes were costly in terms of performance, especially if the tables were not located on a local machine.

LISTING 22.1 ~~PROCESSING~~ PROCESSING USING ACCESS BASIC AS SEEN IN ACCESS 2.0

```
Sub IncreaseQuantity()

    On Error GoTo IncreaseQuantity_Err
    Dim db As DATABASE
    Dim rst As Recordset

    Set db = CurrentDb
    Set rst = db.OpenRecordset("Select OrderId, _
            Quantity From tblOrderDetails", _
            dbOpenDynaset)

    'Loop through recordset increasing Quantity field by 1
    Do Until rst.EOF
        rst.Edit
        rst!Quantity = rst!Quantity + 1
        rst.UPDATE
        rst.MoveNext
    Loop

IncreaseQuantity_Exit:
    Set db = Nothing
    Set rst = Nothing
    Exit Sub

IncreaseQuantity_Err:
    MsgBox "Error # " & Err.Number & ": " & Error.Description
    Resume IncreaseQuantity_Exit
End Sub
```

22

TRANSACTION
PROCESSING

NOTE

 This code, and all the code in this chapter, is located in the CHAP22EX.MDB database on the sample code CD-ROM in the basTrans module.

The same code found in Listing 22.1 performs much differently when run in Access 2000. In addition to any explicit transaction processing you might implement for data-integrity reasons, Access 2000 does its own behind-the-scenes transaction processing. This implicit transaction processing is done solely to improve the performance of your application. As the processing loop in the `IncreaseQuantity` routine executes, Access buffers and then periodically writes the data to disk. In a multiuser environment, Jet (implicitly) commits transactions every 50 milliseconds by default. This period of time is optimized for concurrency rather than performance. If you feel that it is necessary to sacrifice concurrency for performance, you can modify a few Windows registry settings to achieve the specific outcome you want. These settings are covered in the next section.

Although implicit transaction processing, along with the modifiable Windows registry settings, generally gives you better performance than explicit transaction processing, it is not a cut-and-dried situation. Many factors impact the performance benefits gained by both implicit and explicit transaction processing:

- Amount of free memory
- Number of columns and rows being updated
- Size of the rows being updated
- Network traffic

If you plan to implement explicit transaction processing solely to improve performance, you should make sure that you benchmark performance using both implicit and explicit transactions. It is critical that your application-testing environment be as similar as possible to the production environment in which the application will run.

MODIFYING THE DEFAULT BEHAVIOR

Before you learn how to implement transaction processing, take a look at what you can do to modify the default behavior of the transaction processing built in to Access 2000. Three registry settings affect implicit transactions in Access 2000: ImplicitCommitSync, ExclusiveAsnycDelay, and SharedAsyncDelay. These keys are located in the \HKEY_LOCAL_MACHINE\SOFTWARE\Microsoft\Jet\4.0\Engines\Jet 4.0 registry folder.

> **TIP**
>
> You can access the Windows registry using the RegEdit utility. To utilize RegEdit, select the Run option from the Start menu. Then type `RegEdit`.

The ImplicitCommitSync setting determines whether the system waits for a commit to finish before proceeding with application processing. The default is No. This means that the system will proceed without waiting for the commit to finish. You generally won't want to change this setting; using No dramatically improves performance. The danger of accepting the value of No is that you will increase the amount of time during which the data is vulnerable. Before the data is flushed to disk, the user might turn off the machine, compromising the integrity of the data.

The ExclusiveAsyncDelay setting specifies the maximum number of milliseconds that elapse before Jet commits an implicit transaction when a database is opened for exclusive use. The default value for this setting is 2000 milliseconds. This setting does not in any way affect databases that are open for shared use.

The SharedAsyncDelay setting is similar to the ExclusiveAsyncDelay setting. It determines the maximum number of milliseconds that elapse before Jet commits an implicit transaction when a database is opened for shared use. The default value for this setting is 50. The higher this value, the greater the performance benefits reaped from implicit transactions, but the higher the chances that concurrency problems will result. These concurrency issues are discussed in detail in the section "Using Transaction Processing in a Multiuser Environment," later in this chapter.

In addition to the settings that affect implicit transaction processing in Access 2000, an additional registry setting affects explicit transaction processing. The UserCommitSync setting controls whether explicit transactions are completed synchronously or asynchronously. With the default setting of Yes, control doesn't return from a `CommitTrans` statement until the transactions actually are written to disk, resulting in synchronous transactions. When this value is changed to No, a series of changes are queued, and control returns before the changes are complete.

You can modify the values of these registry settings and other Jet settings by using Regedit.exe (the Registry Editor) for Windows 95/98 or RegEdt32.exe for Windows NT. Changes to this section of the registry affect all applications that use the Jet 4.0 Engine. If you want to affect only your application, you can export the Microsoft Jet portion of the registry tree and import it into your application's registry tree. You then can customize the registry settings for your application. To force your application to load the appropriate registry tree, you must set the `INIPath` property of the `DBEngine` object.

A much simpler approach is to set properties of the ADO `Connection` object; you can specify new settings at runtime for all the previously mentioned registry entries as well as additional entries. A further advantage of this approach is that it will modify (temporarily) registry entries for any machine under which your application runs. Any values you change at runtime temporarily override the registry values that are set, enabling you to easily control and maintain specific settings for each application. This code illustrates how you modify the Exclusive and Shared Async Delay settings using properties of the `Connection` object:

```
Sub ChangeOptions()
    Dim cnn As ADODB.Connection
    Set cnn = CurrentProject.Connection

    cnn.Properties("JET OLEDB:Exclusive Async Delay") = 1000
    cnn.Properties("JET OLEDB:Shared Async Delay") = 50
End Sub
```

IMPLEMENTING EXPLICIT TRANSACTION PROCESSING

Now that you are aware of the settings that affect transaction processing, you are ready to learn how to implement transaction processing. Three methods of the `Connection` object (covered in Chapter 12, "What Are ActiveX Data Objects and Data Access Objects and Why Are They Important?") control transaction processing:

- `BeginTrans`
- `CommitTrans`
- `RollbackTrans`

The `BeginTrans` method of the `Connection` object begins the transaction loop. The moment `BeginTrans` is encountered, Access begins writing all changes to a log file in memory. Unless the `CommitTrans` method is issued on the `Connection` object, the changes are never actually written to the database file. After the `CommitTrans` method is issued, the updates are written permanently to the database object. If a `RollbackTrans` method of the `Connection` object is encountered, the log in memory is released. Listing 22.2 shows an example of how transaction processing works under Access 2000. Compare this to Listing 22.1.

LISTING 22.2   TRANSACTION PROCESSING IN ACCESS 2000 USING `BeginTrans`, LOGGING, `CommitTrans`, AND `RollbackTrans`

```
Sub IncreaseQuantityTrans()
    On Error GoTo IncreaseQuantityTrans_Err
    Dim cnn As ADODB.Connection
    Dim rst As ADODB.Recordset
    Dim boolInTrans As Boolean

    boolInTrans = False
    Set rst = New ADODB.Recordset
```

```
    Set cnn = CurrentProject.Connection
    rst.ActiveConnection = cnn
    rst.CursorType = adOpenKeyset
    rst.LockType = adLockOptimistic
    rst.Open "Select OrderId, Quantity From tblOrderDetails"

    'Begin the Transaction Loop
    cnn.BeginTrans
        boolInTrans = True
        'Loop through recordset increasing Quantity field by 1
        Do Until rst.EOF
            rst!Quantity = rst!Quantity + 1
            rst.UPDATE
            rst.MoveNext
        Loop
        'Commit the Transaction; Everything went as Planned
    cnn.CommitTrans
    boolInTrans = False

IncreaseQuantityTrans_Exit:
    Set cnn = Nothing
    Set rst = Nothing
    Exit Sub

IncreaseQuantityTrans_Err:
    MsgBox "Error # " & Err.Number & ": " & Err.Description
    'Rollback the Transaction; An Error Occurred
    If boolInTrans Then
        cnn.RollbackTrans
    End If
    Resume IncreaseQuantityTrans_Exit
End Sub
```

This code uses a transaction loop to ensure that everything completes as planned or not at all. Notice that the loop which moves through the recordset, increasing the Quantity field in each record by 1, is placed in a transaction loop. If all processing in the loop completes successfully, the CommitTrans method executes. If the error-handling code is encountered, the RollbackTrans method is issued, ensuring that none of the changes are written to disk. The boolInTrans variable is used to determine whether the code is within the transaction loop. This ensures that the error handler performs the rollback only if an error occurs within the transaction loop. If the CommitTrans or RollBackTrans method is issued without an open transaction, an error occurs.

LOOKING AT TRANSACTION PROCESSING ISSUES

Before you decide that transaction processing is the best thing since sliced bread, you should keep in mind several issues concerning transaction processing. These issues are outlined in this section.

Realizing That Transactions Occur in a Workspace

Transactions exist in the context of a `Connection` object. The `BeginTrans`, `CommitTrans`, and `RollbackTrans` methods affect all operations on the specific connection. If you want simultaneous, unrelated transactions to be in effect, you must create separate `Connection` objects in which the transactions are applied. Whereas DAO supported transactions that spanned multiple databases, ADO transactions are limited to a specific data source because they exist in the context of a connection.

Making Sure the Data Source Supports Transactions

Not all data sources support transaction processing. Excel and dBase files, for example, do not support transaction processing. Neither do certain back-end ODBC database servers. When in doubt, you can use the Transaction DDL property of the `Connection` object to determine whether the data source supports transaction processing. If the Transaction DDL property exists and is nonzero, the data source supports transaction processing. To determine whether the property exists, query its value. If the property is nonexistent, an error occurs. Listing 22.3 shows an example of how to determine whether an object supports transaction processing.

LISTING 22.3 DETERMINING WHETHER A CONNECTION SUPPORTS TRANSACTION PROCESSING

```
Sub SupportsTransCurrentDB()
    On Error GoTo SupportsTrans_Err
    Dim cnn As ADODB.Connection
    Dim rst As ADODB.Recordset
    Dim boolSupportsTrans As Boolean
    Dim vntValue As Variant

    boolSupportsTrans = False

    Set cnn = CurrentProject.Connection

    Set rst = New ADODB.Recordset
    rst.ActiveConnection = cnn
    rst.CursorType = adOpenKeyset
```

```
    rst.LockType = adLockOptimistic
    rst.Open "tblOrderDetails"

    'Begin the Transaction Loop Only if Recordset
    'Supports Transaction
    On Error Resume Next
    vntValue = cnn.Properties.Item("Transaction DDL")
    If Not Err.Number And _
        cnn.Properties.Item("Transaction DDL").Value <> 0 Then
        boolSupportsTrans = True
        cnn.BeginTrans
    End If
    On Error Goto SupportsTrans_Err

    'Loop through recordset increasing Quantity field by 1
    Do Until rst.EOF
        rst!Quantity = rst!Quantity - 1
        rst.UPDATE
        rst.MoveNext
    Loop

    'Issue the CommitTrans if Everything went as Planned
    'and Recordset Supports Transactions
    If boolSupportsTrans Then
        cnn.CommitTrans
    End If

SupportsTrans_Exit:
    Set cnn = Nothing
    Set rst = Nothing
    Exit Sub

SupportsTrans_Err:

    MsgBox "Error # " & Err.Number & ": " & Err.Description

    'Rollback the Transaction if An Error Occurred
    'and Recordset Supports Transactions
    If boolSupportsTrans Then
        cnn.RollbackTrans
    End If
    Resume SupportsTrans_Exit

End Sub
```

22

**TRANSACTION
PROCESSING**

The code uses a Boolean variable called `boolSupportsTrans` to track whether the connection supports transactions. Notice the statement `On Error Resume Next`. The Transaction DDL property of the `Connection` object is evaluated. If it does not exist, an error occurs. The next statement tests for a nonzero error number and a nonzero property value. Only if the Transaction DDL property for the `Connection` object exists and is nonzero is the `BeginTrans` issued and the `boolSupportsTrans` variable set equal to `True`. The `boolSupportsTrans` variable is evaluated two different times in the remainder of the routine. The `CommitTrans` method is issued only if `boolSupportsTrans` evaluates to `True`. In the error handling, the `RollbackTrans` method is issued only if the `boolSupportTrans` variable is equal to `True`.

Listing 22.4 shows an example where the data source, an Excel spreadsheet, does not support transactions. Notice that the code uses a data source that references the Excel spreadsheet. A recordset is opened using the `Connection` object. The remainder of the code is similar to Listing 22.3.

LISTING 22.4   DETERMINING WHETHER A CONNECTION BASED ON A NON-ACCESS DATA SOURCE SUPPORTS TRANSACTION PROCESSING

```
Sub SupportsTransOtherDB()
    On Error GoTo SupportsTrans_Err
    Dim cnn As ADODB.Connection
    Dim rst As ADODB.Recordset
    Dim boolSupportsTrans As Boolean
    Dim vntValue As Variant

    boolSupportsTrans = False

    Set cnn = New ADODB.Connection
    cnn.Open "DSN=TestXLS;UID=;PWD=;"

    Set rst = New ADODB.Recordset
    With rst
        .ActiveConnection = cnn
        .CursorType = adOpenKeyset
        .LockType = adLockOptimistic
        .Open "tblCustomers"
    End With

    'Begin the Transaction Loop Only if Recordset
    'Supports Transaction

    On Error Resume Next
    vntValue = cnn.Properties.Item("Transaction DDL")
    If Not Err.Number And _
        cnn.Properties.Item("Transaction DDL").Value <> 0 Then
```

```
        boolSupportsTrans = True
        cnn.BeginTrans
    End If
    On Error GoTo SupportsTrans_Err

    'Loop through recordset increasing Quantity field by 1
    Do Until rst.EOF
        rst!City = "Thousand Oaks"
        rst.UPDATE
        rst.MoveNext
    Loop

    'Issue the CommitTrans if Everything went as Planned
    'and Recordset Supports Transactions
    If boolSupportsTrans Then
        cnn.CommitTrans
    End If

SupportsTrans_Exit:
    Set cnn = Nothing
    Set rst = Nothing
    Exit Sub

SupportsTrans_Err:

    MsgBox "Error # " & Err.Number & ": " & Err.Description

    'Rollback the Transaction if An Error Occurred
    'and Recordset Supports Transactions
    If boolSupportsTrans Then
        cnn.Rollback
    End If
    Resume SupportsTrans_Exit

End Sub
```

CAUTION

When dealing with an application that is linked to a data source that does not support transactions, the Transaction DDL property will not evaluate properly. Because when dealing with linked tables, the connection that you use is that of the Access database, the Transaction DDL property will appear to support transactions. This same behavior is exhibited if the Jet Provider is used to connect to the data source. In either case, no error will occur when the `BeginTrans`, `CommitTrans`, or `RollBackTrans` methods are executed. Instead, the process will appear to complete successfully. If a `RollBackTrans` is issued, no rollback occurs and all changes are retained!

Nesting Transactions

Another issue to be aware of with transactions is that you can nest transactions. The hierarchy for nesting is FIFO. The inner transactions always must be committed or rolled back before the outer transactions. After a `CommitTrans` occurs, you cannot undo changes made to that transaction unless it is nested in another transaction that is itself rolled back. The `BeginTrans` method returns a value indicating the level of nesting. A 1 is returned for a top-level transaction, a 2 for a second-level transaction, and so on.

Neglecting to Explicitly Commit Transactions

When a transaction loop is executing, all updates are written to a log file in memory. If a `CommitTrans` is never executed, the changes are, in effect, rolled back. In other words, a `RollbackTrans` is implicit if the changes are never explicitly written to disk with the `CommitTrans` method. This generally works to your advantage. If the power is interrupted or the machine hangs before the `CommitTrans` is executed, all changes are rolled back. This behavior can get you into trouble if you forget the `CommitTrans` method, however. If the connection is closed without the `CommitTrans` method being executed, the memory log is flushed and the transaction is implicitly rolled back.

Checking Available Memory

Another gotcha with transactions occurs when the physical memory on the computer is exhausted by the transaction log. Access 2000 first attempts to use virtual memory. The transaction log is written to the temporary directory specified by the `TEMP` environment variable of the user's machine. This method dramatically slows down the transaction process. If all memory and the `TEMP` disk space are exhausted by the transaction process, an error 2004 results. You must issue a rollback at this point. Otherwise, you are in danger of violating the integrity of the database.

CAUTION

If your code attempts to commit the transaction after a 2004 error has occurred, the Jet Engine commits as many changes as possible, leaving the database in an inconsistent state. The 2004 error is found using the `SQLState` property of the Errors collection of the `Connection` object.

Using Forms with Transactions

Access handles its own transaction processing on bound forms. You cannot control this transaction processing in any way. If you want to use transaction processing with forms, you must create unbound forms or run code with no form interface.

USING TRANSACTION PROCESSING IN A MULTIUSER ENVIRONMENT

In a multiuser environment, transaction processing has implications beyond the protection of data. By wrapping a process in a transaction loop, you ensure that you are in control of all records involved in the process. The cost of this additional control is reduced concurrency for the rest of the users of the application. Listing 22.5 illustrates this scenario.

LISTING 22.5   A SAFE WAY TO DO TRANSACTIONS IN A MULTIUSER ENVIRONMENT THAT SACRIFICES CONCURRENCY

```
Sub MultiPessimistic()
    On Error GoTo MultiPessimistic_Err
    Dim cnn As ADODB.Connection
    Dim rst As ADODB.Recordset
    Dim intCounter As Integer
    Dim intChoice As Integer
    Dim intTry As Integer
    Dim boolInTrans As Boolean


    boolInTrans = False
    Set rst = New ADODB.Recordset
    Set cnn = CurrentProject.Connection

    rst.ActiveConnection = cnn
    rst.CursorType = adOpenKeyset
    rst.CursorLocation = adUseServer
    rst.LockType = adLockPessimistic
    rst.Open "Select OrderId, ProductID, UnitPrice " & _
        "From tblOrderDetails Where ProductID > 50"

    'Begin the Transaction Loop
    cnn.BeginTrans
        boolInTrans = True
```

continues

22

LISTING 22.5   CONTINUED

```
            'Loop through recordset increasing UnitPrice
            Do Until rst.EOF
                'Lock Occurs Here for Each Record in the Loop
                rst!UnitPrice = rst!UnitPrice * 1.1
                rst.UPDATE
                rst.MoveNext
            Loop
            'Commit the Transaction; Everything went as Planned
            'All locks released for ALL records involved in the Process
        cnn.CommitTrans
        boolInTrans = False
        Set cnn = Nothing
        Set rst = Nothing
        Exit Sub

MultiPessimistic_Err:
    Select Case cnn.Errors(0).SQLState
        Case 3260
        intCounter = intCounter + 1
        If intCounter > 2 Then
            intChoice = MsgBox(Err.Description, _
                vbRetryCancel + vbCritical)
            Select Case intChoice
                Case vbRetry
                    intCounter = 1
                Case vbCancel
                    'User Selected Cancel, Roll Back
                    Resume TransUnsuccessful
            End Select
        End If
        DoEvents
        For intTry = 1 To 100: Next intTry
        Resume
        Case Else
            MsgBox "Error # " & Err.Number & ": " & Err.Description
    End Select

TransUnsuccessful:
    If boolInTrans Then
        cnn.RollbackTrans
    End If
    MsgBox "Warning: Entire Process Rolled Back"
    Set cnn = Nothing
```

```
    Set rst = Nothing
    Exit Sub

End Sub
```

The `MultiPessimistic` routine uses pessimistic locking. This means that each time the data within a record is edited, the edited record is locked. If all goes well and no error occurs, the lock is released when the `CommitTrans` is reached. The error-handling code traps for a 3260 error. This error means that the record is locked by another user. The user running the transaction processing is given the opportunity to retry or cancel. If the user chooses Retry, the code once again tries to edit the data within the record. If the user chooses Cancel, a rollback occurs. This cancels the changes made to all the records involved in the process.

Two key points should be made about the `MultiPessimistic` routine. First, as this routine executes, each record involved in the process is locked. This potentially means that all other users will be unable to edit a large percentage, or even any, of the records until the transaction process finishes. This is wonderful from a data-integrity standpoint, but it might not be practical in an environment where users must update data on a frequent basis. It therefore is a good idea to keep transaction loops as short in duration as possible. Second, if any of the lock attempts are unsuccessful, the entire transaction must be canceled. Once again, this might be what you want or need from a data-integrity standpoint, but it might require that all users refrain from editing data while an important process completes.

With optimistic locking, the lock attempt occurs when the `Update` method is issued rather than when the data is edited. This does not make much of a difference; all the records involved in the transaction remain locked until the `CommitTrans` or `RollbackTrans` occurs. The main difference is in the errors for which you must trap. Listing 22.6 shows the code for using optimistic locking in a multiuser environment.

LISTING 22.6 OPTIMISTIC LOCKING IN A MULTIUSER ENVIRONMENT

```
Sub MultiOptimistic()
    On Error GoTo MultiOptimistic_Err
    Dim cnn As ADODB.Connection
    Dim rst As ADODB.Recordset
    Dim intCounter As Integer
    Dim intChoice As Integer
```

continues

LISTING 22.6   CONTINUED

```
Dim intTry As Integer
Dim boolInTrans As Boolean

boolInTrans = False
Set rst = New ADODB.Recordset
Set cnn = CurrentProject.Connection

rst.ActiveConnection = cnn
rst.CursorType = adOpenKeyset
rst.CursorLocation = adUseServer
rst.LockType = adLockOptimistic
rst.Open "Select OrderId, ProductID, UnitPrice " & _
    "From tblOrderDetails Where ProductID > 50"

'Begin the Transaction Loop
cnn.BeginTrans
    boolInTrans = True
    'Loop through recordset increasing UnitPrice
    Do Until rst.EOF
        rst!UnitPrice = rst!UnitPrice * 1.1
        'Lock Occurs Here for Each Record in the Loop
        rst.UPDATE
        rst.MoveNext
    Loop
    'Commit the Transaction; Everything went as Planned
    'All locks released for ALL records involved in the Process
cnn.CommitTrans
boolInTrans = False
Set cnn = Nothing
Set rst = Nothing
Exit Sub

MultiOptimistic_Err:
    Select Case cnn.Errors(0).SQLState
        Case 3197   'Data Has Changed Error
            If rst.EditMode = adEditInProgress Then
                intChoice = MsgBox("Overwrite Other User's Changes?", _
                vbYesNoCancel + vbQuestion)
                Select Case intChoice
                    Case vbCancel, vbNo
                        MsgBox "Update Canceled"
                        Resume TransNotSuccessful
                    Case vbYes
                        rst.UPDATE
                        Resume
                End Select
            End Select
```

```
            End If
        Case 3186, 3260   'Locked or Can't be Saved
            intCounter = intCounter + 1
            If intCounter > 2 Then
                intChoice = MsgBox(Err.Description, _
                            vbRetryCancel + vbCritical)
                Select Case intChoice
                    Case vbRetry
                        intCounter = 1
                    Case vbCancel
                        'User Selected Cancel, Roll Back
                        Resume TransNotSuccessful
                End Select
            End If
            DoEvents
            For intTry = 1 To 100: Next intTry
            Resume
        Case Else
            MsgBox "Error # " & Err.Number & ": " & Err.Description
    End Select

TransNotSuccessful:
    If boolInTrans Then
        cnn.RollbackTrans
    End If
    MsgBox "Warning: Entire Process Rolled Back"
    Set cnn = Nothing
    Set rst = Nothing
    Exit Sub

End Sub
```

Notice that, in the MultiOptimistic routine, the lock occurs each time the Update method is issued. All the locks are released when the CommitTrans is executed. Furthermore, the error handling checks for a 3197 (data has changed) error. The 3197 occurs when the data is changed by another user between the time the Edit method is issued and just before the Update method is issued.

USING TRANSACTION PROCESSING IN A CLIENT/SERVER ENVIRONMENT

When dealing with transactions in a client/server environment, you must consider several additional issues: when and how transactions occur, what types of transactions are supported, and what types of problems can occur.

Implicit Transactions

When explicit transactions are not used, the way in which transactions are committed on the database server depends on what types of commands are being executed. In general, every line of code has an implicit transaction around it. This means that there is no way to roll back an action because it is committed immediately on the database server. The exceptions to this rule are any SQL statements issued that modify data. These SQL statements (UPDATE, INSERT, and APPEND) are executed in batches; a transaction loop is implicitly placed around the entire statement. If any records involved in the SQL statement cannot be updated successfully, the entire UPDATE, INSERT, or APPEND is rolled back.

Explicit Transactions

When explicit transactions are used, ODBC translates the BeginTrans, CommitTrans, and RollbackTrans methods to the appropriate syntax of the back-end server and the transaction processes as expected. The main exception to this rule is when transactions are not supported by the specific back end you are using. Listing 22.7 shows an example of transaction processing with a SQL Server back end.

LISTING 22.7 TRANSACTION PROCESSING WITH A SQL SERVER BACK END

```
Sub TransSQLServer()
    Dim cnn As ADODB.Connection
    Dim cmd As ADODB.Command
    Dim boolInTrans As Boolean

    boolInTrans = False
    Set cnn = New ADODB.Connection
    Set cmd = New ADODB.Command

    cnn.ConnectionString = "Provider=SQLOLEDB; Data Source=Alexis; " & _
        "Initial Catalog=Pubs; User ID=SA; Password="
    cnn.Open

    cnn.BeginTrans
        boolInTrans = True
        cmd.ActiveConnection = cnn
        cmd.CommandText = "UPDATE sales Set qty = qty + 1 " & _
            "Where Stor_ID = '7067';"
        cmd.CommandType = adCmdText
        cmd.Execute
        cmd.CommandText = "Update titles Set price = price + 1 " & _
            "Where Type = 'Business'"
        cmd.CommandType = adCmdText
```

```
        cmd.Execute
    cnn.CommitTrans
    boolInTrans = False

TransSQLServer_Exit:
    Set cnn = Nothing
    Set cmd = Nothing
    Exit Sub

TransSQLServer_Err:
    MsgBox "Error # " & Err.Number & ": " & Err.Description
    If boolInTrans Then
        cnn.Rollback
    End If
    Resume TransSQLServer_Exit
End Sub
```

The `TransSQLServer` routine begins by creating both `Connection` and `Command` object variables. Next, it executes the `BeginTrans` method on the connection. It creates a temporary query definition. The `ConnectionString` property of the `Connection` object is set to point at a SQL Server database called Pubs. The connection is opened using the `Open` method of the `Connection` object. The `BeginTrans` method of the `Connection` object is used to initiate the transaction loop. Several properties are set for the `Command` object, including the `ActiveConnection`, `CommandText`, and `CommandType` property. After these properties are set, the temporary query is executed. The `CommandText` property of the query definition is modified and the query is executed again. If both `Execute` methods complete successfully, the `CommitTrans` method is issued on the `Connection` object. If any error occurs during processing, the `RollbackTrans` method is issued.

TIP

Listing 22.7 provides an example of using transactions when going against data stored in Microsoft SQL Server. Using ADO recordsets to update client/server data is very inefficient. As discussed in Chapter 19, "Client/Server Techniques," it is almost always preferable to update client/server data using stored procedures.

Lock Limits

A potential pitfall when dealing with client/server databases involves lock limits. Many database servers impose strict limits on how many records can be locked concurrently. As you saw in Listings 22.2 and 22.3, a transaction loop can potentially lock a significant number of records. It is important to consider the maximum number of locks supported by your back end when using transaction loops in your VBA code. This problem is eliminated by using stored procedures to update your client/server data.

Negative Interactions with Server-Specific Transaction Commands

You should never use the server-specific transaction commands when building pass-through queries. These server-specific commands can conflict with the `BeginTrans`, `CommitTrans`, and `RollbackTrans` methods, causing confusion and potential data corruption.

PRACTICAL EXAMPLES

Improving the Integrity of the Time and Billing Application Using Transaction Processing

As you continue to develop the Time and Billing application, you might find it necessary to use VBA code to accomplish certain tasks. These tasks might require that several processes complete successfully or not at all. As these situations arise, you should consider placing them in a transaction loop. An example of such a situation is the frmArchivePayments form, as shown in Figure 22.1. frmArchivePayments enables the user to specify a date range. This date range is used as the criterion to determine what data is sent to the tblPaymentsArchive table and removed from the tblPayments table. When this process is run, you want to ensure that the process runs in its entirety or not at all. Listing 22.8 shows transaction loop code suitable for Time and Billing.

FIGURE 22.1

The frmArchivePayments form enables the user to specify a date range of payments to be archived.

LISTING 22.8   A TRANSACTION LOOP SUITABLE FOR THE TIME AND BILLING APPLICATION

```
Sub cmdArchivePayments_Click()
    On Error GoTo Err_cmdArchivePayments_Click

    Dim cnn As ADODB.Connection
    Dim strSQL As String
    Dim boolInTrans As Boolean

    boolInTrans = False

    Set cnn = CurrentProject.Connection

    cnn.BeginTrans
        boolInTrans = True
        strSQL = "INSERT INTO tblPaymentsArchive" & _
            " SELECT DISTINCTROW tblPayments.* " & _
            " FROM tblPayments " & _
            " WHERE tblPayments.PaymentDate Between #" & _
            Me!txtStartDate & _
            "# And #" & _
            Me!txtEndDate & "#;"
        cnn.Execute strSQL
        strSQL = "DELETE DISTINCTROW tblPayments.PaymentDate " & _
            "FROM tblPayments " & _
            " WHERE tblPayments.PaymentDate Between #" & _
            Me!txtStartDate & _
            "# And #" & _
            Me!txtEndDate & "#;"
        cnn.Execute strSQL
    cnn.CommitTrans
    boolInTrans = False

Exit_cmdArchivePayments_Click:
    Exit Sub

Err_cmdArchivePayments_Click:
    MsgBox Err.Description
    If boolInTrans Then
        cnn.RollbackTrans
    End If
    Resume Exit_cmdArchivePayments_Click

End Sub
```

This routine uses the BeginTrans method of the Connection object to initiate a transaction loop. A SQL statement is built, using the values of the txtStartDate and txtEndDate controls on the form as criteria for the SQL statement. This SQL statement adds all records in the specified date range to the tblPaymentsArchive table. The Execute method is applied to the Connection object, using the SQL string as an argument. The SQL string then is modified to build a statement that deletes all records in the specified date range from the tblPayments table. If both SQL statements execute successfully, the CommitTrans method is executed, committing both transactions. If an error occurs, the whole transaction is rolled back.

SUMMARY

If transactions are used properly, you can gain many benefits from them. Transactions help ensure that all parts of a logical piece of work complete successfully or not at all. In some situations, they also can improve performance. You must be aware of several issues when using transactions. The potential pitfalls vary, depending on whether you are issuing a transaction in a multiuser Access environment or in a client/server environment. If you take all mitigating factors into account, you can ensure that transactions provide you with the data integrity you expect from them.

REPLICATION MADE EASY

IN THIS CHAPTER

WHY THIS CHAPTER IS IMPORTANT

Access 95 was the first desktop database that included built-in replication capabilities. Replication has further matured with the introduction of Access 2000; it's a powerful feature that is becoming increasingly important in today's world of mobile and distributed computing. This chapter teaches you about replication and how to implement it through both the user interface and code.

USES OF REPLICATION

Data replication is the capability of a system to automatically make copies of its data and application objects in remote locations. Any changes to the original or data changes to the copies are propagated to all other copies. Data replication allows users to make changes to data offline at remote locations. Changes to either the original or the remote data are synchronized with other instances of the database.

The original database is referred to as the *design master*. Changes to definitions of tables or other application objects can be made only at the design master. The design master is used to make special copies called *replicas*. Although there is only one design master, replicas can make other replicas. The process of the design master and replicas sharing changes is referred to as *synchronization*. The design master and replicas that participate in the synchronization process are collectively referred to as a *replica set*.

To see an example of data replication at work, say you have a team of salespeople who are out on the road all day. At the end of the day, each salesperson logs on to one of the company's Windows NT servers through DUN (Dial-Up Networking) or RAS (Remote Access Services). Each salesperson's transactions are sent to the server. If necessary, any changes to the server data are also sent to the salesperson. In addition to data being replicated, if the developers in the organization are busily adding forms, reports, and modules to the database's master copy, any changes to the application components are also updated in the remote copies as users log on to the system.

This example illustrates just one of the several valuable uses of replication. In a nutshell, data replication is used to improve the availability and integrity of data throughout an organization or enterprise. The practical uses of data replication are many; they can be categorized into five general areas, explained in the following sections.

Sharing Data Among Offices

In today's global economy, it's the norm for companies to have many offices distributed throughout the country, or even the world. Before Access 95, it was difficult to implement an Access application that would support sharing data among several offices. However, with replication, each office can have a replica of the database. Periodically throughout the day, each office can synchronize its changes with corporate headquarters. How often the synchronization happens depends on the frequency required for data at each location to be current at any given moment.

Sharing Data Among Dispersed Users

Sharing data among dispersed users is illustrated by the salesperson example used earlier. This implementation of replication generally involves mobile users who connect to the network after modifying data out on the road. Because only incremental changes are transferred from the design master (the original) to the replicas (the copies), and from the replicas to the design master, this form of replication makes the mobile computing scenario economically feasible.

Reducing Network Load

Replication can be very effective in reducing network traffic loads. The design master can be replicated onto one or more additional servers. Distributed users can then make changes to one of the additional servers, which significantly improves performance by distributing the processing load throughout the network. Changes made to the data on the additional servers can be synchronized with the main server periodically during the day. How often synchronization occurs depends on the need for data to be current at any moment in time.

Distributing Application Updates

Replication is an excellent vehicle for distributing application updates. Design changes can be made only to the design master; therefore, as users throughout the organization log on to synchronize with the design master, any structural changes to the application are sent to the user. This is much more efficient and effective than giving every user an entirely new copy of the application database each time a minor change is made to the application's schema.

Backing Up the Data in Your Application

Many people don't think of replication as a means of backing up application data, but replication is extremely well suited for this task. Ordinarily, to back up an Access database, everyone must log off the system, but that's not necessary with replication. The synchronization process can occur periodically during the day while users are still logged on to the system, and all changes are replicated. Not only is this more efficient than backing up the entire database, it also ensures that you can quickly be up and running on a backup server if there's a problem on a server.

UNDERSTANDING WHEN REPLICATION ISN'T APPROPRIATE

Despite the many positive aspects of replication, it is not appropriate in a few situations, such as when data consistency is critical. If an application requires that data be current at every given moment, it isn't a good candidate for replication. Replication is also not effective when a large volume of existing records are modified throughout the day by many different users. In a situation like this, resolving conflicts that happen when multiple users update the same record wouldn't be practical. Furthermore, you cannot utilize replication if you are using Visual SourceSafe to manage the development process. Finally, you cannot rename or move design masters, and a design master that becomes corrupted can be difficult to recover.

UNDERSTANDING THE IMPLEMENTATION OF REPLICATION

The following steps compose the replication process:

1. Making a database replicable.
2. Creating and distributing replicas.
3. Synchronizing replicas with the design master.
4. Resolving conflicts.

These steps can be done in the following ways:

- Through the Access user interface
- By using the Windows Briefcase
- By using the Replication Manager
- By using ADO code

The steps needed for the replication process, and the alternatives for performing each step, are covered in this chapter. An overview of each alternative is outlined in the following sections.

The Access User Interface

The Access user interface gives you a series of menu items that allow you to perform all the steps of the replication process. The Tools | Replication menu has the following options: Create Replica, Synchronize Now, Partial Replica Wizard, Resolve Conflict, and Recover Design Master. These menu options are covered throughout this chapter.

Briefcase Replication

The Windows Briefcase supplies the foundation Access needs for the replication process. Users can simply drag a database file to the Briefcase to replicate it, make changes to the file while on the road, and synchronize the replica with the design master when they reconnect to the network. This is done because when Access 2000 is installed, it registers a special class ID with the Windows Briefcase. When a database is dragged to the Briefcase, the Briefcase's Reconciler code is called. When the user selects Update Selection or Update All from the Briefcase menu, the Merge Reconciler is called. Briefcase replication is available as an installation option through Windows 95, its successors, and Windows NT 4.0.

The Replication Manager

The Replication Manager is a sophisticated tool that's part of Microsoft Office 2000 Developer. It's a mandatory player in the replication process when you're managing many replicas. Besides providing basic replication functionality, the Replication Manager lets you schedule the synchronization of replicas. In fact, the Replication Manager allows you to manage and intricately control all aspects of the replication process. The Replication Manager is covered in more detail in the section "Using the Replication Manager."

ADO Code

Most aspects of the replication process can also be done by using ADO code, which can be used to make a database replicable, create and synchronize replicas, and get and set properties of a replicable database. ADO can easily be integrated with the other methods of replication. Although it requires the most time and effort on your part, ADO code lets you base replication on events rather than time and give your users a custom user interface for the replication process.

Programs That Support Replication Using ADO

Visual Basic 4.0 and higher, Excel for Windows 95 and higher, and Visual C++ all support replication using Data Access Objects. You can't perform replication with these products by using either the Briefcase or Microsoft Office Developer, however, so it's easier to manage the replication process on a machine that has Access installed.

23

REPLICATION MADE EASY

UNDERSTANDING THE REPLICATION ARCHITECTURE: WHAT MAKES REPLICATION TICK?

Now that you know what replication is and what alternatives you have for implementing it, you're ready to learn about what makes it happen. Six components are responsible for the replication process:

- Tracking Layer
- Microsoft Replication Manager
- Synchronizer
- File System Transport
- Briefcase Reconciler
- Registry Entries

The Tracking Layer

The Tracking Layer refers to the part of the Jet Engine that's capable of tracking and recording all the changes made to the design master and to each of the replicas. It's responsible for making sure changes are available to be transmitted to other replicas.

The Microsoft Replication Manager

The Replication Manager gives you the tools needed to support the replication process. It can also be used to generate reports on synchronization activity.

The Synchronizer

If you use the Briefcase or the Access user interface to manage the replication process, Jet handles the exchange of information between the replicas. If you use the Replication Manager to manage the replication process, the Synchronizer is responsible for monitoring the changes and handling the exchange of data between replicas.

When you're using the Replication Manager, each replica is assigned a Synchronizer. The Synchronizer performs either direct or indirect synchronization between the members of a replica set. When synchronization is initiated, the Synchronizer tries to make a direct connection with the target member of the replica set. If both members of the replica set can be opened simultaneously by the Synchronizer, direct synchronization occurs, which means that changes from one member of the replica set are applied directly to the other member.

If the Synchronizer determines that the target replica set member isn't available, indirect synchronization takes place. There are many reasons why the target replica set member might be unavailable; some possible reasons why a direct connection can't be established include the following:

- The network server where the replica resides is down.
- The computer containing the other replica is logged off the network.
- The other member is currently involved in another synchronization.
- The other member is not in a shared folder.

Regardless of the cause of an indirect synchronization, the Synchronizer for the first member of the replica set leaves a message for the Synchronizer assigned to the member of the unavailable replica set. This message is stored in a shared folder on the network that acts as a drop-box location for the target member. All messages sent while a member of the replica set is unavailable are stored in the drop-box location.

NOTE

If you need to determine whether a direct or indirect synchronization occurred, you can browse the MSysExchangeLog system table. This table, included only in replicated databases, is covered in the section of this chapter titled "System Tables Added to the Database."

The Synchronizer is configured through the Replication Manager user interface and is covered in more detail in the section "Using the Replication Manager."

The File System Transport

The File System Transport is responsible for supplying messaging services to the Synchronizer.

The Briefcase Reconciler

The Briefcase Reconciler is another integral component of the replication architecture. As mentioned, it makes sure that a database is replicable and manages the merging of changes between the Briefcase replica and the Desktop replica.

The Registry Entries

Several Windows Registry entries are responsible for helping with the replication process; a couple are shown in Figure 23.1. Notice the Transporter subkey under the HKEY_LOCAL_MACHINE\SOFTWARE\Microsoft\Jet\4.0 key. This entry contains important path information used by the Replication Manager and the Synchronizer. The Briefcase Reconciler uses entries under HKEY_CLASSES_ROOT\CLSID. Note that although the name has changed to Synchronizer, the key in the registry remains Transporter.

FIGURE 23.1
Replication and the Windows Registry.

UNDERSTANDING REPLICATION TOPOLOGIES

The topology for data synchronization determines which replicas synchronize with each other. The *topology* is essentially a blueprint for how the changes are merged between the members of the replica set. Different topologies are used for different situations, and the topology you choose is determined by your business needs and your organization's design. The synchronization topologies are star, ring, fully connected, linear, and hybrid. (See Figure 23.2.)

Star Topology

With the star topology, a single hub periodically synchronizes with the rest of the replicas. The biggest advantage of this topology is simplicity and ease of programming. Another is that data doesn't have to travel very far. Each replica synchronizes with only one other database, the hub. However, this isn't particularly reliable. If the controlling replica is damaged or unavailable, the synchronization process can't take place. Another disadvantage of the star topology is that the first replica to synchronize with the hub gets no data from the other replicas, but the last replica to synchronize with the hub receives all the data from the others. Issuing two rounds of synchronization can circumvent this problem. Finally, the star topology can't be used with a large number of replicas because the entire load is placed on the hub.

FIGURE 23.2

Examples of replication topologies.

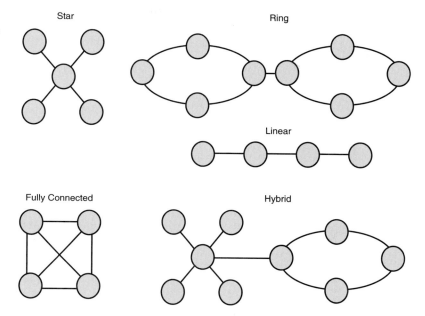

Star

Ring

Linear

Fully Connected

Hybrid

> **NOTE**
>
> The design master must never be a hub. If you designate it as the hub, it's possible for partial design changes to be accidentally synchronized to the rest of the replicas. Instead, place the design master on one of the satellite machines and synchronize design changes with the controlling replica whenever they're complete and fully tested.

Ring Topology

With the ring topology, each computer synchronizes with the next computer in the replication chain. There's no central point of synchronization in this scenario. The major advantage of the ring topology is that the load is distributed throughout the satellite machines. The primary disadvantage is that it might take a long time for changes to be distributed throughout the replicas because there's no central point of synchronization. Furthermore, if one of the replicas in the chain is damaged or unavailable, the replication process stops, but this can be handled by using code that senses the problem and bypasses the unavailable machine.

Fully Connected Topology

When the fully connected topology is used, every replica synchronizes with every other replica. This topology offers several advantages. Its strongest point is that it makes sure data is the most current at any given moment because data is sent directly from each replica to all the other replicas in the replica set. For this reason, it's the best solution when the data must be as current as possible. Another benefit of the fully connected topology is its high level of redundancy. This means that the same data exists in multiple places. Also, because of the low level of *latency* (which means that at any given moment, it's likely the data isn't current) in the fully connected topology, the effect of any one of the replicas failing is minimal. The fully connected topology does have disadvantages, however. It requires the most overhead of any of the topologies because of the network traffic generated as each replica in the set synchronizes with all the others. Furthermore, the replication schedules must be staggered; otherwise, collisions will probably happen as more than one replica tries to synchronize with the same replica.

Linear Topology

The linear topology is similar to the ring topology except that the chain is never completed. For this reason, the linear topology has the highest level of latency. The biggest advantage of the linear topology is the low level of network traffic generated; however, this topology isn't practical for most applications because it takes more time for changes to reach all the replicas in the set.

Hybrid Topology

A hybrid topology is any combination of the other topologies. In a complex application, it's usually not appropriate to use a single topology by itself. By combining the topologies, you can get exactly the results you need. Figure 23.2 illustrates just one example of a hybrid topology—a ring connected with a star. You should experiment with the different configurations to see which topology best balances processing load, network traffic, and data latency.

CHANGES THAT REPLICATION MAKES TO YOUR DATABASE

Replication makes several changes to the database, but they're necessary to manage the demands of the replication process. The following changes are made to a database when it's replicated:

- Fields are added to each replicated table.
- Several system tables are added to the database.
- Properties are added to the database document objects.

- Sequential AutoNumber fields are changed to random AutoNumber fields.
- The size of the database increases.

Fields Added to Each Replicated Table

During the replication process, the Jet Engine determines whether each table has a field with an AutoNumber data type and a ReplicationID field size. If it doesn't find a field meeting these criteria, it adds a field called s_Guid to the table that uniquely identifies each record. It's identical across replicas.

The Jet Engine also adds three additional fields to each table in the database: s_Lineage, s_ColLineage, and s_Generation. The s_Lineage field stores the IDs of replicas that have updated a record and the last version created by those replicas; the s_Generation field stores information about groups of changes. These fields are visible only if you opt to view system objects (use Tools | Options).

System Tables Added to the Database

The Jet Engine also adds several tables to your database that track conflicts, errors, and exchanges made between the replica databases. MSysSideTables and MSysExchangeLog are the most useful of these tables; they can be viewed if you have chosen to view system objects (using Tools | Options).

MSysSidetable tracks tables that have experienced a conflict during the synchronization process. It stores the name of the side table that has the conflicting records.

MSysErrors tracks all unresolved synchronization errors. It's empty when all errors have been resolved. This table can be found in all the replicas.

MSysSchemaProb identifies errors that happened while synchronizing a replica's design. It's visible only if a design conflict has occurred between the user's replica and another replica in the set.

MSysExchangeLog is a local table that stores information about synchronizations that have taken place between the local replica and other members of the replica set.

Properties Added to the Database Objects

Several new properties are added to a replicable database, some of which are available only in VBA code. The database's Replicable property is set to True, and this property cannot be modified after it's set to True. The ReplicaID property is a unique ID assigned to each replica. The DesignMasterID property can transfer the design master status to another database, which is generally done only if the original master becomes irreparably damaged.

23

REPLICATION
MADE EASY

In addition to the properties that apply to the database, two properties can be applied to the tables, queries, forms, reports, macros, and modules in the database: the KeepLocal and Replicable properties. The KeepLocal property, applied to an object before the database is replicated, prevents the object from being copied to the other replicas in the set. The Replicable property, used after a database is replicated, indicates that the object will be replicated.

Changes to Sequential AutoNumber Fields

Another important change made to your tables when replicating a database is that all the Autonumber fields are changed from incremental to random. Existing records aren't affected, but new keys are generated randomly because that reduces conflicts when the databases are synchronized. If all the copies generate sequential keys, you can see that conflicts will happen when you try to merge changes. By randomly generating primary keys, this conflict is much less likely to take place.

Changes to the Size of the Database

When a database is replicated, its size increases because of the added fields and tables. Generally, this increase isn't a problem. If disk space is at a premium, you should consider this aspect of replication before you decide to build replication into your application.

MAKING A DATABASE REPLICABLE

A replicable database is simply a database whose Replicable property has been set to True. If a database hasn't been marked as replicable, you can't replicate it. However, when a database has been flagged as replicable, the Jet Engine makes several changes to it to render it replicable. Until these changes are made, the database isn't recognized as part of a replication set and can't be synchronized with other databases.

When you're ready to replicate a database, you should take the following steps:

1. Flag any objects in the database that you don't want replicated as local by setting their KeepLocal property to True.
2. Make a replication design master by setting the database's Replicable property to True.
3. Make copies of the design master, called replicas.

You can make a database replicable by using the Access user interface, using the Windows Briefcase, using the Replication Manager, or writing code. The following two sections cover using the Access user interface and the Windows Briefcase. Making a database replicable by using the Replication Manager is covered in the section "Using the Replication Manager"; using code is covered in the section "Implementing Replication Using Code."

Rendering a Database Replicable with the Access User Interface

Choose Tools|Replication|Create Replica. Microsoft Access gives you a warning that it must close the database before proceeding. (See Figure 23.3.)

FIGURE 23.3

This dialog box warns you that Access must close the database before converting it to a design master.

After selecting Yes, you see another dialog box asking whether you want Access to make a backup of the original database before continuing. (See Figure 23.4.) It's always a good idea to back up a database before replicating it because a database can't be returned to its nonreplicable state after it's flagged as replicable.

FIGURE 23.4

This dialog box prompts you to have Access create a backup of the database before it's replicated.

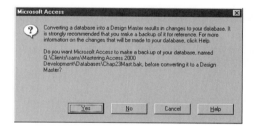

Next, you're prompted for the name and location of your new replica in the Location of New Replica dialog box. (See Figure 23.5.) After you click OK, the new replica is created and the process is finished.

Your original database is converted to a design master, and the replica is assigned the name and location specified in the Location of New Replica dialog box. If the replication process is completed successfully, the dialog box shown in Figure 23.6 appears. Notice that only the design master can accept changes to the database structure (schema).

FIGURE 23.5

The Location of New Replica dialog box allows you to specify a location and name for the replica.

FIGURE 23.6

This dialog box appears after successful replication of a database.

Rendering a Database Replicable with the Windows Briefcase

Instead of using the Access user interface to replicate a database, you can use the Windows Briefcase. All you need to do is drag and drop the database file from Windows Explorer to the Briefcase icon on your desktop; select Make Sync Copy; then you see the dialog box shown in Figure 23.7.

FIGURE 23.7

This dialog box appears after you drag and drop a database to the Briefcase to be replicated.

Except for the final message you get, you see the same series of messages as you do when you choose Replication from the Tools menu in the Access user interface. Only one database can be used to make design changes, such as modifying table structures. The Briefcase dialog box, shown in Figure 23.8, asks which database you want to keep as the design master. Generally, you select the Original Copy rather than the Briefcase Copy. You do this because the briefcase copy is generally used only as a means to add, edit, and delete data when on the road.

FIGURE 23.8

The final dialog box you see during Briefcase replication offers you the choice of which copy you want to use for the design master.

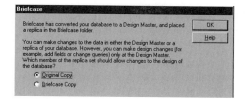

PREVENTING OBJECTS FROM BEING REPLICATED

You might want to prevent specific objects in a replicable database from being replicated if, for example, certain data in your database is confidential or it's unnecessary for most users to see certain data. An employee salary table, for example, might be maintained and used in the master but isn't necessary for any of the replicas. The fewer objects that are replicated, the more effective the synchronization process is.

In the Access user interface, you can check the Make Replicable check box in the Save As dialog when you create a new object, as shown in Figure 23.9 (if unchecked, the new object is local), or you can change the Replicable property of an existing object in its properties sheet, as shown in Figure 23.10. Replicated objects are indicated by an icon of a globe with rotating arrows in the objects lists in the Access database window.

FIGURE 23.9

Making a new object replicable in the Save As dialog.

FIGURE 23.10

Changing an object's Replicable property in its properties sheet.

You can also change the Replicable property by using VBA code or the Replication Manager. To do this, set the KeepLocal property of the specific objects to True. When you try to set the KeepLocal property to True with VBA code, you get an error unless you have already appended the property onto the object. You must, therefore, include error handling in your code to handle this problem. Using the Replication Manager to flag an object as nonreplicable is covered in the section "Replicating a Database with the Replication Manager." The code required to add the KeepLocal property to an object and set its value to True is covered in the section "Implementing Replication Using Code."

CREATING ADDITIONAL REPLICAS

After you have made one replica, you'll probably want to make more. These additional replicas are copies that can be distributed throughout the organization. They can be created by using the Access user interface, the Windows Briefcase, the Replication Manager, or VBA code.

A sales organization, for example, might use multiple replicas for sales reps who take copies of the database along on their notebook computers. Each of these copies must be a replica created by the replication process rather than a copy made by the operating system. Otherwise, the work of each salesperson can't be synchronized with that of the others.

Replicas can be made with any of the four methods mentioned, but additional replicas can also be made from any member of a replica set. Each replica set is independent from all other replica sets. Replicas from different sets can't be synchronized with one another.

Creating Additional Replicas with the Access User Interface

To create additional replicas with the Access user interface, follow these steps:

1. Open the database you want to replicate. You can open either the design master or any replica.
2. Choose Tools | Replication | Create Replica.
3. When prompted, supply a name for the new replica.

Creating Additional Replicas with the Windows Briefcase

You can also make more replicas by dragging and dropping the design master—or any one of the replicas—to the Briefcase. If you drag and drop the design master to the Briefcase, you're prompted with a dialog box asking whether you want the design master or the replica to be placed in the Briefcase.

SYNCHRONIZING REPLICAS

Synchronizing replicas means reconciling all the changes between them. Modified records are changed in all the copies, deleted records are removed from all the replicas, and added records are appended to all the replicas.

The ability to synchronize is what makes data replication useful. Additions, modifications, and deletions are propagated among all the replicas in a set, which lets users see the changes other users made.

As with creating a replica, Access gives you four methods of synchronizing replicas: the Access user interface, the Windows Briefcase, the Replication Manager, or VBA code.

Synchronizing Databases with the Access User Interface

To perform synchronization with the Access user interface, follow these steps:

1. Choose Tools | Replication | Synchronize Now.
2. The Synchronize Database dialog box opens. (See Figure 23.11.) Select the database you want to synchronize with and click OK.

FIGURE 23.11

The Synchronize Database dialog box lets you select the database you want to synchronize with.

3. You're prompted to allow Access to close the database prior to synchronization (see Figure 23.12). If you select Yes, Access closes and reopens the database for you.

FIGURE 23.12

This dialog box confirms that you will allow Access to close the database prior to synchronization.

Synchronizing Databases with the Windows Briefcase

The second way to synchronize replicas is by using the Windows Briefcase. Simply open the Briefcase window and select the database file. On the Briefcase menu, click Update Selection. If you want to synchronize all the replicas in the Briefcase, click Update All to open the Update My Briefcase dialog box. (See Figure 23.13.) Click Update, and the synchronization process is finished.

RESOLVING REPLICATION CONFLICTS

When the Jet Engine tries to synchronize two databases, it might find that the same row has been changed in both databases, so a conflict results that must be handled. The rule is that the database in which the row has changed most often wins. If both rows have changed the same number of times, the winner is chosen randomly. This might sound frightening, but it isn't as bad is it seems because you can let the user know which changes were rejected.

You must know whether two members of the replica set contain conflicting information. Two users out in the field might have entered different information about a sale or a customer, so it's important that the program identify these inconsistencies and have a method for handling them.

If there are conflicts, you're warned about them when you try to open the database that has the conflicts. (See Figure 23.14.) Here, you're given the choice of whether to resolve the conflicts or not.

FIGURE 23.14

This dialog box warns of synchronization conflicts.

If the user selects Yes, the Jet Engine tries to identify the conflicts. After identifying the conflicts, the Microsoft Replication Conflict Viewer dialog box, shown in Figure 23.15, appears. Notice that in this example, the Jet Engine identified a conflict in the tblClients table. The user can either resolve the conflict or postpone the conflict resolution.

FIGURE 23.15

Use the Microsoft Replication Conflict Viewer dialog box to resolve conflicts between tables.

If the user clicks View, another Microsoft Replication Conflict Viewer dialog box opens. (See Figure 23.16.) This dialog box shows the user each record that has a conflict, providing the opportunity to keep existing data, keep revised data, overwrite with conflicting data, or overwrite with revised data.

FIGURE 23.16

In this Resolve Replication Conflicts dialog box, you view and resolve specific conflicts.

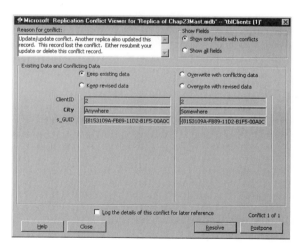

The user can log the details of the conflict for later reference. The user can resolve or postpone the resolution of each conflict. After responding to all conflicts, the user is returned to the Microsoft Replication Conflict Viewer dialog.

> **NOTE**
>
> If you don't want to give your users this level of control over conflict resolution, you can write code to resolve conflicts in any way you want. This is covered in the section "Synchronizing a Database Using Code."

USING THE REPLICATION MANAGER

The Replication Manager is a powerful tool that lets you take full advantage of replication in Access 2000. It's included only with Microsoft Office 2000 Developer, as one of the Developer Tools. The Replication Manager's major benefits include the following:

- Lets you easily replicate a database
- Allows you to easily create additional replicas
- Gives you the ability to synchronize any replicas in the set
- Allows you to schedule automated synchronization
- Gives you the opportunity to view an object's replication history
- Lets you easily manage replication properties
- Offers a way to manage synchronization with replicas at remote sites
- Allows you to perform synchronization over a LAN, an intranet, or the Internet

Running the Replication Manager for the First Time

The Replication Manager can be opened by using a Desktop shortcut or through the Windows Start menu, where it is located in the Microsoft Office 2000 Developer program group. The first time you run the Replication Manager, the Configure Replication Manager Wizard appears. (See Figure 23.17.)

1. Click Next > to start the configuration process and launch the Configure Replication Manager Wizard.

FIGURE **23.17**
*The Configure
Replication
Manager Wizard.*

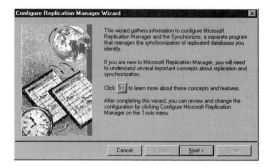

2. This step of the Configure Replication Manager Wizard asks whether you want to support indirect synchronization (see Figure 23.18). With indirect synchronization, a
Synchronizer for each of two replicas opens its own replica locally. A desktop computer
leaves changes in a drop box on the network. When the laptop connects to the network,
the Synchronizer on the laptop finds the changes in its drop-box folder and applies them
to the replica. The notebook leaves its changes in a drop-box folder of the desktop
Synchronizer, which finds the changes and applies them. This is the preferred synchronization method for remote users who aren't always logged on to the network. Make
your selection and click Next.

FIGURE **23.18**
*Selecting a form of
synchronization.*

3. If you choose to support indirect synchronization, the next step of the wizard gives you
some information about Synchronization types. After reading this, click next and the
wizard prompts you for a location for the drop-box folder. (See Figure 23.19.) Select a
folder and click Next.

23

REPLICATION
MADE EASY

FIGURE 23.19

Selecting a location for the Synchronizer to store changes.

4. You're then asked whether the computer on which you're running the wizard is an Internet server. Make your selection and click Next.

5. If you indicate that the computer is an Internet server, the next step asks whether you want to use the Internet server to synchronize replicated databases. If you respond Yes and click Next, you're prompted for the name of the Internet server. Enter the name and click Next. (See Figure 23.20.) The next step asks you to provide a Shared folder and Share name used when synchronizing over the Internet. Click Next and you're prompted for an FTP alias name. Select the FTP alias name and click Next.

FIGURE 23.20

If your computer is an Internet server, here's the place to tell the wizard its partial URL.

6. The next step of the Configure Replication Manager wizard prompts you to designate the order in which the synchronization methods are attempted. The example shown in Figure 23.21 shows that Indirect Synchronization will be attempted. If it does not succeed, Direct Synchronization will be attempted. Finally, Internet Synchronization will be attempted.

7. Select a location for the log file used to record significant events that happen during the synchronization process. (See Figure 23.22.) Click Next.

FIGURE 23.21

Select the order in which each synchronization method is attempted.

FIGURE 23.22

Selecting the name and location for the log file.

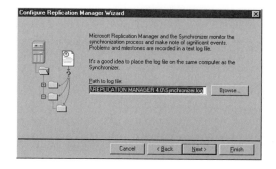

8. The next step of the wizard prompts you for a Synchronizer name. This name is used for an icon and as a descriptive name for the Synchronizer. This step of the wizard also asks whether you want to automatically start the Synchronizer when Windows starts. (See Figure 23.23.) The Synchronizer must be running for scheduled synchronization to take place, so you might want to select this option. Enter a Synchronizer name and indicate whether you want the Synchronizer to automatically start; then click Next.

FIGURE 23.23

Selecting a name for the Synchronizer.

9. Click Finish to complete the process.

23

REPLICATION MADE EASY

After the Configure Replication Manager Wizard is finished, you can either convert a database to a design master or create a new replica. (See Figure 23.24.) You can perform these tasks any time, so you should click Close.

FIGURE 23.24

The Microsoft Replication Manager launches for the first time.

NOTE

If you opted to load the Synchronizer whenever you launch Windows, and you decide that you don't want the Synchronizer to be launched automatically, you must remove the Synchronizer icon from the Windows Startup folder.

Replicating a Database with the Replication Manager

In addition to using the Access user interface and the Briefcase to make a database replicable, you can also use the Replication Manager. It offers additional options, such as designating an object as local. Here are the steps:

1. From the Replication Manager, click the Convert Database to the Design Master toolbar button or choose File | Convert Database to Design Master. The Database to Convert to the Design Master dialog appears. (See Figure 23.25.)

FIGURE 23.25

Select the database you want to convert to a design master.

2. Select a file to convert and click Open.

3. The Convert Database to Design Master wizard appears. Click Next after reading the introductory information.

4. Indicate whether you want to make a backup of the database before converting it to a design master. Then click Next. It's always a good idea to keep a backup of the unreplicated database.

5. Enter a description for the new replica set and click Next. All replicas made from this design master will be members of the replica set you're creating. (See Figure 23.26.)

FIGURE 23.26

Entering a description for the replica set.

6. You're then asked whether you want to make all objects available to the replica set or flag some of them as local. (See Figure 23.27.) If you click Make Some Objects Available to the Entire Replica Set and click the Choose Objects button, the Select Replicated Objects dialog box opens, so you can designate selected objects as local. (See Figure 23.28.) To flag an object as local, clear its check box. Click OK when you're finished.

FIGURE 23.27

Designating whether you want all or just some objects to be replicated.

FIGURE 23.28

*Flagging objects
as local or
replicated.*

7. Next, indicate whether you want the replicas to be read-only. (See Figure 23.29.) The design master is the only place where you can make schema changes. If you want to limit data changes to the design master as well, select the option that makes all replicas read-only. In general, you should keep the default option of I Want to be Able to Create Read/Write Replicas. Click Next after you make a selection.

FIGURE 23.29

*Indicating
whether the data-
base will allow
read/write repli-
cas to be created.*

8. The next step of the wizard asks whether you want to manage synchronization of the design master with the Synchronizer found on the current machine. If you answer No, synchronization must originate by another managed member of the replica set. Make your selection and click Next.

9. Click Finish to complete the wizard; you're then notified of success or warned about any problems that happened during the conversion process.

NOTE

A table can't be designated as local if it's involved in a relationship with a replicated table.

> **NOTE**
>
> When you have more than one replica set, you must use the Managed Replicas tool on the Replication Manager toolbar to view a different replica set. Only one replica set can be viewed at a time.

Creating Replicas with the Replication Manager

Just as you can create replicas by using the Access user interface and the Windows Briefcase, you can also create replicas with the Replication Manager. To do so, follow these steps:

1. Click New Replica on the toolbar; then click Next.
2. Select a source and destination for the replica. The source is the name of the database you're replicating, and the destination is the name of the replica. Click Next
3. Indicate whether you want to be able to make data changes within the replica. Click Next.
4. Indicate whether you want the replica to be managed by the Synchronizer on the current machine. Click Next.
5. Click Finish.

> **NOTE**
>
> If you create a replica of a database managed by a different Synchronizer, you must use the Replication Manager on the other computer to configure the Synchronizer.

Synchronizing Replicas with the Replication Manager

Just as you can synchronize replicas with the Access user interface and the Windows Briefcase, you can also use the Replication Manager by following these steps:

1. From the Replication Manager, click the Synchronize Now tool on the toolbar.
2. The Synchronize Now dialog box opens. (See Figure 23.30.) Here, you can designate details of the synchronization process. When you're finished, click OK to finish the synchronization process.

FIGURE 23.30

The Synchronize Now dialog box allows you to designate details of the synchronization process.

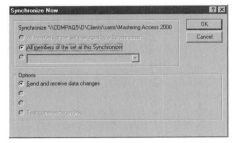

Remote Synchronizations

You might be surprised that the Replication Manager map shows only one machine, even though you have many replicas. One icon appears for each Synchronizer involved in the replica set. Figure 23.31 shows two Synchronizers involved in the replication process: ALEXIS and DELL. The second site was set up by installing the Replication Manager on the second machine. Any replica from the local site can then be moved to the remote site by establishing a connection to the remote site and choosing File | Move Replica. You can locate the managed folder at the remote site and move the replica to the remote site's managed folder.

FIGURE 23.31

The Replication Manager map with two Synchronizers.

After both sites appear on the replication map, you can manage synchronizations by using the join line that connects them. You can right-click on the join line and select Synchronize Now or, to establish a schedule for synchronization, select Edit Schedule. Scheduling synchronization is covered in the next section.

Scheduled Synchronizations

Synchronizations can be scheduled between replicas managed by the same Synchronizer, or between replicas managed by two different Synchronizers. To schedule synchronization between replicas managed by the same Synchronizer, right-click on the icon representing the local Synchronizer and select Edit Locally Managed Replica Schedule. (See Figure 23.32.) From here, you can select the days and times when the replicas synchronize.

FIGURE 23.32

Use the Edit Schedule dialog box to select the days and times when the replicas synchronize.

To schedule the synchronization process between two different Synchronizers, right-click on the join line and select Edit Schedule to open the Edit Schedule dialog box. Here you can schedule the specifics of the synchronization process between the two sites. The shading of each box indicates which Synchronizer initiates that exchange. If the connection can't be made when the exchange is initiated, the drop-box folder keeps a temporary log of the changes. Every 15 minutes, it retries the connection until it's successful.

Reviewing the Synchronization History

The synchronization history can be very useful. Besides giving you an audit trail, it helps you analyze the effectiveness of the topology and synchronization schedule you have selected. Three types of logs are kept by the Replication Manager:

- The local synchronization history
- The remote synchronization history
- The Synchronizer log

To view the local synchronization history, right-click the local machine icon and select View Local Synchronization History. This opens the Synchronization History dialog box. (See Figure 23.33.) It shows you details about the exchange of information between the local replicas.

FIGURE 23.33

Viewing local synchronization history.

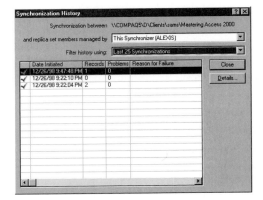

To view the remote synchronization history, select the line joining two Synchronizers and choose View I Synchronization History to open the Synchronization History dialog box. If you want more information about any of the log entries, click Details to open the Synchronization Details dialog box. (See Figure 23.34.)

FIGURE 23.34

The Synchronization Details dialog box shows the details of a synchronization process.

Working with Synchronization Properties

You can also view properties of the selected Synchronizer. To do this, double-click the Synchronizer and the Replica Properties window appears. This tabbed dialog box gives you important information about the selected Synchronizer.

> **NOTE**
>
> Jet 4.0 and Access 2000 support synchronization over the Internet or over an intranet. You place a replica on a server and use the Replication Manager to synchronize, using a standard HTTP connection. This process is covered in Chapter 31, "Access and the Internet."

USING PARTIAL REPLICATION

Jet 3.5 and Access 97 introduced *partial replication*, meaning that only a subset of the data is replicated. This is useful when you have, for example, several salespeople and you want each salesperson to have just his or her own data. However, you want all the salespeople to be able to synchronize their changes with other databases on the network. Partial replicas can be created by using the Partial Replica Wizard, available via the Access user interface or by using VBA code. The procedure for using VBA code to create a partial replica is in the section "Creating a Partial Replica Using Code." The Partial Replica Wizard is covered here. To create a partial replica, follow these steps:

1. Within Microsoft Access, with the database that you want to replicate open, select Tools | Replication | Partial Replica Wizard. The Partial Replica Wizard appears.

2. Designate whether you want to create a new partial replica or to modify an existing partial replica (see Figure 23.35). Click Next.

FIGURE 23.35

Designate whether you want to create a new partial replica or modify an existing partial replica.

3. Designate a name and location for the partial replica. Click Next.

4. Create a filter expression that limits the data contained in the partial replica. To do this, select the table whose data you want to filter. Next select the field that you want to use as criteria and the operator appropriate for the expression. Click Paste. To complete the expression, enter for the expression the value that you want to use to limit the data contained in the partial replica. You can expand or refine the selection using And and Or as appropriate. Figure 23.36 shows a filter expression that creates a partial replica with data only for clients in the state of California. Click Next.

FIGURE 23.36

Designate the filter expression used to limit the data contained in the partial replica.

5. The next step of the Partial Replica Wizard is very important. It allows you to designate additional tables you want to include within the partial replica. Tables that appear bold are related to the table whose criteria you are using to create the partial replica. You must deselect these tables so that only records related to the records in your filter are included in the partial replica. Tables that are not bold are not related to the filtered table with referential integrity enforced. It is up to you whether you want to include the data within these unrelated tables. In Figure 23.37, the check marks have been removed from all the related tables, but the check mark remains for the unrelated table. This means that only related data is included for all the tables where referential integrity is established, whereas the entire tblCompanyInfo table is included.

6. Finally, you can designate whether you want Access to create a report with all the property settings that apply to the partial replica. Make your selection and click Finish.

FIGURE 23.37

Designate what additional data is included in the partial replica.

IMPLEMENTING REPLICATION USING CODE

Most of the replication functions can be implemented by using code, but this isn't the easiest way to manage replication. However, sometimes you might want to implement aspects of the replication process with code so that you can better control the process, and its interface, from within your application.

> **NOTE**
>
> All the examples that follow require the use of the Jet Replication Objects (JRO) object library. To access the JRO object library, you must use Tools | References in the VBE to select the Microsoft Jet and Replication Objects 2.1 Library. The database that will use the JRO library must be open.

Making a Database Replicable by Using Code

The routine shown in Listing 23.1, located in the Chap23Ex database, renders a database replicable by using code.

LISTING 23.1 MAKING A DATABASE REPLICABLE

```
Sub MakeReplicable(strMaster As String)
    Dim rep As JRO.Replica

    Set rep = New JRO.Replica

    rep.MakeReplicable strMaster, True
    Set rep = Nothing
End Sub
```

This routine accepts the path to any database as a parameter. It first creates a JRO Replica object. The MakeReplicable method of the Replica object is used to convert the database to a design master. The MakeReplicable method receives the name of the database that you want to convert to a design master, and an optional parameter that is used to designate whether you want the master to use column-level tracking (discussed in the Note).

NOTE

Prior to Access 2000, conflicts were generated at the record level. This means that if two users made changes to different fields in the same record, a conflict was generated. Access 2000 introduces column-level tracking. This means that if two users make changes to different fields in the same record, a conflict does not occur. Conflicts occur only when two users make changes to the same field in the same record. Column-level tracking is an optional feature that is turned on by default. Column-level tracking can be set only when the database is made replicable.

Flagging an Object as Local

Unless you do something special, all objects in a database are included in the replication process. The code in Listing 23.2 illustrates how to flag a database object as local. It designates the tblEmployee table as local.

LISTING 23.2 FLAGGING AN OBJECT AS LOCAL

```
Sub MakeLocal(strDatabase As String, _
    strName As String, _
    strObjType As String)

    Dim rep As New JRO.Replica

    rep.ActiveConnection = strDatabase
    rep.SetObjectReplicability strName, strObjType, False

    Set rep = Nothing
End Sub
```

The code begins by declaring a JRO Replica object. The ActiveConnection property of the Replica object is set to point at the database whose object you want to flag as local. The

SetObjectReplicability method of the Replica object is used to flag a database object as local. It receives the name of the object you want to flag as local and the type of object you are flagging. Because the code sets the replicability to False, the object is flagged as local.

Creating a Replica Using Code

A new replica can be created with code by using the CreateReplica method of the Replica object. The code appears in Listing 23.3.

LISTING 23.3 MAKING A REPLICA

```
Sub MakeReplica(strMaster As String, strReplica As String)
    Dim rep As JRO.Replica
    Set rep = New JRO.Replica

    rep.ActiveConnection = strMaster
    rep.CreateReplica strReplica, "Replica of " & strMaster
End Sub
```

This code accepts two parameters, the first containing the path and filename for the master, and the second containing the path and filename for the replica. The CreateReplica method is executed on the Replica object. The first parameter to the CreateReplica method is the name of the replica you are creating. The second parameter is the name of the replica. Other optional parameters include the type of replica you want to create, the visibility of the replica, the priority for the replica, and the updateability of the replica.

Types of Replicas

When creating a replica, the ReplicaType parameter is used to designate the type of replica created. A replica can be designated as a design master, a full replica, a partial replica, or a replica that is not replicable.

Visibility of Replicas

Access 2000 and JRO introduce a new property that is used to designate the visibility of a replica. The replica's visibility determines which replicas can synchronize with a given replica. The visibility of a replica can be set only when a replica is created. A replica is designated as global, local, or anonymous. A global replica can synchronize with any replica in its replica set. By default, all replicas are global.

A local replica can synchronize only with its parent. A parent can schedule synchronization with a local replica. The parent proxies replication conflicts and errors for the local replica. A local replica can only create other local replicas. The replicas created by a local replica will share the same parent as the local replica. All other replicas are unaware of a local replica.

An anonymous replica can synchronize only with its parent. Anonymous replicas are appropriate when a replica rarely participates in the synchronization process. The anonymous replica proxies its identity for updates to the publishing replica. Anonymous replicas can create only other anonymous replicas. The child replicas share the same parent as the anonymous replica.

Priority for Replicas

Another new property of a replica is used to indicate the priority of the replica during the synchronization process. If conflicts are encountered during the synchronization process, the replica with the highest priority wins.

Updateability of Replicas

The updateability property of the replica is used to determine whether the data in the replica is updateable. By default, a replica's data is updateable. Setting this property to the constant value jrRepUpdReadOnly designates the data within the replica as read-only.

Creating a Partial Replica Using Code

You can also create a partial replica using VBA code, as appears in Listing 23.5.

LISTING 23.5   CREATING A PARTIAL REPLICA

```
Sub CreatePartialReplica()

    Dim repFull As New JRO.Replica
    Dim repPartial As New JRO.Replica

    repFull.ActiveConnection = "c:\My Documents\MyMaster.mdb"
    repFull.CreateReplica "c:\My Documents\CA Clients.mdb", _
        "Partial Replica of MyMaster", _
        jrRepTypePartial
    Set repFull = Nothing

    repPartial.ActiveConnection = "c:\My Documents\CA Clients.mdb"
    repPartial.Filters.Append "tblClients", jrFilterTypeTable, _
        "State = 'CA'"
    repPartial.Filters.Append "tblProjects", jrFilterTypeRelationship, _
     "ClientProjects"
    repPartial.PopulatePartial "c:\My Documents\MyMaster.mdb"
    Set repPartial = Nothing

End Sub
```

The code begins by establishing a connection to the master. It uses the `CreateReplica` method of the `Replica` object to create a partial replica. A connection is then made to the replica. Two filters are appended to the `Replica` object. The first filter is used to populate the `tblClients` table in the replica with all the clients located in the state of California. The second filter is used to populate the tblProjects table with all the projects associated with clients in the state of California. The `PopulatePartial` method is used to populate the replica with the data designated in the filters.

Synchronizing a Database Using Code

At times, you might want to finish the synchronization process by using VBA code. The routine shown in Listing 23.6 synchronizes the two databases designated as parameters. The constant `jrSyncTypeImpExp` indicates that you want to perform a two-way synchronization. The constant `jrSyncModeDirect` indicates that the synchronization mode is direct.

LISTING 23.6   SYNCHRONIZING TWO DATABASES

```
Sub Synchronize(strDB1 As String, strDB2 As String)
    Dim rep As New JRO.Replica
    rep.ActiveConnection = strDB1
    rep.Synchronize strDB2, jrSyncTypeImpExp, jrSyncModeDirect
    Set rep = Nothing
End Sub
```

Handling Conflicts Using Code

You can also handle conflicts by using code (see Listing 23.7). What you do when a conflict is identified is determined by the business needs of your users.

LISTING 23.7   IDENTIFYING CONFLICTS USING CODE

```
Sub IdentifyConflicts(strConflictDB)
    Dim rep As New JRO.Replica
    Dim rst As ADODB.Recordset

    rep.ActiveConnection = strConflictDB
    Set rst = rep.ConflictTables

    If rst.BOF And rst.EOF Then
        MsgBox "No Conflicts!!!"
    Else
        Do Until rst.EOF
            Debug.Print rst.Fields(0)
```

continues

LISTING 23.7   CONTINUED

```
            rst.MoveNext
        Loop
    End If

End Sub
```

This routine goes through each table, determining whether something is in the table's `ConflictTable` property. If the `ConflictTable` property has something in it, a recordset is opened from the Conflict table. The routine loops through each record of the Conflict table, displaying the value of the first field in the Debug window.

PRACTICAL EXAMPLES

Managing the Time and Billing Application with Replication

You must make a decision about whether it's necessary to implement replication in the Time and Billing application. It could be very useful if, for example, you have many consultants who work in the field and need to enter client, project, billing, and expense information while on the road. Using what you've learned in this chapter, you can make sure all changes made to each consultant's copy of the database are sent to the main server database each time the consultant dials into the office.

Replication can also be used so that the data managed by the Time and Billing application is backed up during the day, which minimizes the chance of data loss or downtime. Finally, you might want to implement replication in the Time and Billing application to distribute the work load over a few servers in your organization.

The potential benefits of using replication with the Time and Billing application are many. With what you have learned in this chapter, you must decide whether replication is appropriate for your application and how it can best be used in your organization.

SUMMARY

Replication is a very complex and robust Access feature. It can be used at the most basic level to synchronize changes between two databases, or, in an enterprisewide application, to synchronize changes between many machines on a WAN (Wide Area Network). The easiest, but least robust, way to implement replication is by using the Access user interface or the Windows Briefcase. However, with the Replication Manager, you can schedule and manage synchronization activity, as well as handle the most complex of replication topologies. Finally, by using code, you can customize the behavior of your application's synchronization activities.

BLACK-BELT PROGRAMMING

PART

IV

IN THIS PART

ADVANCED VBA TECHNIQUES

IN THIS CHAPTER

WHY THIS CHAPTER IS IMPORTANT

The Visual Basic for Applications (VBA) language is extremely rich and comprehensive. VBA is covered throughout this book because it applies to different topics, but this chapter focuses on some advanced application development techniques. These topics include user-defined types, arrays, advanced function techniques, and VBA compilation options. The mastering of these topics helps to ensure your success as a VBA programmer.

WHAT ARE USER-DEFINED TYPES AND WHY WOULD YOU USE THEM?

User-defined types were briefly introduced in Chapter 14, "Error Handling: Preparing for the Inevitable." In Chapter 14, a user-defined type was used to hold pertinent error information. A user-defined type, known as a *struct* or *record*, allows you to create a variable containing several pieces of information. User-defined types are often used to hold information from one or more records in memory. They are also used to hold related information that would otherwise be stored in several unrelated variables. Because each element of a user-defined type can be instructed to hold a particular type of data, each element in the type can be defined to correspond to the type of data stored in a specific field of a table. A user-defined type might look like this:

> **NOTE**
>
> The code snippets that follow are located in the basDataHandling module.

```
Public Type TimeCardInfo
    TimeCardDetailID As Long
    TimeCardID As Long
    DateWorked As Date
    ProjectID As Long
    WorkDescription As String * 255
    BillableHours As Double
    BillingRate As Currency
    WorkCodeID As Long
End Type
```

Notice that the type of data stored in each element has been explicitly declared. The element containing the string WorkDescription has been declared with a length of 255. User-defined types make code cleaner by storing related data as a unit. A user-defined type exists only in memory and is, therefore, temporary. It's excellent for information that needs to be temporarily tracked at runtime. Because it's in memory, it can be quickly and efficiently read from and written to.

Declaring a User-Defined Type

You declare a user-defined type by using a `Type` statement that must be placed in the module's Declarations section. Types can be declared as Public or Private within a standard module. Types can be used, but can't be declared in Form or Report modules.

Creating a `Type` Variable

A `Type` variable is an instance of the type in memory; it must be declared before you can use the type. To declare a `Type` variable, create a `Local`, `Private`, `Module-Level`, or `Public` variable based on the type. Depending on where you place this declaration and how you declare it (`Dim`, `Private`, or `Public`), you determine its scope. The same rules for any other kind of variable apply to `Type` variables. The `Dim` statement in the code that follows creates a variable called `mtypTimeCardData`. If you place this `Dim` statement in the module's General section, it's visible to all routines in that module (notice the `m`, indicating that it is declared at the module level). If you place it in a subroutine or function, it's local to that particular routine:

```
Dim mtypTimeCardData As TimeCardInfo
```

Storing Information from a Record in a Form into a `Type`

After a `Type` variable has been declared, you can store data into each of its elements. The following code in the frmTimeCardHours form stores information from the form into a `Type` variable called `mtypTimeCardData`. The `Type` variable is declared as a `Private` variable in the General Declarations section of the form. The `Type` structure is declared in basDataHandling.

```
Private Sub cmdWriteToType_Click()

    mtypTimeCardData.TimeCardDetailID = Me.TimeCardDetailID
    mtypTimeCardData.TimeCardID = Me.TimeCardID
    mtypTimeCardData.DateWorked = Me.DateWorked
    mtypTimeCardData.ProjectID = Me.ProjectID
    mtypTimeCardData.WorkDescription = Me.WorkDescription
    mtypTimeCardData.BillableHours = Me.BillableHours
    mtypTimeCardData.BillingRate = Me.BillingRate
    mtypTimeCardData.WorkCodeID = Me.WorkCodeID
End Sub
```

The code for this chapter can be found in the CHAP24EX.MDB database on the book's CD-ROM. The advantage of this code is that rather than creating eight variables to store these eight pieces of related information, it creates one variable with eight elements. This method keeps things nice and neat.

Retrieving Information from the Elements of a Type

To retrieve information from your Type variable, simply refer to its name, followed by a period, and then the name of the element. The following code displays a message box containing all the time-card hour information:

```
Private Sub cmdDisplayFromType_Click()
   MsgBox "Timecard Detail ID Is " & _
   mtypTimeCardData.TimeCardDetailID & Chr(13) & _
         "Timecard ID Is " & mtypTimeCardData.TimeCardID & Chr(13) & _
         "Date Worked Is " & mtypTimeCardData.DateWorked & Chr(13) & _
         "Project ID Is " & mtypTimeCardData.ProjectID & Chr(13) & _
         "Work Description Is " & _
          Trim(mtypTimeCardData.WorkDescription) & Chr(13) & _
         "Billable Hours Is " & mtypTimeCardData.BillableHours & _
          Chr(13) & "Billing Rate Is " & _
          mtypTimeCardData.BillingRate & Chr(13) & _
         "Workcode ID Is " & mtypTimeCardData.WorkCodeID
End Sub
```

WORKING WITH CONSTANTS

A *constant* is a meaningful name given to a meaningless number or string. Constants can be used only for values that don't change at runtime. A tax rate or commission rate, for example, might be constant throughout your application. There are three types of constants in Access:

- Symbolic
- Intrinsic
- System-defined

Symbolic constants, created by using the Const keyword, are used to improve the readability of your code and make code maintenance easier. Rather than referring to the number .0875 every time you want to refer to the tax rate, you can refer to the constant MTAXRATE. If the tax rate changes and you need to modify the value in your code, you'll make the change in only one place. Furthermore, unlike the number .0875, the name MTAXRATE is self-documenting.

Intrinsic constantsare built into Microsoft Access; they are part of the language itself. As an Access programmer, you can use constants supplied by Microsoft Access, Visual Basic, and ActiveX Data Objects (ADO). You can also use constants provided by any object libraries you're using in your application.

There are only three system-defined constants, available to all applications on your computer: True, False, and Null.

Defining Your Own Constants

As mentioned, a Symbolic constant is declared by using the `Const` keyword. A constant can be declared in a subroutine or function or in the General section of a Form, Report, or Class module. Unlike in previous versions of Access, constants can be strong-typed in Access 97 and Access 2000. There are several naming conventions for constants. One of them is to use a suitable scoping prefix, the letter *c* to indicate you're working with a constant rather than a variable, and then the appropriate tag for the data type. The declaration and use of a Private constant would look like this:

```
Private Const mccurTaxRate As Currency = .0875
```

The naming convention that I prefer is the use of a scoping prefix and typing the name of the constant in all uppercase. The example given previously is changed to appear as follows:

```
Private Const MTAXRATE as Currency = .0875
```

This code, when placed in a module's Declarations section, creates a Private constant called `MTAXRATE` and sets it equal to `.0875`. Here's how the constant is used in code:

```
Function TotalAmount(curSaleAmount As Currency)
    TotalAmount = curSaleAmount * MTAXRATE
End Function
```

This routine multiplies the `curSaleAmount`, received as a parameter, by the constant `MTAXRATE`. It returns the result of the calculation by setting the function name equal to the product of the two values. The advantage of the constant in this example is that the code is more readable than `TotalAmount = curSaleAmount * .0875` would be.

Scoping Symbolic Constants

Just as regular variables have scope, user-defined constants have scope. In the preceding example, you created a Private constant. The following statement, when placed in a module's Declarations section, creates a Public constant:

```
Public Const GTAXRATE As Currency = 0.0875
```

Because this constant is declared as Public, it can be accessed from any subroutine or function (including event routines) in your entire application. To better understand the benefits of a Public constant, say you have many functions and subroutines, all referencing the constant `GTAXRATE`. Imagine what would happen if the tax rate were to change. If you hadn't used a constant, you would need to search your entire application, replacing the old tax rate with the new tax rate. However, because your Public constant is declared in one place, you can easily go in and modify the one line of code where this constant is declared.

> **NOTE**
>
> By definition, the value of constants can't be modified at runtime. If you try to modify the value of a constant, you get this VBA compiler error:
>
> `Variable Required - can't assign to this expression`
>
> Figure 24.1 illustrates this message box. You can see that an attempt was made to modify the value of the constant called GTAXRATE, which resulted in a compile error.
>
> If you must change the value at runtime, you should consider storing the value in a table rather than declaring it as a constant. You can read the value into a variable when the application loads; then modify the variable if needed. If you choose, you can write the new value back to the table.

FIGURE 24.1

An error message resulting from trying to modify the value of a constant.

Working with Intrinsic Constants

Microsoft Access declares a number of intrinsic constants that can be used in Code, Form, and Report modules. Because they're reserved by Microsoft Access, you can't modify their values or reuse their names; however, they can be used at any time without being declared.

You should use intrinsic constants whenever possible in your code. Besides making your code more readable, they make your code more portable to future releases of Microsoft Access. Microsoft might change the value associated with a constant, but it isn't likely to change the constant's name. All intrinsic constants appear in the Object Browser; to activate it, simply click the Object Browser tool on the Visual Basic toolbar while in the VBE. To view the constants that are part of the VBA language, select VBA from the Object Browser's Project/Library drop-down list. Click Constants in the Classes list box, and a list of those constants are displayed in the Members of 'Constants' list box. (See Figure 24.2.)

FIGURE 24.2

*Using the Object
Browser to view
intrinsic con-
stants.*

In the list shown in Figure 24.2, all the constant names begin with vb. All VBA constants are
prefixed with vb, all ActiveX Data Object constants are prefixed with ad, all Data Access
Object (DAO) constants with db, and all constants that are part of the Access language are prefixed with ac. To view the Access language constants, select Access from the Project/Library
drop-down list and Constants from the Classes list box. To view the ActiveX Data Object constants, select ADODB from the Project/Library drop-down list. The constants are categorized
by their function into various classes (for example, LockTypeEnum, ExecuteOptionEnum).
Select the appropriate class from the Classes list box, and its members appear in the Members
Of... list box.

Another way to view constants is within the context of the parameter you're working with in
the Code window. Right-click after the name of a parameter and select List Constants to display the constants associated with the parameter. This feature is covered in detail in Chapter 7,
"VBA: An Introduction."

WORKING WITH ARRAYS

An *array* is a series of variables referred to by the same name. Each element of the array is dif-
ferentiated by a unique index number, but all the elements must be of the same data type.
Arrays help make coding more efficient. It's easy to loop through each element of an array,
performing some process on each element. Arrays have a lower bound, which is zero by
default, and an upper bound, and all array elements must be contiguous.

The scope of an array can be Public, Module, or Local. As with other variables, this depends
on where the array is declared and whether the Public, Private, or Dim keyword is used.

Declaring and Working with Fixed Arrays

When declaring a *fixed array*, you give VBA the upper bound and the type of data it will contain. The following code creates an array that holds six string variables:

```
Dim astrNames(5) As String
```

Fixed means that this array's size can't be altered at runtime. The following code gives an example of how you can loop through the array:

```
Sub FixedArray()
    Dim astrNames(5) As String
    Dim intCounter As Integer
    astrNames(0) = "Dan"
    astrNames(1) = "Reggie"
    astrNames(2) = "Alexis"
    astrNames(3) = "Joshua"
    For intCounter = 0 To UBound(astrNames)
        Debug.Print astrNames(intCounter)
    Next intCounter
End Sub
```

This code starts by storing values into the first four elements of a six-element array. It then loops through each element of the array, printing the contents. Notice that the For...Next loop starts at zero and goes until the upper bound of the array, which is (5). Because the array is made up of strings, the last two elements of the array contain zero-length strings. If the array was composed of integers, the last two elements would contain zeros.

Another way to traverse the array is to use the For Each...Next construct. Your code would look like this:

```
Sub ArrayWith()
    Dim astrNames(5) As String
    Dim intCounter As Integer
    Dim vntAny As Variant
    astrNames(0) = "Dan"
    astrNames(1) = "Reggie"
    astrNames(2) = "Alexis"
    astrNames(3) = "Joshua"
    For Each vntAny In astrNames
        Debug.Print vntAny
    Next vntAny
End Sub
```

This code declares a Variant variable called vntAny. Instead of using a loop with Ubound as the upper delimiter to traverse the array, the example uses the For Each...Next construct.

> **NOTE**
>
> Many people do not like the fact that by default, the elements of an array are zero based. Fortunately, the VBA language allows you to declare both the lower bound and the upper bound of any array. The syntax looks like this:
>
> ```
> Dir astrNames(1 to 6)
> ```

Declaring and Working with Dynamic Arrays

Often, you don't know how many elements your array needs to contain. In this case, you should consider declaring a *dynamic array*, which can be resized at runtime. Using this type of array can make your code more efficient because VBA preallocates memory for all elements of a fixed array, regardless of whether data is stored in each of the elements. However, if you aren't sure how many elements your array will contain, preallocating a huge amount of memory can be quite inefficient.

To create a dynamic array, you declare it without assigning an upper bound. You do this by omitting the number between the parentheses when declaring the array, as shown in this example:

```
Sub DynamicArray()
    Dim astrNames() As String
    Dim intCounter As Integer
    Dim vntAny As Variant
    ReDim astrNames(1)
    astrNames(0) = "Dan"
    astrNames(1) = "Reggie"
    For Each vntAny In astrNames
        Debug.Print vntAny
    Next vntAny
End Sub
```

However, there's a potential problem when you try to resize the array:

```
Sub ResizeDynamic()
    Dim astrNames() As String
    Dim intCounter As Integer
    Dim vntAny As Variant
    ReDim astrNames(1)
    astrNames(0) = "Dan"
    astrNames(1) = "Reggie"
    ReDim astrNames(3)
    astrNames(2) = "Alexis"
    astrNames(3) = "Joshua"
```

```
        For Each vntAny In astrNames
            Debug.Print vntAny
        Next vntAny
    End Sub
```

You might expect that all four elements will contain data. Instead, the `ReDim` statement reinitializes all the elements, and only elements two and three contain values. This problem can be avoided by using the `Preserve` keyword. The following code behaves quite differently:

```
Sub ResizePreserve()
    Dim astrNames() As String
    Dim intCounter As Integer
    Dim vntAny As Variant
    ReDim astrNames(1)
    astrNames(0) = "Dan"
    astrNames(1) = "Reggie"
    ReDim Preserve astrNames(3)
    astrNames(2) = "Alexis"
    astrNames(3) = "Joshua"
    For Each vntAny In astrNames
        Debug.Print vntAny
    Next vntAny
End Sub
```

In this example, all values already stored in the array are preserved. The `Preserve` keyword brings its own difficulties, though. It can temporarily require huge volumes of memory because during the `ReDim` process, VBA creates a copy of the original array. All the values from the original array are copied to a new array. The original array is removed from memory when the process is complete. The `Preserve` keyword can cause problems if you're dealing with very large arrays in a limited memory situation.

TIP

> Each type of array complements the other's drawbacks. As a VBA developer, you have the flexibility of choosing the right type of array for each situation. Fixed arrays are the way to go when the number of elements doesn't vary widely, but dynamic arrays should be used when the number varies widely and you're sure you have enough memory to resize even the largest possible arrays.

Passing Arrays as Parameters

Many people are unaware that you can pass an array as a parameter to a function or subroutine. The following code provides an example:

```
Sub PassArray()
    Dim astrNames(5) as String
    Dim intCounter As Integer

    Call FillNames(astrNames)
    For intCounter = 0 To UBound(astrNames)
        Debug.Print astrNames(intCounter)
    Next intCounter
End Sub

Sub FillNames(varNameList As Variant)
    varNameList(0) = "Alison"
    varNameList(1) = "Dan"
    varNameList(2) = "Alexis"
    varNameList(3) = "Joshua"
    varNameList(4) = "Amanda"
    varNameList(5) = "Brianna"
End Sub
```

The code begins by declaring a fixed array called astrNames. The FillNames routine is called. It receives the array as a parameter and then populates all its elements. The PassArray routine is then able to loop through all the elements of the array that was passed, displaying information from each element.

ADVANCED FUNCTION TECHNIQUES

The advanced function techniques covered in this section allow you to get the most out of the procedures you build. First, you learn the difference between passing your parameters by reference and passing them by value, and see that the default method of passing parameters isn't always the most prudent method.

The second part of this section shows you how to work with optional parameters, which help you build flexibility into your functions. They let you omit parameters, but named parameters allow you to add readability to your code. Named parameters also shelter you from having to worry about the order in which the parameters must appear. After reading this section, you can build much more robust and easy-to-use functions.

Passing by Reference Versus Passing by Value

By default, parameters in Access are passed by reference. This means that a memory reference to the variable being passed is received by the function. This process is best illustrated by an example:

```
Sub PassByRef()
    Dim strFirstName As String
    Dim strLastName As String
    strFirstName = "Alison"
    strLastName = "Balter"
    Call FuncByRef(strFirstName, strLastName)
    Debug.Print strFirstName
    Debug.Print strLastName
End Sub
Sub FuncByRef(strFirstParm As String, strSecondParm As String)
    strFirstParm = "Bill"
    strSecondParm = "Gates"
End Sub
```

You might be surprised that the `Debug.Print` statements found in the subroutine `PassByRef` print `"Bill"` and `"Gates"`. This is because `strFirstParm` is actually a reference to the same location in memory as `strFirstName`, and `strSecondParm` is a reference to the same location in memory as `strLastName`. This violates the concepts of *black-box processing*, in which a variable can't be changed by any routine other than the one it was declared in. The following code eliminates this problem:

```
Sub PassByVal()
    Dim strFirstName As String
    Dim strLastName As String
    strFirstName = "Alison"
    strLastName = "Balter"
    Call FuncByVal(strFirstName, strLastName)
    Debug.Print strFirstName
    Debug.Print strLastName
End Sub
Sub FuncByVal(ByVal strFirstParm As String, _
ByVal strSecondParm As String)
    strFirstParm = "Bill"
    strSecondParm = "Gates"
End Sub
```

This `FuncByVal` subroutine receives the parameters by value. This means that only the values in `strFirstName` and `strLastName` are passed to the `FuncByVal` routine. The `strFirstName` and `strLastName` variables, therefore, can't be modified by the `FuncByVal` subroutine. The `Debug.Print` statements print `"Alison"` and `"Balter"`.

The following example illustrates a great reason why you might want to pass a parameter by reference:

```
Sub GoodPassByRef()
    Dim blnSuccess As Boolean
    Dim strName As String
    strName = "Microsoft"
    blnSuccess = GoodFunc(strName)
    Debug.Print blnSuccess
End Sub
Function GoodFunc(strName As String)
    If Len(strName) Then
        strName = UCase$(strName)
        GoodFunc = True
    Else
        GoodFunc = False
    End If
End Function
```

In essence, the GoodFunc function needs to return two values. Not only does the function need to return the uppercase version of the string passed to it, but it also needs to return a success code. Because a function can return only one value, you need to be able to modify the value of strName within the function. As long as you're aware of what you're doing and why you're doing it, there's no problem with passing a parameter by reference.

> **NOTE**
>
> I use a special technique to help readers of my code see whether I'm passing parameters by reference or by value. When passing parameters by reference, I refer to the parameters by the same name in both the calling routine and the actual procedure that I'm calling. On the other hand, when passing parameters by value, I refer to the parameters by different names in the calling routine and in the procedure that's being called.

24

ADVANCED VBA TECHNIQUES

After reading this section, you might ask yourself whether it is better to pass parameters by reference or by value. Although in terms of "black-box" processing, it is better to pass by value, code that involves parameters passed by reference actually executes more quickly. As long as you and the programmers that you work with are aware of the potential problems with passing parameters by reference, in general I feel that it is better to pass parameters by reference.

Optional Parameters: Building Flexibility into Functions

Access 97 and Access 2000 allow you to use optional parameters. In other words, it isn't necessary to know how many parameters will be passed. The `ReturnInit` function in the following code receives the second two parameters as optional; then evaluates whether the parameters are missing and responds accordingly:

```
Function ReturnInit(ByVal strFName As String, _
        Optional ByVal strMI, Optional ByVal strLName)
    If IsMissing(strMI) Then
        strMI = InputBox("Enter Middle Initial")
    End If
    If IsMissing(strLName) Then
        strLName = InputBox("Enter Last Name")
    End If
    ReturnInit = strLName & "," & strFName & " " & strMI
End Function
```

This function could be called as follows:

```
strName = ReturnInit("Bill",,"Gates")
```

As you can see, the second parameter is missing. Rather than causing a compiler error, as in earlier versions of Access, this code compiles and runs successfully. The `IsMissing` function, built into Access, determines whether a parameter has been passed. After identifying missing parameters, you must decide how to handle the situation in code. In the example, the function prompts for the missing information, but here are some other possible choices:

- Insert default values when parameters are missing.
- Accommodate for the missing parameters in your code.

Listing 24.1 and Listing 24.2 illustrate how to carry out these two alternatives.

LISTING 24.1   INSERTING DEFAULT VALUES WHEN PARAMETERS ARE MISSING

```
Function ReturnInit2(ByVal strFName As String, _
        Optional ByVal strMI, Optional ByVal strLName)
    If IsMissing(strMI) Then
        strMI = "B"
    End If
    If IsMissing(strLName) Then
        strLName = "Jones"
    End If
    ReturnInit2 = strLName & "," & strFName & " " & strMI
End Function
```

This example uses a default value of `"B"` for the middle initial and a default last name of `"Jones"`. Now take a look at Listing 24.2, which illustrates another method of handling missing parameters.

Listing 24.2 Accommodating for Missing Parameters in Your Code

```
Function ReturnInit3(ByVal strFName As String, _
      Optional ByVal strMI, Optional ByVal strLName)
   Dim strResult As String
   If IsMissing(strMI) And IsMissing(strLName) Then
      ReturnInit3 = strFName
   ElseIf IsMissing(strMI) Then
      ReturnInit3 = strLName & ", " & strFName
   ElseIf IsMissing(strLName) Then
      ReturnInit3 = strFName & " " & strMI
   Else
      ReturnInit3 = strLName & ", " & strFName & " " & strMI
   End If
End Function
```

This example manipulates the return value, depending on which parameters it receives. If neither optional parameter is passed, just the first name displays. If the first name and middle initial are passed, the return value contains the first name followed by the middle initial. If the first name and last name are passed, the return value contains the last name, a comma, and the first name. If all three parameters are passed, the function returns the last name, a comma, a space, and the first name.

Named Parameters: Eliminate the Need to Count Commas

In all the examples you've seen so far, the parameters to a procedure have been supplied positionally. Named parameters allow you to supply parameters without regard for their position, which is particularly useful with procedures that receive optional parameters. Take a look at this example:

```
strName = ReturnInit3("Bill",,"Gates")
```

Because the second parameter isn't supplied, and the parameters are passed positionally, a comma must be used as a placemarker for the optional parameter. This requirement can become unwieldy when you're dealing with several optional parameters. The following example greatly simplifies the process of passing the parameters and also better documents what's happening:

```
strName = ReturnInit3(strFName:= "Bill",strLName:= "Gates")
```

When parameters are passed by name, it doesn't even matter in what order the parameters appear, as shown in the following example:

```
strName = ReturnInit3(strLName:= "Gates",strFName:="Bill")
```

This call to the `ReturnInit3` function yields the same results as the call to the function in the previous example.

> **NOTE**
>
> When using named parameters, each parameter name must be exactly the same as the name of the parameter in the function being called. Besides requiring intimate knowledge of the function being called, this method of specifying parameters has one important disadvantage: If the author of the function modifies a parameter's name, all routines that use the named parameter when calling the function will fail.

WORKING WITH `Empty` AND `Null`

`Empty` and `Null` are values that can exist only for Variant variables. They're different from one another and different from zero or a zero-length string. At times, you need to know whether the value stored in a variable is zero, a zero-length string, `Empty`, or `Null`. You can make this differentiation only with Variant variables.

Working with `Empty`

Variant variables are initialized to the value of `Empty`. Often, you need to know whether a value has been stored in a Variant variable. If a Variant has never been assigned a value, its value is `Empty`. As mentioned, the `Empty` value is not the same as zero, `Null`, or a zero-length string.

It's important to be able to test for `Empty` in a runtime environment. This can be done by using the `IsEmpty` function, which determines whether a variable has the `Empty` value. The following example tests a String variable for the `Empty` value:

```
Sub StringVar()
    Dim strName As String
    Debug.Print IsEmpty(strName) 'Prints False
    Debug.Print strName = "" 'Prints True
End Sub
```

The `Debug.Print` statement prints `False`. This variable is equal to a zero-length string because the variable is initialized as a String variable. All String variables are initialized to a zero-length string. The next example tests a Variant variable to see whether it has the `Empty` value:

```
Sub EmptyVar()
    Dim vntName As Variant
    Debug.Print IsEmpty(vntName) 'Prints True
    vntName = ""
    Debug.Print IsEmpty(vntName) 'Prints False
    vntName = Empty
    Debug.Print IsEmpty(vntName) 'Prints True
End Sub
```

A Variant variable loses its `Empty` value when any value has been stored in it, including zero, `Null`, or a zero-length string. It can become `Empty` again only by storing the keyword `Empty` in the variable.

Working with `Null`

`Null` is a special value that indicates unknown or missing data. `Null` is not the same as `Empty`, nor is one `Null` value equal to another one. Variant variables can contain the special value called `Null`.

Often, you need to know whether specific fields or controls have never been initialized. Uninitialized fields and controls have a default value of `Null`. By testing for `Null`, you can make sure fields and controls contain values.

If you want to make sure that all fields and controls in your application have data, you need to test for `Null`s. This can be done by using the `IsNull` function:

```
Sub NullVar()
    Dim vntName As Variant
    Debug.Print IsEmpty(vntName) 'Prints True
    Debug.Print IsNull(vntName) 'Prints False
    vntName = Null
    Debug.Print IsNull(vntName) 'Prints True
End Sub
```

Notice that `vntName` is equal to `Null` only after the value of `Null` is explicitly stored in it. It's important to know not only how variables and `Null` values interact, but also how to test for `Null` within a field in your database. A field contains a `Null` if data hasn't yet been entered in the field and the field has no default value. In queries, you can test for the criteria `"Is Null"` to find all the records in which a particular field contains a Null value. When dealing with recordsets (covered in Chapter 12, "ADO and DAO: Accessing Data Programmatically"), you can also use the `IsNull` function to test for a `Null` value in a field. Here's an example:

```
Sub LoopProjects()
    Dim rst As ADODB.Recordset
    Set rst = New ADODB.Recordset
```

24

ADVANCED VBA
TECHNIQUES

```
   rst.Open "tblProjects", CurrentProject.Connection
   Do Until rst.EOF
      Debug.Print rst!ProjectID, rst!ProjectName
      If IsNull(rst!ProjectBeginDate) Then
        Debug.Print "Project Begin Date Contains No Value!!"
      End If
      rst.MoveNext
   Loop
End Sub
```

Alternatively, you could use the more compact Nz function to detect Nulls and print a special message:

```
Sub LoopProjects2()
   Dim rst As ADODB.Recordset
   Set rst = New ADODB.Recordset

   rst.Open "tblProjects", CurrentProject.Connection
   Do Until rst.EOF
      Debug.Print rst!ProjectID, rst!ProjectName
      Debug.Print Nz(rst!ProjectBeginDate, _
            "Project Begin Date Contains No Value!!")
      rst.MoveNext
   Loop
End Sub
```

All the concepts of recordset handling were covered in Chapter 12. For now, you need to understand only that this code loops through each record in tblProjects. It uses the IsNull function to evaluate whether the ProjectBeginDate field contains a Null value. If the field does contain a Null, a warning message is printed to the Immediate window. Here is another example:

```
Private Sub Form_Current()
   Dim ctl As Control
   For Each ctl In Controls
      If TypeOf ctl Is TextBox Then
         If IsNull(ctl.Value) Then
            ctl.BackColor = vbCyan
         Else
            ctl.BackColor = vbWhite
         End If
      End If
   Next ctl
End Sub
```

The code in this example (found in the frmProjects form in CHAP24EX.MDB) loops through every control on the current form. If the control is a text box, the routine checks to see whether the value in the text box is Null. If it is, the BackColor property of the text box is set to Aqua; otherwise, it's set to White.

You should know about some idiosyncrasies of Null:

- Expressions involving Null always result in Null. (See the next example.)
- A function that's passed a Null usually returns a Null.
- Null values propagate through built-in functions that return variants.

The following example shows how Null values are propagated:

```
Sub PropNulls()
    Dim rst As ADODB.Recordset

    Set rst = New ADODB.Recordset
    rst.Open "tblProjects", CurrentProject.Connection

    Do Until rst.EOF
        Debug.Print rst!ProjectID, rst!ProjectBeginDate + 1
        rst.MoveNext
    Loop
End Sub
```

Figure 24.3 illustrates the effects of running this routine on a table in which the first and third records contain Null values. Notice that the result of the calculation is Null for those records because the Null propagated within those records.

FIGURE 24.3

The result of running the PropNulls *routine.*

```
Immediate
    1           Null
    2           1/2/96
    3           Null
    4           2/1/96
```

Notice the difference if the value in the field is Empty:

```
Sub EmptyVersusNull()
    Dim rst As ADODB.Recordset

    Set rst = New ADODB.Recordset
    rst.Open "tblProjects", CurrentProject.Connection

    Do Until rst.EOF
```

```
        Debug.Print rst!ProjectID, rst!PurchaseOrderNumber + 10
        rst.MoveNext
    Loop
End Sub
```

In this example, the tblProjects table has four records. The PurchaseOrderNumber for the first record contains a `Null`; for the third record, it contains an `Empty`. Notice the different effects of the two values, as shown in Figure 24.4.

FIGURE 24.4

The result of running the EmptyVersusNull *routine.*

Looking at Figure 24.4, you can see that `Null` printed for the first record, and `Hello` printed for the third record.

NOTE

The `EmptyVersusNull` routine uses a numeric operator (+). As discussed, the effect of `Null` used in a calculation is a resulting `Null`. In text strings, you can use an ampersand (&) instead of a plus (+) to eliminate this problem. Figure 24.5 illustrates the same code with an ampersand to concatenate rather than add. You can see that no `Null` values result from the concatenation.

FIGURE 24.5

The result of changing plus (+) in the EmptyVersusNull *routine to an ampersand (&).*

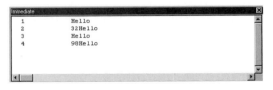

It's very common to create a generic routine that receives any value, tests to see whether it's `Null`, and returns a non-`Null` value. An example is the `CvNulls` function:

```
Function CvNulls(vntVar1 As Variant, vntVar2 As Variant) _
    As Variant
    CvNulls = IIf(IsNull(vntVar1), vntVar2, vntVar1)
End Function
```

This routine would be called as follows:

```
Sub TestForNull(vntSalary As Variant, vntCommission As Variant)
    Dim curTotal As Currency
    curTotal = CvNulls(vntSalary, 0) + CvNulls(vntCommission, 0)
    MsgBox curTotal
End Sub
```

The `TestForNull` routine receives two parameters: `salary` and `commission`. It adds the two values to determine the total of salaries plus commissions. Ordinarily, if the value of either parameter is `Null`, the expression results in `Null`. This problem is eliminated by the `CvNulls` function, which also receives two parameters. The first parameter is the variable being tested for `Null`; the second is the value you want the function to return if the first parameter is determined to be `Null`. The routine combines the `Immediate If` (`IIf`) function and the `IsNull` function to evaluate the first parameter and return the appropriate value.

> **NOTE**
>
> If you simply want to substitute a value for a `Null`, the built-in function `NZ` can be used instead of a user-defined function. The user-defined function offers more functionality, when necessary.

CREATING AND WORKING WITH CUSTOM COLLECTIONS

Earlier in this chapter, I discussed the problems associated with arrays. If you are unsure of the number of elements that the array will contain, fixed arrays can take up large amounts of memory unnecessarily. On the other hand, the resizing of dynamic arrays is rather inefficient. Finally, all the elements of an array must be contiguous and the arbitrary identifier for the array element is meaningless. The answer: custom collections. Custom collections can contain values and objects. You can easily add items to, and remove items from, a collection. Each element in the collection is identified by a meaningful unique key.

In summary, custom collections are similar to arrays, but they offer several advantages:

- Collections are dynamically allocated. They take up memory based only on what's in them at a given time. This is different from arrays, whose size must be either predefined or redimensioned at runtime. When an array is redimensioned, Access actually makes a copy of the array in memory, taking up substantial resources. By using custom collections, you can avoid this consumption of extra resources.

- A collection always knows how many elements it has, and elements can easily be added and removed.
- Each element of a collection can contain a different type of data.
- Elements can be added into any element of a collection.

NOTE

The code examples in this section are found in the basCollections module of the Chap24Ex database.

Creating a Collection

A collection is created using a Collection object. After the Collection object is declared, items can be added to the collection. The code necessary to create a custom collection looks like this:

```
Dim colNames as Collection
```

Adding Items to a Collection

The Add method of the Collection object is used to add items to a custom collection. The Add method receives a value or object reference as its first parameter, and a unique key to that element of the collection as a second parameter. The Add method appears as follows:

```
colNames.Add "Alexis", "Alexis"
```

The code shown previously adds the name Alexis to a collection called colNames. The key to the item in the collection is the name Alexis. In the following code example, the collection colNames is first declared and instantiated. Then several names are added to the custom collection colNames.

```
Sub AddToCollection()
    Dim colNames As Collection
    Set colNames = New Collection
    colNames.Add "Alison", "Alison"
    colNames.Add "Dan", "Dan"
    colNames.Add "Alexis", "Alexis"
    colNames.Add "Joshua", "Joshua"
    colNames.Add "Amanda", "Amanda"
    colNames.Add "Brianna", "Brianna"
End Sub
```

> **CAUTION**
>
> Unlike almost every other array or collection in VBA, custom collections are one-based rather than zero-based. This is a big change if you're used to relying on arrays and collections being zero-based.

Accessing an Item in a Collection

After items have been added to a collection, the `Item` method is used to access them via either their ordinal position, or the key designated when they were added. Accessing an item in a collection using the ordinal position looks like this:

```
Debug.Print colNames.Item(1)
```

Because the `Item` method is the default method of the collection object, the code can be shortened to this:

```
Debug.Print colNames(1)
```

I usually prefer to refer to an item in a collection using its unique key. The code appears as follows:

```
Debug.Print colNames("Alexis")
```

Removing Items from a Collection

The `Remove` method of the Collection object is used to remove items from a collection. The syntax looks like this:

```
colNames.Remove 2
```

The syntax shown previously would remove the second element of the collection. Using the key, the code is changed to this:

```
colNames.Remove "Brianna"
```

You can easily remove all the elements of a collection in one of two ways:

```
Set colNames = New Collection
```

or

```
Set colNames = Nothing
```

Iterating Through the Elements of a Collection

The `For...Each` loop is used to iterate through the items in a collection. The code looks like this:

```
Sub IterateCollection()
    Dim colNames As Collection
    Dim varItem As Variant
    Set colNames = New Collection

    colNames.Add "Alison", "Alison"
    colNames.Add "Dan", "Dan"
    colNames.Add "Alexis", "Alexis"
    colNames.Add "Joshua", "Joshua"
    colNames.Add "Amanda", "Amanda"
    colNames.Add "Brianna", "Brianna"

    For Each varItem In colNames
        Debug.Print colNames(varItem)
    Next varItem
End Sub
```

Notice that in addition to the declaration of the Collection variable, a variant variable is declared. The variant variable is used in the `For...Each` loop to loop through each item in the collection. Notice that the variant variable is used as the subscript within the `For...Each` loop to access a particular item within the collection.

UNDERSTANDING AND EFFECTIVELY USING COMPILATION OPTIONS

Microsoft Access gives you a few alternatives for compilation. Understanding them can help you to decide whether compilation speed or trapping compilation errors is more important to you.

Compile on Demand

By default, VBA compiles your code only when the code in the module changes or when a procedure in one module is called by another module. Although this default setting can dramatically speed the compilation process, it can leave you wondering whether you have a hidden time bomb lurking somewhere in your application.

Here's a typical scenario: You open a form, make some simple changes, save the changes, and close the form. You repeat this process for a few additional forms. You also open a couple of modules to make some equally simple changes. During the testing process, you forget to test one or more of the forms and one or more of the modules. With the Compile On Demand option set to True (its default value), errors aren't identified until the offending code is accessed.

To disable the Compile On Demand feature, choose Tools | Options from the VBE. Click the General tab and remove the check from Compile On Demand. You might notice some degradation in performance each time your code compiles, but this is time well spent.

IMPORTING AND EXPORTING CODE MODULES

The Access 2000 VBE allows you to import code or form modules into, and export code modules from, a database. To export a form or code module, take the following steps:

1. Activate the VBE.
2. Within the Project Explorer window, right-click the object you want to export.
3. Select Export File. The Export File dialog appears.
4. Select a location and name for the exported file and then click Save.

When you export a module, it is exported as an ASCII text file. You can import the text file into another Microsoft Access database, into any other Microsoft Office product (for example, Microsoft Excel), or into a Visual Basic project.

NOTE

If you export a Form module, only the Class module behind the form is exported. No visual aspects of the form are exported.

Just as you can export a text file, you can import a text file. This allows you to add an existing module or form to a project. The file is copied and imported into the database. The original file is unaffected. To import a file into your Access database:

1. Activate the VBE.
2. Within the Project Explorer window, right click and select Import File. The Import File dialog appears.
3. Locate and select the file you want to import, and then click Open.

24

ADVANCED VBA
TECHNIQUES

WORKING WITH PROJECT PROPERTIES

Every database project has user-definable properties. These include:

- The project name
- A description of the project
- The name of the help file associated with the project
- The help context ID associated with the project
- Conditional compilation arguments
- A password associated with the project

To view or modify project properties:

1. Activate the VBE.
2. Select Tools | <project name> Properties. The Project Properties dialog appears (see Figure 24.6).

FIGURE 24.6

The Project Properties dialog.

3. Click the General tab to designate or change any of the general project properties.
4. Click the Protection tab to specify a password for the VBA project.
5. Click OK to close the dialog, accepting the options you have set. You must close the database and reopen it for any security options to take effect.

The Protection options deserve special attention. If you click to select Lock Project for Viewing, the VBA project cannot be viewed or edited by someone who does not have the correct password. If you do not select Lock Project for Viewing, the VBA project can be viewed by anyone, but project properties can be changed only by someone with the correct password.

Putting Advanced Techniques to Use in the Time and Billing Application

The Time and Billing application will put into practice all that you have learned throughout this chapter. The following examples cover the use of Null, intrinsic constants, and type structures.

Examples of Null, the DoCmd Object, and Intrinsic Constants

The following event routine is used to view all the projects associated with the selected client. It illustrates the importance of the ability to work with Null values and intrinsic constants.

```
Private Sub cmdProjects_Click()
On Error GoTo Err_Projects_Click
    If IsNull(Me.txtClientID) Then
        MsgBox "Enter client information before viewing projects form."
    Else
        DoCmd.RunCommand Command:=acSaveRecord
        DoCmd.OpenForm "frmProjects", , , "[ClientID]=" & Me.txtClientID
    End If
Exit_Projects_Click:
    Exit Sub
Err_Projects_Click:
    MsgBox Err.Description
    Resume Exit_Projects_Click
End Sub
```

The routine first invokes error handling (discussed in Chapter 14, "Error Handling: Preparing for the Inevitable"); then uses the IsNull function to test whether a ClientID has been entered. The IsNull function returns a True if the value in the txtClientID control is Null. If it is, an error message is displayed. If the txtClientID control contains a non-Null value, two methods are performed on the DoCmd object.

The first method performed on the DoCmd object is the RunCommand method. This method receives the constant associated with the name of the menu command you want to execute. The use of intrinsic constants makes this code more readable, and the RunCommand method makes it much easier to call menu commands from code.

24

ADVANCED VBA
TECHNIQUES

The second method performed on the DoCmd object is OpenForm, which opens the frmProjects form. Two optional parameters, View and FilterName, are omitted. The fourth parameter, the WhereCondition, is set to the ClientID that's displayed on the Client form.

An Example of Using a Type Structure

Many parts of the Time and Billing application require the company information stored in the tblCompanyInfo table. It would be inefficient to read the data from this table each time the application needs it. It would be much more efficient to read this data once, when the application loads, and store it in a type structure. Because it remains in memory at all times, you can efficiently retrieve it whenever needed. The type structure is defined and a Public Type variable based on the type structure is declared in a module's Declarations section. It looks like this:

```
Type CompanyInfo
    SetUpID As Long
    CompanyName As String * 50
    Address As String * 255
    City As String * 50
    StateProvince As String * 20
    PostalCode As String * 20
    Country As String * 50
    PhoneNumber As String * 30
    FaxNumber As String * 30
    DefaultPaymentTerms As String * 255
    DefaultInvoiceDescription As String
End Type
Public typCompanyInfo As CompanyInfo
```

A subroutine is invoked when the client form (your startup form) is first loaded. This routine populates all the elements of the type structure. The routine looks like this:

```
Sub GetCompanyInfo()

    Dim rs As ADODB.Recordset
    Set db = CurrentDb
    Set rs = New ADODB.Recordset

    rs.Open "tblCompanyInfo, CurrentProject.Connection
    typCompanyInfo.SetUpID = rs!SetUpID
    typCompanyInfo.CompanyName = rs!CompanyName
    typCompanyInfo.Address = rs!Address
    typCompanyInfo.City = rs!City
    typCompanyInfo.StateProvince = rs!StateProvince
    typCompanyInfo.PostalCode = rs!PostalCode
    typCompanyInfo.Country = rs!Country
    typCompanyInfo.PhoneNumber = rs!PhoneNumber
```

```
    typCompanyInfo.FaxNumber = rs!PhoneNumber
    rs.Close
    db.Close
End Sub
```

Don't be concerned with the recordset handling included in this routine. Instead, notice that the value from each field in the first (and only) record of the tblCompanyInfo table is being loaded into the elements of the Global Type variable. Here's an example of how the Type variable is used:

```
Sub PopulateControls()
    txtCompanyName.Value = Trim(typCompanyInfo.CompanyName)
    txtAddress.Value = Trim(typCompanyInfo.Address)
    txtCityStateZip.Value = Trim(typCompanyInfo.City) & ", " & _
        Trim(typCompanyInfo.StateProvince) & _
        "  " & Format(Trim(typCompanyInfo.PostalCode), "!&&&&&-&&&&")
    txtPhoneFax.Value = "PHONE: " & _
        Format(Trim(typCompanyInfo.PhoneNumber), "(&&&)&&&-&&&&") & _
        "        FAX: " & _
        Format(Trim(typCompanyInfo.FaxNumber), "(&&&)&&&-&&&&")
End Sub
```

This routine is called by the `Activate` event of `rptInvoice`. It populates four different controls on the form with the company information retrieved from the elements of the Global Type variable.

SUMMARY

As an Access developer, you spend much of your time writing VBA code. Knowing the tricks and tips of the trade and understanding the more advanced aspects of the language will save you much time and help you streamline your application code.

This chapter shows you tricks and tips you can use to help you effectively navigate the VBA environment and delves into more advanced aspects of the VBA language, such as user-defined types, constants, and arrays. You have seen the important difference between passing parameters by reference and passing them by value, and learned about other advanced function techniques, such as optional and named parameters. Other important topics covered in this chapter include collections, `Empty` versus `Null`, and compilation options. Understanding these valuable aspects of the VBA language will help you get the most out of the code you write.

USING ACTIVEX CONTROLS

IN THIS CHAPTER

ACTIVEX CONTROLS EXPLAINED

A powerful aspect of Access 2000 is its capability to be extensible. In addition to the controls available as part of the product, you can incorporate ActiveX controls on your forms. This means that you aren't limited by what Access supplies, only by the imaginations of third-party developers who design ActiveX controls.

> **NOTE**
>
> Microsoft has renamed *OLE controls* as *ActiveX controls*. You can expect to see these terms used interchangeably.

ActiveX controls support the OLE 2.0 custom control architecture and provide support for 32-bit operating systems. They have their own code, methods, events, and properties. An ActiveX control's functionality is stored in a file with an .OCX extension. This is why ActiveX controls are often referred to as OCXs. A Calendar OCX control comes with Microsoft Access, and additional OCX controls are included in the Microsoft Office 2000 Developer Edition (ODE) Tools and are also available from third-party vendors, such as FMS, Database Creations, Crescent, Sheridan, Far Point, and many others.

Two types of ActiveX controls are available. The first is visible at both design time and runtime; after being placed on a form, it provides a front-end interface that allows the user to directly manipulate the object. One example is the Calendar control in Access 2000. The second type of ActiveX control is visible at design time, but not at runtime; this type of control can, for example, give you access to all Windows common dialog boxes, such as Open, Print, and so on. The control itself isn't visible to the user, but its functionality is available to the user at runtime. Another example is a timer control; it operates within the application, triggering event code to run, but isn't actually visible to the user.

With ActiveX controls, you can easily incorporate more functionality in your applications. For example, if you need to include a calendar on your form, you don't need to worry about how to build your own. Instead, you can include a custom calendar control and modify the calendar's behavior by changing its properties and executing its methods.

INCORPORATING ACTIVEX CONTROLS IN ACCESS 2000

Before you can incorporate an ActiveX control in your application, you must perform three steps:

1. Install the ActiveX control
2. Register the control
3. Add the control to a form

Installing an ActiveX Control

When you buy an ActiveX control, it generally has an installation program that copies the OCX file to your Windows system directory. The name of this directory can vary depending on whether you're running Windows 95, Windows 98, or Windows NT and what you named your Windows directory during your operating system installation.

Registering an ActiveX Control

After you have installed the control, you're ready to register it with Access. Often a control is automatically registered during installation, which is true of the Calendar OCX included with Access, as well as all the OCX controls that come with the Microsoft ODE Tools. OCX controls are registered in the `HKEY_LOCAL_MACHINE\SOFTWARE` class in the Windows Registry. (See Figure 25.1.) In the figure, the Image List control, registered as `ImagelistCtrl`, is selected.

FIGURE 25.1
OCX controls in the Windows Registry.

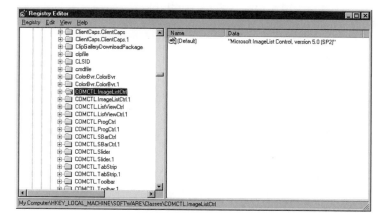

If an ActiveX control isn't registered, you can do so by using the ActiveX Controls dialog box. To open this dialog box, choose Tools | ActiveX Controls. (See Figure 25.2.)

The ActiveX Controls dialog box lists all the ActiveX controls currently registered in Access. To add an ActiveX control to the list, click Register. This opens the Add ActiveX Control dialog box. (See Figure 25.3.)

Make sure that you're pointing to the directory containing the OCX you want to register. The control you're registering must already be installed; if it hasn't been installed, it won't be on the list. Select the OCX you want to register, and click OK. You then return to the ActiveX Controls dialog box, and the control you selected appears on the list of registered controls. You're ready to include the control on a form.

If you no longer plan to use an ActiveX control, you should use the Unregister button, located in the ActiveX Control dialog, which removes the Registry entries for controls you don't use.

Adding ActiveX Controls to Forms

After you have registered an ActiveX control, you can include it on your forms. You do this in one of two ways:

- Select the ActiveX control from the toolbox by clicking the More Controls icon.

- Choose ActiveX Control from the Insert menu when you're in Form or Report Design view.

The More Controls tool shows you all ActiveX controls registered by your system. This includes ActiveX controls that are part of Excel, Visual Basic, and any other application that uses ActiveX controls. Some of these controls won't work properly with Access. To determine which controls you can safely include in your application, read the Access Readme file or contact the vendor of the ActiveX control. The More Controls menu is shown in Figure 25.4.

FIGURE 25.4

The More Controls menu shows you all the ActiveX controls registered on your system.

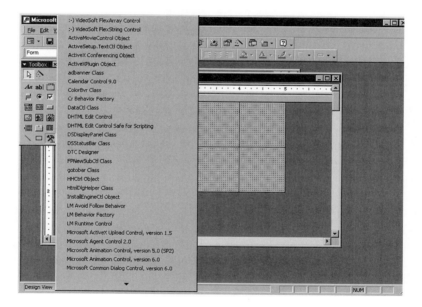

The More Controls menu shows all the ActiveX controls installed on the system. You can also use the Insert menu to select an ActiveX control from the Insert ActiveX Control dialog box. (See Figure 25.5.) After selecting a control from the Select an ActiveX Control list box, the control is placed on the form. You can move the control around the form and size it as needed.

FIGURE 25.5

Use the Insert ActiveX Control dialog box to add an ActiveX control to a form.

After you have placed an ActiveX control on a form, the control is ready to operate in its default format. If you insert the Calendar OCX control in a form and run the form, it looks like Figure 25.6.

FIGURE 25.6

A Calendar OCX, shown in Form view, with no properties explicitly set.

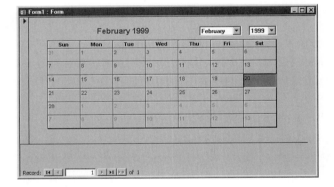

The Calendar control can display all the months of the year, along with the corresponding days for each particular month. So far, you haven't set any properties for the calendar, nor have you written code to respond to any of the calendar's events. Setting an ActiveX control's properties, executing an ActiveX control's methods, and responding to an ActiveX control's events are covered in the following sections.

Understanding and Managing the Control Reference in Your Access Application

When you insert an ActiveX control on a form, Access automatically creates a reference to the control's Type Library that appears in the References dialog box. (See Figure 25.7.) To invoke the References dialog box, choose Tools | References with the Visual Basic Editor active. Note that the full path to the control is stored in this dialog box. For example, Figure 25.7 shows that the Calendar OCX is stored in D:\Program Files\Microsoft Offce\Office. If the OCX is moved, VBA might not be able to resolve the reference. If this happens, you must open the References dialog box and manually remove the check from the reference marked as missing and set a reference to the ActiveX control in its new location.

FIGURE 25.7

Use the References dialog box to add and remove library references.

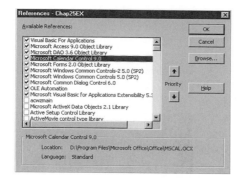

If you're distributing an application with ActiveX controls, the application may or may not work without problems. Access does its best to try to resolve references to ActiveX controls. If the controls are in the Windows\System directory or the directory Access is installed in, Access can automatically resolve the references, even if the application is installed in a different directory on the user's machine than it was on your machine.

Remember, not only do ActiveX controls need to be referenced, but they also need to be registered in the Windows Registry. If you use the Package and Deployment Wizard included with the Microsoft ODE Tools to distribute your application, the OCXs are automatically registered when the user installs your application. If you don't use the Microsoft Office 2000 Package and Deployment Wizard to distribute your application, you must write code to register the ActiveX control, or the user will have to manually register it.

SETTING PROPERTIES OF AN ACTIVEX CONTROL AT DESIGN TIME

The methods, events, and properties associated with each ActiveX control differ. They're specific to that control and are determined by the control's author, and they are used to manipulate the control's appearance and behavior. Each control's methods, events, and properties are in a separate .OCX file.

If you don't modify a control's properties, it functions with its default appearance and behavior. Much of the richness of third-party controls comes from the ability to customize the controls by changing their properties at both design time and runtime. Some controls support *data binding*, which lets you store or display data in a control from an underlying field in a table. Furthermore, the ability to respond to an ActiveX control's events allows you to respond to the user's interaction with the control, and being able to execute the control's methods lets you manipulate the control.

Figure 25.8 shows some of the Calendar control's many properties. As with any control, most of its properties can be set at design time and modified or read at runtime.

FIGURE 25.8

The Calendar control's Property sheet.

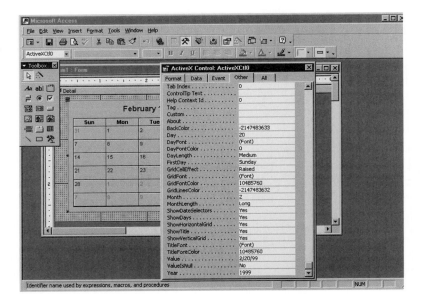

Another way to set properties for a control is to do it graphically by selecting the Custom property from the object's Property sheet; then clicking the build button. For example, if you select the Custom property from the Calendar control's Property sheet and click the build button, the Calendar Control Properties dialog box appears. (See Figure 25.9.) Here, you can modify many of the calendar's attributes, including the first day of the week, whether you want the days of the week to show, and the colors and fonts. The properties shown in this dialog box vary for each control.

TIP

You can access the Control Properties dialog by double-clicking the ActiveX control in the Design view of a form.

FIGURE 25.9

*The Calendar
Control
Properties dialog
box allows you to
set some initial
properties for the
control.*

CODING EVENTS OF AN ACTIVEX CONTROL

Just as the properties of the control can be set or evaluated at runtime, the control's events can
be coded, too. To get a list of all the events associated with an ActiveX control, open the
Procedure box in the Module window. Make sure that the control name for your ActiveX control is listed in the Object box. Figure 25.10 shows all the events for the Calendar control.

FIGURE 25.10

*Viewing the events
of the Calendar
control.*

The Calendar control's AfterUpdate event is triggered when the user selects a date from the
calendar. The following code changes the value of the txtDateSelected text box to the Value

property of the calPickADay control. This code is placed in the Calendar control's AfterUpdate event so that it executes any time the user selects a date on the calendar.

```
Private Sub calPickADay_AfterUpdate()
    txtDateSelected.Value = calPickADay.Value
End Sub
```

 This code—and most of the code in this chapter—is in the CHAP25EX.MDB file on the book's CD-ROM. This example is found in the frmPickADay form.

USING THE CALENDAR CONTROL

The Calendar control is one of the more powerful OCX controls available. Understanding its properties and methods makes it a lot easier to work with; they are covered in the following sections. Most of the examples are found in frmCalPropsAndMethods.

Properties of a Calendar Control

The Day, Month, and Year properties designate the day, month, and year displayed on the calendar. These properties are automatically changed at runtime as the user selects different dates on the calendar. You can modify the values programmatically by using macros or Visual Basic, thereby changing the day, month, or year that's selected.

The Value property is one of the Calendar control's most important properties. It retrieves the selected calendar date or moves the date highlight to a specific day. The following code uses the Value property to display the selected day in a message box:

```
Private Sub cmdDisplayDate_Click()
    MsgBox calSelectADay.Value
End Sub
```

The ValueIsNull property lets you indicate that no date is selected on the calendar. This property is used when you want to make sure that the user explicitly selects a date.

The DayFont and DayFontColor properties specify the font and color for displaying the day titles. The DayFont property is further broken down into the properties Name, Size, Bold, Italic, Underline, and Strikethrough. An individual property can be modified like this:

```
calSelectADay.DayFont.Italic = True
```

You can use the With...End With construct to change several font properties at once:

```
With calSelectADay.DayFont
    .Bold = True
    .Italic = True
    .Name = "Arial"
End With
```

The `DayFontColor` property can be used to easily modify the color of the day titles:

```
calSelectADay.DayFontColor = 16711680
```

The `GridFont` and `GridFontColor` properties are similar to the `DayFont` and `DayFontColor` properties. `GridFont` determines the font type and size attributes for the text in the calendar, and `GridFontColor` indicates the text color in the calendar. For example, the following routine modifies the Bold, Italic, and Name properties of the `GridFont` property and changes the color of the days displayed on the calendar:

```
Private Sub cmdChangeGridFont_Click()
   With calSelectADay.GridFont
      .Bold = True
      .Italic = True
      .Name = "Arial"
   End With
   calSelectADay.GridFontColor = 8388736
End Sub
```

The `DayLength` and `MonthLength` properties designate how you want the day or month titles to be displayed. The available choices for `DayLength` are Short (0), Medium (1), and Long (2). Short displays the day as one character, Medium displays the day as a three-character abbreviation, and Long displays the full day (for example, Monday). The available choices for `MonthLength` are Short (0) and Long (2). Short displays the month as a three-character abbreviation, and Long displays the full month name. The following code specifies both the `DayLength` and `MonthLength` properties as Short:

```
Private Sub cmdChangeLength_Click()
   calSelectADay.DayLength = 0
   calSelectADay.MonthLength = 0
End Sub
```

The `ShowDateSelectors` property indicates whether combo boxes appear at the top of the calendar, allowing the user to select a month and year. This property can be set to `True` or `False`.

The `ShowTitle` property indicates whether the month and year are displayed at the top of the calendar.

The `GridLinesFormat` and `GridLinesColor` properties specify whether the gridlines are raised, sunken, or flat and what color they are.

Methods of a Calendar Control

The Calendar control also has several methods, or actions you can take on the Calendar object. The `NextDay`, `PreviousDay`, `NextWeek`, `PreviousWeek`, `NextMonth`, `PreviousMonth`, `NextYear`, and `PreviousYear` methods all move the control's `Value` property forward or backward by the specified period of time.

Other methods of the Calendar control include the following:

- The `Refresh` method repaints the Calendar control.
- The `Today` method sets the `Value` property to the current date.
- The `AboutBox` method displays the Calendar control's About box.

> **NOTE**
>
> The following examples require controls supplied with the Microsoft Office 2000 Developer Edition. You must have the ODE for the following code samples to run. Also, if you have the ODE, you can distribute these tools royalty free to your users.
>
> If you have the ODE installed and still can't run some of the examples, you might want to check the References dialog box to make sure the controls are properly referenced.

Figure 25.11 shows how the Calendar control works. As you can see, the form, called frmCalendar, lets the user move from day to day, month to month, or year to year. The user can also move to the current day, or even select a date, and then click the Display Orders for Selected Date command button to view all the orders placed on the selected date.

FIGURE 25.11

An example of using the Calendar control.

The code for the Today command button illustrates using the `Today` method:

```
Private Sub cmdToday_Click()
    calPickADay.Today
End Sub
```

Because the Today method is issued on the Calendar control, the selected day will become the current date. The code for the Display Orders for Selected Date command button looks like this:

```
Private Sub cmdOrders_Click()
    frmOrdersByDate.Form.RecordSource = _
        "Select * from qryOrdersByDate Where OrderDate = #" _
        & calPickADay.Value & "#"
End Sub
```

This code changes the subform's RecordSource to include only those records in which the OrderDate is equal to the selected calendar date. The remainder of the code for the frmCalendar form is discussed in the following section.

USING THE UPDOWN CONTROL

The UpDown control is an excellent tool for incrementing and decrementing values. Used in conjunction with other controls, it can easily act as a means to increment and decrement the controls' values. For example, on the frmCalendar form, UpDown objects increment and decrement the selected day, month, and year. Like the Calendar control, the UpDown object has its own built-in properties and methods. Although the properties can be modified on the Other tab of the Properties window, it's easier to modify them by using the UpDown properties dialog box.(See Figure 25.12.) To open it, double-click on the UpDown object whose properties you want to modify.

FIGURE 25.12

The UpDown Properties dialog box.

The `Orientation` property, one of the most important for the `UpDown` object, indicates whether you want the `UpDown` object to be displayed vertically or horizontally. The two most commonly used events of a `UpDown` object are the `UpClick` event and the `DownClick` event; they specify what happens when the user clicks either button of the control. The following code is placed in the `DownClick` event of the updnDay `UpDown` object on frmCalendar. Notice that the code executes a `PreviousDay` method on the calPickADay control, causing the Calendar control to set the focus to the previous day:

```
Private Sub updnDay_DownClick()
    calPickADay.PreviousDay
End Sub
```

The `UpClick` event of the updnDay control uses the `NextDay` method of the calPickADay control to cause the focus to shift to the next day:

```
Private Sub updnDay_UpClick()
    calPickADay.NextDay
End Sub
```

The `DownClick` event of the updnMonth control uses the Calendar control's `PreviousMonth` method to move focus to the same day in the previous month:

```
Private Sub updnMonth_DownClick()
    calPickADay.PreviousMonth
End Sub
```

The `UpClick` event of the updnMonth control uses the Calendar control's `NextMonth` method to move focus to the same day in the next month:

```
Private Sub updnMonth_UpClick()
    calPickADay.NextMonth
End Sub
```

The `DownClick` and `UpClick` events of the updnYear control use the Calendar control's `PreviousYear` and `NextYear` methods to move backward and forward a year in the calendar:

```
Private Sub updnYear_DownClick()
    calPickADay.PreviousYear
End Sub

Private Sub updnYear_UpClick()
    calPickADay.NextYear
End Sub
```

As you can see, by combining the different ActiveX controls, you can create exciting, user-friendly, utilitarian applications.

USING THE STATUSBAR CONTROL

You can use the StatusBar control to quickly and easily add professional-looking status bars to your forms, as shown in the frmCalendar form in Figure 25.11. The StatusBar in the figure has six panels; the first two have been configured to display the current date and time, and the last three display the status of the Caps, Num, and Ins keys.

Properties can be set for the StatusBar control as a whole or for the individual panels. (See Figure 25.13.) The Style property specifies whether you want the status bar to include multiple panels or only a single panel. The SimpleText property is used only for single-panel status bars; it specifies the text in the panel. Finally, the MousePointer property lets you select the type of mouse pointer that appears when it's placed over the StatusBar control.

FIGURE 25.13

The general properties of the StatusBar control.

Each panel of the StatusBar control has properties that affect what that panel looks like and how it performs. The Index property of the panel is used to identify the particular panel. The panel properties are shown in Figure 25.14. The Style property is an important one; it specifies what information is displayed in the panel. It can be set to Text, Caps, Num Lock, Ins, Scroll, Time, Date, or Kana Lock. When set, the control can automatically sense whether the Caps Lock or other keys are active. The Text property indicates the text displayed in the panel when the Style property is set to Text. The value of this property is often modified at runtime to display a specific message to the user. The Alignment property determines whether the information is left-aligned, right-aligned, or centered in the panel, and the Bevel property can be set to None, Insert, or Raised.

FIGURE 25.14

*The StatusBar
panel properties.*

As you insert and remove panels, each panel is assigned an index, and the `Index` property is used to refer to a specific panel at runtime, as shown in this example:

```
Private Sub calPickADay_AfterUpdate()
   If calPickADay.Value = Date Then
      sbrStatus.Panels(3).Text = "TODAY!!!"
   Else
      sbrStatus.Panels(3).Text = ""
   End If
End Sub
```

This code evaluates the `calPickADay` value to see whether it's equal to the current date. If so, the text of the third panel is set to `TODAY!!!`. Otherwise, the third panel's text is set to a zero-length string.

CAUTION

In the Access "world," almost everything is zero-based. Of course, there are exceptions to every rule. The StatusBar control is one of those exceptions—it's one-based. The code in the previous example really does modify the text in the third panel.

USING THE COMMON DIALOG CONTROL

The Common Dialog control is actually like many controls in one. It's used to display the standard Windows File Open, File Save As, Font, Color, and Print common dialog boxes. It's a hidden control that doesn't appear at runtime, but whose properties and methods can be manipulated by using VBA code. The frmCommonAndRich form, shown in Figure 25.15, illustrates using several of the common dialog boxes as well as the Rich Textbox control, covered in the next section.

FIGURE 25.15

The form used to illustrate common dialog and rich text boxes.

The Screen Color and Button Font command buttons illustrate using the Common Dialog control. They invoke the Color and Font common dialog boxes, respectively. The code for the `Click` event of the cmdColor command button looks like this:

```
Private Sub cmdColor_Click()
    dlgCommon.Flags = cdlCCFullOpen
    dlgCommon.ShowColor
    Me.Detail.BackColor = dlgCommon.Color
End Sub
```

The code begins by setting the Common Dialog control's `Flags` property, which is used to specify attributes of the common dialog box. The value of cdlCCFullOpen for the Color common dialog box indicates that the entire Color dialog box, including the portion that lets the user create custom colors, is displayed. The `ShowColor` method, when applied to the Common Dialog control, invokes the Color common dialog box. (See Figure 25.16.) The color the user selects is filled into the `Color` property of the Common Dialog control. This color is used to modify the `BackColor` property of the form's Detail section.

FIGURE 25.16

The Color chooser is part of the Common Dialog box.

The following code uses the `With...End With` loop to change several properties from the Common Dialog box:

```
Private Sub cmdFont_Click()
    Dim ctl As Control
    dlgCommon.Flags = cdlCFScreenFonts
    dlgCommon.ShowFont
    For Each ctl In Controls
        If TypeOf ctl Is CommandButton Then
            With ctl
                .FontName = dlgCommon.FontName
                .FontBold = dlgCommon.FontBold
                .FontItalic = dlgCommon.FontItalic
                .FontSize = dlgCommon.FontSize
            End With
        End If
    Next ctl
End Sub
```

The `Click` event of cmdFont first sets the Common Dialog control's `Flags` property to `cdlCFScreenFonts`. For the Font common dialog box, the value of `cdlCDFScreenFonts` causes the dialog box to list only the screen fonts supported by the user's system. The `ShowFont` method is used to invoke the actual dialog box. (See Figure 25.17.) Using a `With...End With` construct, the code takes each property set in the common dialog box and uses it to loop through the form's Controls collection, modifying the font attributes of each command button.

The File Open, File Save, and File Print common dialog boxes are covered in the next section.

FIGURE 25.17

The Font part of the Common Dialog box allows you to set several font properties at one time.

USING THE RICH TEXTBOX CONTROL

The Rich Textbox control allows you to design a text box for writing code that affects the selected text. Properties that can be specified for the selected text include the `Font`, `Font Size`, `Bold`, and `Italic` properties. You can even add bullet points to the selected text. Furthermore, you can save the contents of the Rich Textbox control in a rich text format (RTF) file and later retrieve it back into the control.

The following code illustrates using several of the Rich Textbox control's properties:

```
Private Sub cmdTextColor_Click()
   dlgCommon.ShowColor
   rtfDocument.SelColor = dlgCommon.Color
End Sub
```

This code uses the Color common dialog box to set the `SelColor` property of the Rich Textbox control. The selected text appears in whatever color the user selects from the common dialog box.

The `Click` event of the cmdTextFont command button sets the `SelFontName`, `SelBold`, `SelItalic`, and `SelFontSize` properties of the Rich Textbox control to the font, style, and size selected in the Font common dialog box:

```
Private Sub cmdTextFont_Click()
   dlgCommon.Flags = cdlCFScreenFonts
   dlgCommon.ShowFont
   With rtfDocument
      .SelFontName = dlgCommon.FontName
      .SelBold = dlgCommon.FontBold
      .SelItalic = dlgCommon.FontItalic
      .SelFontSize = dlgCommon.FontSize
   End With
End Sub
```

The selected attributes are applied only to the selected text.

25

USING ACTIVEX CONTROLS

The Rich Textbox control has a method called `SaveFile` that lets you save the contents of the Rich Textbox control to an RTF file. The code looks like this:

```
Private Sub cmdSave_Click()
   dlgCommon.Filter = "RTF Files (*.rtf)¦*.rtf"
   dlgCommon.ShowSave
   If dlgCommon.FileName = "" Then
      MsgBox "You Must Specify a File Name", vbExclamation, _
         "File NOT Saved!"
   Else
      rtfDocument.SaveFile dlgCommon.FileName
   End If
End Sub
```

The code begins by setting the Common Dialog control's `Filter` property; this filters the filenames displayed in the File Save common dialog box. The `ShowSave` method invokes the Save As common dialog box. (See Figure 25.18.) After the user types in or selects a filename, the Common Dialog control's `FileName` property is filled in with the name of the file that the user specified. If the user clicks Cancel, the `FileName` property contains a zero-length string, and the user is warned that the file wasn't saved.

FIGURE 25.18

The Save As common dialog box allows you to enter a name, a location, and an extension to your file.

As mentioned, you can also retrieve the contents of an RTF file into the control. The code looks like this:

```
Private Sub cmdOpen_Click()
   dlgCommon.FileName = ""
   dlgCommon.Filter = "RTF Files (*.rtf)¦*.rtf"
   dlgCommon.InitDir = CurDir
   dlgCommon.ShowOpen
   If dlgCommon.FileName = "" Then
      MsgBox "You Must Specify a File Name", vbExclamation, _
         "File Cannot Be Opened!"
   Else
      rtfDocument.LoadFile dlgCommon.FileName
   End If
End Sub
```

The Click event of the cmdOpen command button uses the ShowOpen method to invoke the File Open common dialog box. (See Figure 25.19.) If the user selects a file, the Rich Textbox control's LoadFile method uses the Common Dialog control's FileName property as the name of the file to open.

FIGURE 25.19

The Open common dialog box not only lets you specify which files to open, but also allows you to navigate around your computer and network.

Besides being able to open and save the contents of a Rich Textbox control, you can print the control's contents. The Click event of the cmdPrint command button sets the Common Dialog control's Flags property to cdlPDAllPages:

```
Private Sub cmdPrint_Click()
    dlgCommon.Flags = cdlPDAllPages
    dlgCommon.ShowPrinter
    rtfDocument.SelPrint dlgCommon.hDC
End Sub
```

This selects the All option button in the Print dialog box (and deselects the Pages and Selection option buttons.) The ShowPrinter method displays the Print common dialog box. (See Figure 25.20.) The SelPrint method of the Rich Textbox control is then used to print the selected text with the printer selected in the Print common dialog box.

FIGURE 25.20

The Print common dialog box has several options for printing chores.

25

USING ACTIVEX CONTROLS

USING THE TABSTRIP CONTROL

You can use the TabStrip control to conserve screen real-estate by displaying data on different "pages" of the same form. The TabStrip control included in the ODE is the same control you're used to seeing in applications such as Microsoft Word and Microsoft Excel. It's easy to implement this control in your own forms. Figure 25.21 shows a form called frmTabbed that uses the TabStrip control.

FIGURE 25.21

A form that uses the TabStrip control.

As the user clicks on each tab, the appropriate information displays. For example, if the user selects a customer on the Customers tab, and then clicks the Orders tab, all orders for the selected customer are displayed. If the user selects an order on the Orders tab, and then clicks the Order Details tab, all details about the selected order are displayed. The code looks like this:

```
Private Sub tabSelect_Click()
   Select Case Me!tabSelect.SelectedItem.INDEX
      Case 1
         Me!fsubCustomers.Visible = True
         Me!fsubOrders.Visible = False
         Me!fsubOrderDetails.Visible = False
      Case 2
         Me!fsubOrders.Form.RecordSource = _
            "Select * from tblOrders Where CustomerID = '" _
            & Me!fsubCustomers.Form!CustomerID & "';"
         Me!fsubCustomers.Visible = False
         Me!fsubOrders.Visible = True
         Me!fsubOrderDetails.Visible = False
      Case 3
         Me!fsubOrders.Form.RecordSource = _
            "Select * from tblOrderDetails Where OrderID = " _
            & Me!fsubOrders.Form!OrderID & ";"
```

```
            Me!fsubCustomers.Visible = False
            Me!fsubOrders.Visible = False
            Me!fsubOrderDetails.Visible = True
    End Select
End Sub
```

Here's how the code works: After adding a TabStrip control to a form, you can double-click it to view its properties. (See Figure 25.22.) The TabStrip Control Properties dialog box allows you to set properties for the TabStrip control as a whole, as well as for each tab. When the tabs have been added, you can code the TabStrip control's Click event to determine what will happen as the user clicks on each tab.

FIGURE 25.22

The TabStrip control properties dialog box sets initial properties for the TabStrip control.

NOTE

A Tab control is included as a standard control in the Access toolbox, so you don't need to use the ActiveX TabStrip control in your applications. Third-party vendors have Tab controls with more features than Microsoft's. These are all ActiveX-type controls.

Like the StatusBar control, the TabStrip control is one-based. A Case statement is used to evaluate which tab was selected. The frmTabbed form has three subforms: fsubCustomers, fsubOrders, and fsubOrderDetails. When the frmTabbed form is first displayed, only the fsubCustomers subform control is visible. As the user clicks on each tab in the TabStrip control, the appropriate subform is displayed, and the other two subforms are hidden. The RecordSource for fsubOrders is modified at runtime to show only orders for the selected customer from fsubCustomers, and the RecordSource for fsubOrderDetails is modified at runtime to show only the order detail items for the order selected on fsubOrders.

USING THE IMAGELIST CONTROL

The TabStrip control can be enhanced by using an ImageList control, which stores images you'll be using in the form. It's populated at design time with these images. The ImageList control is hidden at runtime, but any of its images can be used in your form.

The frmImageList form, shown in Figure 25.23, is similar to the frmTabbed form, except that each tab has an image that comes from the ImageList control called imgPictures. The properties of the imgPictures ImageList control are shown in Figure 25.24. Notice that three pictures have been inserted. The General tab's size has been set to 16×16, and the tabSelect TabStrip control has been modified to include imgPictures as its ImageList under the General properties tab. The index of each picture in the imgPictures ImageList control has been added as the Image property for each tab in the TabStrip control; the Image property specifies which image in the bound ImageList control should be displayed in the particular tab.

FIGURE 25.23

The frmImageList form, with pictures for tabs.

FIGURE 25.24

The properties of the ImageList control.

LICENSING AND DISTRIBUTION ISSUES

Some OCX controls can be distributed freely, but others have differing levels of restrictions. The licensing policies for a particular OCX control are determined by its vendor.

The licensing rules in effect for an OCX can be enforced by law, which means that improper distribution of the control is a crime. Distributing an OCX control without proper licensing is just like copying a software product illegally.

If you have any questions about licensing a third-party control, consult the vendor who created the control. A one-time fee might be required to freely distribute the OCX; in other cases, you might have to pay a royalty for each copy of the control that's distributed. If you aren't sure whether you want to buy a third-party control, you might want to consult the vendor. Many vendors let potential customers try out their products for a limited period of time. In fact, many of the demo versions are available online.

PRACTICAL EXAMPLES

Implementing ActiveX Controls

ActiveX controls can be used in many places in the Time and Billing application. Use your imagination to determine where controls will enhance the application's usefulness. The following examples illustrate a few potential uses of the ActiveX controls.

Adding a Calendar to the Report Criteria Dialog

One example of an ActiveX control is in the frmReportDateRange dialog box, shown in Figure 25.25. The Calendar control can be used to populate the Beginning Date and Ending Date text boxes.

FIGURE 25.25

Adding the Calendar control to the Report Criteria form.

The code for adding the Calendar control looks like this:

```
Private Sub cmdSetDates_Click()
    On Error GoTo cmdSetDates_Error

    If cmdSetDates.Caption = "Set Beginning Date" Then
        BeginDate = calSetDates.Value
```

```
        cmdSetDates.Caption = "Set Ending Date"
    Else
        EndDate = calSetDates.Value
        cmdSetDates.Caption = "Set Beginning Date"
    End If

    Exit Sub

cmdSetDates_Error:
    MsgBox "Error # " & Err.Number & ": " & Err.Description
    Exit Sub

End Sub
```

Because the same calendar is used to populate the Beginning Date and Ending Date text boxes, the form has a command button with a caption that toggles. The user can select a date, and then click Set Beginning Date. The BeginDate text box is populated with the value selected on the calendar, and the command button's caption is set to display `Set Ending Date.` If the command button's caption says `Set Ending Date` and the user clicks that button, the EndDate text box is filled with the value selected on the calendar, and the command button's caption changes to say `Set Beginning Date.`

SUMMARY

ActiveX controls greatly extend the abilities of Access 2000 and allow you to incorporate more functionality into your applications. These controls are easy to use and extremely powerful. In this chapter you learned how to install, register, and work with ActiveX controls.

Each ActiveX control has its own properties, events, and methods. By modifying properties, reacting to events, and executing methods, you can take advantage of its rich features. Licensing for each ActiveX control varies, so you need to investigate that for each control you want to use to know whether—and under what conditions—you can distribute it to your users.

AUTOMATION: COMMUNICATING WITH OTHER APPLICATIONS

IN THIS CHAPTER

WHY THIS CHAPTER IS IMPORTANT

Windows users have come to expect seamless integration between products. They are not concerned with what product you use to develop their application; they just want to accomplish their task. Often, Microsoft Word, Microsoft Excel, or some other product is best suited for a particular task that your application must complete. It is your responsibility to pick the best tool for the job. This means that you must know how to communicate from your application directly to that tool.

All this means is that you can no longer learn only about the product and language that you select as your development tool. Instead, you must learn about all the other available applications. Furthermore, you must learn how to communicate with these applications—a challenging but exciting feat.

ActiveX automation is the capability of one application to control another application's objects. This means that your Access application can launch Excel, create or modify a spreadsheet, and print it—all without the user having to directly interact with the Excel application. Many people confuse automation with the process of linking and embedding. OLE 1.0 gave you the capability to create compound documents, meaning that you can embed an Excel spreadsheet in a Word document or link to the Excel spreadsheet from within a Word document. This capability was exciting at the time and still is quite useful in many situations, but OLE 2.0 (in addition to everything that OLE 1.0 provides) introduced the capability for one application to actually control another application's objects. With Office 97, Microsoft changed the way users refer to OLE. It became known as *automation* and is an industry standard and a feature of the *Component Object Model* (COM).

Just as you can control other applications using automation, your Access application can be controlled by other applications, such as Excel or a Visual Basic application. This means that you can take advantage of Access's marvelous report writer from your Visual Basic application. In fact, you can list all the Access reports, allow your user to select one, and then run the report—all from within a Visual Basic form.

DEFINING SOME AUTOMATION TERMS

Before you learn how automation works, you need to understand a few automation terms. Automation requires an automation client and an automation server. The *automation client* application is the one that is doing the talking. It is the application that is controlling the server application. Because this book is about Access, most of the examples in this chapter show Access as an automation client, meaning that the Access application is controlling the other application (Excel, Word, and so on). The *automation server* application is the application being controlled. It contains the objects being manipulated. Excel is acting as an automation server when Access launches Excel, makes it visible, creates a new worksheet, sends the results of a query to the worksheet, and graphs the spreadsheet data. It is Excel's objects that are being controlled, Excel's properties that are being changed, and Excel's methods that are being executed.

Another important component of automation is a *type library*; this is a database that lists the objects, properties, methods, and events exposed by an automation server application. Type libraries allow the server application's objects, properties, and methods to be syntax checked by the Access compiler. You also can use a type library to get help on another application's objects, properties, and methods from within Access.

An *object model* of an automation server application contains the set of objects that are exposed to automation client applications. The objects within the object model are called *object types*. When you write automation code, you create and manipulate instances of an object type. These instances are called *objects*.

CAUTION

It is important to be aware of the hardware that automation requires. It is common for a developer using a Pentium II with 128M of RAM to create a really slick application, only to find that it won't run on the 12M 486s owned by the users. Automation craves RAM. The more, the better! I recommend 48M of RAM or more for applications that use automation. It also is important to recognize that automation is not fast, even on the slickest of machines.

DECLARING AN OBJECT VARIABLE TO REFERENCE YOUR APPLICATION

Automation requires that you create object variables that reference application objects. After you create an object variable, you can query and change the object's properties as well as execute its methods.

You can learn about an object's properties and methods using its object libraries. An *object library* contains a listing of all the properties and methods that an object exposes. To be able to view foreign objects from within Access, you first must establish a reference to that application. After a reference is established, you can view that object's properties and methods using the Object Browser. You also can view any modules and classes that the parent object exposes.

To register an object, the Visual Basic Editor (VBE) must be active. With the code window active, choose Tools | References. The References dialog box appears, as shown in Figure 26.1.

FIGURE 26.1

The References dialog box.

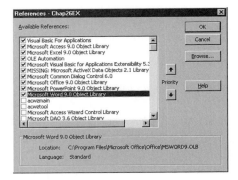

Each time you install a program, the Windows Registry is updated. The References dialog box shows you all the objects that are registered in Windows. (See Figure 26.2.) If you want to link to one of the available objects from within Access, you must enable the check box to the left of the object name. Choose OK. You can browse that object's properties and methods in the Object Browser, as shown in Figure 26.3. As covered in Chapter 8, "Objects, Properties, Methods, and Events Explained," to access the Object Browser, you can choose View | Object Browser, press F2, or click the Object Browser tool while in the Module window. Notice that in Figure 26.3, the Object Browser displays all the classes that belong to the Excel 9.0 object library. The Range class is selected. All the members of the Range class are displayed in the list box at the right. The AutoFill method is selected. Notice that the bottom half of the Object Browser shows all the arguments associated with the AutoFill method of the Range class.

FIGURE 26.2

Registered automation server objects.

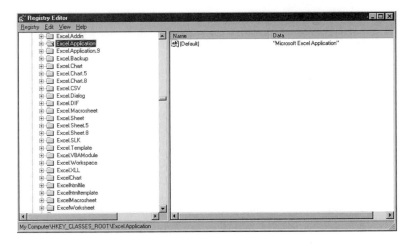

FIGURE 26.3

The Object Browser.

CREATING AN AUTOMATION OBJECT

Before you can talk to an application, you need to know the objects contained within it. You then can use `Dim`, `Private`, or `Public` statements to point to and control various application objects. Each product comes with documentation indicating which objects it supports. You also can view the objects that a product supports by using the Object Browser. After you create an object variable, you can manipulate the object without user intervention.

Declaring an Object Variable

To create an instance of an object, you first must create an object variable that holds a reference to the object. You can do this by using a `Dim` statement:

```
Dim objExcel As New Excel.Application
```

This code creates an object variable pointing to the Excel application object. A new instance of the Excel application is started automatically. This Excel object is part of the Excel application. It can be controlled by VBA using the object variable. Unless instructed otherwise, the instance of Excel is invisible. You can make it visible by using this statement:

```
objExcel.Visible = True
```

Alternatively, you can use two statements to declare and instantiate an object. The code looks like this:

```
Dim objExcel as Excel.Application
Set objExcel = New Excel.Application
```

The Dim statement declares an object variable that is ready to be associated with a running instance of Excel. The Set statement launches Excel and points the object variable at the running instance of Excel. The advantage of this method is that you can better control when the instance of Excel is actually created. If, for example, the declaration is in the General Declarations section of a form, the Set statement can be placed under a command button that is used to launch Excel.

MANIPULATING AN AUTOMATION OBJECT

After you create an instance of an object, you are ready to set its properties and execute its methods. You can talk to the object through the object variable you created. Using this object variable, you can get and set properties and execute methods.

Setting and Retrieving Properties

The objects you will be talking to through automation all have properties. *Properties* are the attributes of the object—the adjectives you use to describe the objects. You can use VBA to inquire about the properties of objects and set the values of these properties. Here are some examples:

```
objExcel.Visible = True
objExcel.Caption = "Hello World"
objExcel.Cells(1, 1).Value = "Here I Am"
```

Each of these examples sets properties of the Excel application object. The first example sets the Visible property of the object to True. The second example sets the Caption of the object to "Hello World". The final example sets the Value property of the Cells object, contained within the Excel object, to the value "Here I Am".

Executing Methods

Properties refer to the attributes of an object, and *methods* refer to the actions you take on the object. Methods are the verbs that apply to a particular object type. Here's an example:

```
objExcel.Workbooks.Add
```

This code uses the Add method to add a workbook to the Excel object.

CONTROLLING EXCEL FROM ACCESS

Before you attempt to talk to Excel, you must understand its object model. Excel gives you an excellent overview of the Excel object model. You can find this model by searching for "object model" in Excel Help. Each object in the model has hypertext links that enable you to obtain specific help on the object, its properties, and its methods.

After you launch Excel, it launches as a hidden window with a `Visible` property of `False`. Destroying the Excel object variable does not cause Excel to terminate. To make things even more complicated, each time you use the `New` keyword within the `Dim` or `Set` statement, a new instance of Excel is launched. This means that it is possible for numerous hidden copies of Excel to be running on a user's machine, which can lead to serious resource problems. If you want to use a running instance of Excel, you can omit the `New` keyword. This has its disadvantages as well. Let's say, for example, that the user of your application has created a large spreadsheet and has not saved it recently. Your application uses an existing instance of Excel, creates a new workbook, prints, and then exits without saving. You might find that your user is very angry about the loss of his or her important work. For this reason, I have found it preferable to suffer the potential resource costs and create my own instance of Excel. If you want to launch Excel invisibly, do your work, and get out, make sure that you terminate Excel upon completion of your code.

Before you execute code that relies on a running copy of Excel, it is important to ascertain that Excel launched successfully. The function shown in Listing 26.1 attempts to launch Excel. If it is successful, `True` is returned from the function. Otherwise, `False` is returned from the function.

LISTING 26.1   THE `CreateExcelObj` SUBROUTINE

```
Function CreateExcelObj() As Boolean
    On Error GoTo CreateExcelObj_Err
    CreateExcelObj = False
    'Attempt to Launch Excel
    Set gobjExcel = New Excel.Application
    CreateExcelObj = True

CreateExcelObj_Exit:
    Exit Function

CreateExcelObj_Err:
    MsgBox "Couldn't Launch Excel!!", vbCritical, "Warning!!"
    CreateExcelObj = False
    Resume CreateExcelObj_Exit
End Function
```

The routine begins by invoking error handling. The return value for the function is initialized to `False`. The routine then attempts to launch Excel. If it is successful, the public variable `gobjExcel` references the running instance of Excel and `True` is returned from the function. If an error occurs, the code within the error handler is executed. A message is displayed and the return value for the function is set to `False`.

CAUTION

To take advantage of the exciting world of automation, all automation server applications must be installed on the user's machine and the user must possess a full license to the server applications. In fact, you will be unable to compile and run the examples contained in the sample database for this chapter unless you have the server applications loaded on your development machine.

The `CreatExcelObj` function is called from the `Click` event of `cmdFillExcel` command button on the frmSimpleExcel form. The application attempts to talk to the Excel object only if the return value of the function is `True`, indicating that Excel was loaded successfully.

```
Private Sub cmdFillExcel_Click()
If CreateExcelObj() Then
      Call FillCells
   End If
End Sub
```

If Excel launches successfully, the `FillCells` subroutine executes, as shown in Listing 26.2.

LISTING 26.2   THE `FillCells` SUBROUTINE

```
Sub FillCells()
    Dim objWS As Excel.Worksheet

    With gobjExcel
        .Workbooks.Add
        Set objWS = gobjExcel.ActiveSheet
        With objWS
            .Cells(1, 1).Value = "Schedule"
            .Cells(2, 1).Value = "Day"
```

```
            .Cells(2, 2).Value = "Tasks"
            .Cells(3, 1).Value = 1
            .Cells(4, 1).Value = 2
        End With
        .Range("A3:A4").SELECT
        .Selection.AutoFill gobjExcel.Range("A3:A33")
        .Range("A1").SELECT
        .Visible = True
    End With
End Sub
```

 You can find this relatively simple routine in frmSimpleExcel, which is part of the CHAP26EX.MDB database file. (See Figure 26.4.) It begins by using the Add method on the Workbooks collection of the Excel object to add a new workbook to the instance of Excel. It then uses Set objWS = poExcel.ActiveSheet to provide a shortcut for talking to the active sheet in the new Excel workbook. Using the objWS object reference, the values of several cells are modified. The AutoFill method is used to quickly fill a range of cells with data. The cursor is returned to cell A1, and the Excel object is made visible. You might wonder what the AutoFill method is; it automates the process of filling a range of cells with a pattern of data. Figure 26.5 shows the results. I mention it here not just to tell you what it is, but also to illustrate an important point: You must know the product you are automating and its capabilities. If you are not familiar with the product from a user's perspective, you will find it extremely difficult to work with the product using automation.

FIGURE 26.4

The form used to launch, communicate with, and close Excel.

Figure 26.5

Using the AutoFill *method to populate a range of cells.*

CLOSING AN EXCEL AUTOMATION OBJECT

After the user clicks the CloseExcel command button, the CloseExcel subroutine is called, as shown in Listing 26.3. The routine first checks to see whether the gobjExcel object variable is still set. If it is, Excel is still running. The DisplayAlerts property of the Excel application object is set to False. This ensures that when the Quit method is executed, Excel will not warn about any unsaved worksheets. This methodology is acceptable because all work was accomplished using a new instance of the Excel application. If you want your work to be saved, you should execute the required code before the Quit method is executed.

Listing 26.3 The CloseExcel Routine

```
Sub CloseExcel()

    If Not gobjExcel Is Nothing Then
        gobjExcel.DisplayAlerts = False
        gobjExcel.Quit
    End If

CloseExcel_Exit:
    Set gobjExcel = Nothing
    Exit Sub
```

```
CloseExcel_Err:
    MsgBox "Error # " & Err.Number & ": " & Err.Description
    Resume CloseExcel_Exit
End Sub
```

CREATING A GRAPH FROM ACCESS

Now that you have learned how to talk to Excel, you are ready to learn how to do something a bit more practical. Figure 26.6 shows a form called frmCreateExcelGraph. The form shows the result of a query that groups the result of price multiplied by quantity for each country. The Create Excel Graph command button sends the result of the query to Excel and produces the graph shown in Figure 26.7. (Listing 26.4 shows the code that produces this graph.)

FIGURE 26.6

The form used to create an Excel graph.

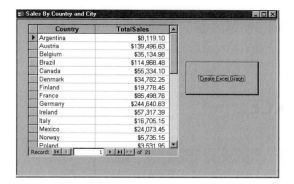

FIGURE 26.7

The result of a query graphed in Excel.

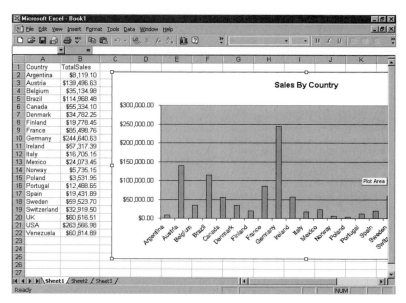

LISTING 26.4 CREATING A GRAPH FROM ACCESS

```
Private Sub cmdCreateGraph_Click()
    On Error GoTo cmdCreateGraph_Err
    Dim rstData As ADODB.Recordset
    Dim rstCount As ADODB.Recordset
    Dim fld As ADODB.Field
    Dim rng As Excel.Range
    Dim objWS As Excel.Worksheet
    Dim intRowCount As Integer
    Dim intColCount As Integer

    'Display Hourglass
    DoCmd.Hourglass True
    Set rstData = New ADODB.Recordset
    rstData.ActiveConnection = CurrentProject.Connection
    Set rstCount = New ADODB.Recordset
    rstCount.ActiveConnection = CurrentProject.Connection

    'Attempt to create Recordset and launch Excel
    If CreateRecordset(rstData, rstCount, "qrySalesByCountry") Then
        If CreateExcelObj() Then
            gobjExcel.Workbooks.Add
            Set objWS = gobjExcel.ActiveSheet
            intRowCount = 1
            intColCount = 1
            'Loop though Fields collection using field names
            'as column headings
            For Each fld In rstData.Fields
                If fld.Type <> adLongVarBinary Then
                    objWS.Cells(1, intColCount).Value = fld.Name
                    intColCount = intColCount + 1
                End If
            Next fld
            'Send Recordset to Excel
            objWS.Range("A1").CopyFromRecordset rstData, 500


            'Format Data
            With gobjExcel
                .Columns("A:B").Select
                .Columns("A:B").EntireColumn.AutoFit
                .Range("A1").Select
                .ActiveCell.CurrentRegion.Select
                Set rng = .Selection
                .Selection.NumberFormat = "$#,##0.00"
```

```
                    'Add a Chart Object
                    .ActiveSheet.ChartObjects.Add(135.75, 14.25, 607.75, 301)_
                      .Select
                    'Run the Chart Wizard
                    .ActiveChart.ChartWizard Source:=Range(rng.Address), _
                        Gallery:=xlColumn, _
                        Format:=6, PlotBy:=xlColumns, CategoryLabels:=1,_
                        SeriesLabels _
                        :=1, HasLegend:=1, Title:="Sales By Country",_
                        CategoryTitle _
                        :="", ValueTitle:="", ExtraTitle:=""
                    'Make Excel Visible
                    .Visible = True
                End With
            Else
                MsgBox "Excel Not Successfully Launched"
            End If
        Else
            MsgBox "Too Many Records to Send to Excel"
        End If
        DoCmd.Hourglass False

cmdCreateGraph_Exit:
    Set rstData = Nothing
    Set rstCount = Nothing
    Set fld = Nothing
    Set rng = Nothing
    Set objWS = Nothing
    DoCmd.Hourglass False
    Exit Sub

cmdCreateGraph_Err:
    MsgBox "Error # " & Err.Number & ": " & Err.Description
    Resume cmdCreateGraph_Exit
End Sub
```

This routine begins by creating several object variables. It then creates two recordsets and sets the ActiveConnection property of each recordset to the connection associated with the current project. It calls a user-defined function called CreateRecordset, located in the basUtils module. The CreateRecordset function receives three parameters: the two recordset object variables and the name of a query. Listing 26.5 shows the CreateRecordset function.

LISTING 26.5 THE `CreateRecordset` FUNCTION

```
Function CreateRecordset(rstData As ADODB.Recordset, _
    rstCount As ADODB.Recordset, _
    strTableName As String)
    On Error GoTo CreateRecordset_Err
    'Create recordset that contains count of records in query
    rstCount.Open "Select Count(*) As NumRecords from " & strTableName
    'If more than 500 records in query result, return false
    'Otherwise, create recordset from query
    If rstCount!NumRecords > 500 Then
        CreateRecordset = False
    Else
        rstData.Open strTableName
        CreateRecordset = True
    End If

CreateRecordset_Exit:
    Set rstCount = Nothing
    Exit Function

CreateRecordset_Err:
    MsgBox "Error # " & Err.Number & ": " & Err.Description
    Resume CreateRecordset_Exit
End Function
```

This function begins by counting how many records are returned by the query name that is passed. If the number of records exceeds 500, the function returns a `False`; otherwise, the function opens a recordset based on the query name that is passed and returns a `True`. This function ensures that only a reasonable number of records is sent to Excel and that a recordset can be opened successfully.

If the `CreateRecordset` function returns a `True`, the remainder of the code in the `Click` event of the `cmdCreateGraph` command button executes. The routine uses the `CreateExcelObj` function to launch Excel. If Excel is opened successfully, a new workbook is created. The routine then loops through each field in the Fields collection of the recordset (the result of the query). The values of the cells in the first row of the worksheet are set equal to the names of the fields in the recordset. Next, the routine uses the `CopyFromRecordset` method of the Excel `Range` object to copy the contents of the recordset `rstData` to cell `A1` in the active worksheet. The data from each row is placed in a different row within the spreadsheet. The data from each column in a particular row is placed in the various columns of the worksheet. OLE object fields (`adLongVarBinary`) are excluded from the process.

After all the data in the recordset is sent to Excel, the routine is ready to create a chart. It moves the cursor to cell A1 and then selects the entire contiguous range of data. It adds a chart object to the worksheet and then uses the Chart Wizard to create a chart. Finally, Excel is made visible so that users can see the fruits of their efforts.

CONTROLLING WORD FROM ACCESS

As you discovered in the preceding section, Excel exposes many objects. Each of these objects can be manipulated separately, using its own properties and methods. Prior to Office 97, this was not true for Word because Word exposed only one object, called Word.Basic. Microsoft Word 97 and Microsoft Word 2000 sport the Visual Basic for Applications language. Both Word 97 and Word 2000 expose many objects just as Excel and other Microsoft products do.

Just like Excel, you can use the Dim statement or Dim as New statement to launch Word. Like Excel, Word launches as a hidden object. The Word application object has a Visible property, which makes the Word object visible. If you create a Word object using automation, Word will not automatically terminate, even if the object variable is destroyed.

Figure 26.8 shows the form called frmMergeToWord, which shows the results of running a query called qryMailMerge. After the user clicks the Merge to Word command button, all the records that are displayed are sent to a Word mail merge and printed. Figure 26.9 shows an example of the resulting document, and Listing 26.6 shows the code that generated this document.

FIGURE 26.8

The data that will be merged to Word.

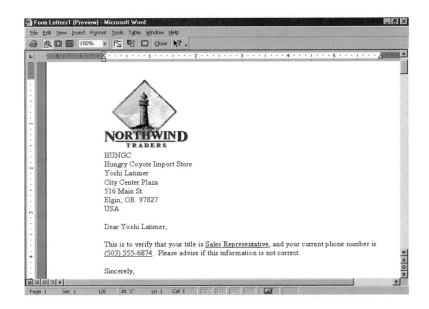

LISTING 26.6   GENERATING A WORD MAIL MERGE DOCUMENT

```
Private Sub cmdMergeToWord_Click()
    On Error GoTo cmdMergeToWord_Err
    DoCmd.Hourglass True
    If CreateWordObj() Then
        With gobjWord
            .Documents.Open "c:\my documents\customerletter.doc"
            DoEvents
            With gobjWord.ActiveDocument.MailMerge
                .Destination = wdSendToNewDocument
                .SuppressBlankLines = True
                .Execute
            End With
            .ActiveDocument.PrintPreview    'Preview
            .Visible = True
        End With
    End If

cmdMergeToWord_Exit:
    DoCmd.Hourglass False
    Exit Sub

cmdMergeToWord_Err:
    MsgBox "Error # " & Err.Number & ": " & Err.Description
```

```
    Set gobjWord = Nothing
    Resume cmdMergeToWord_Exit
End Sub
```

The code begins by presenting an hourglass mouse pointer to the user. This ensures that if the process takes a while, the user knows that something is happening. It then calls the CreateWordObj routine to create a Word object. The CreateWordObj routine is similar to the CreateExcel routine shown earlier in the chapter. The Open method is executed on the Documents collection of the Word object. It opens a document called customerletter in the my documents directory. The customerletter document already has been set up to do a mail merge with the results of a query called qryMerge. The subroutine sets the Destination property of the MailMerge object to a new document. It sets the SuppressBlankLines property to True, and then executes the mail merge with the Execute method. This merges the results of qryMailMerge and creates a new document with the mail-merged letters. The PrintPreview method is executed on the ActiveDocument object so that the merged document is printed. Finally, the Visible property of the Word object is set to True, making Word visible, and the hourglass vanishes.

CONTROLLING POWERPOINT FROM ACCESS

Believe it or not, even PowerPoint can be controlled using automation. You can create a presentation, print a presentation, or even run a slide show directly from Access.

PowerPoint launches as a hidden window. To make PowerPoint visible, you must set the Visible property of AppWindow to True. Destroying the PowerPoint object variable does not terminate the PowerPoint application.

> **NOTE**
>
> You can find details of the PowerPoint object model on the Microsoft Solutions Development Kit CD-ROM. You should review this object model before attempting to communicate with PowerPoint.

The code shown in Listing 26.7 is located under the Click event of the cmdChangePicture command button on frmOLEToPowerPoint, which is shown in Figure 26.10. Figure 26.11 shows the resulting PowerPoint slide.

FIGURE 26.10

The form used to create a PowerPoint slide.

FIGURE 26.11

A PowerPoint slide created using automation.

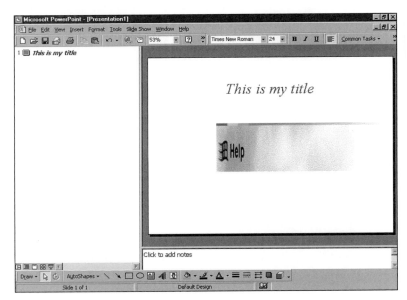

LISTING 26.7 SELECT PICTURE

```
Private Sub cmdChangePicture_Click()
    dlgCommon.ShowOpen
    If Len(dlgCommon.FileName) Then
        olePicture.SourceDoc = dlgCommon.FileName
        olePicture.Action = acOLECreateLink
    End If
End Sub
```

The code in the Click event of cmdChangePicture invokes the File Open common dialog box so that the user can select a picture to be added to the slide. The FileName property returned from this dialog box is used as the SourceDoc property for the automation object. The new picture then is linked to the automation object.

Listing 26.8 shows the routine that creates the PowerPoint slide.

LISTING 26.8 CREATING THE POWERPOINT SLIDE

```
Private Sub cmdMakePPTSlide_Click()

Dim objPresentation As PowerPoint.Presentation
    Dim objSlide As PowerPoint.Slide

    If IsNull(Me.txtTitle) Or Me.olePicture.SourceDoc = "" Then

        MsgBox "A Title Must Be Entered, and a Picture _
        Selected Before Proceeding"

    Else

        'Create instance of PowerPoint application
        Set mobjPPT = New PowerPoint.Application
        'Make instance visible to user
        mobjPPT.Visible = True
        'Add a Presentation
        Set objPresentation = mobjPPT.Presentations.Add
        'Add a Slide
        Set objSlide = objPresentation.Slides.Add(1, ppLayoutTitleOnly)
        'Chage the Slide Background
        objSlide.Background.Fill.ForeColor.RGB = RGB(255, 100, 100)
        'Modify the Slide Title
        With objSlide.Shapes.Title.TextFrame.TextRange
            .Text = Me.txtTitle
            .Font.Color.RGB = RGB(0, 0, 255)
            .Font.Italic = True
        End With
        'Add the OLE Picture
        objSlide.Shapes.AddOLEObject _
            Left:=200, Top:=200, Width:=500, Height:=150, _
            Filename:=olePicture.SourceDoc, link:=True

    End If


cmdMakePPTSlide_Exit:
    Set objPresentation = Nothing
    Set objSlide = Nothing
    Exit Sub

cmdMakePPTSlide_Err:
    MsgBox "Error # " & Err.Number & ": " & Err.Description
    Resume cmdMakePPTSlide_Exit
End Sub
```

The routine begins by creating an instance of PowerPoint. The instance is made visible. A presentation then is added to the PowerPoint object, and a slide is added to the presentation. The background fill of the slide is modified. The text, color, and italic properties of the title object are customized. Finally, the `SourceDoc` property of the `olePicture` object is used to create an automation object, which is added to the slide.

CONTROLLING ACCESS FROM OTHER APPLICATIONS

Many times, you will want to control Access from another application. You might want to run an Access report from a Visual Basic or Excel application, for example. Just as you can tap into many of the rich features of other products (such as Excel) from within Access, you can use some of Access's features from within another program. Fortunately, it is extremely easy to control Access from within other applications.

You can find an overview of the Access object model in Access Help. Unless you are very familiar with the Access object model, you should look at this graphical representation of Access's object model before you attempt to use automation to control Access. Access launches with its `Visible` property set to `False`. You can change the `Visible` property of the application object to `True` to make Access visible.

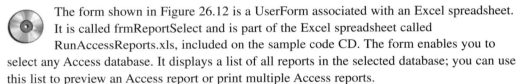

The form shown in Figure 26.12 is a UserForm associated with an Excel spreadsheet. It is called frmReportSelect and is part of the Excel spreadsheet called RunAccessReports.xls, included on the sample code CD. The form enables you to select any Access database. It displays a list of all reports in the selected database; you can use this list to preview an Access report or print multiple Access reports.

FIGURE 26.12

The UserForm that enables you to print Access reports.

Listing 26.9 shows how this UserForm form accomplishes its work.

LISTING 26.9   CREATING A VISUAL BASIC FORM TO PRINT REPORTS

```
Private Sub cmdSelectDatabase_Click()
    dlgCommon.Filter = "*.mdb"
    dlgCommon.ShowOpen
```

```
    If dlgCommon.FileName = "" Then
        MsgBox "You Must Select a File to Continue"
    Else
        Me.txtSelectedDB = _
            dlgCommon.FileName
        Call ListReports
    End If
End Sub

Private Sub ListReports()
    On Error GoTo ListReports_Err
    Dim vntReport As Variant

    If mobjAccess Is Nothing Then
        Set mobjAccess = New Access.Application
    End If

    mobjAccess.OpenCurrentDatabase (Me.txtSelectedDB)

    lstReports.Clear
    For Each vntReport In mobjAccess.CurrentProject.AllReports
        lstReports.AddItem vntReport.Name
    Next vntReport

ListReports_Exit:
    Exit Sub

ListReports_Err:
    MsgBox "Error #" & Err.Number & _
    ": " & Err.Description
    Resume ListReports_Exit
End Sub
```

The `cmdSelectDatabase_Click` event routine sets the `Filter` property of the common dialog control to Access database files. The `ShowOpen` method of the common dialog control is used to display the File Open dialog to the user. After the user selects a file from the dialog, the `ListReports` routine is executed.

The `ListReports` subprocedure begins by creating an instance of the Access application. It uses the `OpenCurrentDatabase` method of the `Access` object to open the Access database selected by the user in the File Open common dialog box. It then loops through the `AllReports` collection of the `CurrentProject` object that is associated with the selected database. The name of each report is added to the list box.

The routine in Listing 26.10 prints the selected reports.

LISTING 26.10 CREATING A NEW INSTANCE OF THE ACCESS APPLICATION OBJECT

```
Private Sub cmdPrint_Click()
    On Error GoTo cmdPreview_Err
    Dim intCounter As Integer
    Dim intPrintOption As Integer
If optPreview.Value = True Then
        intPrintOption = acViewPreview
    ElseIf optPrint.Value = True Then
        intPrintOption = acViewNormal
    End If

    mobjAccess.Visible = True
    For intCounter = 0 To _
        lstReports.ListCount - 1
        If lstReports.Selected(intCounter) Then
            mobjAccess.DoCmd.OpenReport _
            ReportName:=Me.lstReports.List(intCounter), _
            View:=intPrintOption
        End If
    Next intCounter

cmdPreview_Exit:
    Exit Sub

cmdPreview_Err:
    MsgBox "Error #" & Err.Number & _
    ": " & Err.Description
    If Not mobjAccess Is Nothing Then
    mobjAccess.Quit
    End If
    Set mobjAccess = Nothing

    Resume cmdPreview_Exit

End Sub
```

The cmdPrint Click event routine begins by evaluating whether the print or preview option button is selected. The Access application object is made visible. The code then loops through the lstReports list box, printing or previewing each selected report. The OpenReport method is used along with the constant acViewPreview or the constant acViewNormal in order to accomplish this task.

Using Automation to Extend the Functionality of the Time and Billing Application

Many potential applications of automation exist for the Time and Billing application. One of them is discussed in this section.

The form in Figure 26.13 enables users to select a table or query to send to Excel. The form is called frmSendToExcel.

FIGURE 26.13

Exporting a table or query to send to Excel.

The list box on the form is populated with the Callback function shown in Listing 26.11. Notice that the function uses the AllTables and AllQueries collections of the current database to populate the list box, excluding all the system tables.

LISTING 26.11   USING THE Callback FUNCTION TO FILL A LIST BOX

```
Function FillWithTableList(ctl As Control, vntID As Variant, _
      lngRow As Long, lngCol As Long, intCode As Integer) _
      As Variant

    Dim intCounter As Integer
    Static sastrTables() As String
    Static sintNumTables As Integer
    Dim vntRetVal As Variant
    Dim vntData As Variant

    vntRetVal = Null

    Select Case intCode
        Case acLBInitialize           ' Initialize.
            'Determine the Total Number of Tables + Queries
            sintNumTables = CurrentData.AllTables.Count + _
                CurrentData.AllQueries.Count
```

continues

LISTING 26.11   CONTINUED

```
                ReDim sastrTables(sintNumTables - 2)
                'Loop through each Table adding its name to
                'the List Box
                For Each vntData In CurrentData.AllTables
                    If Left(vntData.Name, 4) <> "MSys" Then
                        sastrTables(intCounter) = vntData.Name
                        intCounter = intCounter + 1
                    End If
                Next vntData
                'Loop through each Query adding its name to
                'the List Box
                For Each vntData In CurrentData.AllQueries
                    sastrTables(intCounter) = vntData.Name
                    intCounter = intCounter + 1
                Next vntData
                vntRetVal = sintNumTables
            Case acLBOpen                   'Open
                vntRetVal = Timer            'Generate unique ID for control.
            Case acLBGetRowCount            'Get number of rows.
                vntRetVal = sintNumTables
            Case acLBGetColumnCount         'Get number of columns.
                vntRetVal = 1
            Case acLBGetColumnWidth         'Get column width.
                vntRetVal = -1               '-1 forces use of default width.
            Case acLBGetValue               'Get the data.
                vntRetVal = sastrTables(lngRow)
        End Select
        FillWithTableList = vntRetVal
End Function
```

The Click event of the cmdSendToExcel command button sends the selected table or query to Excel. Listing 26.12 shows this code.

LISTING 26.12   SENDING A TABLE OR QUERY TO EXCEL

```
Private Sub cmdSendToExcel_Click()
    On Error GoTo cmdSendToExcel_Err
    Dim objWS As Excel.Worksheet
    Dim rstData As ADODB.Recordset
    Dim rstCount As ADODB.Recordset
    Dim fld As ADODB.Field
    Dim intColCount As Integer
    Dim intRowCount As Integer

    Set rstData = New ADODB.Recordset
    rstData.ActiveConnection = CurrentProject.Connection
```

```
        Set rstCount = New ADODB.Recordset
        rstCount.ActiveConnection = CurrentProject.Connection

        'Invoke Hourglass
        DoCmd.Hourglass True
        'Try to Create Recordset and Create Excel Object
        If CreateRecordset(rstData, rstCount, lstTables.Value) Then
            If CreateExcelObj() Then
                'Add a Workbook
                gobjExcel.Workbooks.Add
                'Create a Shortcut to the Active Sheet
                Set objWS = gobjExcel.ActiveSheet
                intRowCount = 1
                intColCount = 1
                'Loop through the Fields collection
                'Make each field name a column heading in Excel
                For Each fld In rstData.Fields
                    If fld.Type <> adLongVarBinary Then
                        objWS.Cells(1, intColCount).Value = fld.Name
                        intColCount = intColCount + 1
                    End If
                Next fld
                'Send Recordset to Excel
                objWS.Range("A2").CopyFromRecordset rstData, 500
                gobjExcel.Range("A1").Select
                'Set up AutoFilter
                gobjExcel.Selection.AutoFilter
                gobjExcel.Visible = True
            Else
                MsgBox "Excel Not Successfully Launched"
            End If
        Else
            MsgBox "Too Many Records to Send to Excel"
        End If


cmdSendToExcel_Exit:
    DoCmd.Hourglass False
    Set objWS = Nothing
    Set rstCount = Nothing
    Set rstData = Nothing
    Set fld = Nothing
    Exit Sub

cmdSendToExcel_Err:
    MsgBox "Error # " & Err.Number & ": " & Err.Description
    Resume cmdSendToExcel_Exit
End Sub
```

The routine begins by creating a recordset object using the CreateRecordSet function shown in Listing 24.13. It then attempts to launch Excel. If it is successful, it loops through the Fields collection of the recordset resulting from the selected table or query. It lists all the field names as column headings in Excel. Next, it uses the CopyFromRecordset method of the range object to copy all the field values to the rows in the Excel worksheet. Finally, it issues the AutoFilter method so that the user easily can manipulate the data in Excel, filtering it as necessary. (See Figure 26.14.)

FIGURE 26.14

Using AutoFilter to analyze data sent to Excel.

CAUTION

Although extremely easy to use, the CopyFromRecordset method of the range object has one major limitation. If the table or query used to populate the recordset being sent to Excel contains an OLE object field, the method will fail. There are two solutions to this problem. The most simple solution is to always base the recordset sent to Excel on a query. Do not include any OLE object fields in the query. A second solution is to use a less elegant alternative to the CopyFromRecordset method. Simply loop through the recordset one record at a time. As each record is visited, send it to the appropriate row and column. Because the first method is not only easier to code, but is more optimized, it should be used wherever possible.

LISTING 26.13   CHECKING RECORDSET SIZE

```
Function CreateRecordset(rstData As ADODB.Recordset, _
    rstCount As ADODB.Recordset, _
    strTableName As String)
    On Error GoTo CreateRecordset_Err
    'Create recordset that contains count of records in query
    rstCount.Open "Select Count(*) As NumRecords from " & strTableName
    'If more than 500 records in query result, return false
    'Otherwise, create recordset from query
    If rstCount!NumRecords > 500 Then
        CreateRecordset = False
    Else
        rstData.Open strTableName
        CreateRecordset = True
    End If

CreateRecordset_Exit:
    Set rstCount = Nothing
    Exit Function

CreateRecordset_Err:
    MsgBox "Error # " & Err.Number & ": " & Err.Description
    Resume CreateRecordset_Exit
End Function
```

This routine, found in basOLE, ensures that the recordset is not too large to send to Excel. If the size of the recordset is acceptable, it creates the recordset and returns `True`.

SUMMARY

Automation enables you to control other applications from your Access application, and it enables other programs to control your Access application. This chapter begins by providing an overview of automation and why you might want to use it. It discusses creating an object variable to reference the application you are automating. After the ins and outs of the object variable were explained, you saw numerous examples of manipulating automation objects. You looked at detailed code showing automation involving Excel, Word, and PowerPoint. Finally, you learned about controlling Access from other applications.

The capability to communicate with other applications has become a prerequisite for successful software development. It is extremely important to be aware of the wealth of tools available. The capability to call on other applications' features is helping to make the world document-centric rather than application-centric. This means that users can focus on their tasks and not on how they are accomplishing those tasks. Although automation requires significant hardware and also is rather slow, the benefits it provides often are well worth the price.

898

EXPLOITING THE POWER OF THE WINDOWS API

IN THIS CHAPTER

WHY THIS CHAPTER IS IMPORTANT

One of the richest libraries of programming code functions is supplied by Windows itself. This function library commonly is referred to as the *Windows API* (Application Programming Interface). Fortunately, as VBA programmers, you can tap into the Windows function library by using these built-in Windows functions in your own VBA modules.

Furthermore, you might discover other *dynamic link libraries* (DLLs) that contain functions that would be useful in your applications. These DLLs also are available to you as long as you are properly licensed to use and distribute them.

A *DLL* is a library of procedures that applications can link to and use at runtime. Functions contained in the Windows API and other DLLs can provide your applications with significant added functionality. It is much more efficient to use an external DLL to accomplish a task than to attempt to write a VBA function to accomplish the same task.

DECLARING AN EXTERNAL FUNCTION TO THE COMPILER

To use a DLL function, you must do the following:

- Declare the function to the VBA compiler.
- Call the function.
- Use the return value.

The VBA language is not intrinsically aware of the functions available in external libraries. Declaring a DLL function means making the VBA compiler aware of the name of the function, the library it is located in, the parameters it expects to receive, and the values it expects to return.

If you do not properly declare the library function to the VBA compiler, you receive an error message stating `Sub or Function Not Defined`. User-defined functions and subroutines written in VBA are declared using `Sub` or `Function` keywords. These keywords define the procedures so that VBA can locate the routines when they are called. Functions in a DLL are declared in the same way. After you declare a DLL function to the compiler, Access knows where to locate it, and you can use it throughout your application.

You declare an external function to VBA using a `Declare` statement. You can place `Declare` statements in the Declarations section of a standard module, a standalone class module, or the class module behind a form or report. A `Declare` statement placed in a standard module is immediately available to your entire application. If the `Declare` statement is explicitly declared as private, it is available only to the module in which it was declared. A `Declare` statement placed in the General Declarations section of a standalone class module, or the class module behind a form or report, is available only after the form or report is loaded or after the class is instantiated. Furthermore, a `Declare` statement placed in the General Declarations section of a standalone class module or the module behind a form or report can have only private scope.

You can use a `Declare` statement to declare both subroutines and functions. If the procedure returns a value, you must declare it as a function. If it does not return a value, you must declare it as a subroutine.

A `Declare` statement looks like this:

```
Private Declare Function GetKeyboardType Lib "user32" _
    (ByVal nTypeFlag As Long) As Long
```

This `Declare` statement declares a function called `GetKeyboardType`, which is located in the Windows 9X or Windows NT System folder in a DLL file called user32. It receives a long integer parameter by value and returns a long integer. Notice that this function was declared as private.

NOTE

Remember that the function name and library name are both case sensitive. Unless you explicitly include the path as part of the `Declare` statement, the default system path, the Windows folder, and the Windows System folder are all searched for in the library. Most Windows API functions are contained within the library files user32.exe, gdi32.exe, and kernel32.exe.

Passing by Reference Versus Passing by Value

When a parameter is passed by *reference*, the memory address of the argument is passed to the function. When a parameter is passed by *value*, the actual value of the argument is passed to the function. Unless explicitly told otherwise, VBA passes all parameters by reference. Many library functions expect to receive parameters by value. If such a function is passed a reference to a memory location, it cannot function properly. If you want to pass an argument by value, the `ByVal` keyword must be placed in front of the argument in the `Declare` statement. When calling library functions, you must know the types of arguments a function expects to receive and whether the function expects to receive the parameters by reference or by value. Passing an argument by reference rather than by value, or passing the incorrect data type for an argument, can cause your system to become unstable and even can result in a General Protection Fault (GPF) or Illegal Operation.

Passing String Parameters

String parameters require special handling when being passed to DLL functions. Windows has two ways of storing strings: the BSTR and LPSTR formats. Unless you are dealing with an API call specifically involving object linking and embedding (OLE), the string you are passing to the function is stored in the LPSTR format. DLL functions that receive strings in the LPSTR format cannot change the size of the string they are passed. This means that if a DLL function is passed a small string that it must fill in with a large value, the function simply overwrites another area of memory with the extra characters. This usually results in a GPF or Illegal Operation. The following code demonstrates this point and handles the error that is generated.

```
Sub WinSysDir()
   Dim strBuffer As String
   Dim intLength As Integer
   Dim strDirectory As String

   strBuffer = Space$(160)

   intLength = abGetSystemDirectory(strBuffer, Len(strBuffer))
   strDirectory = Left(strBuffer, intLength)
   MsgBox strDirectory
End Sub
```

> **NOTE**
>
> The code here and most of the code in this chapter is located in CHAP27EX.MDB on your sample code CD-ROM.

Notice that the Space$ function is used to store 160 spaces in the string variable strBuffer. Actually, the Space$ function stores 160 spaces, followed by a null character in the strBuffer variable.

The abGetSystemDirectory Windows API function receives two parameters:

- The buffer that it will fill with the name of the Windows System folder—in this case, strBuffer.

- The length of the buffer that will be filled—in this case, Len(strBuffer). The key here is that the length of the buffer that is passed to the GetSystemDirectory function is more than sufficient to hold the name of the Windows System folder.

The GetSystemDirectory function fills the buffer and returns the length of the string that it actually found. By looking at the left intLength number of characters in the strBuffer variable, you can determine the actual location of the Windows System folder.

The Declare statement for the GetSystemDirectory function looks like this:

```
Declare Function abGetSystemDirectory _
    Lib "kernel32" _
    (ByVal lpBuffer As String, ByVal nSize As Long) _
    As Long
```

Notice the ByVal keyword that precedes the lpBuffer parameter. Because the ByVal keyword is used, Visual Basic converts the string from BSTR to LPSTR format by adding a null terminator to the end of the string before passing it to the DLL function. If the ByVal keyword is omitted, Visual Basic passes a pointer to the function where the string is located in memory. This can cause serious problems.

CAUTION

Windows API calls are fraught with potential danger. To reduce the chances of data loss or database corruption, always save your work before testing a procedure containing an external function call. If the Access application terminates, at least you won't lose your work. In addition, always make sure that your database is backed up. If the Access application terminates and your database is not closed properly, you risk the chance of damage to the database. Regularly backing up ensures that if the database becomes corrupted during testing, you can retrieve the last good version from a backup.

Aliasing a Function

When you declare a function to VBA, you are given the option to alias it, as in the preceding function. An *alias* is a substitute name that you can use to refer to a function. You might want to alias a Windows API function for several reasons:

- A DLL procedure has a name that includes an invalid character.
- A DLL procedure name is the same as a VBA keyword.
- You want to omit the A required by ANSI versions of the API call.
- You want to ensure that you have a unique procedure name in an Access library or application.

- You want to call a DLL procedure referenced by an ordinal number.
- You want to give your API functions a distinctive prefix to prevent conflicts with API declarations in other modules or add-ins.

Reasons for aliasing an API function are discussed in more detail in the following sections.

Function Calls and Invalid Characters

It is not uncommon for a DLL procedure name to contain a character that is not allowed in VBA code. An example is a DLL procedure that begins with an underscore (_); VBA does not allow a procedure name to begin with an underscore. To use the DLL function, you must alias it, as this example shows:

```
Declare Function LOpen _
    Lib "kernel32" _
    Alias "_lopen" _
    (ByVal lpPathName As String, ByVal ReadWrite As Long) _
    As Long
```

Notice that the Windows API function _lopen begins with an underscore. The function is aliased as LOpen for use in the Access application.

DLL Functions with Duplicate Names

The DLL procedure name you want to use might share the same name as a VBA function. You can resolve this conflict only by aliasing the DLL function. The following code aliases a DLL function:

```
Declare Function GetObjectAPI _
    Lib "gdi32" _
    Alias "GetObject" _
    (ByVal hObject As Long, _
    ByVal nCount As Long, _
    lpObject As Any) As Long
```

The GetObject function is part of the Windows API and is a VBA function. When you alias the function, there is no confusion as to whether the API or VBA GetObject function is being called.

Eliminating the A Required by ANSI

Many API function calls have both ANSI and Unicode versions. The ANSI versions of the functions end with an A. You might want to call the ANSI version of a function but prefer to use the name of the function without the A. You can accomplish this by using an alias, as this code shows:

```
Declare Function FindWindow _
    Lib "user32" Alias "FindWindowA" _
    (ByVal lpClassName As Any, ByVal lpWindowName As String) As Long
```

This Declare statement creates an alias of FindWindow for the ANSI function FindWindowA.

> **NOTE**
>
> *Unicode* is a standard developed by the *International Standards Organization* (ISO). It was developed to overcome the 256-character limit imposed by the ANSI character standard. The ANSI standard uses only 1 byte to represent a character, limiting the number of characters to 256. This standard uses 2 bytes to represent a character, allowing up to 65,536 characters to be represented. Access uses Unicode for string manipulation, which can lead to problems with DLL calls. To overcome this problem, you always should call the ANSI version of the API function (the version of the function that ends with an A).

Unique Procedure Names in an Access Library or Module

Sometimes you simply want to ensure that a procedure name in a library you are creating is unique, or you might want to ensure that the code you are writing will not conflict with any libraries you are using. Unless you use the Private keyword to declare each procedure, external function declarations are global throughout Access's memory space. This can lead to potential conflicts, because Access does not allow multiple declarations of the same external routine. For this reason, you might want to place a unique identifier, such as your initials, at the beginning or end of the function declaration, as in this example:

```
Declare Function ABGetWindowsDirectory Lib "kernel32" _
Alias "GetWindowsDirectory" _
(ByVal lpBuffer As String, ByVal nSize As Long) As Long
```

This statement declares the Windows API function GetWindowsDirectory in the library kernel32. The function is aliased as ABGetWindowsDirectory. This function was aliased in order to differentiate it from other calls to the GetWindowsDirectory function that might share this procedure's scope.

Calling Functions Referenced with Ordinal Numbers

Every DLL procedure can be referenced by an ordinal number in addition to its name. In fact, some DLLs use only ordinal numbers and do not use procedure names at all, requiring you to use ordinal numbers when declaring the procedures. When you declare a function referenced by an ordinal number, you should declare the function with the `Alias` keyword, as in this example:

```
Declare Function GetAppSettings _
    Lib "Utilities" _
    Alias "#47" () As Long
```

This code declares a function with an ordinal number 47 in the library called `Utilities`. It now can be referred to as `GetAppSettings` whenever it is called in VBA code.

WORKING WITH CONSTANTS AND TYPES

Some DLLs require the use of constants or user-defined types, otherwise known as *structures* or *parameters*. You must place these in the General Declarations section of your module, along with the `Declare` statements you have defined.

Working with Constants

Constants are used by many of the API functions. They provide you with an English-like way of sending required values to an API function. The constant is used as an alias for a specific value. Here's an example:

```
Global Const SM_CXSCREEN = 0
Global Const SM_CYSCREEN = 1
```

The constant declarations and function declarations are placed in the General Declarations section of a module. When the `GetSystemMetrics` function is called, the `SM_CXSCREEN` and `SM_CYSCREEN` constants are passed as arguments to the function:

```
Sub GetScreenInfo()
   MsgBox "Screen Resolution is : " & _
      GetSystemMetrics(SM_CXSCREEN) & _
      " By " & _
      GetSystemMetrics(SM_CYSCREEN)

End Sub
```

When the `SM_CXSCREEN` constant is passed to the `GetSystemMetrics` function, the horizontal screen resolution is returned; when the `SM_CYSCREEN` constant is passed to the function, the vertical screen resolution is returned.

Working with Types

When working with types, you first must declare the type in the General Declarations section of a module. You then can pass elements of a user-defined type, or you can pass the entire type as a single argument to the API function. The following code shows an example of a `Type` declaration:

```
Type OSVERSIONINFO
    dwOSVersionInfoSize As Long
    dwMajorVersion As Long
    dwMinorVersion As Long
    dwBuildNumber As Long
    dwPlatformId As Long
    strReserved As String * 128
End Type
```

The `Type` structure `OSVERSIONINFO` is declared in the General Declarations section of the module, as shown in Listing 27.1.

LISTING 27.1 DECLARING THE `Type` STRUCTURE OSVERSIONINFO IN THE GENERAL DECLARATIONS SECTION OF THE MODULE

```
Function GetOSInfo()

    Dim OSInfo As OSVERSIONINFO
    Dim strMajorVersion As String
    Dim strMinorVersion As String
    Dim strBuildNumber As String
    Dim strPlatformId As String

    ' Set the length member before you call GetVersionEx
    OSInfo.dwOSVersionInfoSize = Len(OSInfo)
    If GetVersionEx(OSInfo) Then
        strMajorVersion = OSInfo.dwMajorVersion
        strMinorVersion = OSInfo.dwMinorVersion
        strBuildNumber = OSInfo.dwBuildNumber And &HFFFF&
        strPlatformId = OSInfo.dwPlatformId
MsgBox "The Major Version Is:  " & strMajorVersion & vbCrLf & _

        "The Minor Version Is:  " & strMinorVersion & vbCrLf & _

        "The Build Number Is:  " & strBuildNumber & vbCrLf & _
        "The Platform ID Is:  " & _
        IIf(strPlatformId = 1, "Win 95 or Win 98", _
        "Win NT") & vbCrLf
    End If
End Function
```

27

EXPLOITING THE
POWER OF THE
WINDOWS API

In this listing, the statement `Dim OSInfo As OSVERSIONIFO` creates a `Type` variable. The entire structure is passed to the `GetVersionEx` function. The `GetVersionEx` function fills in the elements of the structure with information about the operating system. This information then is retrieved and stored into variables that are displayed in a message box.

Using the Windows API Text Viewer

As you might imagine, `Declare` statements, constant declarations, and type structures can be time consuming and difficult to add to your code modules. Fortunately, the Windows API Text Viewer, a tool that ships with Microsoft Office Developer, helps you complete these tasks. It makes it easy for you to add `Declare` statements, types, and constants required by the Windows API function calls to your code. You can launch the Window API Text Viewer as an add-in to the Access 2000 VBE. To do this, follow these steps:

1. Activate the VBE.
2. Select Add-ins | Add-In Manager. The Add-In Manager appears.
3. Select VBA WinAPI Viewer.
4. Click Loaded/Unloaded.
5. Click Load on Startup if you want the API Viewer to be available each time you launch Access.
6. Click OK.
7. Open the Add-Ins menu. WinAPI Viewer should appear.
8. Select WinAPI Viewer from the Add-Ins menu.

When you first launch the Windows API Text Viewer, it appears as shown in Figure 27.1. You can load a text file or a database file containing declares, types, and constants.

FIGURE 27.1

The Windows API Text Viewer.

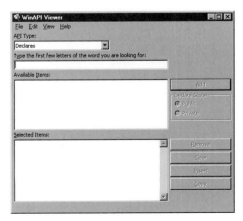

Loading a Text File

Microsoft Office Developer Edition ships with a file called WIN32API.TXT. You can load and browse this file so that you easily can obtain `Declare` statements, type structures, and constants. To load the WIN32API.TXT file into the Windows API Text Viewer, follow these steps:

1. Choose File | Load Text File. The Select a Text API File dialog box appears, as shown in Figure 27.2.

2. Select a text file to load into the viewer and click Open. The WIN API Text viewer appears as in Figure 27.3.

FIGURE 27.2

The Select a Text API File dialog box.

FIGURE 27.3

The WinAPI viewer after loading a text file.

Loading a Database File

After a text file is converted to a database, you should load the database each time you use the Windows API Text Viewer. To load the database file, follow these steps:

1. Choose File | Load Database File. The Select a Jet Database dialog box appears, as shown in Figure 27.4.

2. Select the database you want to load and click Open.

FIGURE 27.4

Use the Select a Jet Database dialog box to specify the database to load into the Text Viewer.

Pasting API Declares, Types, and Constants

Regardless of whether you have loaded a text or a database file, the Windows API Text Viewer appears as shown in Figure 27.5. All the declares for the 32-bit API appear in the Available Items list box. Select each `Declare` statement you want to add to your module and click Add. You can use the API Type drop-down list to view and select types or constants. In Figure 27.6, the `GetVersionEx` and `GetWindow` declares have been added to the Selected Items list. The `SM_CXSCREEN` and `SM_CYSCREEN` constants, as well as the `OSVERSIONINFO` type, also have been added.

FIGURE 27.5

The Windows API Text Viewer after a file has been loaded.

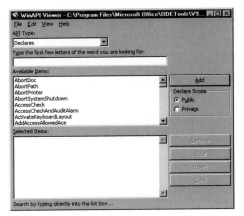

Follow these steps to add the selected items to a module:

1. In the API Text Viewer, click Copy. The selected declares, constants, and types are placed on the Windows Clipboard.

2. Place your cursor in the module where you want the selected declares, constants, and types to be placed.

3. Click Paste. The selected items are pasted into the module, as shown in Figure 27.7.

FIGURE 27.6

The Windows API Text Viewer with several items in the Selected Items list.

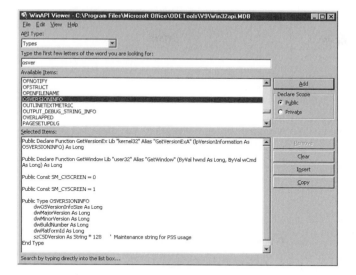

FIGURE 27.7

A module after selected items are pasted into it.

CALLING DLL FUNCTIONS: IMPORTANT ISSUES

After a procedure is declared, you can call it just like any VBA function. The main issue is that you must ensure that you are passing correct values to the DLL. Otherwise, the bad call can cause your application to shut down without warning. In fact, external library calls are very tricky. You therefore should always save your work before you test the calls.

Most DLLs expect to receive standard C strings. These strings are terminated with a null character. If a DLL expects a null-terminated string, you must pass the string by value. The ByVal keyword tells VBA to pass the string as null-terminated.

Although you must pass strings by value, they actually are received by reference. The ByVal keyword simply means that the string is null-terminated. The DLL procedure actually can modify the value of the string, which can mean problems. As discussed in the "Passing String Parameters" section earlier in this chapter, if you do not preallocate space for the procedure to use, it overwrites any memory it can find, including memory currently being used by your application, another application, or even the operating system. You can avoid this problem by making the string argument long enough to accept the longest entry that you think will be placed into the parameter.

EXAMINING THE DIFFERENCES BETWEEN 16-BIT AND 32-BIT APIS

You might be familiar with the 16-bit API from earlier versions of Windows, but you must be aware of some changes when working with the 32-bit API. These changes can cause you significant grief if you are not aware of them:

- Window handles (hWnd properties) now are *long integers* in the 32-bit API. They are *integers* in the 16-bit API.

- Function names are *not* case sensitive in the 16-bit API. They *are* case sensitive in the 32-bit API.

- When working with the 16-bit API, you should reboot whenever you get a GPF because it is likely that the memory of your computer is corrupted. With the 32-bit API, each program runs in its own virtual machine. Therefore, it often is unnecessary to reboot simply because a GPF occurs.

- Data types in the 32-bit API are exactly double what needs to be used in Visual Basic for Applications. This means that if you read C language documentation specifying that a particular API call requires a Double, you should use a Long with the Visual Basic for Applications call to the API function.

USING API FUNCTIONS

The potential uses for API calls are endless. You can use API calls to modify the System menu, obtain system information, or even switch between running applications. In fact, you can accomplish so many things using API calls that entire books are devoted to the topic. The remainder of this chapter covers several of the common uses of API calls.

GETTING INFORMATION ABOUT THE OPERATING ENVIRONMENT

By using Windows API calls, you can get volumes of information about the system environment—including the type of hardware on which the application is running, the amount of memory that exists or is available, and the operating system version under which the application is running. This is just a sampling of the system environment information that you can get via the Windows API.

It is handy and professional to include system information in your application's Help About box. It also is important to include this system information in your error handling and logging because such information can help you diagnose the problem. This is discussed in Chapter 14, "Error Handling: Preparing for the Inevitable."

Figure 27.8 shows a custom About dialog box that includes information about the system environment. This form uses several Windows API calls to get the system information displayed on the form.

FIGURE 27.8

A custom About dialog box illustrating the capability to obtain system information from the Windows API.

Before any of the DLL functions required to obtain this information can be called, all the functions need to be declared to the compiler. This is done in the General Declarations section of the module basUtils. Any constants and type structures used by the DLL calls also must be included in the General Declarations section. Listing 27.2 shows what the General Declarations section of basAPICalls looks like.

LISTING 27.2 THE GENERAL DECLARATIONS SECTION OF BASUTILS

```
Option Compare Database
Option Explicit

Public Const MAX_PATH = 160

Declare Function abGetVersionEx _
  Lib "kernel32" _
   Alias "GetVersionExA" _
   (lpOSInfo As OSVERSIONINFO) As Boolean

Type OSVERSIONINFO
   dwOSVersionInfoSize As Long
   dwMajorVersion As Long
   dwMinorVersion As Long
   dwBuildNumber As Long
   dwPlatformId As Long
   strReserved As String * 128
End Type

'The function GetVersionEx gets information about
'the version of operating system that is currently
'running.  The information is filled into the type
'structure OSVERSIONINFO.

Const SM_CXSCREEN = 0
Const SM_CYSCREEN = 1
Const SM_MOUSEPRESENT = 19

Declare Function abGetSystemMetrics _
   Lib "user32" _
   Alias "GetSystemMetrics" _
   (ByVal nIndex As Long) As Long

'The GetSystemMetrics function uses three constants to
'determine whether a mouse is present, and to determine
'the width and height of the screen.

Type MEMORYSTATUS
   dwLength As Long
   dwMemoryLoad As Long
   dwTotalPhys As Long
   dwAvailPhys As Long
   dwTotalPageFile As Long
   dwAvailPageFile As Long
   dwTotalVirtual As Long
```

```
        dwAvailVirtual As Long
End Type

Declare Sub abGlobalMemoryStatus _
    Lib "kernel32" _
    Alias "GlobalMemoryStatus" _
    (lpBuffer As MEMORYSTATUS)

'The GlobalMemoryStatus function retrieves information
'about current available memory.  It points to a type
'structure called SYSTEM_INFO, filling in its elements
'with relevant memory information.

Type SYSTEM_INFO
    dwOemID As Long
    dwPageSize As Long
    lpMinimumApplicationAddress As Long
    lpMaximumApplicationAddress As Long
    dwActiveProcessorMask As Long
    dwNumberOrfProcessors As Long
    dwProcessorType As Long
    dwAllocationGranularity As Long
    dwReserved As Long
End Type

Declare Sub abGetSystemInfo Lib "kernel32" _
    Alias "GetSystemInfo" _
    (lpSystemInfo As SYSTEM_INFO)

'The GetSystemInfo function returns information about
'the system.  It fills in the type structure SYSTEM_INFO
'with relevant information about the system.

Declare Function abGetWindowsDirectory _
    Lib "kernel32" _
    Alias "GetWindowsDirectoryA" _
    (ByVal lpBuffer As String, _
    ByVal nSize As Long) As Long

'The function GetWindowsDirectory retrieves the name of the
'directory within which Windows is running

Declare Function abGetSystemDirectory _
    Lib "kernel32" _
    Alias "GetSystemDirectoryA" _
```

continues

LISTING 27.2 CONTINUED

```
   (ByVal lpBuffer As String, _
   ByVal nSize As Long) As Long

'The GetSystemDirectory function retrieves the name of the
'directory in which the Windows system files reside.

Declare Function abGetTempPath _
   Lib "kernel32" _
   Alias "GetTempPathA" _
   (ByVal nBufferLength As Long, _
   ByVal lpBuffer As String) As Long

'The GetTempPath function retrieves the name of the
'directory where temporary files are stored

Declare Function abGetCommandLine _
   Lib "kernel32" _
   Alias "GetCommandLineA" () _
   As String
```

As you can see, several type structures, constants, and `Declare` statements are required to obtain all the information that appears on the form. When the form (frmSystemInformation) is opened, all the Windows API functions are called, and the text boxes on the form are filled with the system information. The `Open` event of the form frmSystemInformation calls a subroutine called `GetSysInfo`, which is shown in Listing 27.3.

LISTING 27.3 THE `GetSysInfo` SUBROUTINE

```
Sub GetSysInfo(frmAny As Form)
   Dim intMousePresent As Integer
   Dim strBuffer As String
   Dim intLen As Integer
   Dim MS As MEMORYSTATUS
   Dim SI As SYSTEM_INFO
   Dim strCommandLine As String

   frmAny.txtScreenResolution = abGetSystemMetrics(SM_CXSCREEN) & _
   " By " & abGetSystemMetrics(SM_CYSCREEN)
   intMousePresent = CBool(abGetSystemMetrics(SM_MOUSEPRESENT))
   frmAny.txtMousePresent = IIf(intMousePresent, "Mouse Present", _
   "No Mouse Present")

   'Set the length member before you call GlobalMemoryStatus
   MS.dwLength = Len(MS)
```

```
abGlobalMemoryStatus MS
frmAny.txtMemoryLoad = MS.dwMemoryLoad & "%"
frmAny.txtTotalPhysical = Format(Fix(MS.dwTotalPhys / 1024), _
"###,###") & "K"
frmAny.txtAvailablePhysical = Format(Fix(MS.dwAvailPhys / 1024), _
"###,###") & "K"
frmAny.txtTotalVirtual = Format(Fix(MS.dwTotalVirtual / 1024), _
"###,###") & "K"
frmAny.txtAvailableVirtual = Format(Fix(MS.dwAvailVirtual / 1024), _
"###,###") & "K"

abGetSystemInfo SI
frmAny.txtProcessorMask = SI.dwActiveProcessorMask
frmAny.txtNumberOfProcessors = SI.dwNumberOrfProcessors
frmAny.txtProcessorType = SI.dwProcessorType


strBuffer = Space(MAX_PATH)
intLen = abGetWindowsDirectory(strBuffer, MAX_PATH)
frmAny.txtWindowsDir = Left(strBuffer, intLen)

strBuffer = Space(MAX_PATH)
intLen = abGetSystemDirectory(strBuffer, MAX_PATH)
frmAny.txtSystemDir = Left(strBuffer, intLen)

strBuffer = Space(MAX_PATH)
intLen = abGetTempPath(MAX_PATH, strBuffer)
frmAny.txtTempDir = Left(strBuffer, intLen)

End Sub
```

Now take a look at this subroutine in detail. The subroutine calls the function
GetSystemMetrics (aliased as abGetSystemMetrics). The GetSystemMetrics function is
called three times. The first time, it is sent the constant SM_CXSCREEN, and the second time, it is
sent the constant SM_CYSCREEN. These calls return the horizontal and vertical screen resolutions.
The GetSystemMetrics function, when passed the constant SM_MOUSEPRESENT, returns a logical
True or False indicating whether a mouse is present.

The GlobalMemoryStatus API call fills in a structure with several pieces of information
regarding memory. The elements of the structure are filled with the memory load, total and
available physical memory, and total and available virtual memory.

The GetSystemInfo API call also provides you with valuable system information. It fills in a structure with several technical tidbits, including the active processor mask, number of processors, and the processor type.

Finally, the function calls GetWindowsDirectory, GetSystemDirectory, and GetTempPath. These three functions return the Windows folder, System folder, and temp file path, respectively. Notice that buffer space is preallocated before each call. Because each call returns the length of the folder name retrieved, you then take the characters on the left side of the buffer for the number of characters specified in the return value.

DETERMINING DRIVE TYPES AND AVAILABLE DRIVE SPACE

Often, it is necessary to determine the types of drives available and the amount of space free on each drive. Fortunately, Windows API functions are available to help you to accomplish these tasks. The frmListDrives form lists the type of each drive installed on the system and the amount of free space on each drive, as shown in Figure 27.9. The declarations that are required for the APIs are shown in Listing 27.4.

FIGURE 27.9

The frmListDrives form, showing the type of each drive installed on the system and the amount of free space on each drive.

LISTING 27.4   API DECLARATIONS

```
Public Const DRIVE_UNKNOWN = 0
Public Const DRIVE_UNAVAILABLE = 1
Public Const DRIVE_REMOVABLE = 2
Public Const DRIVE_FIXED = 3
Public Const DRIVE_REMOTE = 4
Public Const DRIVE_CDROM = 5
Public Const DRIVE_RAMDISK = 6

Declare Function abGetDriveType _
    Lib "kernel32" _
    Alias "GetDriveTypeA" _
```

```
      (ByVal nDrive As String) _
   As Long

'The GetDriveType Function returns an integer
'indicating the drive type

Declare Function abGetDiskFreeSpace _
   Lib "kernel32" _
   Alias "GetDiskFreeSpaceA" _
   (ByVal lpRootPathName As String, _
   lpSectorsPerCluster As Long, _
   lpBytesPerSector As Long, _
   lpNumberOfFreeClusters As Long, _
   lpTotalNumberOfClusters As Long) _
As Long

'The GetDiskFreeSpace Function determines the amount of
'free space on the active drive
```

The Click event of the cmdListDrives command button located on frmListDrives calls a subroutine called GetDriveInfo, sending it the txtDrives text box. Listing 27.5 shows the GetDriveInfo procedure.

LISTING 27.5   THE GetDriveInfo PROCEDURE

```
Sub GetDriveInfo(ctlAny As Control)
   Dim intDrive As Integer
   Dim strDriveLetter As String
   Dim strDriveType As String
   Dim strSpaceFree As String

   'Loop through all drives
   For intDrive = 65 To 90 'A through Z
      strDriveLetter = (Chr(intDrive) & ":\")
      'Get Drive Type
      strDriveType = TypeOfDrive(strDriveLetter)
      'Get Space Free
      strSpaceFree = NumberOfBytesFree(strDriveLetter)
      ctlAny.Value = _
         ctlAny.Value & _
         Left(strDriveLetter, 2) & _
         " - " & strDriveType & _
```

continues

LISTING 27.5 CONTINUED

```
            IIf(strDriveType <> "Drive Doesn't Exist", _
                strSpaceFree, "") & _
            vbCrLf
    Next intDrive

End Sub
```

The routine loops through all available drive letters. For each drive letter, two user-defined functions are called: TypeOfDrive and NumberOfBytesFree. Listing 27.6 shows the TypeOfDrive function.

LISTING 27.6 THE TypeOfDrive FUNCTION

```
Function TypeOfDrive(ByVal strDrive As String) As String
    Dim intDriveType As Integer
    Dim strDriveType As String

        intDriveType = abGetDriveType(strDrive)
        Select Case intDriveType
            Case DRIVE_UNKNOWN
                strDriveType = "Type Unknown"
            Case DRIVE_UNAVAILABLE
                strDriveType = "Drive Doesn't Exist"
            Case DRIVE_REMOVABLE
                strDriveType = "Removable Drive"
            Case DRIVE_FIXED
                strDriveType = "Fixed Drive"
            Case DRIVE_REMOTE
                strDriveType = "Network Drive"
            Case DRIVE_CDROM
                strDriveType = "CD-ROM"
            Case DRIVE_RAMDISK
                strDriveType = "RAM Disk"
        End Select
        TypeOfDrive = strDriveType
End Function
```

The TypeOfDrive function receives a drive letter as a parameter. It calls the Windows API function GetDriveType to determine the type of the drive whose drive letter was passed to the function. The GetDriveType function returns a numeric value that indicates the type of the specified drive. The returned value is evaluated with a case statement, and text representing the drive type is returned from the function.

Exploiting the Power of the Windows API

CHAPTER 27

921

27

EXPLOITING THE
POWER OF THE
WINDOWS API

The `NumberOfBytesFree` function determines how many bytes are free on a particular drive, as shown in Listing 27.7.

LISTING 27.7   THE `NumberOfBytesFree` FUNCTION

```
Function NumberOfBytesFree(ByVal strDrive As String) As String
    Dim lngSectors As Long
    Dim lngBytes As Long
    Dim lngFreeClusters As Long
    Dim lngTotalClusters As Long
    Dim intErrNum As Integer

    intErrNum = abGetDiskFreeSpace(strDrive, lngSectors, _
    lngBytes, lngFreeClusters, lngTotalClusters)
    NumberOfBytesFree = " with " & _
        Format((lngBytes * lngSectors) * _
        lngFreeClusters, "#,##0") & _
        " Bytes Free"
End Function
```

This function receives a drive letter as a parameter. It then calls the `GetDiskFreeSpace` Windows API function, sending it the drive letter and several long integers. These long integers are filled in with the information required to determine the number of bytes free on the specified drive.

After the type of drive and number of bytes free are determined, the `GetDriveInfo` procedure concatenates the information with the text contained in a text box on the frmListDrives form. If the drive specified is unavailable, the amount of available disk space is not printed.

PRACTICAL EXAMPLES

Applying What You Have Learned to the Time and Billing Application

You can add some polish to the Time and Billing application by adding a custom About form to the application. You can add the form now and integrate it into the application in Chapter 39, "Distributing Your Application." The frmSystemInformation form has been added to the application and the appropriate declares, constants, and types have been added to basWinAPI. The form and API functionality also can be added to a library so that they will be available to all applications.

SUMMARY

External libraries, referred to as *dynamic link libraries* (DLL), open up the entire Windows API as well as other function libraries to your custom applications. Using external libraries, your applications can harness the power of functions written in other languages, such as C, Delphi, or Visual Basic 6. In this chapter you learned how to declare API functions, type structures, and constants, and how to call Windows API functions. Using the techniques that you learned, you can easily extend beyond the power of Access, harnessing the power of the operating system environment.

EXPLOITING THE POWER OF CLASS MODULES

IN THIS CHAPTER

EXPLORING THE BENEFITS OF CLASS MODULES

Access 2000 offers two types of modules: standard modules and class modules. Access 95 introduced class modules for forms and reports, but Access 97 was the first version of Access to offer the capability to create standalone class modules.

A class module is similar to a code module. The subroutines and functions in the class module become the methods of the class. The `Property Let` and `Property Get` routines become the properties of the class, and the class module's name becomes the name of the custom object. A class module is a great way to encapsulate related functions into a portable, self-contained object. Class modules can help you simplify the process of performing the following tasks:

- Manipulating databases and recordsets
- Calling Windows API functions
- Performing low-level file-handling tasks
- Accessing and modifying the registry

If you regularly open databases and recordsets and traverse those recordsets by using code, you might decide that you want to simplify these tasks. By building class modules, you can more easily access table data.

OBJECT ORIENTATION—AN INTRODUCTION

The world of object orientation is exciting, but it requires a new way of thinking about things. Access 2000 is actually object-based rather than object-oriented. So, what exactly is the difference? The definition of the following terms should help you differentiate between these two concepts:

- Class—A template for an object
- Object—An instance of a class
- Instantiation—The process of creating an object based on a class
- Polymorphism—Multifaced; using the same method and property names with different objects; the properties and methods are implemented differently for different objects
- Subclassing—Building one class based on another
- Inheritance—Refers to the fact that subclasses take on the behavior of their parent classes

VBA, and therefore Access, supports the creation of custom classes and the instantiation of objects based on those classes. Polymorphism can also be "simulated" by using the same property and method names within different classes. VBA does not support subclassing and inheritance. Classes cannot be based on other classes, and therefore, cannot elicit the behavior of other classes. In fact, the reason that polymorphism can only be "simulated" is that true polymorphism can exist only when child classes inherit the properties and methods of their parents.

To make sure that you understand the terms, let's use an analogy. Imagine that you are going to bake some cookies. The cookie cutter is the class, the template for a cookie object. When you use the cookie cutter to create an actual cookie, you instantiate the cookie class to create a cookie object. The cookie has some properties, such as a powdered sugar property, and some methods, such as the bake method. A ham class is a template for a ham object. The ham class also has a bake method. The "code" behind the bake method of the cookie object and the bake method of the ham object are different. This is polymorphism (multifaced) in action. If VBA were object-oriented, the cookie class and the ham class would have been derived from the same parent. Now that you are familiar with some object-oriented terms and concepts, take a look at how custom classes work in VBA.

CREATING AND USING A CLASS MODULE

You can insert a class module in one of three ways:

- With the Database window active, select Insert | Class Module.
- With the Interactive Development Environment active, select Insert | Class Module.
- With the Interactive Development Environment active, right-click the project within the Project Explorer window and select Insert | Class Module from the pop-up menu.

After being inserted, a class module looks like a standard code module (see Figure 28.1). The differences lie in how the variables and procedures in the class module are accessed, as well as in the behavior of the class module.

Adding Properties

The most basic way to add a property to a class module is to use a public variable. For example, the following code shows the declaration of two public variables, `FirstName` and `LastName`. After it is added to a class, each of these variables is considered a property of the class.

```
Public FirstName as String
Public LastName as String
```

FIGURE 28.1

*A new class
module.*

Adding Methods

A function or subroutine placed within a class module is considered a method of the class. The
Speak subroutine that follows acts as a method of the PublicPerson class. It accesses the
FirstName and LastName properties of the class, displaying them in a message box:

```
Public Function Speak()
    MsgBox FirstName & " " & LastName
End Function
```

Instantiating and Using the Class

To utilize the code within a class, you must instantiate an object based on that class. To do that,
you first declare an object based on the class. You then instantiate the object using a Set statement. After you have done that, you can access the properties and methods of the object. The
code looks like this:

```
Sub SingleInstance()
    Dim oPerson As Person
    Set oPerson = New Person

    oPerson.FirstName = "Alison"
    oPerson.LastName = "Balter"
    oPerson.Speak
End Sub
```

The code begins by declaring a `Person` object. The `Set` statement is used to create an instance of the `Person` object. The `FirstName` and `LastName` properties of the instance are set to `Alison` and `Balter`, respectively. The `Speak` method of the object is then executed, displaying the name of the person.

Property Let and Get—Adding Properties the Right Way

Public variables, when used as properties, have the following major disadvantages:

- Using public variables, you cannot create properties that are read-only or write-only.
- You cannot validate what goes into public variables.
- You cannot manipulate the value as the public variable is set.
- You cannot track changes to public variables.

For these reasons, it is prudent to utilize property procedures rather than public variables. With property procedures, you can create custom runtime properties of user-defined objects. After you have defined custom properties, you can use `Property Let` and `Get` to assign values to and retrieve values from custom properties. Custom properties give you more flexibility in creating your applications; you can create reusable objects that expose properties to other objects.

Custom properties are Public by default and are placed in Class, Form, or Report modules, making them visible to other modules in the current database. They aren't visible to other databases.

The `Property Let` routine defines a property procedure that assigns a value to a user-defined object's property. Using a `Property Let` is similar to assigning a value to a Public variable, but a Public variable can be written to from anywhere in the database, with little or no control over what's written to it. With a `Property Let` routine, you can control exactly what happens when a value is assigned to the property. Here's an example:

```
Public Property Let FirstName(ByVal strNewValue As String)
    mstrFirstName = UCase(strNewValue)
End Property
```

You might be thinking this code looks just like a subroutine, and you're somewhat correct. It's a special type of subroutine that executes automatically in response to the change in a custom property's value. The example receives the value the property is changed to as `strNewValue`. The uppercase version of the value is stored in the private variable `mstrFirstName`. The following line of code causes the code in the `Property Let` to execute:

```
FirstName = "Alison"
```

`Property Let` sets the value of a custom property, but `Property Get` defines a property procedure that retrieves a value from a user-defined object's property. This example illustrates how `Property Get` is used:

```
Public Property Get FirstName() As String
    FirstName = mstrFirstName
End Property
```

The `Property Get` routine automatically executes whenever the code tries to retrieve the value of the property. The value stored in the private variable `mstrFirstName` is returned from the `Property Get` procedure. This routine can be executed by retrieving the property from anywhere in the database. The following line of code causes the code in the `Property Get` to execute:

```
MsgBox FirstName
```

The code that follows shows the declaration of the two private variables `mstrFirstName` and `mstrLastName`. The `Property Let` for `FirstName` and the `Property Let` for `LastName` store values into these two private variables. The `Property Get` for `FirstName` and the `Property Get` for `LastName` retrieve the values stored in the private variables.

```
Private mstrFirstName As String
Private mstrLastName As String

Public Property Get FirstName() As String
    FirstName = mstrFirstName
End Property

Public Property Let FirstName(ByVal strNewValue As String)
    mstrFirstName = UCase(strNewValue)
End Property

Public Property Get LastName() As String
    LastName = mstrLastName
End Property

Public Property Let LastName(ByVal strNewValue As String)
    mstrLastName = UCase(strNewValue)
End Property
```

CREATING MULTIPLE CLASS INSTANCES

One of the advantages of class modules is that multiple instances of the class can be created. Each instance maintains its own variables and executes its own code. This is illustrated in the following code:

```
Sub MultipleInstance()
    Dim oPerson1 As Person
    Dim oPerson2 As Person

    Set oPerson1 = New Person
    Set oPerson2 = New Person

    oPerson1.FirstName = "Alison"
    oPerson1.LastName = "Balter"
    oPerson1.Speak
    oPerson2.FirstName = "Dan"
    oPerson2.LastName = "Balter"
    oPerson2.Speak

End Sub
```

Two instances of the `Person` class are created. The first is referred to as `oPerson1` and the second as `oPerson2`. The `FirstName` property of `oPerson1` is set equal to `Alison` and the `LastName` property of `oPerson1` is set equal to `Balter`. The `FirstName` property of `oPerson2` is set equal to `Dan` and the `LastName` property of `oPerson2` is set equal to `Balter`. The `Speak` method displays the name of the correct person in a message box.

THE `Initialize` AND `Terminate` EVENTS

The `Initialize` and `Terminate` events are the two built-in events that execute for a class object. The `Initialize` event executes as the class is instantiated, and the `Terminate` event executes as the class is destroyed.

`Initialize`

The `Initialize` event is generally used to perform tasks such as establishing a connection to a database and initializing variables. The following is an example of the use of the `Initialize` event:

```
Private Sub Class_Initialize()
    FirstName = "Alison"
    LastName = "Balter"
End Sub
```

In this example the default values of the `FirstName` and `LastName` properties of the class are set equal to `Alison` and `Balter`, respectively.

Terminate

The `Terminate` event is generally used to perform the class's cleanup tasks. An example is closing a recordset used by the class. The following is an example of the use of the `Terminate` event:

```
Private Sub Class_Terminate()
    rstCustomer.Close
    Set rstCustomer = Nothing
End Sub
```

WORKING WITH CUSTOM COLLECTIONS

In addition to the collections built into the Access and other object libraries, you can create custom collections. Custom collections are similar to arrays, but they offer several advantages:

- Collections are dynamically allocated. They take up memory based only on what's in them at a given time. This is different from arrays, whose size must be either predefined or redimensioned at runtime. When an array is redimensioned, Access actually makes a copy of the array in memory, taking up substantial resources. By using custom collections, you can avoid that.
- A collection always knows how many elements it has, and elements can easily be added and removed.
- Each element of a collection can contain a different type of data.
- Elements can be added into any element of a collection.

Although collections are very powerful and provide several advantages, it is important that you are aware of their disadvantages, which are as follows:

- Every item in a collection is stored as a variant.
- Although the capability to store a different type of data in each element of a collection can be an advantage, it can also be a disadvantage. If you attempt to treat each item in the collection the same (for example, by accessing the same property in each element of the collection), your code might render an error.

You might wonder why collections are covered in this section. A common use of collections is to house instances of custom objects. An example of such a use is covered in the section of this chapter titled "Using a Collection to Manipulate Multiple Instances of the File Information Class."

Creating a Collection

Defining a custom collection is easy—simply use the `Dim` keyword to create an object of the type `Collection`, as shown here:

```
Dim colSports As New Collection
```

The `Dim` statement tells the compiler you want to declare a variable, and the `As New` keywords indicate that you're creating a new instance of something. Specifically, you're creating a new instance of a `Collection` object. Let's take a look at how you can add items to and remove items from a custom collection.

Adding Items to a Collection

The `Add` method adds a new item to a custom collection. It looks like this:

```
colSports.Add "Basketball"
```

This line of code adds the text "Basketball" to the colSports collection. The `Add` method has three optional arguments: `Key`, `Before`, and `After`. `Key` is a string name you can use to uniquely identify an element; the `Before` and `After` arguments enable you to specify where in the collection the new item will be placed. Here's an example:

```
Sub NewCollection()
    Dim colSports As New Collection
    colSports.Add "Basketball"
    colSports.Add "Skiing"
    colSports.Add "Skating", Before:=1
    colSports.Add "Hockey", After:=2
End Sub
```

This code creates a new collection called colSports and adds two consecutive elements to the collection: Basketball and Skiing. It then adds Skating before Basketball. Skating becomes Element 1 and Basketball becomes Element 2. Finally, it adds Hockey after Element 2 (Basketball).

CAUTION

Unlike almost every other array or collection in VBA, custom collections are one-based rather than zero-based. This is a big change if you're used to relying on arrays and collections being zero-based.

Looping Through the Elements of a Custom Collection

Just as you can loop through built-in collections, you can also loop through a custom collection. The code looks like this:

```
Sub LoopThroughCollection()
   Dim colSports As New Collection
   Dim varSport As Variant
   colSports.Add "Basketball"
   colSports.Add "Skiing"
   colSports.Add "Skating", Before:=1
   colSports.Add "Hockey", After:=2
   For Each varSport In colSports
      Debug.Print varSport
   Next varSport
End Sub
```

This code uses a For Each...Next loop to loop through each element of colSports. Notice that the routine declares a variant variable as the type of object in the collection. This is done so that different types of values can be stored in each object in the collection. Access refreshes any collection when you open a database and specifically refer to it.

Referencing Items in a Collection

When you add an item to a collection, you can specify a custom key for the object. This makes it easy to return to the item in the collection whenever necessary. The following code illustrates how to specify a custom key:

```
Sub CustomKey()
   Dim colSports As New Collection
   colSports.Add "Basketball", "B"
   colSports.Add "Skiing", "S1"
   colSports.Add "Skating", "S2"
   colSports.Add "Hockey", "H"
   Debug.Print colSports.Item("S1")
End Sub
```

This code adds several items to the colSports collection. As each item is added, it's assigned a unique key. Each item in the collection can then be easily accessed by using its unique key. The Item method is often used when adding several instances of a form, such as a Customer form to a collection. The customer ID of each customer is added as the unique key for each form in the collection. This unique identifier enables you to readily return to a specific instance of the Customer form.

Removing Items from a Collection

Removing objects from a custom collection is just as easy as adding them. You use the `Remove` method, which looks like this:

```
Sub RemoveElements()
    Dim colSports As New Collection
    colSports.Add "Basketball"
    colSports.Add "Skiing"
    colSports.Add "Skating"
    colSports.Add "Hockey"
    colSports.Remove 2
End Sub
```

This routine removes Element 2 (Skiing) from the collection.

PRACTICAL EXAMPLES

Class Modules

To best understand how to benefit from the use of class modules, it is beneficial to see them in action. Four examples are covered in this chapter. The first shows the use of a file information class. Each instance of the class is used to house information about a particular file. The second illustrates how the use of a customer class facilitates the process of dealing with customer data. The third is a system information class. It retrieves and then provides information about the computer system. The fourth and final example shows how a custom error class facilitates the process of implementing error handling within your application.

The File Information Class

 It is a common application requirement to be able to extract the drive, path, or short filename from a complete filename. Although obtaining these pieces of information can be accomplished using a standard code module and functions, placing the functions in a class module makes them easier to work with. The `FileInformation` class contained in the Chap28Ex sample database contains four properties: `FullFileName`, `Drive`, `Path`, and `Name`. The `FullFileName` property is set by the user of the class. It contains the complete filename and path of the file whose parts the user wishes to extract. The `Drive`, `Path`, and `Name` properties of the class contain the drive, path, and name of the file specified in the `FullFileName` property. The `Property Let` and `Property Get` procedures, as well as the private variables associated with these properties, are shown in Listing 28.1.

LISTING 28.1   THE PROPERTY DECLARATIONS FOR THE FILE INFORMATION CLASS

```
Private mstrFullFileName As String
Private mstrDrive As String
Private mstrPath As String
Private mstrName As String

Public Property Get FullFileName() As String
   FullFileName = mstrFullFileName
End Property

Public Property Let FullFileName(ByVal strFileName As String)
   Call GetDrive(strFileName)
   Call GetPath(strFileName)
   Call GetName(strFileName)
End Property

Public Property Get Drive() As String
   Drive = mstrDrive
End Property

Public Property Get Path() As String
   Path = mstrPath
End Property

Public Property Get Name() As String
   Name = mstrName
End Property
```

Notice that the `Drive`, `Path`, and `Name` properties have no associated `Property Let` routines. This is because these properties are read-only properties from outside the class. When the `FullFileName` property is set, the `GetDrive`, `GetPath`, and `GetName` routines are executed. Each of these routines populates the appropriate private variables so that they can be retrieved in the `Property Get` routines. The `GetDrive`, `GetPath`, and `GetName` subroutines are shown in Listing 28.2.

LISTING 28.2   THE `GetDrive`, `GetPath`, AND `GetName` ROUTINES RETRIEVE THE DRIVE, PATH, AND SHORT FILENAME OF THE FILE DESIGNATED IN THE `FullFileName` PROPERTY

```
Private Sub GetDrive(ByVal strFile As String)
   mstrDrive = Left$(strFile, _
     InStr(strFile, ":"))
End Sub

Private Sub GetPath(ByVal strFile As String)
    mstrPath = strFile
```

```
    Do While Right$(mstrPath, 1) <> "\"
        mstrPath = Left$(mstrPath, _
        Len(mstrPath) - 1)
    Loop
End Sub

Private Sub GetName(strFile)
   mstrName = Mid$(strFile, _
     Len(mstrPath) + 1)
End Sub
```

The GetDrive routine extracts the characters to the left of the colon, including the colon, thereby extracting the drive. The GetPath routine locates the last backslash in the filename. The string to the left of the last backslash contains the path name. Finally, the GetName routine extracts everything to the right of the last backslash.

Note that the GetDrive, GetPath, and GetName routines are private to the class module. This means that their code cannot be executed from outside the class module. The code shown in Listing 28.3 illustrates how the code within the class module is used.

LISTING 28.3   USING THE FileInformation CLASS

```
Private Sub cmdGetFileInfo_Click()
    Dim oFile As FileInformation

    If IsNull(Me.txtFullFileName) Then
        MsgBox "File Name Must Be Entered"
    Else
        Set oFile = New FileInformation
        oFile.FullFileName = Me.txtFullFileName
        Me.txtDrive = oFile.Drive
        Me.txtPath = oFile.Path
        Me.txtName = oFile.Name
    End If
End Sub
```

This code, found in the frmFileInformation form in Chap28Ex, declares a FileInformation variable. As long as the user has entered a filename, the FileInformation class is instantiated. The FullFileName property is set equal to the value contained in the txtFullFileName text box. This causes the GetDrive, GetPath, and GetName routines to execute, thereby populating the private variables contained within the class. The Drive, Path, and Name property values are then retrieved and placed in text boxes on the form.

Using a Collection to Manipulate Multiple Instances of the File Information Class

The idea of using a collection to manipulate multiple instances of a class may seem odd to you. It is illustrated in Listing 28.4.

LISTING 28.4   USING A COLLECTION TO MANIPULATE MULTIPLE INSTANCES OF THE FileInformation CLASS

```
Sub FileInfoCollection(strDirName As String)
    Dim colFiles As Collection
    Dim objFileInfo As FileInformation
    Dim strFile As String
    Dim vntFile As Variant

    Set colFiles = New Collection

    strFile = Dir(strDirName)
    Do Until Len(strFile) = 0
        Set objFileInfo = New FileInformation
        objFileInfo.FullFileName = strDirName & strFile
        colFiles.Add objFileInfo
        strFile = Dir()
    Loop

    For Each vntFile In colFiles
        Debug.Print vntFile.Drive, vntFile.Path, vntFile.Name
    Next vntFile

End Sub
```

The code receives a directory path (including a trailing backslash) as a parameter. It creates and instantiates a `Collection` object. The `Dir` function is then executed, retrieving the name of the first file in the specified directory. As long as at least one file is found, the code within the `Do Until` loop is executed. An instance of the `FileInformation` class is created. The `FullFileName` property of the instance is then set equal to the directory name concatenated with the filename. The most important line of code in the routine is then executed. It adds the instance of the `FileInformation` class to the collection. This enables the instance to persist. The `Dir` function is then called to retrieve the name of the next file in the specified directory, and the process is repeated until no additional filenames are located.

After all the instances of the `FileInformation` class are added to the collection, the `For...Each` loop is used to iterate through all items in the collection. The `Drive`, `Path`, and

Name properties of each item in the collection are retrieved and printed to the Debug window. Notice that a variant variable must be used to iterate through the elements of the Collection object.

Data Access Class

Building a data access class greatly facilitates the process of dealing with data, particularly when the data within a table is accessed from numerous forms or numerous databases. By encapsulating the data access activities into a class module, you can better ensure that the data is treated consistently by all the forms and applications. Each field within the table becomes a property of the class. This is illustrated by the private declarations and Property Let and Property Get routines shown in Listing 28.5.

LISTING 28.5   THE PRIVATE VARIABLES AND Property Let AND Property Get ROUTINES USED BY THE DATA ACCESS CLASS

```
Private mlngClientID As Long
Private mstrCompanyName As String
Private mstrAddress As String
Private mstrCity As String
Private mconn As ADODB.Connection
Private mrst As ADODB.Recordset
Private mboolAddFlag As Boolean

Public Property Get ClientID() As Long
    ClientID = mlngClientID
End Property

Public Property Get CompanyName() As String
    CompanyName = mstrCompanyName
End Property

Public Property Let CompanyName(ByVal strCompanyName As String)
    mstrCompanyName = strCompanyName
End Property

Public Property Get Address() As String
    Address = mstrAddress
End Property

Public Property Let Address(ByVal strAddress As String)
    mstrAddress = strAddress
```

continues

28

EXPLOITING THE
POWER OF CLASS
MODULES

LISTING 28.5   CONTINUED

```
End Property

Public Property Get City() As String
    City = mstrCity
End Property

Public Property Let City(ByVal strCity As String)
    mstrCity = strCity
End Property

Public Property Get AddFlag() As Boolean
    AddFlag = mboolAddFlag
End Property

Public Property Let AddFlag(ByVal boolAddFlag As Boolean)
    mboolAddFlag = boolAddFlag
End Property
```

The `Initialize` event of the class, shown in Listing 28.6, is responsible for establishing a connection with the database and opening a recordset based on the data in the tblClients table. Notice that the LockType is set to `adLockOptimistic`, and the CursorType is set to `adOpenDynamic`. The combination of these two property settings renders the recordset's data updateable.

LISTING 28.6   THE `Initialize` EVENT ESTABLISHES A CONNECTION TO THE DATA AND OPENS A RECORDSET BASED ON THE TBLCLIENTS TABLE

```
Private Sub Class_Initialize()
    Set mconn = New ADODB.Connection
    Set mrst = New ADODB.Recordset

    mconn.ConnectionString = CurrentProject.Connection
    mconn.Open

    mrst.LockType = adLockOptimistic
    mrst.CursorType = adOpenDynamic
    mrst.Open "tblClients", mconn, Options:=adCmdTable
    Call Scatter
End Sub
```

After the recordset is open, the contents of the first record in the recordset must be available as properties of the class. This is necessary so that the contents of the first record can be displayed in the frmClients form. The Scatter method, shown in Listing 28.7, accomplishes this task.

LISTING 28.7   THE Scatter METHOD TAKES THE CONTENTS OF THE CURRENT RECORD AND PLACES THEM IN MODULE LEVEL VARIABLES

```
Public Sub Scatter()
    With mrst
        mlngClientID = !ClientID
        mstrCompanyName = !CompanyName
        mstrAddress = !Address
        mstrCity = !City
    End With
End Sub
```

The Scatter method simply takes the contents of the fields in the current record (in this case the first record) and stores them in private variables that are accessed by the Property Get and Property Let routines within the class. You might wonder how all this code is initiated. It is initiated by the Load event of the frmClients form, shown in Listing 28.8.

LISTING 28.8   THE Form_Load ROUTINE OF THE FRMCLIENTS FORM CALLS THE Scatter METHOD AND THEN POPULATES THE FORM'S TEXT BOXES

```
Private Sub Form_Load()
    Set mobjClients = New Client
    With mobjClients
        .Scatter
        Me.txtClientID = .ClientID
        Me.txtCompanyName = .CompanyName
        Me.txtAddress = .Address
        Me.txtCity = .City
    End With
End Sub
```

The Load event instantiates the Client class, causing the Initialize event of the class to execute. The Scatter method of the class executes and then the text boxes on the form are populated with the contents of the ClientID, CompanyName, Address, and City properties of the class. The frmClient form, populated with data from the first record in the tblClients table, is shown in Figure 28.2.

FIGURE 28.2

The frmClients form is used to display and manipulate data in the tblClients table.

After the first record is displayed, the user may opt to move to the next record in the recordset. Listing 28.9 shows the click event of the cmdNext command button on the frmClients form.

LISTING 28.9 THE CLICK EVENT OF THE cmdNext COMMAND BUTTON CALLS THE MoveNext METHOD OF THE CLASS AND THEN DISPLAYS THE CONTENTS OF THE CLASS'S PROPERTIES

```
Private Sub cmdNext_Click()
    With mobjClients
        .MoveNext
        Me.txtClientID = .ClientID
        Me.txtCompanyName = .CompanyName
        Me.txtAddress = .Address
        Me.txtCity = .City
    End With
End Sub
```

The cmdNext click event calls the MoveNext method of the class. The MoveNext method is responsible for moving forward from record to record within the class. It uses the module-level recordset object set in the Initialize event of the class. This appears in Listing 28.10.

LISTING 28.10 THE MoveNext METHOD IS RESPONSIBLE FOR MOVING TO AND DISPLAYING THE NEXT RECORD IN THE RECORDSET

```
Public Sub MoveNext()
    With mrst
        If Not .EOF Then
            .MoveNext
            If .EOF Then
                .MoveLast
            End If
        End If
        Call Scatter
    End With
End Sub
```

The MoveNext method first tests to see whether the end of the recordset has been reached. If not, the MoveNext method is used to move to the next record in the recordset. If the end of the recordset is encountered, the code moves back to the last record. The Scatter method is called to update the values of the module-level variables. The cmdNext click event then retrieves these values via the Property Get routines, to update the data displayed on the form.

The cmdPrevious click event of the frmClients form is similar to the cmdNext click event. It appears in Listing 28.11.

LISTING 28.11 THE CLICK EVENT OF THE cmdPREVIOUS COMMAND BUTTON CALLS THE MovePrevious METHOD OF THE CLASS AND THEN DISPLAYS THE CONTENTS OF THE CLASS'S PROPERTIES

```
Private Sub cmdPrevious_Click()
    With mobjClients
        .MovePrevious
        Me.txtClientID = .ClientID
        Me.txtCompanyName = .CompanyName
        Me.txtAddress = .Address
        Me.txtCity = .City
    End With
End Sub
```

The click event of the cmdPrevious command button first calls the MovePrevious method of the class. The MovePrevious method of the class is similar to the MoveNext method. It appears in Listing 28.12.

LISTING 28.12 THE MovePrevious METHOD IS RESPONSIBLE FOR MOVING TO AND DISPLAYING THE PREVIOUS RECORD IN THE RECORDSET

```
Public Sub MovePrevious()
    With mrst
        If Not .BOF Then
            .MovePrevious
            If .BOF Then
                .MoveFirst
            End If
        End If
        Call Scatter
    End With
End Sub
```

28

EXPLOITING THE
POWER OF CLASS
MODULES

The MovePrevious method first tests to see if the record pointer is before the first record in the recordset. If not, the MovePrevious method is used to move to the previous record in the recordset. If the beginning of the recordset is encountered, the code moves forward to the first record. The Scatter method is called to update the values of the module-level variables. These variables are then retrieved by the Property Get routines initiated by the click event of the cmdPrevious command button.

The Client class enables the user to edit the data in the underlying recordset. The user simply enters data into the form's unbound text boxes. After the data is entered, the user clicks Save. The click event of the cmdSave command button is executed. The click event appears in Listing 28.13.

LISTING 28.13   THE CLICK EVENT OF THE CMDSAVE COMMAND BUTTON SAVES THE FORM'S DATA TO THE UNDERLYING RECORDSET

```
Private Sub cmdSave_Click()
    With mobjClients
        .CompanyName = Me.txtCompanyName
        .Address = Me.txtAddress
        .City = Me.txtCity
        .Save
        .AddFlag = False
        Me.txtClientID = .ClientID
    End With
End Sub
```

The code in the click event of the cmdSave command button first sets all the properties of the class to the corresponding text box values. It then executes the Save method of the class (see Listing 28.15).

Before we look at the Save method, it is important to explore the code under the click event of the cmdNew command button (see Listing 28.14). It is very simple. It clears the text boxes on the form, readying them for the entry of the new data. It then sets the value of the AddFlag to True.

LISTING 28.14   THE CLICK EVENT OF THE CMDNEW COMMAND CLEARS ALL THE TEXT BOXES AND SETS THE VALUE OF THE AddFlag PROPERTY TO True

```
Private Sub cmdNew_Click()
    Me.txtClientID = ""
    Me.txtCompanyName = ""
    Me.txtAddress = ""
    Me.txtCity = ""
    mobjClients.AddFlag = True
End Sub
```

In the case of either an edit or an add, the code in the Save method of the class actually writes the data from the new record to disk. This code is shown in Listing 28.15.

Listing 28.15 The Save Method of the Class Calls the Appropriate Routine to Write the Data to Disk

```
Public Sub Save()
    If mboolAddFlag Then
        Call AddNew
    Else
        Call Edit
    End If
End Sub
```

The Save method of the class first determines whether the user is adding or editing data. This is determined by evaluating the mboolAddFlag. The mboolAddFlag is set to True when the Add button is clicked. When editing, the value of the variable is False. If the user is adding the record, the private routine call AddNew is executed. It appears in Listing 28.16.

Listing 28.16 The AddNew Method of the Class Adds the New Record

```
Private Sub AddNew()
    With mrst
        .AddNew
            !CompanyName = mstrCompanyName
            !Address = mstrAddress
            !City = mstrCity
        .Update
        mlngClientID = !ClientID
    End With
End Sub
```

The AddNew method of the class uses the AddNew method of an ADO recordset to populate a new record with the values contained in the private variables. The Update method of the recordset object writes the new data to disk. When the Update method is executed, the value of the AutoNumber field is assigned. The value of the AutoNumber field is stored in the variable called mlngClientID. This variable is retrieved in the click event of cmdSave so that the txtClientID text box contains the appropriate value.

Whereas the AddNew method of the class is responsible for adding the record in the recordset, the Edit method of the class is responsible for updating the data in an existing record. It appears in Listing 28.17.

LISTING 28.17   THE Edit METHOD OF THE CLASS UPDATES THE CONTENTS OF A RECORD

```
Private Sub Edit()
    With mrst
        !CompanyName = mstrCompanyName
        !Address = mstrAddress
        !City = mstrCity
        .Update
    End With
End Sub
```

The Edit method uses the Update method of the ADO recordset to take the values in the module-level variables and write them to disk.

The last data task associated with the cmdClients form provides the user with the capability to delete a record from the recordset. The code behind the Click event of the cmdDelete command button appears in Listing 28.18.

LISTING 28.18   THE Click EVENT OF THE CMDDELETE COMMAND BUTTON CALLS THE Delete METHOD OF THE CLASS

```
Private Sub cmdDelete_Click()
    With mobjClients
        .Delete
        Me.txtClientID = .ClientID
        Me.txtCompanyName = .CompanyName
        Me.txtAddress = .Address
        Me.txtCity = .City
    End With
End Sub
```

This code executes the Delete method of the class. The Delete method is shown in Listing 28.19. It utilizes the Delete method of an ADO recordset to delete the current record from the recordset. After the delete, the record pointer is sitting on the deleted record. The MoveNext method of the class is used to move the record pointer to the next valid record. The Click event of the cmdDelete command button then populates the text boxes on the form with the values of the record that the MoveNext method moved to.

LISTING 28.19 THE Delete METHOD OF THE CLASS DELETES A RECORD FROM THE RECORDSET

```
Public Sub Delete()
    With mrst
        .Delete
        Call MoveNext
    End With
End Sub
```

System Information Class

The process of obtaining system information, such as the amount of drive space free, is usually a somewhat tedious and difficult process. This information is generally available only through the Windows API. Executing Windows API functions is best left to more advanced developers. So how can a junior developer access this important information? If the senior developer encapsulates the complex functionality of the Windows API calls in a class module, the more junior developer can obtain the system information as properties of the class.

The class called SystemInformation is responsible for obtaining information about the hardware, operating system, and system resources. To obtain this information, the following Declare statements, type structure declarations, and constant declarations are included in the General Declarations section of the class module (see Listing 29.20).

LISTING 28.20 THE PRIVATE VARIABLES AND TYPE STRUCTURES REQUIRED BY THE SystemInformation CLASS

```
Private Declare Sub GlobalMemoryStatus _
    Lib "Kernel32" (lpBuffer As MEMORYSTATUS)
Private mlngTotalMemory As Long
Private mlngAvailableMemory As Long
Private mstrOSVersion As String
Private msngOSBuild As Single
Private mstrOSPlatform As String
Private mlngProcessor As Long

Private Type MEMORYSTATUS
    dwLength As Long
    dwMemoryLoad As Long
    dwTotalPhys As Long
```

continues

LISTING 28.20   CONTINUED

```
      dwAvailPhys As Long
      dwTotalPageFile As Long
      dwAvailPageFile As Long
      dwTotalVirtual As Long
      dwAvailVirtual As Long
End Type

Private Declare Function GetVersionEx Lib "Kernel32" _
      Alias "GetVersionExA" (lpOSInfo As OSVERSIONINFO) As Boolean

Private Type OSVERSIONINFO
      dwOSVersionInfoSize As Long
      dwMajorVersion As Long
      dwMinorVersion As Long
      dwBuildNumber As Long
      dwPlatformId As Long
      strReserved As String * 128
End Type

Private Declare Sub GetSystemInfo Lib "Kernel32" _
  (lpSystemInfo As SYSTEM_INFO)

Private Type SYSTEM_INFO
      dwOemID As Long
      dwPageSize As Long
      lpMinimumApplicationAddress As Long
      lpMaximumApplicationAddress As Long
      dwActiveProcessorMask As Long
      dwNumberOrfProcessors As Long
      dwProcessorType As Long
      dwAllocationGranularity As Long
      dwReserved As Long
End Type
```

The SystemInformation class contains six properties. They are TotalMemory, AvailableMemory, OSVersion, OSBuild, OSPlatform, and Processor. All these properties are read-only. They are set within the class and cannot be modified from outside it. The Property Get functions for the six properties are shown in Listing 28.21.

LISTING 28.21 THE Property Get AND Property Let ROUTINES REQUIRED BY THE SystemInformation CLASS

```
Public Property Get TotalMemory() As Long
    TotalMemory = mlngTotalMemory
End Property

Public Property Get AvailableMemory() As Long
    AvailableMemory = mlngAvailableMemory
End Property

Public Property Get OSVersion() As String
    OSVersion = mstrOSVersion
End Property

Public Property Get OSBuild() As Single
    OSBuild = msngOSBuild
End Property

Public Property Get OSPlatform() As String
    OSPlatform = mstrOSPlatform
End Property

Public Property Get Processor() As Long
    Processor = mlngProcessor
End Property
```

All the work is done in the Initialize event of the class. When the class is instantiated, the Initialize event executes all the Windows API functions necessary to obtain the required system information. The Initialize event of the class is shown in Listing 28.22.

LISTING 28.22 THE Initialize EVENT OF THE SYSTEM INFORMATION CLASS EXECUTES THE WINDOWS API FUNCTION REQUIRED TO OBTAIN THE SYSTEM INFORMATION

```
Private Sub Class_Initialize()
    'Get Free Memory
    Dim MS As MEMORYSTATUS
    MS.dwLength = Len(MS)
    GlobalMemoryStatus MS

    mlngTotalMemory = Format(MS.dwTotalPhys, "Standard")
```

continues

LISTING 28.22   CONTINUED

```
    mlngAvailableMemory = Format(MS.dwAvailPhys, "Standard")

    'Get Version Information
    Dim OSInfo As OSVERSIONINFO
    OSInfo.dwOSVersionInfoSize = Len(OSInfo)
    If GetVersionEx(OSInfo) Then
        mstrOSVersion = OSInfo.dwMajorVersion & "." & _
            OSInfo.dwMinorVersion
        msngOSBuild = OSInfo.dwBuildNumber And &HFFFF&
        If OSInfo.dwPlatformId = 0 Then
            mstrOSPlatform = "Windows 95"
        Else
            mstrOSPlatform = "Windows NT"
        End If
    End If

    'Get System Information
    Dim SI As SYSTEM_INFO
     GetSystemInfo SI
    mlngProcessor = SI.dwProcessorType

End Sub
```

The `GlobalMemoryStatus` Windows API function populates the `TotalMemory` and `AvailableMemory` properties. The `GetVersionEX` function is used to set the `OSVersion`, `OSBuild`, and `OSPlatform` properties. Finally, the `GetSystemInfo` function populates the `Processor` property.

Custom Error Handler Class

Implementing error handling within an application can be very tedious, especially if you attempt to place specific error-handling logic in each routine that you write. Chapter 14, "Error Handling: Preparing for the Inevitable," showed you how to create a generic error handler. Although implementing a generic error handler does not mandate the use of a class module, utilizing a class module greatly facilitates the process of implementing error handling within your applications. Listing 28.23 illustrates this point.

LISTING 28.23   A STANDARD ACCESS ROUTINE

```
Sub AnySub()
    Const SUBNAME As String = "AnySub"
    On Error GoTo AnySub_Err

    MsgBox "This is the rest of your code...."
    Err.Raise 11
    MsgBox "We are Past the Error!!"

    Exit Sub

AnySub_Err:
    Dim intAction As Integer

    Set gobjErrorHandler = New ErrorHandler

    With gobjErrorHandler
        .MODULENAME = MODULENAME
        .Routine = SUBNAME
        .ErrorMessage = Err.Description
        .ErrorNumber = Err.Number
        intAction = .ErrorProcess
    End With

    Select Case intAction
        Case gconERR_CONTINUE
            Resume Next
        Case gconERR_RETRY
            Resume
        Case gconERR_EXIT
            Exit Sub
        Case gconERR_QUIT
            Quit
    End Select
End Sub
```

When an error occurs, the ErrorHandler class is instantiated. The Initialize event of the class executes. It appears in Listing 28.24.

LISTING 28.24   THE Initialize EVENT OF THE ErrorHandler CLASS

```
Private Sub Class_Initialize()
    mstrUserName = CurrentUser
    mdatDateTime = Now
End Sub
```

The Initialize event of the class sets the module-level variables mstrUserName and mdatDateTime equal to the CurrentUser and the current date and time, respectively. These variables are used by the UserName and DateTime properties of the class.

After the Initialize event of the class executes, the ModuleName, Routine, ErrorMessage, and ErrorNumber properties of the class are set equal to the value of the constant MODULENAME, the value of the constant SUBNAME, the Description property of the Err object, and the Number property of the Err object, respectively. The Property Let and Property Get routines for the ModuleName, Routine, ErrorMessage, and ErrorNumber properties appear in Listing 28.25.

LISTING 28.25 THE Property Let AND Property Get ROUTINES OF THE CLASS MANIPULATE ERROR INFORMATION

```
Public Property Get MODULENAME() As String
    MODULENAME = mstrModule
End Property

Public Property Let MODULENAME(ByVal strModule As String)
    mstrModule = strModule
End Property

Public Property Get Routine() As String
    Routine = mstrRoutine
End Property

Public Property Let Routine(ByVal strRoutine As String)
    mstrRoutine = strRoutine
End Property

Public Property Get ErrorMessage() As String
    ErrorMessage = mstrErrorMessage
End Property

Public Property Let ErrorMessage(ByVal strErrorMessage As String)
    mstrErrorMessage = strErrorMessage
End Property

Public Property Get ErrorNumber() As Integer
    ErrorNumber = mintErrorNumber
End Property

Public Property Let ErrorNumber(ByVal intErrorNumber As Integer)
    mintErrorNumber = intErrorNumber
End Property
```

As you can see, each `Property Let` routine stores into a module-level variable. The associated `Property Get` routine then retrieves the value from the module-level variable.

The `ErrorProcess` method of the `ErrorHandler` class is then executed. It appears in Listing 28.26.

LISTING 28.26   THE `ErrorProcess` METHOD OF THE `ErrorHandler` CLASS LOGS THE ERROR AND THEN TAKES APPROPRIATE ACTION IN RESPONSE TO THE ERROR

```
Public Function ErrorProcess() As Integer

    Call LogError

    Dim rst As ADODB.Recordset
    Set rst = New ADODB.Recordset
    rst.ActiveConnection = CurrentProject.Connection
    rst.Open "Select Response from tblErrors Where ErrorNum = " & _
        mintErrorNumber, Options:=adCmdText
    If rst.EOF Then
        DoCmd.OpenForm "frmError", WindowMode:=acDialog, _
            OpenArgs:="ErrorHandler"
        ErrorHandler = ERR_QUIT
    Else
        Select Case rst!Response
            Case ERR_QUIT
                DoCmd.OpenForm "frmError", WindowMode:=acDialog, _
                    OpenArgs:="Critical Error:  Application _
                            will Terminate"
                ErrorProcess = ERR_QUIT
            Case ERR_RETRY
                ErrorProcess = ERR_RETRY
            Case ERR_EXIT
                DoCmd.OpenForm "frmError", WindowMode:=acDialog, _
                    OpenArgs:="Severe Error:  Processing Did _
                            Not Complete"
                ErrorProcess = ERR_EXIT
            Case ERR_CONTINUE
                ErrorProcess = ERR_CONTINUE
        End Select
    End If

End Function
```

The routine begins by calling a routine that logs the error that occurred. This error logging routine is called `LogError` and is shown in Listing 28.27. The `LogError` routine utilizes ADO code to add a record to the tblErrorLog table. The record that is added contains all the information about the error that occurred. Notice that the error information is retrieved from the module level variables populated by the `ErrorHandler` class's `Property Let` routines.

After the error is logged, the number of the error that occurred is looked up in the tblErrors table. If it is not found in the tblErrors table, a form is displayed, containing all the critical information about the error that occurred. The value contained in the constant `ERR_QUIT` is returned from the `ErrorHandler` function. If the error number is found in the tblErrors table, the value contained in the Response field is evaluated. If it is the value contained in the constant `ERR_QUIT`, the frmError form is displayed, and the value in the constant `ERR_QUIT` is returned from the `ErrorHandler` function. If the Response field contains the value of the `ERR_RETRY` constant, the `ERR_RETRY` value is returned from the function, without the frmError form being displayed. If the Response field contains the value associated with the `ERR_EXIT` constant, the frmError form is displayed and the `ERR_EXIT` value is returned from the `ErrorHandler` function. Finally, if the value in the Response field is the value associated with the `ERR_CONTINUE` function, no error information is displayed and the `ERR_CONTINUE` value is returned from the `ErrorHandler` function.

LISTING 28.27 THE `LogError` SUBROUTINE USES ADO CODE TO ADD THE ERROR INFORMATION TO TBLERRORLOG

```
Private Sub LogError()
    Dim cnn As ADODB.Connection
    Dim strSQL As String

    strSQL = "INSERT INTO tblErrorLog (ErrorDate, ErrorTime, _
        UserName, ErrorNum, ErrorString, ModuleName, RoutineName) "
    strSQL = strSQL & "SELECT ( #" & DateTime & "#, #" _
                            & mdatDateTime & "#, '" _
                            & mstrUserName & "', " _
                            & mintErrorNumber & ", '" _
                            & mstrErrorMessage & "', '" _
                            & mstrModule & "', '" _
                            & mstrRoutine & "')"

    Set cnn = New ADODB.Connection
    cnn.ConnectionString = CurrentProject.Connection
    cnn.Open
    cnn.Execute strSQL

End Sub
```

All the code contained in the ErrorHandler class is similar to that contained in the basErrorHandler module discussed in Chapter 14. The code has been modified so that it is implemented using properties and methods of a Class object.

SUMMARY

In this chapter, you learned how to implement your application's subroutines and functions as methods of class modules. In doing so, you discovered how complex activities can be encapsulated into class modules, greatly simplifying the implementation of their functionality. After exploring the basics of object orientation and class modules, you saw several practical examples of classes in action. These included a File Information class, a Data Access class, a System Information class, and an Error Handler class. The possible practical application of classes within the business environment are limited only by your imagination!

CREATING YOUR OWN LIBRARIES

IN THIS CHAPTER

WHY THIS CHAPTER IS IMPORTANT

As your knowledge of the VBA language expands and you become more proficient as a VBA programmer, you probably will develop functions and subroutines that you would like all your databases to share. Without the use of library databases, the code in each of your databases is an island unto itself. Although the functions and subroutines within your code modules can be called from anywhere in the same database, these procedures cannot be called from a different database.

Without a shared library of code and other standard objects, you will find yourself copying routines and other database objects from one database to the next. The library database can be used by all your applications and distributed to all your users. A library database is just like any other database; it is simply a collection of procedures and objects that you want to share among numerous databases. The only difference between the library database and other databases is in the way the database is referenced. Instead of opening a library database to use it, you reference it from another database.

Access is highly dependent on library databases. The Table Wizard, Form Wizard, Report Wizard, Database Wizard, Database Splitter, Database Analyzer, and Database Documenter are all examples of tools that reside in library databases. In fact, all the wizards, builders, and menu add-ins you are accustomed to using while developing your applications are all contained within library databases. Wizards, builders, and menu add-ins are covered in Chapter 30, "Using Builders, Wizards, and Menu Add-Ins." This chapter focuses on creating library databases and placing generic functions in a library database to make them available to all your application databases.

PREPARING A DATABASE TO BE A LIBRARY

Creating a library database involves two steps:

1. Writing the functions and creating the objects to be used as a library
2. Loading the database as a library

You begin by creating the generic objects you want to share among your applications. To load the database as a library, you must reference it from another database. This process is covered in the next section.

Before you can reference a database as a library, you need to think about how to construct the database so that it best serves you as a library. Although a library database is just a normal database, planning the design of the library is integral to its success and usefulness. Improper planning can cause anything from extra memory being required to the database malfunctioning.

Structuring Code Modules for Optimal Performance

Library databases contain the general functions that you use in most of your applications. Because of the way Access loads code modules, you must structure your library databases effectively in order to achieve optimal performance.

Access 2.0 loaded all code modules the moment the application loaded. This meant that, when developing an Access 2.0 application, it was not particularly important how you structured your subroutines and functions within the various modules of the database. This situation changed dramatically with Access 95, Access 97, and Access 2000, all which load code modules only if they are needed. In Access 95, Access 97, and Access 2000, if no procedures within a particular module are called, the module is never loaded into memory. On the other hand, if a single subroutine or function is called or if a public variable is referenced, the entire module loads. Therefore, it is crucial that you structure your modules to minimize what is loaded into memory.

These techniques help you structure your modules effectively:

- Separate frequently used procedures from those that are called infrequently.
- Place in the same module procedures that are used together.
- Place in their own modules procedures that are called rarely.
- If the same procedure is called by routines in more than one module, consider duplicating the routine and placing a copy of it in each module. This method prevents an entire module from loading just because a single routine within it is called.
- Place in the same module procedures within a call tree. This is necessary because Access looks at the potential call tree when it loads a module. If a procedure in one module is called from a procedure in another module, both modules are loaded into memory.

Although you generally want as little to load into memory as possible, the opposite is true for commonly used functions. By placing frequently used procedures in the same module, you ensure that they are loaded into memory and can be accessed quickly when they are called. This improves the performance of your application.

Writing Library Code That Runs

Code that runs perfectly within a normal database might not run as expected when it is part of a library database. One good example is the CurrentDB function. As you have seen throughout this book, the CurrentDB function is a commonly used function that enables you to reference the current database. You would think that the CurrentDB function references the database in which the code is running, but this is actually not the case. The CurrentDB function specifically references the database that is active in the user interface. If a library function refers to

CurrentDB, it does not refer to itself; instead, it refers to the application database that is calling the library function. If you want to refer to the library database, you must use the CodeDB function. The CodeDB function always refers to the database in which the code is running. You must decide whether CurrentDB or CodeDB is applicable for each situation.

Compiling the Library

It is important to compile a library database before you distribute it. This ensures that it provides optimal performance. If library code is not compiled, it compiles each time it is accessed, which significantly degrades the performance of your application. The compilation process and its benefits are discussed in detail in Chapter 15, "Optimizing Your Application." After you complete all changes to the library database, select Debug|Compile. You must choose this command each time you make changes to the library database.

CREATING A REFERENCE

A *reference* is Access's way of locating a library database so that it can use the code in it. You can establish references in four ways:

- Create a library reference
- Create a runtime reference
- Create an explicit reference
- Use VBA code

> **TIP**
>
> Much of the text that follows refers to the Windows Registry. You can access the Windows Registry using the RegEdit utility. To utilize RegEdit, select the Run option from the Start menu. Then type RegEdit.

Creating a Library Reference

You create a library reference by adding the library to the Menu Add-ins section of the Windows Registry, as shown in Figure 29.1. The Menu Add-ins section is located in the HKEY_LOCAL_MACHINE\SOFTWARE\Microsoft\Office\9.0\Access\Menu Add-Ins key. This type of reference is limited because it allows the functions of the library database to be invoked only as an add-in. Creating a library reference is covered in more detail in Chapter 30.

FIGURE 29.1

Viewing the Menu Add-ins section of the Windows Registry.

Creating a Runtime Reference

Creating a runtime reference involves establishing a reference to the library at runtime using the Run method of the Application object. This method of creating a reference actually opens the library database and executes the specified function. It uses OLE automation to accomplish this task.

The major advantage of this technique is that the library code is not loaded into memory until it is used. Furthermore, this technique does not require that additional modules in the call stack be loaded into memory unless they are called explicitly. Creating a runtime reference does have a few disadvantages, though:

- The library database must have an MDA extension.
- The library database must be located in the path specified in the AddInPath key in the Windows Registry. The AddInPath key is located in the HKEY_LOCAL_MACHINE\SOFTWARE\Microsoft\Office\9.0\Access\Wizards subdirectory of the Windows Registry, as shown in Figure 29.2.

Calling a Function from a Library at Runtime

The code in Listing 29.1 illustrates how to call a function in a library. Notice that the IsLoaded function is being called from the library. This code is located in the CHAP29EX.MDB database on the sample code CD-ROM.

FIGURE 29.2

Viewing the AddInPath key of the Windows Registry.

LISTING 29.1   CALLING A FUNCTION IN A LIBRARY

```
Sub AppRun()
    If Application.Run("Chap29Lib.IsLoaded", "frmCustomers") Then
        MsgBox "Customers Form is Loaded"
    Else
        MsgBox "Customers Form is NOT Loaded!!"
    End If
End Sub
```

This code uses the Run method of the Application object to call a function called IsLoaded, which is located in the CHAP29LIB.MDA library. This file must be referenced with an explicit reference (see "Creating an Explicit Reference," later in this chapter) or be located in the directory specified in the AddInPath key of the Windows Registry. Notice the explicit reference to the name of the library in which the function is located. When using this method of loading a library (without an explicit reference), the library name must be specified.

Using the LoadOnStartup Key

You can add a LoadOnStartup key to the Windows Registry. This key provides a means for Access to load a type library when the database is loaded. A type library is not an actual module, but more a blueprint of what the module looks like. It displays the functions and constants for a specific module. This is helpful because Access can look up functions without having to actually load the module in which the function is located. This key is not automatically created for you. To create the LoadOnStartup key and add an entry to it, follow these steps:

1. Choose Run from the Windows Start menu.

2. Type `RegEdit` and click OK; this launches the Registry Editor.

3. Open the Registry tree until you see HKEY_LOCAL_MACHINE\SOFTWARE\Microsoft\Office\9.0\Access\Wizards.

4. Click the Wizards entry.

5. Choose Edit | New | Key. A new key is added.

6. Type `LoadOnStartup` as the name of the new key.

7. With LoadOnStartup selected, choose Edit | New | String Value.

8. Type the full name and path of the library as the name of the new string value.

9. Choose Edit | Modify.

10. Type `rw` for the value.

Figure 29.3 shows an example of a completed entry that references the library in the c:\Libraries directory: CHAP29LIB.MDA.

FIGURE 29.3

Referencing a library using the Registry Editor.

The module and procedure lists of library databases listed under the LoadOnStartup key are loaded when Access is started. When you use the `Run` method (discussed in the "Creating a Library Reference" section), Access searches for the specified procedure in the loaded or referenced libraries. If it does not find the procedure, Access searches any databases listed in the LoadOnStartUp key. Because the module and procedure lists of databases listed under the key become available when Access is started, Access searches the list and then locates and loads the required library.

As you can see, the LoadOnStartUp key can reap the benefits of `Application.Run` by using the type library. This is beneficial because the functions can be checked without loading the actual module until it is referenced explicitly through code.

NOTE

The LoadOnStartUp key is not a panacea. Loading the type library when Access is loaded does slow down the initial load time for your application. Furthermore, the memory occupied by the type information is used regardless of whether the library functions actually are accessed. You must decide whether either of these facts is an issue.

Creating an Explicit Reference

The most common type of reference by far is an explicit reference. This type of reference is created from any code module in the database referencing the library. To create an explicit reference, follow these steps:

1. Choose a module from the database container window and click the Design button to open the Design view of the module.

2. Choose Tools | References from the VBE menu. The References dialog box appears, as shown in Figure 29.4.

FIGURE 29.4

The References dialog box.

3. Click the Browse button.

4. Select Microsoft Access Databases (*.mdb) or Add-ins (*.mda) from the Files of Type drop-down.

5. Locate the library database you want to reference.

6. Click Open to close the Add References dialog box.

7. Click OK to close the References dialog box.

When you add a library database to the References dialog box, Access loads the database as a library when you make a call to the library from your code. You can call a library routine just as you would call any subroutine or function. You then can use code in the library database to open forms and other objects stored in the library. Access does not actually load the library database into memory until code in the active application database calls a function or subroutine that is located in the library.

Explicit library references impose a few limitations:

- The references you add in a database are available only to that database. Therefore, you must add the library reference to each application database that needs to use the library.

- The explicit path to the reference is stored in the database. This means that, if the library is moved, the reference cannot be resolved. Exceptions to this rule are covered later in this section.

When a function is called that is in a library that cannot be located, the message shown in Figure 29.5 appears. This box indicates that Access cannot find the project or library containing the procedure. The References dialog box shows the library as missing, as shown in the sixth line of the Available References list box in Figure 29.6.

FIGURE 29.5

A warning message indicating that the library database cannot be located.

FIGURE 29.6

The References dialog box with a library flagged as missing.

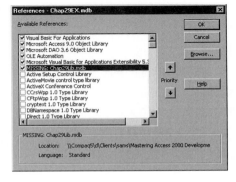

Although Access might not be able to find a library database that has been moved, it does its best to resolve library references. By default, Access looks in these places to attempt to resolve a library reference:

- The absolute path of the library
- The relative path to the library
- The directory where Access is installed
- The Windows path (Windows and Windows\System folders)
- The path located in the RefLibPaths key of the Windows Registry

Although most of these locations are self-explanatory, a couple of them require further explanation. If the library is not located in exactly the same location on the user's machine as it is on your machine, Access searches the relative path to the library next. This means that if the library is placed in the same directory as the database that is referencing it, or in the same relative location, the library database is found. Suppose your application database is located in c:\AccessApps\Sales. The library database is located in c:\AccessApps\Sales\Libraries. The user installs the application in c:\SalesApp with the library installed in c:\SalesApp\Libraries. In this case, Access can resolve the reference to the library.

Another trick when dealing with library databases is to use the RefLibPaths key of the Windows Registry. If a key called RefLibPaths exists in the Windows Registry, Access also searches the paths specified under RefLibPaths in an attempt to resolve any references. To use this trick, follow these steps:

1. Create a RefLibPaths key under the HKEY_LOCAL_MACHINE\SOFTWARE\Microsoft\Office\9.0\Access subdirectory, if it does not already exist.
2. With the key selected, choose Edit | New | String Value.
3. Type the name of the library database as the name of the new string value.
4. Choose Edit | Modify.
5. Type the name of the path containing the library as the value.
6. Repeat steps 2 through 5 for each library you are referencing.

This is a good method to use if you will be distributing an application containing several library databases. You can select a location for the library databases and then reference that location in the Windows Registry. You even can create the Registry entries programmatically by using Windows API calls or the VBA `SaveSetting` statement. Figure 29.7 shows the RefLibPath key with an entry for the Chap29Lib.mdb library.

FIGURE 29.7

The RefLibPath key of the Windows Registry.

TIP

You can use the Setup Wizard to create the RefLibPaths key in the Windows Registry. This is the easiest way to create the RefLibPaths entry, but it requires that you distribute your application using the Setup Wizard.

Creating a Reference Using VBA Code

With Access 2000 comes the capability to create library references using VBA code. You use the `AddFromFile` method to accomplish this task. The `AddFromFile` method is applied to the References collection. The References collection is similar to other collections used within Access, and provides a hook to the references associated with a database. The `AddFromFile` method of the References collection accepts a string as a parameter. The string contains the name of the library reference you are adding. Listing 29.2 shows the code to pass in a library name and then add a reference to it.

LISTING 29.2 LOCATING AND REFERENCING LIBRARIES IN CODE

```
Function CreateLibRef(strLibName)
    Dim ref As Reference
    On Error GoTo CreateLibRef_Err
    ' Create new reference
    Set ref = References.AddFromFile(strLibName)
    CreateLibRef = True
```

continues

LISTING 29.2   CONTINUED

```
Exit_CreateLibRef:
    Exit Function
CreateLibRef_Err:
    Dim intAnswer As Integer
    Dim strLocation As String
    intAnswer = MsgBox("Library Not Found, Attempt to Locate?", _
        vbYesNo, "Error")
    If intAnswer = vbYes Then
        strLocation = InputBox("Please Enter the Location of the Library")
        Resume
    Else
        CreateLibRef = False
        GoTo Exit_CreateLibRef
    End If

End Function
```

The routine begins by invoking an error handler. A reference object is then set to the result of the `AddFromFile` method being executed on the References collection. If the `AddFromFile` method executes successfully, the reference is created and the function returns a `True` condition. Otherwise, the user is asked whether he wants to locate the library database. If he responds affirmatively, he is prompted for the location of the library database and the code attempts once again to establish the reference. If he opts not to supply a location, the routine terminates, returning a `False` condition.

DEBUGGING A LIBRARY DATABASE

You can open a library database and test it just like any other database. Although you always should begin testing the library functions this way, it also is important that you give the database a test drive as a library. In other words, after you eliminate any bugs from the database, you should reference it from another database and test it as a library database.

If you need to make changes to a library database while accessing it from another database, you easily can do so by following these steps:

1. Make sure that the library database is referenced from Tools | References as mentioned earlier in "Creating an Explicit Reference."
2. Click the Object Browser tool from the Module Design window.
3. From the Project/Library drop-down menu, select the library database that contains the code you want to modify. (See Figure 29.8.)

FIGURE 29.8

Using the Object Browser to modify a library database.

4. Select the class you want to modify from the Classes list box.

5. Select the member you want to modify from the Members list box.

6. Click View Definition (the button with the arrow pointing toward the box), or double-click the member whose code you want to view. You are placed in the correct module and procedure of the library database. You now can make changes to the code in the database as required.

SECURING AN ACCESS LIBRARY

Many people develop Access libraries for mass distribution in the retail market. Whether you are marketing a library database or just distributing it in your organization or to your clients, you should consider securing your library code. This protects the library code from being modified or copied by unauthorized individuals. It is highly advisable to secure your library if you plan to distribute it—not only for the sake of securing your intellectual property, but to avoid the headache of some user who tries to alter the code and then calls you for support. Security issues are covered in detail in Chapter 33, "Database Security Made Easy."

PRACTICAL EXAMPLES

Building a Library for Your Application

Now that you are familiar with library databases and what they offer, try extracting all the generic functions from the Time and Billing application and placing them in a library database. This section presents a step-by-step roadmap to accomplishing this task.

> **NOTE**
>
> This process already has been completed for CHAP29.MDB. The associated library database is called CHAP29LIBRARY.MDA. If you want to complete this process as an exercise, copy CHAP26.MDB and complete the outlined steps.

To extract the generic functions from the Time and Billing application and place them in a library database, follow these steps:

1. Create a new database that will become the library database. Import the basUtils, basGenericErrorHandler, and basWinAPI modules as well as the frmError form into the library database.

2. Remove three routines from basUtils within the library database: `RunReport`, `GetCompanyInfo`, and `CreateInstances`. Assume that these routines are specific to the application database and should not be moved to become a part of the library.

3. Choose Debug | Compile to ensure that you do not get any compile errors in the library database.

4. Open the application database.

5. Remove basGenericErrorHandler, basWinAPI, and frmError from the application database.

6. Remove six subroutines from basUtils in the application database: `IsLoaded`, `FlipEnabled`, `ImportantKey`, `AreTablesAttached`, `LastOccurence`, and `TryAgain`.

7. Choose Tools | References to reference the library database.

8. Choose Debug | Compile to ensure that you do not get any compile errors in the application database.

9. Test the application to ensure that it runs successfully. To properly check all aspects of the application, you need to introduce an error to test the error-handling routines. Rename the CHAP19DATA.MDB database to test the linking routines.

You should move one more database element to the library database: the Report Selection Criteria form. This form is generic and can be used by many of the applications you create.

Follow these steps to move the frmReportDateRange form to the library database:

1. Open the library database and import the frmReportDateRange form.

2. Create a module called basGenericForms and add the `OpenReportDateRange` subroutine to the module. Because you cannot open a form in a library database directly, you must create a routine within the library database that opens the form.

3. Open the application database and remove the frmReportDateRange form.

4. Modify the appropriate objects within the application database like this:

```
Sub OpenReportDateRange(strOpenArg As String)
    DoCmd.OpenForm "frmReportDateRange", , , , , acDialog, _
        strOpenArg
End Sub
```

You must modify three reports in the application database to accommodate the movement of the frmReportDateRange form to a library database: rptProjectBillingsByWorkCode, rptClientBillingsByProject, and rptEmployeeBillingsByProject. The Open event of rptProjectBillingsByWorkCode should be modified to look like this:

```
Private Sub Report_Open(Cancel As Integer)
    Call OpenReportDateRange("rptProjectBillingsByWorkCode")
    If Not IsLoaded("frmReportDateRange") Then
        Cancel = True
    End If
End Sub
```

Instead of opening the form directly, which would not work because the form is in a library database, you must call the OpenReportDateRange library routine. The OpenReportDateRange library routine is responsible for opening the form. The strOpenArg parameter to the OpenReportDateRange subroutine is used as the OpenArgs parameter for the frmReportCriteria form. You must make similar changes to the rptClientBillingsByProject and rptEmployeeBillingsByProject reports. You should modify the Open event of the rptClientBillingsByProject report to look like Listing 29.3.

LISTING 29.3 MODIFYING THE Open EVENT OF THE RPTCLIENTBILLINGSBYPROJECT REPORT

```
Private Sub Report_Open(Cancel As Integer)
    Call OpenReportDateRange("rptClientBillingsByProject")
    If Not IsLoaded("frmReportDateRange") Then
        Cancel = True
    Else
        Select Case Forms!frmReportDateRange!optDetailLevel.Value
            Case 1
                Me.Caption = Me.Caption & " - Summary Only"
                Me!lblTitle.Caption = Me.lblTitle.Caption & " - _
                Summary Only"
                Me.Detail.Visible = False
```

continues

29

CREATING YOUR
OWN LIBRARIES

LISTING 29.3   CONTINUED

```
            Case 2
                Me.Caption = Me.Caption & " - Detail Only"
                Me!lblTitle.Caption = Me.lblTitle.Caption & " - _
                  Detail Only"
                Me.GroupHeader0.Visible = False
                Me.GroupFooter1.Visible = False
                Me!CompanyNameDet.Visible = True
            Case 3
                Me.Caption = Me.Caption & " - Summary and Detail"
                Me!lblTitle.Caption = Me.lblTitle.Caption & _
                " - Summary and Detail"
                Me!CompanyNameDet.Visible = False
        End Select
    End If
End Sub
```

Modify the Open event of the rptEmployeeBillingsByProject report to look like this:

```
Private Sub Report_Open(Cancel As Integer)
    Call OpenReportDateRange("rptEmployeeBillingsByProject")
    If Not IsLoaded("frmReportDateRange") Then
        Cancel = True
    End If
End Sub
```

After you move the generic features of the application to the library database, you can try to build another application database and use the same library features.

SUMMARY

Library databases enable you to create libraries of code, forms, reports, and other objects that will be shared by multiple databases. Library databases facilitate the application development process by enabling you to easily centralize the development of common code libraries. You also can use these databases to incorporate add-ins, wizards, and builders into your applications and development environment (covered in Chapter 30).

This chapter began by defining a library database. It then walked you through all the steps required to prepare a database to become a library database. You can use several methods to reference a library database. The chapter discussed each method, highlighting the pros and cons of each. After you reference a library database, the debugging process begins. This chapter highlighted how easy it is to debug an Access 2000 library database. Finally, it provided you with practical examples of how you can use library databases in your applications.

Library databases can greatly facilitate the application development process, enabling you to easily implement sophisticated functionality into all your applications. Although the process of designing library databases can be intimidating at first, a well-planned library database can shave hours off the application development and maintenance processes.

USING BUILDERS, WIZARDS, AND MENU ADD-INS

IN THIS CHAPTER

WHY THIS CHAPTER IS IMPORTANT

Add-ins are tools that extend the functionality of Access. They enhance the Access environment by making difficult tasks easier, automating repetitive tasks, and adding enhanced functionality. You can design add-ins for yourself or for others in your organization to use. You even might want to distribute add-ins as part of your application so that your users can build their own database objects. If you are really ambitious, you might decide to build an add-in for sale in the Access third-party market.

Microsoft Access supports three types of add-ins: builders, wizards, and menu add-ins. Each has its own advantages and uses. When you begin the process of designing an add-in, you must decide whether it will be a builder, wizard, or menu add-in. This decision affects how you design the add-in as well as how you install it. This chapter defines and shows you how to design and install each type of add-in.

USING BUILDERS

A *builder* is an add-in that helps users construct an expression or another data element. Builders most often are used to help users fill in a property of a database object. Builders generally consist of a single dialog box that appears after the user clicks the ellipsis to the right of the property on the Property sheet. An example of a builder is the Expression Builder that appears when users are setting the control source of a text box on a form. Access supports three types of builders:

- Property builders
- Control builders
- Expression builders

Looking At Design Guidelines

When designing your own builder, you should be consistent with the builders that are part of Access. You therefore must learn about the standards for an Access builder. To design builders that are consistent with the built-in builders, keep a few guidelines in mind:

- Set the `AutoCenter` property of the Builder form to `Yes`.
- Remove record selectors and navigation buttons.
- Remove scrollbars.
- Be consistent about the placement of objects on the form. Place the OK and Cancel buttons in the same place in each builder you create, for example.
- Design the forms as dialog boxes.

Creating a Builder

Now that you are familiar with some general design guidelines for builders, you are ready to design your first builder. What a builder does is completely up to your imagination. For illustration, this section begins with a simple builder that prompts users to select the special effect for a text box. Three overall steps are required to create the builder:

1. Write a builder function.

2. Design a builder form.

3. Register the builder.

The following sections go over each of these steps in detail.

Writing a Builder Function

 The *builder function* is the function Access calls each time the builder is launched. It launches the builder form and then returns a value to the appropriate property. Listing 30.1 is an example of a builder function. It is located in CHAP30LIB.MDA in the basBuilders module on the accompanying CD-ROM.

LISTING 30.1 CREATING A BUILDER FUNCTION

```
Function SpecialEffect(strObject As String, _
          strControl As String, _
          strCurrentValue As String)

   On Error GoTo SpecialEffect_Err
   DoCmd.OpenForm FormName:="frmSpecialEffect", _
                WindowMode:=acDialog, _
                OpenArgs:=strCurrentValue
   If SysCmd(acSysCmdGetObjectState, acForm, _
          "frmSpecialEffect") = acObjStateOpen Then
      Select Case Forms!frmSpecialEffect.optSpecialEffect.Value
         Case 1
            SpecialEffect = "Flat"
         Case 2
            SpecialEffect = "Raised"
         Case 3
            SpecialEffect = "Sunken"
         Case 4
            SpecialEffect = "Etched"
         Case 5
            SpecialEffect = "Shadowed"
```

continues

LISTING 30.1   CONTINUED

```
        Case 6
            SpecialEffect = "Chiseled"
    End Select
    DoCmd.Close acForm, "frmSpecialEffect"
Else
    SpecialEffect = strCurrentValue
End If

SpecialEffect_Exit:
    Exit Function

SpecialEffect_Err:
    MsgBox "Error # " & Err.Number & ": " & Err.Description
    Resume SpecialEffect_Exit
End Function
```

A builder function must receive three preset arguments and must return the value that will become the value for the property being set. The three preset arguments follow:

- strObject— The name of the table, query, form, report, or module on which the builder is operating.
- strControl—The name of the control to which the property applies.
- strCurrentValue— The current property value.

Although the names of the arguments are arbitrary, their data types, positions, and content cannot be changed. Access automatically fills in the values for the three arguments.

The SpecialEffect function opens the form called frmSpecialEffect. It opens the form in Dialog mode, passing it the current value of the property as the OpenArgs value. Figure 30.1 shows the frmSpecialEffect form.

The following code is located in the Click event of the cmdOkay command button on the form:

```
Private Sub cmdOK_Click()
    Me.Visible = False
End Sub
```

Notice that the code sets the Visible property of the form to False. The code placed behind the cmdCancel command button looks like this:

```
Private Sub cmdCancel_Click()
    DoCmd.Close
End Sub
```

This code closes the frmSpecialEffect form.

FIGURE 30.1

The Special Effect builder form.

After the user clicks OK or Cancel, the code within the SpecialEffect function continues to execute. The function uses the SysCmd function to determine whether the frmSpecialEffect form is loaded. You also can use the user-defined IsLoaded function to accomplish this task. If the frmSpecialEffect form still is loaded, the user must have selected a special effect and clicked OK. Because the form still is open, the function can determine which option button the user selected.

The Case statement within the SpecialEffect function evaluates the value of the optSpecialEffect option group found on the frmSpecialEffect form. It sets the return value for the function equal to the appropriate string, depending on the option button that the user of the builder selects. If the user of the builder selects the second option button (with a value of 2), for example, the SpecialEffect function returns the string "Raised". After the option button value is evaluated and the return value is set, the frmSpecialEffect form no longer is needed, so it is closed.

If the user chooses Cancel from the frmSpecialEffect form, the SysCmd function returns False, and the return value of the SpecialEffect function is set equal to strCurrentValue, the original property value. The property value therefore is not changed.

Designing a Builder Form

Although you have seen the code behind the Click event of the OK and Cancel buttons on the frmSpecialEffect form, you have not learned about the design of the form or the idea behind this builder. Ordinarily, when the Special Effect property is set from the Property window, no wizard exists to assist with the process. Although the process of setting the Special Effect property is quite simple, the main problem is that it is difficult to remember exactly what each special effect looks like. The custom special effect builder is designed with this potential problem in mind. It enables users of the builder to see what each special effect looks like before deciding which effect to select.

The properties of the form are quite simple. The Modal property of the form is set to Yes. The record selectors, navigation buttons, and scrollbars have been removed. The AutoCenter property of the form has been set to True. Six text boxes have been added to the form. The special effect of each text box has been set to a different style. An option group has been added to the form. This group has a different value, depending on which option button was selected. The Default property of the OK command button has been set to Yes, making the OK button the default choice. The Cancel property of the Cancel command button was set to Yes, ensuring that if the user presses Esc, the code behind the Cancel button executes. The code behind the Click events of the OK and Cancel buttons was shown in the preceding section. Listing 30.2 shows one more piece of code that enhances this builder.

LISTING 30.2 ENHANCING THE BUILDER

```
Private Sub Form_Load()
    'Set the Value of the Option Group
    'To the Current Value of the Property
    Select Case Me.OpenArgs
        Case "Flat"
            Me.optSpecialEffect.Value = 1
        Case "Raised"
            Me.optSpecialEffect.Value = 2
        Case "Sunken"
            Me.optSpecialEffect.Value = 3
        Case "Etched"
            Me.optSpecialEffect.Value = 4
        Case "Shadowed"
            Me.optSpecialEffect.Value = 5
        Case "Chiseled"
            Me.optSpecialEffect.Value = 6
    End Select
End Sub
```

This subroutine is placed in the Load event of the builder form. It sets the value of the option group to the current value of the property (passed in as an OpenArg).

Although the frmSpecialEffect form is not particularly exciting, it illustrates quite well that you can design a form of any level of complexity to facilitate the process of setting a property value. So far, though, you have not provided an entry point to the builder. If you select the Special Effect property, no ellipsis appears. You do not yet have access to the builder.

Registering a Builder

Before you can use a builder, you must register it. You can register a builder in two ways:

- Manually add the required entries to the Windows Registry.
- Set up the library database so that the Add-in Manager can create the Windows Registry entries for you.

Manually Adding Entries to the Windows Registry

Adding the required entries to the Windows Registry involves four steps:

1. If no Registry key exists for the property for which you are designing a builder, add the property as a subkey under Property Wizards.
2. Add an additional subkey for the builder.
3. Add four predefined Registry values for the key.
4. Set the proper data value for each value name.

The four value names that must be created for the subkey are Can Edit, Description, Function, and Library. Table 30.1 describes these value names for the Registry subkey.

TABLE 30.1 VALUES FOR THE REGISTRY SUBKEY

Value Name	Value Type	Purpose
Can Edit	DWORD	Allows the builder to operate on and modify an existing value.
Description	String	Specifies a subkey description that appears in the dialog box, which is invoked automatically if more than one builder exists for a property.
Function	String	Name of the builder function.
Library	String	Name of the library containing the builder function.

Now that you have an overview of the steps involved in the process, you are ready to walk through the steps in detail. The following steps set up the builder called SpecialEffect, which is contained in the library database CHAP30LIB.MDA in the folder c:\AccessLibs:

1. To invoke the Registry Editor, choose Start | Run from the task bar. Type `regedit` and click OK. This invokes the Registry Editor.

2. Locate the HKEY_LOCAL_MACHINE\SOFTWARE\Microsoft\Office\9.0\Access\ Wizards\Property Wizards key, as shown in Figure 30.2.

FIGURE 30.2

The Property Wizards Registry key.

3. Determine whether a subkey exists with the name of the property for which you are creating a builder (in this case, SpecialEffect). If so, skip to step 6.

4. Choose Edit | New | Key.

5. Type the property name as the name for the new key (in this case, `SpecialEffect`).

6. With the new key selected, choose Edit | New | Key again.

7. Type a descriptive name for your builder (in this case, `SpecialEffectBuilder`).

8. Choose Edit | New | DWORD Value.

9. Type `Can Edit` as the value name.

10. Choose Edit | New | String Value.

11. Type `Description` as the value name.

12. Choose Edit | New | String Value.

13. Type `Function` as the value name.

14. Choose Edit | New | String Value.

15. Type `Library` as the value name.

16. Double-click the Can Edit value name. The Edit DWORD Value dialog box appears, as shown in Figure 30.3.

FIGURE 30.3

The Edit DWORD Value dialog box.

17. Enter 1 for the value data and click OK.

18. Double-click the Description value name. The Edit String dialog box appears, as shown in Figure 30.4.

FIGURE 30.4

The Edit String dialog box.

19. Enter the description you want the user of the builder to see if more than one builder is assigned to the property (in this case, `Special Effect Builder`). Click OK.

20. Double-click the Function value name. Enter the name of the builder function (in this case, `SpecialEffect`). Click OK.

21. Double-click the Library value name. Enter the name and location of the library database (in this case, `C:\Windows\Application Data\Microsoft\Addins`). You do not have to enter the path if the library is located in the Access folder.

30

USING BUILDERS, WIZARDS, AND MENU ADD-INS

Figure 30.5 shows the completed Registry entries. The builder now should be ready to use. To test the builder, you need to exit and relaunch Access. If all the Registry entries are created successfully, you can use the builder. To test the builder, open any database (not the library database), create a new form, and add a text box. Select Special Effect from the Format tab of the Properties window. An ellipsis appears to the right of the Special Effect drop-down, as shown in Figure 30.6. If you click the ellipsis, the builder form appears. Select a special effect and click OK. The special effect you selected now appears in the Special Effect property.

FIGURE 30.5

The completed Registry entries required to add the builder.

FIGURE 30.6

Using the custom builder.

NOTE

If you do not follow exactly the format for the value names, the message `Invalid add-in entry for 'SpecialEffectBuilder'` appears, as shown in Figure 30.7. You must correct the Registry entry.

FIGURE 30.7

This error message appears if the Registry entry is invalid.

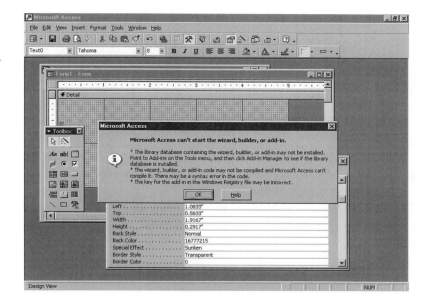

Automating the Creation of Registry Entries

The alternative to editing the Windows Registry manually is to set up the library database so that the Add-in Manager can create the Registry entries for you. This involves adding a table to the library database. The table must be called USysRegInfo. Follow these steps:

1. Tables that begin with USys or MSys are considered system tables and by default are hidden. The first step is to show system tables. With the library database open, choose Tools|Options. From the View tab, click System Objects. Click OK. Figure 30.8 shows the database with Tables selected in the Objects list.

FIGURE 30.8

The Tables tab with system objects visible.

2. The next step is to import an existing USysRegInfo table. To do this, right-click within the database window and select Import. Using the Import dialog box, move to the \Program Files\Microsoft Office\Office\1033 folder and locate the ACWZMAIN.MDE file. This is a library file that ships with Access. Select the ACWZMAIN.MDE file and click Import.

3. The Import Objects dialog box appears, as shown in Figure 30.9. Locate and select the USysRegInfo table and click OK. A copy of the USysRegInfo table is added to your library database.

FIGURE 30.9

Using the Import Objects dialog box to add the USysRegInfo table to your library database.

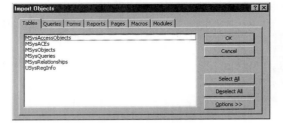

4. Double-click to open the USysRegInfo table in the database window.

5. Delete any existing entries in the table.

6. Specific entries must be added to the USysRegInfo table. Figure 30.10 shows these entries, and Table 30.2 explains them. Add the entries and close the table.

FIGURE 30.10

The completed table with entries for Registry.

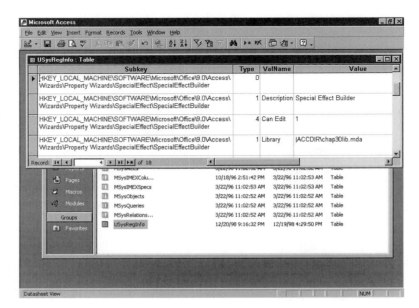

7. Open the database that references the add-in.

8. Choose Tools | Add-ins | Add-in Manager. The Add-in Manager dialog box appears, as shown in Figure 30.11.

FIGURE 30.11

The Add-in Manager dialog box.

9. Click the Add New button to launch the Open dialog box. Here, you can browse for your add-in or select it from within the default folder.

10. Locate the add-in that you want to add and click OK. The add-in you select is added to the Add-in Manager dialog box and is selected for you.

11. Click Close. You now are ready to use the add-in.

TABLE 30.2   THE STRUCTURE OF THE USysRegInfo TABLE

Field Name	Description
SubKey	Name of the subkey value in the Registry where the value you are adding is located.
Type	Type of subkey value you are creating (String, Binary, or DWORD).
ValName	Value name for the entry.
Value	Value associated with the value name.

USING WIZARDS

A *wizard* consists of a series of dialog boxes; it provides a step-by-step interface to creating a database object. The wizard shields users from the complexities of the process. You probably are familiar with wizards such as the Form Wizard, the Report Wizard, and the Database Wizard. Access 2000 supports the development of several types of custom wizards:

- Table wizards
- Query wizards

- Form wizards
- Report wizards
- Property wizards
- Control wizards

Looking at Design Guidelines

Wizard design guidelines are almost identical to builder design guidelines. The main difference is that wizards generally present the user with multiple modal dialog boxes, whereas a builder generally consists of a single modal dialog box. All the data requirements for the wizard must be met before the user can close the last dialog box.

Creating a Wizard

 Creating a wizard is more complex than creating a builder. A wizard generally requires a multipage form and code that creates database objects. Consider a wizard that creates a simple form. The wizard comprises two modal dialog boxes, shown in Figures 30.12 and 30.13. The first dialog box asks the user for a form caption, form name, and message to appear on the new form. The second dialog box enables the user to add OK and Cancel buttons to the form. The multipage form and all the code that enables it to work are in the CHAP30LIB.MDA database on the accompanying CD-ROM.

FIGURE 30.12
Step 1 of the custom Form Wizard.

Each page of the wizard contains code to ensure that it operates successfully. The form is called frmGetFormInfo. The first page of this multipage form gives the user the opportunity to choose Cancel, Next, or Finish. The code for the Cancel button looks like this:

```
Private Sub cmdCancel1_Click()
    DoCmd.Close
End Sub
```

FIGURE 30.13

Step 2 of the custom Form Wizard.

This code closes the wizard form. No other actions are taken because the process is being canceled. If the user clicks Next, this code executes:

```
Private Sub cmdNext1_Click()
   DoCmd.GoToPage 2
   Me.Caption = "My Form Wizard - Step 2"
End Sub
```

This code moves to the second page of the form and changes the caption of the form to indicate that the user is on step 2 of the wizard. The code under the Finish button looks like this:

```
Private Sub cmdFinish1_Click()
   If CreateCustomForm() Then
      MsgBox "Form Created Successfully"
      DoCmd.Close
   Else
      MsgBox "Unable to Create Form"
   End IfEnd Sub
```

This code calls a function called `CreateCustomForm`, which is responsible for building the actual form. The details of the `CreateCustomForm` function are discussed later in this section. If the function returns `True`, the wizard form is closed and a message is displayed indicating that the process was successful. Otherwise, a message is displayed indicating that the form was not created successfully and the user remains in the wizard. The second page of the form contains similar subroutines. The code under the Back button looks like this:

```
Private Sub cmdBack2_Click()
   DoCmd.GoToPage 1
   Me.Caption = "My Form Wizard - Step 1"
End Sub
```

This code moves back to the first page of the form. If the user chooses Cancel, this code executes:

```
Private Sub cmdCancel2_Click()
   DoCmd.Close
End Sub
```

This code closes the form, taking no further action. If the user clicks Finish, the `Click` event code of the `cmdFinish2` command button executes:

```
Private Sub cmdFinish2_Click()
   Call cmdFinish1_Click
End Sub
```

This code calls the code under the `Click` event of the `cmdFinish1` command button.

The `CreateCustomForm` function (located in the basWizards module of the library database), as seen in Listing 30.3, contains the code that actually builds the new form.

LISTING 30.3   THE `CreateCustomForm` FUNCTION BUILDS THE FORM

```
Function CreateCustomForm() As Boolean

   On Error GoTo CreateCustomForm_Err

   Dim frmNew As Form
   Dim ctlNew As Control

   'Create a New Form and Set Several of Its Properties
   Set frmNew = CreateForm()
   frmNew.Caption = Forms!frmGetFormInfo.txtFormCaption
   frmNew.RecordSelectors = False
   frmNew.NavigationButtons = False
   frmNew.AutoCenter = True

   'Create a Label Control on the New Form
   'Set Several of Its Properties
   Set ctlNew = CreateControl(frmNew.Name, acLabel)
   ctlNew.Caption = Forms!frmGetFormInfo.txtLabelCaption
   ctlNew.Width = 3000
   ctlNew.Height = 1000
   ctlNew.Top = 1000
   ctlNew.Left = 1000

   'Evaluate to See if the User Requested an OK Command Button
   'If They Did, Add the Command Button and Set Its Properties
   'Add Click Event Code for the Command Button
```

```
    If Forms!frmGetButtons.chkOK.Value = -1 Then
        Set ctlNew = CreateControl(frmNew.Name, acCommandButton)
        ctlNew.Caption = "OK"
        ctlNew.Width = 1000
        ctlNew.Height = 500
        ctlNew.Top = 1000
        ctlNew.Left = 5000
        ctlNew.Name = "cmdOK"
        ctlNew.Properties("OnClick") = "[Event Procedure]"
        frmNew.Module.InsertText "Sub cmdOK_Click()" & vbCrLf & _
            vbTab & "DoCmd.Close acForm, """ & _
            Forms!frmGetFormInfo.txtFormName & _
            """" & vbCrLf & "End Sub"
    End If


    'Evaluate to See if the User Requested a Cancel Command Button
    'If They Did, Add the Command Button and Set Its Properties
    'Add Click Event Code for the Command Button
    If Forms!frmGetButtons.chkCancel.Value = -1 Then
        Set ctlNew = CreateControl(frmNew.Name, acCommandButton)
        ctlNew.Caption = "Cancel"
        ctlNew.Width = 1000
        ctlNew.Height = 500
        ctlNew.Top = 2000
        ctlNew.Left = 5000
        ctlNew.Name = "cmdCancel"
        ctlNew.Properties("OnClick") = "[Event Procedure]"
        frmNew.Module.InsertText "Sub cmdCancel_Click()" & vbCrLf & _
            vbTab & "MsgBox(""You Canceled!!"")" & vbCrLf & "End Sub"
    End If


    'If the User Entered a Form Name, Save the Form
    If Not IsNull(Forms!frmGetFormInfo.txtFormName) Then
        DoCmd.Save , Forms!frmGetFormInfo.txtFormName
    End If


    'Return True If No Errors
    CreateCustomForm = True
    Exit Function

CreateCustomForm_Err:
    MsgBox "Error # " & Err.Number & ": " & Err.Description
    CreateCustomForm = False
    Exit Function
End Function
```

The code begins by creating both form and control object variables. The form object variable is set to the return value from the `CreateForm` function. The `CreateForm` function creates a new form object. Several properties of the new form object are set: `Caption`, `RecordSelectors`, `NavigationButtons`, and `AutoCenter`. Next, the function uses the `CreateControl` function to create a new label. A reference to the new label is called ctlNew. The `Caption`, `Width`, `Height`, `Top`, and `Left` properties of the new label are set. If the user indicated that he or she wanted an OK button, a new command button is created. The `Caption`, `Width`, `Height`, `Top`, `Left`, `Name`, and `Properties` properties are all set. The `InsertText` method is used to insert code for the `Click` event of the command button. If the user requested a Cancel button, the same properties are set. Finally, if the user indicated a name for the new form, the `Save` method is used to save the new form object.

> **NOTE**
>
> Several functions exist to create and delete forms, reports, form controls, and report controls. You can use ADO code to create, modify, and delete tables and queries. Using the functions and ADO code, you can manipulate database objects any way you want. ADO is covered in Chapter 12, "ADO and DAO: Accessing Data Programmatically."

Getting the Wizard Ready to Go

Like a builder, a wizard needs to be added to the Windows Registry before it can be used. You can do this by modifying the Registry directly or by adding entries to the USysRegInfo table. Figure 30.14 shows the completed Registry entry for the custom Form Wizard.

Notice that the function name is `MyCustomForm`. This is the entry point to the wizard. The Library key designates the name of the library add-in database containing the entry point function. The Description key specifies what appears in the New Object dialog box. Finally, the Index key designates the order in which the wizard is displayed in the list in the New Object dialog box. The `MyCustomForm` function, located in the basWizards module, simply calls the frmGetFormInfo form, initiating the wizard process:

```
Function MyCustomForm(strRecordSource As String) As Variant
    DoCmd.OpenForm FormName:="frmGetFormInfo", WindowMode:=acDialog
End Function
```

FIGURE 30.14

Registry entries for the custom Form Wizard.

USING MENU ADD-INS

A *menu add-in* is a general-purpose tool that enables you to perform a task that generally affects multiple objects or Access itself. The Database Splitter and Database Documenter are examples of menu add-ins. You access menu add-ins through the Add-ins submenu of the Tools menu.

Looking at Design Guidelines

Menu add-ins are available to the user whenever the Tools menu is available. Menu add-ins are not context sensitive like wizards and builders. Therefore, they should in no way rely on what the user is doing at a particular moment.

Creating a Menu Add-In

Creating a menu add-in is just like creating a wizard. The difference is in how you install the add-in. The menu add-in must be registered under HKEY_LOCAL_MACHINE\SOFTWARE \Microsoft\Office\9.0\Access\Menu Add-Ins. You can accomplish the registration process by modifying the Registry directly or by using the USysRegInfo table. Figure 30.15 shows the Registry with the correct entries to run the Form Wizard, created earlier in this chapter, as an add-in. Figure 30.16 shows how you can automate the registration process by using the

USysRegInfo table. Three entries are included in the USysRegInfo table. All three entries designate the proper place in the Registry tree to add the new key. The first entry contains the subkey and a type of zero. The second entry contains the value name `Expression` and the name of the entry point function as the value. Notice that the expression name is preceded by an equal (=) sign and is followed by parentheses. The quotation marks within the parentheses are required because this particular entry-point function requires an argument. The third and final entry contains the value name `Library` and the name of the library as the value. This is all you need to do to turn a wizard into a menu add-in.

FIGURE 30.15

Registry entries for the menu add-in.

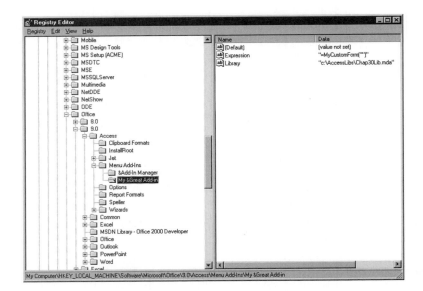

FIGURE 30.16

The USysRegInfo entries for the menu add-in.

Designing Your Own Add-Ins

The types of builders, wizards, and menu add-ins that you create depend on your specific needs. To reinforce what you have learned, this section includes the step-by-step process for creating a builder to help you add validation text messages. When you invoke the builder, the Choose Builder dialog box shown in Figure 30.17 appears. This dialog box appears because you will design two builders: one that enables the user to select from a list of polite messages and another that enables the user to select from rude messages. If the user selects Polite Validation Text Builder, the dialog box in Figure 30.18 appears. If the user selects Rude Validation Text builder, the dialog box in Figure 30.19 appears.

FIGURE 30.17

The Choose Builder dialog box.

FIGURE 30.18

The polite messages builder.

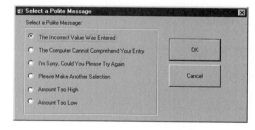

FIGURE 30.19

The rude messages builder.

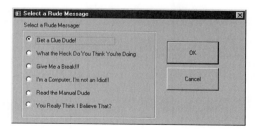

The first entry-point function is located in basBuilders and is shown in Listing 30.4.

LISTING 30.4 THE FIRST ENTRY-POINT FUNCTION

```
Function ValidTextPolite(strObject As String, _
            strControl As String, _
            strCurrentValue As String)

    On Error GoTo ValidTextPolite_Err
    DoCmd.OpenForm FormName:="frmPolite", _
                WindowMode:=acDialog, _
                OpenArgs:=strCurrentValue
    If SysCmd(acSysCmdGetObjectState, acForm, _
            "frmPolite") = acObjStateOpen Then
        Select Case Forms!frmPolite.optPolite.Value
            Case 1
                ValidTextPolite = "The Incorrect Value Was Entered"
            Case 2
                ValidTextPolite = "The Computer Cannot Comprehend Your Entry"
            Case 3
                ValidTextPolite = "I'm Sorry, Could You Please Try Again"
            Case 4
                ValidTextPolite = "Please Make Another Selection"
            Case 5
                ValidTextPolite = "Amount Too High"
            Case 6
                ValidTextPolite = "Amount Too Low"
        End Select
        DoCmd.Close acForm, "frmPolite"
    Else
        ValidTextPolite = strCurrentValue
    End If

ValidTextPolite_Exit:
    Exit Function

ValidTextPolite_Err:
    MsgBox "Error # " & Err.Number & ": " & Err.Description
    Resume ValidTextPolite_Exit
End Function
```

The ValidTextPolite function receives all the parameters required by a builder function. The function opens frmPolite modally, passing it the current validation text value of the selected control as the OpenArg. If the user selects a value from the frmPolite form and clicks OK, the selected value is evaluated and the appropriate text is returned from the ValidTextPolite function. The return value becomes the validation text of the selected control. Listing 30.5 shows the Load event of frmPolite.

LISTING 30.5   THE Load EVENT OF FRMPOLITE

```
Private Sub Form_Load()
    'Set the Value of the Option Group
    'To the Current Value of the Property
    Select Case Me.OpenArgs
            Case "The Incorrect Value Was Entered"
                Me.optPolite.Value = 1
            Case "The Computer Cannot Comprehend Your Entry"
                Me.optPolite.Value = 2
            Case "I'm Sorry, Could You Please Try Again"
                Me.optPolite.Value = 3
            Case "Please Make Another Selection"
                Me.optPolite.Value = 4
            Case "Amount Too High"
                Me.optPolite.Value = 5
            Case "Amount Too Low"
                Me.optPolite.Value = 6
        End Select

End Sub
```

This code ensures that the value of the option button on the frmPolite form reflects the text that currently is entered in the Validation Text property of the current control. The ValidTextRude entry point function is similar to ValidTextPolite. Listing 30.6 shows the ValidTextRude entry-point text function; it is located in basBuilders.

LISTING 30.6   THE ValidTextRude ENTRY-POINT FUNCTION

```
Function ValidTextRude(strObject As String, _
            strControl As String, _
            strCurrentValue As String)

    On Error GoTo ValidTextRude_Err
    DoCmd.OpenForm FormName:="frmRude", _
                WindowMode:=acDialog, _
                OpenArgs:=strCurrentValue
    If SysCmd(acSysCmdGetObjectState, acForm, _
            "frmRude") = acObjStateOpen Then
        Select Case Forms!frmRude.optRude.Value
            Case 1
                ValidTextRude = "Get a Clue Dude"
            Case 2
                ValidTextRude = "What the Heck do You Think You're Doing?"
```

continues

30

USING BUILDERS,
WIZARDS, AND
MENU ADD-INS

LISTING 30.6 CONTINUED

```
            Case 3
                ValidTextRude = "Give Me a Break!!"
            Case 4
                ValidTextRude = "I'm a Computer, I'm not an Idiot!!"
            Case 5
                ValidTextRude = "Read the Manual Dude"
            Case 6
                ValidTextRude = "You Really Think I Believe That?"
        End Select
        DoCmd.Close acForm, "frmRude"
    Else
        ValidTextRude = strCurrentValue
    End If

ValidTextRude_Exit:
    Exit Function

ValidTextRude_Err:
    MsgBox "Error # " & Err.Number & ": " & Err.Description
    Resume ValidTextRude_Exit
End Function
```

The Load event of frmRude is similar to the Load event of frmPolite, as Listing 30.7 shows.

LISTING 30.7 THE Load EVENT OF FRMRUDE

```
Private Sub Form_Load()
    'Set the Value of the Option Group
    'To the Current Value of the Property
    Select Case Me.OpenArgs
        Case "Get a Clue Dude!"
            Me.optRude.Value = 1
        Case "What the Heck Do You Think You're Doing"
            Me.optRude.Value = 2
        Case "Give Me a Break!!"
            Me.optRude.Value = 3
        Case "I'm a Computer, I'm not an Idiot!!"
            Me.optRude.Value = 4
        Case "Read the Manual Dude"
            Me.optRude.Value = 5
        Case "You Really Think I Believe That?"
            Me.optRude.Value = 6
    End Select

End Sub
```

To create the builder, design both forms so that they look like the ones in Figures 30.18 and 30.19. Include code for the `Load` event of each form as listed previously. The code behind the OK button of each form sets the `Visible` property of the form to `False`. The code behind the Cancel button on each form closes the form. Make sure that you name the option groups `optPolite` and `optRude` so that the code runs properly for each form. You can place the two entry-point functions, `ValidTextPolite` and `ValidTextRude`, in any code module in the library database. The last step involves registering the two builders. The entries in USysRegInfo, shown in Figure 30.20, accomplish the task of registering the builder the first time that the add-in is selected through the Add-ins dialog box. This table is located in CHAP30LIB.MDA.

FIGURE 30.20

Registry entries for the polite and rude builders.

SUMMARY

By creating builders, wizards, and add-ins, you can enhance the development environment for yourself and your users. You even can add wizards so that your users can build their own queries, forms, or reports on-the-fly without a full copy of Access. Your wizard simply needs to prompt the user for the appropriate information and then build the objects to your specifications. What you can do with wizards, builders, and add-ins is limited only by your imagination.

ACCESS AND THE INTERNET

CHAPTER

31

IN THIS CHAPTER

WHAT'S NEW WITH ACCESS AND THE INTERNET

Access 2000 has many features that make it easier to develop Internet and intranet-aware applications. You can develop applications that publish dynamic or static information on the Internet or on your organization's intranet. The Hyperlink field type enables you to store Internet and intranet addresses in your Access tables, and form hyperlinks make it easy to jump to Internet and intranet addresses directly from your forms. New features of Access 2000 include data access pages. Data access pages enable you to quickly and easily create Web views of your database. This chapter explores the power of Access and its integration with the Internet and intranets. Chapter 32, "Utilizing Data Access Pages," is devoted entirely to the creation of active data pages.

SAVING DATABASE OBJECTS AS HTML

Probably one of the most basic but powerful features in Access is the capability to save database objects as HTML (HyperText Markup Language) documents. Table data, query results, form datasheets, forms, and reports can all be published as HTML. Each of these objects is covered in the following sections.

Saving Table Data as HTML

When saving table data to HTML, you can store it in the HTML file format so that it can be easily published on the Web. Just follow these steps:

1. Click Tables in the Objects list of the Database window.
2. Click to select the table whose data you want to save as HTML.
3. Choose File | Export to open the Export Table dialog box.
4. Use the Save As Type drop-down list to select HTML documents.
5. Select a file name and location for the HTML document.
6. Click Save to finish the process.

The file is exported to HTML and can be viewed from any Web browser. (See Figure 31.1.) You can also view the HTML source, as shown in Figure 31.2.

FIGURE 31.1

The tblCustomers table saved as HTML.

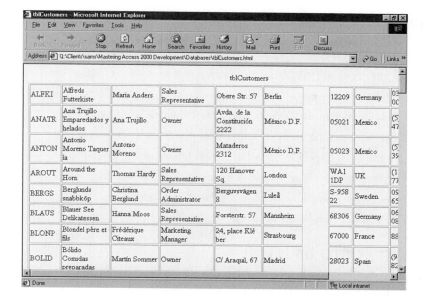

FIGURE 31.2

Viewing the source of the tblCustomers table's HMTL file.

Saving Query Results as HTML

The capability to save query results as HTML means you don't need to save all fields and all records to an HTML file. In fact, you can even save the results of Totals queries and other complex queries as HTML. Saving the result of a query as HTML is similar to saving a table as HTML:

1. Click Queries in the Objects list of the Database window.
2. Click to select the query whose results you want to save as HTML.
3. Choose File | Export to open the Export Query dialog box.
4. Use the Save As Type drop-down list to select HTML documents.
5. Select a file name and location for the HTML document.
6. Click Save to finish the process.

Saving Forms as HTML

Only a form's datasheet can be saved as HTML because an HTML file is a static file. It doesn't change as the data in the database changes, nor can the data in the HTML file be modified. To save a form's datasheet as HTML, follow these steps:

1. Click Forms in the Objects list of the Database window.
2. Click to select the form whose results you want to save as HTML.
3. Choose File | Export to open the Export Form dialog box.
4. Use the Save As Type drop-down list to select HTML documents.
5. Select a file name and location for the HTML document.
6. Click Save; this opens the HTML Output Options dialog box.
7. Select an optional HTML template that's applied to the HTML document. By selecting an HTML template, you can easily maintain a consistent look for your Web publications. Click OK.

Saving Reports as HTML

Reports and their formatting can be saved as HTML, too, which is an elegant way to publish data on an Internet or intranet site. To publish a report as HTML, just follow these steps:

1. Click Reports in the Objects list of the Database window.
2. Click to select the report whose results you want to save as HTML.
3. Choose File | Export to open the Save As dialog box.
4. Use the Save As Type drop-down list to select HTML documents.

5. Select a file name and location for the HTML document.

6. Click Save to open the HTML Output Options dialog box.

7. Select an optional HTML template that's applied to the HTML document. Click OK.

Figure 31.3 shows a report published as HTML. Because the report is a multipage report, several HTML files are generated. Each page of the report is linked, and the user can easily navigate from page to page by using the First, Previous, Next, and Last hyperlinks automatically generated during the Save process.

FIGURE 31.3

Viewing the rptCustomersWeb report as HTML.

LINKING TO HTML FILES

Just as you can link to dBase tables, Paradox tables, or ODBC data sources, you can also link to HTML files by following these steps:

1. Right-click within the Database window and select Link Tables; this opens the Link dialog box.

2. Use the Files of Type drop-down list to select HTML documents.

3. Select the HTML file you want to link to and click Link. The Link HTML Wizard appears. (See Figure 31.4.)

4. In the wizard's first step, indicate whether the first row of data contains column headings. You can also see Access's proposed layout for the linked table.

FIGURE 31.4

The first step of the Link HTML Wizard.

5. Click Advanced to designate specifics about the linked table. The Link Specification dialog box opens. (See Figure 31.5.) Here you can select which fields you want to include in the linked table, date delimiters, and other specifics of the linked file. Make your selections and click OK.

FIGURE 31.5

In the Link Specification dialog box, you designate specifics about the linked table.

6. Click Next to proceed with the Link HTML Wizard. In the next step, you select a field name and data type for each field in the HTML file. Make your selections and click Next.

7. In the wizard's last step, you supply a table name for the linked table. Make your selection and click Finish.

8. You then see a message that the table linked successfully. The table appears in the Database window with a special icon indicating that it's an HTML file. (See Figure 31.6.)

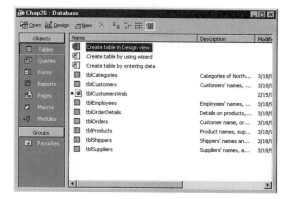

FIGURE 31.6

*The Database
window with a
linked HTML
document.*

The linked HTML file can be browsed, queried, and reported on just like any other table. However, none of the data in the linked file can be modified.

IMPORTING HTML FILES

The data in an HTML file can be imported so that it becomes exactly like any other Access table; follow these steps to import an HTML file:

1. Right-click within the Database window and select Import; this opens the Import dialog box.

2. Use the Files of Type drop-down list to select HTML documents.

3. Select the HTML file you want to import and click Import to open the Import HTML Wizard. This wizard is almost identical to the Link HTML Wizard.

4. In the wizard's first step, you indicate whether the first row of data contains column headings. You can also see Access's proposed layout for the imported table.

5. Click Advanced to designate specifics about the imported table. The Import Specification dialog box opens. Here you can select which fields you want to include in the imported table, date delimiters, and other specifics of the imported file. Make your selections and click OK.

6. Click Next to go to the next step. Here, you have the choice of importing the data into a new table or adding it to an existing table. Make your selection and click Next.

7. In the next step, select a field name and data type for each field in the HTML file. You can also designate whether you want Access to create an index for the field and even whether you want to exclude the field entirely. Make your selections and click Next.

8. Next, the wizard lets you designate a primary key for the imported table. If you prefer, you can have Access supply the primary key. (See Figure 31.7.) Make your selection and click Next.

FIGURE 31.7

Designating a primary key for your new table.

9. In the wizard's last step, supply a table name for the linked table. If you're concerned about whether the imported table is normalized, you can have Access launch the Table Analyzer after the import is finished. Make your selections and click Finish.

10. You then see a message that the table imported successfully; it appears in the Database window just as any other Access table does.

DECIDING BETWEEN STATIC AND DYNAMIC HTML FORMATS

Many people don't understand the differences between publishing static and dynamic data. *Static data* doesn't change. If you want to publish information that rarely, if ever, changes, you should create a static Web page; the techniques for doing so have been covered in the beginning of this chapter. The data output for each of the methods discussed so far is static and can be changed only by republishing the data and resubmitting it to the Web.

Dynamic data, on the other hand, does change. You should save your data in the dynamic format when you know it will change frequently and your Web application needs to store and retrieve live data from your application by using a form. To publish dynamic Web data you have several choices. Active data pages, covered in Chapter 32, "Utilizing Data Access Pages," are one solution. As chapter 32 discusses, active data pages are targeted toward Internet, rather than intranet applications. For Internet applications, you can output the object to either the ASP file format or the IDC/HTX file format instead of an HTML file.

ASP stands for Active Server Page. Active Server is a component of Microsoft Internet Information Server 3.0 and later versions. The .ASP file contains the following:

- ODBC connection information, such as the data source name, user name, and password
- One or more queries in the form of SQL statements
- Template directives for layout of the resulting HTML file
- VBScript code containing references to Active Server controls

With an ASP file, you publish the object and install it. The Microsoft Internet Information Server, at the request of the Web browser, runs VBScript code and calls the Active Server controls. It then opens up the database by using the ODBC driver and the .ASP file, runs the queries stored in the .ASP file, and merges the results and HTML tags in the .ASP file into an HTML file. The HTML file is then sent back to the Web browser for display.

When you select the IDC/HTX file format, two files are created. The .HTX file—an HTML extension file—has all the formatting tags and instructions needed so that the query's results can be formatted. The .IDC file—an Internet Database Connector file—contains a SQL statement and other information needed by the Microsoft Internet Information Server so that it can connect to an ODBC data source, such as your Access database file (.MDB). The ODBC data source name, user name, and password are all stored in the .IDC file, but no data is stored in it.

After you have published a database object and installed it on the Web by using a Web document publishing server, such as the Microsoft Internet Information Server (IIS), IIS opens the Access database by using the ODBC driver and the .IDC information file on request from a Web browser. It runs the query stored in the .IDC file and merges the result and the .HTX file into an HTML file that's sent back to the Web browser for display.

WORKING WITH ACTIVE SERVER PAGES (.ASP FILES)

The following steps are required to output data to an ASP file:

1. Select the database object you wish to export.
2. Select File | Export. The Export table dialog appears.
3. Select Microsoft Active Server Pages from the Save as Type drop-down list. Click Save. The Microsoft Active Server Pages Output Options dialog appears (see Figure 31.8.)
4. Click Browse to select an HTML template, if desired.
5. Specify an ODBC data source. This data source must be established in the Windows Control Panel and is used by the Web server to access data within the Access database.
6. Designate the user and password under which the connection will be made.
7. Click OK to output the .ASP file.

FIGURE 31.8

The Microsoft Active Server Pages Output Options dialog enables you to designate required options to output your database object in the .ASP file format.

WORKING WITH HTX/IDC FILES

The following steps are required to output data to HTX/IDC files:

1. Select the database object you want to export.

2. Select File | Export. The Export table dialog appears.

3. Select Microsoft IIS 1-2 from the Save as Type drop-down list and click Save. The HTX/IDC Output Options dialog appears (see Figure 31.9.)

4. Click Browse to select an HTML template, if desired.

5. Specify an ODBC data source. This data source must be established in the Windows Control Panel and used by the Web server to access data within the Access database.

6. Designate the user and password under which the connection will be made.

7. Click OK to output the .htx and .idc files.

FIGURE 31.9

The HTX/IDC Output Options dialog enables you to designate required options to output your database object in the HTX/IDC file format.

TESTING ASP AND HTX/IDC FILES

Because both the ASP format and the IDC/HTX file formats utilize server-side processing to output an HTML document, you must take the following steps to test the files on your Web server:

1. Install the appropriate software on the computer that will act as the Web server (i.e. Microsoft Internet Information Server.)

2. Create a folder under the root directory of the Web server.

3. Define privileges for the folder. Make sure that you include Execute privileges for IIS 3.0 or Script privileges for IIS 4.0 and above.

4. Copy the ASP or IDC/HTX files to the folder. Make sure that you copy any related files, such as graphics or linked files.

5. Define an ODBC data source that points at the database containing the data you wish to publish. Make sure that the data source is defined as a System DSN on the Web server and that the data source name (DSN) matches the data source that you designated in the Microsoft Active Server Pages Output options or HTX/IDC Output options dialog. Make sure that the username and password match the username and password entered in the User to Connect As and Password for User text boxes of the Microsoft Active Server Pages Output options or HTX/IDC Output options dialog.

6. Because the ASP and IDC/HTX file formats both utilize server-side processing, the HTTP protocol must be used when testing them. Notice that in Figure 31.10, the HTTP protocol is used to process the tblCustomers.idc file. The Web address used within the browser to process the IDC file is `http://presario/customerdata/tblcustomers.idc`.

> **NOTE**
>
> Although both the ASP and IDC/HTX file formats are covered in this chapter, they are not equally represented in current technologies. Whereas the ASP technology is being used more and more and is highly supported within Microsoft Visual InterDev 6.0, the IDC/HTX format is supported by Microsoft only for purposes of backward compatibility. You should carefully consider whether it is prudent to utilize the IDC/HTX technology.

FIGURE **31.10**

*The HTTP proto-
col is used to
access ASP and
IDC/HTX files on
a Web server.*

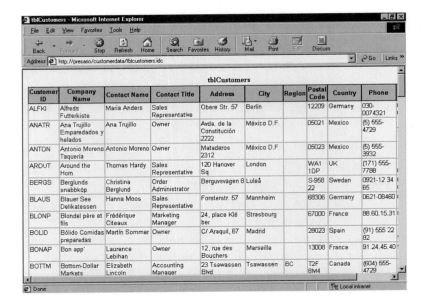

WORKING WITH HTML TEMPLATES

HTML templates help give all your Web pages a consistent look. They enable you to effort-
lessly enhance the appearance of any Web page and add navigation to your Web application.
HTML templates can include logos, background images, and standard navigation buttons.

An HTML template is a file that includes HTML tags and tokens unique to Access. These tags
and tokens tell Access where to insert data. When you output a datasheet, form, or report to an
HTML file, you can specify a template that's applied to the object. If you specify a template
file when you output an object to a dynamic HTML format, it's merged with the .HTX or .ASP
file during the output operation. Figure 31.11 shows the tblCustomers.idc file formatted with
the cajun.htm file that ships with Microsoft Office.

FIGURE 31.11

*The
tblCustomer.idc
file formatted with
the cajun.htm
template.*

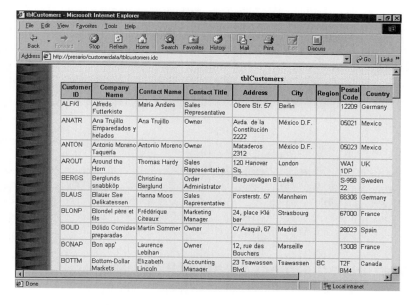

SENDING DATA TO AN FTP OR HTTP SERVER

Sometimes you need to import, link to, or export a database object to or from an FTP or HTTP server. *FTP*—File Transfer Protocol—is a protocol that enables you to transfer files over the Internet without a network server connection. HyperText Transfer Protocol (HTTP) is a behind-the-scenes Internet protocol that lets a client machine view documents written in HTML and other formats over the Internet. The techniques for importing, linking to, and exporting objects to an FTP server are covered in the following sections.

Importing or Linking to Data on FTP and HTTP Servers

The processes of importing and linking to FTP and HTTP servers are similar, so they're covered together in this section. Here's the steps to follow:

1. To import or link to data on an FTP server, right-click within the Database window.

2. Select Import to import data or Link Tables to link data; this opens the Import or Link dialog box.

3. Select HTML Documents from the Files of Type drop-down.

4. To import or link to data on an HTTP server, type the Internet address—
   `http://www.mcgpc.com/employee.html`, for example—in the File Name box. If you prefer, you can click the arrow to the right of the Look In box, then click Internet Locations
   (FTP). Click to select the location of the item you want.

5. Click Import to import the HTML document or Link to link to the HTML document.
   Follow the steps of the wizard to proceed with the import or linking process.

> **NOTE**
>
> A linked HTML table is actually a snapshot of the original data source, so you don't
> see any updates made to the original table while it's open. To refresh the local copy
> of the HTML table, you must close and reopen the table. Furthermore, because the
> data is a snapshot, the linked data is not updateable from within Microsoft Access.

Exporting an Object to an FTP Server

Exporting a database object to a database server is essentially copying through the Internet; to
do that, follow these steps:

1. Right-click a table within the Database window and select Export. The Export Table dialog opens.

2. Click to open the drop-down list to the right of the Save In box and select FTP
   Locations.

3. Click to select the FTP location and then click Export.

TAKING ADVANTAGE OF HYPERLINKS

Hyperlinks in Access 2000 are extremely powerful. They enable you to jump from your application to an Internet, intranet, or file location. Hyperlinks can be stored in table fields or
placed directly on forms and reports.

Storing Hyperlinks in Tables

Using the new Hyperlink field type, you can easily store URLs (addresses to Internet or
intranet sites) and UNCs (addresses to files on a local area network or a local hard disk) in
your tables' records. To create a Hyperlink field, select Hyperlink from the Data Type drop-
down list while viewing a table's design. Data stored in the field is used as a hyperlink
address.

Placing Hyperlinks on Forms and Reports

Although the Hyperlink field type enables you to associate URLs and UNCs with each record in a table, the capability to place hyperlinks on forms and reports lets your users easily navigate from your forms and reports to other parts of your application and to URL and UNC locations. Hyperlinks can be added to command buttons, labels, and image controls because each of these controls has a Hyperlink Address and Hyperlink SubAddress property. (See Figure 31.12.) The Hyperlink Address property contains the actual URL or UNC, and the Hyperlink SubAddress property specifies a particular location in the URL or UNC. For example, if the UNC points to an Access database, the Hyperlink SubAddress might point to a form in the database.

FIGURE 31.12

Command buttons, labels, and image controls have Hyperlink Address and SubAddress properties.

The easiest way to specify the Hyperlink Address and SubAddress properties is to click in the Hyperlink Address property and then click the Build button; this opens the Insert Hyperlink dialog box. Here, you can click Browse to find both the Hyperlink Address and Hyperlink SubAddress. The properties are automatically filled in for you. (See Figure 31.13.)

FIGURE 31.13

Use the Insert Hyperlink dialog box to easily specify the Hyperlink Address and Hyperlink SubAddress properties.

INTRODUCING THE WEB TOOLBAR

The Web toolbar controls all the tools you need to navigate and enables you to quickly and easily do the following:

- Navigate from page to page
- Refresh the current page
- Search the Web
- Add items to favorites
- Navigate to favorites
- Move to a specific URL

Just like any other toolbar, it can be activated any time to make navigating the Web easier.

IMPLEMENTING REPLICATION OVER THE INTERNET

The Access 2000 Replication Manager can be installed on an Internet or intranet server so that you can configure replicas to synchronize with replicas on the server. The replica on the Internet or intranet server is considered the *hub* because all other replicas synchronize with it.

During synchronization, each client machine makes an HTTP connection with an Internet or an intranet server. Direct synchronizations can't be performed over the Internet; instead, an FTP folder on the server acts as a drop-box folder for an indirect synchronization. It works like this:

1. The client machine builds a message file containing all the design and data changes made since the replicas were last synchronized.
2. This message file is placed in the FTP file location on the Internet or intranet server.
3. The Synchronizer on the Internet or intranet server applies the changes to its local replica, and then it builds a message file with all the design and data changes made since the client and server replicas were last synchronized. These changes are also placed in the FTP file location.
4. The server sends the message file's name and location back to the client workstation.
5. The client then transfers the message file from the server to the client workstation by using FTP. All the changes specified in the message file are applied to the client replica. The client machine doesn't need to have a Synchronizer because Jet and Windows DLLs handle the synchronization.

SUMMARY

It's easy to integrate Access and the Internet or with an intranet. Access enables you to easily publish database objects to the Web and import HTML data from the Web. In fact, you can even create dynamic Web pages! Using data access pages, covered in the next chapter, you can even build forms that display and update live data directly from a browser. Access 2000 helps bring your data to the continually evolving information superhighway—the possibilities are endless!

USING DATA ACCESS PAGES

IN THIS CHAPTER

UNDERSTANDING DATA ACCESS PAGES

Data access pages are new to Access 2000. Using data access pages, you can quickly and easily create a Web view of your data. Data access pages are extremely flexible and scalable. The simplest data access page can be created as easily as any Access form. On the other hand, using the Microsoft Script editor (MSE), you can turn your data access pages into powerful Web pages. Probably the biggest downside of data access pages is that they must be viewed on a machine with Internet Explorer 5 and Microsoft Office installed. This makes data access pages an excellent candidate for intranet applications, but not for Internet applications.

> **TIP**
>
> Data Access Pages can be run over an Internet or intranet if the client has IE5/Office Extensions.

CREATING DATA ACCESS PAGES

Data access pages are created in one of the following four ways:

- Using AutoPage
- Using a wizard
- From an existing Web page
- From scratch

Creating a Data Access Page Using the AutoPage Feature

To create a data access page using AutoPage, follow these steps:

1. Click Pages in the list of objects in the Database window.
2. Click the New button in the Database window. The New Data Access Page dialog appears.
3. Choose the table or query on which the data access page will be based.
4. Select AutoPage: Columnar from the list of options for creating a data access page (see Figure 32.1).
5. Click OK. The data access page is created (see Figure 32.2).

FIGURE 32.1

The New Data Access Page dialog allows you to select the method you want to use to create a data access page.

FIGURE 32.2

A data access page based on the tblClients table using the AutoPage feature.

Creating a Data Access Page Using a Wizard

To create a data access page using a wizard, follow these steps:

1. Click Pages in the list of objects in the Database window.
2. Double-click the Create Data Access Page By Using Wizard option. The Page Wizard appears (see Figure 32.3).

FIGURE 32.3

Selecting the table or query and the fields that you want to include in the data access page.

3. Select the table or query on which you want to base the data access page. In Figure 32.3, the tblClients table is selected.

4. Select the fields that you want to appear on the data access page. In Figure 32.3 the ClientID, CompanyName, ContactFirstName, ContactLastName, ContactTitle, OfficePhone, IntroDate, and HomePage fields are selected. Click Next to continue.

5. Add any desired grouping levels to the page (see Figure 32.4). It is important to note that if you add grouping levels to the page, the created page is read-only. Click Next to continue.

FIGURE 32.4

Adding grouping levels to a data access page.

6. Select a sort order for the records included on the page (see Figure 32.5.) In the figure, the page is sorted by the ContactLastName field combined with the ContactFirstName field. Click Next to continue.

FIGURE 32.5

Selecting a sort order for the records on a page.

7. The last page of the wizard asks you for a title for the page. Enter the title and then designate whether you want to open the page or modify the page's design. Click Finish to complete the process. Figure 32.6 shows the completed page in Design view. Figure 32.7 shows the completed page in Page view.

FIGURE 32.6

A completed data access page in Design view.

FIGURE 32.7

A completed data access page in Page view.

Data access pages are *not* stored in your database file or project. Instead, data access pages are saved as HTML files. To save a data access page, follow these steps:

1. Click Save on the toolbar. The Save as Data Access Page dialog appears (see Figure 32.8).

2. Enter the name of the HTML document. In the figure, the name is entered as pagClients.

3. Click Save.

FIGURE 32.8

The Save as Data Access Page dialog allows you to select a name and location for the saved HTML document.

Although the data access page is saved as a separate document, it appears in the Database window (see Figure 32.9). Notice in the figure that a ToolTip appears, indicating the name and location of the saved HTML document. When the data access page is opened from within Microsoft Access, it appears as a window within the Access environment. To view the page as it will appear in a browser, right-click the page in the Database window and select Web Page Preview.

FIGURE 32.9

A completed data access page appears as an object in the Database window.

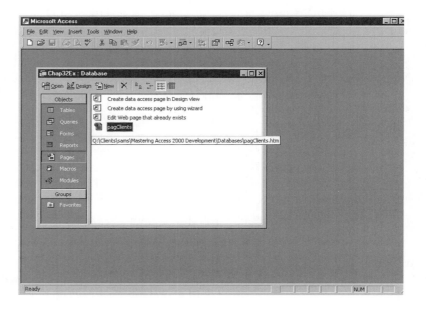

Creating a Data Access Page from an Existing Web Page

You might already have an HTML document that you have created. Fortunately, Access 2000 allows you to base a new data access page on an existing HTML document. To create a data access page from an existing Web page, follow these steps:

1. Click Pages in the list of objects in the Database window.

2. Double-click the Edit Web Page That Already Exists wizard option. The Locate Web Page dialog appears (see Figure 32.10).

FIGURE 32.10

The Locate Web Page dialog allows you to open an existing HTML document for editing within the Access Environment.

3. Select an existing HTML document and click Open. You can now edit the page right within the Microsoft Access environment.

Creating a Data Access Page from Scratch

Although the Data Access Page Wizard is very powerful, there are times when you will want to build a data access page from scratch. To do this, follow these steps:

1. Click Pages in the list of objects in the Database window.

2. Double-click the Create Data Access Page In Design View option. A blank data access page appears (see Figure 32.11).

3. Add controls to the data access page and set their properties.

FIGURE 32.11

When the Create Data Access Page in Design View option is used, a blank data access page appears.

You might wonder how to associate a table from your database with a data access page that you build from scratch. The process differs somewhat from the process of associating a form with data. The process is as follows:

1. Click the Field List tool on the toolbar. The Field List window appears (see Figure 32.12).

FIGURE 32.12

The Field List window allows you to easily add table and query fields to your data access pages.

2. Notice that the Field List window shows two expandable lists: one with the tables in the database, and the other with the queries in the database (see Figure 32.13).

FIGURE 32.13

The expanded Field List window shows you all the tables and queries within the current database.

3. To add all fields from an existing table or query to the data access page, drag an entire table or query from the field list to the data access page.

4. To add specific fields from a table or query to the data access page, expand the field list to display the desired table or query and then drag and drop individual fields to the data access page. In Figure 32.14, selected fields have been added from the tblEmployee table to the data access page.

FIGURE 32.14

A data access page containing selected fields from the tblEmployees table.

MODIFYING IMPORTANT PROPERTIES OF A DATA ACCESS PAGE

Just as a form or report has properties, so does a data access page. Many of the properties are similar to those of forms and reports. The most important properties are discussed here.

To modify the properties of a data access page, you must first make sure that the page is selected. The easiest way to select the page is to click its title bar. Among the most important properties of a data access page are its Data properties. These appear in Figure 32.15, and the most important properties are discussed here.

FIGURE 32.15

The Data properties of a data access page allow you to control the behavior of the data underlying the data access page.

The `DataEntry` Property

The first property is the `DataEntry` property. By default, the `DataEntry` property is `False`. This means that when the data access page is viewed from within Microsoft Access or within a browser, all records in the underlying data source are available. When changed to True, records can be added but existing data cannot be seen (see Figure 32.16).

FIGURE 32.16
The DataEntry property allows you to specify whether existing records are available.

The MaxRecords Property

The MaxRecords property allows you to designate the number of records that a connection sends to the local computer. If this property is not set properly, extremely large volumes of data can travel over the Internet or over an intranet to the user's browser. This can cause severe performance problems. It is therefore a good idea to set this number to the maximum number of records that you feel are appropriate for a user to retrieve.

The RecordsetType Property

The RecordsetType property can be set to dscUpdatableSnapshot or to dscSnapshot. If dscUpdatableSnapshot is selected, the data in the resulting data access page is editable. If dscSnapshot is selected, the data is rendered view-only.

The UseRemoteProvider Property

The UseRemoteProvider property determines whether the data source control uses the Microsoft Remote Data Services provider for data connections. This property can be set to True only for pages that are read from a Microsoft Internet Information Server using an HTTP or HTTPS (secure) address. When used, the Microsoft Remote Data Services provider fetches data by passing the HTTP or HTTPS request to Microsoft Internet Information Server (IIS). IIS makes the OLE DB connection to the database.

MODIFYING THE RECORD NAVIGATION CONTROL PROPERTIES

By default, the record navigation control on a data access page allows you to perform the following tasks:

- Move to the next, previous, first, and last record
- Move to a new record
- Delete an existing record
- Save changes to a record
- Cancel changes made to a record
- Sort in ascending or descending order
- Filter data shown on the data access page

There are times when it is not appropriate for all these features to be available. To customize the properties of the record navigation control, you must first select it. To do this, click the control while in Design view of the page. The most important properties are available within the Other tab (see Figure 32.17).

FIGURE 32.17

The Other tab of the properties window allows you to change the most important properties of the record navigation control.

The `RecordSource` Property

Probably the most important property of a record navigation control is its `RecordSource` property. The `RecordSource` property is used to designate the table or query that underlies the data access page.

The `ShowNextButton`, `ShowPrevButton`, `ShowFirstButton`, and `ShowLastButton` Properties

The `ShowNextButton`, `ShowPrevButton`, `ShowFirstButton`, and `ShowLastButton` properties allow you to designate whether the next, previous, first, and last buttons appear on the record navigation control. These properties allow you to determine how the user can move through records included in the data access page. You can set each of these properties individually. For example, you can opt to include the previous and next buttons, but not the first and last buttons.

The `ShowNewButton` Property

The `ShowNewButton` property allows you to determine whether the new button appears on the record navigation control. If included, the user clicks this button to add a new record to the data underlying the data access page. If excluded, unless you provide your own custom add button, the user is unable to add new records from within the data access page.

The `ShowDelButton` Property

The `ShowDelButton` property allows you to determine whether the delete button appears on the record navigation control. If included, the user clicks this button to delete the current record. If excluded, unless you provide your own custom delete button, the user is unable to delete records from within the data access page.

The `ShowSaveButton` Property

The `ShowSaveButton` property allows you to determine whether the save button appears on the record navigation control. If included, the user clicks this button to commit changes made to the controls on the data access page. If excluded, the user can save data by moving to another record after making her changes.

The `ShowUndoButton` Property

The `ShowUndoButton` property allows you to determine whether the undo button appears on the record navigation control. If included, the user clicks this button to undo changes made to the current record. If excluded, the user can still undo changes to a record using his Escape key.

The `ShowSortAscendingButton` and `ShowSortDescendingButton` Properties

The `ShowSortAscendingButton` and `ShowSortDescendingButton` properties allow you to determine whether the sort ascending and sort descending buttons appear on the record navigation control. If included, the user clicks within the field that she wants to sort on and then clicks the appropriate button to sort in ascending or descending order. The data is sorted by the field that the user selected. If excluded, the user is unable to sort the data contained within the data access page.

The `ShowToggleFilterButton` Property

The `ShowToggleFilterButton` property allows you to determine whether the filter button appears on the record navigation control. If included, the user clicks within the field he wants to filter on and then clicks the tool. The data underlying the data access page is filtered based on the contents of the current field for the current record. For example, in Figure 32.18, the data is filtered so that just the system analysts appear. If the `ShowToggleFilterButton` is excluded from the record navigation control, the user is unable to filter the data underlying the data access page (unless you provide this functionality via a custom command button).

FIGURE 32.18

*The
ShowToggleFilter
Button property
allows you to fil-
ter the data
shown in the data
access page.*

CREATING GROUPED DATA ACCESS PAGES

Grouping records on a data access page is similar to grouping records on a report. Grouped data access pages have the following advantages over grouped reports:

- Current data is always displayed within the data access page.
- Unlike reports, data access pages are interactive. This means that using a grouped data access page, a user can filter, sort, and view just the records she wants.
- When grouped data access pages are sent via email, the recipient is presented with current data each time he opens the message.

To create a grouped data access page, follow these steps:

1. Click Pages in the list of objects in the Database window.
2. Double-click the Create Data Access Page By Using Wizard option. The Page Wizard appears.
3. Select the table or query on which you want to group the data (the "one" side).
4. Select the fields from the first table or query that you want to appear on the data access page.
5. Select the table or query on which you want to base the "many" side of the data access page.
6. Select the fields from the second table or query that you want to appear on the data access page. In Figure 32.19, the ProjectName field is selected from the tblProjects table (the one side of the relationship). The DateWorked, BillableHours, and BillingRate fields are selected from the tblTimeCardHours table. Click Next to continue.

FIGURE 32.19

To create a grouped data access page, first select fields from multiple tables.

7. Select the fields you want to group by. In Figure 32.20, the data is grouped by the ProjectName field. Click Next.

8. Select how you want the data to be sorted within the grouping. Click Next.

9. Enter the title for the page and click Finish.

The resulting page appears in Figure 32.21. As you can see, the data automatically appears collapsed. Furthermore, only one project name (the one side of the relationship) appears at a time. Both of these aspects of a grouped data access page are easily modified via properties of the group.

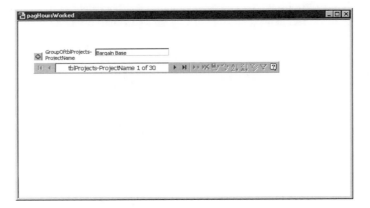

The properties of the group are shown in Figure 32.22. When the Expanded by Default property is set to Yes, it automatically displays the data within a grouping (see Figure 32.23). The Data Page Size property allows you to designate the maximum number of records to show at a time for a particular grouping level. In Figure 32.24, the Data Page Size property of the second-level grouping is set to three. This means that up to three detail records appear within each grouping level.

FIGURE 32.22

Using the properties of a group, you can control group attributes.

FIGURE 32.23

The Expanded by Default property of a group allows you to designate whether data at a group level automatically appears in an expanded format.

FIGURE 32.24

The Data Page Size property of a group allows you to designate the maximum number of detail records that appear at a time within a particular group.

32

USING DATA ACCESS PAGES

AUGMENTING DATA ACCESS PAGES WITH VBSCRIPT

One of the powers of data access pages is in your ability to customize them beyond what the data access page designer allows. The Microsoft Script Editor (MSE) allows you to create scripts that extend the functionality of your data access pages. Using the MSE, you create scripts behind the events of objects on the data access page.

To open the MSE and create script behind a data access page, follow these steps:

1. Create a data access page.

2. Use the Toolbox tool on the toolbar to display the toolbox (see Figure 32.25).

FIGURE 32.25

Using the Toolbox, you can add controls to your data access page.

3. Add a control, such as a command button, to the data access page. Use the ID property to rename the control, if desired.

4. Right-click the control and select Microsoft Script Editor. The Microsoft Development Environment (MDE) appears (see Figure 32.26).

FIGURE 32.26

The Microsoft Script Editor allows you to write code in response to events generated within your data access pages.

5. Locate the Script Outline window. You might need to select View | Other Windows | Script Outline Window, use the Ctrl+Alt+S keystroke combination, or click the Script Outline tab to activate the Script Outline window. When the Script Outline window is active, click the plus sign to view Client Objects & Events.

6. Locate the object that you just added.

7. Click the plus sign to view the events associated with the object. In Figure 32.27, the events associated with the command button called cmdSayHello are displayed in the Script Outline window.

FIGURE 32.27

Click the plus sign within the Script Outline window to view the events associated with an object.

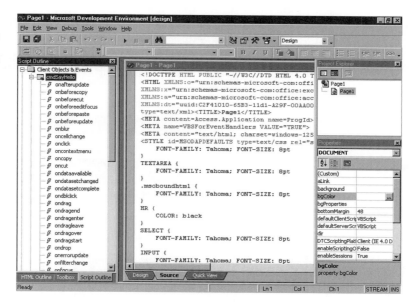

8. To insert an event routine, double-click the name of the event that you want to code. An event handler is inserted for the event. In Figure 32.28, a script block is inserted for the onclick event of the command button called cmdSayHello.

9. Write code that executes in response to the event. In Figure 32.29, the MsgBox statement is used to display the message "Hello" when someone clicks the cmdSayHello command button.

FIGURE 32.28

A script block for the onclick *event of the* cmdSayHello *command button.*

FIGURE 32.29

VBScript code that displays the message "Hello" *when the* onclick *event of the* cmdSayHello *command button occurs.*

Important Data Access Page Events

As you have seen, scripts included for data access pages are written in event handlers attached to objects on a page. As in an Access form, an event handler (or event routine) is a subroutine or function that is automatically triggered in response to something happening to an object. Some important events that you can code include the following:

- The OnRowEnter event of the Document object fires after the current record changes but before fields are populated for the new record.

- The OnRowExit event of the Document object occurs before the current record changes. This event is commonly used to perform record-level validations.

- The BeforeCollapse event of a section occurs before the section is collapsed.

- The BeforeExpand event of a section occurs before a section is expanded.

- The BeforeNextPage, BeforePreviousPage, BeforeFirstPage, and BeforeLastPage events of the page navigation control occur before the navigation control navigates to the next, previous, first, and last pages, respectively. All these events can be canceled by setting the info.return value of the event to False.

- The Current event fires after a section becomes the current section.

- The DataPageComplete event fires when all data binding is completed after a page open, navigation, or expansion.

As with the events of a form or a report, it is important to explore and learn about the events of a page so that you know where to place your code.

VBScript Versus VBA

Because Internet Explorer 5.0 cannot interpret VBA, scripts that you write must be in the VBScript language. VBScript is a subset of the VBA language. The following are important differences between VBA and VBScript that you should be aware of:

- All variables are variants. This means that Dim statements cannot include types.

- Arguments (parameters) to subroutines and functions cannot have types.

- Many built-in functions available in VBA are not available in VBScript.

- Intrinsic constants such as vbYesNo are not available in VBScript. If you want to include constants in your code, you will have to declare them yourself.

VBScript Versus JavaScript

Scripts that you write behind your data access pages can be written in either VBScript or in JavaScript. If you are accustomed to writing VBA code, you will probably find VBScript much easier to learn than JavaScript. On the other hand, if you are experienced at developing Web pages using JavaScript, you will probably want to continue writing your scripts in JavaScript. The following are some important differences between VBScript and JavaScript:

- VBScript is better supported by the data access page object model. This means that certain page events are not recognized if coded in JavaScript.

- JavaScript is case sensitive, making it more difficult to write than VBScript.

PRACTICAL EXAMPLES

Applying What You Have Learned to the Time and Billing Application

Consider some of the forms in the Time and Billing application that you would like to have available on your intranet site. Try building these forms as data access pages and modifying any code so that it is written in VBScript rather than VBA.

SUMMARY

Data access pages are a valuable new addition to Access 2000. Using data access pages, you can quickly and easily build HTML documents based on the data in your database. These pages can be displayed on any machine running Internet Explorer 5 and Microsoft Office 2000. As with forms and reports, you can quickly and easily build a data access page using a wizard. After a data access page is built, you can customize it to your needs. This customization can include adding VBScript or JavaScript that executes in response to events that occur for controls on the page.

ADDING POLISH TO YOUR APPLICATION

PART

V

IN THIS PART

DATABASE SECURITY MADE EASY

IN THIS CHAPTER

WHY THIS CHAPTER IS IMPORTANT

After you design and develop a sophisticated application, you should ensure that the integrity of the application and the data it maintains are not violated. Microsoft Access gives you several options for securing your database. These options range from a very simple method of applying a password to the entire database, to applying varying levels of security to each and every object in the database. The more intricate your security solution, the more difficult it is to implement. Fortunately, you can tailor the complexity of the security you implement to the level of security required by each particular application.

IMPLEMENTING SHARE-LEVEL SECURITY: ESTABLISHING A DATABASE PASSWORD

The simplest, yet least sophisticated, method of implementing security is to assign a password to the overall database. This means that every person who wants to gain access to the database must enter the same password. After a user gains access to the database, all the database's objects are available to that user. This type of security is referred to as *share-level security*.

Share-level security is the simplest and quickest security to set up. With almost no effort, the database and its objects are secured. This method of security is quite adequate for a small business where the users of the database want to ensure that no unauthorized people can obtain access to the data, but each person who does have access to the database has full access to all its objects.

To assign a database password, follow these steps:

1. Open the database to which you want to assign a password. To assign a database password, you must open the database exclusively. To accomplish this, select Open Exclusive from the Open drop-down of the Open dialog.

2. Choose Tools | Security | Set Database Password. The Set Database Password dialog box appears, as shown in Figure 33.1.

3. Type and verify the password and click OK. The password is case sensitive.

After you assign a password to a database, users are prompted for a password each time they open the database. The Password Required dialog box appears each time the database is opened, as Figure 33.2 shows.

After users enter a valid password, they gain access to the database and all its objects. In fact, users even can remove the password by choosing Tools | Security | Unset Database Password. The Unset Database Password dialog box only requires that users know the original password. (See Figure 33.3.)

FIGURE 33.1

The Set Database Password dialog box.

FIGURE 33.2

The Password Required dialog box.

FIGURE 33.3

The Unset Database Password dialog box.

This section outlines all there is to know about setting a database password. Although these passwords are extremely easy to understand and implement, they also are extremely unsophisticated. As you can see, users either have or do not have access to the database, and it is very easy for any user who has access to the database to modify or unset its password.

33

DATABASE
SECURITY MADE
EASY

CAUTION

If you forget the password associated with a database, there is absolutely no way that you will gain access to the database and its objects. It therefore is extremely important that you carefully maintain a list of the passwords associated with each database.

NOTE

To assign a password to a database, users must be able to open the database exclusively. You can grant or deny users the right to open a database exclusively by using the User and Group Permissions dialog box. Assigning rights that permit or deny users or groups exclusive open rights is covered in the "Step 11: Assigning Rights to Users and Groups" section of this chapter.

ENCRYPTING A DATABASE

Before moving on to the more sophisticated methods of securing a database, it is important that you understand what any method of security does and does not provide for you. No matter how well you learn about and implement the techniques in this chapter, you will not be protected against someone attempting to read the data contained in your database. It is important that you are aware that even after you secure a database, someone with a disk editor can view the contents of the file. Although the data in the file will not appear in an easy-to-read format, the data is there and available for unauthorized individuals to see.

You might be feeling discouraged and asking yourself, "Why bother with security?" Do not despair! Fortunately, Access enables you to encrypt a database. The encryption process renders the data in the database indecipherable from data in word processors, disk utilities, and other products capable of reading text. When a database is encrypted, no one can decipher any of its data.

A database can be encrypted using the standard Access menus or by writing a VBA subroutine. In either case, the database you are encrypting must not be open. To encrypt a database using Access's standard menus, follow these steps:

1. Choose Tools | Security | Encrypt/Decrypt Database.

2. The Encrypt/Decrypt Database dialog appears. Select the file you want to encrypt and click OK.

3. You are prompted for the name of the encrypted database. If you select the same name as the existing file, Access deletes the original decrypted file after it determines that the encryption process is successful.

> **NOTE**
>
> It is always a good idea to back up the original database before you begin the encryption process. This ensures that if something goes awry during the encryption process, you won't lose your data.

> **NOTE**
>
> You also can encrypt or decrypt a database file by using code. This is covered in Chapter 34, "Advanced Security Techniques."

When you encrypt a database, the entire database (not just the data) is encrypted. As you access the data and the objects in the database, Access needs to decrypt the objects so that users can use them and then encrypt them again when users are finished accessing them. Regardless of the method of encryption you use, the encrypted database degrades performance by about 15 percent. Furthermore, encrypted databases usually cannot be compressed by most disk-compression software utilities because compression software usually relies on repeated patterns of data. The encryption process is so effective at removing any patterns that it renders most compression utilities ineffective. You need to decide whether this decrease in performance and the inability to compress the database file is worth the extra security that encryption provides.

ESTABLISHING USER-LEVEL SECURITY

For most business environments, share-level security is not sufficient. Therefore, it is necessary to take a more sophisticated approach toward securing the objects in your database. User-level security enables you to grant specific rights to users and groups in a workgroup. This means that each user or group can have different permissions on the same object. With this method of security, each user begins by entering a username and password. The Jet Engine validates the username and password and determines the permissions associated with the user. Each user maintains his or her own password, which is unrelated to the passwords of the other users.

With this method of security, users belong to groups. You can assign rights at the group level, the user level, or both. Users inherit the rights of their least restrictive group. This is highlighted by the fact that security is always on. By default, all users get rights to all objects because every user is a member of the group called Users. By default, this group is given all rights to all objects. If you have not implemented security, all users are logged on as the Admin user, who is a member of the Users group and the all-powerful Admins group. The Jet Engine determines that the Admin user has no password and therefore does not display an opening logon screen. Because members of the Users and Admins groups get rights to all objects by default, it appears as though no security is in place.

With user-level security, you easily can customize and refine the rights to different objects. One set of users might be able to view, modify, add, and remove employee records, for example. Another set of users might be able to view only employee information. The last group of users might be allowed no access to the employee information, or they might be allowed access only to specific fields (such as name and address). The Access security model easily accommodates this type of scenario.

The major steps to implementing user-level security follow (each step is developed in detail later in the chapter):

1. Use the Workgroup Administrator to establish a new system database.
2. Start Access and change the Admin user's password to a non-null password.
3. Create a new user who will be the administrator of the database.
4. Make the user a member of the Admins group.
5. Exit and restart Access, logging on as the new system administrator.
6. Remove the Admin user from the Admins group.
7. Assign a password to the new system administrator.
8. Open the database you want to secure.
9. Run the Security Wizard.
10. Create users and groups consisting of members of the workgroup defined by the system database.
11. Assign rights to users and groups for individual objects.

> **NOTE**
>
> Many of the steps previously outlined can be accomplished using the User-Level Security Wizard. Although the Security Wizard is a powerful tool, it does not provide the same level of flexibility afforded to you when you perform the steps yourself. In this chapter, I therefore focus on performing the steps without the Security Wizard and then cover it in detail in the section of the chapter titled "Step 9: Running the Security Wizard." Throughout the chapter, I designate which steps are performed by the Security Wizard.

Step 1: Creating a Workgroup

The first step to establishing user-level security involves setting up a workgroup. Then you can define groups and users who belong to that workgroup and assign rights to those groups and users. Before you learn how to create groups and users, it is important for you to understand that groups and users are defined only in the context of a specific workgroup. Think of a workgroup as a group of users in a multiuser environment who share data and applications.

When you establish a new workgroup, Access creates a *workgroup information file*; this is where a unique identifier for the workgroup (called a WID), users, groups, and passwords are stored for a particular workgroup. All application databases can share the same workgroup file, or you can maintain separate workgroup files for different application databases.

Understanding the Workgroup: The System.mdw File

As mentioned in the preceding section, user and group security information is stored in a workgroup information file. The default name for this file is System.mdw. Each application database is associated with a specific workgroup information file. This combination of the information stored in the workgroup information file and the information stored in the database grants or denies individual users access to the database or to the objects in it. Multiple databases can share the same workgroup information file. The workgroup information file contains the following elements:

- The name of each user and group
- The list of users who make up each group
- The encrypted logon password for each user who is defined as part of the workgroup
- Each user's and group's unique *security identifiers* (SIDs)

A SID is a machine-generated binary string that uniquely identifies each user or group. The system database contains the names and SIDs of the groups and users who are members of that particular workgroup and, therefore, share a system database.

Actually, you can create many workgroup information files. The name of the workgroup information file currently being used is stored in the Windows Registry. You can view it under HKEY_LOCAL_MACHINE in the key called \HKEY_LOCAL_MACHINE\SOFTWARE\ Microsoft\Office\9.0\Access\Jet\4.0\Engines\. (See Figure 33.4.)

FIGURE 33.4

Viewing the current system information file in the Windows Registry.

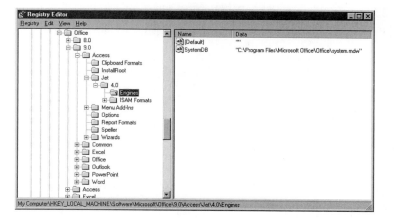

> **TIP**
>
> You can access the Windows registry using the RegEdit utility. To utilize RegEdit, select the Run option from the Start menu. Then type `RegEdit`.

Establishing a Workgroup

One way to establish a new workgroup is using the Workgroup Administrator. The Workgroup Administrator is a separate program that you execute outside Microsoft Access. To launch the Workgroup Administrator, you must choose Run from the Start menu and browse to find the Wrkgadm.exe file. Of course, you can add a desktop shortcut to execute this file more conveniently.

> **TIP**
>
> If you are unsure where the Wrkgadm.exe file is located, you can use the Windows Explorer to locate the file.

After you enter the Workgroup Administrator, you see the Workgroup Administrator dialog box, as shown in Figure 33.5.

FIGURE 33.5

The Workgroup Administrator dialog box.

From the Workgroup Administrator dialog box, you can create a new workgroup or you can join one of the existing workgroups. If you click Create, you see the Workgroup Owner Information dialog box shown in Figure 33.6.

In the Workgroup Owner Information dialog box, you can enter a name, an organization, and a case-sensitive workgroup ID that will be used to uniquely identify the workgroup to the system. If you do not establish a unique workgroup ID, your database is not secure. As you will see, anyone can find out your name and organization. If you do not establish a workgroup ID, anyone can create a new system information file with your name and company, rendering any security that you implement totally futile.

It is important that you record and store all workgroup information in a very safe place so that you can re-create it in an emergency. After entering the workgroup owner information, click OK. The Workgroup Information File dialog box appears, prompting you for the name and location of the workgroup information file, as shown in Figure 33.7.

FIGURE 33.6

The Workgroup Owner Information dialog box.

FIGURE 33.7

The Workgroup Information File dialog box.

The Workgroup Information File dialog box enables you to enter the name and location of the workgroup file. After you type the name of a new workgroup file and click OK, you are asked to confirm the information, as shown in Figure 33.8. You are given one final opportunity to change any information. Click OK to confirm the information. Next, you are notified that the workgroup has been created successfully. You then can click Exit to close the Workgroup Administrator.

33

DATABASE
SECURITY MADE
EASY

FIGURE 33.8

The Confirm Workgroup Information dialog box.

You can use the Security Wizard, covered later in this chapter, to create a new Workgroup Information file. The Security Wizard will prompt you for the information necessary to create the Workgroup Information file. It doesn't matter whether you opt to create a Workgroup Information file using the Workgroup Administrator, or with the Security Wizard, the results are the same.

Joining a Different Workgroup

If different groups of users in your organization work with entirely different applications, you might find it appropriate to create multiple workgroup information files. In order to access a database that has been secured properly with a specific workgroup information file, the database must be accessed while the user is a member of that workgroup. If the same user requires access to more than one database, each associated with a different workgroup information file, it might be necessary for the user to join a different workgroup. This can be accomplished by using the Workgroup Administrator or by using a desktop shortcut that associates a specific database with a workgroup file. Desktop shortcuts are covered in Chapter 39, "Distributing Your Application." To join a different workgroup using the Workgroup Administrator, follow these steps:

1. Launch the Workgroup Administrator.
2. Click the Join button. The Workgroup Information File dialog box appears.
3. Locate the name of the workgroup file you want to join. You can click the Browse button to help you locate the workgroup file.
4. Click OK. You are notified that you successfully joined the workgroup, as Figure 33.9 shows.
5. Click Exit to close the Workgroup Administrator.

FIGURE 33.9
Confirmation that a workgroup was joined successfully.

Step 2: Changing the Password for the Admin User

After creating a new workgroup, you are ready to change the logon for the workgroup by adding a password for the Admin user. This is necessary so that Access will prompt you with a Logon dialog box when you launch the product. If Admin has no password, the Logon dialog box never appears. Without a Logon dialog box, you will never be able to log on as yourself.

To change the password for the Admin user, launch Access and select Tools | Security | User and Group Accounts. The User and Group Accounts dialog appears. It does not matter what database you are in when you do this. In fact, you do not need to have any database open because the password that you are creating applies to the workgroup information file rather than to a database.

The User and Group Accounts dialog box enables you to create and delete users and assign their group memberships. It also enables you to create and delete groups and invoke a logon password for Microsoft Access.

> ### CAUTION
>
> It is important to understand that even if you access this dialog box from a specific database, you are setting up users and groups for the entire workgroup. This means that if you assign a password while you are a member of the standard SYSTEM.MDW workgroup, and others on your network share the same system workgroup file, you will be extremely surprised when everyone on your network is prompted with a logon dialog box when they attempt to launch Microsoft Access. If you do not want this to occur, you must create a new system workgroup file before establishing security.

When you are sure that you are a member of the correct workgroup and are viewing the User and Group Accounts dialog box, you are ready to assign a password to the Admin user. Click the Change Logon Password tab of the User and Group Accounts dialog box to select it, as shown in Figure 33.10.

FIGURE 33.10

*The Change
Logon Password
dialog box.*

Assign a new password and verify it. (There is no old password unless you think of the old password as blank.) Then click Apply to establish a password for the Admin user. You are now ready to create a new user who will administrate the database.

If you choose to use the Security Wizard to secure your database, it changes the password for the Admin user. This ensures that the Logon dialog appears when the workgroup file created by the Security Wizard is used.

Step 3: Creating an Administrative User

After you assign a password to Admin, you are ready to create a new administrative user. You accomplish this from within the User and Group Accounts dialog. Access comes with two predefined groups: the Admins group and the Users group. The Admins group is the System Administrator's group account. This group automatically contains a member called Admin. Members of the Admins group have the irrevocable power to modify user and group memberships and clear user passwords, so anyone who is a member of the Admins group is all powerful within your system. The Admins group must contain at least one member at all times.

It is extremely important to create a unique workgroup ID from the Workgroup Administrator. Otherwise, members of other workgroups can create their own workgroup files and grant themselves permissions to your database's objects. Furthermore, it is important to ensure that the Admin user does not own any objects and is not given any explicit permissions. Because the Admin user is the same across all workgroups, all objects that Admin owns or has permissions to are available to anyone using another copy of Microsoft Access or Visual Basic.

The system also comes with a predefined Users group. This is the default group composed of all user accounts. All users automatically are added to the Users group and cannot be removed from this group. The Users group automatically is given all permissions to all objects. As with the Admin user, the Users group is the same across all workgroups. It therefore is extremely important that you take steps to remove all rights from the User's group, thereby ensuring that the objects in the database are secured properly. Fortunately, the Security Wizard, covered later in this chapter, accomplishes the task of removing all rights from the User's group. Because rights cannot be removed from the Admins group and the Admin user is the same across all workgroups, another user must be created. This new user will be responsible for administrating the database.

To create a new user to administrate the database, click the Users tab of the User and Group Accounts dialog. If you closed the dialog after the last step, choose Tools | Security | User and Group Accounts. Just like when you assigned a password for the Admin user, it does not matter which database you are in when you do this; it is only important that you are a member of the proper workgroup. Remember that you are defining a user for the workgroup—not for the database. The Users tab of the User and Group Accounts dialog box is shown in Figure 33.11.

To establish a new administrative user, click New. The New User/Group dialog box appears, as shown in Figure 33.12.

The New User/Group dialog box enables you to enter the username and a unique personal ID. This personal ID is not a password. The username and personal ID combine to become the encrypted SID that uniquely identifies the user to the system. Users create their own passwords when they log on to the system.

FIGURE 33.11

The User and Group Accounts dialog box.

FIGURE 33.12

The New User/Group dialog box.

The Security Wizard allows you to create one or more Administrative users for your database. In fact, the Security Wizard automatically creates a user called Administrator. This user becomes the owner of the database.

33

Step 4: Making the Administrative User a Member of the Admins Group

The next step is to make the new user a member of the Admins group. To do this, select the Admins group from the Available Groups list box, and then click Add with the new user selected in the Name drop-down list box. The new user should appear as a member of the Admins group, as shown in Figure 33.13.

FIGURE 33.13

Adding the new user to the Admins group.

If you use the Security Wizard, the user called Administrator is automatically added to the Admins group. Of course, you can also add other users to the Admins group.

Step 5: Exiting Access and Logging On as the System Administrator

You now are ready to close the User and Group Accounts dialog box and exit Access. Click OK. Exit Access and attempt to run it again. After attempting to open any database (or if you create a new database), you are prompted with the Access Logon dialog box shown in Figure 33.14.

FIGURE 33.14

The Access Logon dialog box.

Log on as the new system administrator. You do not have a password at this point; only the Admin user has a password. At this point, it still does not matter which database is open.

Step 6: Removing the Admin User from the Admins Group

Before you continue, you should remove the Admin user from the Admins group. Remember that the Admin user is the same in every workgroup. Because the Admins group has all rights to all objects in the database (including the right to assign permissions to and remove permissions from other users and objects), if you do not remove Admin from the Admins group, your database will not be secure. To remove the Admin user from the Admins group, follow these steps:

1. Select Tools | Security | User and Group Accounts.
2. Make sure the Users tab is selected.
3. Select the Admin user from the Name drop-down list box.
4. Select Admins from the Member Of list box.
5. Click Remove. The User and Group Accounts dialog box appears as shown in Figure 33.15.

FIGURE 33.15

Removing Admin from the Admins group.

If you use the Security Wizard to secure your database, the Admin user is automatically removed from the Admins group. In fact, the Security Wizard does not make the Admin user a member of any group besides Users (the group to which all users must be members).

Step 7: Assigning a Password to the System Administrator

Now that you are logged on as the new Administrator, you should modify your password. If you have closed the User and Group Accounts dialog, choose Tools | Security | User and Group Accounts. Click the Change Logon Password tab. Remember that you can assign a password only for the user whom you are logged on as.

One of the really cool aspects of the Security Wizard is that it allows you to assign passwords for all users who are members of the workgroup. This saves you a lot of time and effort when establishing a large number of users.

Step 8: Opening the Database You Want to Secure

After all this work, you finally are ready to actually secure the database. Up to this point, it did not matter which database you had open. Everything you have done so far has applied to the workgroup rather than to a particular database. Open the database you want to secure. At the moment, the Admin user owns the database, and members of the Users group have rights to all objects in the database.

Step 9: Running the Security Wizard

Unless you are creating a brand new database after you perform all the preceding steps, the first thing you should do to secure an existing database is to use the Security Wizard. The Security Wizard allows you to perform the following tasks:

- Create a Workgroup Information file
- Designate the database objects you want to secure
- Assign a password for the Visual Basic project
- Select from predefined groups that the wizard creates
- Assign desired rights to the Users group
- Create users
- Assign users to groups
- Create a backup, unsecured copy of your database

To run the Security Wizard, choose Tools | Security | User Level Security Wizard. The first step of the Security Wizard dialog box appears, as shown in Figure 33.16.

FIGURE 33.16

The first step of the Security Wizard prompts you to select an existing workgroup file or create a new workgroup information file.

The first step of the Security Wizard prompts you to select an existing workgroup information file or create a new workgroup information file. Click Next to proceed to the second step of the Security Wizard (pictured in Figure 33.17). The second step prompts you to provide required information about the workgroup information file that you are creating. You are asked to enter a File Name, a Workgroup Identifier or WID, your name, and your company name. You can designate the new workgroup file as the default workgroup file on your computer, or you can have Access create a shortcut to the secured database, including the name and path to the workgroup file.

FIGURE **33.17**

The second step of the Security Wizard prompts you to enter required information about the workgroup file.

The third step of the Security Wizard, shown in Figure 33.18, allows you to select the objects you want to secure. Notice that you can secure all objects, or you can opt to secure specific tables, queries, forms, reports, or macros. Modules, including the code behind forms and reports, are secured separately. The fourth step of the Security Wizard allows you to provide a Visual Basic Environment (VBE) password. This VBE password secures the VBA project containing all the code modules in the database, including the code behind the forms and reports.

FIGURE **33.18**

The third step of the Security Wizard allows you to select the objects you want to secure.

The fifth step of the Security Wizard, pictured in Figure 33.19, allows you to easily create group accounts. If your security needs match those predefined by one of the default groups, you can save yourself a significant amount of time by allowing the Security Wizard to create the necessary groups for you. Examples of predefined groups are read-only users who can read all data but cannot modify data or the design of database objects, as well as project designers who can edit all data and the design of application objects but cannot modify the structure of tables or relationships.

FIGURE 33.19

The fifth step of the Security Wizard allows you create groups from a list of pre-defined group accounts.

In the sixth step of the Security Wizard, shown in Figure 33.20, you designate what permissions, if any, you want to grant to the Users group. It is important to remember that *all* users are members of the Users group. Therefore, any permissions that you grant to the Users group are granted to all the users of your application. As a general rule, I recommend not granting any rights to the Users group. It is better to assign rights to other groups and then make specific users members of those groups.

FIGURE 33.20

In the sixth step of the Security Wizard, you can grant specific rights to the Users group.

The seventh step of the Security Wizard allows you to define the users who will use your database. In this step of the wizard, you supply each user's name, a password, and a unique Personal ID or PID (see Figure 33.21). To add a user, enter the name, password, and PID and then click Add This User to the List. To delete a user, click the user you want to delete and then click Delete User from List. Click Next when you are finished defining all users.

FIGURE 33.21

The seventh step of the Security Wizard allows you to define the users of your database.

In the next step of the Security Wizard, you assign the users created in step seven to the groups designated in step five. To assign a user to a group, click Select a User and Assign the User to Groups. Next select a user from the Group or User Name drop-down. Then click to add the selected user to any of the predefined groups (see Figure 33.22).

FIGURE 33.22

The eighth step of the Security Wizard allows you to assign users to groups.

The final step of the Security Wizard prompts you to enter the name of the backup copy of the unsecured database. After you click Finish, the existing database is secured and the original unsecured database is given the name designated for the backup.

The owner of a database cannot be changed and always has rights to everything in the database. Because Admin is the owner of the database and is the same in all workgroups, Access must copy all the database objects to a new, secure database owned by the new user. The wizard is intelligent enough to create a new secure database with the original database name and create a backup with the name that you designate. Access in no way modifies the existing, unsecured database. When the process is completed, the security report shown in Figure 33.23 appears.

FIGURE 33.23

The One-step Security Wizard Report is the result of a successfully completed Security Wizard process.

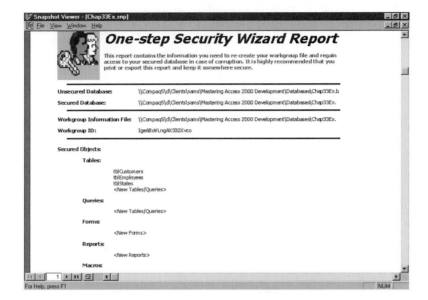

After completion, the Security Wizard provides you with a report containing detailed information about the workgroup it created, the objects it secured, and the groups and users it created. The new copy of the database is owned by the new system administrator. All rights have been revoked from the Users group.

When you close the report, you are prompted to save it as a snapshot so that you can view it again later. Because the report contains valuable information about the workgroup and the secured database, I strongly suggest that you save the report. If you do save the report, make sure that you save it in a very safe place. Armed with the information contained in the report, a savvy user could violate the security of your database.

Step 10: Creating Users and Groups

Any time after you establish and join a workgroup, you can establish the users and groups who will be members of the workgroup. Users represent individual people who will access your database files. Users are members of groups. Groups are categories of users who share the same rights. Rights can be assigned at the user level or at the group level. Administratively, it is easier to assign all rights at the group level. However, this involves categorizing access rights into logical groups and then assigning users to those groups.

If groups have been set up properly, the administration of the system is greatly facilitated. If rights of a category of users need to be changed, they can be changed at a group level. If a user is promoted and needs additional rights, you can make that user a member of a new group. This is much easier than trying to maintain separate rights for each user.

You can add, modify, and remove users and groups by using front-end interface tools, as well as through VBA code. This chapter covers how to maintain users and groups using the front-end interface tools. Chapter 34, "Advanced Security Techniques," covers how to maintain users and groups by using code.

Regardless of how you choose to define groups and users, you generally should create groups and then assign users to the appropriate groups. It is important to evaluate the structure of the organization as well as your application before you begin the mechanical process of adding the groups and users.

Adding Groups

To add a new group, follow these steps:

1. First make sure that you are a member of the correct workgroup. With or without any database open, select Tools | Security | User and Group Accounts.
2. Click the Groups tab of the User and Group Accounts dialog box.
3. Click New. The New User/Group dialog box appears.
4. Type the name of the group and enter a PID that uniquely identifies the group.
5. Click OK.
6. Repeat steps 3–5 for each group you want to add.

CAUTION

The *personal identification* (PID) is a case-sensitive, alphanumeric string that can be from four to 20 characters in length. In combination with the user or group name, the PID uniquely identifies the user or group in a workgroup. Personal identification numbers should be stored in a very safe place. In the hands of the wrong person, access to the PID can lead to a breach of security. On the other hand, if the database is damaged and an important PID is not available, the data and objects in the database will not be accessible, even to the most legitimate users.

Adding Users

To add users through the user interface, follow these steps:

1. Choose Tools | Security | User and Group Accounts.
2. Click the Users tab if it is not already selected.
3. Click New. The New User/Group dialog box appears.
4. Enter the name of the user and the PID associated with the user. Remember that this is not a password; instead, it combines with the username to create a unique identifier for the user.
5. Click OK.
6. Repeat steps 3–5 for each user you want to define.

Assigning Users to the Appropriate Groups

Before you proceed with the final step, assigning rights to users and groups, you should make each user a member of the appropriate group. A user can be a member of as many groups as you choose, but remember that each user gets the rights of his or her most forgiving group. In other words, if a user is a member of both the Admins group and a group with read-only access to objects, the rights of the Admins group prevail. To assign each user to the appropriate groups, follow these steps:

1. Choose Tools | Security | User and Group Accounts.
2. Click the Users tab if it is not already selected.
3. From the Name drop-down list box, select the user for whom you want to create group membership.
4. Double-click the name of the group to which you want to add the user, or single-click the group and click the Add button.
5. Repeat steps 3 and 4 for each user to whom you want to assign group membership.

Figure 33.24 shows a user named Dan who has been added to the Full Permissions group.

> **NOTE**
>
> Remember that the users and groups you create are for the workgroup as a whole—not just for a specific database.

FIGURE 33.24

Assigning a user to the appropriate group.

Step 11: Assigning Rights to Users and Groups

So far, you have created groups and users but you haven't given any of your groups or users rights to objects in the database. The key is to assign specific rights to each group, and then to make sure that all users are members of the appropriate groups. After that, you can assign each group specific permissions to the objects in your database. User and group information is maintained in the system database; permissions for objects are stored in system tables in the application database (MDB) file. After you establish a workgroup of users and groups, you must assign rights to specific objects in your database by following these steps:

1. Make sure the database containing the objects you want to secure is open.

2. Choose Tools | Security | User and Group Permissions. The dialog box shown in Figure 33.25 appears. Notice that as you click on each user in the User/Group Name box, as indicated by the check boxes in the Permissions section of the dialog box, you see that only the Administrator has rights to any objects. The Security Wizard automatically removed all permissions from the user named Admin. If you select the Groups option button, you see that only the Admins group has any rights (if you have previously run the Security Wizard and added other users and groups they will have rights as well).

3. To assign rights to a group, select the Groups option button. All the available groups appear in the User/Group Name box.

4. From the Object Type drop-down list, select the type of object you want to secure.

5. From the Object Name list box, select the names of the objects to which you want to assign rights. You can select multiple objects by pressing the Ctrl and Shift keys.

6. Enable the appropriate Permissions check boxes to select permissions for the objects. The types of available permissions are discussed in the text that follows.

7. Repeat steps 4–6 for all objects to which you want to assign rights.

FIGURE 33.25

*The User and
Group
Permissions
dialog box.*

In order to assign permissions appropriately, it is important that you understand the types of permissions that are available in addition to what each type of permission allows the user to do. Table 33.1 lists the types of permissions available.

TABLE 33.1 ASSIGNING PERMISSIONS

Permission	Allows User To
Open/Run	Open a database, form, or report; or run a macro.
Open Exclusive	Open a database with exclusive access.
Read Design	View tables, queries, forms, reports, macros, and modules in Design view.
Modify Design	View and change the design of tables, queries, forms, reports, macros, and modules.
Administer	Set the database password, replicate the database, and change startup properties (when the user has administer permission of a database). Have full access to the object and its data (when the user has administer permission of a database object—such as a table, query, form, report, macro, or module). Assign permissions for that object to other users (when the user has administer permissions for an object).

Permission	Allows User To
Read Data	View the data in a table or query.
Update Data	View and modify table or query data. Cannot insert and delete records, however.
Insert Data	Add records to a table or query.
Delete Data	Delete records in a table or query.

Some of these permissions implicitly include associated permissions. A user cannot update data in a table if he or she does not have the rights to read the data and the design of the table in which that data is located, for example.

PROVIDING AN ADDITIONAL LEVEL OF SECURITY: CREATING AN MDE

Access 2000 offers an additional level of security through the creation of an MDE file. An *MDE file* is a database file with all editable source code removed. This means that all the source code behind the forms, reports, and modules contained in the database is eliminated. An MDE file offers additional security because the forms, reports, and modules in an MDE file cannot be modified. Other benefits of an MDE file include a reduced size and optimized memory usage. To create an MDE file, follow these steps:

1. Open the database on which the MDE file will be based.
2. Choose Tools | Database Utilities | Make MDE File. The Save MDE As dialog box appears.
3. Select a name for the MDE and click OK.

Before you dive into MDEs, it is important that you are aware of the restrictions they impose. If you plan ahead, these restrictions probably will not cause you too many problems. On the other hand, if you enter the world of MDEs unaware, they can cause you much grief. You should consider these restrictions:

- The design of the forms, reports, and modules in an MDE file cannot be viewed or modified. In fact, new forms, reports, and modules cannot be added to an MDE. It therefore is important to keep the original database when you create an MDE file. This is where you will make changes to existing forms, reports, and modules and add new forms, reports, and modules. When you are finished, you simply rebuild the MDE.

- Because you must rebuild the MDE every time changes are made to the application, the front-end/back-end approach is best when dealing with MDE files. This means that the tables are contained in a standard Access database and the other objects are stored in the

MDE file. You therefore can rebuild the MDE without worrying about the reconciliation of data.

- You cannot import or export forms, reports, or modules to or from an MDE.

- You cannot change code by using properties or methods of the Access or VBA object models because MDEs contain no code.

- You cannot change the database's VBA project name.

- You cannot convert an MDE to future versions of Access. It will be necessary to convert the original database and then rebuild the MDE file with the new version.

- You cannot add or remove references to object libraries and databases from an MDE file. Also, you cannot change references to object libraries and databases.

- Every library database that an MDE references also must be an MDE. This means that if Database1 references Database2, which references Database3, all three databases must be stored as MDEs. You first must save Database3 as an MDE, reference it from Database2, and then save Database2 as an MDE. You then can reference Database2 from Database1, and finally save Database1 as an MDE.

- A replicated database cannot be saved as an MDE. The replication first must be removed from the database. This is accomplished by removing the replication system tables and properties from the database. The database then can be saved as an MDE and the MDE can be replicated and distributed as a replica set. Any time changes must be made to the database, they must be made to the original database, resaved as an MDE file, and then redistributed as a new replica set.

- Any security that applies to a database will follow through to an MDE file created from it. To create an MDE from a database that already is secured, you first must join the workgroup information file associated with the database. You must have Open/Run and Open Exclusive permissions to the database. You also must have Modify Design and Administer permissions to all tables in the database, or you must own all tables in the database. Finally, you must have Read Design permissions on all objects contained in the database.

- If error handling is not added to code within an MDE, and an error occurs, no error message appears.

- If you want to remove security from the database, you must remove the security from the original database and rebuild the MDE.

As long as you are aware of the restrictions associated with MDEs, they can offer you many benefits. In addition to the natural security they provide, the size and performance benefits they offer are significant.

> **TIP**
>
> A great use for MDEs is for demo versions of your applications. Performance of MDEs is excellent, but more importantly, by using VBA code MDEs can easily be rendered both time- and data-limited.

LOOKING AT SPECIAL ISSUES

Although the discussion of security so far has been quite thorough, a couple of issues surrounding the basics of security have not yet been covered. They include additional issues with passwords, understanding how security works with linked tables, understanding and working with object ownership, and printing security information. These topics are covered in this section.

Passwords

When you create a user, no password is assigned to the user. Passwords can be assigned to a user only when that user has logged on to the system. The System Administrator cannot add or modify a user's password. It is important to encourage users to assign themselves a password the first time they log on to the system. Using VBA code, the users can be forced to assign themselves a password. This is covered in Chapter 24, "Advanced VBA Techniques." Alternatively, the administrator of the database can log on as each user, assigning them a password.

Although you cannot assign a password to a user or modify the user's password, you can remove a user's password. This is necessary when a user forgets his or her password. To clear a user's password, follow these steps:

1. With or without a database open, choose Tools | Security | User and Group Accounts.
2. From the Names drop-down list, select the user whose password you want to clear.
3. Click Clear Password to clear the user's password.

Security and Linked Tables

When you design your application with two databases (one for tables and the other for the remainder of the application objects), it is necessary for you to secure both databases. Securing only the linked tables is not sufficient!

A potential problem still exists. If a user has access to add, delete, and modify data from your application, that user can open the database containing the data tables from outside your application and modify the data without going through the forms and reports you designed. One solution to this problem is to revoke all rights from the tables. Base all forms and reports on queries that have the Run Permissions property set to Owner's. This provides users with the least opportunity to modify the data from outside your system.

Ownership

Remember that the user who creates the database is the database's owner. This user retains irrevocable rights to the database. You cannot change the owner of a database; you can change only the ownership of objects in the database. You can change the owner of the database if you have rights to its objects by creating a new database and importing all the objects from the other database. You can accomplish this by using the Security Wizard.

By default, the creator of each object in the database is its owner. To change the ownership of an object in the database, follow these steps:

1. With the appropriate database open, choose Tools | Security | User and Group Permissions.

2. Click the Change Owner tab to select it, as shown in Figure 33.26.

FIGURE 33.26

Changing an object's ownership.

3. From the Object Type list box, select the objects whose ownership you want to change. You can press Ctrl and Shift to select multiple objects.

4. Select the Groups or Users option button.

5. Select the name of the group or user who will become the new owner of the objects.

6. Click Change Owner.

7. Repeat steps 3–7 for all objects for which you want to assign new ownership.

Printing Security

You can print a list of each user and the groups he or she is a member of by following these steps:

1. With the appropriate database open, choose Tools | Security | User and Group Accounts.
2. Click Print Users and Groups. The Print Security dialog box appears, as shown in Figure 33.27.

FIGURE 33.27

The Print Security dialog box.

3. Select the Both Users and Groups, Only Users, or Only Groups option button.
4. Click OK.

NOTE

You can print the rights to different objects by using the Database Documenter. This is covered in Chapter 35, "Documenting Your Application."

PRACTICAL EXAMPLES

Securing the Time and Billing Application

Now that you have learned the steps involved in properly securing an Access database, you can apply the steps to the Time and Billing application:

1. To begin, launch the Workgroup Administrator (Wrkgadm.exe). Click the Create button to create a new workgroup.
2. Enter your name and organization. Enter TimeBillApp as the Workgroup ID, as shown in Figure 33.28. Click OK.

FIGURE 33.28

*Entering informa-
tion for a new
workgroup.*

Workgroup Owner Information

The new workgroup information file is identified by the name,
organization, and case-sensitive workgroup ID you specify.

Use the name and organization information below, or enter a
different name or organization. If you want to ensure that your
workgroup is unique, also enter a unique workgroup ID of up to 20
numbers or letters.

Name: Alison Balter

Organization: Marina Consulting Group LLC

Workgroup ID: TimeBillApp

OK   Cancel

3. Call the workgroup database `Time.MDW`. Click OK. Confirm the path to the new workgroup, as shown in Figure 33.29.

FIGURE 33.29

*Specifying a name
and path for a
new workgroup
information file.*

Confirm Workgroup Information

Please confirm that the information you have typed is correct. If it is correct, choose
the OK button. Choose the Change button to retype any of the information.

Important: Store this information in a safe place. If you need to recreate the workgroup
information file, you must supply the exact same information.

Name: Alison Balter

Company: Marina Consulting Group LLC

Workgroup ID: TimeBillApp

Workgroup Information File: Q:\CLIENTS\SAMS\MASTERING ACCESS 2000
                            DEVELOPMENT\DATABASES\TIME.MDW

OK   Change

4. Exit the Workgroup Administrator and launch Access.

5. Choose Tools | Security | User and Group Accounts.

6. Click New and add a user named `PCGuru`. Give PCGuru a personal ID of `HeadCheese`, as
   shown in Figure 33.30. Click OK.

FIGURE 33.30

*Entering the name
and personal ID
of a new user.*

7. Click Add >> to add PCGuru to the Admins group, as shown in Figure 33.31.

8. Click the Change Logon Password tab to select it.

9. Assign a new password of `NoPower` to the Admin user and click Apply.

10. Click the Users tab.

11. From the Name drop-down list, select Admin.

12. Remove Admin from the Admins group, as shown in Figure 33.32.

FIGURE **33.31**

Adding a user to a group.

FIGURE **33.32**

Removing a user from a group.

13. Exit and restart Access. Open the Chap33 database and log on as PCGuru (with no password).

14. Choose Tools | Security | User and Group Accounts.

15. Click the Change Logon Password tab to select it.

16. Assign PCGuru the password of TheGuru.

17. Choose Tools | Security | User-Level Security Wizard.

18. Select Modify My Current Workgroup Information File. Click Next.

19. Click Next, accepting that you want to secure all objects.

20. Click to add the groups Read-Only Users and UpdateData Users. Click Next.

21. Click Next to accept that the Users group should not have any permissions.

22. Add the following users: Dan, Alexis, Brendan, Amanda, and Mimi. Assign any personal IDs and passwords that you want. Click Next.

23. Add Dan and Alexis to the Update Data group. Add Mimi and Amanda to the Read-Only Users group. Add Brendan to the Admins group. Click Next.

24. Enter a name for the backup copy of your database and click Finish.

25. Exit Access and log back on as each of the various users. Attempt to read, modify, add, and delete records from the tblClients and tblProjects tables. Ensure that security has been implemented as planned.

Don't forget that if the tables are linked, you need to go into the linked database to secure those tables.

SUMMARY

The security system in Access 2000 is quite robust but also somewhat complex. Using Access security, you can fully secure a database and all its objects. As a developer, you might want to prevent people from modifying the objects in your database. Furthermore, you might want to restrict certain users from viewing certain data, using specific forms, or running certain reports.

This chapter walks you through all the steps required to properly secure a database. It begins by showing you how to set up a database password and how to encrypt a database. It then covers all the details of implementing user-level security.

Invoking user-level security first involves setting up a workgroup using the Workgroup Administrator. You then must create an administrative user and make that user a member of the Admins group. Next, you change the password for the Admin user and remove the Admin user from the Admins group. You then exit Access, log on as the System Administrator, and assign yourself a password. All these steps are covered in detail in this chapter. In addition, this chapter walks you through the process of using the Security Wizard to perform many of the necessary tasks for you, such as changing the owner of the database from Admin to the new Administrator and revoking all permissions from the Users group. This ensures that the database is truly secure. The final step is to assign permissions for groups and/or users to the objects that reside in your newly secured database. The chapter also covers this very powerful process.

ADVANCED SECURITY TECHNIQUES

IN THIS CHAPTER

WHY THIS CHAPTER IS IMPORTANT

You might not always be available to set up security for the users of your application. Of course, one alternative is to make sure that they purchase their own copies of Access and then to instruct them on how to maintain security implementing the user interface. Access security is very complex, though, so this solution is not particularly practical. In fact, if you are distributing your application to a large group of users, this option is an impossibility. Fortunately, you can build into your application code the capability to maintain all aspects of security directly. It is important that you provide your administrative users with the capability to establish and maintain security for their workgroups. This involves building a front-end interface to all the security functionality provided by Access. Behind the scenes, you can use ActiveX Data Object (ADO) code to implement the security functionality.

MAINTAINING GROUPS USING CODE

Chapter 33, "Database Security Made Easy," discusses the importance of creating logical groups of users and then assigning rights to those groups. The administrator of your application might want to add or remove groups after you have distributed your application. You can use group ADOs to create and manage group accounts at runtime.

Adding a Group

You add a group using the Append method of the Groups collection. The Groups collection is part of the ADOX Catalog object. Figure 34.1 shows a form that enables users to add and remove groups.

FIGURE 34.1

This form enables administrative users to add and remove groups.

 This form is named frmMaintainGroups and is included in the CHAP34EX.MDB database located on the sample code CD-ROM. Listing 34.1 shows the code under the Add button.

LISTING 34.1   ADDING A GROUP

```
Private Sub cmdAdd_Click()
    Dim boolSuccess As Boolean
    If IsNull(Me.txtGroupName) Then
        MsgBox "You Must Fill In Group Name Before Proceeding"
    Else
        boolSuccess = CreateGroups()
        If boolSuccess Then
            MsgBox "Group Created Successfully"
        Else
            MsgBox "Group Not Created"
        End If
    End If
End Sub
```

This code tests to ensure that entries have been made for the Group Name. If so, the CreateGroups function is called. Based on the return value from CreateGroups, the user is notified whether the group was created successfully. Listing 34.2 uses the Append method of the Groups collection to add a new group to the workgroup.

LISTING 34.2   THE CreateGroups FUNCTION ADDS A GROUP

```
Function CreateGroups() As Boolean

    On Error GoTo CreateGroups_Err

    Dim cat As ADOX.Catalog

    CreateGroups = True

    Set cat = New ADOX.Catalog
    cat.ActiveConnection = CurrentProject.Connection

    cat.Groups.Append (Me.txtGroupName)

CreateGroups_Exit:
    Set cat = Nothing
    Exit Function

CreateGroups_Err:
    MsgBox "Error # " & Err.Number & ": " & Err.Description
    CreateGroups = False
    Resume CreateGroups_Exit
End Function
```

34

ADVANCED
SECURITY
TECHNIQUES

The function uses a `Catalog` variable. The `Catalog` variable is part of the Microsoft ADO Extension for DDL and Security (ADOX). You must reference the ADOX library before you can use the `Catalog` variable. The example sets the `ActiveConnection` property of the `Catalog` variable to the connection associated with the current project. After the connection is established, the `Append` method of the Groups collection of the `Catalog` object is used to append the group. The `Append` method of the Groups collection receives one parameter, the name of the group. The `Append` method, when applied to the Groups collection, adds a new group to the catalog. The function uses the value in `txtGroupName` as the name of the group to add. After running this routine, you can verify that a new group has been added to the workgroup by choosing Tools | Security | User and Group Accounts. The newly created group should appear in the group drop-down list on the group page.

Removing a Group

The code to remove a group is very similar to the code required to add a group. Listing 34.3 shows the code under the `cmdRemove` command button.

LISTING 34.3   REMOVING A GROUP

```
Private Sub cmdRemove_Click()
   Dim boolSuccess As Boolean
   If IsNull(Me.txtGroupName) Then
      MsgBox "You Must Fill In Group Name Before Proceeding"
   Else
      boolSuccess = RemoveGroups()
      If boolSuccess Then
         MsgBox "Group Removed Successfully"
      Else
         MsgBox "Group Not Removed"
      End If
   End If
End Sub
```

This routine ensures that the group name has been filled in and then calls the `RemoveGroups` function. An appropriate message is displayed, indicating whether the group was removed successfully. Listing 34.4 shows the `RemoveGroups` function.

LISTING 34.4   THE RemoveGroups FUNCTION REMOVES A GROUP

```
Function RemoveGroups()
   On Error GoTo RemoveGroups_Err

   Dim cat As ADOX.Catalog

   RemoveGroups = True

   Set cat = New ADOX.Catalog
   cat.ActiveConnection = CurrentProject.Connection
   cat.Groups.Delete Me.txtGroupName.Value

RemoveGroups_Exit:
   Set cat = Nothing
   Exit Function

RemoveGroups_Err:
   If Err.Number = 3265 Then
      MsgBox "Group Not Found"
   Else
      MsgBox "Error # " & Err.Number & ": " & Err.Description
   End If
   RemoveGroups = False
   Resume RemoveGroups_Exit

End Function
```

The RemoveGroups function uses the Delete method of the Groups collection of the Catalog object, using the value in txtGroupName as the name of the group to remove. If the group does not exist, an error number 3265 results. An appropriate error message appears.

USING CODE TO MAINTAIN USERS

Not only might you want to maintain groups using code, but you might also want to maintain users with code. You can employ user data access objects to create and manage user accounts at runtime. The frmMaintainUsers form shown in Figure 34.2 illustrates this process.

FIGURE 34.2

This form enables administrative users to add and remove users.

34

ADVANCED
SECURITY
TECHNIQUES

Adding Users

You add a user by using the Append method of the Users collection of the Catalog object. The frmMaintainUsers form, also contained in CHAP34EX.MDB, contains a command button named cmdAddUsers that adds a user. Listing 34.5 shows the code for this.

LISTING 34.5   ADDING A USER

```
Private Sub cmdAdd_Click()
    Dim boolSuccess As Boolean
    If IsNull(Me.txtUserName) Then
        MsgBox "You Must Fill In User Name Before Proceeding"
    Else
        boolSuccess = CreateUsers(Me.txtUserName.Value, _
            Nz(Me.txtPassword.Value, ""))
        If boolSuccess Then
            MsgBox "User Created Successfully"
        Else
            MsgBox "User Not Created"
        End If
    End If
End Sub
```

This code checks to ensure that the username has been filled in and then calls the CreateUsers function shown in Listing 34.6.

NOTE

The CreateUsers function, and all functions included in this chapter, is found in the basSecurity module in the Chap34Ex.mdb sample database.

LISTING 34.6   THE CreateUsers FUNCTION CREATES A USER

```
Function CreateUsers(UserName as String, _
    Password as String) As Boolean

    On Error GoTo CreateUsers_Err

    Dim cat As ADOX.Catalog

    CreateUsers = True

    Set cat = New ADOX.Catalog
```

```
    cat.ActiveConnection = CurrentProject.Connection
    cat.Users.Append UserName, Password

CreateUsers_Exit:
    Set cat = Nothing
    Exit Function

CreateUsers_Err:
    MsgBox "Error # " & Err.Number & ": " & Err.Description
    CreateUsers = False
    Resume CreateUsers_Exit
End Function
```

This routine creates a `Catalog` variable. It sets the `ActiveConnection` property of the `Catalog` object to the connection associated with the current project. It then invokes the `Append` method of the Users collection of the `Catalog` object to add the user to the catalog. The values in the `txtUserName` and `txtPassword` controls are passed to the `Append` method as arguments. The `Append` method is applied to the Users collection of the catalog to add the user to the collection of users in the catalog.

Assigning Users to a Group

So far, you have added a user, but you have not given the user group membership. Next, take a look at how you can add a user to an existing group. Listing 34.7 shows the code behind the `cmdAssign` button on the frmMaintainUsers form.

LISTING 34.7   ASSIGNING A USER TO A GROUP

```
Private Sub cmdAssign_Click()
    Dim boolSuccess As Boolean
    If IsNull(Me.txtUserName) Or IsNull(Me.txtGroupName) Then
      MsgBox "You Must Fill In User Name and Group Name Before Proceeding"
    Else
        boolSuccess = AssignToGroup(Me.txtUserName.Value, _
           Me.txtGroupName.Value)
      If boolSuccess Then
         MsgBox "User Successfully Assigned to Group"
      Else
         MsgBox "User Not Assigned to Group"
      End If
    End If
End Sub
```

34

ADVANCED
SECURITY
TECHNIQUES

This code ensures that both the `txtUserName` and `txtGroupName` text boxes are filled in and then calls the `AssignToGroup` function that attempts to assign the user to the specified group. Listing 34.8 shows the `AssignToGroup` function.

LISTING 34.8   THE `AssignToGroup` FUNCTION ASSIGNS A USER TO A GROUP

```
Function AssignToGroup(UserName as String, _
   GroupName as String)
    On Error GoTo AssignToGroup_Err

    Dim cat As ADOX.Catalog
    AssignToGroup = True

    Set cat = New ADOX.Catalog
    cat.ActiveConnection = CurrentProject.Connection
    cat.Groups.Append GroupName
    cat.Users(UserName).Groups.Append _
        GroupName

AssignToGroup_Exit:
    Set cat = Nothing
    Exit Function

AssignToGroup_Err:
    Select Case Err.Number
        Case -2147467259 'Group already exists
            Resume Next
        Case 3265
            MsgBox "Group Not Found"
        Case Else
            MsgBox "Error # " & Err.Number & ": " & Err.Description
    End Select
    AssignToGroup = False
    Resume AssignToGroup_Exit

End Function
```

This code creates a `Catalog` object variable. The `ActiveConnection` property of the `Catalog` object is set to the `Connection` property of the current project. The `Append` method of the Groups collection of the `Catalog` object is used to add the group to the Groups collection of the catalog. If the group already exists, the resulting error is ignored. Finally, the `Append` method is applied to the Groups collection of the `User` object of the `Catalog` object to add the user to the group. Notice that the username is supplied as the `Item` of the Users collection that is being referenced (the `UserName` parameter). The group that the user is appended to is supplied by the value specified as the `GroupName` parameter.

Removing Users from a Group

Just as you will want to add users to groups, you also will want to remove them from groups. The code in Listing 34.9 is located under the cmdRevoke command button on the frmMaintainUsers form.

LISTING 34.9   REMOVING A USER FROM A GROUP

```
Private Sub cmdRevoke_Click()
   Dim boolSuccess As Boolean
   If IsNull(Me.txtUserName) Or IsNull(Me.txtGroupName) Then
     MsgBox "You Must Fill In User Name and Group Name Before Proceeding"
   Else
      boolSuccess = RevokeFromGroup(Me.txtUserName.Value, _
         Me.txtGroupName.Value)
      If boolSuccess Then
         MsgBox "User Successfully Removed from Group"
      Else
         MsgBox "User Not Removed to Group"
      End If
   End If
End Sub
```

This code ensures that the name of the user and group are filled in on the form and then calls the RevokeFromGroup function, which is shown in Listing 34.10.

LISTING 34.10   THE RevokeFromGroup FUNCTION REMOVES A USER FROM A GROUP

```
Function RevokeFromGroup(UserName as String, _
   GroupName as String)
   On Error GoTo RevokeFromGroup_Err

   Dim cat As ADOX.Catalog

   RevokeFromGroup = True

   Set cat = New ADOX.Catalog
   cat.ActiveConnection = CurrentProject.Connection
   cat.Users(UserName).Groups.Delete _
      GroupName

RevokeFromGroup_Exit:
```

34

**ADVANCED
SECURITY
TECHNIQUES**

continues

LISTING 34.10   CONTINUED

```
    Set cat = Nothing
    Exit Function

RevokeFromGroup_Err:
    If Err.Number = 3265 Then
        MsgBox "Group Not Found"
    Else
        MsgBox "Error # " & Err.Number & ": " & Err.Description
    End If
    RevokeFromGroup = False
    Resume RevokeFromGroup_Exit

End Function
```

This procedure establishes a `Catalog` object and points its `Connection` property to the connection associated with the current project. It then removes the specified user from the group by performing the `Delete` method on the Groups collection of the `User` object. Notice that the `Item` of the Users collection referenced is specified in the parameter `UserName`, which is passed from the text box `txtUserName`, and the group the user is deleted from is specified by the parameter `GroupName`, which is passed from the `txtGroupName` text box.

Removing Users

Sometimes you want to remove a user entirely. The `cmdRemove` command button on the frmMaintainUsers form accomplishes this task, as shown in Listing 34.11.

LISTING 34.11   DELETING A USER

```
Private Sub cmdRemove_Click()
    Dim boolSuccess As Boolean
    If IsNull(Me.txtUserName) Then
        MsgBox "You Must Fill In User Name Before Proceeding"
    Else
        boolSuccess = RemoveUsers(Me.txtUserName.Value)
        If boolSuccess Then
            MsgBox "User Removed Successfully"
        Else
            MsgBox "User Not Removed"
        End If
    End If
End Sub
```

This code needs only a username to proceed. If a username has been supplied, the RemoveUsers function is called, as shown in Listing 34.12.

LISTING 34.12   THE RemoveUsers FUNCTION DELETES A USER

```
Function RemoveUsers(UserName as String)
   On Error GoTo RemoveUsers_Err

   Dim cat As ADOX.Catalog

   RemoveUsers = True

   Set cat = New ADOX.Catalog
   cat.ActiveConnection = CurrentProject.Connection
   cat.Users.Delete UserName

RemoveUsers_Exit:
   Set cat = Nothing
   Exit Function

RemoveUsers_Err:
   If Err.Number = 3265 Then
      MsgBox "User Not Found"
   Else
      MsgBox "Error # " & Err.Number & ": " & Err.Description
   End If
   RemoveUsers = False
   Resume RemoveUsers_Exit

End Function
```

The RemoveUsers function issues the Delete method on the Users collection of the catalog. This removes the user from the workgroup.

LISTING ALL GROUPS AND USERS

Figure 34.3 shows an enhanced version of the frmMaintainUsers form. It is named frmMaintainAll. The frmMaintainAll form, located in CHAP34EX.MDB, enables the user to add and remove users, assign users to groups, and assign passwords to users. The Groups and Users text boxes have been replaced with combo boxes so that the user can view and select from existing users and groups.

FIGURE 34.3

This form enables administrative users to maintain users, groups, and passwords.

Listing All Groups

The ListGroups function is the callback function used to populate the cboGroups combo box. Callback functions are covered in detail in Chapter 9, "Advanced Form Techniques." Listing 34.13 gathers a list of existing groups in the workgroup.

LISTING 34.13 THE ListGroups FUNCTION CREATES A LIST OF ALL GROUPS

```
Function ListGroups(ctl As Control, vntID As Variant, _
        lngRow As Long, lngCol As Long, intCode As Integer) _
        As Variant

    Dim cat As ADOX.Catalog
    Dim grp As ADOX.Group

    Dim intCounter As Integer
    Static sastrGroups() As String
    Static sintNumGroups As Integer
    Dim varRetVal As Variant

    varRetVal = Null

    Select Case intCode
        Case acLBInitialize          ' Initialize.
            Set cat = New ADOX.Catalog
            cat.ActiveConnection = CurrentProject.Connection
            sintNumGroups = cat.Groups.Count
            ReDim sastrGroups(sintNumGroups - 1)
            For Each grp In cat.Groups
                sastrGroups(intCounter) = grp.Name
                intCounter = intCounter + 1
            Next grp
            varRetVal = sintNumGroups
        Case acLBOpen                 'Open
            varRetVal = Timer          'Generate unique ID for control.
```

```
        Case acLBGetRowCount            'Get number of rows.
            varRetVal = sintNumGroups
        Case acLBGetColumnCount         'Get number of columns.
            varRetVal = 1
        Case acLBGetColumnWidth         'Get column width.
            varRetVal = -1              '-1 forces use of default width.
        Case acLBGetValue               'Get the data.
            varRetVal = sastrGroups(lngRow)
    End Select
    ListGroups = varRetVal
End Function
```

The gist of the ListGroups function is that it uses the Count property of the Groups collection of the catalog to determine how many groups are contained in the catalog. This number is used by the callback function to designate how many rows will appear in the combo box. Notice the line For Each grp In cat.Groups. This code loops through each group object in the Groups collection of the catalog. The Name property of the Group object is added to the combo box.

Listing All Users

Listing all users is very similar to listing all groups, as shown in Listing 34.14.

LISTING 34.14   THE ListUsers FUNCTION CREATES A LIST OF ALL USERS

```
Function ListUsers(ctl As Control, vntID As Variant, _
        lngRow As Long, lngCol As Long, intCode As Integer) _
        As Variant

    Dim cat As ADOX.Catalog
    Dim usr As ADOX.User
    Dim intCounter As Integer
    Static sastrUsers() As String
    Static sintNumUsers As Integer
    Dim varRetVal As Variant

    varRetVal = Null

    Select Case intCode
        Case acLBInitialize          ' Initialize.
            Set cat = New ADOX.Catalog
            cat.ActiveConnection = CurrentProject.Connection
            sintNumUsers = cat.Users.Count
            ReDim sastrUsers(sintNumUsers - 1)
```

34

continues

LISTING 34.14 CONTINUED

```
        For Each usr In cat.Users
            sastrUsers(intCounter) = usr.Name
            intCounter = intCounter + 1
        Next usr
        varRetVal = sintNumUsers
    Case acLBOpen                  'Open
        varRetVal = Timer          'Generate unique ID for control.
    Case acLBGetRowCount           'Get number of rows.
        varRetVal = sintNumUsers
    Case acLBGetColumnCount        'Get number of columns.
        varRetVal = 1
    Case acLBGetColumnWidth        'Get column width.
        varRetVal = -1             '-1 forces use of default width.
    Case acLBGetValue              'Get the data.
        varRetVal = sastrUsers(lngRow)
    End Select
    ListUsers = varRetVal
End Function
```

This code looks at the Count property of the Users collection of the Catalog object to determine how many users exist. The For Each usr In wrk.Users line loops through each user in the Users collection. The name of each user is added to an array that is used to populate the cboUsers combo box.

WORKING WITH PASSWORDS

Many times, the administrative user needs to add, remove, or modify users' passwords. By using the user interface, you can modify only the password of the user currently logged in; by using code, however, you can modify any user's password, as long as you have administrative rights to do so.

Assigning Passwords to Users

The frmMaintainAll form enables the administrative user to assign a password to the user selected in the combo box. Listing 34.15 shows the code to assign a new password for a user.

LISTING 34.15 CHANGING A USER'S PASSWORD

```
Private Sub cmdPassword_Click()
    Dim boolSuccess As Boolean
    If IsNull(Me.cboUserName.Value) Then
        MsgBox "You Must Fill In User Name and Password Before Proceeding"
```

```
    Else
        boolSuccess = AssignPassword()
        If boolSuccess Then
            MsgBox "Password Successfully Changed"
        Else
            MsgBox "Password Not Changed"
        End If
    End If
End Sub
```

This routine ensures that a username has been entered and then calls the `AssignPassword` function, located in the frmMaintainAll form, as shown in Listing 34.16.

LISTING 34.16   THE `AssignPassword` FUNCTION CHANGES A USER'S PASSWORD

```
Function AssignPassword()
    On Error GoTo AssignPassword_Err

    Dim cat As ADOX.Catalog
    Set cat = New ADOX.Catalog
    cat.ActiveConnection = CurrentProject.Connection

    AssignPassword = True

    cat.Users(Me.cboUserName.Value).ChangePassword _
        "", Nz(Me.txtPassword.Value)

AssignPassword_Exit:
    Set cat = Nothing
    Exit Function

AssignPassword_Err:
    MsgBox "Error # " & Err.Number & ": " & Err.Description
    AssignPassword = False
    Resume AssignPassword_Exit

End Function
```

The `AssignPassword` function uses the `ChangePassword` method of the `User` object specified in the cboUserName combo box, which is part of the Users collection. The first parameter, the old password, is left blank intentionally. Members of the Admins group can modify anyone's password but their own without having to know the old password. The second parameter, the new password, is the value entered in the txtPassword text box. The `Nz` function sets the new password to a zero-length string if the administrative user did not supply a new password.

Listing Users Without Passwords

Many times, an administrative user simply wants to obtain a list of all users who do not have passwords. This list can be obtained quite easily by using VBA code and ADOs. Figure 34.4 shows the frmMaintainPasswords form, which is located in the CHAP34EX.MDB database.

FIGURE 34.4

This form enables administrative users to view users without passwords.

When the form is loaded, the list box uses a callback function to display a list of all users who do not have passwords. Listing 34.17 shows the code for the frmMaintainPasswords form.

LISTING 34.17 LOCATING USERS WITHOUT PASSWORDS

```
Function ListUsers(ctl As Control, vntID As Variant, _
       lngRow As Long, lngCol As Long, intCode As Integer) _
       As Variant

   On Error GoTo ListUsers_Err

   Dim cat As ADOX.Catalog
   Dim conn As ADODB.Connection
   Dim usr As ADOX.User
   Dim intCounter As Integer
   Dim boolNoPass As Boolean
   Static sastrUsers() As String
   Static sintNumUsers As Integer
   Dim varRetVal As Variant

   varRetVal = Null

   Select Case intCode
      Case acLBInitialize          ' Initialize.
         Set cat = New ADOX.Catalog
         cat.ActiveConnection = CurrentProject.Connection
         sintNumUsers = cat.Users.Count
         ReDim sastrUsers(sintNumUsers - 1)
```

```
        For Each usr In cat.Users
            boolNoPass = True
            Set conn = New ADODB.Connection
            conn.Open CurrentProject.Connection, usr.Name, ""
            If boolNoPass Then
                sastrUsers(intCounter) = usr.Name
                intCounter = intCounter + 1
            End If
        Next usr
        varRetVal = sintNumUsers
      Case acLBOpen                     'Open
        varRetVal = Timer               'Generate unique ID for control.
      Case acLBGetRowCount              'Get number of rows.
        varRetVal = sintNumUsers
      Case acLBGetColumnCount           'Get number of columns.
        varRetVal = 1
      Case acLBGetColumnWidth           'Get column width.
        varRetVal = -1                  '-1 forces use of default width.
      Case acLBGetValue                 'Get the data.
        varRetVal = sastrUsers(lngRow)
    End Select
    ListUsers = varRetVal

ListUsers_Exit:
    Set cat = Nothing
    Set usr = Nothing
    Exit Function

ListUsers_Err:
    If Err.Number = -2147217843 Then
        boolNoPass = True
        Resume Next
    Else
        MsgBox "Error # " & Err.Number & ": " & Err.Description
        Resume ListUsers_Exit
    End If
End Function
```

The meat of the code is in the For...Each loop. The code loops through each user in the Users collection. It begins by setting the value of the boolNoPass flag to True. It creates a new catalog and attempts to log on to the new catalog by using the Name property of the current user object and a password that is a zero-length string. If an error occurs, the error-handling code sets the boolNoPass flag to False. The -2147467259 error means that the password was not valid, indicating that the user must have a password because the logon was not successful. If the logon was successful, the user must not have a password and therefore is added to the list box.

Ensuring That Users Have Passwords

You might want to ensure that users who log on to your application have a password. You can accomplish this by using the code in Listing 34.18.

LISTING 34.18 ENSURING THAT YOUR APPLICATION'S USERS HAVE PASSWORDS

```
Function AutoExec()
    Dim cat As ADOX.Catalog
    Dim usr As ADOX.User
    Dim strPassword As String

    Set cat = New ADOX.Catalog
    cat.ActiveConnection = CurrentProject.Connection
    Set usr = cat.Users(CurrentUser)
    On Error Resume Next
    usr.ChangePassword "", ""
    If Err.Number = 0 Then
        strPassword = InputBox("You Must Enter a Password _
            Before Proceeding", "Enter Password")
        If strPassword = "" Then
            DoCmd.Quit
        Else
            usr.ChangePassword "", strPassword
        End If

    End If
    AutoExec = True
End Function
```

The AutoExec function can be called from the startup form of your application. It points a User object variable to CurrentUser. It accomplishes this by using the return value from the CurrentUser function as the user to look at in the Users collection. The CurrentUser function returns a string containing the name of the current user.

When an object variable is pointing at the correct user, the code attempts to set a new password for the user. When modifying the password of the current user, both the old password and the new password must be supplied to the ChangePassword method of the User object. If the old password is incorrect, an error occurs. This indicates that the user has a password and nothing special needs to happen. If no error occurs, you know that no password exists, so the user is prompted for a password. If the user does not supply a password, the application quits. Otherwise, a new password is assigned to the user.

NOTE

You can find an example of the usefulness of this function in the basUtils module in the Chap34ExNoPass.MDB database located on your sample code CD-ROM.

ASSIGNING AND REVOKING PERMISSIONS TO OBJECTS USING CODE

Often, you will want to assign and revoke object permissions using code. Once again, you easily can accomplish this by using ADO code. The form in Figure 34.5 is named frmTableRights and is located in the CHAP34EX.MDB database.

FIGURE 34.5

This form enables administrative users to assign rights to groups.

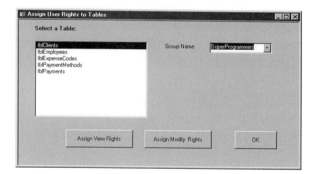

The code in Listing 34.19 assigns view rights for the table selected in the Select a Table list box to the group selected in the Group Name drop-down list.

LISTING 34.19 ASSIGNING VIEW RIGHTS

```
Private Sub cmdViewRights_Click()
    Dim cat As ADOX.Catalog

    Set cat = New ADOX.Catalog
    cat.ActiveConnection = CurrentProject.Connection

    cat.Groups(Me.cboGroupName.Value).SetPermissions _
        Me.lstTables.Value, _
```

34

ADVANCED
SECURITY
TECHNIQUES

continues

LISTING 34.19   CONTINUED

```
            ObjectType:=adPermObjTable, _
            Action:=adAccessSet, _
            Rights:=adRightRead
End Sub
```

The SetPermissions method of the Group object is used to establish the permissions for the
table. The rights for the table are granted to the group specified in the cboGroupName combo
box. The table to which the rights are granted is designated in the lstTables list box. The
object type to which the rights are assigned is designated in the ObjectType parameter. The
constant adPermObjTable is used to specify the object type as a table. The Action parameter is
used to designate the type of action being taken. The constant adAccessSet is used to indicate
that the rights are being established. The Rights parameter is used to specify the rights being
granted. The constant adRightRead is used to assign read rights to the table. Table 34.1 lists
the permission constants for queries and tables.

TABLE 34.1   THE PERMISSION CONSTANTS FOR QUERIES AND TABLES

Permission Constant	Grants Permission To
adRightDelete	Delete rows from the table or query.
adRightInsert	Insert new rows into the table or query.
adRightReadDesign	Read the definition of the table or query.
adRightUpdate	Modify table or query data.
adRightRead	Read data stored in the table or query. Also, implicitly grants read permission to the definition of the table or query.
adWriteDesign	Alter the definition of the table or query.
adRightWithGrant	Grant permissions for the object.
adRightAll	All rights to the object.

Listing 34.20 shows an example in which the adRightRead constant is combined with the
adRightUpdate constant using a bitwise OR. The adRightUpdate constant does not imply that
the user also can read the table definition and data. As you might guess, it is difficult to edit
data if you cannot read it. You therefore must combine the adRightRead constant with the
adRightUpdate constant in order to allow the user or group to read and modify table data.

LISTING 34.20   MODIFYING USER RIGHTS

```
Private Sub cmdModifyRights_Click()
    Dim cat As ADOX.Catalog
```

```
    Set cat = New ADOX.Catalog
    cat.ActiveConnection = CurrentProject.Connection

    cat.Groups(Me.cboGroupName.Value).SetPermissions _
        Me.lstTables.Value, _
        ObjectType:=adPermObjTable, _
        Action:=adAccessSet, _
        Rights:=adRightRead Or adRightUpdate
End Sub
```

ENCRYPTING A DATABASE USING CODE

Chapter 33 shows how you can encrypt a database by using the user interface. If a database is not encrypted, it is not really secure because a savvy user can use a disk editor to view the data in the file. If you have distributed your application with the runtime version of Access and you want to give your user the ability to encrypt the database, you must write ADO code to accomplish the encryption process. The code looks like this:

```
Sub Encrypt(strDBNotEncrypted As String, strDBEncrypted As String)
    Dim je As New JRO.JetEngine

    je.CompactDatabase SourceConnection:="Data Source=" _
     & strDBNotEncrypted & ";", _
        DestConnection:="Data Source=" & strDBEncrypted & _
        "; Jet OLEDB:Encrypt Database=True"
End Sub
```

This subroutine receives two parameters. The first is the name of the database that you want to encrypt. The second is the name you want to assign to the encrypted database. The `CompactDatabase` method is issued on the `JetEngine` object. This method receives two parameters: the name of the original database to encrypt and the name for the new encrypted database. Notice that the data source for the destination includes information indicating that you want to encrypt the database being compacted.

ACCOMPLISHING FIELD-LEVEL SECURITY USING QUERIES

In itself, Access does not provide field-level security. You can achieve field-level security by using queries, though. Here's how it works. You do not provide the user or group with any rights to the table that you want to secure. Instead, you give the user or group rights to a query containing only the fields that you want the user to be able to view. Ordinarily, this would not

34

ADVANCED
SECURITY
TECHNIQUES

work because if users cannot read the tables underlying a query, they cannot read the data in the query result.

The trick is in a query option named `WITH OWNERACCESS OPTION`. The `WITH OWNERACCESS OPTION` of a query grants the user running the query the rights possessed by the owner of the query. The Staff group, for example, has no rights to the tblEmployees table. The Supervisors group has Read Design, Read Data, and Update Data permissions to the tblEmployees table. The qryEmployees query is owned by the Supervisors group, as shown in Figure 34.6. Figure 34.7 shows the query itself. Notice in Figure 34.7 that the `Run Permissions` property has been set to `Owner's`. Figure 34.8 shows the resulting SQL. Notice the `WITH OWNERACCESS OPTION` clause at the end of the SQL statement. When any member of the Staff group (who has no other rights to tblEmployees) runs the query, that member inherits the Supervisor group's ability to read and modify the table data.

FIGURE 34.6

The query owned by the Supervisors group.

FIGURE 34.7

The Design view of a query with Run Permissions *set to* Owner's.

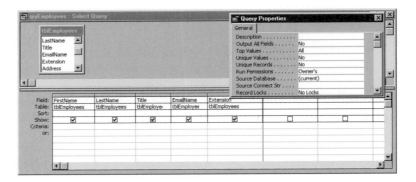

FIGURE 34.8

The SQL view of a query with Run Permissions *set to* Owner's.

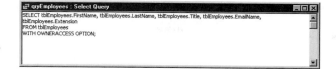

PROHIBITING USERS AND GROUPS FROM CREATING OBJECTS

You might want to prevent the members of a workgroup from creating new databases or creating specific database objects. Preventing users from creating databases or other objects can be accomplished only by using VBA code.

Prohibiting Users and Groups from Creating Objects

You might want to prohibit users from creating specific types of objects. For example, you might want to prevent them from creating new tables, queries, or other objects in your application or data database file. Listing 34.21 illustrates this process.

LISTING 34.21   PROHIBITING USERS FROM CREATING OTHER OBJECTS

```
Sub NoTables(strGroupToProhibit)
   On Error GoTo NoTables_Err
   Dim cat As ADOX.Catalog

   Set cat = New ADOX.Catalog
   cat.ActiveConnection = CurrentProject.Connection
   cat.Tables.Refresh

   cat.Groups(strGroupToProhibit).SetPermissions Null, _
      adPermObjTable, adAccessDeny, adRightCreate


NoTables_Exit:
   Set cat = Nothing
   Exit Sub

NoTables_Err:
   MsgBox "Error # " & Err.Number & ": " & Err.Description
   Resume NoTables_Exit


End Sub
```

34

ADVANCED
SECURITY
TECHNIQUES

The code uses the `SetPermissions` method of the Groups collection of the `Catalog` object to set permissions for new tables. The parameters used in the example deny table creation rights for the group specified in the call to the function.

ACCOMPLISHING PROHIBITED TASKS BY LOGGING ON AS A DIFFERENT USER

Although you might not want particular users to be able to accomplish particular tasks, you might at times want to go behind the scenes and accomplish the task for them. As you saw in the preceding section, you can prohibit a user or group from creating new tables and queries. This is fine, except when you run into a situation in which your code requires that a temporary table be created. In this situation, you can temporarily log on as a different user, perform the process, and then log off.

SECURING CLIENT/SERVER APPLICATIONS

It is important to understand that security for client/server applications must be applied on the back-end database server. You can request logon IDs and passwords from users at runtime and pass them to the database server as part of the connection string, but Access security itself does nothing in terms of interacting with client/server data. Any errors returned from the back end must be handled by your application.

SECURITY AND REPLICATION

Database security cannot be implemented on replicated databases. Only user-level security can be implemented. All the replicas inherit the security applied to the Design Master. Replicate only the database file. Never replicate the security information file (System.mdw). Instead, make sure that exactly the same security information file is available at each location where the replica is used. You can do this by copying the file to each location.

A user must have administer permission on a database to perform the following tasks:

- Converting a nonreplicable database into a replicable database
- Making a replica of the Design Master
- Making a local object replicable
- Making a replicable object local

Applying Advanced Techniques to Your Application

The advanced techniques you build in to the Time and Billing application depend on how much responsibility you want to give the application for implementing security. You might want to implement security from outside the application rather than build it directly into the application. You can add all the forms contained in CHAP34EX.MDB directly into the Time and Billing application if you want. Also, you can add the code in the AutoExec routine (covered in the section "Ensuring That Users Have Passwords") into the Time and Billing application so that you force users running the application to assign themselves a password.

SUMMARY

The security features available in Access are extremely rich. Being able to implement security using both code and the user interface gives you immense power and flexibility when implementing security in your application.

This chapter begins with a look at maintaining users and groups using code. Next, you learned about using code to assign and maintain passwords, as well as determining whether a user has a password. You also learned about assigning and revoking permissions to objects using code, as well as many other advanced techniques that give you full control over security in your application.

Security requires a lot of planning and forethought. You must make decisions about what groups to define and which rights you will assign to each group. Also, you must decide what features you will build in to your application using VBA code. This chapter illustrates how you can build all aspects of security directly into the user interface of your application.

34

DOCUMENTING YOUR APPLICATION

IN THIS CHAPTER

WHY THIS CHAPTER IS IMPORTANT

Back in the days of mainframes and very formal centralized management information systems (MIS) departments, documentation was a mandatory requirement for the completion of an application. Today, it seems as though all types of people are developing applications: administrative assistants, CEOs, sales managers, MIS professionals, and so on. To make matters worse, many of us who consider ourselves MIS professionals never received any formal systems training. Finally, the demand to get an application up and running and then to move on to the next application is more prevalent than ever. As a result of all these factors, it seems that documentation has gone by the wayside.

Despite all the reasons why documentation doesn't seem to happen, it is as important to properly document your application today as it was in the mainframe days. Documentation provides you and your users with these benefits:

- It makes the system easy for you and others to maintain.
- It helps state the purpose and function of each object in the application.

This chapter covers the various ways in which you can document your application. It shows you how you can document your application objects, as well as your application code.

PREPARING YOUR APPLICATION TO BE SELF-DOCUMENTING

Fortunately, Access ships with an excellent tool to assist you with the process of documenting your database: the Database Documenter. Although this tool can be used without any special preparation on your part, a little bit of work as you build the components of your application can go a long way toward enhancing the value of the output supplied by the Database Documenter.

Documenting Your Tables

The Database Documenter prints all field and table descriptions entered in the design of a table. Figure 35.1 shows a table in Design view. Notice the descriptions for the ClientID and StateProvince fields. These descriptions provide additional information that is not readily obvious by looking at the field names. The Table Properties window also contains a Description property. This property is included in the documentation for the table when it is printed in the Database Documenter.

FIGURE 35.1

Documenting a table by including descriptions of each field and using the Table Properties box.

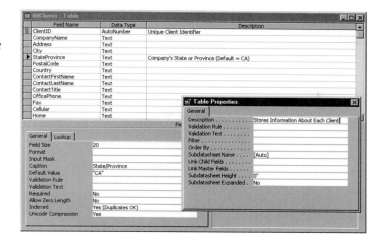

In addition to enhancing the output from the Database Documenter, entering a table description also assists you and the users of your database when working with the tables in the database. Figure 35.2 shows the Database window after descriptions are entered for the tables in the database. Notice that the description of each table appears in the Database window.

FIGURE 35.2

The Database window with table descriptions.

Documenting Your Queries

Just as you can enhance the output that the Database Documenter provides for tables, you also can enhance the output the Database Documenter provides for queries. Figure 35.3 shows the Query Properties window. As you can see, the Description property is filled in with a detailed description of the purpose of the query. Figure 35.3 shows the description of a query, and Figure 35.4 shows the description of an individual column in a query. Both the query and field descriptions are included in the output provided by the Database Documenter.

FIGURE 35.3

Documenting a query using the Description property.

FIGURE 35.4

Documenting a column in a query.

Documenting Your Forms

Documentation is not limited to table and query objects. A form has a `Description` property. It cannot be accessed from the Design view of the form, though. To view or modify the Description property of a form, follow these steps:

1. Make the Database window the active window.

2. Right-click the form for which you want to add a description.

3. Choose Properties. The Object Properties dialog box appears, as shown in Figure 35.5.

4. Enter a description in the Description text box.

5. Click OK. The description you entered appears in the Database window, as shown in Figure 35.6, and it also appears in the output from the Database Documenter.

FIGURE 35.5

You can use the Object Properties dialog box to document each object in the database.

FIGURE 35.6

The Database window with a description of a form.

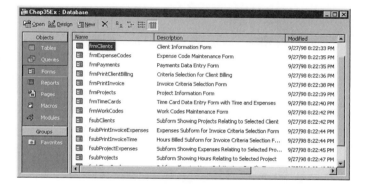

Documenting Your Reports

Reports are documented in exactly the same manner as forms. Reports have a Description property that must be entered in the Object Properties dialog box. Remember that to access this dialog box, you right-click the object in the Database window and then choose Properties.

Documenting Your Macros

Macros can be documented in significantly more detail than forms and reports. You can document each individual line of the macro, as shown in Figure 35.7. Not only does this provide documentation in the Database Documenter, but also macro comments become code comments when you convert a macro to a Visual Basic module. In addition to documenting each line of a macro, you can add a description to the macro. As with forms and reports, to accomplish this, right-click the macro from the Database window and choose Properties.

35

DOCUMENTING YOUR APPLICATION

FIGURE 35.7

Documenting a macro by including a description of what each line of the macro does.

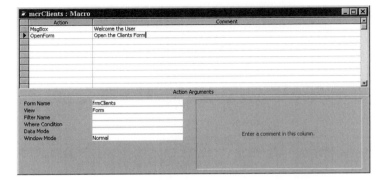

Documenting Your Modules

I cannot emphasize enough how important it is to document your modules. You accomplish this by using comments. Of course, not every line of code needs to be documented. I document all areas of my code that I feel are not self-explanatory. Comments assist me when I revisit the code to make modifications and enhancements. They also assist anyone who is responsible for maintaining my code. Finally, they provide the user with documentation about what my application is doing. Comments print with your code modules, as shown later in this chapter in the section "Using the Database Documenter." As with the other objects, you can right-click a module to assign a description to it.

Using Database Properties to Document the Overall Database

In addition to enabling you to assign descriptions to the objects in the database, Microsoft Access enables you to document the database as a whole. You do this by filling in the information included in the Database Properties window. To access a database's properties, choose File | Database Properties or right-click the title bar of the Database window and choose Database Properties. The Database Properties dialog box appears, as shown in Figure 35.8. As you can see, it is a tabbed dialog box; tabs include General, Summary, Statistics, Contents, and Custom.

Descriptions of the tabs in the Database Properties dialog box follow:

- **General**—The General tab displays general information about your database. This includes the date the database was created, when it was last modified, when it was last accessed, its location, its size, its MS-DOS name, and its file attributes. None of the information on the General tab can be modified.

Figure 35.8

The Database Properties window showing the General properties of a database.

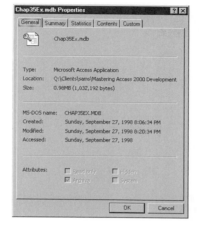

• **Summary**—The Summary tab, shown in Figure 35.9, contains modifiable information that describes the database and what it does. This tab includes the database title, its subject, and comments about the database. It also includes the *hyperlink base*—a base address used for all relative hyperlinks inserted in the database. It can be an Internet address (URL) or a filename path (UNC).

Figure 35.9

The Summary tab of the Database Properties window.

• **Statistics**—The Statistics tab contains statistics of the database, such as when it was created, last modified, and last accessed.

• **Contents**—The Contents tab, shown in Figure 35.10, includes a list of all the objects contained in the database.

FIGURE 35.10

The Contents tab of the Database Properties window.

• **Custom**—The Custom tab enables you to define custom properties associated with the database. This is useful when you are dealing with a large organization with numerous databases, and you want to be able to search for all the databases containing certain properties.

USING THE DATABASE DOCUMENTER

The Database Documenter is an elegant tool that is part of the Access application. It enables you to selectively produce varying levels of documentation for each of the objects in your database. To use the Database Documenter, follow these steps:

1. Make sure that the Database window is the active window.

2. Choose Tools | Analyze | Documenter. The Documenter dialog box appears, as shown in Figure 35.11.

FIGURE 35.11

You can use the Database Documenter dialog box to designate which objects you want to document.

3. Click the appropriate tab to select the type of object you want to document. To document a table, for example, click the Tables tab.

4. Enable the check box to the left of each object that you want to document. You can click the Select All command button to select all objects of the selected type.

5. Click the Options button to refine the level of detail provided for each object. Depending on which object type is selected, different options are displayed. Database Documenter options are covered in the next section of this chapter.

6. Repeat steps 3–5 to select all database objects that you want to document.

7. Click OK when you are ready to produce the documentation.

TIP

To document all objects in the database, click the All Object Types tab and then click Select All.

CAUTION

Access can take quite a bit of time to produce the requested documentation, particularly if numerous objects are selected. For this reason, you should not begin the documentation process if you will soon need your computer to accomplish other tasks. This is because, while Access is processing this task, switching to another application becomes difficult if not impossible—how difficult depends on the amount of RAM installed on your system, as well as the type of processor (CPU) installed on your computer and its speed.

NOTE

To document the properties of the database or the relationships between the tables in the database, click the Current Database tab and select Properties or Relationships.

After you select all the desired objects and options and click OK, the Object Definition window appears. You can use this Print Preview window to view the documentation output for the objects you selected. (See Figure 35.12.) This Print Preview window is just like any other Print Preview window; you can view each page of the documentation and send the documentation to the printer.

FIGURE 35.12

The Object Definition Print Preview window.

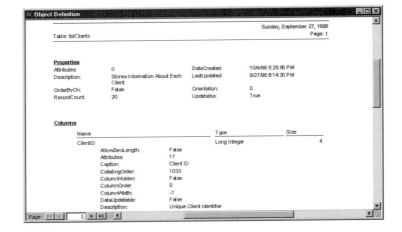

Using the Documenter Options

By default, the Database Documenter outputs a huge volume of information for each selected object. Each control on a form is documented, for example, including every property of the control. It is easy to produce 50 pages of documentation for a couple of database objects. Besides being a tremendous waste of paper, though, this volume of information is overwhelming to review. Fortunately, you can refine the level of detail provided by the Documenter for each category of object you are documenting. Just click the Options button in the Database Documenter dialog box.

Figure 35.13 shows the Table Definition options. Notice that you can specify whether you want to print table Properties, Relationships, and Permissions by User and Group. You also can indicate the level of detail you want to display for each field: Nothing; Names, Data Types, and Sizes; or Names, Data Types, Sizes, and Properties. For table indexes, you can opt to include Nothing; Names and Fields; or Names, Fields, and Properties.

FIGURE 35.13

You can use the Print Table Definition dialog box to designate which aspects of a table's definition are documented.

If you select the Queries tab and then click Options, the Print Query Definition dialog box appears, as shown in Figure 35.14. Here, you can select the level of detail to be output for the selected queries. You can choose whether to include Properties, SQL, Parameters, Relationships, and Permissions by User and Group for the query. You also can select the level of detail to include for each column of the query and for the indexes involved in the query.

FIGURE 35.14

You use the Print Query Definition dialog box to designate which aspects of a query's definition are documented.

The Form and Report options are similar to one another. Figure 35.15 shows the Print Form Definition dialog box. Here, you can specify whether you want to print Properties, Code, and Permissions by User and Group for the form. For each control on the form, you can choose to print Nothing, the Names of the controls, or the Names and Properties of the controls. The Print Report Definition dialog box offers the same options. Both the Print Form Definition dialog and the Print Report Definition dialog offer a Properties command button. The Properties button is used to designate the categories of properties that are printed. You can opt to print Other properties, Event properties, Data properties, or Format properties. Utilizing this feature allows you to hone in on the specific categories of properties that you are interested in.

FIGURE 35.15

You use the Print Form Definition dialog box to designate which aspects of a form's definition are documented.

For macros, you can choose whether you want to print macro Properties, Actions and Arguments, or Permissions by User and Group. For modules, you can choose to view Properties, Code, and Permissions by User and Group.

As you can see, the Database Documenter gives you great flexibility in the level of detail it provides. Of course, if you haven't filled in the properties of an object (for example, the description), it does you no good to ask the Documenter to print those properties.

Producing Documentation in Other Formats

After you produce the documentation and it appears in the Object Definition Print Preview window, you can output it to other formats. From the Print Preview window, choose File | Export. The Export Report dialog box appears, as shown in Figure 35.16. Notice that you can output the documentation to Microsoft Excel, HTML, Text Files, a Rich Text Format file, or a Snapshot format. Enter the filename, select the Save As type, and then click Save. If you select the AutoStart check box from the Export Report dialog box, the Documenter creates the file and then launches you into the appropriate application. The application launched depends on your Registry entries. If Microsoft's Internet Explorer (IE) is the application associated with the file extension HTML, for example, AutoStart launches IE with your Documenter output loaded when you output to an HTML file. Similarly, if you choose a Microsoft Excel file format and Excel is associated through the Registry with XLS file types, AutoStart launches Excel with the output loaded in Excel when the process is complete. The same holds true for the other file types—RTF and TXT and their respective Registry associations, which usually are Word and Notepad.

FIGURE 35.16

You use the Export Report dialog box to designate the type of file to which the object definition will be output.

WRITING CODE TO CREATE YOUR OWN DOCUMENTATION

Most of the time, the options provided by the Database Documenter are sufficient. At times, you won't like the format the Database Documenter selects—or, more important, you might want to document properties of the database objects not available through the user interface. In these situations, you can choose to enumerate the database objects using code and output them to a custom report format.

Using ADO, you can enumerate any of the objects in your database. Listing 35.1 shows an example.

LISTING 35.1 USING ADO TO ENUMERATE THE TABLE OBJECTS IN A DATABASE

```
Sub EnumerateTables()

    Dim conn As New Connection
    Dim adoCat As New ADOX.Catalog
    Dim adoTbl As New ADOX.Table
    Dim strSQL As String

    DoCmd.SetWarnings False
    Set conn = CurrentProject.Connection
    adoCat.ActiveConnection = conn

    For Each adoTbl In adoCat.tables
        If adoTbl.Type = "Table" Then
            strSQL = "INSERT INTO tblTableDoc" _
                & "(TableName, DateCreated, LastModified) " _
                & "Values (""" & adoTbl.Name & """, #" _
                & adoTbl.DateCreated & "#, #" _
                & adoTbl.DateModified & "#) "

            DoCmd.RunSQL strSQL
        End If
    Next adoTbl
    DoCmd.SetWarnings True
End Sub
```

The EnumerateTables routine, located in the basDocument module of CHAP35EX.MDB on your sample code CD-ROM, documents various information about the tables in the database. It uses the ADOX catalog and table objects and a For...Each loop to loop through all the table definitions in the database. For each table in the

35

database, it determines whether the table's type property is set to "Table", indicating that it is a standard table (as opposed to a system table or a query). It then executes a SQL statement, inserting all the requested information about the table definition into a table called tblTableDoc. This table then can be used as the foundation for a report. Of course, when you use appropriate For...Each loops and properties, along with the ADOX object model, *any* information about *any* of the objects in the database can be obtained using the same technique.

PRACTICAL EXAMPLES

Applying What You Learned to the Time and Billing Application

Practice using various options in the Database Documenter for the Time and Billing application. As you change the options for each object type, view the output differences. If you are particularly ambitious, try writing some code to enumerate the objects of the database.

SUMMARY

Documentation is a necessary part of the application development process; fortunately, Microsoft Access makes it very easy. This chapter covers the object Description properties Access provides, as well as the extremely powerful Database Documenter. The chapter also highlights how you can create your own documentation using data Access objects and custom reports. Using any combination of the techniques covered in the chapter, you can produce very complete documentation for all aspects of your application.

MAINTAINING YOUR APPLICATION

IN THIS CHAPTER

WHY THIS CHAPTER IS IMPORTANT

Although you don't need to do too much to maintain an Access database, you must know about an important technique that will help to ensure that your databases are maintained as effectively as possible. The technique you should be familiar with is compacting. *Compacting* a database means removing unused space from a database (MDB file). The compacting process, and the ways you can accomplish it, are covered in this chapter.

COMPACTING YOUR DATABASE

As you and the users of your application work with a database, the database grows in size. In order to maintain a high state of performance, Access defers the removal of discarded pages from the database until you explicitly compact the database file. This means that as you add data and other objects to the database and remove data and objects from the database, the disk space that was occupied by the deleted objects is not reclaimed. This results not only in a very large database (MDB) file, but it also ultimately means a degradation in performance as the physical file becomes fragmented on disk. Compacting a database accomplishes these tasks:

- Reclaims all space occupied by deleted data and database objects.

- Reorganizes the database file so that the pages of each table in the database are contiguous. This improves performance because, as the user works with the table, the data in the table is located contiguously on the disk.

- Resets counter fields so that the next value will be one more than the last *undeleted* counter value. If, while testing, you add many records that you delete just prior to placing the application in production, compacting the database resets all the counter values back to 1.

- Re-creates the table statistics used by the Jet Engine when queries are executed and marks all queries to be recompiled the next time they are run. These are two very important related benefits of the compacting process. If indexes have been added to a table or the volume of data in the table has been dramatically changed, the query won't execute efficiently. This is because the stored query plan Jet uses to execute the query is based on inaccurate information. When the database is compacted, all table statistics and the query plan for each query are updated to reflect the current state of the tables in the database.

TIP

It is a good idea to defragment the hard drive that a database is stored on before performing the compact process. The defragmentation process ensures that as much contiguous disk space as possible is available for the compacted database.

> **NOTE**
>
> In earlier versions of Access, the repair process was a separate utility from the compact process. With Access 2000, there is no longer a separate repair process. The compact and repair processes both occur when a database is compacted. When you open a database in need of repair, you are prompted to compact the database.

To compact a database, you can use one of four methods:

- Use commands provided in the user interface.
- Click an icon you set up for the user.
- Set up the database so that it is compacted whenever you close it.
- Use the `CompactDatabase` method.

Regardless of which method you select for the compact procedure, the following conditions must be true:

- The user performing the compact procedure must have the rights to open the database exclusively.
- The user performing the compact procedure must have Modify Design permission for all tables in the database.
- The database must be available to be opened for exclusive use. This means that no other users can be using the database.
- The drive or network share the database is located on cannot be read-only.
- The file attribute of the database cannot be set to read-only.
- Enough disk space must be available for both the original database and the compacted version of the database. This is true even if the database is compacted to a database by the same name.

> **CAUTION**
>
> It is a good idea to back up the database before attempting to compact it. It is possible for the compact process to do further damage to the database. Also, do not use the compact process as a substitute for carefully following backup procedures. The compact process is not always successful. Nothing is as foolproof as a fastidiously executed routine backup process.

> **NOTE**
>
> If, at any time, Access detects that a database is damaged, you are prompted to repair the database. This occurs when you attempt to open, compact, encrypt, or decrypt the damaged database. At other times, Access might not detect the damage. Instead, you might suspect that damage has occurred because the database behaves unpredictably. This is when you should first back up and then perform the compact process, using one of the methods covered in this chapter.

Using the User Interface

The Access user interface gives users a fairly straightforward interface to the compact operation. To compact the currently open database, choose Tools | Database Utilities | Compact and Repair Database. The current database then is closed, compacted, and reopened.

To compact a database other than the currently open database, follow these steps:

1. Close the open database.

2. Choose Tools | Database Utilities | Compact and Repair Database. The Database to Compact From dialog box appears, as shown in Figure 36.1.

FIGURE 36.1

The Database To Compact From dialog box.

3. Select the database you want to compact and click Compact. The Compact Database Into dialog box appears, as shown in Figure 36.2.

36

FIGURE 36.2
*The Compact
Database Into
dialog box.*

4. Select the name for the compacted database. This can be the same name as the original database name, or it can be a new name (if you are compacting a database to the same name, make sure that it is backed up). Click Save.

5. If you select the same name, you are prompted to replace the existing file. Click Yes.

Using a Shortcut

A very simple way to give users a way to compact a database is to create an icon that performs the compact process. This is accomplished using the /Compact command-line option. The /Compact command-line option compacts the database without ever opening it. The shortcut looks like this:

```
c:\MSOffice\Access\Msaccess.exe c:\Databases\TimeAndBilling.MDB /Compact
```

This syntax can be followed by a space and the name of a destination database if you do not want the current database to be overwritten by the compacted version. If you do not include a path for the destination database, it is placed in the My Documents folder by default. The shortcut can be created automatically for you using the Setup Wizard that ships with the Office 2000 Developer. This is covered in Chapter 39, "Distributing Your Application."

To create a shortcut yourself, follow these steps:

1. Open the folder where your application is installed.
2. Right-click the application (MDB) icon for your database.
3. Choose Create Shortcut.
4. Right-click the shortcut you just created.
5. Choose Properties.
6. Click the Shortcut tab.
7. Modify the shortcut to appear with the syntax shown in the previous example.

Whenever the Database Is Closed

Using the environmental setting Compact on Close, you can designate that specific databases are compacted whenever they are closed. A database is compacted upon close only if Access determines that the size will be reduced by at least 256KB. To set the Compact on Close environmental setting:

1. Open the database that you want to affect. Select Tools | Options.
2. Click the General tab of the Options dialog.
3. Click the Compact on Close check box.

> **NOTE**
>
> Although set in Tools | Options, the Compact on Close setting applies only to the database that is open when the option is selected. This allows you to selectively designate which databases are compacted when they are closed.

> **CAUTION**
>
> Remember that all the conditions that must be met for a database to be compacted apply when the database is designated to compact on close. For example, if other users are in the database when someone tries to close it, the user trying to close the database will receive an error.

Using Code

Using the `CompactDatabase` method, you can compact a database using code. The `CompactDatabase` method is performed on a member of the Microsoft Jet and Replication Objects (JRO), the `JetEngine` object. It receives a source connection string and a destination connection string as parameters. These connection strings are used to designate the source and destination databases, respectively. The `Source Connection` and `Destination Connection` parameters are also used for the following purposes:

- To change the locale of the database
- To encrypt or decrypt the database
- To convert the database from an older Jet version to a new version
- To specify the user ID and password

Maintaining Your Application

CHAPTER 36

1119

36

MAINTAINING
YOUR
APPLICATION

The `Locale Identifier` property of the `Destination Connection` parameter is used to determine the collating order in which the data in the compacted database will be sorted. This option is used when you are working with a database in which the data is stored in another language and you want the data to be collated in a particular language.

The `Jet OLEDB:Encrypt Database` property of the `Destination Connection` parameter is used to specify whether you want the compacted database to be encrypted. If you do not specify this property, the compacted database will have the same encryption status as the original source database.

The `Jet OLEDB:Engine Type` property of the `Source Connection` parameter is used to designate the version of the source database to open. The `Jet OLEDB:Engine Type` property of the `Destination Connection` parameter is used to designate the version of the new database that is created. If omitted, the version of the source and destination databases is the same.

Finally, the `User ID` and `Password` properties of the `Source Connection` parameter enable you to supply the name of the user and the user's password for a database that is password protected.

The following code, contained in the basUtils module of Chap36Ex.MDB, compacts and encrypts a database called Chap36Big.MDB:

```
Sub CompactDB()
    Dim je As New JRO.jetengine

    If Len(Dir("c:\my documents\Chap36Small.mdb")) Then
        Kill "c:\my documents\Chap36Small.mdb"
    End If

    je.CompactDatabase _
      SourceConnection:="Data Source=c:\my documents\Chap36Big.mdb", _
      DestConnection:="Data Source=c:\my documents\Chap36Small.mdb; " & _
      "Jet OLEDB:Encrypt Database=True"

End Sub
```

The compacted database will be called Chap36Small.MDB. During the compact process, the database is also encrypted.

In order for this code to execute successfully, remember that the Chap36Big database must be closed and the user running the code must have the right to open the database exclusively. Furthermore, the user must have Modify Design Permissions for all tables in the database. Finally, because the `CompactDatabase` method is performed on the JRO JetEngine object, you must include a reference to the Microsoft Jet and Replication Objects 2.1 Library. This library is not referenced by default when you create a new Access database. You must use Tools | References to reference the JRO object library.

SUMMARY

The compact process should be performed regularly—especially on databases containing your application data. The compact process provides major benefits in terms of both performance and conservation of disk space. The more activity that occurs on a database, the more frequently it should be compacted. Although the compact process should be considered an important part of the database maintenance process, remember that there is absolutely no substitute for proper backup techniques.

THE MICROSOFT OFFICE DEVELOPER

IN THIS CHAPTER

DISTRIBUTING YOUR APPLICATION: AN INTRODUCTION

Distribution of your applications is only one of the capabilities of MOD—but it is a very important one. Developers often design applications that will be distributed to many users. The most basic distribution option is to require each user to purchase a copy of Access and then simply provide each user with a copy of the database (MDB) files required for the application. The developer then can go to each user and configure the application appropriately.

Although distributing an application by copying it to each user's machine does not require much specialized knowledge on the part of the developer, it generally is not very practical. For one thing, it often is prohibitively expensive for each user of the application to own a copy of Access. Additionally, in many situations, the developer is distributing an application to users who are dispersed throughout the country or even the world. Some of these applications might include ActiveX controls, which might not be installed on users' computers.

Many Access applications are mass-marketed to hundreds or even thousands of users. It is very impractical to require such a user base to own Microsoft Access or to properly install the application (including the ActiveX controls) without a professional setup program. Finally, without Microsoft Office Developer (MOD), it is much more difficult for you as a developer to provide the user with the professional look and feel you want your application to have. For these reasons, most developers must purchase MOD and learn how to take advantage of what it offers.

LOOKING AT MOD

Microsoft Office Developer (MOD) is a version of Microsoft Office that includes all the components of Office Premium plus a rich set of developer tools and applications. MOD enables you to package and distribute professional-looking applications without requiring your users to purchase Access for each computer running the application, and to add extra functionality to your applications in the form of ActiveX controls and custom data reports. Additionally, MOD includes a set of tools that enhance the development environment (some of which had to be purchased separately in previous versions of Office). There are three major categories of MOD components:

- Office 2000 Developer Tools
- Developer Applications
- MSDN Help

Additionally, some miscellanous components don't explicitly appear on the MOD setup screens:

- Printed developer documentation and sample code
- A set of 32-bit ActiveX controls, some of them data-bound
- The Microsoft Development Engine (MSDE)
- Data Binding Manager and Data Environment Designer
- COM Add-in Designer and Visual Studio Templates
- Access Runtime

Developer Applications

The Developer Applications are (as the name implies) major applications or SDKs that let you manage your development work more efficiently or add extra functionality to your applications. Each application must be installed separately from the Developer Applications screen of MOD setup; none is installed by default.

Visual SourceSafe and Visual SourceSafe Integration

The Visual SourceSafe tool enables developers to share and secure source code. When used in a team development environment, Visual SourceSafe enables developers to check out and work on specific aspects of an application. As a bonus, Visual SourceSafe provides version control, including the capability to roll back to prior builds of an application. Visual SourceSafe and its rich functionality are fully integrated into the Access 2000 development environment. Visual SourceSafe is covered in detail in Chapter 38, "Managing Application Development with Visual SourceSafe."

HTML Help Workshop

The HTML Help Workshop significantly eases the pain associated with the process of building custom Help into your applications. A successor to the Windows Help Workshop included with previous editions, this version assists with the process of authoring Help in the new HTML format. The HTML Workshop includes a screen capture utility that facilitates the process of capturing screen shots.

Answer Wizard Builder

The Answer Wizard Builder (part of the Answer Wizard SDK) lets you create a custom Answer Wizard index that contains your custom Help topics, so your custom topics are displayed along with the standard Help topics in the Office Assistant. This builder is most suitable for use in add-ins you create.

Microsoft Agent SDK

The Microsoft Agent SDK lets you create custom animated characters (similar to the Office Assistant characters) to use in your own applications.

Developer Tools

The Developer Tools are installed as a package. Although you have the option of deselecting some of them during installation, they are all useful, so I would recommend installing the entire set. Before you can use these tools, you must set them up in the Add-in Manager, as described in the following, using the Code Librarian as an example:

1. Select Tools | Add-Ins | Add-In Manager. The Add-In Manager dialog box appears (see Figure 37.1).

FIGURE 37.1

Activating the VBA Code Librarian as an add-in.

2. Click to select Code Librarian in the list of Available Add-Ins.

3. Click Loaded/Unloaded to load the Code Librarian add-in.

4. If you want to load the Code Librarian each time you launch Access, click Load on Startup.

5. Click OK to exit the Add-In Manager dialog box.

To save time, you might want to activate all the Developer Tools you anticipate using at one time; otherwise, you will have to activate each one separately before using it.

Code Librarian

The VBA Code Librarian helps you create reusable code. It accomplishes this by providing a centralized database that teams of developers share—or just for your own personal use. The VBA Code Librarian ships with a large database of prewritten code, and you can add code of your own to help you create standardized applications. You can even add entire databases of your own code libraries.

Using the Code Librarian

After you have loaded the VBA Code Librarian, you are ready to use it. Follow these steps to use the Code Librarian:

1. Select Code Librarian from the Add-Ins menu. The Code Librarian launches as a separate application (see Figure 37.2).

FIGURE 37.2

The Code Librarian window.

2. To open a code library, click the Open tool on the toolbar or select Open from the File menu. The Open dialog box appears (see Figure 37.3).

FIGURE 37.3

The Open dialog box enables you to select the code library with which you want to work.

3. Select the library that you want to open and click Open. As shown in Figure 37.4, the code library opens and its contents are displayed in the Code Librarian window.

Working with Existing Functions in the Code Library

Follow these steps to view and use functions already included in the code library:

1. Select the desired code library from the list of code libraries that appear in the Code Library pane. The functions contained in the library appear in the right pane. In Figure 37.4, the Date/Time/Interval code library is selected.

FIGURE **37.4**

The Codelib.mdb code library ships with the MOD and contains a wealth of sample functions.

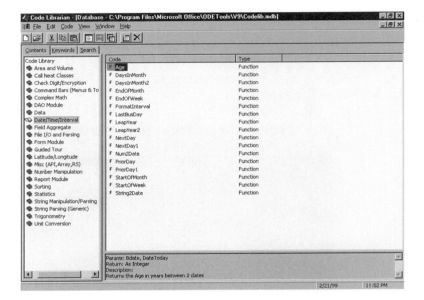

2. To view, copy, or edit a library function, click to select the function in the code pane, and then click the View Code tool on the toolbar. If you prefer, select Code|Modify, or double-click the function whose code you want to work with. A tabbed window appears. The first tab, the Code tab, shows you the code contained in the function. In Figure 37.5, the Age function is selected.

FIGURE **37.5**

The Code tab of the Code Librarian window shows you the code contained within the library function.

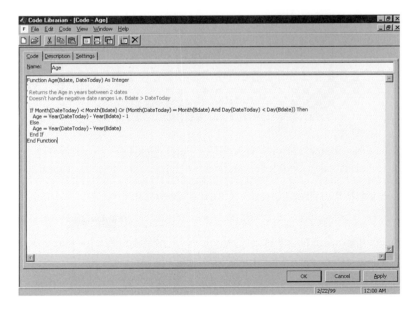

3. Modify the function's code if you want.

4. To insert the function's code into the active Access module, at the cursor position, click the Insert Code to Module toolbar tool. Alternatively, click Copy Code to Clipboard and then paste the code into your Access project where you want it.

5. Click the Description tab to view or modify information about the parameters, return value, and other descriptive information about the function. The Description tab appears in Figure 37.6.

FIGURE 37.6

The Description tab of the Code Librarian enables you to view and modify descriptive information about the function.

6. The Settings tab, pictured in Figure 37.7, enables you to categorize the functions that you place within the library. Details of using the Settings tab are covered in the section "Designating Settings for Your Library Functions," later in this chapter.

FIGURE 37.7

The Settings tab of the Code Librarian enables you to categorize and associate keywords with the select library function.

Creating New Code Libraries

In addition to working with existing code libraries, you will probably want to create new code libraries. Take the following steps to create a new code library:

1. Click the New button on the Code Librarian toolbar, or select New from the File menu. The New dialog appears.

2. Use the Look-In drop-down list to select a location for the library.

3. Type the name of the library in the File Name text box.

4. Click Open to create the library.

Adding Functions to a Code Library

So far, this chapter has discussed how to work with existing library functions. This section discusses how to create new library functions. To create a new library function, follow these steps:

1. Click the Add New Code tool on the toolbar, or select New from the Code menu. The Code tab of the Code Librarian is activated (see Figure 37.8).

FIGURE 37.8

The Code tab of the Code Librarian is used to add code to the new library function.

2. Enter a name for the function within the Name text box.

3. Add the code for the function in the large text box that appears under the Name text box. Click Apply to accept the function. A completed function appears in Figure 37.9.

4. Click the Description tab, and add any descriptive information to the library function (see Figure 37.10).

5. Click the Settings tab. Enter settings as described in the following section.

FIGURE 37.9

The function CSZ has been added as a library function.

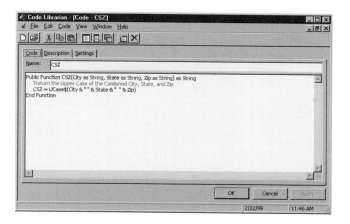

FIGURE 37.10

Use the Description tab of the Code Librarian to provide descriptive information for the function.

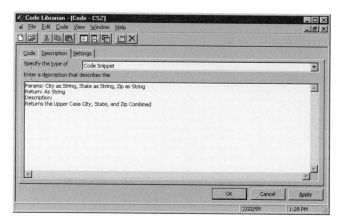

Designating Settings for Your Library Functions

To help organize the functions in your library, you can categorize them and associate keywords with them. To add your library functions to a category, follow these steps:

1. Activate the function you want to work with as covered in the section of the chapter titled "Working with Existing Functions in the Code Library."

2. Click to select the Settings tab.

3. Click Add to create a new category. The Add Category dialog box appears (see Figure 37.11).

FIGURE 37.11

Use the Add Category dialog to associate a library function with an existing category.

4. Click New. The Code Librarian-New Categories dialog appears (see Figure 37.12).

FIGURE 37.12

The New Categories dialog is used to add new categories to your library.

5. Enter the name for the new category.

6. Click Add to add the category.

7. Enter any additional categories, clicking Add for each one.

8. When you're finished adding new categories, click Close. You are returned to the Add Category dialog.

9. Select the category within which you want to place the library function. Click Add.

10. Select any additional categories within which you want to place the library function, clicking Add for each category.

11. Click Close when you are finished. The function is added to the selected categories.

You can also associate keywords with your library functions. To accomplish this, follow these steps:

1. Activate the function you want to work with as covered in the section of the chapter titled "Working with Existing Functions in the Code Library."

2. Click to select the Settings tab.

3. Click Add to create a new keyword. The Add Keyword dialog box appears (see Figure 37.13).

FIGURE 37.13

Use the Add Keyword dialog box to add new keywords and associate them with your library functions.

37

4. Enter the name for the new keyword.

5. Click New to add the keyword.

6. Type the names of any additional keywords, clicking New for each one.

7. Select the category within which you want to place the library function. Click Add.

8. Select any additional keywords with which you want to associate the library function, clicking Add for each keyword.

9. Click Close when you are finished. The selected keywords are associated with the function.

VBA Code Commenter

The VBA Code Commenter enables you to quickly and easily add standardized comments to your programming code. To accomplish this, it provides customizable templates that you apply to your procedures. To use the VBA Code Commenter, you must first activate it as an add-in using the Add-In Manager as you did for the Code Librarian.

After you have loaded the VBA Code Commenter, you are ready to use it.

1. Select VBA Code Commenter from the Add-Ins menu. The VBA Code Commenter dialog box appears (see Figure 37.14).

FIGURE 37.14

The VBA Code Commenter dialog box enables you to designate the options that are used when comments are inserted into your code.

2. Click to designate whether you want to add comments to the current procedure, to all procedures in the current module, or to all procedures in the current project.
3. Enter the name of the file containing the Code Header template.
4. Provide the name and initials of the author.
5. Click Show Template to view the template, if you want. The Show Template dialog appears (see Figure 37.15). Click Close when you're finished viewing the template.

FIGURE 37.15

The Show Template dialog box enables you to preview the template to be used to comment your code.

6. Click OK when you are ready to generate the comments. An example of comments entered by the VBA Code Commenter appears in Figure 37.16. Remember that you can customize the Code Header template to modify the generated comments to your specific needs.

FIGURE 37.16

Comments inserted into your code vary depending on the template used.

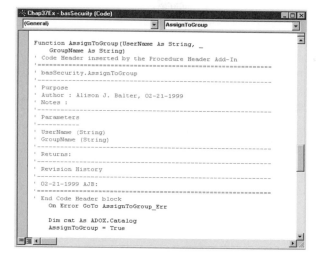

VBA Error Handler

The VBA Error Handler automates the process of adding standardized error-handling code to your applications. Using this tool, you can add error-handling code at the module, procedure, and project levels. First activate the VBA Error Handler, if necessary, using the Add-In Manager. To use it, follow these steps:

1. Select VBA Error Handler from the Add-Ins menu. The VBA Error Handler dialog appears (see Figure 37.17).

FIGURE 37.17

The VBA Error Handler dialog enables you to designate the options that are used when error handling is inserted into your code.

2. Click to designate whether you want to add error handling to the current procedure, to all procedures in the current module, or to all procedures in the current project.

3. Enter the name of the file that contains the Error Handling template.

4. Designate whether you want to update existing error handlers with the template.

5. Provide the name and initials of the author.

6. Click Show Template to view the template, if you want. The Show Template dialog appears (see Figure 37.18). Click Close when you're finished viewing the template.

FIGURE 37.18

The Show Template dialog enables you to preview the template to be used to add error handling to your code.

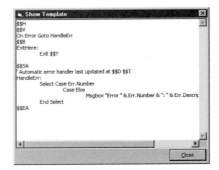

7. Click OK when you are ready to generate the error-handling code. An example of error handling created by the VBA Error Handler appears in Figure 37.19. Remember that you can customize the Error Handling template to modify the generated error handling to your specific needs.

FIGURE 37.19

Error handling inserted into your code varies depending on the template used.

VBA String Editor

The VBA String Editor enables you to quickly and accurately build strings of text and variables for expressions of various kinds, including SQL statements and scripts. After you create them, you can easily embed these strings in your VBA code. To use the VBA String Editor, you must first activate it as an add-in using the technique described for the Code Librarian. After you have loaded the VBA String Editor, you are ready to use it. To use it, select String Editor from the Add-Ins menu. The VBA String Editor dialog appears (see Figure 37.20).

FIGURE 37.20

The VBA String Editor helps you construct strings of text and variables for use in code.

The String Editor automatically puts quotation marks, spaces, carriage return constants, and other syntactical elements into strings, such as the strings displayed in message boxes or strings printed in the Immediate window by `Debug.Print` statements. Instead of worrying about getting the quotes, spaces, and constants just right, just type the whole expression, omitting the syntactical elements, mark the variables with a toolbar button, and paste the expression into your code. All the parsing is done automatically, even inserting the vbCrLf carriage return and line feed constant where you broke the line of text.

For example, if you type the following line and mark the variables using the toolbar button

```
strFirstName strLastName lived at strStreetAddress on dteOrderDate
```

the expression is transformed into

```
strFirstName & " " & strLastName & " lived at " & strStreetAddress & _
" on " & dteOrderDate
```

Multi-Code Import/Export

To use the Multi-Code Import/Export feature, you must first activate it as an add-in using the technique described for the Code Librarian. Once installed, this feature lets you select multiple items to import or export from a project in a single pass, rather than process each item separately. To export several objects, select Multi-Code Export from the Add-Ins menu. The Multi-Code Export window opens, as shown in Figure 37.21.

Click the Export button to export the selected objects to files; after they are exported you will get a confirmation dialog. You can export standard or class modules to .BAS or .CLS files, UserForms to .FRM files, and designers (data environments and data reports) to .DSR files.

Importing multiple objects into a project works in a similar way. Select Multi-Code Import from the Add-Ins menu. A Multi-Code Import dialog opens. Click its Browse button to open a Select Files to Import dialog box in which you can select multiple files to import into your project, as shown in Figure 37.22.

FIGURE 37.21

Exporting several objects from a project using the Multi-Code Export dialog box.

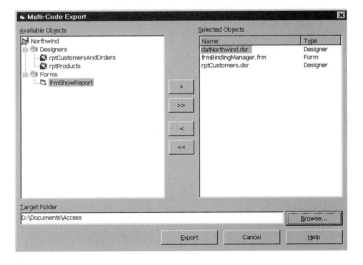

FIGURE 37.22

Importing several objects into a project using the Multi-Code Import dialog.

As you can see, the Multi-Code Import/Export utilities aren't restricted to code alone. Using these tools, you can save UserForms and data reports as files that can be transferred to another computer (or another developer) and imported into other VBA projects.

VBA Package and Deployment Wizard

The Package and Deployment Wizard enables you to easily create distribution disks containing all the files necessary to run your application. The Package and Deployment Wizard creates a very professional-looking setup program that your users will run when they want to install your application. Using the Package and Deployment Wizard, you can customize what is included with your application. However, it omits some of the Access-specific functionality that was available in the Access 97 Setup Wizard, and lacks functionality for dealing with installations involving other Office applications. The Package and Deployment Wizard is covered in detail in Chapter 39, "Distributing Your Application."

VBA WinAPI Viewer

The WinAPI Viewer facilitates the process of including the `Declare` statements, `Type` declarations, and `Constant` declarations required for you to use DLL functions in your applications. MOD ships with several files that contain API declarations, in both database and text format. When these files are loaded into the WinAPI Viewer, they enable you to select `Declare` statements, `Type` declarations, and `Constant` declarations and then copy them into your modules with the click of a mouse. This time-saving tool is discussed in detail in Chapter 27, "Exploiting the Power of the Windows API."

Miscellaneous MOD Components

The components described in the following sections aren't listed by name in MOD Setup, but they include some of the most significant new features of MOD. The data management components in particular offer substantial new functionality. Runtime lets you distribute your applications to users who don't have Access on their computers, and the MSDE provides better connectivity to SQL Server 7.0.

The Microsoft Data Engine

The Microsoft Data Engine (MSDE) is a database engine (an alternative to the Jet Engine) that provides 100 percent code compatibility with SQL Server 7.0. It is optimized for five users and has a 2GB database size limit. You might think of MSDE as an intermediate stage between an Access database and full SQL Server 7.0. You can distribute the MSDE to your users royalty free. Using the MSDE, you can easily develop scaleable database applications so that the application you build today with the MSDE can be moved to an enterprisewide client/server environment when the scope of the application increases.

Data Tools and Designers

The data tools described in the following sections are brand new tools for Office that greatly enhance your ability to display Access data on UserForms in various Office applications. The Data Environment Designer, data reports, data-bound ActiveX controls (including the ADO Data Control), and the Data Binding Manager can be used together to present Access or other data in a read-only format on Office UserForms to add extra functionality to Office applications you create.

The MOD designers are tools used to work with data sources and prepare reports using the data. To use them, you must activate them because by default, they are not activated. To do this, open the VBE window, select File I Insert, and then select Components. The Components dialog opens. Click its Designers tab and check the designers you want to use. When you close this dialog box you will see several new selections on the Insert menu in a new project: Addin Class, Data Report, and Data Environment.

Data Environment Designer

The Data Environment Designer lets you easily create connections to data sources and make linked commands under the connections (commands correspond to recordsets) using a graphical environment. To use this designer, follow these steps:

1. Select New Project from the File menu in the VBE window.

2. Click the Empty Project icon to create a new project, as shown in Figure 37.23.

FIGURE 37.23

Creating a new project.

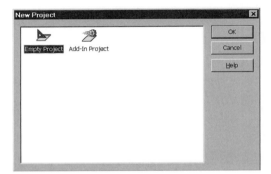

3. With the new project highlighted, select Data Environment from the Insert menu. You will see a new Connection object called Connection1. Name it `conNorthwind` using the Name property in its properties sheet (see Figure 37.24).

FIGURE 37.24

Creating a new data environment.

4. Right-click the connection and select Properties.

5. On the properties sheet's Provider tab, select the Microsoft Jet 4.0 OLE DB Provider (see Figure 37.25).

FIGURE 37.25

Selecting the Jet 4.0 OLE DB Provider.

6. On the Connection tab, select a database (say, the Northwind sample database) from a standard File Open dialog. Figure 37.26 shows the Northwind database selected as the data source for the data environment.

FIGURE 37.26

Selecting the Northwind database as the report's data source.

7. Click OK to close the dialog (the advanced options generally can be left at the default settings).

8. With the connection highlighted, click the Add Command button on the toolbar.

9. Open the command's properties sheet.

10. A new command is created, called Command1; rename it comProducts (see Figure 37.27).

FIGURE 37.27

Creating a new command for the data report.

11. On the General tab, select Table as the database object.

12. Select the Products table from the Object Name drop-down list.

13. Click OK to close the dialog.

After you have set up your connection string, you can drag it to a data report (see the next section). This designer is a great help in setting up connection strings, sparing the developer the pain of constructing them manually using an extremely cryptic syntax.

The Data Report Designer produces a report laid out much like an Access report, with Header, Footer, and Detail sections. To create a report, follow these steps:

1. Select Data Report from the Insert menu in a project (for example, the one you just created).

2. A new report opens, with a DataReport control separated into sections like an Access report, as shown in Figure 37.28. Name the report rptProducts.

3. Drag the previously created comProducts command to the report's Detail section. Figure 37.29 shows the fields in the command on the report.

FIGURE 37.28

The newly created data report.

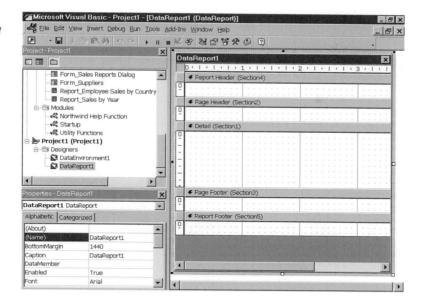

FIGURE 37.29

Fields from the Northwind Products table on the data report.

4. Set the report's Data Member property to the name of the command. This property is not available in the properties sheet in MOD report designers, so instead of setting the property in the interface, open the report's code module and enter the following procedure:

```
Private Sub DataReport_Initialize()
    Set rptProducts.DataSource = datNorthwind
    rptProducts.DataMember = "comProducts"
End Sub
```

5. Switch to the Immediate window, and type the following line of code (or place it on the Click event of a command button on a UserForm):

```
rptProducts.Show
```

6. The report displays in a small, non-resizable window, as shown in Figure 37.30.

FIGURE 37.30

A data report displaying data from the Northwind Products table.

Data reports can be published to the Web or printed, previewed, or exported to an HTML or text file. They don't have as many design tools as Access reports, and they lack even a single level of Undo. However, they are useful if your reporting needs aren't too complicated.

ActiveX Controls

MOD includes a set of ActiveX controls (over and above those provided with Office Premium), many of which (unlike earlier versions) are now capable of binding to data. That is, they can be assigned a data source and automatically display data from the source, without complicated programming. Two of the most useful data-bound ActiveX controls are the Hierarchical FlexGrid control, which enables you to easily represent hierarchical data; and the Data Repeater control, which enables you to easily repeat ActiveX controls so you can create a scrollable set of records.

The MOD controls are listed in Table 37.1. The data-bound ones are indicated by an asterisk.

TABLE 37.1 MOD ACTIVEX CONTROLS

Control Name	Usage
*ADO Data Control	Binds to data in a table or other data source; used to supply data to other controls.
Animation	Displays silent audio/video interleaved (AVI) clips.
Common Dialog	Displays one of several Windows dialogs, such as the File Open and Colors dialogs.
Chart Control	Displays data in a chart format, similar to an Excel chart.
CoolBar	Creates user-configurable Internet Explorer-style toolbars.
*Data Report	Used with the Data Report Designer to place fields of data on a report.
*DataCombo	A data-bound combo box.
*DataGrid	A data-bound data sheet.
*DataList	A data-bound list box.
DateTimePicker	Displays a pop-up calendar and saves the selected date to a field.
FlatScrollbar	Works like the Windows scrollbar, with several style choices.
*Hierarchical Flexgrid	Displays data from linked tables, similar to the new sub-datasheet feature in Access.
ImageCombo	Similar to a combo box, except that you can include images with the list items.
ImageList	Stores a list of images that can be displayed in other controls, such as the TreeView control.
Internet Transfer	Lets you connect to Web sites and FTP sites.
ListView	Displays data as ListItem objects, which can have an associated icon. Can be used to display an expanded view of a TreeView control node.
MonthView	Displays a fixed-size calendar showing one or more months at a time. Users can select a single date or a range of dates.
ProgressBar	Graphically represents the progress of a transaction.

continues

TABLE 37.1   CONTINUED

Control Name	Usage
Rich Textbox	Displays Rich Text with color, emphasis, and different fonts.
Slider	A bar with a thumb control (similar to a Windows scrollbar). The user moves the thumb to adjust a value.
StatusBar	Displays information about the status of various application components.
SysInfo	Detects system events such as desktop resizing or resolution changes. Also can display operating system or version information.
Tabbed Dialog	Presents several pages of information with tabs for selecting a page.
TabStrip	A strip of tabs used to define multiple pages for a window or dialog.
ToolBar	Contains a collection of buttons used to create a toolbar for an application.
TreeView	Displays data in a hierarchical tree, like the Windows Explorer.
UpDown	Increments or decrements a number (this control is used in many of the built-in Windows and Office dialogs).
Winsock	Lets you connect to a remote computer using either the UDP or TCP protocol.

These controls help you build highly professional applications with minimal effort. As an example, the following steps walk you through creating a data-bound DataGrid control on a UserForm that could be used in any Office application; these steps use Word.

1. Open the Word VBE window and create a new UserForm in the VBE window.

2. Right-click the Control toolbox and open the Additional Controls dialog. Select the Microsoft ADO data control, as shown in Figure 37.31.

3. Place an ADO data control on the form, as shown in Figure 37.32. Name it ocxADO.

4. Double-click the (Custom) selection in the control's properties sheet to open the control's special properties sheet (see Figure 37.33).

Figure 37.31

Adding the ADO data control to the Control toolbox.

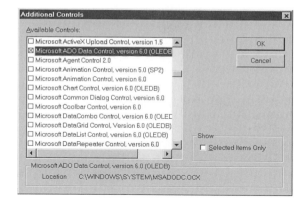

Figure 37.32

Inserting an ADO data control onto a UserForm.

Figure 37.33

The Property Pages dialog of an ADO control.

5. Select the Use Connection String option, and click the Build button next to it to open the Data Link Properties dialog.

6. In the properties sheet's Provider tab, select the Microsoft Jet 4.0 OLE DB Provider, as shown in Figure 37.34.

FIGURE 37.34

Selecting the Jet 4.0 provider in an ADO control's Data Link Properties dialog.

7. On the Connection tab, select the Northwind sample database from a standard File Open dialog.

8. Click OK to close this dialog. Back on the properties sheet's General page, you will see the connection string for the new connection, as shown in Figure 37.35.

FIGURE 37.35

The connection string for the data source.

9. On the RecordSource page, select the adCmdTable command type.

10. From the Table or Stored Procedure Name drop-down list, select the table you want to use as a record source, as shown in Figure 37.36.

FIGURE 37.36

Selecting the Northwind Employees table to use as a record source for the data report.

11. Click OK to close the dialog (the advanced options generally can be left at the default settings).

12. Set the control's Visible property to False (the VCR buttons are not functional in the VBA interface for this control).

13. Place a Microsoft DataGrid control on the form, using the same technique as for the ADO control (refer to step 2).

14. Double-click the form to open its code module, and select its Initialize event.

15. Enter the following line of code for the Initialize event (where ocxFlexGrid is the name of the DataGrid control, and ocxADO is the name of the ADO data control):

```
Private Sub UserForm_Initialize()
    Set ocxFlexGrid.DataSource = ocxADO
End Sub
```

16. Click the Run button to run the form; the DataGrid displays data from the selected Northwind table, as shown in Figure 37.37.

ActiveX custom controls are covered in detail in Chapter 25, "Using ActiveX Controls."

FIGURE 37.37

Data from a Northwind table displayed in a DataGrid control on a Word UserForm.

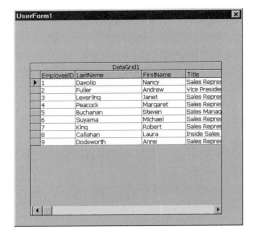

COM Add-In Designer and Visual Studio Templates

The COM Add-In Designer enables you to create standalone COM DLLs. (A COM add-in is a DLL registered so that it can be loaded by Office 2000 applications.) When they're created, these DLLs are used from within the Visual Basic for Applications development environment, where they augment the functionality of the standard development environment. COM add-ins (unlike Access, Word, or Excel add-ins) are available to all Office applications, not just to one. COM add-ins can be built in VB 5.0 or higher, Office 2000 VBA, C++, or J++. More information on building COM add-ins can be obtained at `http://msdn.microsoft.com/developer/`.

Access Runtime

The royalty-free runtime license provided with MOD enables your users to take advantage of your application and all it provides without owning their own copy of Access. When running your application with the Access runtime version, your users cannot directly create new database objects. Furthermore, they do not have access to the Database window, built-in toolbars, numerous menu items, and several other features that are part of the full Access product. In many situations, you don't want the user to have access to all these features. Instead, you want to provide your users with a very complete, fully integrated application that only you will be responsible for modifying. Furthermore, you want to provide all this to your users without requiring them to purchase Access for every computer running your application. The MOD, with its royalty-free runtime license, enables you to do exactly that.

Replication Manager

The *Replication Manager* tool enables you to manage replication in your custom application. This highly powerful, very sophisticated tool contains a runtime version that can be distributed with your applications. The Replication Manager is covered in detail in Chapter 23, "Replication Made Easy."

Printed Developer Documentation and Sample Code

To many people's surprise, Access does not include a printed language reference or an object model guide as standard equipment. Although such documentation is available online, many developers prefer to view their documentation in print. Both the *Office Programmer's Guide* and the *Microsoft Office Object Model Guide* are included as hard copy with the MOD.

37

THE MICROSOFT
OFFICE
DEVELOPER

PRACTICAL EXAMPLES

Distributing the Time and Billing Application

 The completed Time and Billing application, found on your sample code CD-ROM as CHAP37.MDB, has been modified to include comments and standard error handling. The comments were added using the VBA Code Commenter, and the standard error handling was added using the VBA Error Handler. In Chapter 39, "Distributing Your Application," custom toolbars and menu bars will be added to the application's forms and reports. Startup options will be set and the application will be fully tested under the runtime version of the product. All that is left is to properly secure the application to meet the specific needs of your organization and to deploy the application.

SUMMARY

Microsoft Office Developer contains a host of valuable tools. Some of these tools, such as the Access Runtime, the Replication Manager, and ActiveX controls provide runtime functionality. Others, such as Visual SourceSafe, the VBA Code Librarian and the VBA Code Commenter, assist with the development process. In this chapter, you learned the role of each tool in Microsoft Office Developer. After reading the chapter, you should be comfortable using the add-in tools available within the development environment.

MANAGING APPLICATION DEVELOPMENT WITH VISUAL SOURCESAFE

IN THIS CHAPTER

WHY THIS CHAPTER IS IMPORTANT

Visual SourceSafe is a tool you can use to manage the development of an Access application being worked on by a team of developers. After a database has been placed under SourceSafe control, each object must be checked out before it's modified. After the changes to the object have been made, the object is checked in so that other developers can see the changes. At any time, you can get the following information about the objects in the database:

- Which objects are checked out
- A history of everything that has happened to an object
- The differences between two versions of an object

Using Visual SourceSafe, you can easily revert an object to a previous version or merge different versions of an object. Visual SourceSafe is not only a tool for teams of developers, but also for an individual developer who wants to keep every version of each object in an application. It's a phenomenal tool that helps make Access a serious developer environment.

HOW DO I INSTALL VISUAL SOURCESAFE?

Visual SourceSafe can be used only with the Microsoft Office 97 Developer Edition of Access and Microsoft Office 2000 Developer. It is included with Microsoft Office 2000 Developer as one of the developer applications. It's also included as part of the Enterprise edition of Visual Basic, or it can be bought as a standalone product. In fact, Visual SourceSafe isn't the only source-code control product that can be used with Office 2000 Developer. Instead, Office Developer supplies a software source code control component that can integrate various source-code control products into Access. To integrate Visual SourceSafe or another version control product into Access, you need to install both the MOD Developer Tools (in particular, the Developer Add-ins and ActiveX Controls component) and the client part of your version control product.

To install Visual SourceSafe from Office 2000 Developer, select Visual SourceSafe 6.0 from the Developer Applications screen of the Setup program, and click the Install button. Follow the onscreen instructions to install VSS, selecting one of these three installation options:

- Shared database server
- Custom
- Stand-alone

In addition to installing VSS from Office 2000 Developer or Visual Basic, Enterprise Edition, you also need the Source Code Control integration that is part of the Office 2000 Developer Tools selection. If you installed the entire set of Developer Tools when installing Office 2000

Developer, you have this feature; otherwise, run Office 2000 Developer setup again, and on the Developer Tools setup screen, select the Developer Addins and ActiveX Controls selection (this selection includes VSS integration). Click Continue and follow the onscreen instructions to install this feature. This sets up the Visual SourceSafe client. After you install Visual SourceSafe and the VSS integration tool, you'll see a SourceSafe entry under the Tools menu, displaying the following options:

- Create Database from SourceSafe Project
- Add Database to SourceSafe
- Run SourceSafe
- Options

The Create Database from SourceSafe Project menu item allows you to create a local database from an existing Visual SourceSafe project. The Add Database to SourceSafe option creates a Visual SourceSafe project from the open database. The Run SourceSafe option runs the Visual SourceSafe Explorer. Finally, the Options menu item lets you configure different Visual SourceSafe options. Each of these menu items is covered in the following sections.

USING VISUAL SOURCESAFE: AN OVERVIEW

When you want to place a database under SourceSafe control, you create it from a SourceSafe project; this database becomes the master copy. Each developer works on a local copy of the database, and no objects in the database can be modified until they're checked out. When a developer checks out an object, it's copied from Visual SourceSafe into the local database. No other developers see changes made to the object until it's checked back in. When the developer checks the object back in, it's copied from the local database to the Visual SourceSafe project.

With the exception of modules, only one person can check out an object at a time. This means that two people can't make changes to any other types of objects under SourceSafe control simultaneously. Multiple developers, however, can check out modules. When you check a module back in, your changes are merged with any changes other developers have made since you checked the module out.

THE LOGISTICS OF MANAGING A PROJECT WITH VISUAL SOURCESAFE

The first step you must take when you decide to place an object under SourceSafe control is to add the host database to SourceSafe. You can then begin to check objects in and out and to use the product's features. The following sections explain in more detail how to work with Visual SourceSafe.

Adding a Database to Visual SourceSafe

When you're ready to place an application under SourceSafe control, take the following steps:

1. If you are not already set up as a VSS user, run the Visual SourceSafe 6.0 Admin selection from the Microsoft Visual SourceSafe program group, and follow the onscreen instructions to add yourself as a user.

2. Choose Tools | SourceSafe | Add Database to SourceSafe.

3. A dialog box opens, indicating that Visual SourceSafe must close the database before it can be placed under SourceSafe control. (See Figure 38.1.) Click Yes to continue.

FIGURE 38.1

This dialog box notifies you that the database must be closed for it to be added to SourceSafe control.

4. The Visual SourceSafe Login appears (See Figure 38.2.) Enter your login information for the user you just created, and click OK.

FIGURE 38.2

The Login dialog requires that you successfully log in before placing a database under SourceSafe control.

5. After successfully logging on, the Add to SourceSafe Project dialog box appears. (See Figure 38.3.) The name of the database is selected as the name for the SourceSafe Project.

FIGURE 38.3

Use the Add to SourceSafe Project dialog box to select a project name.

6. Click OK to accept the project name. You're then prompted to create the project. (See Figure 38.4.)

FIGURE 38.4

The dialog box asking whether you want to create the project.

7. Click Yes to create the project; this opens the Add Objects to SourceSafe dialog box. (See Figure 38.5.) Here you can determine which database objects you want to place under SourceSafe control. By default, each object in the database is selected. You can deselect specific objects or deselect all objects; then select just the objects you want. When you're finished, click OK.

FIGURE 38.5

The Add Objects to SourceSafe dialog box lets you specify which objects you want to add to SourceSafe control.

8. SourceSafe notifies you as it exports each object to SourceSafe. (See Figure 38.6.) When it's done, the warning shown in Figure 38.7 tells you that you don't have the Data and Misc. objects checked out. This means that any changes you make to local tables are lost the next time you check out or get the latest version of these objects. You can prevent this by always checking the Other: Data and Misc. Objects selection when adding objects to a VSS project.

FIGURE 38.6

Including an object in Visual SourceSafe by exporting from the host database.

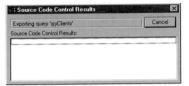

FIGURE 38.7

This warning message tells you that you don't have the Data and Misc. objects checked out.

9. Click OK to complete the process. Looking at the Database window, you should see that each object has a lock that remains until you have checked out an object. (See Figure 38.8.)

FIGURE 38.8

The Database window of a database under SourceSafe control with all objects locked.

After you add a database to SourceSafe control, the SourceSafe submenu expands to include many options needed to manage a SourceSafe project. (See Figure 38.9.) These options are covered throughout the remainder of this chapter.

FIGURE 38.9

The Visual SourceSafe menu gives you several options for managing a Visual SourceSafe Project.

38

VISUAL
SOURCESAFE

Understanding the Objects Placed Under SourceSafe Control

Each query, form, report, macro, and module is stored as a separate text file in Visual SourceSafe. When you add an object to SourceSafe control, it's exported to a text file and copied into the Visual SourceSafe project. When you check out an object, it's copied to a temporary location on your machine and then imported into the Access database on your machine as a query, form, report, macro, or module.

All other database objects (tables, relationships, command bars, database properties, startup properties, import/export specs, VBA project references, the VBA project name, and conditional compilation arguments) are stored in one Access MDB file that Visual SourceSafe treats as a binary file. These objects can't be checked out individually.

As mentioned, all queries, forms, reports, macros, and modules are stored as text files and the rest of the objects are stored in one binary file. Table 38.1 shows each object type and the extension the object is stored with when it gets added to Visual SourceSafe.

TABLE 38.1   FILE EXTENSIONS FOR VISUAL SOURCESAFE FILES

Object	Extension
Queries	ACQ
Forms	ACF
Reports	ACR
Macros	ACS
Modules	ACM
Tables, relationships, and miscellaneous objects	ACB

Creating a Database from a SourceSafe Project

The developer who adds a database to SourceSafe can continue to work on the original copy. Other developers who want to work on the application must create their own local copies of the database. To do that, follow these steps:

1. Add each developer as a VSS user, using the Visual SourceSafe 6.0 Admin selection in the Microsoft Visual SourceSafe program group.

2. Choose Tools | SourceSafe | Create Database from SourceSafe Project from the menu to open the Create Local Project from SourceSafe dialog box. (See Figure 38.10.)

FIGURE 38.10

In the Create Local Project from SourceSafe dialog box, you select a project used to create a local database copy.

3. Log on to VSS (if necessary).

4. Select a project and click OK. You're prompted for a folder where your local copy of the database will be placed.

5. Select an existing folder and click OK; this returns you to the SourceSafe project dialog box.

6. Click OK to create the database. During the process, the Source Code Control Results window keeps you apprised of the progress (See Figure 38.11.) When Access is done creating the local objects, the Source Code Control Results window says Completed.

FIGURE 38.11

The Source Code Control Results window shows you the status of the database creating process.

The Visual SourceSafe Toolbar

The VSS toolbar shown in Figure 38.12 gives you a selection of buttons that give you one-click access to various VSS features. These buttons let you add objects to SourceSafe, get the latest version of an object, check objects in and out, share objects, show the History or Differences window, and run SourceSafe with the same functionality as using the menu commands, as described in the following sections.

FIGURE 38.12

The Visual SourceSafe toolbar in floating mode.

Checking In and Checking Out Database Objects

After a database has been added to Visual SourceSafe, you can't modify any of the objects you designated as controlled by SourceSafe without first checking them out. You check out the

38

VISUAL
SOURCESAFE

objects you want to modify, make changes to them, and check them back in when you're finished. The easiest way to check out a single object is to right-click it and select Check Out. If
you want to check out multiple objects, click Check Out on the VSS toolbar or choose
Tools | SourceSafe | Check Out; this opens the Check Out Object(s) from SourceSafe dialog
box. (See Figure 38.13.) Here you can select all the objects you want to check out. When you
return to the Database window, the objects you checked out have a check mark next to them.
(See Figure 38.14.)

FIGURE 38.13

*Use the Check
Out Objects from
SourceSafe dialog
box to designate
which database
objects you want
to check out.*

FIGURE 38.14

*The Database
window adds an
icon to show
which objects in a
database have
been checked out.*

If you try to modify the design of an object that is not controlled by Visual SourceSafe, you
don't get any error messages, so everything proceeds as usual. On the other hand, if you try to
modify the design of an object that is controlled by Visual SourceSafe but hasn't been checked
out, the error message in Figure 38.15 appears. As you can see, you're given the choice of
checking out the object, opening the object as read-only and not checking it out, or canceling.

FIGURE 38.15

The error message you see when you try to modify the design of an object that hasn't been checked out.

You can check in one object or check in several objects simultaneously. To check in objects, right-click any object that's checked out and select Check In (or select the object and click Check In on the VSS toolbar); this opens the Check In Objects to SourceSafe dialog box. (See Figure 38.16.) Click to select any objects you want to check in, then click OK. The objects you checked in once again appear in the Database window with a padlock icon, indicating that they can't be modified without being checked out.

FIGURE 38.16

Use the Check In Objects to SourceSafe dialog box to designate which checked-out objects you want to check in.

38

VISUAL
SOURCESAFE

TIP

If you check out an object and realize that you made a mistake, you can right-click the object and choose Undo Check Out to quickly check it back in.

Getting the Latest Version

While you're working on the database, the objects in your local copy might not be updated with changes other users have made to the objects. To see these changes, you must get the object's latest version from the SourceSafe project. To do this with one object, right-click the object and select Get Latest Version or select the object and click Get Latest Version on the VSS toolbar; for multiple objects, choose Tools | SourceSafe | Get Latest Version. The Get Objects from SourceSafe dialog box appears, allowing you to select the objects you want.

Adding Objects to Visual SourceSafe

Depending on how you have configured Visual SourceSafe, you might be prompted to add new objects to SourceSafe control. If you add objects to your database and don't place them under SourceSafe control, you can always opt to add them later. To do this, choose Tools | SourceSafe | Add Object(s) to SourceSafe or click Add Objects to SourceSafe on the VSS toolbar. The Add Objects to SourceSafe dialog box opens, showing you all the objects in your local database that haven't been added to SourceSafe control.

> **TIP**
>
> To control whether new objects are automatically placed under SourceSafe control, choose Tools | SourceSafe | Options. Pick the option you want from the Add Objects to Source Control when Adding Them to Microsoft Access drop-down list.

Refreshing an Object's Status

When looking at the Database window, you can't be sure that the icons indicating an object's status accurately reflect the object's current state. To refresh the icons in the Database window, choose Tools | SourceSafe | Refresh Object Status.

LEVERAGING THE POWER OF VISUAL SOURCESAFE

Not only does Visual SourceSafe help to manage the process of several developers working on an application simultaneously, but it also helps you manage versions of your application. It does this by showing you the differences between the checked-out version of an object and the version stored in the Visual SourceSafe project, by allowing you to view an object's history, and by letting you revert to an object's previous version.

Showing Differences Between Modules

One of the more powerful aspects of Visual SourceSafe is its ability to show the differences between the checked-out version of an object and the version in the SourceSafe project. These differences show you what you've done since you checked the object out. To view the differences, choose Tools | SourceSafe | Show Differences. First the Difference Options dialog opens, where you can select display options, and then the Differences window opens, which lets you easily jump from difference to difference within the object. Deleted lines are blue, changed lines are red, and added lines are green.

Showing an Object's History

Often, it helps to view everything that's transpired in an object; for example, you might want to see who checked out each object and when. To see an object's history, first click to select the object; then choose Tools | SourceSafe | Show History. First you get a History Options dialog (see Figure 38.17), where you enter From, To, and User information. The From and To boxes accept dates, versions, or labels, and the User box accepts a valid VSS user name.

FIGURE 38.17

The History Options dialog box, filled in with dates.

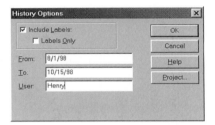

The History Options dialog box enables you to designate options for the history information that you view. VSS tracks changes by internal version, date, or user-designated labels. Labels generally are the most useful way to track changes because you can use meaningful phrases like 2.01, First Beta, or Approved for Company-Wide Distribution.

Click OK after making your selections. The History of File dialog box opens, which shows you the versions of the object, who performed each action on the object, the date the action was performed, and what the action was (see Figure 38.18). From the History of File dialog box, you can do the following:

- View each version of the object

FIGURE 38.18

The History of File dialog allows you to view just about everything that has happened to an object.

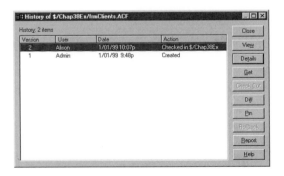

- See the details of each action taken on the object
- Get the object's current version from the Visual SourceSafe project
- See the differences between two versions of the object
- Pin a specific version of a file to the current project, ensuring that the file can't be changed when shared
- Roll back to a previous version of the object
- Get a report of everything that has transpired with the object

Reverting to an Object's Previous Version

Visual SourceSafe also enables you to roll back to previous versions of an object. This is particularly useful if things have gone seriously awry and you want to start over in a version where conditions were more stable. You can revert to an object's previous version from the History of File dialog box. Select the version you want to roll back to and click Rollback. You're warned that your actions are irreversible. If you select Yes, the object is rolled back to the selected version.

CHANGES VISUAL SOURCESAFE MAKES TO ACCESS'S BEHAVIOR

Visual SourceSafe alters Access's behavior; therefore, the following sections explain these changes so they don't take you by surprise.

The Compact Command

Before you distribute a database, you should always compact it. When you try to compact a database that's under SourceSafe control, you're asked whether you want to remove the database from SourceSafe control. When you respond Yes, Access goes through each object in the database and removes all SourceSafe properties.

Opening a Database

When you open a database that's under SourceSafe control, it's always opened exclusively. This prevents more than one developer from modifying objects in the local database at a given time.

When you open a database, you can opt to have Access automatically refresh all objects from the SourceSafe project, you can be prompted on whether you want to refresh all objects, or you can opt not to have Access automatically refresh any objects. To modify this option, choose Tools | SourceSafe | Options and use the Get Latest Checked In Version of Objects When Opening a Database drop-down list to designate your choice.

Closing a Database

When closing a database, you can choose to have Access automatically check in all objects, to prompt you on whether you want to check in all objects, or not to have Access check in any objects. This option is found under Tools | SourceSafe | Options. Use the Check In Objects When Closing the Database drop-down list to select your choice.

Opening an Object in Design View

Each time you check out an object, Access determines whether it has been checked out already. If the object hasn't been checked out by another user, you're asked whether you want to check it out. If you respond No, Access opens the object as read-only. If the object has been checked out by another user, and it's a module, you're warned that another user has the object checked out and you get the option of checking the object out. Your changes will be merged with the other user's changes later. If you try to check out any object other than a module, and it has already been checked out by another user, you're warned that you can just view the object as read-only in Design view.

Saving a New Object or Using Save As on an Existing Object

When you save a new object, or choose File | Save As for an existing object, you can designate whether the new object is placed under SourceSafe control. Designating what happens when a new object is saved is accomplished by choosing Tools | SourceSafe | Options. You can have Access automatically place the object under SourceSafe control, you can have Access prompt you for your choice, or you can tell Access not to place the object under SourceSafe control. Use the Add Objects to Source Control When Adding Them to Microsoft Access drop-down list to make your selection.

Renaming an Object

When you rename an object that's under SourceSafe control, Access automatically reflects the name change in the source control project. An object can't be renamed while checked out by another user.

> **NOTE**
>
> If you want to rename tables, command bars, and other objects that are part of the binary file, you must first check out Data and Misc. objects because changes to the former objects will affect the latter.

38

VISUAL
SOURCESAFE

Deleting an Object

When you delete an object, you can have Visual SourceSafe display a message box asking whether you want to remove the object from the SourceSafe project, you can have Access automatically remove the object from the SourceSafe project, or you can opt for Access not to remove the object from the SourceSafe project. This option can be configured by choosing Tool | SourceSafe | Options in the Remove Objects From Source Control When Deleting Them From Microsoft Access drop-down list.

GETTING HELP FOR VISUAL SOURCESAFE

If you installed VSS Help as part of the MSDN Help Library that comes with Office 2000 Developer, you can open extensive Help books on VSS either from Help buttons on VSS screens or directly from the MSDN Help library, as shown in Figure 32.19.

FIGURE 38.19

The Visual SourceSafe Help topics.

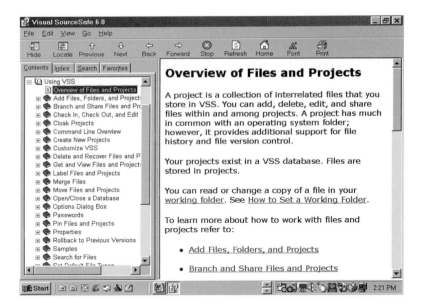

UNDERSTANDING THE LIMITATIONS OF VISUAL SOURCESAFE

Although Visual SourceSafe is a powerful product, it does impose some limitations you should be aware of. Only Access 97 and Access 2000 databases can be placed under Visual SourceSafe control, and user and group permissions can't be set when an object is under

SourceSafe control. In fact, when you add a database to SourceSafe control, *all user and group permissions are removed! Furthermore, you can't put replicated databases under source code control, and you can't move, rename, or copy the local version of the database and continue working with it under SourceSafe control.* To move a database, you must first check in all objects, delete the local database, and then re-create it in the new location.

PRACTICAL EXAMPLES

Putting the Time and Billing Application Under SourceSafe Control

There are two reasons why you might want to place the Time and Billing application under SourceSafe control. First, multiple developers might be working on the project; second, you might want to keep track of changes made to each object to reserve the option of rolling back to a previous version of an object.

SUMMARY

Visual SourceSafe is a powerful product for both the individual developer and members of a development team. It helps you manage group development and versioning of the objects in a database. Furthermore, it integrates seamlessly with Microsoft Access 2000 and is fairly easy to use. In my opinion, most, if not all, Access databases should be placed under SourceSafe control while they're being developed.

38

VISUAL SOURCESAFE

DISTRIBUTING YOUR APPLICATION

IN THIS CHAPTER

WHY THIS CHAPTER IS IMPORTANT

Many developers are responsible for designing applications that will be distributed to many users. The most basic distribution option is to require each user to purchase a copy of Access and then simply provide each user with a copy of the database (MDB) files required for the application. The developer then can go to each user and configure the application appropriately.

Although distributing an application by copying it to each user's machine does not require much specialized knowledge on the part of the developer, it generally is not very practical. For example, in many situations, the developer is distributing an application to users who are dispersed throughout the country or even the world. Many Access applications are mass marketed to hundreds or even thousands of users. In these situations, it is mandatory to use a professional setup program to properly install the application. For these reasons, most developers distribute their applications using the Package and Deployment Wizard, an important component of the Microsoft Office Developer Edition.

INTRODUCING THE PACKAGE AND DEPLOYMENT WIZARD

The Package and Deployment Wizard enables you to easily create distribution disks containing all the files necessary to run your application. The Package and Deployment Wizard creates a highly professional-looking setup program that your users will run when they want to install your application. Using the Package and Deployment Wizard, you can customize what is included with your application. You can even provide your users with the familiar Standard, Compressed, and Custom options that they have come to know from installing other Microsoft products.

LOADING THE PACKAGE AND DEPLOYMENT WIZARD ADD-IN

Before you can use the Package and Deployment Wizard, you must activate the Package and Deployment Wizard add-in. To do this:

1. Activate the VBE (Visual Basic Development Environment).
2. Select Add-in Manager from the Add-in menu. The Add-in Manager dialog appears (see Figure 39.1).

FIGURE 39.1

The Add-in Manager dialog allows you to load the Package and Deployment Wizard.

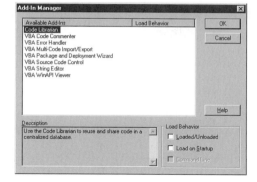

3. Select VBA (Visual Basic for Applications) Package and Deployment Wizard.

4. Click to select the Loaded/Unloaded check box.

5. Click Load on Startup if you want the wizard to be loaded each time that you launch Access.

6. Click OK. The Package and Deployment Wizard should now appear as an option under the Add-ins menu (see Figure 39.2).

FIGURE 39.2

The Add-in menu after the Package and Deployment Wizard add-in has been activated.

39

DISTRIBUTING YOUR APPLICATION TO RUN WITH A FULL COPY OF ACCESS

Many developers distribute their applications to end users who own and have installed Microsoft Access. These users might be responsible for designing their own ad hoc queries and reports. For these users, it is important that you properly secure your application, provide the users of your application with only the functionality you want included in your application, and give professional polish to your application.

Many of the topics in this chapter apply to your application whether you are distributing the application to users with the Access runtime version or with the full copy of Access. You probably should include a switchboard, custom menu bars, and custom toolbars in your application, for example, whether you are distributing your application with the runtime version or for use under the full version of Access.

USING FULL VERSIONS VERSUS RUNTIME VERSIONS OF ACCESS

Many people have the misconception that using the Package and Deployment Wizard and distributing your application using the Access runtime version somehow means that the application is compiled. This is not the case at all! In fact, if the database is not secured properly, anyone can install his or her own copy of Access and modify the application's data and other objects just as you can. Using the Package and Deployment Wizard and distributing your application with the Access runtime version does not modify the database in any way. It simply gives you the license to freely distribute the engine required to run your application.

Actually, the engine is not even a modified version of the Access executable! The MSACCESS.EXE file that you distribute is the same as the MSACCESS.EXE that you use to build your application. When you use the Package and Deployment Wizard to create installation disks for your users, the same MSACCESS.EXE that you use is copied to the installation disks. So how can there be any difference between the retail and runtime versions of Access?

When the user installs your application, the MSACCESS.EXE is copied to the user's machine. During this process, the installation program checks a Windows Registry licensing key to see whether the user owns a copy of Access. If the licensing key indicates that the user does not own a copy of Access, or if the key does not exist, the licensing key (which is a set of numbers and letters) is updated to indicate that the user will be using the runtime version of the product. When Access executes and the runtime licensing key is found, the product launches in runtime mode.

When the runtime licensing key is found, Access behaves differently than when the full licensing key is found. If you are not aware of the differences, you will be quite surprised when certain aspects of your application no longer function as expected. The following is a list of the limitations of the runtime versions of the product:

- The Database window is hidden.
- Design views are hidden.
- Built-in toolbars are not supported.
- Some menu items are not available.
- Certain keys are disabled.

Hidden Database Window

When users launch your application using the runtime version of Access, the Database window is not visible. It's actually there, but it is hidden because its colors are set to the same colors as the Windows background color. This means that you can interact with the Database window using code, but the users of your application will be unable to interact with the Database window directly.

The fact that the Database window is hidden tends to be a double-edged sword. On one hand, it prevents most users from modifying the objects in your application. On the other hand, it puts the responsibility on you to build a complete interface for your application. Remember that, for you as a developer, the Database window is a starting point. You must provide a different starting point and navigational tools for your users to maneuver throughout your application.

Hidden Design Views

The users of your application won't directly have access to any design views, which means that they are unable to create or modify tables, queries, forms, reports, macros, or modules. You still can get to all this functionality through code, though. You can build a wizard that enables your users to define all aspects of a query or some other object, for example, and then build the query (or other object) using ADO (ActiveX Data Objects) code. Again, this helps protect your application from novice users, but it puts the pressure on you to ensure that your application provides its users with all the functionality they need.

Built-In Toolbars Not Supported

All built-in toolbars are completely unavailable with the runtime version of Access, which means that you must design your own toolbars and attach them to your forms and reports as appropriate. This is covered in the "Adding Custom Menus and Toolbars" section of this chapter.

39

DISTRIBUTING
YOUR
APPLICATION

Unavailable Menu Items

Built-in toolbars are not supported at all when using the runtime version of Access, but menus are simply modified after the runtime key is found. Many menu items are hidden in the runtime version. These hidden menu items prevent users from making changes to your application.

Although many of the menu commands are hidden from the user, they can be accessed by using the DoMenuItem command. In other words, the functionality is there, but it is simply hidden from your users.

Disabled Keys

Several keystrokes are unavailable to your users when they run your application with the runtime version of Access. Table 39.1 lists these keystrokes.

TABLE 39.1   DISABLED KEYS

Keys	Function
Ctrl+Break	Halts macro and code execution
Shift (when opening the database)	Prevents execution of the AutoExec macro and ignores Startup properties
Alt+F1/F11	Displays the Database window
F12	Displays the Save As dialog box
Shift+F12	Saves a database object
Ctrl+G	Displays the Debug window
Ctrl+F11	Toggles between custom and built-in toolbars

As you can see, these are keys that you would rarely, if ever, want your users to use. You might consider the disabling of these keystrokes a positive side effect of using the runtime version of the product.

PREPARING YOUR DATABASE FOR USE WITH THE ACCESS RUNTIME VERSION

Several steps are required to prepare your database for use with the Access runtime version. Although many of these steps are mandatory when distributing your application with the runtime version, they also are good as a general practice when developing a polished application. To prepare your application for use with the Access runtime version, follow these steps:

- Create the application.
- Create Help files and associate the Help topics with the application's objects, if desired.
- Test and debug the application.
- Run and test the application with the /Runtime command line argument.
- Run the Package and Deployment Wizard.
- Deploy the application.
- Package and distribute the application.

Creating the Application

You must be concerned about several things when designing an application for use with the Access runtime version. Although the following items are niceties in any application, they are a mandatory aspect of developing an application for use with the Access runtime version:

- Build the application around forms.
- Build error handling into the application.
- Build custom menus and toolbars into the application.
- Set startup options for the application.
- Properly secure the application.

Building the Application Around Forms

The first step when creating the application with runtime distribution in mind is to build the application around forms. This means that everything in the application needs to be forms driven. Your application generally should begin by displaying a Main Switchboard. The Main Switchboard then can navigate the user to additional switchboards such as a Data Entry Switchboard, Reports Switchboard, Maintenance Switchboard, and so on. An alternative is to display the most commonly used form when the application launches. Menu and toolbar items can then be used to navigate to other parts of your application. For example, if the application's main purpose is to maintain membership information for a union, the startup form would be the membership form. Other forms, such as the member payments form, would be accessed via a menu attached to the membership form. This second option is my personal favorite.

Building Error Handling into the Application

It is imperative that you build error handling into your application. If an error occurs when someone is using the runtime version of Access and no error handling is in place, an error message is displayed and the user instantly is returned to the Windows desktop. Therefore, it is crucial that you build error handling into all your routines. Creating a generic error handler to assist you with this task is covered in Chapter 14, "Error Handling: Preparing for the Inevitable."

Adding Custom Menus and Toolbars

As mentioned earlier in this chapter, limited versions of the standard Access menus are available under the Access runtime version, but toolbars are not available at all. You therefore must provide your users with whatever menu bar and toolbar functionality the application requires.

As discussed in Chapter 9, "Advanced Form Techniques," you can attach a menu bar to a form using the Menu Bar property of the form (see Figure 39.3). When a specific menu bar is associated with a particular form or report, the menu appears whenever the form or report becomes the active window. It generally is easier to base a form or report's menu on one of the standard Access menus and then add or remove menu items as appropriate.

FIGURE 39.3

The Menu Bar property of a form.

You must build each toolbar that you want to use with your application. As covered in Chapter 9, you can specify the toolbar that you want to be visible with your form or report by using the Toolbar property of the form or report. At times, you might prefer to control the toolbars that display by using code. By using this method, you can give the users access to your own toolbars or custom toolbars at will. Listing 39.1 shows the code placed in the `Activate` event of the form or report.

Listing 39.1 CODE FOR THE `Activate` EVENT

```
Private Sub Form_Activate()
On Error GoTo Err_Form_Activate
    Call ToolBarShow("tbrMainForm", True)
    Me.fsubClients.Requery

Exit_Form_Activate:
    Exit Sub

Err_Form_Activate:
    MsgBox Err.Description
    Resume Exit_Form_Activate
End Sub
```

The `Activate` event of the frmClients form calls a user-defined procedure called `ToolbarShow`. It passes the `ToolbarShow` routine two parameters: the name of the toolbar it will affect and a Boolean variable indicating whether the specified toolbar should be shown or hidden. Listing 39.2 shows the `ToolBarShow` routine.

Listing 39.2 THE `ToolBarShow` ROUTINE

```
Sub ToolBarShow(strToolbar As String, fShow As Boolean)
   DoCmd.ShowToolbar strToolbar, _
        IIf(fShow, acToolbarYes, acToolbarNo)
   DoCmd.ShowToolbar "Form View", _
        IIf(fShow, acToolbarNo, acToolbarWhereApprop)
End Sub
```

The `ToolBarShow` routine is one routine that handles both the showing and hiding of custom toolbars. It receives a string and a Boolean variable. The `Showtoolbar` method, contained in the `DoCmd` object, sets the toolbars visible or hidden. The command does this by taking the name of the toolbar and a Boolean value (both are passed in as parameters) and toggling the visible property for that toolbar to `True` for visible or `False` for hidden, depending on which was passed into the function. If the `ToolBarShow` routine is passed the string `tbrMainForm` and the Boolean `True`, for example, it shows the `tbrMainForm` toolbar.

In case the application will run in both the retail and runtime versions of Access, you should ensure that the standard toolbar is hidden when the form is active. The second `ShowToolbar` method indicates that the Form View toolbar will be hidden if you are displaying the custom toolbar and will be shown, where appropriate, if you are hiding the custom toolbar. The `Deactivate` event of the form looks like this:

```
Private Sub Form_Deactivate()
    Call ToolBarShow("tbrMainForm", False)
End Sub
```

This routine hides the `tbrMainForm` toolbar and shows the Form View toolbar where appropriate.

Clearly, it is important that you perform all the menu and toolbar handling required by your application. This ensures that all menu bars and toolbars are available when they should be, and *only* when they should be.

Setting Startup Options

Access 2000 provides you with several startup options that enable you to control what happens to your application when it is loaded. Figure 39.4 shows the Startup dialog box, which includes the Advanced options. Table 39.2 lists each option in the Startup dialog box.

FIGURE 39.4

The Startup dialog box.

TABLE 39.2 STARTUP OPTIONS

Option	Function
Application Title	Sets the `AppTitle` property, which displays a custom title in the application title bar.
Application Icon	Sets the `AppIcon` property, which displays a custom icon in the application title bar.

Option	Function
Menu Bar	Sets the `StartupMenuBar` property, which specifies the custom menu bar displayed by default when the application is loaded.
Allow Full Menus	Sets the `AllowFullMenus` property, which allows or restricts the use of Access menus.
Allow Default Shortcut Menus	Sets the `AllowShortcutMenus` property, which allows or restricts the use of standard Access shortcut menus (menus accessed with a right click).
Display Form/Page	Sets the `StartupForm` property, which specifies the form displayed when the application is loaded.
Display Database Window	Sets the `StartupShowDBWindow` property, which determines whether the Database window is visible when the application is opened.
Display Status Bar	Sets the `StartupShowStatusBar` property, which determines whether the status bar is visible when the application is opened.
Shortcut Menu Bar	Sets the `StartupShortcutMenuBar` property, which specifies a menu bar displayed by default as the shortcut (right click) menu bar.
Allow Built-in Toolbars	Sets the `AllowBuiltInToolbars` property, which indicates whether built-in toolbars are available to your users.
Allow Toolbar/Menu Changes	Sets the `AllowToolbarChanges` property, which determines whether your users can customize toolbars in the application.
Use Access Special Keys	Sets the `AllowSpecialKeys` property, which determines whether the user can use keys such as F11 to display the Database window, Ctrl+F11 to toggle between custom and built-in toolbars, and so on.

As you might have guessed, many of these options apply only when you are running the application under the full version of Access (as opposed to the runtime.) You do not need to set the Display Database Window property, for example, if your application will be running only under the runtime version of Access. The Database window is never available under the runtime version of the product, so this property is ignored when the application is run under the runtime version. Nevertheless, I like setting these properties to ensure that the application behaves as I want it to under *both* the retail and runtime versions of the product.

All the properties can be set by using the Startup dialog box or by using code. If you use code, you must make sure that the property exists for the `Database` object before you set it. If the property does not exist, you must append the property to the `Database` object.

39

DISTRIBUTING
YOUR
APPLICATION

Only users with Administer permission for the database can modify the Startup properties. If you want to ensure that certain users cannot modify the startup options of the database, you must ensure that they do not have Administer permissions.

 As part of the startup options for your database, you should determine what code, if any, is run when the application is loaded. You can accomplish this in one of two ways. You can start the application with an AutoExec macro and then issue a RunCode action to execute a VBA procedure. The other option is to designate a Startup form for the application and then call a custom AutoExec routine from the Open event of the Startup form. I *always* use the second option because it provides you with more control, and you can include error handling in the code module behind the startup form, whereas an AutoExec macro cannot contain error handling. The code shown in Listing 39.3 is called from the Open event of the Startup form for the Time and Billing application. This code, and the rest of the code in this chapter, is located in the CHAP39.MDB database file on the sample code CD-ROM.

LISTING 39.3   SETTING OPTIONS FROM A STARTUP FORM ROUTINE

```
Sub AutoExec(frmAny As Form)
    On Error GoTo AutoExec_Err:

    'Optional Test for Runtime Version
    If Not SysCmd(acSysCmdRuntime) _
        And CurrentUser <> "Admin" Then
        MsgBox "You aren't allowed here"
    End If

    DoCmd.OpenForm "frmSplash"
    DoEvents
    DoCmd.Hourglass True

    If Not VerifyLink Then
        If Not Relink Then
            MsgBox "You Cannot Run This App Without Locating Data Tables"
            DoCmd.Close acForm, "frmSplash"
            DoCmd.Quit
        End If
    End If

    Call GetCompanyInfo
    DoCmd.Hourglass False
    If IsLoaded("frmSplash") Then
        DoCmd.Close acForm, "frmSplash"
```

```
        End If
        Exit Sub

AutoExec_Err:
        DoCmd.Hourglass False
        MsgBox "Error # " & Err.Number & ": " & Err.Description
        Exit Sub
End Sub
```

This generic routine receives any form as a parameter. It uses the OpenForm method to open a form called frmSplash. Then it issues a DoEvents command to give the form time to open. An hourglass mouse pointer is displayed and the routine calls a user-defined function that ensures that the database tables are linked successfully. This VerifyLink routine is covered in the "Automating the Process of Linking to Tables" section of this chapter. If the VerifyLink function returns False, the Relink function is executed in an attempt to re-establish the broken link. The Relink function is covered in the same section as the VerifyLink routine. If the Relink function is unsuccessful, users are warned that they cannot run the application. The frmSplash form is closed and the application is exited. As long as the tables' links were established successfully, the AutoExec routine proceeds to call a routine called GetCompanyInfo, where it loads frequently used information into an array. The hourglass mouse pointer is removed and the splash screen is unloaded.

Securing the Application

Don't fool yourself! Remember that the runtime version of Access in no way secures your application. It simply provides you with royalty-free distribution. You must perform all the same measures to secure your application under the runtime version of Access that you perform under the retail version of the product. The bottom line is that you must take measures to secure your application if you want it and its data to be secure. The basics of security are covered in Chapter 33, "Database Security Made Easy," and the intricacies of security are covered in Chapter 34, "Advanced Security Techniques." Distributing your application as an MDE provides an additional level of security while improving performance and decreasing the size of the database file. MDE files are covered in the next section.

Distributing Your Application as an MDE

The process of creating an MDE file compiles all modules, removes all source code from your database, and compacts the destination database. All code will run, but the user will be unable to modify forms, reports, and modules. Besides protecting the objects in your database, this process reduces the size of the database and some of the overhead associated with it, thereby

39

improving application performance. Creating and distributing an MDE file is not as simple as it might appear at first glance. Chapter 32, "Using Data Access Pages," covers the process of creating an MDE file and the important issues that surround this new Access file format.

Adding Custom Help to the Application

To add polish to your application and ensure that the help you provide to your users applies to what they are looking at in your application, you must provide a custom Help file. In essence, adding help to your application involves creating an .RTF file and other supporting files, and using the Windows Help Workshop to build a compiled Help file. You then must add help to the various objects in your application. There are many excellent tools available that can assist you to add custom help to your applications.

Testing and Debugging the Application

Before you even bother trying to run your application under the runtime version, you should fully test and debug the application under the retail version of the product. When you are fairly confident that you have all the kinks worked out of the application, you are ready to test it in the runtime environment.

Running and Testing the Application with the `/Runtime` Command-Line Switch

If you have the Microsoft Office 2000 Developer tools installed, Microsoft provides you with a very easy way to test an application to see how it will perform under the runtime version of Access without having to actually create distribution disks. You can do this by using the `/Runtime` command-line switch. The `/Runtime` switch forces Access to load in runtime mode. Here's how it works:

```
c:\program files\microsoft office\office\msaccess.exe
➥c:\databases\chap39.mdb /runtime
```

After you load the application with the `/Runtime` switch, you should once again test all aspects of the application. At times, you might want to test to see whether the application has been launched with the runtime or retail version of the product. You can accomplish this with the following code:

```
If Not SysCmd(acSysCmdRuntime) _
    And CurrentUser <> "Admin" Then
    MsgBox "You aren't allowed here"
End If
```

The SysCmd function, when passed the constant acSysCmdRuntime, checks to see whether the application was launched using the runtime version of Access. In this case, if the program was run with the retail version of Access and CurrentUser is not Admin, a message is displayed indicating that the user is not allowed. Of course, you easily could modify this routine to check for other users and to quit the application if an unauthorized person attempts to launch the application without the runtime version of the product.

TIP

If you want to simulate the runtime environment on the machine of a user who has Access installed, you must copy the file mso9rt.dll to the directory on the user's machine called \program files\common files\microsoft shared\vba\vba6.

Running the Package and Deployment Wizard

After you have fully tested and prepared your application for distribution, you are ready to run the Package and Deployment Wizard. The Package and Deployment Wizard walks you through all the steps required to build distribution disks that include all the components your application needs to run. You launch the Package and Deployment Wizard from VBE.

1. Activate the VBE.

2. Select Package and Deployment Wizard from the Add-ins menu. The Package and Deployment Wizard starting dialog box appears, as shown in Figure 39.5.

FIGURE 39.5

The Package and Deployment Wizard Welcome dialog box.

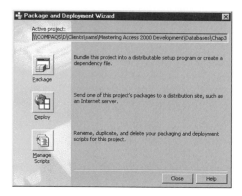

Viewing the Introductory Screen

The Package and Deployment Wizard starting dialog box displays the name of the active project that will be prepared. It gives you the opportunity to:

- Bundle your project into a distributable setup program
- Create a dependency file
- Send the packaged application to a distribution site
- Rename, delete, and duplicate packaging and deployment scripts

The first step is to bundle the project into a distributable setup program. Click the Package button to begin the process. A dialog appears, informing you of the steps that Access is taking to build the setup program (see Figure 39.6).

Figure 39.6

The Package and Deployment Wizard keeps you apprised of its progress as it builds the setup program.

Selecting the Type of Package You Want to Create

The second step of the Package and Deployment Wizard prompts you to select the type of package you want to create (see Figure 39.7). Standard Setup Package is used to create a package that is installed by the Setup.exe program. Dependency File is used to create a list of all the runtime components required by your application. You will generally select Dependency File only when you are using another setup program to deploy your application. Select the appropriate package type and click Next.

Selecting the Folder Where Your Package Will Be Assembled

The third step of the Package and Deployment Wizard prompts you for the folder where your package will be assembled. You can assemble the package on a local or network drive. Make your selection and click Next. If you select an existing folder, your are prompted that files in the folder might be overwritten. You can click Yes to proceed, or No to select another folder.

FIGURE 39.7

The second step of the Package and Deployment Wizard prompts you for the type of package you want to create.

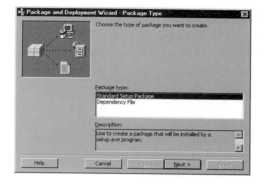

Missing Dependency File Information

The fourth step of the Package and Deployment Wizard lists all files for which dependency information could not be found (see Figure 39.8). This list does not necessarily indicate a problem. It simply means that no dependency information was available for the listed files. It is possible that the listed files have no dependencies. If the file is an Access file, it appears in bold. You can click Scan to search the file for dependencies. If you are certain that a file has no dependencies, you can click its check box to permanently mark it as having no dependencies. When you are satisfied with the list, click OK.

FIGURE 39.8

The fourth step of the Package and Deployment Wizard lists all files for which dependency information could not be found.

You might be prompted with an additional dialog that displays a list of files for which dependency information might be out-of-date. Again, to proceed, click OK. If you want to cancel the Package and Deployment process, click Cancel.

Adding Files to be Included on the Distribution Disks

The fifth step of the Package and Deployment Wizard enables you to specify files that you want to add to the setup disks, as shown in Figure 39.9. The types of files you might opt to add using this dialog box include the following:

- Application databases
- Data databases
- Library files
- ActiveX controls (OCX files)
- Icon files
- Splash screens
- Help files
- Registry files
- License files
- Office documents
- Remote server files
- Any other special files that you need distributed

FIGURE 39.9

Adding files to the setup disks.

Follow these steps to add a file:

1. In the Package and Deployment Wizard dialog box, click Add. The Add File dialog box appears.

2. Locate the file you want to add and click Open.

3. Click to select Include Access Runtime if you want to deploy your application using the runtime.

4. When you are done adding all required files, click Next.

Designating Cab Options

A cab file is a compressed container file (cabinet file) for your application's files. In the sixth step of the Package and Deployment Wizard, you can opt to create a single cab file or to create multiple cab files (see Figure 39.10). A single cab file is appropriate for a network installation, whereas multiple cab files are appropriate for a floppy disk installation. If you select multiple cab files, you should select a cab file size appropriate for the type of disks you plan to use. When ready, click Next.

FIGURE 39.10

Selecting whether you want to create one or multiple cab files.

Choosing the Title for Your Installation

In the seventh step of the Package and Deployment Wizard, you can select an installation title for your application (see Figure 39.11). This title appears on the splash screen. You can also designate a program to be run when the installation is finished. Click Next.

FIGURE 39.11

Selecting a title for your installation.

39

Selecting Start Menu Items to be Created

In the eighth step of the Package and Deployment Wizard, you can designate Start menu groups and items that are created during the installation process (see Figure 39.12). Click New Group to create a new group and New Item to create a new item. If you opt to create a new item, the Start Menu Item Properties dialog appears (see Figure 39.13). Designate the Name, Target, and Start In path for the item. Click OK to return to the Start Menu Items form. Click Properties to modify the Name, Target, and Start In path for any existing shortcuts. Click Remove to remove a shortcut. Click Next when you're finished designating all options.

FIGURE 39.12

Selecting start menus groups and items that are created during the installation process.

FIGURE 39.13

Specify the Name, Target, and Start In path for start menu items that you create.

Selecting Install Locations for Included Files

In the ninth step of the Package and Deployment Wizard, you can designate the install location for the listed files (see Figure 39.14). Click within the Install Location column of the file you want to modify, and then change the file location. Click Next when done modifying the location of all files.

FIGURE 39.14

Selecting the installation location for the application.

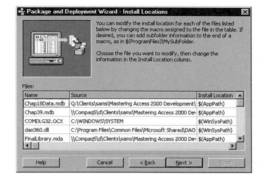

Designating Files to be Marked as Shared

In the tenth step of the Package and Deployment Wizard, you can designate your application files as shared (see Figure 39.15). You should do this for any of your application files that are used by more than one program. Shared files are removed *only* if all files using them are removed. To mark a file as shared, click its check box. Click Next when ready to proceed.

FIGURE 39.15

Click the check boxes of any of your application's files that you want to designate as shared.

Specifying a Script Name

The final step of the Package and Deployment Wizard prompts you to enter a script name (see Figure 39.16). All the settings that you have designated are saved under the script name. The script name can be used to recreate the setup at any time. Click Finish when ready to create the package. You are notified as each step of the setup process is completed (see Figure 39.17). When the setup process is complete, a Packaging report appears (see Figure 39.18). This report contains important information about the status of the packaging process. Click Save Report to save the report as a file, if desired. Click Close when done. You are returned to the opening step of the Package and Deployment Wizard, where you can opt to immediately deploy your application, if desired.

39

DISTRIBUTING YOUR APPLICATION

FIGURE 39.16
Enter a script name and click finish to create the package.

FIGURE 39.17
Access notifies you of each step in the setup it takes in completing the package.

FIGURE 39.18
When the packing process is complete, a packaging report appears.

Deploying the Application

Before you can begin installing the application on workstations, you must deploy your project's packages to a distribution site. Once again, this is accomplished using the Package and Deployment Wizard. Complete the following steps:

1. From the opening window of the Package and Deployment Wizard (see Figure 39.5), select Deploy.

2. In the first step of the Deploy Wizard, you select the package to deploy. Click Next when ready.

3. The second step of the Deploy portion of the Package and Deployment Wizard allows you to designate the type of deployment you want to perform. You can deploy to a folder, or via the Web (see Figure 39.19). The steps that follow differ, depending on your selection. Click Next after you make your selection.

FIGURE 39.19

You can opt to deploy to a folder or via the Web.

4. If you select Folder, the third step of the Package and Deployment Wizard prompts you to designate where you want to deploy the package. You can deploy locally, or to a network. Make your selection and click Next.

5. In the final step of the Deploy phase of the Package and Deployment Wizard, you designate a name for the deployment script (see Figure 39.20). This script is used for future deployments of the package. When ready, click Finish.

6. When the process is complete, a Deployment report appears. Click Save Report if you want to save the report. Click Close when done. You are returned to the opening screen of the Package and Deployment Wizard.

39

DISTRIBUTING YOUR APPLICATION

FIGURE 39.20

Designate a name for the deployment script and click Finish.

Distributing the Application

The most important thing you must do when packaging and distributing your application is to test the application on a machine that has never had a copy of Access or any Access runtime application installed. This ensures that your application includes all required components. I like to keep a "virgin" machine available for testing my application setups. Here's what I do:

1. Back up the Windows and Windows\System folders on the machine.
2. Install my application.
3. Test my application.
4. Delete my application.
5. Delete everything in the Windows\System folder.
6. Restore the Windows System folder from backup.

By following these steps, I ensure that I always have a "clean" machine on which to test my application. Obviously, it is imperative that you test *all* aspects of your application on the machine on which you performed the installation from your Setup disks.

> **TIP**
>
> Several third-party software packages are available to help you to easily backup and restore your Windows installation. A popular package is Ghost, available from Symantec.

When you are ready to test the Setup process, follow these steps:

1. Select Run from the Windows Start menu.

2. In the Run dialog box, locate the Setup files that the Deploy portion of the Package and Deploy Wizard created, as shown in Figure 39.21. Click OK.

FIGURE 39.21

Selecting Run from the Start menu.

3. After being notified of the setup's progress, the Application Setup dialog box appears, as shown in Figure 39.22.

FIGURE 39.22

The Application Setup Welcome dialog box.

4. Click OK to continue.

5. Select a location for the application installation (see Figure 39.23).

FIGURE 39.23

Selecting a location for the program installation.

6. Click the command button to install the application to the specified directory. The Choose Program Group dialog box appears. Select a program group and click Continue.

39

DISTRIBUTING
YOUR
APPLICATION

The installation process is completed. If you opted during the Package and Deployment Wizard to create desktop shortcuts, they are created automatically when the Setup program is executed.

LOOKING AT OTHER ISSUES

Two additional issues have not yet been covered regarding the distribution of your application. The first issue involves ensuring that the application database can establish any links that it has to external tables. The second issue involves the prospect of using replication to effectively distribute changes to your application.

Automating the Process of Linking to Tables

Access hard codes locations for table links. This means that if you install your application on another machine, unless the other machine has exactly the same folder structure as you do on your machine, the tables will not link successfully. The code shown in Listing 39.4 checks to see whether the required tables are available. If they are not found in the expected location, the routine attempts to locate them in the same folder as the application database. If they still cannot be found, the user is given an opportunity to locate the files. If they *still* cannot be found, the application terminates.

LISTING 39.4　THE LinkTables ROUTINE

```
Sub LinkTables()
    On Error GoTo LinkTables_Err:

    'Optional Test for Runtime Version
    If Not SysCmd(acSysCmdRuntime) _
        And CurrentUser <> "Admin" Then
        MsgBox "You aren't allowed here"
        Exit Sub
    End If

    DoCmd.Hourglass True

    If Not VerifyLink Then
        If Not Relink(CurrentProject.FullName, True) Then
            Me.dlgCommon.ShowOpen
            If Not Relink(Me.dlgCommon.FileName, False) Then
                MsgBox "You Cannot Run This App Without _
                    Locating Data Tables"
                DoCmd.Close acForm, "frmSplash"
                DoCmd.Quit
```

```
            End If
        End If
    End If

    Call GetCompanyInfo
    DoCmd.Hourglass False
    Exit Sub

LinkTables_Err:
    DoCmd.Hourglass False
    MsgBox "Error # " & Err.Number & ": " & Err.Description
    Exit Sub

End Sub
```

The routine begins by executing a function called `VerifyLink`. The `VerifyLink` function is shown in Listing 39.5 and is found in the FinalLibrary.MDA file on the sample code CD. It first creates an ADOX `Catalog` object. It sets the `ActiveConnection` property of the `Catalog` object to the `Connection` property of the `CurrentProject`. The `CurrentProject` object returns a reference to the database using the library, rather than to the library itself. The heart of the routine is the `For...Next` loop. It loops through each `Table` object in the `Tables` collection of the `Catalog` object. If the table is linked, it attempts to reference the first field in the table. If an error occurs, the table link must be broken. The error number is non-zero, and the routine exits the `For...Next` loop. Because the function returns whether or not the error number is equal to zero, `False` is returned if an error occurs, and `True` is returned if no error occurs.

LISTING 39.5   THE `VerifyLink` FUNCTION

```
Function VerifyLink() As Boolean
    'Verify connection information in linked tables.

    'Declare Required Variables
    Dim cat As ADOX.Catalog
    Dim tdf As ADOX.Table
    Dim strTemp As String

    'Point Database object variable at the current database
    Set cat = New ADOX.Catalog

    With cat
```

continues

39

LISTING 39.5   CONTINUED

```
        Set .ActiveConnection = CurrentProject.Connection

        'Continue if links are broken.
        On Error Resume Next

        'Open one linked table to see if connection
        'information is correct.
        For Each tdf In .Tables
            If tdf.Type = "LINK" Then
                strTemp = tdf.Columns(0).Name
                If Err.Number Then
                    Exit For
                End If
            End If

        Next tdf
    End With

    VerifyLink = (Err.Number = 0)

End Function
```

If the `VerifyLink` function returns a `False`, the `Relink` function is executed. The `Relink` function is shown in Listing 39.6. It receives two parameters. The first parameter is the name of the database the function will attempt to link to. The second parameter is a Boolean variable that is used to designate whether the database is considered the default database.

The function begins by modifying the status bar. It then creates a `Catalog` object and an instance of a custom class called `DBInfo`. The `ActiveConnection` property of the `Catalog` object is set equal to the `Connection` property of the current project. Next the `FullName` property of the `DBInfo` class is set equal to the name of the file that is passed as a parameter to the function. The `DBInfo` class extracts the path and the filename from the full filename. Just as with the `VerifyLink` function, the `ReLink` function uses a `For...Next` loop to loop through all the tables in the database. As it loops through each table, it attempts to establish a link to a database with the name passed as parameter to the `Relink` function.

This is where the `DefaultData` parameter comes into play. The first time that the `LinkTables` routine calls the `Relink` function, it passes the name and path of the application database as the first parameter, and `True` for the second parameter. The `Relink` function then attempts to link to a database located in the same folder as the application database, but with the word *Data* appended to the end of the filename. For example, if the application database is named

Membership, the Relink function looks for a database called MembershipData in the same location as the application database. If it is successful, it returns True, and if it is unsuccessful, it returns False. I use this method to attempt to re-establish the link because I commonly place both the application and data databases on a client's network, both in the same folder. When I do this, I employ a naming convention where the data database has the same name as the application database, but with the word *Data* appended to it.

If no data database with the expected filename is found in the folder where the application database is located (False was returned from the Relink function), the LinkTables routine uses the Common Dialog control to display a File Open dialog. This gives the user the opportunity to locate the data database. The filename and path that the user selects in the dialog is passed to the Relink routine, along with False as the second parameter. Because the user has selected the file that he or she believes contains the data, there is no reason to append the word *Data* onto the filename. Once again the Relink routine loops through the tables collection of the Catalog object, attempting to re-establish the broken links. If successful, it returns True, and if unsuccessful, it returns False. If False is returned from the second call to the Relink function, the LinkTables routine exits the Access application.

LISTING 39.6   THE Relink FUNCTION

```
Function ReLink(strDir As String, DefaultData As Boolean) _
    As Boolean

    ' Relink a broken linked Access table.

    Dim cat As ADOX.Catalog
    Dim tdfRelink As ADOX.Table
    Dim oDBInfo As DBInfo
    Dim strPath As String
    Dim strName As String
    Dim intCounter As Integer
    Dim vntStatus As Variant


    vntStatus = SysCmd(acSysCmdSetStatus, "Updating Links")

    Set cat = New ADOX.Catalog
    Set oDBInfo = New DBInfo

    With cat
        .ActiveConnection = CurrentProject.Connection
        oDBInfo.FullName = strDir
```

continues

LISTING 39.6   CONTINUED

```
    strPath = oDBInfo.FilePathOnly
    strName = Left(oDBInfo.FileName, InStr(oDBInfo.FileName, ".") - 1)

    On Error Resume Next
    Call SysCmd(acSysCmdInitMeter, "Linking Data Tables", _
                    .Tables.Count)

  For Each tdfRelink In .Tables
      intCounter = intCounter + 1
      Call SysCmd(acSysCmdUpdateMeter, intCounter)
      If .Tables(tdfRelink.Name).Type = "LINK" Then
          tdfRelink.Properties("Jet OLEDB:Link Datasource") = _
          strPath & strName & IIf(DefaultData, "Data.Mdb", ".mdb")
      End If
      If Err.Number Then
            Exit For
      End If
  Next tdfRelink
End With

Call SysCmd(acSysCmdRemoveMeter)

vntStatus = SysCmd(acSysCmdClearStatus)

ReLink = (Err = 0)

End Function
```

Using Replication to Efficiently Distribute Your Application

You might not want to rebuild and redistribute Setup disks each time you change the design of your application database. Not only is this time-consuming, but also it is difficult to ensure that each user runs the Setup process in order to obtain the application database. If your organization is networked, it generally is much more effective to distribute application updates using replication. This involves making design changes to the Design Master and then synchronizing with a hub after the changes are completed and tested properly. Replication is covered in detail in Chapter 23, "Replication Made Easy."

Distributing the Time and Billing Application

 The completed Time and Billing application, found on your sample code CD-ROM as CHAP39.MDB, has been modified to prepare it for distribution. Switchboards have been added to assist the user with the process of navigating throughout the application. Error handling has been built into most of the application's routines. Custom toolbars and menu bars have been added to the application's forms and reports. Startup options have been set. The application has been fully tested under the runtime version of the product. All that is left is to properly secure the application to meet the specific needs of your organization and to build the Setup disks.

SUMMARY

The process of preparing an application for distribution actually starts in the planning stages of the application. It involves everything from providing a means by which the users of the application can navigate from task to task, to preparing the distribution disks. It also involves important steps such as properly securing the application to ensure that the integrity of its data and objects are maintained, and building in a solid error handler to ensure that all errors are handled gracefully. Remember that whether your users will be running your application using the retail or runtime version of Access, by using the techniques you learned in this chapter, you can add professional polish and pizzazz to any application.

39

1200

APPENDIXES

PART

VI

IN THIS PART

TABLE STRUCTURES

IN THIS APPENDIX

This appendix gives you a complete listing of all the tables included in the Time and Billing application. Each table includes the following:

- A list of the field names, types, and lengths of each field in the table
- A detailed list of the properties associated with each field in the table

THE TBLCLIENTS TABLE

This table stores pertinent information about each client, such as the company name, contact name, and phone numbers.

TABLE A.1 THE TBLCLIENTS TABLE

Field Name	Type	Size (Bytes)
ClientID	Number (Long)	4
CompanyName	Text	50
Address	Text	255
City	Text	30
StateProvince	Text	20
PostalCode	Text	20
Country	Text	20
ContactFirstName	Text	30
ContactLastName	Text	50
ContactTitle	Text	50
OfficePhone	Text	30
Fax	Text	30
Cellular	Text	30
Home	Text	30
EMailAddress	Text	30
ReferredBy	Text	30
AssociatedWith	Text	30
IntroDate	Date/Time	8
DefaultRate	Currency	8
Notes	Memo	(Varies)
HomePage	Hyperlink	

TABLE A.2 THE FIELD PROPERTIES FOR EACH FIELD IN THE TBLCLIENTS TABLE

Property	Value
ClientID	**Number (Long)**
Allow Zero Length	False
Attributes	Fixed Size, Auto-Increment
Caption	Client ID
Collating Order	General
Column Hidden	False
Column Order	Default
Column Width	Default
Ordinal Position	0
Required	False
Source Field	ClientID
Source Table	tblClients
CompanyName	**Text**
Allow Zero Length	False
Attributes	Variable Length
Caption	Company Name
Collating Order	General
Column Hidden	False
Column Order	Default
Column Width	Default
Display Control	Text Box
Ordinal Position	1
Required	True
Source Field	CompanyName
Source Table	tblClients
Address	**Text**
Allow Zero Length	False
Attributes	Variable Length

continues

TABLE A.2   CONTINUED

Property	Value
Collating Order	General
Column Hidden	False
Column Order	Default
Column Width	Default
Display Control	Text Box
Ordinal Position	2
Required	False
Source Field	Address
Source Table	tblClients
City	**Text**
Allow Zero Length	False
Attributes	Variable Length
Collating Order	General
Column Hidden	False
Column Order	Default
Column Width	Default
Display Control	Text Box
Ordinal Position	3
Required	False
Source Field	City
Source Table	tblClients
StateProvince	**Text**
Allow Zero Length	False
Attributes	Variable Length
Caption	State/Province
Collating Order	General
Column Hidden	False
Column Order	Default
Column Width	Default

Property	Value
Default Value	"CA"
Display Control	Text Box
Ordinal Position	4
Required	False
Source Field	StateProvince
Source Table	tblClients
PostalCode	**Text**
Allow Zero Length	False
Attributes	Variable Length
Caption	Postal Code
Collating Order	General
Column Hidden	False
Column Order	Default
Column Width	Default
Display Control	Text Box
Ordinal Position	5
Required	False
Source Field	PostalCode
Source Table	tblClients
Country	**Text**
Allow Zero Length	False
Attributes	Variable Length
Collating Order	General
Column Hidden	False
Column Order	Default
Column Width	Default
Display Control	Text Box
Ordinal Position	6
Required	False
Source Field	Country
Source Table	tblClients

A

TABLE
STRUCTURES

continues

TABLE A.2   CONTINUED

Property	Value
ContactFirstName	**Text**
Allow Zero Length	False
Attributes	Variable Length
Caption	Contact First Name
Collating Order	General
Column Hidden	False
Column Order	Default
Column Width	Default
Display Control	Text Box
Ordinal Position	7
Required	False
Source Field	ContactFirstName
Source Table	tblClients
ContactLastName	**Text**
Allow Zero Length	False
Attributes	Variable Length
Caption	Contact Last Name
Collating Order	General
Column Hidden	False
Column Order	Default
Column Width	Default
Display Control	Text Box
Ordinal Position	8
Required	False
Source Field	ContactLastName
Source Table	tblClients
ContactTitle	**Text**
Allow Zero Length	False
Attributes	Variable Length

Property	Value
Caption	Contact Title
Collating Order	General
Column Hidden	False
Column Order	Default
Column Width	Default
Display Control	Text Box
Ordinal Position	9
Required	False
Source Field	ContactTitle
Source Table	tblClients
OfficePhone	**Text**
Allow Zero Length	False
Attributes	Variable Length
Caption	Office Phone
Collating Order	General
Column Hidden	False
Column Order	Default
Column Width	Default
Display Control	Text Box
Input Mask	!\(999\)000\-0000
Ordinal Position	10
Required	False
Source Field	OfficePhone
Source Table	tblClients
Fax	**Text**
Allow Zero Length	False
Attributes	Variable Length
Collating Order	General
Column Hidden	False

continues

A

TABLE STRUCTURES

TABLE A.2 CONTINUED

Property	*Value*
Column Order	Default
Column Width	Default
Display Control	Text Box
Input Mask	!\(999\)000\-0000
Ordinal Position	11
Required	False
Source Field	Fax
Source Table	tblClients
Cellular	**Text**
Allow Zero Length	False
Attributes	Variable Length
Collating Order	General
Column Hidden	False
Column Order	Default
Column Width	Default
Display Control	Text Box
Input Mask	!\(999\)000\-0000
Ordinal Position	12
Required	False
Source Field	Cellular
Source Table	tblClients
Home	**Text**
Allow Zero Length	False
Attributes	Variable Length
Collating Order	General
Column Hidden	False
Column Order	Default
Column Width	Default

Property	Value
Display Control	Text Box
Input Mask	!\(999\)000\-0000
Ordinal Position	13
Required	False
Source Field	Home
Source Table	tblClients
EMailAddress	**Text**
Allow Zero Length	False
Attributes	Variable Length
Caption	E-Mail Address
Collating Order	General
Column Hidden	False
Column Order	Default
Column Width	Default
Display Control	Text Box
Ordinal Position	14
Required	False
Source Field	EMailAddress
Source Table	tblClients
ReferredBy	**Text**
Allow Zero Length	False
Attributes	Variable Length
Caption	Referred By
Collating Order	General
Column Hidden	False
Column Order	Default
Column Width	Default
Display Control	Text Box
Ordinal Position	15

continues

TABLE A.2   CONTINUED

Property	Value
Required	False
Source Field	ReferredBy
Source Table	tblClients
AssociatedWith	**Text**
Allow Zero Length	False
Attributes	Variable Length
Caption	Associated With
Collating Order	General
Column Hidden	False
Column Order	Default
Column Width	Default
Display Control	Text Box
Ordinal Position	16
Required	False
Source Field	AssociatedWith
Source Table	tblClients
IntroDate	**Date/Time**
Allow Zero Length	False
Attributes	Fixed Size
Caption	Intro Date
Collating Order	General
Column Hidden	False
Column Order	Default
Column Width	Default
Default Value	=Date()
Ordinal Position	17
Required	True
Source Field	IntroDate

Property	Value
Source Table	tblClients
Validation Rule	<=Date()
Validation Text	Date Entered Must Be On Or Before Today
DefaultRate	**Currency**
Allow Zero Length	False
Attributes	Fixed Size
Caption	Default Rate
Collating Order	General
Column Hidden	False
Column Order	Default
Column Width	Default
Decimal Places	255
Default Value	125
Format	Currency
Ordinal Position	18
Required	False
Source Field	DefaultRate
Source Table	tblClients
Validation Rule	Between 75 And 150
Validation Text	Rate Must Be Between 75 and 150
Notes	**Memo**
Allow Zero Length	False
Attributes	Variable Length
Collating Order	General
Column Hidden	False
Column Order	Default
Column Width	Default
Ordinal Position	19
Required	False
Source Field	Notes
Source Table	tblClients

continues

TABLE A.2   CONTINUED

Property	Value
HomePage	**Hyperlink**
Allow Zero Length	False
Attributes	Variable Length
Caption	Home Page
Collating Order	General
Column Hidden	False
Column Order	Default
Column Width	Default
Ordinal Position	20
Required	False
Source Field	HomePage
Source Table	tblClients

THE TBLCOMPANYINFO TABLE

This table stores information about your company, including address and default payment terms.

TABLE A.3   THE tblCOMPANYINFO TABLE

Field Name	Type	Size (Bytes)
SetupID	Number (Long)	4
CompanyName	Text	50
Address	Text	255
City	Text	50
StateProvince	Text	20
PostalCode	Text	20
Country	Text	50
PhoneNumber	Text	30
FaxNumber	Text	30
DefaultPaymentTerms	Text	255
DefaultInvoiceDescription	Memo	(varies)

TABLE A.4 THE PROPERTIES OF EACH FIELD INCLUDED IN THE tblCompanyInfo TABLE

Property	*Value*
SetupID	**Number (Long)**
Allow Zero Length	False
Attributes	Fixed Size, Auto-Increment
Caption	SetupID
Collating Order	General
Column Hidden	False
Column Order	Default
Column Width	Default
Ordinal Position	0
Required	False
Source Field	SetupID
Source Table	tblCompanyInfo
CompanyName	**Text**
Allow Zero Length	False
Attributes	Variable Length
Caption	Company Name
Collating Order	General
Column Hidden	False
Column Order	Default
Column Width	Default
Display Control	Text Box
Ordinal Position	1
Required	False
Source Field	CompanyName
Source Table	tblCompanyInfo
Address	**Text**
Allow Zero Length	False
Attributes	Variable Length

continues

A

TABLE STRUCTURES

TABLE A.4   CONTINUED

Property	Value
Collating Order	General
Column Hidden	False
Column Order	Default
Column Width	Default
Display Control	Text Box
Ordinal Position	2
Required	False
Source Field	Address
Source Table	tblCompanyInfo
City	**Text**
Allow Zero Length	False
Attributes	Variable Length
Collating Order	General
Column Hidden	False
Column Order	Default
Column Width	Default
Display Control	Text Box
Ordinal Position	3
Required	False
Source Field	City
Source Table	tblCompanyInfo
StateProvince	**Text**
Allow Zero Length	False
Attributes	Variable Length
Caption	State/Province
Collating Order	General
Column Hidden	False
Column Order	Default
Column Width	Default
Display Control	Text Box

Property	Value
Ordinal Position	4
Required	False
Source Field	StateProvince
Source Table	tblCompanyInfo
PostalCode	**Text**
Allow Zero Length	False
Attributes	Variable Length
Caption	Postal Code
Collating Order	General
Column Hidden	False
Column Order	Default
Column Width	Default
Display Control	Text Box
Input Mask	00000\-9999
Ordinal Position	5
Required	False
Source Field	PostalCode
Source Table	tblCompanyInfo
Country	**Text**
Allow Zero Length	False
Attributes	Variable Length
Collating Order	General
Column Hidden	False
Column Order	Default
Column Width	Default
Display Control	Text Box
Ordinal Position	6
Required	False
Source Field	Country
Source Table	tblCompanyInfo

continues

A

TABLE STRUCTURES

TABLE A.4   CONTINUED

Property	Value
PhoneNumber	**Text**
Allow Zero Length	False
Attributes	Variable Length
Caption	Phone Number
Collating Order	General
Column Hidden	False
Column Order	Default
Column Width	Default
Display Control	Text Box
Input Mask	!\(999") "000\-0000
Ordinal Position	7
Required	False
Source Field	PhoneNumber
Source Table	tblCompanyInfo
FaxNumber	**Text**
Allow Zero Length	False
Attributes	Variable Length
Caption	Fax Number
Collating Order	General
Column Hidden	False
Column Order	Default
Column Width	Default
Display Control	Text Box
Input Mask	!\(999") "000\-0000
Ordinal Position	8
Required	False
Source Field	FaxNumber
Source Table	tblCompanyInfo

Property	Value
DefaultPaymentTerms	**Text**
Allow Zero Length	False
Attributes	Variable Length
Caption	Default Payment Terms
Collating Order	General
Column Hidden	False
Column Order	Default
Column Width	Default
Display Control	Text Box
Ordinal Position	9
Required	False
Source Field	DefaultPaymentTerms
Source Table	tblCompanyInfo
DefaultInvoiceDescription	**Memo**
Allow Zero Length	False
Attributes	Variable Length
Caption	Default Invoice Description
Collating Order	General
Column Hidden	False
Column Order	Default
Column Width	Default
Ordinal Position	10
Required	False
Source Field	DefaultInvoiceDescription
Source Table	tblCompanyInfo

THE TBLEMPLOYEES TABLE

This table includes relevant employee information, such as name, address, and billing rate.

TABLE A.5   THE TBLEMPLOYEES TABLE

Field Name	Type	Size (Bytes)
EmployeeID	Number (Long)	4
FirstName	Text	50
LastName	Text	50
Title	Text	50
EmailName	Text	50
Extension	Text	30
Address	Text	255
City	Text	50
StateOrProvince	Text	20
PostalCode	Text	20
Country	Text	50
HomePhone	Text	30
WorkPhone	Text	30
BillingRate	Currency	8

TABLE A.6   THE PROPERTIES OF EACH FIELD INCLUDED IN THE TBLEMPLOYEES TABLE

Property	Value
EmployeeID	**Number (Long)**
Allow Zero Length	False
Attributes	Fixed Size, Auto-Increment
Caption	Employee ID
Collating Order	General
Ordinal Position	0
Required	False
Source Field	EmployeeID
Source Table	tblEmployees
FirstName	**Text**
Allow Zero Length	False
Attributes	Variable Length

Property	Value
Caption	First Name
Collating Order	General
Ordinal Position	1
Required	False
Source Field	FirstName
Source Table	tblEmployees
LastName	**Text**
Allow Zero Length	False
Attributes	Variable Length
Caption	Last Name
Collating Order	General
Ordinal Position	2
Required	False
Source Field	LastName
Source Table	tblEmployees
Title	**Text**
Allow Zero Length	False
Attributes	Variable Length
Collating Order	General
Ordinal Position	3
Required	False
Source Field	Title
Source Table	tblEmployees
EmailName	**Text**
Allow Zero Length	False
Attributes	Variable Length
Caption	Email Name
Collating Order	General
Ordinal Position	4

continues

A

TABLE STRUCTURES

TABLE A.6   CONTINUED

Property	Value
Required	False
Source Field	EmailName
Source Table	tblEmployees
Extension	**Text**
Allow Zero Length	False
Attributes	Variable Length
Collating Order	General
Ordinal Position	5
Required	False
Source Field	Extension
Source Table	tblEmployees
Address	**Text**
Allow Zero Length	False
Attributes	Variable Length
Collating Order	General
Ordinal Position	6
Required	False
Source Field	Address
Source Table	tblEmployees
City	**Text**
Allow Zero Length	False
Attributes	Variable Length
Collating Order	General
Ordinal Position	7
Required	False
Source Field	City
Source Table	tblEmployees

Property	Value
StateOrProvince	**Text**
Allow Zero Length	False
Attributes	Variable Length
Caption	State/Province
Collating Order	General
Ordinal Position	8
Required	False
Source Field	StateOrProvince
Source Table	tblEmployees
PostalCode	**Text**
Allow Zero Length	False
Attributes	Variable Length
Caption	Postal Code
Collating Order	General
Input Mask	00000-9999
Ordinal Position	9
Required	False
Source Field	PostalCode
Source Table	tblEmployees
Country	**Text**
Allow Zero Length	False
Attributes	Variable Length
Collating Order	General
Ordinal Position	10
Required	False
Source Field	Country
Source Table	tblEmployees

continues

A

TABLE STRUCTURES

TABLE A.6   CONTINUED

Property	Value
HomePhone	**Text**
Allow Zero Length	False
Attributes	Variable Length
Caption	Home Phone
Collating Order	General
Input Mask	!(999) 000-0000
Ordinal Position	11
Required	False
Source Field	HomePhone
Source Table	tblEmployees
WorkPhone	**Text**
Allow Zero Length	False
Attributes	Variable Length
Caption	Work Phone
Collating Order	General
Input Mask	!(999) 000-0000
Ordinal Position	12
Required	False
Source Field	WorkPhone
Source Table	tblEmployees
BillingRate	**Currency**
Allow Zero Length	False
Attributes	Fixed Size
Caption	Billing Rate
Collating Order	General
Decimal Places	2
Format	Currency
Ordinal Position	13
Required	False
Source Field	BillingRate
Source Table	tblEmployees

THE TBLERRORLOG TABLE

This table logs all application errors encountered while using the Time and Billing application, including error number and the name of the routine and module where the error occurred.

TABLE A.7 THE TBLERRORLOG TABLE

Field Name	Type	Size (Bytes)
ErrorSeq	Number (Long)	4
ErrorDate	Date/Time	8
ErrorTime	Date/Time	8
UserName	Text	30
ErrorNum	Number (Integer)	2
ErrorString	Text	30
Module	Text	50
Routine	Text	50

TABLE A.8 THE PROPERTIES AND VALUES ASSOCIATED WITH EACH FIELD IN THE TBLERRORLOG TABLE

Property	Value
ErrorSeq	**Number (Long)**
Allow Zero Length	False
Attributes	Fixed Size, Auto-Increment
Collating Order	General
Column Hidden	False
Column Order	Default
Column Width	Default
Description	Unique Identifier for the Error
Ordinal Position	0
Required	False
Source Field	ErrorSeq
Source Table	tblErrorLog

continues

A

TABLE
STRUCTURES

TABLE A.8   CONTINUED

Property	Value
ErrorDate	**Date/Time**
Allow Zero Length	False
Attributes	Fixed Size
Collating Order	General
Column Hidden	False
Column Order	Default
Column Width	Default
Description	Date that the Error Occurred
Format	Medium Date
Ordinal Position	1
Required	False
Source Field	ErrorDate
Source Table	tblErrorLog
ErrorTime	**Date/Time**
Allow Zero Length	False
Attributes	Fixed Size
Collating Order	General
Column Hidden	False
Column Order	Default
Column Width	Default
Description	Time that the Error Occurred
Format	Long Time
Ordinal Position	2
Required	False
Source Field	ErrorTime
Source Table	tblErrorLog
UserName	**Text**
Allow Zero Length	False
Attributes	Variable Length

Property	Value
Collating Order	General
Column Hidden	False
Column Order	Default
Column Width	Default
Description	Name of the User
Display Control	Text Box
Ordinal Position	3
Required	False
Source Field	UserName
Source Table	tblErrorLog
ErrorNum	**Number (Integer)**
Allow Zero Length	False
Attributes	Fixed Size
Collating Order	General
Column Hidden	False
Column Order	Default
Column Width	Default
Decimal Places	255
Default Value	0
Description	VBA Error Code
Display Control	Text Box
Ordinal Position	4
Required	False
Source Field	ErrorNum
Source Table	tblErrorLog
ErrorString	**Text**
Allow Zero Length	False
Attributes	Variable Length
Collating Order	General

continues

TABLE A.8   CONTINUED

Property	Value
Column Hidden	False
Column Order	Default
Column Width	Default
Description	VBA Error Description
Display Control	Text Box
Ordinal Position	5
Required	False
Source Field	ErrorString
Source Table	tblErrorLog
Module	**Text**
Allow Zero Length	False
Attributes	Variable Length
Collating Order	General
Column Hidden	False
Column Order	Default
Column Width	Default
Description	Module in Which the Error Occurred
Display Control	Text Box
Ordinal Position	6
Required	False
Source Field	Module
Source Table	tblErrorLog
Routine	**Text**
Allow Zero Length	False
Attributes	Variable Length
Collating Order	General
Column Hidden	False
Column Order	Default
Column Width	Default

Property	Value
Description	Routine in Which the Error Occurred
Display Control	Text Box
Ordinal Position	7
Required	False
Source Field	Routine
Source Table	tblErrorLog

THE TBLERRORS TABLE

This table gives you information about how your application should respond to error numbers.

TABLE A.9   THE TBLERRORS TABLE

Field Name	Type	Size (Bytes)
ErrorNum	Number (Long)	4
Response	Number (Long)	4

TABLE A.10   THE PROPERTIES AND VALUES ASSOCIATED WITH EACH FIELD IN THE TBLERRORS TABLE

Property	Value
ErrorNum	**Number (Long)**
Allow Zero Length	False
Attributes	Fixed Size
Collating Order	General
Column Hidden	False
Column Order	Default
Column Width	Default
Decimal Places	255
Default Value	0
Description	Number of the Error
Display Control	Text Box

continues

TABLE A.10   CONTINUED

Property	Value
Ordinal Position	0
Required	False
Source Field	ErrorNum
Source Table	tblErrors
Response	**Number (Long)**
Allow Zero Length	False
Attributes	Fixed Size
Collating Order	General
Column Hidden	False
Column Order	Default
Column Width	Default
Decimal Places	255
Default Value	0
Description	Action to Take
Display Control	Text Box
Ordinal Position	1
Required	False
Source Field	Response
Source Table	tblErrors

THE TBLEXPENSECODES TABLES

This table contains all the valid expense codes used in the Time and Billing application.

TABLE A.11   THE tblExpenseCodes

Field Name	Type	Size (Bytes)
ExpenseCodeID	Number (Long)	4
ExpenseCode	Text	30

TABLE A.12 THE FIELD PROPERTIES OF THE tblEXPENSECODES TABLE

Property	Value
ExpenseCodeID	**Number (Long)**
Allow Zero Length	False
Attributes	Fixed Size, Auto-Increment
Caption	Expense Code ID
Collating Order	General
Ordinal Position	0
Required	False
Source Field	ExpenseCodeID
Source Table	tblExpenseCodes
ExpenseCode	**Text**
Allow Zero Length	False
Attributes	Variable Length
Caption	Expense Code
Collating Order	General
Ordinal Position	1
Required	False
Source Field	ExpenseCode
Source Table	tblExpenseCodes

THE TBLPAYMENTMETHODS TABLE

This table lists the valid payment methods.

TABLE A.13 THE tblPAYMENTMETHODS TABLE

Field Name	Type	Size (Bytes)
PaymentMethodID	Number (Long)	4
PaymentMethod	Text	50
CreditCard	Yes/No	1

A

TABLE A.14   THE FIELD PROPERTIES OF THE TBLPAYMENTMETHODS TABLE

Property	Value
PaymentMethodID	**Number (Long)**
Allow Zero Length	False
Attributes	Fixed Size, Auto-Increment
Caption	Payment Method ID
Collating Order	General
Ordinal Position	0
Required	False
Source Field	PaymentMethodID
Source Table	tblPaymentMethods
PaymentMethod	**Text**
Allow Zero Length	False
Attributes	Variable Length
Caption	Payment Method
Collating Order	General
Ordinal Position	1
Required	False
Source Field	PaymentMethod
Source Table	tblPaymentMethods
CreditCard	**Yes/No**
Allow Zero Length	False
Attributes	Fixed Size
Caption	Credit Card?
Collating Order	General
Format	Yes/No
Ordinal Position	2
Required	False
Source Field	CreditCard
Source Table	tblPaymentMethods

THE TBLPAYMENTS TABLE

This table stores client payment information, such as the amount and date of payment for particular projects.

TABLE A.15   THE TBLPAYMENTS TABLE

Field Name	Type	Size (Bytes)
PaymentID	Number (Long)	4
ProjectID	Number (Long)	4
PaymentAmount	Currency	8
PaymentDate	Date/Time	8
CreditCardNumber	Text	30
CardholdersName	Text	50
CreditCardExpDate	Date/Time	8
PaymentMethodID	Number (Long)	4

TABLE A.16   THE FIELD PROPERTIES OF THE TBLPAYMENTS TABLE

Property	Value
PaymentID	**Number (Long)**
Allow Zero Length	False
Attributes	Fixed Size, Auto-Increment
Caption	Payment ID
Collating Order	General
Column Hidden	False
Column Order	Default
Column Width	Default
Ordinal Position	0
Required	False
Source Field	PaymentID
Source Table	tblPayments

continues

A

TABLE STRUCTURES

TABLE A.16 CONTINUED

Property	Value
ProjectID	**Number (Long)**
Allow Zero Length	False
Attributes	Fixed Size
Caption	Project ID
Collating Order	General
Column Hidden	False
Column Order	Default
Column Width	Default
Decimal Places	255
Display Control	Text Box
Ordinal Position	1
Required	False
Source Field	ProjectID
Source Table	tblPayments
PaymentAmount	**Currency**
Allow Zero Length	False
Attributes	Fixed Size
Caption	Payment Amount
Collating Order	General
Column Hidden	False
Column Order	Default
Column Width	Default
Decimal Places	2
Format	Currency
Ordinal Position	2
Required	False
Source Field	PaymentAmount
Source Table	tblPayments

Property	Value
PaymentDate	**Date/Time**
Allow Zero Length	False
Attributes	Fixed Size
Caption	Payment Date
Collating Order	General
Column Hidden	False
Column Order	Default
Column Width	Default
Format	Short Date
Input Mask	99/99/00
Ordinal Position	3
Required	False
Source Field	PaymentDate
Source Table	tblPayments
CreditCardNumber	**Text**
Allow Zero Length	False
Attributes	Variable Length
Caption	Credit Card #
Collating Order	General
Column Hidden	False
Column Order	Default
Column Width	Default
Display Control	Text Box
Ordinal Position	4
Required	False
Source Field	CreditCardNumber
Source Table	tblPayments
CardholdersName	**Text**
Allow Zero Length	False
Attributes	Variable Length

continues

TABLE A.16 CONTINUED

Property	Value
Caption	Cardholder Name
Collating Order	General
Column Hidden	False
Column Order	Default
Column Width	Default
Display Control	Text Box
Ordinal Position	5
Required	False
Source Field	CardholdersName
Source Table	tblPayments
CreditCardExpDate	**Date/Time**
Allow Zero Length	False
Attributes	Fixed Size
Caption	Card Exp. Date
Collating Order	General
Column Hidden	False
Column Order	Default
Column Width	Default
Format	Short Date
Input Mask	99/99/00
Ordinal Position	6
Required	False
Source Field	CreditCardExpDate
Source Table	tblPayments
PaymentMethodID	**Number (Long)**
Allow Zero Length	False
Attributes	Fixed Size
Bound Column	1
Caption	Payment Method ID

Property	Value
Collating Order	General
Column Count	3
Column Heads	False
Column Hidden	False
Column Order	Default
Column Width	Default
Column Widths	0;1440;0
Decimal Places	255
Display Control	Combo Box
Limit To List	True
List Rows	8
List Width	1
Ordinal Position	7
Required	False
Row Source Type	Table/Query
Row Source	SELECT DISTINCTROW tblPaymentMethods.* FROM tblPaymentMethods ORDER BY tblPaymentMethods.PaymentMethod;
Source Field	PaymentMethodID
Source Table	tblPayments

THE TBLPROJECTS TABLE

This table stores information about each project, including a cost estimate and important dates.

TABLE A.17 THE tblPROJECTS TABLE

Field Name	Type	Size (Bytes)
ProjectID	Number (Long)	4
ProjectName	Text	50
ProjectDescription	Memo	-
ClientID	Number (Long)	4

continues

A

TABLE A.17 CONTINUED

Field Name	Type	Size (Bytes)
PurchaseOrderNumber	Text	50
ProjectTotalEstimate	Currency	8
EmployeeID	Number (Long)	4
ProjectBeginDate	Date/Time	8
ProjectEndDate	Date/Time	8

TABLE A.18 THE FIELD PROPERTIES OF THE tblProjects TABLE

Property	Value
ProjectID	**Number (Long)**
Allow Zero Length	False
Attributes	Fixed Size, Auto-Increment
Caption	Project ID
Collating Order	General
Column Hidden	False
Column Order	Default
Column Width	Default
Ordinal Position	0
Required	False
Source Field	ProjectID
Source Table	tblProjects
ProjectName	**Text**
Allow Zero Length	False
Attributes	Variable Length
Caption	Project Name
Collating Order	General
Column Hidden	False
Column Order	Default
Column Width	Default
Display Control	Text Box

Property	Value
Ordinal Position	1
Required	True
Source Field	ProjectName
Source Table	tblProjects
ProjectDescription	**Memo**
Allow Zero Length	False
Attributes	Variable Length
Caption	Project Description
Collating Order	General
Column Hidden	False
Column Order	Default
Column Width	Default
Ordinal Position	2
Required	False
Source Field	ProjectDescription
Source Table	tblProjects
ClientID	**Number (Long)**
Allow Zero Length	False
Attributes	Fixed Size
Bound Column	1
Caption	Client ID
Collating Order	General
Column Count	2
Column Heads	False
Column Hidden	False
Column Order	Default
Column Width	Default
Column Widths	;14400
Decimal Places	255

continues

TABLE A.18 CONTINUED

Property	Value
Default Value	0
Display Control	Combo Box
Limit To List	True
List Rows	8
List Width	1
Ordinal Position	3
Required	True
Row Source Type	Table/Query
Row Source	SELECT DISTINCTROW [tblClients].[ClientID], [tblClients].[CompanyName] FROM [tblClients];
Source Field	ClientID
Source Table	tblProjects
PurchaseOrderNumber	**Text**
Allow Zero Length	False
Attributes	Variable Length
Caption	Purchase Order Number
Collating Order	General
Column Hidden	False
Column Order	Default
Column Width	Default
Display Control	Text Box
Ordinal Position	4
Required	False
Source Field	PurchaseOrderNumber
Source Table	tblProjects
ProjectTotalEstimate	**Currency**
Allow Zero Length	False
Attributes	Fixed Size

Property	Value
Caption	ProjectTotalEstime
Collating Order	General
Column Hidden	False
Column Order	Default
Column Width	Default
Decimal Places	255
Default Value	0
Format	Currency
Ordinal Position	5
Required	False
Source Field	ProjectTotalEstimate
Source Table	tblProjects
EmployeeID	**Number (Long)**
Allow Zero Length	False
Attributes	Fixed Size
Caption	Employee ID
Collating Order	General
Column Hidden	False
Column Order	Default
Column Width	Default
Decimal Places	255
Default Value	0
Display Control	Text Box
Ordinal Position	6
Required	False
Source Field	EmployeeID
Source Table	tblProjects
ProjectBeginDate	**Date/Time**
Allow Zero Length	False
Attributes	Fixed Size

continues

TABLE A.18   CONTINUED

Property	Value
Caption	Project Begin Date
Collating Order	General
Column Hidden	False
Column Order	Default
Column Width	Default
Ordinal Position	7
Required	False
Source Field	ProjectBeginDate
Source Table	tblProjects
ProjectEndDate	**Date/Time**
Allow Zero Length	False
Attributes	Fixed Size
Caption	Project End Date
Collating Order	General
Column Hidden	False
Column Order	Default
Column Width	Default
Ordinal Position	8
Required	False
Source Field	ProjectEndDate
Source Table	tblProjects

THE TBLTIMCARDEXPENSES TABLE

This tables stores necessary information for billable project expenses, such as the date and amount of the expense.

TABLE A.19   THE TBLTIMECARDEXPENSES TABLE

Field Name	Type	Size (Bytes)
TimeCardExpenseID	Number (Long)	4
TimeCardID	Number (Long)	4
ExpenseDate	Date/Time	8
ProjectID	Number (Long)	4
ExpenseDescription	Text	255
ExpenseAmount	Currency	8
ExpenseCodeID	Number (Long)	4

TABLE A.20   THE FIELD PROPERTIES OF THE TBLTIMECARDEXPENSES TABLE

Property	Value
TimeCardExpenseID	**Number (Long)**
Allow Zero Length	False
Attributes	Fixed Size, Auto-Increment
Caption	Time Card Expense ID
Collating Order	General
Column Hidden	False
Column Order	Default
Column Width	Default
Ordinal Position	0
Required	False
Source Field	TimeCardExpenseID
Source Table	tblTimeCardExpenses
TimeCardID	**Number (Long)**
Allow Zero Length	False
Attributes	Fixed Size
Caption	Time Card ID
Collating Order	General
Column Hidden	False
Column Order	Default

continues

TABLE A.20   CONTINUED

Property	Value
Column Width	Default
Decimal Places	255
Display Control	Text Box
Ordinal Position	1
Required	False
Source Field	TimeCardID
Source Table	tblTimeCardExpenses
ExpenseDate	**Date/Time**
Allow Zero Length	False
Attributes	Fixed Size
Caption	Expense Date
Collating Order	General
Column Hidden	False
Column Order	Default
Column Width	Default
Format	Short Date
Input Mask	99/99/00
Ordinal Position	2
Required	False
Source Field	ExpenseDate
Source Table	tblTimeCardExpenses
ProjectID	**Number (Long)**
Allow Zero Length	False
Attributes	Fixed Size
Bound Column	1
Caption	Project ID
Collating Order	General
Column Count	3
Column Heads	False

Property	Value
Column Hidden	False
Column Order	Default
Column Width	Default
Column Widths	0;1020;3156
Decimal Places	255
Display Control	Combo Box
Limit To List	True
List Rows	8
List Width	3
Ordinal Position	3
Required	False
Row Source Type	Table/Query
Row Source	SELECT DISTINCTROW tblProjects.* FROM tblProjects ORDER BY tblProjects.ProjectName;
Source Field	ProjectID
Source Table	tblTimeCardExpenses
ExpenseDescription	**Text**
Allow Zero Length	False
Attributes	Variable Length
Caption	Expense Description
Collating Order	General
Column Hidden	False
Column Order	Default
Column Width	Default
Display Control	Text Box
Ordinal Position	4
Required	False
Source Field	ExpenseDescription
Source Table	tblTimeCardExpenses

continues

TABLE A.20 CONTINUED

Property	Value
ExpenseAmount	**Currency**
Allow Zero Length	False
Attributes	Fixed Size
Caption	Expense Amount
Collating Order	General
Column Hidden	False
Column Order	Default
Column Width	Default
Decimal Places	2
Format	Currency
Ordinal Position	5
Required	False
Source Field	ExpenseAmount
Source Table	tblTimeCardExpenses
ExpenseCodeID	**Number (Long)**
Allow Zero Length	False
Attributes	Fixed Size
Bound Column	1
Caption	Expense Code ID
Collating Order	General
Column Count	2
Column Heads	False
Column Hidden	False
Column Order	Default
Column Width	Default
Column Widths	0;2880
Decimal Places	255
Display Control	Combo Box
Limit To List	True
List Rows	8

Property	Value
List Width	2
Ordinal Position	6
Required	False
Row Source Type	Table/Query
Row Source	SELECT DISTINCTROW tblExpenseCodes.* FROM tblExpenseCodes ORDER BY tblExpenseCodes.ExpenseCode;
Source Field	ExpenseCodeID
Source Table	tblTimeCardExpenses

THE TBLTIMECARDHOURS TABLE

This table stores a record of billable hours for a project, including dates and billing rates.

TABLE A.21 THE tblTimeCardHours Table

Field Name	Type	Size (Bytes)
TimeCardDetailID	Number (Long)	4
TimeCardID	Number (Long)	4
DateWorked	Date/Time	8
ProjectID	Number (Long)	4
WorkDescription	Text	255
BillableHours	Number (Double)	8
BillingRate	Currency	8
WorkCodeID	Number (Long)	4

TABLE A.22 THE FIELD PROPERTIES OF THE tblTimeCardHours Table

Property	Value
TimeCardDetailID	**Number (Long)**
Allow Zero Length	False
Attributes	Fixed Size, Auto-Increment
Caption	Time Card Detail ID

continues

A

TABLE STRUCTURES

TABLE A.22   CONTINUED

Property	Value
Collating Order	General
Column Hidden	False
Column Order	Default
Column Width	Default
Ordinal Position	0
Required	False
Source Field	TimeCardDetailID
Source Table	tblTimeCardHours
TimeCardID	**Number (Long)**
Allow Zero Length	False
Attributes	Fixed Size
Caption	Time Card ID
Collating Order	General
Column Hidden	False
Column Order	Default
Column Width	Default
Decimal Places	255
Display Control	Text Box
Ordinal Position	1
Required	False
Source Field	TimeCardID
Source Table	tblTimeCardHours
DateWorked	**Date/Time**
Allow Zero Length	False
Attributes	Fixed Size
Caption	Date Worked
Collating Order	General
Column Hidden	False
Column Order	Default

Property	Value
Column Width	Default
Format	Short Date
Input Mask	99/99/00
Ordinal Position	2
Required	False
Source Field	DateWorked
Source Table	tblTimeCardHours
ProjectID	**Number (Long)**
Allow Zero Length	False
Attributes	Fixed Size
Bound Column	1
Caption	Project ID
Collating Order	General
Column Count	3
Column Heads	False
Column Hidden	False
Column Order	Default
Column Width	Default
Column Widths	0;1020;3156
Decimal Places	255
Display Control	Combo Box
Limit To List	True
List Rows	8
List Width	3
Ordinal Position	3
Required	False
Row Source Type	Table/Query
Row Source	SELECT DISTINCTROW tblProjects.* FROM tblProjects ORDER BY tblProjects.ProjectName;
Source Field	ProjectID
Source Table	tblTimeCardHours

continues

TABLE A.22   CONTINUED

Property	Value
WorkDescription	**Text**
Allow Zero Length	False
Attributes	Variable Length
Caption	Work Description
Collating Order	General
Column Hidden	False
Column Order	Default
Column Width	Default
Display Control	Text Box
Ordinal Position	4
Required	False
Source Field	WorkDescription
Source Table	tblTimeCardHours
BillableHours	**Number (Double)**
Allow Zero Length	False
Attributes	Fixed Size
Caption	Billable Hours
Collating Order	General
Column Hidden	False
Column Order	Default
Column Width	Default
Decimal Places	255
Display Control	Text Box
Ordinal Position	5
Required	False
Source Field	BillableHours
Source Table	tblTimeCardHours

Property	Value
BillingRate	**Currency**
Allow Zero Length	False
Attributes	Fixed Size
Caption	Billing Rate
Collating Order	General
Column Hidden	False
Column Order	Default
Column Width	Default
Decimal Places	2
Format	Currency
Ordinal Position	6
Required	False
Source Field	BillingRate
Source Table	tblTimeCardHours
WorkCodeID	**Number (Long)**
Allow Zero Length	False
Attributes	Fixed Size
Bound Column	1
Caption	Work Code ID
Collating Order	General
Column Count	2
Column Heads	False
Column Hidden	False
Column Order	Default
Column Width	Default
Column Widths	0;2880
Decimal Places	255
Display Control	Combo Box
Limit To List	True

continues

TABLE A.22   CONTINUED

Property	Value
List Rows	8
List Width	2
Ordinal Position	7
Required	False
Row Source Type	Table/Query
Row Source	SELECT DISTINCTROW tblWorkCodes.* FROM tblWorkCodes ORDER BY tblWorkCodes.WorkCode;
Source Field	WorkCodeID
Source Table	tblTimeCardHours

THE TBLTIMECARDS TABLE

This table stores time card information for each employee.

TABLE A.23   THE TBLTIMECARDS TABLE

Field Name	Type	Size (Bytes)
TimeCardID	Number (Long)	4
EmployeeID	Number (Long)	4
DateEntered	Date/Time	8

TABLE A.24   THE FIELD PROPERTIES OF THE TBLTIMECARDS TABLE

Property	Value
TimeCardID	**Number (Long)**
Allow Zero Length	False
Attributes	Fixed Size, Auto-Increment
Caption	Time Card ID
Collating Order	General
Column Hidden	False
Column Order	Default
Column Width	Default

Property	Value
Ordinal Position	0
Required	False
Source Field	TimeCardID
Source Table	tblTimeCards
EmployeeID	**Number (Long)**
Allow Zero Length	False
Attributes	Fixed Size
Bound Column	1
Caption	Employee ID
Collating Order	General
Column Count	3
Column Heads	False
Column Hidden	False
Column Order	Default
Column Width	Default
Column Widths	0;2000;700
Decimal Places	255
Display Control	Combo Box
Limit To List	True
List Rows	8
List Width	2
Ordinal Position	1
Required	False
Row Source Type	Table/Query
Row Source	SELECT tblEmployees.EmployeeID, [LastName] & ", " & [FirstName] AS EmployeeName, tblEmployees.BillingRate FROM tblEmployees ORDER BY [LastName] & ", " & [FirstName];
Source Field	EmployeeID
Source Table	tblTimeCards

continues

TABLE A.22 CONTINUED

Property	Value
DateEntered	**Date/Time**
Allow Zero Length	False
Attributes	Fixed Size
Caption	Date Entered
Collating Order	General
Column Hidden	False
Column Order	Default
Column Width	Default
Format	Short Date
Input Mask	99/99/00
Ordinal Position	2
Required	False
Source Field	DateEntered
Source Table	tblTimeCards

THE TBLWORKCODES TABLE

This table supplies valid work codes for the application.

TABLE A.25 THE TBLWORKCODES TABLE

Field Name	Type	Size (Bytes)
WorkCodeID	Number (Long)	4
WorkCode	Text	30

TABLE A.26 THE FIELD PROPERTIES OF THE TBLWORKCODES TABLE

Property	Value
WorkCodeID	**Number (Long)**
Allow Zero Length	False
Attributes	Fixed Size, Auto-Increment
Caption	Work Code ID

Property	Value
Collating Order	General
Ordinal Position	0
Required	False
Source Field	WorkCodeID
Source Table	tblWorkCodes
WorkCode	**Text**
Allow Zero Length	False
Attributes	Variable Length
Caption	Work Code
Collating Order	General
Ordinal Position	1
Required	False
Source Field	WorkCode
Source Table	tblWorkCodes

NAMING CONVENTIONS

This appendix gives you suggestions for naming variables and other database objects. The suggested standards are based on the Reddick VBA Naming Conventions (RBVA).

When creating variable names, it's important for you to make the type and intended use of each variable clear and self-documenting. Here are a few rules to follow:

- Remember to always make variable names mixed case, with each word or abbreviation in the variable name capitalized.
- Don't use underscore characters in your variable names.
- Abbreviate variable names only when it's necessary.
- Make the beginning of each variable name describe the type of data it contains.

Following these conventions will go a long way toward keeping your code concise and readable. The format for an object is

`[prefixes]tag[BaseName[Suffixes]]`

A *prefix* appears in lowercase and is used to indicate additional information, such as the scope of a variable. The *tag* also appears in lowercase. It is a short set of characters that indicates the type of an object. The *BaseName* is used to indicate what the object represents. The first letter of each word in the *BaseName* is capitalized. *Suffixes*, when used, provide additional information about the meaning of the *BaseName*. An example of a name for an object is

`mstrFirstName`

The Prefix m is used to indicate that the variable appears at the module level. The tag str is used to indicate that the variable contains a string. The BaseName FirstName indicates that the variable holds a first name. Table B.1 recommends prefixes for Access object tags.

TABLE B.1 ACCESS OBJECT-NAMING CONVENTIONS

Prefix	Control Type	Example
app	Application	appInfoBase
chk	CheckBox	chkReadOnly
cbo	ComboBox	cboLanguages
cmd	CommandButton	cmdRefreshTable
ctl	Control	ctlAny
ctls	Controls	ctlsAll
ocx	CustomControl	ocxCalendar
dcm	DoCmd	dcmOpenForm
frm	Form	frmDataEntryView

Prefix	Control Type	Example
frms	Forms	frmsClientsAndOrders
img	Image	imgHeadShot
lbl	Label	lblShowAllCheckBox
lin	Line	linDivider
lst	ListBox	lstLastTenSites
bas	Module	basErrorControl
ole	ObjectFrame	oleWorksheet
opt	OptionButton	optReadOnly
fra	OptionGroup (frame)	fraColorSchemes
brk	PageBreak	brkTopOfForm
pal	PaletteButton	palBackgroundColor
prps	Properties	prpsActiveForm
shp	Rectangle	shpHidableFrame
rpt	Report	rptOrders
rpts	Reports	rptsTodaysChanges
scr	Screen	scrSecondSplashScreen
sec	Section	secOrderDetail
fsub	Subform	fsubBillableHours
rsub	SubReport	rsubTopFiveSales
txt	TextBox	txtAdditionalNotes
tgl	ToggleButton	tglShowFormatting

Table B.2 lists prefix tags for standard variable types, as well as the storage space required by each.

TABLE B.2 STANDARD VARIABLE DATA TYPE TAGS

Prefix	Data Type	Storage	Example
byte or byt		1 Byte	byteArray
bool or f	Boolean	2 bytes	boolSecurityClear
int	Integer	2 bytes	intLoop
lng	Long	4 bytes	lngEnv

continues

TABLE B.2   CONTINUED

Prefix	Data Type	Storage	Example
sng	Single	4 bytes	sngValue
dbl	Double	8 bytes	dblValue
cur	Currency	8 bytes	curCostPerUnit
dat	Date and Time	8 bytes	datStartTime
obj	Object	varies	objActiveObject
str	String	1 byte per character	strFirstName
stf	String (fixed length)	10 bytes + 1 byte per char	stfSocNumber
var	Variant	16 bytes + 1 byte per char	varInput

The Jet Engine uses objects you might need to refer to in VBA code. Table B.3 lists the Data Access Objects (DAO) object types and their standard naming prefixes.

> **NOTE**
>
> Naming conventions for ADO objects were unavailable at the time of this writing.

TABLE B.3   JET OBJECT/COLLECTION PREFIXES

Prefix	Object Type
cnt	Container
cnts	Containers
db	Database
dbs	Databases
dbe	DBEngine
doc	Document
docs	Documents
err	Error

Prefix	*Object Type*
errs	Errors
fld	Field
flds	Fields
grp	Group
grps	Groups
idx	Index
idxs	Indexes
prm	Parameter
prms	Parameters
pdbe	PrivDBEngine
prp	Property
prps	Properties
qry (or qdf)	QueryDef
qrys (or qdfs)	QueryDefs
rst	Recordset
rsts	Recordsets
rel	Relation
rels	Relations
tbl (or tdf)	TableDef
tbls (or tdfs)	TableDefs
usr	User
usrs	Users
wrk	Workspace
wrks	Workspaces

In addition to the standard notations for variables, there are variable notations for scope and lifetime. These should be placed at the beginning of the variable, before any other prefix. Table B.4 lists the scope and lifetime prefixes.

TABLE B.4   PREFIXES FOR SCOPE AND LIFETIME

Prefix	Description
(none)	Local variable, procedure-level lifetime
s	Local variable, program-level lifetime (static variable)
m	Private (module) variable, program-level lifetime
g	Public (global) variable, program-level lifetime

Table B.5 lists general naming convention tags for the Database window objects.

TABLE B.5   TAGS FOR DATABASE WINDOW OBJECTS

Prefix	Object Type
tbl	Table
qry	Query
frm	Form
rpt	Report
mcr	Macro
bas	Module

There are two sets of naming conventions you can use when naming specific Database window objects: Either use the prefix for the general object prefix from the table, or supply one of the more descriptive tags listed in Table B.6.

TABLE B.6   TAGS FOR SPECIFIC DATABASE WINDOW OBJECTS

Prefix	Suffix	Object Type
tlkp	Lookup	Table (lookup)
qsel	(none)	Query (select)
qapp	Append	Query (append)
qxtb	XTab	Query (crosstab)
qddl	DDL	Query (DDL)
qdel	Delete	Query (delete)
qflt	Filter	Query (filter)
qlkp	Lookup	Query (lookup)
qmak	MakeTable	Query (make table)

Prefix	Suffix	Object Type
qspt	PassThru	Query (SQL pass-through)
qtot	Totals	Query (totals)
quni	Union	Query (union)
qupd	Update	Query (update)
fdlg	Dlg	Form (dialog)
fmnu	Mnu	Form (menu)
fmsg	Msg	Form (message)
fsfr	Subform	Form (subform)
rsrp	SubReport	Form (subreport)
mmnu	Mnu	Macro (menu)

INDEX

Other Related Titles

F. Scott Barker's Microsoft Access 2000 Power Programming
F. Scott Barker
ISBN: 0-672-31506-8
$49.99 US/$74.95 CAN

Visual Basic 6 Unleashed
Rob Thayer
ISBN: 0-672-31309-X
$39.99 US/$59.95 CAN

Microsoft SQL Server 7.0 Unleashed
Greg Mable, et al.
ISBN: 0-672-31227-1
$49.99 US/$74.95 CAN

Peter Norton's Complete Guide to Windows 98
Peter Norton
ISBN: 0-672-31230-1
$29.99 US/$44.95 CAN

Windows 98 Unleashed
Paul McFedries
ISBN: 0-672-31235-2
$34.99 US/$52.95 CAN

Peter Norton's Complete Guide to PC Upgrades, Second Edition
Peter Norton
ISBN: 0-672-31483-5
$29.99 US/$44.95 CAN

Windows NT Server 4 Unleashed, Second Edition
Jason Garms
ISBN: 0-672-31249-2
$49.99 US/$74.95 CAN

Windows NT Workstation 4 Unleashed
Paul Cassel, et al.
ISBN: 0-672-31081-3
$49.99 US/$74.95 CAN

COM/DCOM Unleashed
KeyTek, Inc.
ISBN: 0-672-31352-9
$39.99 US/$59.95 CAN

Programming Windows 98/NT Unleashed
Viktor Toth
ISBN: 0-672-31353-7
$49.99 US/$74.95 CAN

Roger Jenning's Database Developer's Guide with Visual Basic 6
Roger Jennings
ISBN: 0-672-31063-5
$59.99 US/$89.95 CAN

Microsoft Access 2000 Development Unleashed
Stephen Forte, Tom Howe, and James Ralston
ISBN: 0-672-31291-3
$49.99 US/$74.95 CAN

Sams Teach Yourself Microsoft SQL Server 7.0 in 21 Days
Richard Waymire and Rick Sawtell
ISBN: 0-672-31290-5
$39.99 US/$59.95 CAN

SAMS
www.samspublishing.com

All prices are subject to change.

"FREE" Access 2000 Interactive Training Included On Alison Balter's Mastering Access 2000 Development CD

...Inside You'll Get 40 Minutes of Interactive Access Development Instruction—FREE

Thanks to Macmillan Publishing you can learn critical Access Development topics within minutes. You'll gain a whole new perspective of how easy learning can be.

Installation:
1. Place the Disk in your CD Drive 2. From the "Start" menu click "Run..."
3. Type the letter designation for "d:\setup") (for example if your CD drive is "D" type; "d:\3rdparty\Keystone\setup")
4. Click "OK" and follow the instructions on your monitor.

Please Enjoy Your FREE Training

From KeyStone Learning Systems.

Learn from the Best Alison Balter

For over 13 years customers keep coming back because of Alison Balter. Her knowledge and gift for teaching makes learning Access Development a cinch. It's a shade away from live one-on-one instruction. You'll discover just how well versed in Access 2000 development Alison is, after all she wrote the book.

Convenient

With this training you'll have precious insights right at your fingertips. This precision training is so good in fact, you'll wonder how you ever got along without it.

Seeing is Believing

Along with this FREE CD we're offering as an added bonus the entire six level course for only $399.95. (reg.$499.95) That's six hours of training at the lowest price ever. Call toll free 800-581-7610 today or visit our web site at www.klscorp.com. All KeyStone training comes with a 100% money-back-guarantee!

Technical Support:

Phone: 1-800-801-0952

email: techsupport@klscorp.com

KEYSTONE
LEARNING SYSTEMS

1-800-581-7610

2241 South Larsen Parkway
Provo, Utah 84606

www.klscorp.com/access2000

KCBA# A299